JUDAISM FROM CYRUS TO HADRIAN

VOLUME TWO

JUDAISM FROM CYRUS TO HADRIAN

VOLUME TWO:
THE ROMAN PERIOD

Lester L. Grabbe

FORTRESS PRESS   MINNEAPOLIS

JUDAISM FROM CYRUS TO HADRIAN
Volume Two: The Roman Period

Old Testament scripture quotations are from *The TANAKH: The New JPS Translation According to the Traditional Hebrew Text*, copyright © 1985 by the Jewish Publication Society. Used by permission.

New Testament scripture quotations are from The Revised Standard Version of the Bible, copyright © 1946, 1952, 1971 by the Division of Christian Education of the National Council of the Churches of Christ in the USA. Used by permission.

Scripture quotations from the Apocrypha are from The Revised Standard Version Apocrypha, copyright © 1957 by the Division of Christian Education of the National Council of the Churches of Christ in the USA. Used by permission.

Interior design by Publishers' WorkGroup
Cover design by Spangler Design Team
Cartography by Parrot Graphics

Library of Congress Cataloging-in-Publication Data

Grabbe, Lester L.
  Judaism from Cyrus to Hadrian / Lester L. Grabbe.
    p. cm.
  Includes bibliographical references and index.
  Contents: v. 1. The Persian and Greek periods—v. 2. The Roman period.
  ISBN 0–8006–2620–6 (v. 1)—ISBN 0–8006–2621–4 (v. 2)
  1. Jews—History—586 B.C.–70 A.D.—Sources. 2. Jews—History—586 B.C.–70 A.D.—Historiography. 3. Jews—History—168 B.C.–135 A.D.—Sources. 4. Jews—History—168 B.C.–135 A.D.—Historiography. 5. Judaism—History—Post-exilic period, 586 B.C.–210 A.D.—Sources. 6. Judaism—History—Post-exilic period, 586 B.C.–210 A.D.—Historiography. I. Title.
DS121.65.G68   1991
933—dc20   91–36738
                                                          CIP

The paper used in this publication meets the minimum requirements of American National Standard for Information Sciences—Permanence of Paper for Printed Library Materials, ANSI Z329.48-1984.

Manufactured in the U.S.A.   AF 1-2621
  96   95   94   93   92   1   2   3   4   5   6   7   8   9   10

SUMMARY OF CONTENTS: VOLUMES 1 AND 2

CONTENTS:
VOLUME TWO

CONTENTS

ABBREVIATIONS

When used before an author's name or page number, an asterisk refers to items listed in the bibliography at the beginning of that particular chapter.

AASOR	Annual of the American Schools of Oriental Research
AAWG	*Abhandlungen der Akademie der Wissenschaften zu Göttingen*
AB	Anchor Bible
Adver. pagan.	Orosius, *Adversus paganos*
AfO	Archiv für Orientforschung
AGAJU	Arbeiten zur Geschichte des antiken Judentums und des Urchristentums
AHR	American Historical Review
AJA	*American Journal of Archaeology*
AJAH	*American Journal of Ancient History*
AJBA	*Australian Journal of Biblical Archaeology*
AJP	*American Journal of Philology*
AJS Review	*American Jewish Studies Review*
AJSL	*American Journal of Semitic Languages and Literature*
ALGHJ	Arbeiten zur Literatur und Geschichte des hellenistischen Judentums
AnBib	Analecta biblica
ANET	J. B. Pritchard (ed.), *Ancient Near Eastern Texts*
AnOr	Analecta orientalia
ANRW	*Aufstieg und Niedergang der römischen Welt*
AOAT	Alter Orient und Altes Testament
AOS	American Oriental Series
Appian	
Bell. Civ.	*Bella civilia*
Syr.	*Syriakē*

ASOR Sp. Vol.	American Schools of Oriental Research Special Volume
ASTI	*Annual of the Swedish Theological Institute*
Athen. Polit.	Aristotle, *Athenian Politeia*
ATR	*Anglican Theological Review*
AUSS	*Andrews University Seminary Studies*
b.	son of (Hebrew *ben*; Aramaic *bar*)
b. Avod. Zara	Babylonian Talmud, *Avoda Zara*
b. B. Batra	Babylonian Talmud, *Baba Batra*
b. Qid.	Babylonian Talmud, *Qiddussin*
b. Sanh.	Babylonian Talmud, *Sanhedrin*
b. Suk.	Babylonian Talmud, *Sukka*
b. Ta'an.	Babylonian Talmud, *Ta'anit*
b. Yeb.	Babylonian Talmud, *Yebamot*
b. Yoma	Babylonian Talmud, *Yoma* (= *Kippurim*)
BA	*Biblical Archaeologist*
BAR	*Biblical Archaeology Review*
BASOR	*Bulletin of the American Schools of Oriental Research*
B.C.E.	Before the Common Era (= B.C.)
Beh. Inscr.	*Behistun Inscription*
BETL	Bibliotheca ephemeridum theologicarum lovaniensium
Bib	*Biblica*
BibOr	Biblica et orientalia
BJRL	*Bulletin of the John Rylands University Library of Manchester*
BJS	Brown Judaic Studies
BO	*Bibliotheca orientalis*
BSOAS	*Bulletin of the School of Oriental and African Studies*
BTB	*Biblical Theology Bulletin*
BWANT	Beiträge zur Wissenschaft vom Alten und Neuen Testament
BZ	*Biblische Zeitschrift*
BZAW	Beihefte zur *ZAW*
CAH	*Cambridge Ancient History*
CBQ	*Catholic Biblical Quarterly*
CBQMS	Catholic Biblical Quarterly—Monograph Series
CCL	Corpus Christianorum, Series Latina
CCS	Cincinnati Classical Studies
CCWJCW	Cambridge Commentaries on Writings of the Jewish and Christian World 200 B.C. to A.D. 200
CD	*Damascus Document*

C.E.	Common Era (= A.D.)
CHCL	P. E. Easterling, et al. (eds.), *Cambridge History of Classical Literature* (1982–85)
CHI	*Cambridge History of Iran*
CHJ	W. D. Davies and L. Finkelstein (eds.), *Cambridge History of Judaism*
Collect.	Solinus, *Collectanea*
Com. in Dan.	Jerome, *Commentary on Daniel*
ConBNT	Coniectanea biblica, New Testament
ConBOT	Coniectanea biblica, Old Testament
CPJ	V. A. Tcherikover, et al., *Corpus papyrorum Judaicarum*
CRAIBL	*Comptes rendus de l'Académie des inscriptions et belles-lettres*
CRINT	Compendia rerum iudaicarum ad novum testamentum
CSCO	Corpus scriptorum christianorum orientalium
CSCT	Columbia Studies in Classical Texts
CSEL	Corpus scriptorum ecclesiasticorum latinorum
Dial. Trypho	Justin Martyr, *Dialogue with Trypho*
DJD	Discoveries in the Judaean Desert
EB	Etudes bibliques
Eccl. Rabba	*Ecclesiastes Rabbah*
ECL	Early Christian Literature
EI	Eretz-Israel
EJ	*Encyclopaedia Judaica*
Eng.	English text
Eusebius	
Chron.	*Chronicle*
Hist. eccl.	*Historia ecclesiastica*
Praep. evang.	*Praeparatio evangelica*
FRLANT	Forschungen zur Religion und Literatur des Alten und Neuen Testaments
FS	Festschrift
GCS	Griechischen christlichen Schriftsteller
Gen. Rab.	*Genesis Rabbah*
GLAJJ	M. Stern, *Greek and Latin Authors on Jews and Judaism*
GRBS	*Greek, Roman, and Byzantine Studies*
GTA	Göttinger theologische Arbeiten
Hadr.	*Hadrian* (in *Scriptores Historiae Augustae*)
HAR	*Hebrew Annual Review*
HAT	Handbuch zum Alten Testament
HdA	Handbuch der Archäologie

HdO	Handbuch der Orientalisk
Ḥev	Naḥal Ḥever texts
Ḥev Ep	Ḥever Epistles
Ḥev Ep gr	Ḥever Epistles (in Greek)
Hist. nat.	Pliny, *Naturalis historia*
HR	*History of Religions*
HSCP	*Harvard Studies in Classical Philology*
HSM	Harvard Semitic Monographs
HSS	Harvard Semitic Studies
HTR	*Harvard Theological Review*
HTS	Harvard Theological Studies
HUCA	*Hebrew Union College Annual*
ICC	International Critical Commentary
IDB	G. A. Buttrick (ed.), *Interpreter's Dictionary of the Bible*
IDBSup	Supplementary volume to *IDB*
IEJ	*Israel Exploration Journal*
INJ	*Israel Numismatic Journal*
Int	*Interpretation*
IOS	*Israel Oriental Society*
ITQ	*Irish Theological Quarterly*
JAAR	*Journal of the American Academy of Religion*
JANES	*Journal of the Ancient Near Eastern Society of Columbia University*
JAOS	*Journal of the American Oriental Society*
JBL	*Journal of Biblical Literature*
JCS	*Journal of Cuneiform Studies*
JEA	*Journal of Egyptian Archaeology*
JES	*Journal of Ecumenical Studies*
JHS	*Journal of Hellenic Studies*
JJS	*Journal of Jewish Studies*
JLBM	G.W.E. Nickelsburg, *Jewish Literature between the Bible and the Mishnah*
JNES	*Journal of Near Eastern Studies*
Josephus	
Ag. Ap.	*Against Apion*
Ant.	*Antiquities*
War	*War of the Jews*
JQR	*Jewish Quarterly Review*
JR	*Journal of Religion*
JRS	*Journal of Roman Studies*
JSHRZ	Jüdische Schriften aus hellenistisch-römischer Zeit

JSJ	*Journal for the Study of Judaism in the Persian, Hellenistic and Roman Period*
JSNT	*Journal for the Study of the New Testament*
JSOT	*Journal for the Study of the Old Testament*
JSOTSS	Journal for the Study of the Old Testament—Supplement Series
JSP	*Journal for the Study of the Pseudepigrapha*
JSPSS	Journal for the Study of the Pseudepigrapha—Supplementary Series
JSS	*Journal of Semitic Studies*
JTS	*Journal of Theological Studies*
JWSTP	M. E. Stone (ed.), *Jewish Writings of the Second Temple Period*
KAI	H. Donner and W. Röllig, *Kanaanäische und aramäische Inschriften*
KAT	Kommentar zum Alten Testament
LCL	Loeb Classical Library
Lives	Plutarch, *Parallel Lives*
LXX	Septuagint
m. Avot	Mishnah tractate *Avot*
m. Mig.	Mishnah tractate *Megilla*
m. Rosh ha-Shan.	Mishnah tractate *Rosh ha-Shana*
m. Shab.	Mishnah tractate *Shabbat*
m. Suk.	Mishnah tractate *Sukka*
m. Ta'an.	Mishnah tractate *Ta'anit*
Meg. Ta'an.	*Megillat Ta'anit*
MGWJ	*Monatsschrift für Geschichte und Wissenschaft des Judentums*
MSS	Manuscripts
MT	Masoretic Text
Mur.	Wadi Murabba'at texts
Nab. Chron.	*Nabonidus Chronicle*
NCB	New Century Bible
NEB	New English Bible
NHS	Nag Hammadi Studies
NIGTC	New International Greek Testament Commentary
NovT	*Novum Testamentum*
NovTSup	Novum Testamentum, Supplements
NTS	*New Testament Studies*
OCD	*Oxford Classical Dictionary*
OTL	Old Testament Library

ABBREVIATIONS

OTP	J. H. Charlesworth (ed.), *The Old Testament Pseudepigrapha*
OTS	*Oudtestamentische Studien*
PAAJR	*Proceedings of the American Academy of Jewish Research*
PEQ	*Palestine Exploration Quarterly*
Philo	
Congr.	*De congressu eruditionis gratia*
Flaccum	*In Flaccum*
Gaium	*Legatio ad Gaium*
Hyp.	*Hypothetica*
Probus	*Quod omnis probus liber sit*
PSI	*Pubblicazioni della Società Italiana, Papiri Greci et Latini*
PVTG	Pseudepigrapha Veteris Testamenti graece
PW	Pauly-Wissowa, *Real-Encyclopädie der classischen Altertumswissenschaft*
PWSup	Supplement to *PW*
P. Zen.	Zenon papyri
Qumran Scrolls	
CD	*Damascus Document*
1QH	*Thanksgiving Hymns*
1QM	*War Scroll*
1QpHab	*Habbakuk Commentary*
1QS	*Community Rule (Manual of Discipline)*
1QSa	*Appendix A to 1QS (Rule of the Congregation)*
4QMMT	*Halakic Letter*
4QpNah	*Commentary on Nahum*
4QpPsa	*Commentary on Psalm 37*
11QMelch	*Melchizidek text*
11QT	*Temple Scroll*
RB	*Revue biblique*
REG	*Revue des études grecs*
REJ	*Revue des études juives*
RevQ	*Revue de Qumran*
RSR	*Religious Studies Review*
RSV	Revised Standard Version
SANE	Studies on the Ancient Near East
SAWH	*Sitzungsbericht der Akademie der Wissenschaften zu Heidelberg*
SBAW	*Sitzungsberichte der bayerischen Akademie der Wissenschaften*
SBLASP	SBL Abstracts and Seminar Papers

SBLBMI	SBL The Bible and Its Modern Interpreters
SBLDS	SBL Dissertation Series
SBLMS	SBL Monograph Series
SBLRBS	SBL Resources for Biblical Study
SBLSBS	SBL Sources for Biblical Study
SBLSCS	SBL Septuagint and Cognate Studies
SBLSP	SBL Seminar Papers
SBLTT	SBL Texts and Translations
SBT	Studies in Biblical Theology
SC	Sources chrétiennes
Schürer	E. Schürer, *The History of the Jewish People in the Age of Jesus Christ* (rev. G. Vermes, et al.)
SCI	*Scripta Classica Israelica*
SEG	*Supplementum epigraphicum Graecum*
SFSJH	South Florida Studies in Jewish History
SibOr	*Sibylline Oracle*
SJLA	Studies in Judaism in Late Antiquity
SNTSMS	Society for New Testament Studies Monograph Series
SPAW	Sitzungberichte der preussischen Akademie der Wissenschaften
SPB	Studia postbiblica
SPHS	Scholars Press, Hommage Series
SPSH	Scholars Press, Studies in the Humanities
SR	*Studies in Religion/Sciences religieuses*
SSAW	Sitzungsbericht der sachischen Akademie der Wissenschaften
STDJ	Studies on the Texts of the Desert of Judah
Suetonius	
Claud.	*Claudius*
Tib.	*Tiberius*
SUNT	Studien zur Umwelt des Neuen Testaments
SVTP	Studia in Veteris Testamenti pseudepigrapha
t. Hag.	Tosefta, *Hagiga*
t. Shab.	Tosefta, *Shabbat*
Tacitus	
Ann.	*Annals*
Hist.	*Histories*
TAPA	*Transactions of the American Philological Association*
TDNT	G. Kittel and G. Friedrich (eds.), *Theological Dictionary of the New Testament*
TLZ	*Theologische Literaturzeitung*
TSAJ	Texte und Studien zum antiken Judentum

ABBREVIATIONS

TSSI	J.C.L. Gibson, *Textbook of Syrian Semitic Inscriptions*
TT	Texts and Translations
TU	Texte und Untersuchungen
TWAT	G. J. Botterweck and H. Ringgren (eds.), *Theologische Wörterbuch zum Alten Testament*
VigChr	*Vigiliae christianae*
VigChrSupp	VigChr, Supplements
VT	*Vetus Testamentum*
VTSup	Vetus Testamentum, Supplements
WBC	Word Bible Commentary
WHJP	*World History of the Jewish People*
WMANT	Wissenschaftliche Monographien zum Alten und Neuen Testament
WUNT	Wissenschaftliche Untersuchungen zum Neuen Testament
y. Ned.	Jerusalem Talmud, *Nedarim*
y. Sanh.	Jerusalem Talmud, *Sanhedrin*
y. Ta'an.	Jerusalem Talmud, *Ta'anit*
YCS	*Yale Classical Studies*
ZA	*Zeitschrift für Assyrologie*
ZAW	*Zeitschrift für die alttestamentliche Wissenschaft*
ZDMG	*Zeitschrift der deutschen morganländischen Gesellschaft*
ZDPV	*Zeitschrift des deutschen Palästina-Vereins*
ZNW	*Zeitschrift für die neutestamentliche Wissenschaft*
ZPE	*Zeitschrift für Papyrologie und Epigraphik*

6

THE ROMAN CONQUEST
AND HEROD THE GREAT
(63 B.C.E.–6 C.E.)

6.1 BIBLIOGRAPHICAL GUIDE

Avi-Yonah, M., ed. *The Herodian Period* (1975).
CAH. Vol. 10, *The Augustan Empire, 44 B.C.–A.D. 70* (1934).
Cary, M., and H. H. Scullard. *A History of Rome* (1975).
Crawford, M. H. *The Roman Republic* (1978).
Kasher, A. *Jews, Idumaeans, and Ancient Arabs* (1988).
Kraft, R. A., and G.W.E. Nickelsburg, eds. *Early Judaism and Its Modern Interpreters* (1986).
Otto, W. "14) Herodes I." PWSup (1913) 2.1–202.
Schalit, A. *König Herodes: Der Mann und sein Werk* (1969).
Schürer: 1.243–335, 353–57.
Scullard, H. H. *From the Gracchi to Nero* (1982).
Stern, M. Review of *King Herod,* by A. Schalit (1960 Heb. ed.). *JJS* 11 (1960) 49–58.
Wells, C. M. *The Roman Empire* (1984).
Will, E. *Histoire politique du monde hellénistique (323–30 av. J.-C.* 2 vols. (1979–82).

The major study of Herod and his reign is the monumental work by Schalit (cf. the detailed review by Stern of Schalit's earlier Hebrew edition). The older study by Otto still has value, however, even if some of his theories have long been rejected. Both attempt to evaluate Herod as fairly as possible, *sine ira et studio,* in contrast to both many older works and more recent ones which parrot the prejudices of the sources and tradition. Avi-Yonah has a number of valuable essays on the whole period, although the material was about a decade old when the English edition appeared. Although Kasher writes specifically on the Arabs, his study impinges considerably on particular episodes of Judean history during this time. For general information on the Jews and Judaism of the period, see Kraft/Nickelsburg.

On the broader background, the most up-to-date general work on

Roman history is Cary/Scullard (the more detailed survey by Scullard is becoming outdated, as there has been little change in the text since 1959, although the bibliographies and notes have been updated). Brief but enlightening are Wells and Crawford. Will also continues his history as far as the earlier part of this period (to 30 B.C.E.). Unfortunately, the new edition of *CAH* is not yet available for this period of Roman history, but the older volume is still useful. See especially the chapter on Herod by Momigliano (*CAH:* 10.316–39).

6.2 SOURCES

6.2.1 Josephus

Laqueur, R. *Der jüdische Historiker Flavius Josephus* (1920).
Momigliano, A. "Josephus as a Source for the History of Judaea." *CAH* (1934) 10.884–87.
Shutt, R.J.H. *Studies in Josephus* (1961).
Stern, M. "The Greek and Roman Literary Sources." *The Jewish People in the First Century* (1974) 1.18–36.

There is strong consensus that Josephus's principal source for the reign of Herod the Great was Nicolaus of Damascus (6.2.2). Josephus quotes him by name occasionally (e.g., *Ant.* 14.1.3 §9; 14.6.4 §104) and once takes him to task for excessive praise of Herod (*Ant.* 16.7.1 §§183–86), which hints at Josephus's dependence on Nicolaus. There are also other indications that Nicolaus was Josephus's source.

1. Josephus's record is detailed for that period for which Nicolaus gave a thorough account, that is, the lives of Antipater and Herod the Great. At precisely the point at which Nicolaus ceased his history of the Jews (shortly after Herod's death), Josephus's record suddenly becomes very skimpy.
2. The account in *War* is often quite favorable to Antipater (father of Herod), as well as to Herod for the early part of his reign. In *Antiquities*, where other sources are also cited and clearly used, greater criticism of Herod comes to the fore.
3. Josephus is generally antagonistic to Antigonus (son of Aristobulus II), who was a rival to Herod.
4. Josephus is hostile to Antipater among the possible successors to Herod, as Nicolaus is said to have been.

5. The attitude and interest Josephus exhibits is sometimes more characteristic of a Greek than of a Jewish writer (e.g., benefactions by
Herod for the Olympic games [*War* 1.21.12 §426]).

Although *War* is definitely the shorter account, the narrative in *Antiquities* is parallel for the earlier part of Herod's life down to his submission
to Augustus in 30 B.C.E. (6.4.7.3). After that, however, there are often
substantial differences between the accounts in arrangement and bulk
and sometimes also in the actual outline of events (e.g., the circumstances of the execution of Mariamme [6.4.9.4]). These differences make
it difficult to determine precisely what Josephus got from Nicolaus and
what comes from other accounts and from his own embellishments. Many
think that the *War* more directly relies on Nicolaus and is therefore closer
to the Damascene's history. Laqueur developed the theory that *War* is
more favorable to Herod and therefore more directly reliant on Nicolaus,
whereas *Antiquities* represents a thoroughgoing anti-Herodian revision.
Laqueur's view has been combatted by Marcus (6.3.3).

Whereas *War* seems to rely on Nicolaus almost entirely, *Antiquities*
makes abundant use of the lost history of Strabo (6.2.4.1). Strabo's history
is quoted several times (e.g., *Ant.* 14.3.1 §§35–36; 14.7.2 §§111–18) but
probably also serves as the source of information that is found in *Antiquities* but not in *War*. Josephus indicates, however, that both Strabo and
Nicolaus were quite similar for the history of much of this period (*Ant.*
13.12.6 §347; 14.6.4 §104), not because one borrowed from the other but
because both used some of the same basic sources (Schürer: 1.26).

In the last century and the earlier part of this century, it was common
to argue that Josephus took much of his material not directly from Nicolaus, Strabo, and so forth but from an intermediary source (cf. the survey
in *Otto: 6–15; Laqueur). This approach is not popular now, for several
reasons: (1) such intermediate sources are usually hypothetical rather
than historically attested; (2) there is no reason why Josephus could not
have used many of his major sources directly; (3) the theory assumes that
contradictions, diversity of opinions, and differences of evaluation must
come from the source, rather than being Josephus's own contributions to
his historical writing; and (4) the lack of consensus among scholars about
these supposed intermediate sources does not inspire confidence in the
attempts to identify them. This is not to say that Josephus was always
directly acquainted with his quoted sources, because he clearly referred
to certain writers known to him only secondhand (e.g., *Ant.* 1.3.9 §108).

Although the account of Herod's reign in *Antiquities* 15–17 is much
longer than that in *War*, this does not appear to be due predominantly to

additional information. Much of the longer work is marked by rhetorical embellishment and dramatic expansion, often referred to as "novelistic elements": descriptions of the thoughts of the characters, additional dialogue and speech, expansion by means of inessential detail that may come from imagination rather than a greater knowledge, and Josephus's personal views. It is possible that Josephus conversed with Hasmonean descendants and thus had more anecdotal information available. Most of the additional bulk, however, does not increase the factual content of the narrative and, consequently, gives the impression of being Josephus's literary invention. The other chief difference is that this section of the *War* tends to be topical, whereas *Antiquities* 15–17 gives a basically chronological narrative. For example, the accounts of Herod's building projects and territories are a unit in *War*, whereas they are split up and presented in chronological fashion in *Antiquities*.

6.2.2   Nicolaus of Damascus

For a general introduction to Nicolaus, see 5.2.5. As he was for the Hasmonean period, Nicolaus is Josephus's principal source for Herod's rule, both in *War* and *Antiquities*. This seems to be universally agreed, but when it comes to a detailed picture of how Josephus used Nicolaus, there is wide diversity of opinions (see 6.2.1).

6.2.3   Psalms of Solomon

Hann, R. R. "The Community of the Pious: The Social Setting of the Psalms of Solomon." *SR* 17 (1988) 169–89.
JLBM: 203–12.
JWSTP: 573–74.
Schürer: 3.192–97.

A group of eighteen psalmic writings have come down to us in Greek and Syriac, although the original language is generally agreed to be Hebrew. The language is often general, covering themes familiar from the canonical Psalms. There are historical allusions, however, which put the general date for the collection as a whole in the period following Pompey's conquest of Jerusalem in 63 B.C.E. The collection refers to Pompey and his fate at the hands of Caesar (Pss Sol 17:7-18). Psalms 17 and 18 have elicited considerable discussion because they talk of an idealized king, like David, who is larger than life but still very much human. These chapters are obviously important for the subject of messianic expectations during this general period (8.3.5).

6.2.4 Greco-Roman Historians

Lesky, A. H. *A History of Greek Literature* (1966).

For a discussion of sources for Roman history, see *CAH*: 10.866–76. Specific references to Jews and Judaism in the Greco-Roman writers are catalogued in *GLAJJ*. For a recent introduction to the Greek and Latin writings of this period, including the histories, see *CHCL*. Useful older works include Lesky and *OCD*.

6.2.4.1 Strabo

For a general introduction to Strabo, see 5.2.13.1. Strabo's extant *Geography* has a lengthy section on Judea, including a bit of its history, in book 16. His most important account was his *History*, however, and this is no longer extant. It was an important source for Josephus, from whom most of the quotations of it come (6.2.1). According to Josephus (*Ant.* 13.12.6 §347; 14.6.4 §104), Strabo and Nicolaus told basically the same story, which suggests that they depended on a common source.

6.2.4.2 Livy

For a general introduction to Livy, see 5.2.13.2. As one of the Augustan historians, Livy (ca. 60 B.C.E. to 12–14 C.E.) wrote a history of Rome from its beginnings to 9 B.C.E. Of the original 142 books, only 35 have survived: books 1 to 10 of the early history and 21 to 45 on the Second Punic War and the Macedonian and Syrian wars. He is often thought to be an important source for Cassius Dio, however, and therefore a secondhand source for the Herodian period. In quality of historical writing many would rank Livy alongside Tacitus but behind Ammianus Marcellinus, Polybius, and Thucydides.

6.2.4.3 Cassius Dio

For a general introduction to Dio, see 5.2.13.4. For the Herodian period, his books 37 to 54 (65–10 B.C.E.) are fully extant, and book 55 (9 B.C.E.–

8 C.E.) is preserved in abbreviated form. Much of Roman history for the Herodian period is covered by the portion of Dio's history that has been preserved in full, a fortunate accident of history.

6.2.4.4 Appian

For a general introduction to Appian, see 5.2.13.3. For background on the period leading up to and during Herod's reign, the most important part of his history is the section on the Roman Civil War (*Bell. Civ.* 13–18).

6.2.4.5 Suetonius

Suetonius (ca. 69 to after 122 C.E.) is chiefly known for his *Lives of the Twelve Caesars* (Julius to Domitian), which often provides valuable information. Unfortunately, many of his data are given typologically rather than chronologically, and he was fond of filling up space with scandalous anecdotes. As a longtime civil servant, he had the opportunity to gather firsthand information on the Roman emperors. Where he quotes actual documents, as in his life of Augustus, he is extremely important. However, none of the later lives shows the same use of original documents, suggesting that he had no access to such information after finishing his life of Augustus. (Suetonius was dismissed from his post by Hadrian in 121/122 C.E.) Although he often serves as an important source, it is not always easy to evaluate his material, and what he says should be carefully compared with other writers, such as Tacitus, where extant.

6.2.5 Archeology, Coins, Epigraphy

Avi-Yonah, M. "Archaeological Sources." *The Jewish People in the First Century* (1974) 1.46–62.
Barag, D., and D. Flusser. "The Ossuary of Jehohanah, Granddaughter of the High Priest Theophilus." *IEJ* 36 (1986) 39–44.
Isaac, B. "A Donation for Herod's Temple in Jerusalem." *IEJ* 33 (1983) 86–92.
Kloner, A. "A Tomb of the Second Temple Period at French Hill, Jerusalem." *IEJ* 30 (1980) 99–108.
Kuhn, H.-W. "Zum Gekreuzigten von Giv'at ha-Mivtar: Korrektur eines Versehens in der Erstveröffentlichung." *ZNW* 69 (1978) 118–22.
Kuhnen, H.-P. *Palästina in griechisch-römischer Zeit* (1990).
Levine, L. I. "Archaeological Discoveries from the Greco-Roman Era." *Recent Archaeology in the Land of Israel* (1981) 75–88.
Meshorer, Y. *Ancient Jewish Coinage.* Vol. 2: *Herod the Great through Bar Cochba* (1982).

————. "Jewish Numismatics." *Early Judaism and Its Modern Interpreters* (1986) 211–20.

Meyers, E. M., and A. T. Kraabel. "Archaeology, Iconography, and Nonliterary Written Remains." *Early Judaism and Its Modern Interpreters* (1986) 175–210.

Naveh, J. "An Aramaic Tomb Inscription Written in Paleo-Hebrew Script." *IEJ* 23 (1973) 82–91.

Rosenthal, E. S. "The Giv'at ha-Mivtar Inscription." *IEJ* 23 (1973) 72–81.

Sokoloff, M. "The Giv'at ha-Mivtar Aramaic Tomb Inscription in Paleo-Hebrew Script and Its Historical Implications." *Immanuel* 10 (1980) 38–46.

Strange, J. F. "Late Hellenistic and Herodian Ossuary Tombs at French Hill, Jerusalem." *BASOR* 219 (1975) 39–67.

Yadin, Y. "Epigraphy and Crucifixion." *IEJ* 23 (1973) 18–22.

Zias, J., and E. Sekeles. "The Crucified Man from Giv'at ha-Mivtar: A Reappraisal." *IEJ* 35 (1985) 22–27.

For general comments on archeology, see 1.1.1. The main effort at synthesis is Kuhnen. This can be supplemented by Avi-Yonah, Levine, and, most recently, articles in *Kraft/Nickelsburg (Meshorer 1986; Meyers/Kraabel), as well as Schürer (1.6–16), which gives an important summary of secondary sources and collections on archeology, numismatics, and inscriptions. A good deal of archeological work has been done on individual building projects by Herod, including much in the city of Jerusalem; for these, see 6.4.9.2.

For a detailed study of Herodian coinage, see Meshorer (1982: 2.5–34; also, briefly, 1986). Bronze coins were issued throughout Herod the Great's reign, although only one series was dated, that with "year 3." These differ from the undated coins in that they have various symbols taken from Roman coins. Meshorer has argued that "year 3" does not refer to the third year of Herod's kingship but to the third year from when he became tetrarch in 42 B.C.E. Therefore, Meshorer dates the coins to 40 B.C.E., when Herod had not yet ousted Antigonus from Jerusalem. In Meshorer's view the good quality of the coins and the Roman symbols were meant by Herod as propaganda devices against Antigonus, who was also issuing his own coins (6.4.7.1); that is, they served as ideological weapons in the struggle of the two men for the control of the Judean people. Once Herod was in control, he no longer used the Roman symbols and left the coins undated; the quality of the coins also deteriorated.

A further question is why Herod did not issue silver coins. Some have used his failure to do so as evidence of his subservience to Rome; however, other client kingdoms of lower standing in Roman eyes (e.g., the Nabateans) issued silver coinage. Meshorer argues that Herod did indeed coin in silver but that these coins were the Tyrian shekels. The Tyrian coins were minted in very pure silver. With the introduction of Roman coins of a lesser quality, the shekels ceased to be issued by Tyre. We find, however, that Tyrian coins continued to be issued to the year 66 C.E., although from 18 B.C.E. they show specific differences from the previous minting, including an inferior style. Meshorer has proposed the following explanation: the Tyrian shekels were the official coinage used in the Jerusalem temple. When Tyre ceased to mint them, Herod obtained permission to continue issuing them internally to meet the needs of the temple. Thus Herod took over the Tyrian model (with slight modifications) in 18 B.C.E., and his successors continued to issue them until the war with Rome broke out in 66 C.E.

Herod's coins, even the early issues with Roman symbols, have no human representations on them. The inscriptions are in Greek only, with the simple designation "(belonging to) Herod the king" (*hērōdou basileōs, hērōdēs basileus*). Archelaus's issues are basically imitations of his father's, although he has adopted certain symbols of his own for some of them. The inscriptions on Archelaus's coins (only in Greek) read "(belonging to) Herod the ethnarch" (*hērōdou ethnarchou, hērōdēs ethnarchēs*). Archelaus carried the name Herod, as is also attested by Cassius Dio (55.27.6).

6.3 HISTORICAL STUDIES

6.3.1 Status after Pompey's Conquest

Braund, D. C. "Gabinius, Caesar, and the *publicani* of Judaea." *Klio* 65 (1983) 241–44.
Jones, A.H.M. *The Cities of the Eastern Roman Provinces* (1971).
Kanael, B. "The Partition of Judea by Gabinius." *IEJ* 6 (1956) 98–106.
Magie, D. *Roman Rule in Asia Minor, to the End of the Third Century after Christ* (1950).
Momigliano, A. "Richerche sull' organizzazione della Giudea sotto il dominio romano (63 a. C.–70 d. C.)." *Annali della Scuola Normale Superiore di Pisa, Classe di Lettere* 3 (1934) 183–221, 347–96.
Sherwin-White, A. N. *Roman Foreign Policy in the East, 168 B.C. to A.D. 1* (1984) 226–34.
Smallwood, E. M. "Gabinius' Organisation of Palestine." *JJS* 18 (1967) 89–92.
Williams, R. S. "The Role of Amicitia in the Career of A. Gabinius (Cos. 58)." *Phoenix* 32 (1978) 195–210.

After his conquest, Pompey reorganized the administration of various areas in what is known as his "settlement of the East" (Magie: 1.268–78). Of the conquered territories, Judea was one of those most affected. Judea was not attached to Syria, as it might have been, but was allowed to maintain a separate identity and its own rule. In addition Hyrcanus retained the office of high priest, which included some civil authority. Nonetheless, the country was reduced essentially to the old boundaries of Judah as they had been in Persian times (Jones: 256–59). The conquered Hellenistic cities were, for the most part, restored to their old constitutions, although for many of them this did not come about in practical terms until later, under Gabinius. The following were taken from Jewish control: Dora, Strato's Tower, Arethusa, Apollonia, Joppa, Jamnia, Azotus, Anthedon, Gaza, Raphia, and Ascalon on the coast; Marisa in Idumea; Samaria; Scythopolis; Abila, Hippos, Gadara, Pella, and Dium in Transjordan. A number of the cities in the interior were grouped with others that had not been under Jewish rule to form the league known as the Decapolis.

Pompey's settlement may have seemed unfortunate from the Jewish point of view at the time, but it was mild compared to the drastic reorganization under Gabinius. The significance of Gabinius's further division is not explained by Josephus (*War* 1.8.5 §170; *Ant.* 14.5.4 §91), but it has usually been interpreted as a way of bringing the potentially rebellious province to heel by a process of divide and conquer (*Schalit: 30–33; *WHJP*: 7.39–43). The continual rebellions led by Aristobulus and his sons clearly had a good deal of popular support. Instead of quietly shouldering the yoke of Roman rule, Judea looked to be a continuing problem. Something had to be done, and the solution was one that had already worked in Macedonia. From the conqueror's point of view it was effective, although the consequences for the conquered could eventually be disastrous, bringing economic ruin by commercial isolation of the various parts of the country.

Gabinius's solution was to divide the country into five administrative councils (*synodoi, synedria*), with centers at Jerusalem, Jericho, Amathus in Transjordan, Sepphoris in Galilee, and "Gadara." The identification of the last-named city is disputed, although Kanael argues that it should logically be a city of Idumea, the name perhaps a corruption of "Adora" (102–4). (This assumes that Idumea was included in the territory left to Judea, which some scholars do not accept.) Josephus does not discuss the makeup of these councils in detail, although he states that the country was once again an "aristocracy" (*Ant.* 11.4.8 §111, probably meaning a theocracy [2.3.1]), which pleased many Jews. Therefore, the membership of the councils was presumably made up of persons (many of priestly origin) willing to cooperate with Roman rule.

Kanael has argued against this explanation. Far from being an attempt to cow the Jews, Gabinius's division of the country was meant to unify them behind Hyrcanus. Gabinius was planning to invade Parthia and needed a united Judea. The fivefold division was a means of providing administrative centers in the face of the growing opposition to Hyrcanus and support for the sons of Aristobulus. One argument in support of Kanael's thesis is that Gabinius's divisions seem to correspond basically to those under Herod's later rule. However, regardless of whose explanation is correct, Gabinius left his arrangements in effect for only a few years, perhaps because they were not succeeding. After another revolt in 55 B.C.E., he more or less turned the administration over to Antipater: "Gabinius then proceeded to Jerusalem, where he reorganized the government in accordance with Antipater's wishes" (*War* 1.8.7 §178; cf. *Ant.* 14.6.4 §103).

Judea continued to pay tribute (6.3.7). It has often been argued (following Momigliano: 187–89) that Gabinius took the process of tax collection out of the hands of the Roman tax farmers (*publicani*) and made it the responsibility of the Jews themselves. It now seems likely, however, that the *publicani* were not removed until later, probably by a decree from Caesar in about 47 B.C.E. (Braund). In any case, Gabinius seems to have shown a degree of restraint in his administration and not to have robbed the province, for Josephus commends him as "having performed great and brilliant deeds during his term as governor" (*Ant.* 14.6.4 §104).

6.3.2 Ancestry of Herod

Schalit, A. "Die frühchristliche Überlieferung über die Herkunft der Familie des Herodes." *ASTI* 1 (1962) 109–60.

Josephus, the main source for the life of Herod, states that Herod's father, Antipater, was an Idumean (*War* 1.6.2 §123; *Ant.* 14.1.3 §8). Therefore, it is commonplace to state that Herod was only partly Jewish or even that he was a foreigner ruling over Judea (cf. *Ant.* 14.15.2 §403). Several points should be made about this.

1. Other traditions give a different ancestry for Herod, such as the Christian tradition that Antipater was from Ascalon (Justin Martyr, *Dial. Trypho* 52; Julius Africanus, as quoted by Eusebius, *Hist. eccl.* 1.7.11). Most scholars who deal with the subject consider the Christian tradition to be unlikely (Schalit 1962; *Schalit: 677), and Julius Africanus's statement that Antipater was a slave in Apollo's temple indeed looks like slander. By contrast, Josephus writes, "Nicolas of Damascus, to be sure, says that his [Antipater's] family belonged to

the leading Jews who came to Judaea from Babylon. But he says this in order to please Antipater's son Herod" (*Ant.* 14.1.3 §9). Josephus's argument that Nicolaus said this only out of a desire to flatter Herod is a double-edged sword, because his own version could arise from a desire to slander the Herodian family. Furthermore, it is difficult to see why Herod would be pleased to be linked with Babylonian Jews if Nicolaus's account were not true. Why should Herod feel ashamed of Idumean ancestry?

2. The Idumean area was one of those forcibly converted by John Hyrcanus (*Ant.* 13.9.1 §§257–58). Exactly why he was able to succeed in this is not stated, but one explanation is that there were already a good many Jews—or at least a strong Jewish influence—in the area (6.3.6). Therefore, Herod's family could have been Jews who simply lived in the Idumean area; the indication is that at the very least they were Jewish converts.

3. Antipater is said to have married an "Arabian" woman named Cypros (*War* 1.8.9 §181), although she is said to have been taken "from among" (*para*) the Idumeans (*Ant.* 14.7.3 §§121). Whether she was Jewish by religion is not stated.

4. *Testament of Moses* 6:2-6, a passage normally interpreted as referring to Herod, accuses him among other things of being a nonpriest. Nothing is said, however, about his being a foreigner or non-Jew.

5. Herod appears to have lived as a Jew (6.4.9.5).

6.3.3 Relationship of Antipater and Hyrcanus

Laqueur, R. *Der jüdische Historiker Flavius Josephus* (1920).

Hyrcanus is often depicted as the tool of Antipater, who was the real head of state. Laqueur argues that Josephus gives two different pictures, in *War* making Hyrcanus simply a titular head but in *Antiquities* showing him to be the one in charge, with Antipater only doing his bidding (because Josephus was more anti-Herodian in the latter work). Laqueur's thesis has been strongly opposed by Marcus, who combats it in regular footnotes in his LCL translation of *Antiquities* 14 (pp. 500–501, 514, 531, 600–601). Nevertheless, although there are passages that do not support Laqueur's thesis (*Ant.* 14.6.3 §101; 14.11.4 §283), there are others in the data that seem to agree with his conclusions (*War* 1.8.7 §175 // *Ant.* 14.6.2 §99; *Ant.* 14.8.1 §127 // *War* 1.9.3 §§187–88; *Ant.* 14.8.1 §§131–32 // *War*

1.9.4 §190; cf. *Ant*. 14.8.5 §144 // *War* 1.10.3 §199). Laqueur therefore may have a point about a difference of approach in the two works, although he probably overpresses the evidence.

Laqueur argues that Hyrcanus was rather different from the description Josephus gave of a retiring individual who preferred a quiet life (*War* 1.5.1 §109; *Ant*. 13.16.1 §407); rather, Laqueur maintains, Hyrcanus was much stronger and more ambitious than assumed (134–36). Schalit also disagrees insofar as Hyrcanus's actions are those of an ambitious individual but evaluates his leadership capacity much as Josephus did (*15–17; *WHJP*: 7.37–38). One can easily agree that Hyrcanus was ambitious, but more difficult is the question of whether he was as ineffectual as presented (*War* 1.5.1 §109; 1.10.4 §203; *Ant*. 13.16.1 §407; 14.9.2 §158) and whether Antipater was the real boss. Are we too much at the mercy of Josephus's own evaluation (which may ultimately come from Nicolaus)? Nevertheless, whatever Hyrcanus's abilities, it seems he was no match for Antipater and especially for Herod. One must also admit, however, that Herod was an exceptional individual.

6.3.4   Administration under Herod

Avi-Yonah, M. *The Holy Land from the Persian to the Arab Conquests* (1966) 86–101.

———. "Historical Geography of Palestine." *The Jewish People in the First Century* (1974) 1.91–113.

Braund, D. *Rome and the Friendly King: The Character of Client Kingship* (1984).

Herod ruled as a client king (or friendly king) of Rome. Client kings were not uncommon during the late republic and early empire, especially as long as the boundaries of the empire continued to expand (Braund). Client kingship was useful to the Romans because the client kingdom served as a buffer to the areas not under Roman control and could be called upon to render military aid when needed. Furthermore, Rome did not have to expend valuable resources in administration and the posting of legions on a permanent basis, because the client kingdom took care of its own administration and defended its borders under normal circumstances.

Herod began his reign with the much-reduced state of Judea, as it was left after Pompey's redistribution of territory. In the early years of Herod's rule Cleopatra gained some of his territory, although she allowed him to lease it back: the coastal cities and the oasis of Jericho (*War* 1.18.5

§§361–62; *Ant.* 15.4.1–2 §§94–96). After the battle of Actium, when he went over to Octavian, he was given Judea, Samaria, and Idumea (areas which he already governed); the land appropriated by Cleopatra; and the Greek cities of Gadara, Hippus, Joppa, Gaza, Anthedon, and Strato's Tower (*War* 1.20.3 §396; *Ant.* 15.7.3 §217). Octavian only retained Ascalon. Later, in 23 B.C.E., Augustus added to Herod's territories Trachonitis, Batanea, and Auranitis (*War* 1.20.4 §398; *Ant.* 15.10.1 §§343–48), and in 20 B.C.E., Gaulanitis, Paneas, and the Ulatha region (*War* 1.20.4 §400; *Ant.* 15.10.3 §360).

Thus, by the end of his reign Herod controlled a state reaching from southern Lebanon to the Negev and from the Mediterranean to Transjordan. It was an area basically as large as that under Alexander Janneus and probably as large as anything Solomon had governed. The population was not homogeneous but composed of Jews, Samaritans, Greeks, Syrians, and Arabs. The administration varied from area to area because of historical as well as pragmatic factors. The various sorts of administration were:

1. Greek cities. Each of these was supervised by a commissioner, or *stratēgos* (cf. *Ant.* 15.7.9 §254). Attached to Gaba, Heshbon, and perhaps Azotus were military colonies (cleruchies), administered much as they had been under Ptolemaic and Seleucid rule (see 4.3.1).
2. Jewish section of the kingdom. The old Hasmonean division into provinces (*meris*), which were subdivided into toparchies, which in turn were further subdivided into villages, was apparently maintained. All administrative officials were appointed directly by the king.
3. Jerusalem held a unique position. A Sanhedrin still existed in name, apparently, but we have no record of decisions made by it once Herod had become king (cf. 7.3.2.3). When the king was not there himself, a *stratēgos* was responsible for affairs of state (*War* 1.33.3 §652; 2.1.3 §8; *Ant.* 17.6.3 §156; 17.9.1–2 §§209–10).

Herod ruled as a typical Hellenistic monarch under Roman domination. He was the quintessential client king who was often in the company of the emperor, the emperor's family, and high Roman officials, whether in his own kingdom, in Rome, or elsewhere. He periodically traveled to Rome and parts of its eastern empire. His children were educated in Rome. In addition to his enormous internal building program, he provided for a number of projects in various parts of the old Greek areas (6.4.9.2).

6.3.5 Chronology of Herod's Reign

Barnes, T. D. "The Date of Herod's Death." *JTS* 19 (1968) 204–9.
Bernegger, P. M. "Affirmation of Herod's Death in 4 B.C." *JTS* 34 (1983) 526–31.
Bickerman, E. J. *Chronology of the Ancient World* (1980).
Bruggen, J. van. "The Year of the Death of Herod the Great." *Miscellanea Neotestamentica* (1978) 1–15.
Edwards, O. "Herodian Chronology." *PEQ* 114 (1982) 29–42.
Filmer, W. E. "The Chronology of the Reign of Herod the Great." *JTS* 17 (1966) 283–98.
Grabbe, L. L. "Maccabean Chronology: 167–164 or 168–165 B.C.E.?" *JBL* 110 (1991) 59–74.
Stern, M. "Chronology." *The Jewish People in the First Century* (1974) 1.62–68.

Precise dates for every aspect of Herod's reign cannot be determined for certain, and it is not always important to do so for general purposes. Several dates, however, are crucial not only to the framework of his reign but also to the correct chronology of the later history of Judah.

6.3.5.1 Appointment as King

There are basic data for dating the time of Herod's appointment as king. First, it occurred during the consulships of Domitius Calvinus (his second) and Asinius Pollio (*Ant.* 14.14.5 §389), which were in 40 B.C.E. Second, Antony and Octavian were in cooperation at the time, but there had been a good deal of friction between them for several years until the pact of Brundisium in September–October 40 B.C.E. Third, according to Appian (*Bell. Civ.* 5.75.319), Herod was made king of the Idumeans and Samaritans in 39 B.C.E.

The third point might seem to contradict the dating of 40 B.C.E. (Filmer: 285). However, the first two points appear to be conclusive for the year 40, even though Josephus has been known to make errors when he dated according to consulships (e.g., *Ant.* 14.1.2 §4). The last point can probably be reconciled with these, because it relates to activities of Antony after he left Rome, whereas Herod's appointment was earlier, while Antony was still in Rome; furthermore, the statement in Appian is about Herod as ruler over Samaria and Idumea, not Judea. This could be interpreted as a reference to territories added to Herod's realm once Antony came to the region (Stern: 1.63–64).

6.3.5.2 Conquest of Jerusalem

The conquest of Jerusalem has traditionally been placed in 37 B.C.E., but there has been considerable discussion about the time of year in which it occurred. Recently, it has been argued that the date should be 36 B.C.E. (Filmer). The basic data we have about the conquest are that it occurred (1) during either the consulships of Marcus Agrippa and Caninius Gallus (*Ant.* 14.16.4 §487), which would put it in 37 B.C.E., or those of Claudius and Norbanus (Cassius Dio 49.23.1), which would make it 38 B.C.E.; (2) in the 185th Olympiad (*Ant.* 14.16.4 §487), which covered 1 July 41 to 30 June 37 B.C.E.; (3) twenty-seven years after the capture of the city under Pompey in 63 B.C.E. (*Ant.* 14.16.4 §487); (4) in the "third month" (*Ant.* 14.16.4 §487; 14.4.3 §66) or the "fifth month" (*War* 1.18.2 §351); (5) on the "Fast Day" (*Ant.* 14.16.4 §487) or the Sabbath day (Cassius Dio 49.22.4; 37.16.4); and (6) during a "sabbatical year" (*Ant.* 14.16.2 §475).

Despite Filmer, the date 37 B.C.E. seems to be firm, not only because the consuls (as given by Josephus) are correct but also because Mark Antony invaded Parthia with a large army in the spring of 36 B.C.E. A large Roman force also aided Herod during his siege, and it is unlikely that such would have been available in 36 (Stern: 1.67). Furthermore, from what is known of the sabbatical year cycle at that time, the sabbatical year mentioned by Josephus would have been from autumn 38 to autumn 37 (Grabbe). Although Josephus's figure of twenty-seven years after Pompey suggests 36 B.C.E., this could be either a miscalculation on his part or perhaps inclusive reckoning (counting both the starting year and ending year in the total). (Cassius Dio's consuls seem to be an error [*GLAJJ* 2.361]; in any case, Dio does not support Filmer.)

More difficult is the time of year. Josephus's Olympic year assignation suggests the siege would have been finished by the end of June; however, a number of Josephus's Olympic year datings are incorrect in this part of *Antiquities*, if he was counting from summer to summer, as is normally done. Nevertheless, there was no consistent reckoning for the start of the Olympic year in antiquity, and some authors counted from the autumn instead of the summer (cf. Bickerman: 76). The start of the siege, however, was definitely in the 185th Olympiad, even if counted from June, which could also be a source of confusion. What does the "third month" mean, and what about the "fifth month" mentioned elsewhere? The "third month" actually seems to be an error: it correctly belongs to Pompey's siege and has probably been accidentally inserted here (Stern: 1.66). The siege would therefore have begun at the end of winter and lasted five months, which would put the conquest of Jerusalem sometime in mid-summer of 37 B.C.E.

Josephus's statement that the fall of Jerusalem was on the "day of the fast" is puzzling. Although this normally refers to the Day of Atonement in his usage, the "fifth month" just noted does not accord with this. It has been widely accepted that here Josephus has mistakenly interpreted his source (probably Strabo). Among pagan writers it was common to refer to the Sabbath as a fast day. That the city fell on a weekly Sabbath is stated by Cassius Dio. If Strabo or another source referred to the Sabbath by the designation "fast day," then it would be perfectly understandable that Josephus misunderstood this as Yom Kippur. Therefore, a Sabbath in midsummer 37 B.C.E. seems to be the correct time of the city's capture.

6.3.5.3 Herod's Death

Although Herod's death has generally been placed just before Passover in 4 B.C.E., this has not been accepted by everyone. Filmer has recently attempted to redate it to 1 B.C.E., whereas both Edwards and Bernegger have recognized some of the difficulties with the figures in Josephus. The data for the time of Herod's death are (1) an eclipse of the moon occurred shortly before his death (*Ant.* 17.6.4 §167); (2) after certain activities relating to attempts to cure his ailment, he died, just before Passover (*War* 2.1.3 §10; *Ant.* 17.9.3 §213); and (3) he had ruled thirty-seven years since being declared king and thirty-four years over Jerusalem (*War* 1.33.8 §665; *Ant.* 17.8.1 §191).

Much of the discussion has centered on Josephus's placing of the eclipse and the Passover that followed Herod's death. Several recent studies, however, have pointed out that the subsequent reigns of Herod's sons were definitely counted from about 4 B.C.E. (Edwards; van Bruggen). Attempts at a solution are made difficult by disputes over how the years were counted. For example, it has usually been assumed that the Jewish year was reckoned as beginning with Nisan, but van Bruggen has argued that a Tishri beginning fits the data better. Because most scholars have accepted the eclipse of 4 B.C.E., the major problem has been to fit all the activities after the eclipse in the time before the Passover, which came one month later. Indeed, the argument that it was not possible to do so made Filmer try for another dating, but van Bruggen seems to have disposed of this problem (6–8). Therefore, the other data combine to confirm the date of Nisan (March-April) 4 B.C.E. for Herod's death. (Edwards's argument for a year or so later is partly based on the interpretation of a coin dated to "year 3," which he assumes to refer to Herod's conquest of Jerusalem; this assumption appears to be erroneous [6.2.5].)

6.3.6 The Idumeans, Arabs, and Nabateans

Bowersock, G. W. *Roman Arabia* (1983).
Kasher, A. "Gaza during the Greco-Roman Era." *Jerusalem Cathedra* 2 (1982) 63–78.

———. *1988.

Meshorer, Y. *Nabataean Coins* (1975).

Negev, A. "The Nabateans and the Provincia Arabia." *ANRW 2* (1977) 8.520–686.

Rappaport, U. "Les Iduméens en Egypte." *Revue de philologie, d'histoire et de littératures anciennes.* 3d series, 43 (1969) 73–82.

Wenning, R. "Das Nabatäerreich: seine archäologischen und historischen Hinterlassenschaften." In H. P. Kuhnen, *Palästina in griechisch-römischer Zeit* (1990) 367–415.

Beyond statements in the Old Testament and some archeological information, we know little about the Idumeans (Edomites) or the various Arab tribes before the Greek period (see 2.3.5.4 for information on them during the Persian period). In the early Greek period we already have evidence of Hellenization in specific areas of Idumea, although it was probably most intensive in cities such as Marisa (4.2.8). It is during the Maccabean period that the Idumeans are frequently mentioned. They made up one of the "surrounding nations" which harrassed the rebel Jewish state under Judas and against which he fought, taking Hebron and Marisa (1 Macc 5:3, 65-68; 5.4.4). We then skip forward to the reign of John Hyrcanus and a strange episode, the conversion of the Idumeans to Judaism:

> Hyrcanus . . . after subduing all the Idumaeans, permitted them to remain in their country so long as they had themselves circumcised and were willing to observe all the laws of the Jews. And so, out of attachment to the land of their fathers, they submitted to circumcision and to making their manner of life conform in all other respects to that of the Jews. And from that time on they have continued to be Jews. (*Ant.* 13.9.1 §§257–58)

This is puzzling, not so much because of what was done by the Hasmoneans—they were trying to clear the borders of expanded Judea from idolatry—but because the effects of the conversion lasted. Forced conversion does not usually represent a change of mind, and, if possible, those compelled carry on their original religion covertly and revert to it openly as soon as they can. This did not happen with the Idumeans. Although we know of the occasional individual who intended to return to the ancestral religion (e.g., Costobarus [*Ant.* 15.7.9 §§253–55]), the Idumeans as a whole supported the Jews in their later wars with the Romans. For example, in the "war of Varus" (ca. 4 B.C.E.) Idumea revolted along with Jerusalem (*War* 2.5.2-3 §§72–79). Attested in even greater detail is the participation of several thousand Idumeans in the defense of Jerusalem during the 66–70 war (7.4.13.3).

Why did the conversion of the Idumeans succeed? Kasher (*46–77) has dealt with the question at length (drawing on the work of a number of predecessors, which is available only in Hebrew). Although there are some problems with his argumentation in places (e.g., he attempts to use late talmudic and even post-talmudic sources to show the Jewish attitude toward conversion in the second century B.C.E.), he covers most of the important issues. His conclusion is that the Idumeans assimilated to Judaism voluntarily, perhaps by agreement between Hyrcanus and the Idumean leadership. Part of this agreement would have been to place an Idumean (the father of Antipater [5.4.11]) as governor of the territory. Not all Idumeans may have accepted willingly the decision made on their behalf by the leadership, and therefore conversion may have been forced on some. Nevertheless, that the Idumeans retained their Judaism is strong evidence that the conversion was more or less voluntary and did not represent a major change for most inhabitants of the area. Not all the following points are from Kasher, but he has further discussion on most of them.

1. The Idumeans normally practiced circumcision, so enforced circumcision would have been irrelevant for most of them (apart from, perhaps, a few Hellenized Idumeans who had forgone the traditional rite).
2. Strabo says nothing about forced conversion but only that the Idumeans "joined the Judaeans, and shared in the same customs with them" (*Geog.* 15.2.34). (See below for a similar statement about the Itureans, which suggests for both cases not a compulsion by force but an agreed adoption.)
3. It may be that some Jews had always lived in Idumea and influenced the Edomites who settled there. It seems that there was considerable Jewish influence—from whatever source—long before the activities of Hyrcanus I.
4. Josephus's source for his statement that Hyrcanus compelled the Idumeans to accept circumcision was likely Nicolaus of Damascus. As a non-Jew and no particular friend of the Hasmoneans, Nicolaus may have interpreted the event—however achieved—in a negative way, as if done under compulsion.

Kasher also argues that Hellenistic urbanization intensified under the Seleucids after Antiochus IV and that the Idumeans felt hostility to this, which would have speeded up the assimilation process. The cogency of this argument is debatable; at least, it needs further support. That the Idumeans, like the Jews and other natives, may have felt treated as inferiors by the citizens of the Hellenistic cities would not be surprising, but whether that would create solidarity is another question. The Jews as a whole do not seem to have been drawn closer to neighboring peoples as a result of Hellenistic urbanization. (Is this another example of blaming problems on that all-purpose scapegoat, Hellenization?)

Under Aristobulus I, the Arabic tribe of the Itureans is likewise said to have been converted to Judaism: "He . . . compelled the inhabitants, if they wished to remain in their country, to be circumcised and live in accordance with the laws of the Jews" (*Ant.* 13.11.3 §318). Josephus, however, also quotes as his source Timagenes, who gives a slightly different version: "This man . . . brought over to them a portion of the Ituraean nation, whom he joined to them by the bond of circumcision." Thus the original source does not suggest compulsion. One must also keep in mind that the Itureans involved were those in Galilee, which had been predominantly in Jewish hands since the Persian period (*Kasher: 80–83). In sum, the conversion of these Itureans (those in Jewish territory, only a part of the tribe) seems to have been similar to that of the Idumeans and not primarily under compulsion.

The Arab tribe known as the Nabateans first appears in historical records at the time of the Diadochi. In about 312 B.C.E. Antigonus attempted without success to subdue them (Diodorus 19.94–100). They were also alleged to engage in piracy during this and perhaps even later times (Diodorus 3.43.5; Strabo 16.4.8). Otherwise, little is known about the Nabateans until the time of Antiochus IV and the wars of the Maccabees. The list of the Nabatean kings is as follows, although some of the dates are no more than approximate. It is also possible that one or two other names should be added to the list, but their existence has only been suspected, because they are not clearly attested in any historical sources.

> Aretas I (ca. 168 B.C.E.)
> (Rabel I? [ca. 150 B.C.E.?])
> Aretas II (ca. late second century B.C.E.)
> Obodas I (ca. 90 B.C.E.)
> Aretas III (ca. 75 B.C.E.)
> Malichus I (ca. 60–30 B.C.E.)
> Obodas II (30–9 B.C.E.)
> Aretas IV (9 B.C.E.–40 C.E.)
> Malichus II (40–70 C.E.)
> Rabel II (70–106 C.E.)
> Roman province of Arabia created (106 C.E.)

The Maccabees had hostilities with a number of Arab tribes or families (e.g., 1 Macc 9:36-42; 2 Macc 12:10-12) but seem to have been on good terms with the Nabateans for the most part (1 Macc 5:25-26; 9:35). The Nabatean king at the time of the Maccabees was Aretas I (2 Macc 5:8). In the late second century, under Aretas II, the Nabateans began to assert themselves as the Seleucid Empire threatened to break up, pushing into Moab and Gilead. They had benefited from profits of the overland trade from southern Arabia (the *Arabia Felix* of the Romans) from an early stage. As the empire broke up, the Nabateans consolidated power, and it became obvious to them (if it had not already been so) that possession of certain territory would have given them greater control and profits. Not surprisingly, this brought them into conflict with the Hasmoneans.

Most of the important references to the Nabateans, Idumeans, and Arabs in their interaction with Judea are mentioned in the "Synthesis" sections of chapters 5 through 7, which should be consulted for details. Alexander Janneus fought with Aretas II over Gaza (Kasher 1982), which would have been important as a center for the caravan trade (*Ant.* 13.13.3 §360). Janneus was subsequently defeated by Obodas I, Aretas's successor, but still managed to control certain towns in Moab (*Ant.* 13.15.4 §397; 14.1.4 §18). Under Aretas III, however, matters improved for the Nabateans. He occupied Damascus for a time, defeated Janneus, included the title "Philhellene" on his coins, and was able to take advantage of the internecine struggles between Hyrcanus II and Aristobulus II (5.4.11). The intervention of Pompey in the region brought Aretas III difficulties, as it did many other small kingdoms. Scaurus, the new governor of Syria, was sent against the Nabateans. In the end, they had to pay a large tribute payment to the Romans to retain their freedom, and Scaurus minted a coin alleging his victory over Aretas. The Nabateans also gave up territories along the Phoenician coast but obtained some of the Iturean area in compensation, the Romans no doubt thus creating a deliberate rivalry between the two Arab groups (*Kasher: 114–15). Malichus I supported the Parthians when they invaded the Syro-Palestinian area (40 B.C.E.) and was punished by the Romans with a payment of tribute. His refusal to pay brought about a war with Herod (6.4.7.3). His death marks the end of the formative period of the Nabatean kingdom.

The so-called Middle Nabatean Period (30 B.C.E.–70 C.E.) saw the northern Nabatean settlements in the Hauran become important. Little is known of the kings during this period, despite the importance of this period for Nabatean history. The reign of Obodas II seems to have been generally prosperous. During his reign, the Romans sent an ill-fated expedition to Arabia under Aelius Gallus. One of the causes of the failure was alleged to be the treachery of Syllaeus (one of Obodas's ministers, who acted as guide to the expedition), although this is disputed by Bowersock (47–48). Syllaeus was also a thorn in the side to Herod (6.4.9.3). It was the next king, Aretas IV, who succeeded in getting rid of Syllaeus, with Herod's help. Some evidence suggests that there was a three-year period not long after Herod's death when Aretas's kingdom was annexed by Rome (Bowersock: 54–57). If so, then the Romans must have decided a client kingdom was preferable to a new province at this time. During Aretas's long reign, there is evidence of the flourishing of Nabatean culture and urbanization of the people (Bowersock: 57–65). Hegra also shows evidence of development, which may have occurred because of concerns that Nabatea proper might have to be abandoned to the Romans. Aretas's daughter was married to Herod Antipas, which created a major conflict when Antipas divorced her (7.4.4). A final point is one of the apostle Paul's statements, which suggests that Aretas was in control of Damascus at about 40 c.e. Although this is not otherwise known, it seems quite possible (Bowersock: 68–69).

We know little of Malichus II except that he sent troops to help Titus against the Jewish rebels in 67 c.e. (*War* 3.4.2 §68). It has been suggested that Malichus's reign and that of Rabel II saw a marked decline in parts of the Nabatean kingdom, especially in the southern region, caused by encroaching nomadic Arab tribes who destroyed or reduced Nabatean settlements in the Negev and in Arabia (Negev: 639–40). However, this interpretation has also been denied with the claim that the prosperity of Aretas's reign continued (Bowersock: 72–74). Nevertheless, there was a shift of the balance of power to the northern parts of the kingdom, as is indicated by the change of capital from Petra to Bostra. We also find that, for whatever reasons, the use of irrigation for agriculture climbed sharply under Aretas IV and Malichus, reaching a peak under Rabel.

The final event for the period of time covered here was the annexation of the Nabatean kingdom as the Roman province of Arabia in 106 c.e. The exact reason for this is uncertain, but it seems to be part of the general policy of expansion under Trajan (9.4.7). Nabatea was about the only client kingdom remaining in the region. The annexation does not seem to have been all that important to the Romans, because the surviving sources make little of it. Nevertheless, Roman military units were sent to protect the southern border, as inscriptions in the region of Hegra and to the south show. Although Petra had the title of "metropolis of Arabia," the actual capital and administrative center seems to have been Bostra.

6.3.7 Socioeconomic and Demographic Factors

Applebaum, S. "Economic Life in Palestine." *The Jewish People in the First Century* (1976) 2.631–700.

———. "Judaea as a Roman Province: The Countryside as a Political and Economic Factor." *ANRW* 2 (1977) 8.355–96.

———. "The Troopers of Zamaris." *Judaea in Hellenistic and Roman Times* (1989) 47–65.

Braund, D. *Rome and the Friendly King: The Character of Client Kingship* (1984).

Broshi, M. "The Role of the Temple in the Herodian Economy." *JJS* 38 (1987) 31–37.

Heichelheim, F. M. "Roman Syria." *An Economic Survey of Ancient Rome* (1938) 4.121–257.

Kippenberg, H. G. *Religion und Klassenbildung im antiken Judäa* (1982) 110–25.

Momigliano, A. "Richerche sull' organizzazione della Giudea sotto il dominio romano (63 a. C.–70 d. C.)." *Annali della Scuola Normale Superiore di Pisa. Classe di Lettere* 3 (1934) 183–221.

The return of Judea to foreign domination was no doubt demoralizing to many Jews, but it paled alongside the practical, socioeconomic consequences. Although the Hasmonean policy of expansion placed burdens of taxation on the people and certain traditional "royal lands" had probably been reappropriated by the later Maccabean rulers, this was more than offset by the land made available in the newly annexed territories (*Schalit: 171–72, 702–3). Fertile farmland in the areas of Transjordan, the coastal plain, and especially Galilee was a real boost to the Jewish population, even though the native populations were not generally ousted. Furthermore, the sphere of commerce had been broadened by the ports now in Jewish possession.

Much of this was lost in the Pompeian settlement. The Greek cities were restored to nominal independence (6.3.1) and whole tracts of land were removed from Judean rule. Although statements on the subject are rare, there are hints that many Jewish small farmers were affected. Those who had been given appropriated lands in the conquered territories under the Hasmoneans were now turned out and had to make their living as landless tenants or day laborers. It has also been suggested that this was a time when the Jewish population had reached a peak (Applebaum 1977: 361–62). If so, then a glut of unemployed workers suddenly dumped on the market would have created enormous hardships for a certain stratum of the population. There is no way of confirming this—or at least quantifying it—so it remains no more than speculative (cf. 1.2.2), but this might have been one of the factors in the popular military support which

Aristobulus and his sons were able to muster in the series of revolts which they instigated after 63 B.C.E. Josephus wrote that just after taking Jerusalem, Pompey "reinstated Hyrcanus as high priest, in return for his enthusiastic support shown during the siege, particularly in detaching from Aristobulus large numbers of the rural population (*to kata tēn chōran plēthos*) who were anxious to join his standard" (*War* 1.7.6 §153).

Roman rule also brought in a war indemnity, as well as various taxes and other expropriations to help finance the Roman military endeavors. The exact rate of tax imposed by Pompey is uncertain but seems to have been to some extent relieved by a decree of Julius Caesar in 48 B.C.E., as quoted by Josephus:

> Gaius Caesar, Imperator for the second time, has ruled that they shall pay a tax for the city of Jerusalem, Joppa excluded, every year except in the seventh year. . . . And that in the second year they shall pay the tribute at Sidon, consisting of one fourth of the produce sown. (*Ant.* 14.10.6 §§202–3)

The problem is to know from Caesar's phraseology precisely what the tax rate was. Heichelheim concluded that it was a tax of 25 percent paid every second year of a sabbatical cycle, that is, 12.5 percent for six years out of seven (235). Schalit, however, argues that the normal tax was 20 percent most years, with no tax in the seventh year but the tax for the year after the sabbatical being 25 percent (*779–81). This illustrates the difficulty in determining firm figures from the data preserved in the literary sources.

This unsettled period also brought other demands for funds at various times, not least because of the Roman Civil War. While governor of Judea, Crassus robbed the temple of 2,000 talents plus all the golden vessels to finance his campaign against Parthia (6.4.3). Some years later, in 43, Cassius placed a special tribute of 700 talents on Judea to raise funds for his fight against Antony (*War* 1.11.2 §220; *Ant.* 14.11.2 §272). Therefore, the quarter century between Pompey and Herod's kingship would have been difficult at the best of times, but it was further complicated by the wars and fighting in the area through this time. Herod's rule was therefore not a totally unwelcome event from an economic point of view. Although he collected his share of taxes, he ended the long period of fighting and brought in an extended time of peace. He also brought back under his own rule most of the areas that had been under Hasmonean control, including the ports and commercial centers.

The real gains came in 30 B.C.E. and later, when the coastal cities, temporarily lost to Cleopatra under Mark Antony's governorship, were restored by Octavian, along with particular Greek cities. In 23 and 20

B.C.E. territories north of Galilee were added to Herod's domain. These were an important boost to the economy because of Herod's policy of developing some of the sparsely populated areas in these territories by bringing in settlers and opening up the land to cultivation. For example, he founded the city of Phasaelis in a wilderness area, which was then reclaimed through irrigation projects (*Ant.* 16.5.2 §145; cf. *Schalit: 324–25). Later, when he acquired the territory of Trachonitis, he again brought in new settlers (*Ant.* 17.2.1–2 §§23–27). The original settlers were from Babylon, but many other Jews joined them (Applebaum 1989).

Books on Herod's rule generally emphasize the crushing burden of taxation placed on the inhabitants of Judea (e.g., Applebaum 1976: 2.664–67; 1977: 8.377). The weight of taxation was not evenly distributed and some felt it much more acutely than others, but there have been other evaluations of the economic situation under Herod, even given his enormous building program (cf. Momigliano: 351–57). First, the income from his territories was about one thousand talents per year (*Ant.* 17.11.4 §§317–20), not necessarily a large sum when compared with the size of the territory and such economically productive elements as ports and trade centers. Agrippa I had an income of equal size or perhaps even larger from a territory slightly smaller than Herod's (*Ant.* 19.8.2 §352), yet he was said to have been popular with the people. Second, Herod did a great deal to increase the economic prosperity of the region. This was especially true in the areas that he opened up to cultivation, as noted above. Third, the building program within the country was itself a stimulus to the economy by providing work for many Jews. (Indeed, when work on the Jerusalem temple ceased in the 60s C.E., it created a problem by making so many people unemployed all at once [*Ant.* 20.9.7 §§219–23].) Fourth, it has been suggested that a large part of Herod's building program was paid out of the revenue from the annual half-shekel contribution from each Jew in the Diaspora, which brought in large sums each year (Broshi). The question is whether such money would be available to Herod for such projects; however, it should be noted that Agrippa II evidently used the temple fund to pave Jerusalem when he alleviated the unemployment caused by the end of work on the temple (*Ant.* 20.9.7 §222). Therefore, Schalit can with good reason argue that the Jews were better off economically at the end of Herod's reign than at the beginning (*322–28).

The opposition to Herod may be due more to social than economic factors. As Kippenberg has noted, the Roman administration began a taxation process that bypassed the traditional aristocracy (113–15). Under the Seleucids, the aristocracy had been responsible for collecting and paying taxes to the administration. During Hasmonean rule, any taxes were still bound tightly to the high priestly aristocracy. Roman control took away this traditional power base by leaving the aristocracy out of the process altogether, and Herod's method of collecting taxes continued the Roman arrangement. In addition, he took away the power of the aristocratic Sanhedrin (cf. 7.3.2.3). Although it probably continued in name, it seems to have had little practical power, because nothing more is heard of it during his reign. Therefore, not only those on whom the heaviest weight of taxation fell but also the (priestly) aristocracy, the class that in previous times had always been a part of the government, were disenchanted with Herodian rule.

One of the vexing questions is whether Herod paid tribute to Rome, that is, whether the Jews had to shoulder a Roman tax in addition to those paid to Herod's own treasury. Well-known scholars have argued that regular tribute to Rome was paid (Momigliano: 348–51; *Schalit: 161–62; Applebaum 1976: 2.661–62; Applebaum 1977: 373), but others have opposed the idea (Schürer: 1.317; *Otto: 55). The recent study by Braund has argued that client kings did not generally pay regular tribute, although some were required to pay a fixed war indemnity and all could be called upon to supply provisions and auxiliaries when needed for the Roman army in their area (63–66). Although he admits that the case of Judea is problematic, he thinks that the argument from silence is important: although there is plenty of material in which such a tribute would logically have been mentioned, no reference is made to one after Herod became king. Further, the "absence of conclusive evidence is made all the more significant by the fact that certain non-royal states—notably the Macedonian and Illyrian republics—are definitely known to have paid tribute to Rome" (66).

6.4 SYNTHESIS

6.4.1 Overview

With Pompey's capture of Jerusalem in 63 B.C.E., it was a cruel blow to many Jews for their country to be returned to its previous borders and to be once again subordinate to another power; yet it was more or less inevitable. Throughout its history Israel had been able to thrive and maintain independence only when the imperial powers that were centered in Mesopotamia, Egypt, and, later, the West were in decline. Solomon's rule—such as it was—flourished because it fell at a time when both

Assyria and Egypt were in a trough. Israel's geographical position was such that it did not have the resources to build and maintain an empire but would always be squeezed between the great powers to the north and south. The independence achieved under the Hasmoneans, although an extraordinary achievement, could only be temporary. Josephus blames Hyrcanus and Aristobulus for Israel's loss of independence because of their internecine warfare (*Ant.* 14.4.5 §77), but if it had not been that, then it would have been something else: it was only a matter of time until the country came under Roman domination. Those with vision would have seen this and made the best of the situation. The Hasmoneans did not have this vision—the family of Antipater did. Hyrcanus prospered as long as he allowed Antipater to take the lead; Aristobulus and his family butted against the Roman wall until it broke them.

The government of Judea was restored to its position as a theocracy, in place of the monarchy which it had become under the Hasmoneans. The country was again under foreign rule, with important social and economic consequences. The next thirty years were primarily shaped by the collapse of the Roman Republic and its civil wars, events in which Judea and its leaders were heavily involved. Although Hyrcanus was the high priest (and later ethnarch) initially, Antipater and his offspring dominated the next seventy years and more of Jewish history. Antipater's son Herod, who possessed outstanding military and political skills, later rose to become the most important member of a remarkable family. The first years of Roman rule saw a series of governors (Scaurus, Gabinius, Crassus) until the defeat of the Pompeian forces by Caesar in 48 B.C.E. At that time Antipater and Hyrcanus were rewarded by Caesar for their support. Cassius was in command of the region after Caesar's assassination until he was defeated and killed by the forces of Antony and Octavian in 42. Mark Antony then took charge of the region and controlled it for more than a decade, until his own defeat by his erstwhile ally Octavian.

Under Antony and Octavian, Herod proved to be an extremely useful ally of the Romans and was declared king after the Parthian takeover of Palestine in 40. Only a few years after he had retaken Jerusalem and established his rule, the battle of Actium in 31 found Herod on the losing side. Nevertheless, he was confirmed in his kingship by Octavian and became close friends with the emperor and his family. Much of positive value can be seen in Herod's rule, when all considerations are taken into account, although the last part of his reign was clouded by sordid events within his family and by his own reactions to them. With his death in 4 B.C.E., Archelaus became the principal successor, although with only the title of ethnarch, but his rule soon came to an end with disgrace and exile. In 6 C.E. Judea once again became a Roman province.

6.4.2 The Roman Republic to Caesar's Assassination (63–44 B.C.E.)

The weaknesses of the Roman republican system of government were already showing up soon after the Third Punic War (5.4.1.2). The widening cracks led finally to collapse not long after Pompey's conquest of the East. While Pompey was fighting in the Greek areas, the political scene in Rome was dominated by such individuals as Caesar, Crassus, and Cicero. A major issue was the bad feeling between the knights (*equites*) and the Senate, which Cicero was trying to mediate. Pompey's return to Rome from the East was followed shortly afterward, in 60 B.C.E., by the formation of what is often called the First Triumvirate of Pompey, Crassus, and Caesar (thought by Cicero and others to be the main cause of the Civil War a decade later).

Caesar was elected consul in 59 and secured command of all of Gaul and Illyricum. After he took up his post, political infighting seemed to presage a major breach between the triumvirs; however, the triumvirate was renewed in a conference at Luca in 55, only to break up in 54 when Crassus was killed in a foolish attack on Parthian territory. Further, the personal bond between Caesar and Pompey was severed when Pompey's wife (Caesar's daughter) died. The stage was then set for confrontation between the two. With his many military successes, it became clear that Caesar's imminent return to Rome could provoke physical conflict with Pompey. Therefore, a motion was passed by the Senate in late 50 that both individuals give up their military commands. When extremists among the conservatives refused to accept this, Pompey was called to come to the rescue of the republic. Not surprisingly, Caesar was not ready to accept Pompey as the dominant politician and tried to negotiate a more satisfactory solution. Finally, the Senate issued an ultimatum to Caesar, who answered by his famous crossing of the Rubicon River, which initiated the Civil War in early 49.

With the Senate behind him and control of Italy and most of the empire, Pompey may have seemed to be in a strong position. Caesar had only one legion and control of Gaul. However, Pompey was hampered by having only two legions in Italy, and they were legions that Caesar had loaned to him initially and thus were of doubtful loyalty. Caesar quickly added further troops to his own when he defeated the governor of Transalpine Gaul. Attempts at negotiation failed, and Pompey retreated to Greece, which left Caesar in control of Italy. Caesar's first task was to take Spain, which he did quickly, although in the meantime the task force he sent to Africa was soundly defeated. Caesar returned to Rome where he was given a dictatorship, which enabled him to enact necessary measures, but he then gave it up after holding it only eleven days.

When Caesar crossed to Greece early in 48, Pompey had assembled a large force of both troops and ships. The first engagements were indecisive, partly because Pompey could be resupplied by ships, whereas Caesar had to find provisions by land. The decisive battle was at Pharsalus. Pompey escaped to Egypt with a small company but as soon as he landed was killed by the men of Ptolemy XII. Caesar followed and spent the winter in Alexandria, where Cleopatra, the sister of Ptolemy and joint ruler of Egypt, became his mistress. At first Ptolemy supported Caesar, but then he turned against him. In the spring of 47 enough troops had joined Caesar to enable him to defeat Ptolemy and replace him with his younger brother Ptolemy XIII, who now reigned jointly with Cleopatra. After a brief campaign in Asia Minor, Caesar returned to Rome in mid-47. (For events in Judah during the fight between Caesar and Pompey, see 6.4.3.)

Caesar, now dictator a second time, still had Pompeian forces in Africa to deal with. The campaign against them was conducted in the winter and spring of 46, followed by one against Pompey's sons in Spain toward the end of the year. Caesar's return to Rome was his final one. After being elected consul (for the fifth time) with Antony in 44, he was appointed dictator for life. A month later he was killed in a conspiracy whose aim was the restoration of the republic, an impossible ideal.

6.4.3 Jews under Roman Administration

Sources: Josephus, *War* 1.8.1–10.4 §§159–202; *Ant.* 14.5.1–9.1 §§80–157.

As soon as Judah was brought under Roman rule in 63, Pompey's subordinate Scaurus invaded the territory of Aretas III, the Nabatean king (6.3.6). Pompey had been planning to inspect the Nabatean situation when he was interrupted by the events in Judea. Antipater's farsightedness was immediately evident, because he took the opportunity to be mediator between Aretas and the Romans. No doubt his previous experience made him the ideal person to do this, but it is also characteristic of him that he benefited so often from such opportunities. With Antipater's help, the Romans quickly concluded the war. Later, when Gabinius was governor, Antipater and Hyrcanus provided him with grain for a campaign into Egypt; in addition, they persuaded the Jews near Pelusium, who were guards over the entrance to Egypt, to join the Romans as allies.

The shortsightedness of the Hasmoneans was soon demonstrated in several attempts by Aristobulus and his son Alexander (and later Alexander's brother Antigonus) to lead revolts and reestablish their rule. The first attempt was by Alexander at the time that Gabinius was appointed governor of Syria (57 B.C.E.). Hyrcanus did not have the strength to withstand Alexander. There was plenty of sympathy for a native ruler, even if the figures are altogether exaggerated, and Alexander is said to have been able to recruit ten thousand heavy infantry and fifteen hundred cavalry. He had several fortifications and was even attempting to rebuild the walls of Jerusalem, which had been thrown down by Pompey, when the Romans intervened. Fighting alongside the Romans were Antipater's own picked troops. After a major defeat in battle, Alexander withdrew to the fortress at Alexandrium, where he was besieged by Gabinius. Eventually, he asked for terms and was granted them, although Gabinius demolished his fortresses.

The next year Aristobulus, with his son Antigonus, escaped from Rome and led a new rebellion. As a former priest-king, he had no trouble in gaining a large following. Indeed, Peitholaus, the "legate" (*hypostratēgos*) of Jerusalem, deserted to him with a thousand men; presumably, Peitholaus was a Jew, although this is nowhere stated. Aristobulus intended to refortify Alexandrium, but Gabinius came against him too quickly. Aristobulus dismissed all those in his following who did not have the proper equipment, but he is still alleged to have had eight thousand armed troops to take a stand against the Romans, indicating the large following collected in this short time. Unfortunately, the outcome was completely predictable and Aristobulus was returned to Rome as a prisoner.

His two sons were released by the Senate, however, because Gabinius had promised this to their mother when negotiating to have the fortresses surrendered. Their release soon proved to be a mistake, because Alexander revolted a second time. Antipater acted as mediator and managed to persuade many Jews to abandon Alexander; nevertheless, he was still left with a large army (said to be thirty thousand, no doubt grossly exaggerated), with which he met the Romans near Mount Tabor, but again it was to no avail.

The next governor of Judea was Crassus, the triumvir, noted by Josephus only for robbing the temple of its gold. Unlike Pompey, who had not touched the temple treasure or precious vessels, Crassus made off with two thousand talents in money as well as the rest of the golden objects in the sanctuary. The purpose of this appropriation was to help pay for Crassus's ill-conceived expedition against Parthia, where he met his death (54 B.C.E.). He was succeeded by his quaestor Cassius, whose main concern was to hold back the Parthians, who were pushing west as a result of their victory over Crassus. Josephus relates two things about Cassius: he took the city of Taricheae in Galilee and enslaved thirty thousand Jews, and he executed Peitholaus at the instigation of Antipater. The

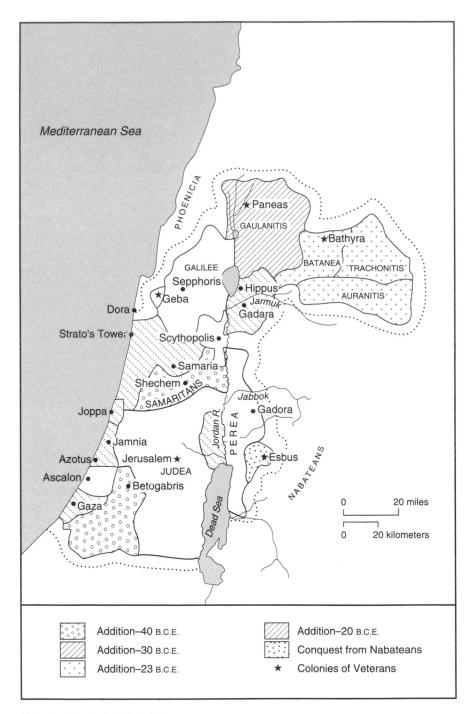

Map 5. Herod's Kingdom

exact reason for the first episode is not given, although one wonders whether it might not be related to the second, because Peitholaus's crime was that he was trying to continue Aristobulus's revolt. Was the taking of Taricheae a part of the suppression of this revolt?

At this point the Roman Civil War began, in 49 B.C.E. Caesar released Aristobulus from prison with the intention of putting him at the head of two legions; the plan was thwarted, however, when Pompey's adherents poisoned Aristobulus before he even left Rome. Likewise, his son Alexander was executed in Antioch at Pompey's orders, but Antigonus and his two sisters were taken under the protection of Ptolemy the Iturean (*Ant.* 14.7.4 §126; *War* 1.9.2 §§185–86). Josephus says nothing about the activities of Antipater and Hyrcanus at this time; perhaps they wisely bided their time to see which way the war went. After Pompey's death in 48, however, Antipater quite decisively took Caesar's side and distinguished himself by aiding in Mithridates' capture of Egypt. This was done diplomatically, by persuading the Jews in Onias's district to support Caesar and allow his army through, as well as by military prowess, in which Antipater showed both outstanding personal bravery and strategic ability in battle.

Caesar rewarded Antipater and Hyrcanus for their usefulness. Hyrcanus was confirmed in the priesthood and Antipater given Roman citizenship. These honors were increased when Antigonus, Aristobulus's son, foolishly accused Antipater and Hyrcanus before Caesar: Hyrcanus was raised to ethnarch of Judah (but seems to have been called "king" by the Jews themselves [*War* 1.10.4 §§202–3; 1.10.9 §214; *Ant.* 14.8.5 §§148, 151; 14.9.1 §157; 14.9.3 §165; 14.9.4 §§168, 172]) and Antipater made "procurator" (*epitropos*) of Judea. Permission was also given to rebuild the walls of Jerusalem, which had been in ruins since Pompey's siege.

6.4.4 Octavian and Antony (44–40 B.C.E.)

After the assassination of Julius Caesar, Antony, as consul, led the opposition to the conspirators. The conspirators had sufficient support to prevent any immediate retribution, but Antony skillfully manipulated public opinion against them by publishing Caesar's will and through his funeral oration. Thus two of the most important conspirators, Brutus and Cassius, were forced to leave Rome, leaving Antony basically in charge. He had been joined by the young Octavian, Caesar's grandnephew, but Antony was bitter because Caesar's will had named Octavian as Caesar's heir, not Antony. This led Cicero and some others to look to Octavian as a possible champion. One of the parties to the conspiracy had been the governor of Cisalpine Gaul, Decimus Brutus. When he refused to relinquish his territory to Antony, the latter besieged him. This gave Cicero the chance to persuade the Senate to send an army against Antony, with Octavian as one of the commanders.

Antony was defeated, but the Senate now made the mistake of snubbing Octavian. When Octavian was refused a consulship, he marched on Rome to take the office by force. In the meantime, Antony was joined by the former consul Lepidus, and the two of them took Cisalpine Gaul from Decimus Brutus. Things now rapidly turned against the republicans. The amnesty against the murderers of Caesar was revoked. Octavian met with Antony and Lepidus in November 43 to form the Second Triumvirate, essentially a dictatorship of the three men. Death sentences were passed on several hundred senators, including Cicero, and a large number of knights. Brutus and Cassius had been awarded command of Asia Minor and Syria respectively before the amnesty was revoked. Cassius had taken advantage of his position to collect tribute in Judea. When they lost their amnesty, he and Brutus joined forces and crossed to Greece, where Octavian and Antony met them at Philippi. Defeated in two separate battles, both Cassius and Brutus committed suicide.

The empire was now essentially divided between Octavian and Antony, although Lepidus was to have Africa if it was thought appropriate later. Nevertheless, there was friction between the two major leaders from the beginning. Antony went to the East to raise funds and organize the region, but when he returned to Italy in 40 he was refused admission, for which he blamed Octavian. Whatever the reason for the misunderstanding, what seemed like imminent war was averted with some difficulty. Instead, in October 40 Octavian and Antony agreed to the Treaty of Brundisium, which gave Italy and the West to Octavian, the East to Antony, and Africa to Lepidus. It was just at this time that the Parthians overran Palestine and put Antigonus on the throne.

6.4.5   Early Career of Herod

Gilboa, A. "The Intervention of Sextus Julius Caesar, Governor of Syria, in the Affair of Herod's Trial." *Scripta Classica Israelica* 5 (1979/80) 185-94.

Sources: Josephus, *War* 1.10.4–14.4 §§203–85; *Ant.* 14.9.2–14.4 §§158–385.

6.4.5.1   Governor of Galilee

When Herod was quite young (probably about twenty-five years old, although only fifteen according to *Ant.* 14.9.2 §158), he was appointed governor (*stratēgos*) of Galilee, while his older brother Phasael was placed over Jerusalem (ca. 48 B.C.E.). Herod's energy and leadership ability were quickly demonstrated by one of his first acts, which was to catch and execute Ezekias (Hezekiah), a bandit leader, along with many of his men. This earned Herod the favor of the Syrians in the area, because Ezekias had been a serious threat to them, and it brought him to the attention of the Syrian governor, Sextus Caesar. In attempting to emulate his younger brother through sound rule, Phasael gained the goodwill of the people of Jerusalem. Because of his own actions and those of his sons, Antipater was respected by the nation and allowed to exercise the authority that in name belonged to Hyrcanus (see 6.3.3).

Not surprisingly, opposition soon developed to the growing power of Antipater's family. Herod was singled out as a special target for attack. Although Hyrcanus's exact attitude at first is unclear, the constant criticism and lobbying by some of the leading Jews eventually goaded him into calling Herod to account before the Sanhedrin. The pretext was his execution of Ezekias without benefit of a trial before the Sanhedrin. Herod's response was a model of sagacity: he complied with the call but came with a bodyguard large enough to show that he was not intimidated but not so large as to imply a threat to Hyrcanus. The precise course of the trial is unclear, because Josephus gives accounts that may be interpreted in three or four ways. What does seem clear is that Sextus Caesar sided with Herod, sending instructions to Hyrcanus for the charges to be dropped, and that Herod decided to consult Sextus in Damascus. The reason for Sextus's intervention is probably that as a Roman citizen, Herod did not have to stand trial before a local court (Gilboa). In any case, Sextus gave greater authority to Herod, making him governor of Coele-Syria and Samaria. Whether Herod was ordered to appear before the Sanhedrin a second time, as Josephus states, is problematic because of Josephus's other statements; however, it does seem that Herod was intent on attacking Jerusalem with an army in revenge for his treatment, only being dissuaded by the wiser counsel of Antipater and Phasael.

6.4.5.2 Death of Antipater

In 46 Bassus, a supporter of Pompey, assassinated Sextus Caesar and took control of the area. When Julius Caesar's forces arrived, Antipater and his sons aided them against Bassus. After Julius's assassination in 44, Cassius came to take over the Roman forces in the area. The war with Bassus continued, except that Murcus now led the fight against him. Cassius ended the struggle between Bassus and Murcus and enlisted the two generals and their forces behind himself. Cassius's next step was to impose tribute on the whole of Syria to raise funds for the coming war, with responsibility for collecting from the different regions apportioned to various individuals. Herod was the first to produce his quota, winning Cassius's favor by this and other acts of friendship. Another Jewish leader, Malichus, gained Cassius's disfavor and would have been executed had not Antipater intervened with a large gift to Cassius.

Malichus rewarded Antipater by plotting against him. The exact reason is unclear: on one occasion (*War* 1.11.3 §223) Josephus implies that it was for Malichus to make way for his own ambition, whereas in his other account (*Ant.* 14.11.3 §277) it is stated that Malichus wanted to secure Hyrcanus's rule. Malichus is said to have used Hyrcanus as a tool on several occasions and could have supported Hyrcanus with the ultimate intent of using him as a puppet (*War* 1.11.7 §232; *Ant.* 14.11.6 §290), in which case Malichus may simply have wanted to do what Antipater had been doing for years. Why he should have been so ungrateful to Antipater is not explained, although one must always be aware that Antipater's solicitude may have been greatly exaggerated in Josephus's source. It could be a straightforward case of Malichus's ambition, as Josephus implies. Such a charge is easy to make and hard to refute because it is plausible, but one wonders whether there is more to the incident than is told.

Whatever the cause of Malichus's opposition to Antipater, he is said to have eventually succeeded in poisoning Antipater. Herod was persuaded by Phasael's argument that they should bide their time about taking revenge. Later, when Malichus tried to keep Herod and his troops out of Jerusalem on one occasion, Herod simply ignored the message which came through Hyrcanus. He then wrote to Cassius for permission to get rid of Malichus, which Cassius was happy to give. When Malichus was in Tyre, Herod got his revenge: he had him executed for planning to return to Jerusalem and raise a revolt against the Romans while Cassius was preoccupied with his war against Antony.

There were also others with plans. The international situation was such that several revolts broke out at the same time. As soon as Cassius left Syria, a Jewish general, Helix, attacked Phasael. Herod was unable to help because of illness, but Phasael managed without his brother. Hyrcanus is said to have sided with Helix and to have turned a number of fortresses over to Malichus's brother; these Herod retook as soon as he recovered. Antigonus, the son of Aristobulus II, had been allowed to return to the area and was aided by Marion, the ruler of Tyre. Herod led the campaign against them with considerable success: he defeated not only Antigonus but also Marion, who had invaded Galilee.

Herod and Hyrcanus do not seem to have been particularly affected by their support of Cassius in the fight against Antony and Octavian. After Cassius's defeat and death, Antony came to take over rulership of the East (42 B.C.E.). An embassy of leading Jews met him and accused Herod and Phasael of governing the country with Hyrcanus as a mere puppet. Antony ruled in favor of the two brothers, not only because of his personal regard for Herod but also, allegedly, because of a large bribe. The opposition did not cease, however, and two more delegations came before Antony with accusations. When the second of the three made their charges, Antony asked Hyrcanus who were the better rulers of the nation, and the latter indicated Herod and Phasael (presumably, the choice was between the two brothers and the "leading Jews" who made up the delegation). The result was that Antony made Herod and his brother tetrarchs while imprisoning a handful of their opponents. The last delegation was much larger, a thousand men, but by this time Antony was losing patience, and he eventually ended up executing a large number of them. It must be recognized, however, that the size of the group and its attitude indicated the beginnings of a revolt.

6.4.5.3 The Parthians Take Palestine

The Parthian invasion of Syria and Palestine in 40 B.C.E. was the opportunity for Herod's opponents. Antigonus once more planned to take over Judah, this time with Parthian aid, and many Jews flocked to his banner. After a brief skirmish near Carmel, Antigonus besieged some opponents in the palace in Jerusalem. Evidently, Phasael was not in Jerusalem at the time, because he and Herod came to intervene in the siege. It was basically a standoff until Pentecost (Feast of Weeks), when many came to Jerusalem for the festival. Quite a few of these seem to have joined Antigonus at this time, although Herod beat off another concerted attack. This time the Parthians intervened in the person of Pacorus, a Parthian general who claimed to be coming to help settle the fight. Phasael received him cordially and even agreed to go with Hyrcanus to the region of Tyre to discuss matters with the Parthian satrap Barzaphranes, against the advice of Herod who remained in Jerusalem.

Herod's suspicions proved right, for Phasael and Hyrcanus were taken prisoner by the Parthians. The plan was to capture Herod as well, but, already wary, he received news of what had happened to Phasael and avoided the trap. Instead, he collected his family and followers and fled Jerusalem in the middle of the night to Idumea, leaving his immediate family with a guard in Masada and scattering the rest around the country. He made his way to Petra with the thought of raising ransom money for his brother from Malichus I, but Malichus refused and ordered him out of his territory. Herod then pushed toward Egypt. It was on the way there that he received word of what had happened: the Parthians had given the throne to Aristobulus, who had mutilated Hyrcanus's ears so that he could no longer be high priest. Phasael had committed suicide.

Herod hurried on to Alexandria and took a ship for Rome, even though it was midwinter and therefore a dangerous time to sail. At Rome he was well received by Antony and Octavian. They determined that the best way to oppose Antigonus and the Parthians was to make Herod king. So it was in late 40 or early 39 that the Senate received Herod and declared him king of Judea.

6.4.6 Octavian and Antony (40–31 B.C.E.)

Once his differences with Antony were temporarily sorted out, Octavian could turn to dealing with the pockets of Pompeian supporters who still resisted the new regime. Pompey's son Sextus Pompeius had built up a power base in Sicily and Sardinia. Octavian asked for help from Antony, but this was not immediately forthcoming, so Octavian turned to his equestrian ally Marcus Agrippa. Nevertheless, the triumvirate was renewed in 37 for another four years. Sextus Pompeius was defeated in 36 by the combined forces of Octavian and Lepidus, but when Lepidus claimed Sicily for himself, Octavian removed him from the office of triumvir. Octavian and Antony had been the principal rivals for some time, but Lepidus's removal made this all the more plain.

Antony's major task was to deal with the Parthians who had overrun Syria in 40. In 39 Antony pushed the Parthians back beyond the Euphrates. By this time he had become involved with Cleopatra, who had done away with her brother Ptolemy XIV to reign as sole ruler. In 37 he sent his wife Octavia (Octavian's sister) back to Italy, although not divorcing her, and openly acknowledged his children by Cleopatra. With her financial support he invaded Parthia in 36 in a disastrous campaign that cost him a third of his force. His successful invasion and capture of Armenia in 34 hardly made up for this loss.

Antony's involvement with Cleopatra was becoming a propaganda weapon for Octavian, who was also strengthening his position by espousing traditional Italian values and customs. When Antony proclaimed Cleopatra's son Caesarion as Caesar's legitimate son and "king of kings," ruling jointly over Egypt with Cleopatra as "queen of kings," it was an additional factor to make Rome question Antony's judgment. When the official triumviral powers lapsed in 33, Octavian laid aside his title, although

Antony did not. In the developing crisis, Octavian largely had the support of Italy and the western provinces. A proclamation was issued removing Antony's powers and declaring war on Cleopatra.

The decisive battle was at Actium in September 31 B.C.E. Although Antony seemed to have a strong fleet, the battle was quickly given up. Antony and Cleopatra sailed back to Alexandria with a few ships, and most of their fleet came into Octavian's hands. Because Octavian had to see to his veterans, it was another year before he pursued Antony to Egypt. At that time Antony, deserted by his troops, committed suicide. Cleopatra was taken prisoner but also committed suicide in captivity. After a century of continual civil war, Rome was finally at peace again.

6.4.7 First Phase of Herod's Reign (40–30 B.C.E.)

Sources: Josephus, *War* 1.15.1–20.3 §§286–393; *Ant.* 14.14.5 §386—15.6.7 §195.

6.4.7.1 Fight for Jerusalem

After being declared king by the Senate, Herod immediately returned to the East and gathered an army to fight Antigonus. In the meantime, his brother Joseph held Masada against the enemy. Ventidius, the Roman general in the area, was supposed to give aid to Herod but did nothing because of alleged bribery by Antigonus; instead, he left his subordinate Silo with a body of troops encamped near Jerusalem. Antigonus was able to suborn Silo as he had Ventidius.

At this point it was well into 39 B.C.E. Galilee as a whole went over to Herod; however, before he could relieve Masada, he had to take Joppa, which had turned against him. After securing Idumea and sending his relatives to Samaria, Herod came against Jerusalem. An attempt was made to thwart the siege by Silo, who claimed that his men did not have enough food, but Herod quickly remedied the situation and, to ensure secure supplies in the future, took Jericho and garrisoned it. Galilee, Idumea, and Samaria were by this time firmly in Herod's hand, and he was able to winter his troops in these districts. Although it is difficult to assess Antigonus's strength, he evidently had areas of support in Palestine, as well as a line of influence to Silo. Herod did not rest even in the winter; he took Sepphoris, which had been in Antigonus's hands, and then used the opportunity to go against certain "brigands" (*lē̦stas*) in the area. Exactly who these were is not stated, although they seem to have

349

had considerable strength and to have required a good deal of force and ingenuity to dislodge. Some of them may have been ordinary bandits, but others were probably groups in opposition to Roman and Herodian rule (cf. *Ant.* 14.15.6 §§432–33; 8.2.12). As soon as Herod left, some Galileans revolted and killed the commander Herod had left in charge. Although the context is not clear, it may have been some of the "bandits" who promoted the revolt.

By this time it was 38, and the Roman commander Machaeras was sent to help Herod; however, he only blundered and at one point even killed many of Herod's supporters. Herod was determined to go to Antony, who was besieging Samosata on the Euphrates, and complain. Machaeras managed to talk him out of the complaint, but Herod made his journey anyway and gave help to Antony. With the siege won, Antony dispatched further troops to Herod's aid. As he was on his way back, however, Herod learned that his brother Joseph had foolishly taken to the field against some of Antigonus's forces and had been massacred. Immediately following this, Galilee and, apparently, Idumea (the reading "Judea" in *Ant.* 14.15.10 §450 seems to be an error) had revolted. Herod had his revenge, retaking Galilee and Jericho and finally killing Antigonus's commander who had brought about Joseph's death. Antigonus himself withdrew to Jerusalem.

The exact length of the siege of Jerusalem and the time of the city's fall are uncertain. There were, in effect, two generals: Herod, at the head of his own army, and Sossius, who had been sent by Antony in command of the Roman force. After beginning the siege, Herod showed his disdain for the enemy by going to Samaria to fetch his betrothed, Mariamme, Hyrcanus's granddaughter, and marry her. With the size of the besieging army (thirty thousand, according to *Ant.* 14.16.1 §468), the outcome was quite predictable; nevertheless, the defenders fought ferociously. When the attackers finally broke through, none of the defenders was spared; indeed, the Jews of Herod's army were as determined to leave no living opponents as the Romans. Antigonus surrendered, however, and was taken prisoner. Herod had two concerns: to keep his non-Jewish troops from violating the temple and to prevent wholesale looting of the city. He managed the latter only by promising generous gifts from his own purse to all the officers and men, a promise that he was quick to fulfill.

The siege had begun sometime in the spring of 37 B.C.E. According to *War* 1.18.2 §351, the city fell only in the fifth month of the siege; according to *Ant.* 14.16.4 §487, in the third. The statement that the city was conquered on the Day of Atonement exactly twenty-seven years after its fall to Pompey seems stylized and rather suspicious; more likely, it was conquered sometime in the summer of 37 (6.3.5.2). Antigonus was executed by Antony in Antioch, thus bringing the Hasmonean kingly rule to an end. That Antigonus can be considered the last of the Hasmonean kings is indicated by his many coins, which give his title in Hebrew as "Mattathias the high priest and the *hever* of the Jews" (*mttyh hkhn hgdl whbr hyhwdym*) but in Greek as "King Anti(gonus)" (*basileōs anti* [cf. 6.2.5]).

6.4.7.2 Troubles with Cleopatra

Up to this point, Josephus's two accounts are very much parallel, with for the most part only slight differences of detail. *War*, however, skims over the next six years to get to the battle of Actium. The *Antiquities* gives a detailed account but one permeated with anti-Herodian statement and innuendo, giving reason to suspect a source different from Nicolaus of Damascus for this section.

Herod had a number of troubles caused by Cleopatra, who not only wanted to take over control of Palestine but also seems to have disliked Herod personally. Fortunately, Antony was well disposed toward Herod, despite his infatuation with Cleopatra; this, along with skillful diplomacy on Herod's part, managed to keep Herod's throne and kingdom for him, even though some territories were taken from him. Cleopatra's designs were not only on Judea but also on Arabia and other territories. She was given an area in Coele-Syria by Antony when she first pressed him for land (*Ant.* 15.3.8 §79). Later, he added territories in Arabia and Jericho, which Herod leased back from her, along with a large section of the coast of Palestine and Phoenicia (*Ant.* 15.4.1–2 §§94–96).

Complicating matters was Herod's domestic situation. Hyrcanus had been released by the Parthians and was invited to return to Judea by Herod. He could not be high priest because of his mutilation, and Herod appointed to the office Ananel, who was from a priestly family in Babylon. This angered Hyrcanus's daughter Alexandra, who thought that her son Aristobulus should have been given the office. She appealed to Cleopatra to use her influence on Antony. Herod decided the best course of action was to accede, and he appointed Aristobulus, who was only seventeen. When a year later Aristobulus was drowned while swimming at the palace in Jericho, Alexandra wrote to Cleopatra accusing Herod of his murder. Cleopatra persuaded Antony to summon Herod to answer the charges, but Herod was cleared by Antony.

6.4.7.3 On the Losing Side

The year 31 B.C.E. marked the final showdown between Antony and Octavian. According to Josephus, Herod was ready to aid Antony in any way possible, but fortunately for the king, Antony did not feel he needed Herod at the battle of Actium. Instead, Antony sent him to fight the Arabs, who were refusing to pay the tribute owed. Josephus says that this was at Cleopatra's instigation because she thought she would gain, whichever one lost (*Ant.* 15.5.1 §110), but even though this scenario is widely accepted (e.g., *Schalit: 122), there is reason to be skeptical (*Kasher: 135–49). It seems very unlikely that Antony would have refused help if it had come. The fight with the Arabs (despite some difficulties) was rather convenient for Herod in light of subsequent events: it made sure that he was otherwise engaged when the time came for the battle between Antony/Cleopatra and Octavian. A politician as astute as Herod could no doubt see what was coming, with the odds very much against Antony's succeeding. He also knew that if Antony was successful, then Cleopatra's full fury might well be unleashed on him. In addition, there are signs that a year or two before Actium he was preparing to take any steps needed to survive in the new order.

The Nabatean king at this time was Malichus I (6.3.6). Initially, Herod was successful; then one of Cleopatra's generals unexpectedly intervened on the side of the Arabs and helped them to defeat the Jews. Herod was able to carry on the fight only by guerrilla tactics for a time. But after a large earthquake did considerable damage in Judah (spring of 31 B.C.E.), the Arabs thought they could conquer the demoralized country. As it happened, the Judean army had not been much injured by the earthquake, so Herod was able to inflict a decisive defeat on the Arabs.

Antony's defeat at Actium in September 31 B.C.E. left Herod on the losing side. The question was what action he should take. Typically, he made a bold stroke: sometime in the spring of 30 B.C.E. he sailed to meet Octavian at Rhodes. Herod appeared before the Roman victor without his crown but otherwise with regal demeanor and candidly stated that he had supported Antony as a faithful ally and would have been at Actium if Antony had not given orders to the contrary. He placed his crown before Caesar but would serve him just as staunchly as he had Antony, if allowed to. There were probably a number of reasons why Octavian was happy to restore Herod's crown and confirm his rule, not least his past record and his administrative ability. Furthermore, it was Octavian's policy to leave Antony's client rulers in power once they had acknowledged his sovereignty. Nevertheless, one suspects that Octavian admired in Herod's action the same courage and sheer guts that he himself possessed. Whatever one might think of Herod in other respects, he was able to lead in a crisis.

6.4.8 Reign of Augustus (31 B.C.E.–14 C.E.)

Millar, F., and E. Segal, eds. *Caesar Augustus* (1984).

The genius of Augustus's reign was that he acted as a constitutional monarch while maintaining the outward trappings of the republic. Further, the machinery of government was so well designed that it was not only passed on in a smooth transition at his death but continued to work and keep the peace at home—for the most part—for another two centuries. He worked with the Senate and was careful to treat it with respect, but he also created it in his own image, weeding out potential opposition by reducing the number of senators and filling vacancies with his supporters. He worked through the offices and powers voted to him by the Senate and even declined honors on occasion. Nevertheless, there was no question in all this that he was the head of government whose source of power was ultimately the legions under his command.

The first desire of the people was for peace, and the veterans wanted their rewards of discharge and land. Therefore, after taking Egypt in 30, Octavian did not attempt to invade Parthia, as many expected he would. Instead, in a welcome respite from fighting, he returned to Rome and began the task of building a stable government. His military career was by no means at an end, and he spent much of the next four decades of rule away from Rome in different areas of the empire. Nevertheless, his greatest achievements were civil, governmental, and domestic, with most of the fighting on the frontiers being conducted by subordinates. He reduced the number of legions from sixty to twenty-eight, a number more or less retained under later rulers.

On his return to Rome in 29, Octavian celebrated his triumph and began a program of public building. The treasury captured from Egypt was very helpful in financing this and thus useful in maintaining his popular support. He closed the temple of Janus, which signified the return of peace. It was now the time for reform of the government, which he began immediately, although the reform effort was to continue and develop throughout the rest of his life.

Things were sufficiently in progress that he was able to make a bold but calculated move in early 27 to renounce all his powers and offices before the Senate. The senators would not hear of it. Finally, after a show of reluctance, he accepted authority over the provinces of Spain, Gaul, and Syria, and also remained consul, a position he had held each year up to then. Accepting administration over these provinces may have seemed rather less than the rule one associates with an emperor; however, most of the legions were stationed in these areas, and their commanders were Octavian's men. Thus, his carefully planned move was such that he could keep the forms of the republic while maintaining his actual power of supreme ruler. Additional bonuses were that he was voted the name

"Augustus," declared *princeps* or first citizen, and the sixth month was named "August" in his honor. This agreement between emperor and people is referred to as the First Settlement.

Shortly after the First Settlement, Augustus left Rome for three years to conduct campaigns and other activities in Gaul and Spain. A conspiracy discovered shortly after his return showed that there were still those ready to challenge or oppose his authority, but he weathered such challenges successfully. He became very ill and, afraid he might not survive, made provision for Agrippa to succeed him. Fortunately, he recovered and had the chance to carry out his plans, but, in another tactical move, he decided to resign his consulship. This made way for others to hold the office and reduced the opportunity for resentment at the permanency of his consulship. As a result, the Senate voted him two new powers. It decreed that (1) his *imperium* would not cease to operate within the city boundary; and (2) he possessed the *maius imperium proconsulare*, which gave him authority even over the governors of senatorial provinces. These powers meant that he could give command to any administrator or military official anywhere in the empire and expect to be obeyed. Further, he was voted a tribunate without some of the restrictions normally inherent in the office. This so-called Second Settlement conferred civil, provincial, and military authority practically without limit, which continued to be the basis of the rule of the emperors who succeeded him. The secret of Augustus's smooth governance lay in the tact and restraint with which he used these almost unlimited powers.

Marcus Agrippa was sent to the East in 23, where he began a friendship with Herod. Despite famine in Rome, which he dealt with without accepting a dictatorship, Augustus himself visited the East for three years (22–19 B.C.E.). Augustus's organization and solidification of government was such that a celebration was made in 17, proclaiming the new age that Augustus had founded. Agrippa was again in the East in 14, not long before his early death, where his friendship with Herod became close. Throughout most of his reign, Herod kept in close touch with Augustus and was able to maintain a good relationship with the emperor, as well as with other members of the family.

6.4.9 The Rest of Herod's Reign (30–4 B.C.E.)

Sources: Josephus, *War* 1.20.3–33.9 §§393–673; *Ant.* 15.6.7 §195—17.8.3 §199.

6.4.9.1 New Territories

Augustus came through Palestine some months after confirming Herod in his kingship and on his way to retaking Egypt (30 B.C.E.). Herod not only entertained him and his troops lavishly but also made available ample provisions for the march across the desert; he was similarly unsparing in expense on Augustus's return from Egypt. As no doubt intended, Augustus concluded that Herod was being generous beyond his means and rewarded him with additional territories. Throughout most of his reign Herod enjoyed the close friendship and confidence of Augustus and was honored with titles and other accoutrements of status, as well as further grants of territory.

The expansion of Herod's kingdom took place over a decade or so (*War* 1.20.3–4 §§396–400; *Ant.* 15.7.3 §217; 15.10.1 §343; 15.10.3 §360). Initially, in 30 B.C.E., Herod received back the territories taken away by Cleopatra, plus land southeast of the Sea of Galilee (Gadara, Hippo) and some coastal cities (Gaza, Anthedon, Strato's Tower [Caesarea]). (He is also said to have received Samaria and Joppa at this time, but the former had probably already been restored by Antony [Appian, *Bell. Civ.* 5.75.319] and the latter by Julius Caesar [*Ant.* 14.10.6 §202].) Some years later (ca. 23 B.C.E.) he was awarded territories northeast of the Sea of Galilee (Trachonitis, Batanea, Auranitis) and, finally (ca. 20 B.C.E.), land north of the Sea of Galilee, connecting Galilee with Trachonitis (including modern Huleh and Paneas [Caesarea-Philippi]). These gifts do not just represent Roman greatness of heart toward Herod. Judea was a frontier kingdom, and it was known that Herod would take great care for its security, thus also keeping a vital link in the Roman boundary safe from barbaric encroachment (see 6.4.9.2).

6.4.9.2 Magnificent Buildings

Applebaum, S. "The Beginnings of the Limes Palaestinae." *Judaea in Hellenistic and Roman Times* (1989) 132–42.

Ben-Dor, M. "Herod's Mighty Temple Mount." *BAR* 12, no. 6 (Nov./Dec. 1986) 40–49.

Geva, H. "The 'Tower of David'—Phasael or Hippicus?" *IEJ* 31 (1981) 57–65.

Gichon, M. "Idumea and the Herodian Limes." *IEJ* 17 (1967) 27–42.

Goldschmidt-Lehmann, R. P. "The Second (Herodian) Temple: Selected Bibliography." *Jerusalem Cathedra* 1 (1981) 336–59.

Levine, L. I. *Roman Caesarea* (1975).

Mazar, B. "Herodian Jerusalem in the Light of the Excavations South and South-West of the Temple Mount." *IEJ* 28 (1978) 230–37.

Netzer, E. "The Hasmonean and Herodian Winter Palaces at Jericho." *IEJ* 25 (1975) 89–100.

————. "The Winter Palaces of the Judean Kings at Jericho at the End of the Second Temple Period." *BASOR* 228 (1977) 1–13.

————. *Greater Herodium* (1981).

Netzer, E., et al. "Symposium: Herod's Building Projects." *Jerusalem Cathedra* 1 (1981) 48–80.

Raban, A., ed. *The Harbours of Caesarea Maritima*. Vol. 1: *The Site and the Excavations* (1989).

Richardson, P. "Religion and Architecture: A Study in Herod's Piety, Power, Pomp and Pleasure." *Bulletin of the Canadian Society of Biblical Studies* 45 (1985) 3–29.

————. "Law and Piety in Herod's Architecture." *SR* 15 (1986) 347–60.

Tsafrir, Y. "The Desert Fortresses of Judaea in the Second Temple Period." *Jerusalem Cathedra* 2 (1982) 120–45.

Wilkinson, J. "The Streets of Jerusalem." *Levant* 7 (1975) 118–36.

Yadin, Y., ed. *Jerusalem Revealed* (1975).

One of the major achievements of Herod's rule was his building program, which was spectacular even by Roman standards. It had two aspects, the civic/personal and the military/defensive, although some works had elements of both connected with them. Dating these buildings is not easy, partly because Josephus lists them all together in the *War*, without any chronological framework. A rough chronology is given in *Antiquities*, but the precise dates are not always clear even in this work. A further problem is that sometimes more than one date is given for the same project. Herod's first project (although the *War* states that it occurred only in the 192d Olympiad, ca. 10–9 b.c.e.) was the inauguration of tetrennial games in honor of Augustus, for which he built a theater and a large amphitheater in Jerusalem (*Ant.* 15.8.1–2 §§267–79; *War* 1.21.8 §415). There was also a hippodrome (*Ant.* 17.10.2 §255). The decoration of the theater caused a disturbance among certain Jews who thought the decorations included human images; Herod was able to defuse the tension by letting the individuals concerned see for themselves that this was not so.

The fortifications of the realm were naturally important. Herod's palace in the upper city of Jerusalem was comprised of two buildings, called Caesareum and Agrippeum after Augustus and Agrippa (*War* 1.21.1 §402; *Ant.* 15.9.3 §318), and one of the protective towers was called Phasael after Herod's brother, who had been killed by the Parthians (*War* 1.21.9 §418; *Ant.* 16.5.2 §144). To protect the temple he built a fortress, called Antonia, after Mark Antony (*War* 1.21.1 §401; *Ant.* 15.8.5 §292). South of Jerusalem he created the fortress of Herodium (named for himself) by artificially raising a hill to an even greater height (*War* 1.21.10 §§419–21; *Ant.* 15.9.4 §§323–25). Near Jericho he constructed a fortress, named Cypros after his mother (*War* 1.21.9 §417; *Ant.* 16.5.2 §143). These all formed part of a fortification system on the border with Arabia that prefigured the *limes Palaestina* (Roman frontier defense system) of later centuries (*Kasher: 152–56; Applebaum; Gichon; cf. Tsafrir). Included in this system were the preexisting fortresses of Masada, Macherus, and Alexandrium, which Herod also strengthened and improved (*War* 7.8.3–4 §§280–303; 7.6.2 §§171–77; *Ant.* 16.2.1 §13). Exactly why this was thought necessary, since the Nabateans were nominally Roman allies, is uncertain.

Next, probably in about 27–25 B.C.E., Herod rebuilt Samaria, renaming it Sebaste, the Greek equivalent of "Augustus" (*War* 1.21.2 §403; *Ant.* 15.8.5 §§292–93, 296–98). On the coast the old city of Strato's Tower was rebuilt with a magnificent artificial harbor and called Caesarea, again after Augustus (*War* 1.21.5–7 §§408–14; *Ant.* 15.8.5 §293; 15.9.6 §§331–41). The work on Caesarea finished in Herod's twenty-eighth year (ca. 10–9 B.C.E.), although it is said to have taken ten years (*Ant.* 16.5.1 §136) or twelve years (*Ant.* 15.9.6 §341). It was later to be the seat of the Roman government of Palestine. In addition to these works, which also served as a part of the system of fortifications, Herod built a number of other sites, which he named after Roman friends or family members. The village of Anthedon, which had been destroyed in warfare, was rebuilt under the name Agrippium (*War* 1.21.8 §416) or Agrippias (*Ant.* 13.13.3 §357). North of Jericho, probably in the last years of his reign, he built a city named Phasaelis after his brother (*War* 1.21.9 §418; *Ant.* 16.5.2 §145). In the Plain of Sharon, north of Joppa, a new town was founded with the name Antipatris after his father, Antipater (*War* 1.21.9 §417; *Ant.* 16.5.2 §§142–43).

One of the most important projects, and the one that would have done the most to endear Herod to the Jewish people, was the restoration and rebuilding of the temple at Jerusalem (*War* 1.21.1 §401; *Ant.* 15.11.1–7 §§380–425). In *War* the rebuilding is dated to his fifteenth year but in *Antiquities*, to his eighteenth. The care with which this project was carried out and the enormous cost involved (apparently paid for by Herod himself) suggest that its alleged fame throughout the Roman Empire was not exaggerated. The work of building could be done only by priests and had to be carried out in such a way as to maintain the dignity of the house and not disrupt the regular cultic services.

6.4.9.3 Conflicts with the Arabs

Marcus Agrippa was sent to Asia Minor in 14 B.C.E. to place a king friendly to the Romans on the throne of Cappadocia. Herod persuaded him to visit Jerusalem and gave him a magnificent welcome in the autumn of that year. The next spring Herod sailed to Pontus to join him, and they made a lengthy return journey by land together. The Jews of Ionia appealed to Herod for help with regard to certain local infringements on their practice of religion. He made representation to Agrippa about the matter and gained a hearing for the Jews' petition. The result was that Agrippa confirmed their traditional religious rights. In honor of his friendship with Agrippa and the accomplishments of the visit, Herod remitted one-fourth of the taxes for one year. Unfortunately, Agrippa died only a year later in 12 B.C.E.

The next major event was a conflict with the Arabs, which occurred near the end of Herod's reign in 10–9 B.C.E. (*Ant*. 16.9.1–4 §§271–99; 16.10.8–9 §§335–55; only the last part is in *War* 1.29.3 §§574–77). A group of men from Trachonitis had traditionally supplemented their living by brigandage. When Herod took over rule, he put a stop to this, so that they had to earn their living only by farming. This caused problems because the soil was poor and also because it probably went against their traditional way of life. While Herod was in Rome, a revolt developed, which was quickly put down, but about forty of the leaders fled to Arabia. Although the Arab king was Obodas II, the real power behind the throne was Syllaeus (*Ant*. 16.7.6 §220), who gave refuge to the brigands and allowed them to raid Judea and Coele-Syria from a secure base in Arabian territory. To add insult to injury, Syllaeus reneged on repayment of a loan from Herod to Obodas. Part of the problem may have been personal, because Syllaeus had once been betrothed to Herod's sister Salome, but the marriage had been prevented by Herod's insistence that Syllaeus convert to Judaism (*Ant*. 16.7.6 §224–25; 17.1.1 §10).

Herod was unable to stop the raiders by normal methods and finally lost patience. He consulted with the Roman governors of Syria, Saturninus and Volumnius. They supported him and agreed that he would be justified in taking his army into Arabia, a serious offense for one Roman client king against another. Herod was wholly successful, destroying the brigand stronghold and capturing the defenders, although he was attacked by an Arab force and killed its commander in defending himself. On the diplomatic front, however, he was outwitted by Syllaeus, who had set off for Rome before Herod's military actions. Putting his case before Augustus, Syllaeus was able to convince him against Herod to the extent that the emperor would not even receive a delegation from Herod to give his side of the event. This was serious for Herod, who had enjoyed Augustus's support and friendship up to this point.

Herod could do nothing but endure the raids and the general humiliation for a period of time. Then Obodas died and Aretas IV took the throne. This action irritated Augustus, whose permission should normally have been sought for the succession; furthermore, it meant that the

Arabian camp was now divided. Herod tried once more to present his case by sending his assistant Nicolaus of Damascus to Augustus. This time the emperor heard Herod's case and was persuaded by Nicolaus, who not only was an effective orator but also had the support of Aretas's faction in his charges against Syllaeus. Augustus had Syllaeus executed and became reconciled with Herod; apparently, he was even of a mind to add Arabia to Herod's domain but decided against it because of Herod's family troubles. So he confirmed Aretas on the throne, although rebuking him for his boldness in taking the kingship without first receiving Roman confirmation. (We have Nicolaus's own account of this episode preserved in a fragment of his *Life*; see *GLAJJ*: 1.250–60.)

6.4.9.4 Family Quarrels

Ladouceur, D. J. "The Death of Herod the Great." *Classical Philology* 76 (1981) 25–34.

Most of the rest of Josephus's narrative about Herod (in both *War* and *Antiquities*) is taken up with the rather unedifying spectacle of family jealousies, hates, intrigues, and executions. The problem for the historian is how to evaluate this information. It is the stuff not of history but of soap opera. This does not mean that many of the events described did not actually take place or even did not occur as recounted. But woven into the narrative is continual moral evaluation, assigning of motives, descriptions of states of mind, and general pseudopsychoanalysis. To take this at face value— as many writers unfortunately have done—is to treat the stuff of romance as if it were straightforward history. Most of the data can be summarized fairly briefly and lose nothing by conciseness. In some cases there is good reason to question the accounts because Josephus contradicts himself, but even where he does not, one can point out what is said without necessarily supposing that it represents a high degree of accuracy.

The first episode in this business was the execution of his wife Mariamme, the daughter of Hyrcanus. Two separate scenarios are given, dated several years apart, so that determining which (if either) is correct is not easy. According to *War* 1.22.2–4 §§436–44, the other women of the household began intriguing against Mariamme, accusing her of adultery. Then when Herod was away in 29 B.C.E., he entrusted her to his brother-in-law Joseph, leaving instructions that Joseph was to slay her if Herod died, because he could not bear the thought of her marrying another man. But Joseph told her of these instructions, and on Herod's return Mariamme confronted him with this information. He assumed that she could have gained access to it only if she had been intimate with Joseph. Therefore, he had them both executed. A similar episode is found in *Ant.* 15.3.5–9 §§62–87, except that it is dated to Herod's trial before Antony (ca. 34 B.C.E.) and in it only Joseph was executed, not Mariamme. A little later (*Ant.* 15.6.5 §§183–86; 15.7.1–4 §§202–34), however, another, similar incident is narrated, but the culpable man is Herod's Iturean servant Soemus. The time is about 29 B.C.E., and both Mariamme and Soemus are executed. Because of the great similarity, it seems likely that Josephus had two versions of the same event and included both in the *Antiquities*. One might draw some significance from the fact that the time of Mariamme's execution is the same in both accounts, even though the co-accused is different; however, Josephus does not seem reliable on chronological matters when he departs from the framework of Nicolaus of Damascus, which he seems to do more in *Antiquities* than in *War*.

Intrigues among Herod's relatives also eventually led to the execution of Alexander and Aristobulus, Mariamme's two sons by Herod (*War* 1.23.1–27.6 §§445–551). They received their education in Rome and were likely heirs to Herod's kingdom, but having returned to Judah (ca. 18 B.C.E.), they seem to have been very resentful about the treatment of their mother. The accounts in Josephus generally portray them simply as rather bitter young men who spoke up when it would have been wiser to keep silent, rather than as guilty of actual plots against Herod's life. A further complication was the question of their half-brother Antipater, son of Herod's first wife, Doris. Their indiscretions resulted in Herod's recalling Antipater from the exile to which he and his mother had been sent and showing him various favors. Once Antipater was present in court, rivalry was inevitable between the potential heirs, especially because Antipater was the firstborn, even though he was not considered the heir after Herod married Mariamme. According to Josephus, who is probably following Nicolaus's bias here, Antipater was the principal instigator of charges, rumors, and lies against the sons of Mariamme.

Events first came to a head in about 12 B.C.E., when Herod finally took Alexander (according to *War*; *Antiquities* also includes Aristobulus) to be accused before Augustus in Rome. The outcome of this was a reconciliation of Herod and his son(s), even to the extent of their being declared joint heirs with Antipater when Herod returned to Jerusalem. The reports of plottings against Herod did not cease, and, to make matters worse, the actions of Alexander's wife also aroused the resentment of Herod's sister Salome. At one point, three of Herod's personal servants who were eunuchs admitted to sexual relations with Alexander and reported his intimate talk, which suggested that he would be ruling instead of Herod before long. After further inquiries, Herod had Alexander imprisoned.

This time Alexander's father-in-law, Archelaus, king of Cappadocia, managed to reconcile him with Herod. Finally, after several more years filled with suspicion, charges, and reports, Herod imprisoned Alexander and Aristobulus and wrote to Augustus for permission to punish them. This was allowed, although only after a trial before the Roman governor of Syria and the leading rulers and aristocrats of the area. Herod was granted a condemnation and had his two sons executed in about 6 B.C.E.

Antipater is alleged by Josephus, probably following Nicolaus, to be the chief plotter not only against Mariamme's two sons but also against Herod. Because of Nicolaus's anti-Antipater bias, it is difficult to know whether to give credence to this charge, even though it is not by any means implausible. In any event, the family intrigues were supposed to have continued even after the executions. Some Pharisees also became involved and were executed by Herod when he found them out (*Ant.* 17.2.4 §§41–44). Herod fell out with his brother Pheroras and exiled him to his tetrarchy. Not long afterward, when Pheroras died, his freedmen reported to Herod their suspicions that he had been poisoned. Investigation by Herod supposedly found evidence of this, pointing ultimately at Antipater, who happened to be in Rome. Confirmation came in Antipater's alleged accusations against Herod's sons Archelaus and Philip. Herod recalled Antipater from Rome and imprisoned him. After Antipater's trial, in which he was found guilty, messengers were sent to Augustus to obtain permission to carry out punishment.

By this time it was late 5 or early 4 B.C.E. Herod became seriously ill, and his health steadily worsened. From Josephus's sequence of events, it appears that the illness lasted only a few months, although the precise progress of the disease is unclear. The description of it is horrendous, but part or even much of this could be a literary concoction; one should be careful in taking the description at face value to the point of trying to determine the precise affliction, as has sometimes been done (cf. Ladouceur). Herod's attempts to find a cure or even relief from the pain were unsuccessful.

On one occasion, rumor had it that Herod was dead. Two religious teachers, Matthias and Judas, put their disciples up to removing the golden image of an eagle that Herod had placed over the temple gate. The two men and many of their followers were executed. Although it is often alleged that Matthias and Judas were Pharisees, Josephus nowhere states this but only describes them as learned in the law, hardly an exclusive preserve of the Pharisees. An eclipse of the moon followed their execution, probably the one of March 4 B.C.E. Shortly after this, Augustus's letter arrived, which allowed Antipater's execution. Only a few days after the execution was carried out, Herod died of his illness; he was near the age of seventy. The time was shortly before Passover, that is, late March or early April, in 4 B.C.E. (see 6.3.5.3).

6.4.9.5 Assessment of Herod's Reign

Davies, W. D., and D. C. Allison. *The Gospel according to Saint Matthew* (1988).
Feldman, L. H. *Josephus and Modern Scholarship (1937–1980)* (1984).
France, R. T. "Herod and the Children of Bethlehem." *NovT* 21 (1979) 98–120.
Richardson, P. "Law and Piety in Herod's Architecture." *SR* 15 (1986) 347–60.
Schalit, A. "A Clash of Ideologies: Palestine under the Seleucids and Romans." *The Crucible of Christianity* (1969) 47–76.

Herod has been such a notorious and controversial figure that any evaluation of him is very difficult. One must consider against what standard his reign is to be assessed: Other Greco-Roman despots? The Hasmonean rulers? Some golden ideal of kingship? Ancient views of Herod were generally negative and have gone a long way to shape the modern ones. Perhaps one of the labels that has had the most influence in later Christian history is "slaughterer of the innocents."

According to Matt 2:16-18, Herod asked the magi to tell him the location of the baby born king of the Jews. When they would not, he is alleged to have slain all males in Bethlehem who were two years old and younger. Some histories and commentaries still take this at face value, but it is a piece of legend, probably Christian, although whether it was meant consciously to be anti-Herodian or only to demonstrate opposition to the Christ child seems uncertain. The legendary nature of the story is indicated by (1) the whole context of men from the East, following a star; (2) the idea that Herod would have taken their mission to find a newborn "king of the Jews" seriously; (3) the fact that Josephus, who has many distinctly anti-Herodian passages and even outright slander, says nothing about such an occurrence (e.g., the criticisms of Herod by a Jewish delegation before Augustus do not use such an example, even though it would have been an unparalleled example of cruelty and despotic rule; see *War* 2.6.2 §§84–86; *Ant.* 17.11.2 §§304–10); (4) the fact that no other writer mentions what would surely be a point of interest to any Roman reader about this Jewish king; and (5) the common motifs found in a variety of accounts of the birth of important religious figures. It has been argued that the origin of many of the motifs of this section of Matthew lie in the Moses haggadic traditions (Davies/Allison: 192–94, 264–66; contra France).

Modern scholarship has presented a mixed picture of Herod. To its credit, there are those who have attempted to present a positive side of the man, but probably the majority of accounts take much of Josephus's assessment at face value (cf. the summary in Feldman: 278–87). Such views can be summed up by the title of Sandmel's book, *Herod: Profile of a Tyrant* (1967). The autocratic and even tyrannical aspect of Herod's rule can be taken for granted, but such is the nature of one-ruler states throughout history. The question is to what extent his rule should be characterized by the negative aspects and to what extent these are countered by other, more positive features. Schalit attempts a revision of the negative view (*1969; cf. Shalit 1969). It would hardly be classified as a whitewash, but it does go a long way toward pointing out the positive features of Herod's rule that not only helped the Jews in many ways during his lifetime but paved the way for his descendants (such as Agrippa I and Agrippa II) to act as advocates for the Jewish people on a number of occasions.

One thing to keep in mind in any discussion is that the bulk of the accounts which have come down to us are either hostile or neutral; favorable portraits of Herod, such as that by Nicolaus of Damascus, have not survived intact. Jewish legend and tradition have been much along the lines of Josephus's rather biased picture. In a tragic stereotype which probably owes much to Nicolaus, Josephus presents Herod as a man who had extraordinary good fortune in his rise to the throne and in his rule; countering this, as if a divine law, were the misfortunes that arose from his own family. There is undoubtedly truth in this binary opposition, but one must keep in mind that Josephus and, probably, Nicolaus used a literary device which may have forced conformity of some of the data to the scheme. Herod's problems within his own family occasioned the anecdote that ascribes to Augustus the statement "I would rather be Herod's pig [Greek, *hys*] than his son [Greek, *huios*]" (Macrobius, *Saturnalia* 2.4.11). The ascription does not have to be correct to illustrate the tradition about Herod preserved in the non-Jewish world. But even if Augustus said such a thing, it could hardly have escaped his notice that he experienced similar troubles within his own family during his long reign. Therefore, Herod was not the only capable ruler whose competence changed remarkably as he passed from the throne room into the living quarters.

As a Hellenistic monarch and a client king under Rome, Herod was probably exceptional in his accomplishments and his generosity toward the general Hellenistic culture. His exercise of power was not particularly arbitrary by the standards of the time, and his exactions from his own people were no more burdensome than those in other kingdoms. Furthermore, he respected the religious sentiment in the Jewish areas of his territory. When confronted by the delegation that accused him of putting pagan images in the Jerusalem theater, he showed them that they had simply misunderstood. His coinage was aniconic. He rebuilt the Jerusalem temple, turning it into one of the outstanding edifices of the Roman world. The only significant religious violation that some could point to was the installment of a golden eagle over the temple entrance.

Indeed, the point must be made that, by all indications, Herod considered himself a Jew. It is common to label him a "foreigner" because sources such as Josephus identify him as an Idumean: "a half-Jew" (*Ant.* 14.15.2 §403). But apart from the question of descent, which is not an easy one (6.3.2), he regarded himself—and was regarded by the Romans, if the anecdotes are true—as a Jew. Notice the following considerations:

1. His respect for Jewish customs. There are no examples of his blatant disregard for them. Even in the midst of a tirade about the introduction of "foreign" and "unlawful" customs by Herod, Josephus has to admit that this did not really involve a breach of Jewish law, as Herod himself demonstrated to his critics (*Ant.* 15.8.1–2 §§267–79).
2. His coins with no human images on them (6.2.5).
3. His requirement that a Nabatean convert to Judaism before being allowed to marry Herod's sister Salome (*Ant.* 16.7.6 §§221–25).
4. The amount of money and interest he put into the Jerusalem temple.
5. His fortress at Herodium, considered by many to have contained a synagogue (although this is not accepted by everyone; see 8.3.3). Even his most private quarters at Masada used no offensive motifs in the skillful decorations (cf. Richardson).

No one of these points by itself is decisive; each one individually could be explained differently, but they have a cumulative effect. Unfortunately, the tendency is to judge Herod by an artificial standard because of prejudice against him. For example, no one seems to question the Jewish identity of Agrippa I, yet all his coins outside Judea have human portraits on them, whereas his grandfather Herod did not use human images on any of his coins. Why should the one incident be ignored to Agrippa's benefit, whereas the positive association with Herod is dismissed as mere politics? It has sometimes been alleged that Herod would not have been considered Jewish because his mother was not Jewish; however, this seems anachronistic, because the matrilineal descent of Jewishness is a later development. In Herod's own time Jews seem to have regarded the ethnicity of the father to be the important factor (8.3.2).

On the economic side, it is often stated that Herod burdened his subjects with taxes. All rulers taxed their subjects, and this would always weigh heavily on the poor and politically impotent, but there is no indication that Herod's taxes were greater than those of previous or later rulers (6.3.7). On the contrary, his rule probably relieved some of the burden, in that the taxes placed by the Romans in the period between 63 and 40 were crushing, partly because of war expenses and partly because a good deal of territory was taken away from Jewish control. Under Herod most of this territory was regained; in addition, he opened up new land to cultivation in certain desolate regions. In addition, it now seems clear that Herod did not pay regular tribute to the Romans (despite the assertion in many standard works that he did).

Further on the financial side, he was able to defuse criticism at various times by acts of generosity to his own people. He prevented the soldiers from looting Jerusalem when it fell in 37 B.C.E. by rewarding them from his own pocket (6.4.7.1). He relieved a famine at considerable expense to himself, which silenced his critics and established general goodwill even among many who had been hostile (*Ant.* 15.9.1–2 §§299–316). In honor of his meeting with Agrippa, he rescinded one-fourth of the taxes for the year 12 B.C.E., which is said to have won over a large assembly consisting of the people of Jerusalem and many from the country (*Ant.* 16.2.5 §§64–65). The enormous expenses of the temple building supposedly came from his own coffers (*Ant.* 15.11.1 §§380).

Nevertheless, one would hardly call Herod a benevolent monarch. He governed as absolute ruler and could be completely ruthless in suppressing opposition (*Ant.* 15.10.4 §§365–72). At the beginning of his rule, he made the Sanhedrin completely impotent—as far as any check on his activities is concerned—by executing a number of its members and cowing the rest (6.4.5.1; 7.3.2.3). Although the Sanhedrin was subordinate to the Hasmonean rulers, it does seem to have functioned as a form of restraint on them, whereas it ceased to have any political function under Herod, as far as can be determined. But was Herod worse than other monarchs of the time—whether local potentates, monarchs of sizable kingdoms, or even the Roman emperor himself? Was he really any different from the Hasmonean rulers before him?

It is very difficult to judge public opinion in the days before scientific polls (and perhaps even since!). There were those who detested Herod and his rule, but to extrapolate beyond that and say that he was unpopular with the Jews—as is so often done—is to go beyond our knowledge. We do not know that he was any more unpopular than, for example, Alexander Janneus. Some who were critical of Herod changed their minds, at least temporarily, according to statements in Josephus. Specific groups and individuals, not least the temple priests and personnel, evidently benefited from his rule. Much of his contribution to building projects elsewhere in the Hellenistic world may have been primarily ego-centric but would still have helped the reputation of the Jews, who were often criticized during this time for their unusual customs. Herod also was able to intercede with the Roman authorities on occasion on behalf of certain Jewish communities (e.g., *Ant.* 16.2.3–5 §§27–65). Any judgment on Herod must consider the positive aspects of his reign, as well as the negative. There lies the final question: Whatever his faults, was Herod's rule not preferable to that of direct Roman rule? Some thought not at the time of his death, but what about in the decades after 6 C.E., when Judea was once again a Roman province?

6.4.10 Archelaus as Ethnarch (4 B.C.E.–6 C.E.)

Sources: Josephus, *War* 2.1.1–7.4 §§1–116; *Ant.* 17.8.4–13.5 §§200–355.

Archelaus, as the heir named in Herod's final will, arranged a magnificent funeral. He also refused to accept the crown until it was confirmed by Augustus; however, to ingratiate himself with the people, he agreed to a number of demands for concessions on taxes and for the release of some prisoners. The thing he wanted most was peace in the realm until he had time to go to Rome. This was not to be, however, for complaints about the two teachers and others who had been executed over the golden eagle incident soon led to gatherings of crowds with demands for revenge. Attempts to get them to disperse quietly merely led to riots, and the only recourse was the use of considerable force. The result was the slaying of three thousand people during the Passover festival and the cutting short of the festivities.

Archelaus was now able to set out for Rome. He was not the only one to do so; his rivals and opponents also hied themselves to the capital to put their cases before Augustus. Archelaus seemed to be in the best position, not only because of Herod's last will but also because he had already taken charge of matters in Judah. He had with him Herod's famed rhetorician Nicolaus of Damascus to put his case. Nevertheless, Antipas had been named in an earlier will, made when there was no question of Herod's sanity, and his case was aided by Salome's opposition to Archelaus.

No sooner had the various contenders for the throne left the country than the murmurings and discontent already manifested in Judea broke into open rebellion once more, at the celebration of Pentecost. The Roman legion in Jerusalem, led by Sabinus, was besieged within the palace. Some of Herod's veterans in Idumea also revolted. A variety of bands and even royal pretenders arose in the countryside (see 8.2.12), looting and pillaging not only the Herodian and Roman possessions but also those of other Jews. The Syrian governor Varus received Sabinus's urgent requests for help and immediately marched south with his two legions, collecting further reinforcements as he went. He captured and burned Sepphoris and several fortified villages on the way. This seems to have taken the fight out of the rebels, because they fled as soon as he came in sight of Jerusalem. The people of Jerusalem quickly admitted the Romans and disclaimed any responsibility for what had happened. Varus rounded up as many of the rebels as he could find in the countryside; many of these were imprisoned, but about two thousand of the chief instigators were crucified. The large contingent of Idumean soldiers also surrendered and most were pardoned, although the leaders were sent to Rome for trial before Augustus. Thus the War of Varus, as it came to be called, came fairly quickly to an end, although certain of the rebel bands continued to cause problems and were not suppressed for some years. The war itself remained for a long time in Jewish popular memory (cf. the *Seder Olam Rabbah* [Ratner, ed.: p. 145]).

The various claims of members of the Herodian family were being presented to Augustus when news of the rebellion came to Rome. Augustus heard the speeches and defenses of both sides but postponed a decision. About the time that Varus put an end to the revolt, a further delegation arrived in Rome. Varus had given permission for a group of fifty leading Jews to present another alternative to Caesar: that the Jewish nation be given autonomy under Roman rule rather than have a Herodian ruler (although according to a fragment of Nicolaus, *Life*, they would accept Antipas's rule as second best [*GLAJJ*: 1.250–60]). The speech before Augustus not only accused Herod of cruel and profligate rule that had impoverished the nation but also charged Archelaus with high-handed actions even before he had been declared king. Nicolaus of Damascus opposed this with a speech defending the memory of Herod and supporting Archelaus.

Augustus took several days to make up his mind after hearing the various sides. His final decision was to split Herod's realm, giving Judea, Idumea, and Samaria to Archelaus, along with the title "ethnarch," not "king" (although the hope was held out that the latter title might eventually come if Archelaus showed himself a worthy ruler). Antipas received Perea and Galilee, whereas Batanea, Trachonitis, and Auranitis went to Philip; both received the title of tetrarch. The income of some cities was given to Salome, although her estates remained under Archelaus's jurisdiction. Other relatives received monetary gifts, but Caesar also divided up among the other heirs the enormous legacy left to himself and kept only a few personal mementos of Herod.

Of Archelaus's reign as ethnarch we know little. Josephus's principal source, Nicolaus, evidently ended with the division of Herod's kingdom, and he simply had little other information available. He only relates that Archelaus divorced his wife and married Alexander's widow; that he had a dream, which an Essene interpreted correctly, about his impending removal from rule; and that in his tenth year Augustus deposed him and exiled him to Gaul. The precise reason for the last event is not given, only that both Jews and Samaritans complained of his "brutality" (*ōmos* [*War* 2.7.3 §111]) or "cruelty and tyranny" (*ōmotēta, tyrannida* [*Ant.* 17.13.2 §342]). Beyond this, about all we have are coins that show that he had the name Herod (*hērōdēs ethnarchos* [6.2.5]). This handful of data hardly constitutes a history of Archelaus's reign.

7

PROVINCE, KINGDOM, PROVINCE— AND THE WAR WITH ROME (6–74 C.E.)

7.1 BIBLIOGRAPHICAL GUIDE

CAH. Vol. 10, *The Augustan Empire, 44 B.C.–A.D. 70* (1934).
Cary, M., and H. H. Scullard. *A History of Rome* (1975).
Cohen, S.J.D. *Josephus in Galilee and Rome* (1979).
Garnsey, P., and R. Saller. *The Roman Empire: Economy, Society, and Culture* (1987).
Garzetti, A. *From Tiberius to the Antonines* (1974).
Goodman, M. *The Ruling Class of Judaea* (1987).
Jeremias, J. *Jerusalem in the Time of Jesus* (1969).
Kraft, R. A., and G.W.E. Nickelsburg, eds. *Early Judaism and Its Modern Interpreters* (1986).
Rajak, T. *Josephus: The Historian and His Society* (1983).
Schürer: 1.336–53, 357–513.
Schwartz, D. R. *Agrippa I* (1990).
Schwartz, S. *Josephus and Judaean Politics* (1990).
Scullard, H. H. *From the Gracchi to Nero* (1982).
Smallwood, E. M. *The Jews under Roman Rule* (1981) 144–330.
Wacher, J. *The Roman Empire* (1987).
Wells, C. M. *The Roman Empire* (1984).

Two major works cover this period of Jewish history, Schürer and Smallwood (the latter had the benefit of the first volume of Schürer). CRINT covers this period, but there are a number of problematic essays, as well as some good ones (see the Preface). The new edition of *CHJ* has not yet reached the Roman period. The volume by Jeremias is very useful, although it relies too much on rabbinic literature for first-century Jewish society (1.1.4). D. R. Schwartz addresses a number of problems important for this chapter, as well as the life of Agrippa I. The historian Josephus is extremely important for this period, having been a participant in the 66–70 war, and his two versions of his own activities give an important insight into his methods of working (7.2.1). For his accounts, see the analysis by Cohen; contrast the more credulous approach of Rajak. S. Schwartz's recent study of Josephus and the priesthood is also important for several sections of this chapter. His study overlaps to some extent with Goodman (on which see 7.3.10).

For general Roman history, the most up-to-date survey is probably Cary/Scullard. Although Scullard has a more recent bibliography and updated notes, the text itself has been little altered since 1959. The semi-popular volume by Wells is brief but readable and stimulating. A more detailed look at the individual emperors, beginning with Tiberius, is Garzetti. Garnsey/Saller and Wacher give up-to-date discussions of various aspects of the Roman Empire. The new edition of *CAH* has not reached this far, but the old edition is still informative on general Roman history.

7.2 SOURCES

7.2.1 Josephus

*Cohen.
———. "Masada: Literary Tradition, Archaeological Remains, and the Credibility of Josephus." *JJS* 33 (1982) 385–405.
Ladouceur, D. J. "Josephus and Masada." *Josephus, Judaism and Christianity* (1987) 95–113.
Mazar, B. "Josephus Flavius and the Archaeological Excavations in Jerusalem." *Josephus, the Bible, and History* (1989) 325–29.
*Rajak.
*Schwartz, S.
Vidal-Naquet, P. "Flavius Josèphe et Masada." *Revue historique* 260 (1978) 3–21.

Josephus had a detailed source (probably Nicolaus of Damascus) for his history during the Hasmonean and Herodian rule, up to the death of Herod and the execution of his will (4 B.C.E.). After that, his account is extremely abbreviated. The *War* gives a brief account of Archelaus's reign as ethnarch (4 B.C.E.–6 C.E.) and the making of Judea into a Roman province; then it skips, without comment, the next twenty years to the governorship of Pilate (26–36 C.E.). *Antiquities* is not much better, although it adds a few details about the situation surrounding the census of Quirinius and Coponius and also lists the governors between Coponius and Pilate. Both works demonstrate that Josephus's knowledge of the period between Herod's death and the 30s was extremely skimpy. Exactly what his sources were is unclear. Beginning with the reign of Caligula (about the time of Josephus's own birth) both accounts become fuller, although, again, we seldom know his sources.

War and *Antiquities* do not differ greatly in essential content, although the latter is much more detailed and contains a good deal that is rather peripheral to Jewish history. Insofar as it parallels *Antiquities*, *War* generally narrates events in a concise manner, giving the impression that Josephus either did not have a great deal of information or was in a hurry to reach the beginning of the war with Rome, or perhaps both. Where *Antiquities* parallels *War*, it tends to be lengthier; although some of this extra length is manifestly rhetorical padding, there are frequently more data, showing that Josephus had welcome additional information. There are occasional contradictions in detail (e.g., Abila was said to have been given to Agrippa II by Claudius in *Ant.* 20.7.1 §138 but by Nero in *War* 2.13.2 §252), but these are not usually of major significance. Much of the extra bulk of *Antiquities* comes from discursive sections on subjects that may be of interest in themselves but are not so important for Jewish history: Parthian history (18.2.4 §§39–52; 18.4.4–5 §§96–105); Tiberius's suppression of Isis worship (18.3.4 §§65–80); the death and succession of Tiberius (18.6.8–10 §§205–27); the events surrounding the assassination of Caligula (19.1.1–3.4 §§1–235); and the succession of Nero (20.8.1–3 §§148–57). In addition, two major sections in *Antiquities* relate marginally to Jewish history but seem to be more hero tales than history in most of their content: the story of a Jewish robber band in Mesopotamia (18.9.1–9 §§310–79) and the rule and conversion of the reigning dynasty in Adiabene (20.2.1–4.3 §§17–96).

Although the first and last parts of the *Life* mention some events in Josephus's personal life before the war and after the fall of Jerusalem, most of it (7–74 §§28–411) essentially parallels the time covered in *War* 2.20.3 §562—3.2.4 §34, that is, about November 66 to May 67 C.E. The two accounts agree in broad outline but differ significantly in some details. More importantly, the aims and emphasis are rather different in the two. The *Life* was written in response to an account of the war by Justus of Tiberias, which was in part quite critical of Josephus (65 §§336–39), so Josephus had the dual aim of defending himself and blackening the character of Justus. Therefore, whereas Justus is hardly mentioned in the *War*, in the *Life* he and his family are presented as almost single-handedly responsible for the war and the victory of the Romans (9 §41)! Such blatant prejudices are not hard to spot. More difficult is knowing to which account to give priority when they differ on the chronology of events or details of data.

This brings up the issue of the relationship of the two accounts, which is still being debated. Cohen has recently adapted an older suggestion to argue that both accounts are based on a *hypomnēma* (a set of detailed notes) which Josephus wrote up soon after the war in preparation for his first work, the *War* (*80–83). Josephus's purpose was rather different when he wrote the two narratives, which accounts for the differences between them. In the part of the *War* which tells about his own deeds, he is presenting himself primarily as the ideal general, although he also distances himself from the "brigands" who, he alleges, were the chief cause of the revolt (*Cohen: 235–36). In the *Life*, as already noted, he was both defending himself against the specific charge that he was in favor of the revolt from the beginning and attacking Justus, with his account slanted accordingly; nevertheless, because he was following a somewhat neutral set of notes, the *Life* may at times preserve a more accurate statement than the *War*. For example, it appears that the *Life* is arranged more chronologically than the *War*, in which Josephus was sometimes more interested in topological matters.

It has often been suggested that archeology confirms Josephus's account. In some cases this is true, especially with regard to his purely topographical descriptions. As so often, however, things are not quite so simple (cf. Ladouceur; Mazar). The siege of Masada is a good example of the historical difficulties in relating Josephus's account to the archeological information. Cohen (1982) has now done a study of the problems of interpretation, showing that a claim of straightforward confirmation is facile (cf. Vidal-Naquet).

7.2.2 Philo of Alexandria

Box, H. *Philonis Alexandrini In Flaccum* (1939).

Dillon, J. *The Middle Platonists* (1977).

Goodenough, E. R. *An Introduction to Philo Judaeus* (1962).

Goodenough, E. R., with H. L. Goodhart. *The Politics of Philo Judaeus* (1938).

Grabbe, L. L. *Etymology in Early Jewish Interpretation* (1988).

Hay, D. M. "Philo's References to Other Allegorists." *Studia Philonica* 6 (1979/80) 41–75.

Hilgert, E. "Bibliographia Philoniana 1935–1981." *ANRW* 2 (1984) 21.1.47–97.

Mayer, G. *Index Philoneus* (1974).

Mendelson, A. *Philo's Jewish Identity* (1988).

Radice, R., and D. T. Runia. *Philo of Alexandria: An Annotated Bibliography 1937–1986* (1988).

Sandmel, S. "Palestinian and Hellenistic Judaism and Christianity: The Question of the Comfortable Theory." *HUCA* 50 (1979a) 137–48.

———. *Philo of Alexandria: An Introduction* (1979b).

Schürer: 3.809–89.

Schwartz, D. R. "Philo's Priestly Descent." *Nourished with Peace* (1984) 155–71.
Smallwood, E. M. *Philonis Alexandrini Legatio ad Gaium* (1961).
Terian, A. *Philonis Alexandrini De Animalibus* (1981).

Philo (ca. 20 B.C.E.–50 C.E.) was a member of the leading Jewish family in Alexandria. His brother Alexander was alabarch (controller of customs) and leader of the Jewish community and probably one of the wealthiest private individuals in the Roman Empire. A nephew, Tiberius Julius Alexander, entered the Roman military and eventually became procurator of Judah and then governor of Egypt (7.4.9.3). A number of scholars over the years have even suggested that Philo was of a priestly family (most recently argued by Schwartz). In his influential position in the Jewish community, Philo was chosen to head a delegation to the emperor Caligula in 39 C.E., to plead the cause of the Alexandrian Jews against the Greek citizenry, which was persecuting them (7.3.5).

Most of Philo's writings are commentaries on the Pentateuch and contain few direct historical data. An exception to this generalization are the two tractates, *Legatio ad Gaium* and *In Flaccum* (Smallwood; Box). The tractate *Flaccum* describes the events in Alexandria in 38–39 C.E. that led to a major persecution of the Jewish community by the dominant Greeks. It is named after the Roman governor of Egypt, who was alleged to have cooperated in the pogrom against the Jews. *Gaium* describes the mission to Rome and the emperor to gain relief, the new threat in the plan to place a statue of Caligula in the Jerusalem temple (7.3.6), and the resolution of the problem.

One of the points debated over the years has been Philo's place within Judaism. Rather than being used as a primary datum, he has not infrequently been judged according to one's preconception about what is or is not a proper Jew (cf. Sandmel 1979a: 137–38). Therefore, some have dismissed Philo because he too was Hellenized, whereas others, who recognized his loyalty to Judaism, attempted to argue that he was Hellenized only on the surface but that his ideas were "native Palestinian." Mendelson's balanced study should help bury a lot of rubbish about the man Philo. First, it is now generally recognized that Philo was thoroughly Hellenized, the Hellenistic Jew par excellence. His writings show a good Greek education, he was an Alexandrian citizen (although most Jews were not [7.3.7]), and he shows knowledge of the gymnasium and the games given in the arena (*Congr.* 74–76; *Probus* 26, 141). His theology is a version of Middle Platonism (Dillon: 139–83). He admired the intellectual side of Greek culture and was fully at home in it.

Nevertheless, Philo was also a loyal Jew who believed firmly in the Jewish practices which set the Jews off from Gentiles (circumcision, dietary regulations, festivals); indeed, he even believed these practices were worth dying for (Mendelson: 74–75). He argued strongly against those who would treat such things as purely allegorical or symbolic without the need to practice them. He also sat uneasily within the Greek society which he so admired, because there were many things in it that his Judaism could not abide (e.g., idolatry). His Jewish beliefs and his opposition to intermarriage thus set him off from the Greeks whose intellectual company he might otherwise have sought.

One detail emerging from a study of Philo is the multiplicity of groups or, perhaps, factions at Alexandria (see Hay). These groups are differentiated primarily in terms of their exegesis, which makes it difficult to pin down other characteristics and to know whether they formed organized sects; however, one group is often labeled the "extreme allegorists," because they argued that one did not necessarily have to keep the traditional laws once the true allegorical meaning was understood. Philo was definitely opposed to this approach.

An enormous amount of scholarship has been produced on Philo, which is only touched on here. For general introductions to Philo, see Sandmel (1979b) and Goodenough (1962). The full bibliographical listing by Hilgert and the annotated bibliography by Radice/Runia are important tools for further study. Most of Philo's works are conveniently translated in LCL (for an exception, see Terian). Although there is no full concordance to Philo as yet, the index by Mayer partially fills this gap.

7.2.3   Justus of Tiberias

Gelzer, H. *Sextus Julius Africanus und die byzantinische Chronographie*. 2 vols. (1885–98).

Holladay, C. R. "Justus of Tiberias." *Fragments from Hellenistic Jewish Authors* (1983) 1.371–89.

Luther, H. *Josephus und Justus von Tiberias* (1910).

Rajak, T. "Justus of Tiberias." *Classical Quarterly* 23 (1973) 345–68.

———. "Josephus and Justus of Tiberias." *Josephus, Judaism, and Christianity* (1987) 81–94.

Ruhl, F. "Justus von Tiberias." *Rheinisches Museum* 71 (1916) 289–308.

Schalit, A. "Josephus und Justus: Studien zur Vita des Josephus." *Klio* 26 (1933) 67–95.

The other Jewish historian of this period is Justus, who belonged to one of the leading families of Tiberias which became reluctantly caught up in the Jewish war. Sometime after the war Justus served as a secretary to Agrippa II. Then, apparently in the early 90s, he issued a history of the revolt that gave a rather different account from Josephus's and also attacked Josephus (or, at least, was interpreted by Josephus as attacking him). Josephus replied to Justus in his *Life*, which is in part a counter-attack against Justus and his family. Unfortunately, much of what we know of Justus's work is gleaned from Josephus's *Life*; otherwise, only several quotations survive (Holladay). A work on the history of the kings of Israel may have formed the earlier part of the same book or perhaps another book altogether. Gelzer has argued that much of the history and chronology in the work of the Christian writer Julius Africanus is derived from Justus (1.20, 258–65). If so, then Justus may have written a history that could be considered with some justification as a rival to Josephus's, but the extant data are simply too few to make any certain estimate of the loss to scholarship.

7.2.4 Other Jewish Writings

Other Jewish writings are probably to be dated during the century preceding the fall of Jerusalem. The major problem is that specific historical events are seldom referred to, whereas those that are may be subject to dispute as to which were in the author's mind. This literature is extremely important for the history of religious thought among the Jews, but the problems with dating sometimes make its precise contribution to the history of Judaism rather uncertain. For a detailed discussion of this literature, see Schürer 3, *JWSTP*, and *JLBM*.

7.2.5 New Testament Writings

Epp, E. J., and G. W. Macrae. *The New Testament and Its Modern Interpreters* (1989).
Kümmel, W. G. *Introduction to the New Testament* (1975).
Neill, S., and T. Wright. *The Interpretation of the New Testament 1861–1986* (1988).

The scholarly literature on the New Testament is enormous, and no attempt is made here to survey it. Rather, a brief introduction from the point of view of the historian is given, with specific literature left to be cited in the individual studies where New Testament passages are relevant (e.g., Sanhedrin [7.3.2.3; 7.3.2.4]; Pharisees [8.2.2]). Although much of the New Testament is of potential value for the study of Judaism before and after 70, references to Judaism in the Pauline and deutero-

Pauline corpus usually have in mind non-Palestinian communities. There-fore, the discussion here is limited to the Gospels and the Acts of the Apostles. For a further discussion of scholarship and bibliography on all these points, see Kümmel, Neill/Wright, and Epp/Macrae. Some recent works on the Gospels and Acts are also given below.

7.2.5.1 Gospels

Brown, R. E. *The Gospel according to John I–XII* (1966).
———. *The Gospel according to John XIII–XXI* (1970).
Davies, W. D., and D. C. Allison. *The Gospel according to Saint Matthew* (1988–).
Fitzmyer, J. A. *The Gospel according to Luke I–IX* (1981).
———. *The Gospel according to Luke X–XXIV* (1985).
Guelich, R. A. *Mark 1—8:26* (1989).
Neirynck, F. "Recent Developments in the Study of Q." *Logia* (1982) 29–75.

As students of the New Testament are well aware, the traditions in the Gospels about Jesus and the early church represent a complex body of data, and there is considerable disagreement over how it is to be eval-uated for historical and biographical reconstruction. Few question that actual figures and events lie at the core of the preserved traditions, and most accept that particular facts about the historical Jesus in his first-century context can be extracted from the Gospels. Even when a tradition is suspect with regard to the life of Jesus, it may still tell us something about the Judaism of his time. Nevertheless, the Gospels also seem to reflect the age of their composition, which is post-70 for all of them, the 80s or 90s for Luke, the same or later for Acts, and as late as the turn of the century for the Fourth Gospel. Also to be taken into consideration is the bias of writings that form both an apology for Christianity and a polemic against those seen as enemies, including various Jewish groups or even "the Jews" as an undifferentiated entity (in the case of John).

The theory of Gospel origins favored by a majority of New Testament scholars is still the two-source theory: that Matthew and Luke chiefly used Mark and Q (Davies/Allison: 1.97–127; Epp/Macrae: 245–69; Neirynck). This is despite the wide debate in recent years and the fact that some scholars prefer other explanations (e.g., the Griesbach hypoth-esis or the rejection of Q). Therefore, priority is usually given to Mark and Q as the most likely to represent the pre-70 situation. Nevertheless, the issue is not so simple. The fact that Mark and perhaps also Q were probably written after 70 suggests that either may give a picture very much colored by the post-70 situation, rather than the actual realities of the time of Jesus. Furthermore, it is now recognized that even the Fourth

Gospel, probably the latest of the canonical Gospels, may contain independent traditions (e.g., the passion narrative) and is not to be dismissed by the historian (although many find Brown's approach somewhat credulous).

7.2.5.2 Acts of the Apostles

Brawley, R. L. *Luke-Acts and the Jews: Conflict, Apology, and Conciliation* (1987).
Haenchen, E. *The Acts of the Apostles* (1971).
Hemer, C. J. *The Book of Acts in the Setting of Hellenistic History* (1989).
Hengel, M. *Acts and the History of Earliest Christianity* (1979).
Lüdemann, G. *Early Christianity according to the Traditions in Acts* (1989).
Mattill, A. J., Jr. "The Value of Acts as a Source for the Study of Paul." *Perspectives on Luke-Acts* (1978) 76–98.
Mills, W. E., ed. *A Bibliography of the Periodical Literature on the Acts of the Apostles* (1986).
Plümacher, E. "Lukas als griechischer Historiker." PWSup (1974) 14.235–64.
Schreckenberg, H. "Flavius Josephus und die lukanischen Schriften." *Wort in der Zeit* (1980) 179–209.

Acts often mentions Jewish institutions and Jews, including some important figures of Jewish history. It is potentially an important source for the historian. The problem is the lack of agreement among New Testament scholars as to the book's general reliability (see Mattill for a summary). Although there has perhaps been a trend to see Acts as fairly reliable and more in the genre of historical writing in recent years, those pressing the issue (e.g., Hengel) have weakened their position by a somewhat polemical treatment that does not always deal with the issues important for a full historical evaluation. Hengel, in his actual analysis of the text (as opposed to his theoretical statements, which are often rather dogmatic), shows a critical approach whose results are sometimes as severe against the historicity of Acts as those against which he inveighs in other parts of his monograph. A useful summary of the situation is given by Lüdemann (1–18). (I ignore here the special pleadings from those whose stance is predetermined by fundamentalist presuppositions; unfortunately, the work of Hemer, although very learned in some respects, ultimately falls into this category.)

In some cases, Luke clearly has good information that accords well with Josephus and other first-century sources. Even if he is writing only a "historical novel" about the early church, his references to Judaism and other contemporary phenomena could still be accurate; therefore, the question of his knowledge of pre-70 Judaism does not necessarily stand or fall with his reliability about the history of the early church. In contrast, along with some important and accurate data (e.g., on Gamaliel I [8.2.2.4]) he also shows shocking ignorance of some fairly basic details of history (e.g., the census of Quirinius [7.3.1]; and he refers to Agrippa I as "Herod" [7.4.6]). Therefore, he will be used as a source but cautiously and critically.

7.2.6 Greco-Roman Writers

Lesky, A. H. *A History of Greek Literature* (1966).

For a discussion of sources for Roman history, see *CAH*: 10.866–76. Specific references to Jews and Judaism in the Greco-Roman writers are catalogued in *GLAJJ*. For a recent introduction to the Greek and Latin writings of this period, including the histories, see *CHCL*. Useful older works include Lesky and *OCD*. For the *Acta Alexandrinorum*, see 7.3.5.

7.2.6.1 Tacitus

Syme, R. *Tacitus* (1958).

No doubt Cornelius Tacitus (ca. 56 to after 115 c.e.) was one of the major Roman historians. In general academic quality he probably ranked alongside Livy, although behind Ammianus Marcellinus, of the writers in Latin (for the definitive general assessment of him as a historian, see Syme). For the first century of the Common Era he is extremely important where extant; unfortunately, his writings are preserved intact only in part, but the lost portions of his work for this period are probably known at second hand through Cassius Dio (7.2.6.2), who seems to have used Tacitus as a source. Although Tacitus does occasionally refer to the Jews and Jewish history directly (see *GLAJJ*: 2.1–93 for texts and commentary), his main use is as a source for Roman history. His two principal historical works are the *Histories* and the *Annals*. *Histories* apparently covered the period 69 c.e. to the reign of Domitian, but we now have only books 1 to 4 and part of book 5, which record events only for the year 69/70. The *Annals* originally covered the reigns of Tiberius to Nero, but the reign of Caligula and portions of the reigns of Claudius and Nero have now been lost (books 1 to 6 and 11 to 16 are preserved). Tacitus exhibits the pro-senatorial and anti-imperial bias which is found in such writers as Dio and Suetonius. Therefore, the one-sided, negative picture of particular emperors needs correction; nevertheless, where extant he is still the major source of reliable data and is preferable to the anecdotal accounts of Suetonius.

7.2.6.2 Cassius Dio

For a general introduction to Dio, see 5.2.13.4. Most of books 55 to 60 are preserved, covering 9 B.C.E.–46 C.E. Only medieval epitomes of books 61 to 69 have come down to us, covering 47–138 C.E.

7.2.6.3 Suetonius

For a general introduction to Suetonius, see 6.2.4.5. He wrote of the lives of all the emperors from Augustus to Domitian.

7.2.6.4 Plutarch

For a general introduction to Plutarch, see 2.2.6.8. Although a number of his *Lives* for this part of the Roman period have been lost, preserved are *Galba* and *Otho*.

7.2.7 Inscriptions and Judean Desert Manuscripts

Bagatti, B., and J. T. Milik. *Gli scavi del "Dominus Flevit" (Monte Oliveto-Gerusalemme)* (1958).
Benoit, P., et al. *Les grottes de Murabba'ât* (1961).
Fitzmyer, J. A., and D. J. Harrington. *A Manual of Palestinian Aramaic Texts* (1978).
Koffmahn, E. *Die Doppelurkunden aus der Wüste Juda* (1968).
Lichtenstein, H. "Die Fastenrolle: Eine Untersuchung zur jüdisch-hellenistischen Geschichte." *HUCA* 8–9 (1931–32) 257–351.
Patrich, J. "Inscriptions araméennes juives dans les grottes d'El-'Aleiliyât: Wadi Suweinit (Naḥal Michmas)." *RB* 92 (1985) 265–73.
Puech, E. "Inscriptions funéraires palestiniennes: tombeau de Jason et ossuaires." *RB* 90 (1983) 481–533.
Tov, E., et al. *The Greek Minor Prophets Scroll from Naḥal Ḥever* (1990).
Yadin, Y. "The Excavation of Masada—1963/64: Preliminary Report." *IEJ* 15 (1965a) 1–120.
———. *The Ben Sira Scroll from Masada* (1965b).
———. *Masada* (1966).

The bulk of the Dead Sea Scrolls relate to the Qumran community (see 5.2.6.1). However, in another section of the Judean desert, Wadi

Murabba'at, were found documents in Hebrew, Aramaic, and Greek, from both the period before the First Revolt and the time of Bar Kokhba. These have all been published (Benoit, et al.) with photos, transcription, (French) translation, and commentary. A more recent edition of the Aramaic material, with English translation and bibliography, is found in Fitzmyer/Harrington (texts 38–50). The pre-70 documents are the following (see 9.2.4.2 for the post-70 material): a note of indebtedness from 56 C.E. (Mur 18 = DJD 2.100–104), a writ of divorce (Mur 19 = DJD 2.104–9, date uncertain), a contract of marriage (Mur 21 = DJD 2.114–17), an unidentified narrative (Mur 72 = DJD 2.172–74), a list of names of persons (Mur 74 = DJD 2.175–77), and perhaps another note of indebtedness (Mur 32 = DJD 2.149–50). See Tov, et al. for the important Greek Scroll of the Minor Prophets from the Judean desert.

Written material of various sorts was found at Masada, although most of it has been published by Yadin only in preliminary form except for the Ben Sira material (1965a; 1965b; 1966). Some volumes of the definitive edition have been announced by the Israel Exploration Society. One of the most poignant of the inscriptions is found in Patrich and was evidently written by refugees from the Romans in the First Revolt, in the face of impending capture and death. It reads, "Joezer [the writer?] has been taken; the guards have entered" (yw'zr 't'qr 'lw[wt] mṭrn).

Another document which may go back to the first century of the Common Era is the *Megillat Ta'anit*, although the copies preserved are medieval. This is a listing of days on which one should not fast, which indicates the dates of events important for Jewish history. The difficulty is that there is little agreement on the particular event represented by many of the dates. Only the brief Aramaic text is early; the accompanying Hebrew commentary is much later and generally of little use for historical purposes. The basic edition is that of Lichtenstein, although it has been republished with bibliography and English translation in Fitzmyer/Harrington (text 150).

Many ossuary inscriptions are known from around the turn of the era. For a sampling of these, see Bagatti/Milik and Puech, as well as Fitzmyer/Harrington for those in Aramaic (texts 69–148). On their religious significance, see 8.2.16. For an older collection of Jewish inscriptions of all sorts, see *CIJ*.

7.2.8 Archeology and Coins

Avigad, N. "The Burial-Vault of a Nazirite Family on Mount Scopus." *IEJ* 21 (1971) 185–200.

————. "The Burnt House Captures a Moment in Time." *BAR* 9, no. 6 (Nov./ Dec. 1983) 66–72.

————. *Discovering Jerusalem* (1984).

Avi-Yonah, M. "The Third and Second Walls of Jerusalem." *IEJ* 18 (1968) 98–125.

Ben-Arieh, S., and E. Netzer. "Where Is the Third Wall of Agrippa I?" *BA* 42 (1979) 140–41.

Hachlili, R. "A Jerusalem Family in Jericho." *BASOR* 230 (1978) 45–56.

————. "The Goliath Family in Jericho: Funerary Inscriptions from a First Century A.D. Jewish Monumental Tomb." *BASOR* 235 (1979) 31–65.

Hachlili, R., et al. "The Genealogy of the Goliath Family." *BASOR* 235 (1979) 66–73.

Isaac, B. "A Donation for Herod's Temple in Jerusalem." *IEJ* 33 (1983) 86–92.

Kuhnen, H.-P. *Palästina in griechisch-römischer Zeit* (1990).

Laperrousaz, E.-M. "Le problème du 'premier mur' et du 'deuxième mur' de Jérusalem après la réfutation décisive de la 'minimalist view.' " *Hommage à Georges Vajda* (1980) 13–35.

Levine, L. I. "Archaeological Discoveries from the Greco-Roman Era." *Recent Archaeology in the Land of Israel* (1981) 75–88.

Lifshitz, B. "Notes philologiques et epigraphiques." *SCI* 2 (1975) 97–112.

McNulty, I. B. "The North Wall Outside Jerusalem." *BA* 42 (1979) 141–44.

Mazar, B., et al. *Beth She'arim*. 3 vols. (1973–76).

Meshorer, Y. *Ancient Jewish Coinage*. Vol. 2: *Herod the Great through Bar Cochba* (1982).

————. "Jewish Numismatics." *Early Judaism and Its Modern Interpreters* (1986) 211–20.

Meyers, E. M., and A. T. Kraabel. "Archaeology, Iconography, and Nonliterary Written Remains." *Early Judaism and Its Modern Interpreters* (1986) 175–210.

Meyers, E. M., and J. F. Strange. *Archaeology, the Rabbis and Early Christianity* (1981).

Meyshan, J. "The Coinage of Agrippa the First." *IEJ* 4 (1954) 186–200.

Netzer, E. "Ancient Ritual Baths (*Miqvaot*) in Jericho." *Jerusalem Cathedra* 2 (1982) 106–19.

Schein, B. E. "The Second Wall of Jerusalem." *BA* 44 (1981) 21–26.

Shanks, H. "The Jerusalem Wall That Shouldn't Be There." *BAR* 13, no. 3 (May/June 1987) 46–57.

Wilkinson, J. "The Streets of Jerusalem." *Levant* 7 (1975) 118–36.

Yadin, Y., ed. *Jerusalem Revealed* (1975).

For general bibliography, see 1.1.1. A survey of the period is now given by Kuhnen. See also Meyers/Kraabel, Meyers/Strange, and Levine. On numismatics, see Meshorer and Meyshan. One of the best-known sites for this period is Jerusalem, although the excavations are still in progress. One topic of continuing interest and controversy is the location of its various walls, on which there is as yet no general agreement (Avi-Yonah; Ben-Arieh/Netzer; Laperrousaz; McNulty; Schein; Shenks).

Both the tetrarchs Herod Antipas and Philip minted coins. Some of the issues of Antipas have the name "Tiberias," in honor of the city which he founded. Through most of his rule the inscription (always in Greek) is "of Herod the tetrarch" (*hērōdou tetrarchou*). However, in his final year coins bear the words "Herod the tetrarch" in the nominative (*hērōdēs tetrarchēs*) and the additional inscription "to Gaius Caesar Germanicus" (*gaiō kaisar germanikō*). These were evidently issued in honor of the emperor Caligula, at a time when Antipas was making a bid for the title "king"; instead, he was removed from his office and exiled (7.4.4). Philip was the first Herodian ruler to use human representations on his coinage. Not only does his own portrait appear but also those of Augustus and Tiberius. One coin type has the head of Augustus and Livia with the inscription "of the Augustuses" (*sebastōn*).

When Agrippa I took over Philip's tetrarchy in 37 c.e., he also issued coins with his own portrait. There arc also portraits of the young Agrippa II on the rcverse of some of the coins, with the inscription "Agrippa, son of the king" or "Agrippa, son of King Agrippa" (*agrippa huiou basileōs, agrippa huiou basileōs agrippa*). A number of coins honor Caligula and members of his family. Under Claudius there were issues with the emperor's portrait and the inscription "Tiberius Caesar Augustus Germ(anicus)" (*tiberios kaisar sebastos germ*). One series, issued soon after Claudius became emperor, included the inscription "treaty of friendship and alliance of the great King Agrippa with Augustus Caesar [Claudius] and the people of Rome" (*orkia bas[ileōs] me[galou] agrippa pr[os] seb[astou] kais[aros] k[ai] dēmo[u] rōm[aiōn] phili[a] k[ai] summach[ia] aut[ou]*). The inscriptions with Agrippa's name vary: "of Agrippa the king" (*agrippa basileōs*), "King Agrippa" (*basileus agrippas*), "King Agrippa, Caesar's friend" (*bas[ileus] agrippa philokaisar*), and the like. One coin recently found is claimed to have "Herod" (*hērō[dēs]*) as part of the name (Meshorer 1982: 2.55–57), but this turns out to be a reference to Agrippa's brother, Herod of Chalcis (7.4.6). Only one series of Agrippa's coins was issued at Jerusalem and evidently intended for use in Judea itself. These have no portraits, are all dated to "year 6" (42 c.e.), and have Jewish symbols (three ears of grain, a canopy). However, the inscription is in Greek (*agripa* [sic] *basileōs*), although it has evidently been simplified from the one normally used by Agrippa at this time, "the great king Agrippa, friend of Caesar" (*basileus megas agrippas philokaisar*).

Agrippa II's coins present a problem of chronology. Some coins have two dates; some of those in honor of Vespasian and Titus are dated to the time of Domitian. It is now generally agreed that the double dates are counted from 56 and 61 c.e., respectively. The Flavian coins with single dates should be dated from 61, according to Meshorer (1982: 2.69–73).

During his long reign, Agrippa issued a variety of coins, many of them in honor of the current emperor (Nero, Vespasian, Titus, Domitian), but it is now agreed that he also broke precedent by issuing coins in honor of Vespasian and Titus after their deaths. He was also the first to issue Jewish coins with a Latin inscription. One, the "Judaea Capta" coin, has the bust of Titus and the inscription "the ruler Titus Caesar" (*autokr[atōr] ti[tos ka]isar*) and was issued on the twentieth anniversary of the fall of Jerusalem. One coin has an inscription which gives Agrippa's name "Marcus" on it. The coins come to an end with "year 35" (95/96 c.e.). This happens to mark the end of Domitian's reign, so whether they ended because of Agrippa's death or for reasons relating to the situation in Rome is debatable.

During the 66–70 revolt, the Jews issued their own coinage. This seems to have begun immediately in late 66, which was designated "year 1" on the coins. The designs on the first few coins are crudely formed but quickly improve. The basic issue was the silver "Jerusalem shekel," which took the place of the Tyrian shekel that had been used to that time (6.2.5). Also minted were silver half-shekels and quarter-shekels, as well as bronze coins of smaller denominations. The inscriptions are in the paleo-Hebrew script. On the coins of year 1 are the inscriptions "shekel of Israel" (*šql yśr'l*) and "holy Jerusalem" (*yrwšlm qdšh*). These also appear on years 2 to 5 (the latter inscription in slightly improved form: *yrwšlym hqdwšh*). On years 2 and 3 appears the further slogan "freedom of Zion" (*ḥrt/ḥrwt ṣywn*). This is replaced in year 4 by the phrase "for the redemption of Zion" (*lg'lt ṣywn*). Symbols used include the chalice, a branch with three pomegranates, a vessel (often referred to as an "amphora"), a vine branch, and the four species of plant associated with the Festival of Tabernacles, or Sukkot (*lulav, etrog,* myrtle, willow).

7.3 HISTORICAL STUDIES

7.3.1 Administration as a Roman Province

Bleckmann, F. "Die erste syrische Statthalterschaft des P. Sulpicius Quirinius." *Klio* 17 (1920/21) 104–12.

Dessau, H. "Zu den neuen Inschriften des Sulpicius Quirinius." *Klio* 17 (1920/21) 252–58.

Fitzmyer, J. A. *The Gospel according to Luke I–IX* (1981) 399–405.

Marshall, I. H. *The Gospel of Luke* (1978) 97–104.

Moehring, H. R. "The Census in Luke as an Apologetic Device." *Studies in New Testament and Early Christian Literature* (1972) 144–60.

Safrai, Z. "The Administrative Structure of Judea in the Roman and Byzantine Periods." *Immanuel* 13 (1981) 30–38.

Speidel, M. P. "The Roman Army in Judaea under the Procurators: The Italian and the Augustan Cohort in the Acts of the Apostles." *Ancient Society* 13/14 (1982/83) 233–40.

Stern, M. "The Province of Judaea." *The Jewish People in the First Century* (1974) 1.308–76.

Syme, R. "The Titulus Tiburtinus." *Akten des VI. Internationalen Kongresses für Griechische und Lateinische Epigraphik* (1973) 585–601.

Wiseman, T. P. "The Census in the First Century b.c." *JRS* 59 (1969) 59–75.

———. " 'There Went Out a Decree from Caesar Augustus. . . .' " *NTS* 33 (1987) 479–80.

As a client kingdom under Herod's rule, Judah's administration and finances were organized from within, not directly by the Romans. When it became a Roman province, Judah became liable for its share of the tax burden, some of which was collected directly by the Romans (6.3.7). As soon as Archelaus had been exiled, the reorganization of the kingdom into a province began under the direction of the Syrian governor Quirinius and the Judean governor Coponius (*War* 2.8.1 §117; *Ant.* 18.1.1 §§1–10). One of the main tasks was the census of people and property, because taxation was determined by the number of people in the household, including slaves, and by the property possessed by each person. This was evidently quite new to the Jews, who "were at first shocked to hear of the registration of property" (*Ant.* 18.1.1 §3). On the Roman taxation in Palestine, see 7.3.10.

There would probably be little discussion of this if the Gospel of Luke did not appear to put this census-taking at a time when Herod was still ruling, instead of under Quirinius (Luke 2:1-5). In the last century or so, a good deal has been written on the subject, both defending Luke's accuracy and arguing that he was simply mistaken. It is now generally agreed that Luke was in error and wrongly associated the birth of Jesus with the census of Quirinius. Those who continue to defend Luke's statement have usually done so for apologetic reasons, and their arguments have been ingenious rather than cogent (e.g., Marshall). There are four reasons for judging Luke in error (for bibliography and a thorough discussion, see Schürer: 1.399–427; for more data, see Fitzmyer; cf. Smallwood: 568–71).

1. Quirinius is known from Josephus and other sources to have been procurator of Syria in 6 c.e. The Tiburtinus inscription was once interpreted to suggest that Quirinius had been legate in Syria twice, but that interpretation is now considered mistaken (Syme). Although a complete list of Roman procurators of Syria cannot be

reconstructed with absolute certainty, Quirinius was not there earlier than 6 C.E.

2. No census would have been conducted under Herod because he was directly responsible for levying tribute (if there was any; see 6.3.7) and for its collection from his subjects. It would have been an unprecedented interference in his internal affairs and a clear undermining of his authority for the Roman governor to have conducted a census while he was ruling.

3. Conducting a census was normal when a kingdom became a province, so the "census under Quirinius" in 6 C.E., as described by Josephus, is precisely what a historian would have expected to find.

4. Luke also appears to have been mistaken in referring to a universal census and in suggesting that people had to return to their home cities for such. Censuses were conducted at different times, as needed, in different parts of the empire. The whole of the empire would not have been polled in any case: for example, by the Augustan age Italy was free of taxation and conscription and therefore not subject to census for such things. Further, one's property was assessed at the area of residence, not the area of birth. Because the purpose of the census was taxation, the logical place to determine property was where one lived, not where one was born (especially if the latter place was distant). However, Wiseman (1987) has recently noted that in 6 C.E. Augustus introduced a 5 percent inheritance tax that was binding on all Roman citizens, which would have required that a new census be taken. Luke's statements do not accord with Augustus's tax either, but it might help explain how he became confused on the subject.

Judea was at this time under the overall control of a Roman governor. It was Roman policy, however, to allow the natives to regulate themselves according to their own constitution. The result was that the high priest and Sanhedrin again became the major institution of government in those areas not reserved by the Roman governor for himself (7.3.2). As Josephus says, "After the death of these kings [Herod and Archelaus], the constitution became an aristocracy, and the high priests were entrusted with the leadership of the nation" (*Ant.* 20.10.5 §251). Judea was once more a theocracy; however, too much had happened for it to revert to the institutions of an earlier era (7.3.10), and troubles soon began.

Although Josephus states that Judea was attached to Syria (*Ant.* 17.13.5 §355), this was true only in the sense that the legate of Syria could always intervene if he thought it necessary (cf. *Ant.* 18.4.2 §88; Tacitus, *Ann.* 2.42.5). Under normal circumstances, however, the Judean governor w autonomous. Judea belonged in the class of imperial province which had a governor of equestrian rather than consular rank (Egypt was similar in this). The governor bore the title of "prefect" (*praefectus*) until Agrippa's reign, as is shown by the Tiburtinus inscription (Syme). The center of Roman administration was Caesarea (Tacitus, *Hist.* 2.78.4). The four legions for the area were stationed in Syria. The force in Judea seems to have been composed of auxiliary troops consisting of five cohorts of soldiers plus a squadron (*ala*) of cavalry, about three thousand men in all (*Ant.* 19.9.2 §§361–66). These had apparently originated as Herod's own internal army, which then passed to the Romans after Archelaus's deposition. It has often been stated that, contrary to Acts 10:1, no Italian troops were stationed in Judea at this time (Schürer: 1.365); however, Speidel has recently argued that the account in Acts is correct (cf. also Stern: 1.327–28).

Although the term "Judea" continued in common usage to refer to the area that had formed Herod's empire, the Roman province of Judea proper was a much reduced area. Perea, Galilee, and the territories northwest of the Sea of Galilee (Trachonitis, Batanea, Auronitis) had already been removed and given to Philip and Herod Antipas to govern. Samaria was also removed at this time, and Idumea was attached to Judea, losing its separate identity. The whole province of Judea-Idumea was subdivided into eleven toparchies (*War* 3.3.5 §§54–56; cf. Pliny, *Hist. nat.* 5.14.70): Jerusalem, Gophna, Acrabeta, Thamna, Lydda, Emmaus, Pella (Bethleptenpha in *War* 4.8.1 §445), Idumea, Engeddi, Herodium, and Jericho.

7.3.2 The High Priests and the Sanhedrin

7.3.2.1 General

Even under Persian and Greek rule, the Sanhedrin (*gerousia, boulē*) was an important institution in the governance of Judea (2.3.1; 4.3.1). Throughout its history the high priest was at its head. With independence under the Hasmoneans, the Sanhedrin came into its own as the supreme authority over the Jewish nation, along with the high priest, who now served also as the ruling monarch. Whether the Sanhedrin was only an advisory body to the high priest or whether it had powers in its own right is still a matter of debate, although a good guess is that sometimes one condition and sometimes the other obtained during its history. The kingship of Herod changed the positions of the Sanhedrin and high priest considerably. Whereas the Romans took the position of an occupying power which left the internal structures more or less intact, Herod served as a native king with absolute powers. Although the high priest continued as the chief religious figure of the nation, he held this office only at the sufferance of Herod. The Sanhedrin, although still in existence under Herod, ceased to have any real function at all, as far as one can tell from the little information that can be gleaned from the sources (7.3.2.3; 6.4.3).

Therefore, the establishment of Judea as a Roman province actually revived the power of the high priest and the Sanhedrin to some extent. Although the territory under jurisdiction of the institution was radically reduced, the Sanhedrin had a real function once there was no king. The governor of Judea maintained strong control over internal affairs, but he would not intrude in some areas where Herod would not have hesitated to interfere. In two areas the Roman governors took a direct hand: they held the power to set up or depose high priests, just as Herod had done, and they kept control of the high priestly garments, which were given out only for the annual festivals and then taken back each time.

7.3.2.2   High Priests from Pompey to Vespasian

Hölscher, G. *Die Hohenpriesterliste bei Josephus und die evangelische Chronologie* (1940).

Schwartz, D. R. "Ishmael ben Phiabi and the Chronology of Provincia Judaea." *Tarbiz* 52 (1982/83) 177–200 (Heb.) + V-VI (Eng. summary).

Neither the office of high priest nor the Sanhedrin can be discussed in isolation. The high priest was essential for the performance of certain aspects of the cult, but his real importance was as president of the Sanhedrin (see below). According to a list at the end of Josephus's *Antiquities*, twenty-eight high priests held the office after Hyrcanus II, before it completely ceased (20.10.5 §250). These data were probably taken from a specific source, perhaps from the temple archives, but Josephus does not list the actual names at this point. Names of high priests currently serving are given in the earlier narratives of *War* and *Antiquities*; these add up to twenty-eight, suggesting that Josephus has given a complete recital of those who held office. There are sporadic statements which contain names not listed in his basic narrative (Jesus b. Sapphia [*War* 2.20.4 §566]; Neus [*War* 2.20.4 §566]; Matthias b. Boethus [*War* 4.9.11 §574; 5.13.1 §527]), but the difficulty seems to be caused by Josephus's use in these cases of the term *archiereus* for individuals of the high priestly family rather than for holders of the high priesthood itself (some have emended Neus to Ananias). The twenty-eight high priests named by Josephus follow, the accompanying dates being no more than approximations in many cases (cf. Schürer: 2.229–32; *Jeremias: 377–78; Hölscher: 9–19):

Appointed by Herod the Great

1. Ananel, said to be from Babylon (37–36; 34–? B.C.E.): *Ant.* 15.2.4 §22; 15.3.1 §§39–41.
2. Aristobulus b. Alexander (35 B.C.E.): *Ant.* 15.3.1 §41; 15.3.3 §§51–56; cf. 20.10.5 §§247–48.
   (Ananel a second time: 34–? B.C.E.).
3. Jesus b. Phiabi (?–24 B.C.E.): *Ant.* 15.9.3 §322.
4. Simon b. Boethus, of an Alexandrian family (24–5 B.C.E.): *Ant.* 15.9.3 §§320–22; 17.4.2 §78; cf. 18.5.1 §109; 19.6.2 §297.
5. Matthias b. Theophilus (5–4 B.C.E.): *Ant.* 17.4.2 §78; 17.6.4 §§164–67.
6. Joseph b. Ellemus: *Ant.* 17.6.4 §§165–66.
7. Joazar b. Boethus (4 B.C.E.; ?–6 C.E.): *Ant.* 17.6.4 §164; 17.13.1 §339; 18.1.1 §3; 18.2.1 §26.

Appointed by Archelaus

8. Eleazar, brother of Joazar (4 B.C.E.–?): *Ant.* 17.13.1 §§339, 341.
9. Jesus b. See: *Ant.* 17.13.1 §341.
   (Joazar a second time: ?–6 C.E.).

Appointed by Quirinius

10. Ananus (or Annas) b. Seth (6–15 C.E.): *Ant.* 18.2.1 §26; 18.2.2 §34; cf. 20.9.1 §197; Luke 3:2; John 18:13-24; Acts 4:6.

Appointed by Valerius Gratus (15–26 C.E.)

11. Ishmael b. Phiabi (15–16 C.E.): *Ant.* 18.2.2 §34.
12. Eleazar b. Ananus (16–17 C.E.): *Ant.* 18.2.2 §34.
13. Simon b. Camithus (17–18 C.E.): *Ant.* 18.2.2 §34.
14. Joseph Caiaphas (18–36 C.E.): *Ant.* 18.2.2 §35; 18.4.3 §95; cf. Matt. 26:3, 57; Luke 3:2; John 11:49; 18:13, 14, 24, 28; Acts 4:6.

Appointed by Vitellius (35–39 C.E.)

15. Jonathan b. Ananus (36–37 C.E.): *Ant.* 18.4.3 §95; 18.5.3 §123; cf. 19.6.4 §313. On his later activities and his murder, see *War* 2.12.5–6 §§240–43; 2.13.3 §256; *Ant.* 20.8.5 §§162–63.
16. Theophilus b. Ananus, brother of Jonathan (37–41 C.E.): *Ant.* 18.5.3 §123.

Appointed by Agrippa I (41–44 C.E.)

17. Simon Cantheras b. Boethus (41–? C.E.): *Ant.* 19.6.2 §297; 19.6.4 §313.

18. Matthias b. Ananus, brother of Jonathan: *Ant.* 19.6.4 §316.
19. Elionaeus b. Cantheras: *Ant.* 19.8.1 §342.

Appointed by Herod of Chalcis (44–48 C.E.)

20. Joseph b. Camei (or b. Camoedi or b. Camudus): *Ant.* 20.1.3 §16; 20.5.2 §103. There is a difficulty here because he is said to have succeeded Cantheras, although we know of no high priest by that name. Either there is a mistaken reference for Elionaeus b. Cantheras or Cantheras should be added to the list, although the latter would give a total number of high priests different from Josephus's.
21. Ananias b. Nedebaeus (ca. 47–59 C.E.?; Schwartz argues that his term ended in 49 C.E.): *Ant.* 20.5.2 §103; cf. 20.6.2 §131; *War* 2.12.6 §243; Acts 23:2; 24:1. On his subsequent life and murder, see *War* 2.17.6 §429; 2.17.9 §§441–42; *Ant.* 20.9.2–4 §§206–13.

Appointed by Agrippa II (50–66 C.E.)

22. Ishmael b. Phiabi (59–61 C.E.?; Schwartz argues his term began in 49 C.E.): *Ant.* 20.8.8 §179; 20.8.11 §§194–95. He may have been executed in Cyrene (cf. *War* 6.2.2 §114).
23. Joseph Cabi b. Simon the high priest (61–62 C.E.): *Ant.* 20.8.11 §196; cf. *War* 6.2.2 §114.
24. Ananus b. Ananus (62 C.E.); *Ant.* 20.9.1 §§197–203. On his murder, see *War* 2.20.3 §563; 2.22.1–2 §§648–53; 4.3.7–5.2 §§151–325; *Life* 38–39 §§193–96; 44 §216; 60 §309.
25. Jesus b. Damnaeus (62–63 C.E.): *Ant.* 20.9.1 §203; 20.9.4 §213; cf. *War* 6.2.2 §114.
26. Jesus b. Gamaliel (63–64 C.E.): *Ant.* 20.9.4 §213; 20.9.7 §223. For his activities and murder during the war, see *War* 4.3.9 §160; 4.4.3–5.2 §238–325; *Life* 38 §193; cf. 41 §204.
27. Matthias b. Theophilus (65–? C.E.): *Ant.* 20.9.7 §223; cf. *War* 6.2.2 §114.

Appointed during the Revolt by "the People"

28. Phanni (or Phanasus) b. Samuel, not of a high priestly family (67–68 C.E.): *War* 4.3.8 §155; *Ant.* 20.10.1 §227.

7.3.2.3   Organization of the Sanhedrin

Goodblatt, D. "Sanhedrin." *Encyclopedia of Religion* (1987) 13.60–63.
Mantel, H. *Studies in the History of the Sanhedrin* (1961).
———. "Sanhedrin." *IDBSup* (1976) 784–86.
Neusner, J. *Judaism: The Evidence of the Mishnah* (1981).

Rivkin, E. "Beth Din, Boule, Sanhedrin: A Tragedy of Errors." *HUCA* 46 (1975) 181–99.

Tcherikover, V. A. "Was Jerusalem a 'Polis'?" *IEJ* 14 (1964) 61–78.

From Josephus and other contemporary sources comes a unified picture of the Sanhedrin and the function of the high priest within it, even though many details of its structure and operation are unknown. The problem comes when the attempt is made to take account of the information in the Mishnah tractate *Sanhedrin* and other passages of rabbinic literature, in which one finds a rather different institution, made up mainly of rabbinic sages and presided over by the rabbinic *nāśî'* ("patriarch"). Various attempts have been made to reconcile the two pictures, one of the most popular being to assume there were two Sanhedrins, one a purely religious council dominated by the sages and the other a political institution presided over by the high priest (e.g., Mantel; cf. Rivkin). These attempts at harmonization are completely wrong-headed according to recent advances in the study of rabbinic literature (1.1.4). No part of the mishnaic tractate *Sanhedrin* seems to have originated in the pre-70 period (Neusner: 62, 95–97, 143–50) or, indeed, at any time before the Ushan period (post-135). The rabbinic Judaism of the post-70 period developed its own institutions to meet the needs of a Judaism without a temple or state. The picture in the Mishnah most likely represents a later rabbinic institution, although it is up to rabbinic scholars to judge to what extent an actual institution, as opposed to an idealized one, is being described. For the pre-70 institution, we must use contemporary sources such as Josephus; although it is possible that some genuine remembrance of the pre-70 Sanhedrin is preserved in rabbinic literature, it would be difficult or impossible to be sure that this is so in any given instance. Methodologically, therefore, it is probably best to ignore the rabbinic data in any reconstruction and simply to admit our ignorance where the early sources do not provide the necessary data for a full picture. (Interestingly, this methodological point is basically accepted in the initial treatment in Schürer [2.219] but is then ignored when details of the structure of the Sanhedrin are discussed, with most of the data taken straight from the later rabbinic sources [2.223–26].)

Early sources (decree of Antiochus III [5.3.1; 5.4.2]; 1 Macc 14:20, 28; 2 Macc 4:44; 11:27) as well as later ones (Acts 4:5-8, 23; 5:21-34; 22:30—23:7; *Ant.* 20.9.1 §§200–203) all give a reasonably consistent picture of a gerousia (council) presided over by the high priest. Its exact composition is not clear but is usually listed as priests, "elders" (*presbyteroi*, probably nonpriestly members of the aristocracy), and temple scribes. Under the Hasmoneans the high priest as quasi- or actual king probably dominated the council to a greater extent than perhaps he had in earlier periods. We have no examples in which the high priest's authority was challenged in any way by the gerousia. After the Roman conquest the high priest had little political power; however, we are told of several instances in the two decades before Herod became king in which the council attempted to assert political control, at least in some areas. The most notable instance is the attempted trial of Herod for the execution of certain bandits whom he had captured (6.4.5.1).

After Herod took power he exacted his revenge by having members of the Sanhedrin executed (*Ant.* 14.9.4 §175). Although Josephus says "all" were murdered, this is probably only hyperbole; but it is possible that the majority of those sitting on the council were assassinated. There is a brief reference to evidence for Hyrcanus's treachery having been shown to the Sanhedrin not long after this (*Ant.* 15.6.2 §173), but afterward we hear no more of the council during Herod's reign, suggesting that it existed in name only, with little more than rubber-stamp powers. However, once Judea became a Roman province in 6 C.E., the way was open for the Sanhedrin, with the high priest at its head, to take a more active role in politics. The Romans took from Herod the prerogative of appointing and deposing high priests, although the priests were chosen only from the traditional families. The reason for Roman control seems to be that the high priest did have some actual powers, and problems could arise if the Romans did not keep the office in the hands of individuals they felt able to trust. The right to appoint and depose high priests was restored to Agrippa I when he became king. After his death it did not revert to the Romans but instead went to Herod of Chalcis, and on his death to Agrippa II (*Ant.* 20.1.3 §§15–16).

7.3.2.4 The Competence of the Sanhedrin

Bammel, E. "Die Blutgerichtsbarkeit in der römischen Provinz Judäa vor dem ersten jüdischen Aufstand." *JJS* 25 (1974) 35–49.

Bickerman, E. J. "The Warning Inscriptions of Herod's Temple." *JQR* 37 (1946/47) 387–405.

Blinzler, J. *The Trial of Jesus* (1959).

———. *Der Prozess Jesus* (1969).

Braund, D. C. *Augustus to Nero: A Sourcebook on Roman History 31 B.C.–A.D. 68* (1985).

Catchpole, D. R. *The Trial of Jesus: A Study in the Gospels and Jewish Historiography from 1770 to the Present Day* (1971).

Lémonon, J.-P. *Pilate et le gouvernement de la Judée* (1981).

Lichtenstein, H. "Die Fastenrolle: Eine Untersuchung zur jüdisch-hellenistischen Geschichte." *HUCA* 8–9 (1931–32) 257–351.

Safrai, S. "Jewish Self-Government." *The Jewish People in the First Century* (1974) 1.377–419.

Sherwin-White, A. N. *Roman Society and Roman Law in the New Testament* (1963).

———. "The Trial of Jesus." *Historicity and Chronology in the New Testament* (1965) 97–116.

Winter, P. *On the Trial of Jesus* (1974).

One of the most hotly disputed points with regard to the Sanhedrin under Roman rule is whether it had the power of capital punishment. Scholars have arrayed themselves on both sides of the question (see, most recently, Lémonon: 74–97). Although some continue to argue that the Sanhedrin could try and execute people (*Smallwood: 149–50; Winter: 110–30; Safrai: 1.397–99), the present trend is to question the council's capital powers, if not actually to deny them (Sherwin-White 1963: 35–43; Blinzler 1959: 157–63 = 1969: 229–44; Schürer: 2.218–23; Catchpole: esp. 236–54; Bammel; Lémonon: 74–97). The arguments involved in the debate can be summarized as follows:

1. Although the Romans usually allowed the continuation of local customs and administration in new provinces, the power of capital punishment was jealously reserved in the hands of the Roman governor (sometimes referred to in discussions by the Latin term *jus gladii*, perhaps anachronistically: Sherwin-White 1963: 9–10; Schürer: 1.368). A good example of this is the decrees of Augustus in 6 b.c.e., regarding the situation in Cyrene. Although the governor could use carefully selected juries in capital cases, he did not have to: "With regard to any disputes that may arise among Greeks in the province of Cyrenaica, excepting capital cases—in these the provincial governor must himself act and judge or appoint a panel of jurors" (Braund: 180).

2. Coponius, the first governor appointed over Judea after it became a province (6 c.e.), was specifically said to "have from Caesar the power to execute" (*mechri tou kteinein labōn para Kaisaros exousian* [*War* 2.8.1 §117]).

3. An important passage in Josephus suggests that the Sanhedrin had no authority to execute:

> Ananus [the high priest] thought that he had a favourable opportunity because Festus was dead and Albinus was still on the way. And so he convened the judges of the Sanhedrin and brought before them a man named James, the brother of Jesus who was called the Christ, and certain others. He accused them of having transgressed the law and delivered them up to be stoned. Those of

the inhabitants of the city who were considered the most fair-minded . . . secretly sent to King Agrippa urging him, for Ananus had not even been correct in his first step, to order him to desist from any further such actions. Certain of them even went to meet Albinus, who was on his way from Alexandria, and informed him that Ananus had no authority to convene the Sanhedrin without his consent. (*Ant.* 20.9.1 §§200–203)

This implies two possibilities: (1) that the Sanhedrin could not even meet without Roman consent, which seems an extreme interpretation of the passage, and (2) that the Sanhedrin could not meet to try capital crimes unless the Roman governor authorized it, which is more likely (Catchpole: 241–44). Josephus does not suggest that the limitation on the council's power was anything new. Therefore, even if it was not a single, consistent policy under Roman rule, the implication is that at least during 44–66 C.E. the Sanhedrin had to have Roman consent to try and carry out capital sentences.

4. The inscription over the gate of the Jerusalem temple forbade non-Jews to enter on pain of death: "No foreigner may go inside the enclosure around the temple or the forecourt; whoever is caught (doing so) will be the cause of his own death which will follow" (Bickerman: 388). This inscription is also referred to by Josephus (*War* 6.2.4 §124–28; *Ant.* 15.11.5 §417) and Philo (*Gaium* 212). This might suggest that the power to try and execute for such an offense was within Jewish jurisdiction. However, the wording more likely suggests a warning not of legal liabilities but of practical consequences, for instance, lynching by a mob of loyal Jews outraged at such a desecration (Bickerman: 394–98). Nevertheless, even if it envisages a legal trial of the offender, it is obviously meant as an exception to the normal processes of law, because it would include Roman citizens over whom local judges normally had no power. That this is an exception is indicated by Titus's statement, quoted in *War* 6.2.4 §126: "And did we not permit you to put to death any who passed it, even were he a Roman?" The special exemption in this case simply confirms that capital punishment was not normally allowed by the native subjects.

5. A number of rabbinic passages are often cited. The question of those describing the general powers and functioning of the Sanhedrin is discussed above (7.3.2.3). Several speak of a period of forty years before the destruction of Jerusalem, when the Sanhedrin had no power of capital punishment (*y. Sanh.* 1.1, 18a; 7.2, 24b; cf. *b. Sanh.* 41a; *b. Avod. Zara* 8b). Although this might be genuine historical memory, there are reasons to discount these passages on

either side of the argument: (1) the figure of forty years is such a stereotypical one that it becomes very suspect; (2) as already noted, any references to the Sanhedrin in rabbinic literature are doubtful in their accuracy for the pre-70 period; and (3) the power to execute was kept in the hands of Herod and Archelaus during their reigns; the Romans would most likely have taken it over in 6 c.e. when Judea became a province, as the commission of Coponius explicitly states (see above), not in about 30 c.e., as the rabbinic passages imply. Consistency requires one to avoid using rabbinic material one way or the other in the argument.

6. *Megillat Ta'anit* 6 reads as follows: "On the 22nd day (of Elul) they began again to execute the wicked" (text in Lichtenstein: 336). The problem is that the particulars of the historical event are not discussed in the original text, but the wording of the passage in question strongly suggests the events in 66 c.e., when the Romans were first routed. If so, then it is reasonable to interpret the second part of the quotation as a resumption of capital trials by the native tribunal. Despite the reasonableness of these arguments, however, they still remain conjectural and provide at most a supplementary argument.

7. A New Testament text often cited to prove that the Sanhedrin was not competent to condemn to death is John 18:31: "Pilate said, 'Take him away and try him by your own law.' The Jews answered, 'We are not allowed to put any man to death.'" The problem with attempting to prove anything from this statement is that it comes from the latest of the Gospels and has no parallel in the Synoptics. Did the fourth evangelist have an actual tradition, or was he simply interpreting from the general tradition, as he so often does? The major positive argument is that the passion tradition in general seems to be in harmony with the view that the Jews needed Roman approval; that is, the Synoptic accounts seem to presuppose what John states explicitly. In addition, the Fourth Gospel also seems to have had an independent passion narrative.

8. A number of sources suggest that persons could be tried and convicted of capital crimes; however, if we exclude rabbinic literature, most of the examples are from the New Testament. Apart from John 7:53—8:11, these accounts center on the persecution of Christians (Acts 5:33-40; 6:12; 7:54-58). This entails two problems. The first is whether examples in the Gospels and the Acts of the Apostles are based on contemporary evidence or are not simply unreliable Christian tradition, with decades of development and embellishment behind them. The second problem is to what extent such stories of

Christian persecution and martyrdom can be trusted at all, especially for the early period of church history.

Acknowledging the later persecutions against the Christians, is it likely that the Jews, Greeks, or Romans engaged in continual persecution against and assault on the Christians in the early years, as is suggested? Can we believe that in its first weeks of existence the church had its leaders hauled before the Sanhedrin and commanded not to teach (Acts 4:1-21), even barely escaping the death penalty (Acts 5:33-40)? Or that members of the Sanhedrin participated in mob action against the Christian preacher Stephen (Acts 6:12—7:1; 7:54-58)? It is difficult to take these accounts at face value.

When such dubious examples are eliminated, however, what evidence exists is in favor of the Romans denying to the Sanhedrin the right to inflict capital punishment, at least without the Romans' express permission. Because of the sporadic nature of the evidence, this conclusion cannot be as firm as others for this period. Nevertheless, even though a degree of uncertainty must be admitted, the evidence presently available would deny the competence of the Sanhedrin to try capital cases without Roman authorization.

7.3.3 Governorship of Pilate

Lémonon, J.-P. *Pilate et le gouvernement de la Judée: Textes et monuments* (1981).
Levick, B. *Tiberius the Politician* (1976).

The events under Pilate's governorship as a whole are discussed at 7.4.3, but this section looks at two points that warrant a detailed discussion.

7.3.3.1 Pilate as a Tool of Sejanus

According to Philo (*Gaium* 159–60; *Flaccum* 1; cf. Eusebius, *Hist. eccl.* 2.5.7), an anti-Semitic policy was pursued by Sejanus, the right-hand man of Tiberius. From this it has often been concluded that Pilate's actions in Palestine reflected the same anti-Jewish attitude because, it is also argued, he was a protégé of Sejanus. This conclusion has now been opposed for three reasons (Levick: 136–37; Lémonon: 275–77).

1. It is a part of Philo's apologetic aim to contrast Tiberius with Caligula; therefore, he attempts to shift the blame for anything which

might discredit his portrayal of Tiberius. Because it was known that Jews were expelled from Rome in 19 c.e. at Tiberius's order, the emperor could be relieved of responsibility by blaming Sejanus as the bad influence that brought about this decision.

2. There is actually no evidence of a direct connection between Pilate and Sejanus.

3. Because Tiberius's policy was to keep the provinces quiet, it is unlikely that Pilate would have deliberately stirred up trouble, however powerful a patron he might have had. The episode with the shields (see 7.3.3.2) can be better explained as a clumsy attempt to show his loyalty at a time of uncertainty, which all officials must have experienced after Sejanus's fall.

7.3.3.2 The Gilded Shields Episode

Davies, P. S. "The Meaning of Philo's Text about the Gilded Shields." *JTS* 37 (1986) 109–14.

Fuks, G. "Again on the Episode of the Gilded Roman Shields at Jerusalem." *HTR* 75 (1982) 503–7.

Maier, P. L. "The Episode of the Golden Roman Shields at Jerusalem." *HTR* 62 (1969) 109–21.

Philo, ostensibly quoting a letter of Agrippa I, refers to an episode during the governorship of Pilate wherein some shields dedicated on behalf of Tiberius were introduced into Herod's palace in Jerusalem by Pilate (*Gaium* 299–305). Even though there was only a dedication inscription and there were no images on the shields, the Jews were affronted and complained bitterly. When they petitioned Tiberius, he ordered Pilate to remove the shields to a temple dedicated to the emperor outside Jewish territory. Although Josephus mentions an incident involving the Roman standards (*War* 2.9.2–3 §§169–74; *Ant.* 18.3.1 §§55–59), it is now generally accepted that Philo's statement refers to a separate incident, about which Josephus is silent. Why did the aniconic shields cause such offense to the Jews? Several answers have been offered, not all of them satisfactory:

1. Several scholars have suggested that the mere presence of objects dedicated to the Roman emperor was an offense to the Jews. However, this is not a good explanation because (1) sacrifices were offered daily in the temple on behalf of the emperor (Philo, *Gaium* 157, 317; Josephus, *War* 2.10.4 §197; *Ag. Ap.* 2.6 §77), and (2) shields of dedication honoring the emperor were found in many synagogues

in Egypt (Philo, *Gaium* 133). Maier has accepted this point but goes on to state, "We have to do here instead with an extremely sensitive, hyper-orthodox reaction against an unpopular foreign governor" (118). If this explanation is correct, however, then Philo would have seen its weakness and refrained from pressing the point.

2. Lémonon (214–17) connects the reaction with the fact that the shields were of the sort that usually bore the portrait of a person, which was here replaced with the dedication inscription. Again, Lémonon's seems a weak argument for Philo to use and does not very well explain why the Jews were so upset as to complain to the emperor himself.

3. Fuks has suggested that the dedication inscription referred to Tiberius as the "son of the divine Augustus" (*divi Augusti filius*), as his inscriptions often did. Against this, Davies has pointed out that less than one-third of Tiberius's known inscriptions contain "divine" in reference to Augustus (111). Davies also suggests that Philo's emphasis is on the dedication itself, rather than the content of the inscription (see point 4). Despite Davies's objections, which certainly have a point, Fuks still seems to have given a reasonable, possible explanation.

4. According to Davies, Philo's wording shows that the objection was not to the shields themselves or even to the specific words of the inscription but to the dedication ceremony. That is, the inscription made it clear that the shields had been dedicated on behalf of Tiberius to Roman gods in a pagan ceremony, and it was to this that the Jews objected. This is an ingenious and cogent explanation, although Fuks's suggestion seems a good alternative; indeed, the two are not mutually exclusive.

7.3.4 Expulsions of the Jews from Rome

Haenchen, E. *The Acts of the Apostles* (1971).
Moehring, H. R. "The Persecution of the Jews and the Adherents of the Isis Cult at Rome A.D. 19." *NovT* 3 (1959) 293–304.

Exactly when the Jewish community in Rome was founded is not known, although an expulsion in 139 B.C.E. shows that there were Jews in Rome by this time (Valerius Maximus 1.3.3; cf. *GLAJJ*: 1.358–60). The community received an important boost in numbers after the conquest of Jerusalem by Pompey in 63 B.C.E. A large number of Jews were taken to Rome as slaves and, when many of these or their descendants were manumitted, remained to expand the community. It was Roman custom to tolerate various religions as long as they behaved themselves. So it was that when the political associations (*collegia*) were banned at various times (e.g., 46 B.C.E.), the synagogues were specifically exempted because they could have fallen under the definition of collegia (*Ant*. 14.10.8 §§213–16). The Romans generally tolerated Judaism and did not interfere with it.

A major confrontation arose in 19 C.E. during the reign of Tiberius (*Ant*. 18.3.5 §§81–84; cf. Tacitus, *Ann*. 2.85.4; Suetonius, *Tib*. 36; Cassius Dio 57.18.5), that led to an expulsion of Jews from Rome. A Roman matron who had converted to Judaism was cheated by Jewish con artists. According to Josephus, the whole community suffered because of the actions of four rogue Jews; however, the situation was probably more complicated than that. More likely there had been a considerable number of converts among the Roman upper class, possibly even through active proselytizing (as is stated by Dio). On the one hand, this went against the rules under which Judaism was permitted, that is, that it in turn had to respect Roman custom and religion. On the other hand, it was a red flag to Tiberius, who was not fond of Oriental cults and had violently suppressed Isis worship earlier the same year after a similar incident (Moehring). Contrary to the impression made by Josephus's rhetoric, only police measures were taken against noncitizens: about four thousand young men were conscripted into the military and sent to Sardinia to fight bandits, but Jews who were Roman citizens were in no way affected.

Expulsion also took place under Claudius. The question is whether there were two expulsions or only one, and when one or both occurred (*Smallwood: 210–16; *GLAJJ*: 2.114–17; *D. R. Schwartz: 94–96). Cassius Dio refers to an edict in 41 by which the Jews were deprived of the right of assembly because of their large number, although he makes the specific point that they were not expelled (60.6.6). Suetonius refers to an undated expulsion caused by riots over "Chrestus" (*Claud*. 25.4). This is usually taken to be a reference to Christians, which would suggest a late date because a conflict between Jews and Christians was not likely to have occurred as early as 41. Acts 18:2 suggests that sometime around 50, Aquila and Priscilla had only recently been forced to leave Rome with other Jews. The patristic writer Orosius quotes Josephus to the effect that an expulsion took place in 49 C.E. (*Adver. pagan*. 7.6.15–16); however, Orosius is not at all reliable, and it seems unlikely that he had access to a passage of Josephus lost to us. (On Orosius, see 9.2.2.2.)

Smallwood concludes that the sources "cannot convincingly be conflated into a single episode" (*215), and there must have been more than one event. The problem is that the sources are difficult to evaluate. For example, Smallwood accepts the reliability of Acts 18:2, but there is reason to be suspicious of it (cf. Haenchen: 538–39). Furthermore, Smallwood's arguments that something may have happened in 41 are not very solid (cf. *D. R. Schwartz: 94–96). Claudius was not happy with the Jewish community in Alexandria, as is evident from his letter (7.3.7), but he was also severe with the Alexandrians. Philo's statement that Augustus did not expel the Jews does not necessarily hint that Claudius is about to do so (contra *Smallwood: 214). Although Acts 18:2 may not be reliable, it seems unlikely that the Christian community would have grown large enough to cause conflict with the Jewish community as early as 41; a date toward the end of Claudius's reign seems more reasonable in the light of Suetonius's comment (although we are not bound by the date 49, for the reasons just noted). D. R. Schwartz, who prefers one expulsion in 41, does not seem to present any new evidence. The difficulty that his dating presents in light of Dio's statement is not discussed, and his argument against 49 does not require the adoption of 41. Therefore, the firm data point to a single expulsion toward the end of Claudius's reign, although more than one is by no means out of the question.

7.3.5 Troubles of the Alexandrian Community

CPJ: 2.25–107.

Kasher, A. *The Jews in Hellenistic and Roman Egypt: The Struggle for Equal Rights* (1985).

Musurillo, H. A., ed. *The Acts of the Pagan Martyrs: Acta Alexandrinorum* (1954).

*Schwartz, D. R.: 96–106.

Tcherikover, V. *Hellenistic Civilization and the Jews* (1959) 296–332, 409–15.

Jews had settled in Egypt probably by pre-exilic times (2.2.2). Various statements in Josephus and elsewhere refer to Jews and Jewish communities in Egypt through the Ptolemaic and Seleucid periods. The Jewish community in Alexandria had a long history. Although Josephus's statement that it began with Alexander's conquest is unlikely, the community may well have its origins as early as the time of Ptolemy I (4.4.3). We have no indication of any major difficulties between the Jewish community and the Greek inhabitants of the city until Roman times, when a sea change in attitude seems to have taken place. The Greek citizens of Alexandria had enormous pride in their ancestry and tradition, and the Roman takeover was a great blow to their prestige and self-esteem. Further, the leaders of Judea (Hyrcanus II and Antipater) had contributed a good deal to the conquest of Egypt and had gained the Roman goodwill as a result (6.4.3). Although most of the Jews were not citizens of Alexandria (7.3.7), they nevertheless shared special privileges with citizens which the native Egyptians did not. This seems to have been the foundation of anti-Semitism in Egypt, which increased with time.

The earliest indications of this anti-Semitic attitude are literary (7.3.8), but no concerted action seems to have been taken until the reign of Caligula. At that time the events in Alexandria were closely tied up with the issue of citizenship (7.3.7) and with Caligula's attempt to place his statue in the Jerusalem temple (7.3.6). The main sources for the sequence of events are Philo's *Flaccum* and *Gaium*, both of which are apologetic works and thus have special problems of reliability (7.2.2). However, they can be supplemented by Josephus (*Ant.* 18.8.1 §§257–60) and by material in the papyri.

Conflict came to a head in 38 c.e., probably in large part because of Jewish agitation for citizenship or at least special privileges for their community (7.3.7). The two leaders of the gymnasium, the center of Greek cultural life, were Isidorus and Lampo. They put great pressure on the Roman governor, Flaccus, to remove the special privileges of the Jews. Then Agrippa I visited the city in August, on his way to take up his new kingdom, and inflamed the situation. Official anti-Jewish measures were put in force, although the popular mob may have taken them beyond what Flaccus intended: synagogues were closed (or, in some cases, destroyed) and all Jews were ghettoized by being forced to live in the Delta area (one of the five districts) of the city. This finally led to riots against the Jews in which much Jewish property was destroyed, and many Jews were killed or given humiliating public punishment. Order was restored only when Flaccus was sent to stand trial before Caligula and replaced by Pollio in October.

Thus far Philo's account in *Flaccum* has provided the basic narrative. There is a hiatus until Philo describes a bit about his actual embassy to Rome, and events must be pieced together from a few bits of data. The peace established was an uneasy one, apparently, and permission was requested by the Jewish community to send an embassy to Caligula. Permission was granted for the Jewish as well as the Greek community to do so, and Philo headed the delegation which left in the winter (*Gaium* 190), but whether it was in 38/39 or 39/40 is uncertain. The mission was overtaken by such events as Caligula's plans to place his statue in the temple, however, and does not appear to have achieved a full hearing. On Caligula's death, the tables were turned, because the Jews seem to have been the ones who rioted this time (*Ant.* 19.5.2 §§278–79). A report was sent to Claudius by the prefect. Finally, the delegations led by Philo and his Alexandrian opponents were heard by Claudius, who affirmed the traditional Roman policy of religious and ethnic tolerance. It has been suggested (Kasher: 263–74) that his decree is the one referred to by Josephus (*Ant.* 19.5.2 §280–85), although that document seems to have been worked over to suit Jewish apologetic concerns (7.3.7).

At this point, matters become rather complicated. Evidently, a second Alexandrian delegation arrived to present its case with regard to the latest riots, along with another Jewish delegation. We have no external record of the delegations, however, or of the hearing before Claudius. All we have is Claudius's letter, from which the external events must be reconstructed (7.3.7). Again, Claudius affirmed Jewish rights regarding religion but warned them about agitating for citizenship or special privileges. Peace was restored, but much of the bitterness remained and was passed on to future generations, until it culminated in the revolt under Trajan (9.4.8). It seems that two of the Alexandrian delegation, Isidorus and Lampo, were tried before Claudius and perhaps even executed by him. A legendary memory of these Alexandrian "martyrs" was preserved in the *Acta Alexandrinorum* (Musurillo).

7.3.6 Caligula's Attempt to Place His Statue in the Temple

Bilde, P. "The Roman Emperor Gaius (Caligula)'s Attempt to Erect His Statue in the Temple of Jerusalem." *Studia Theologica* 32 (1978) 67–93.

Reggiani, C. K. "I rapporti tra l'impero romano e il mondo ebraico al tempo di Caligola secondo la 'Legatio ad Gaium' di Filone Alessandrino." *ANRW* 2 (1984) 21.1.554–86.

*Schwartz, D. R.: 77–89.

Smallwood, E. M. "The Chronology of Gaius' Attempt to Desecrate the Temple." *Latomus* 16 (1957) 3–17.

———. "Philo and Josephus as Historians of the Same Event." *Josephus, Judaism, and Christianity* (1987) 114–29.

Zeitlin, S. "Did Agrippa Write a Letter to Gaius Caligula?" *JQR* 56 (1965/66) 22–31.

The emperor Caligula's (Gaius's) attempt to place his statue into the temple at Jerusalem is a monumental event in the religious history of Judah. Had he succeeded, his action would have been the equivalent of the desecration under Antiochus IV; only its failure has kept it from full notoriety. Still, as with the actions of Antiochus, major questions arise about the course of events and the motivation of the chief instigator, Caligula himself. There are three versions of the story, two in Josephus and one in Philo. Although all three agree in broad outline, there are both significant and minor differences. Therefore, each version should be examined separately.

According to *War* 2.10.1–5 §§184–203, Caligula's decision was simply a part of the hubris with which he conducted himself as a god. No other reason is given and the events are only summarized. Petronius, the Syrian legate, was sent from Antioch with the task of carrying out the order to erect the statue in the temple. He was met at Ptolemais by a large crowd of Jews, who begged him to desist. Leaving his soldiers and the statues [*sic*] there, he went to Tiberias and held an audience with the people and the leading figures of the nation, attempting to show them the senselessness of defiance because they could not win against Rome. But when the people proved intractable and Petronius saw that they were not sowing the ground even though it was time to do so, he agreed to write to Caligula despite the personal risk. Caligula's response was the threat of execution, but the death of the emperor saved both Petronius and the Jews.

Antiquities 18.8.2–9 §§261–309 has a similar account with some important differences. Josephus precedes this version with an account of the delegation from the Alexandrian Jewish community, led by Philo (§§257–60). Caligula decided to set up his image in Jerusalem because he saw himself disrespected by the Jews alone of all his subjects. The description in *Antiquities* of the course of events in Syria is much like the account in *War*, although the former has been expanded by means of speeches and other dramatic devices. When Petronius decided to risk writing to Caligula for a cancellation of the project, God sent a sign in the form of unexpected rain after a long drought. The reason for abandoning the project was not Caligula's premature death, however, but Agrippa's petition to Caligula, an event not even hinted at in the *War*. Because of his regard for Agrippa, Caligula wrote to Petronius cancelling his plans, but when he afterward received Petronius's letter of Jewish resistance, he became angry and ordered Petronius to commit suicide. Fortunately, that letter was held up until after news of Caligula's death had reached Petronius.

A further account, the most detailed of all, is found in Philo's *Gaium* 184–338. According to Philo, Caligula saw the Jews as his enemies (256), because they were the only ones who refused to accept his self-deification (115). In Jamnia (Yavneh), which had a mixed population of Jews and others (199–202), some of the pagan population erected an altar to Caligula, but it was torn down by Jews. In retaliation, Caligula proposed setting up his own statue in the Jerusalem temple, a plan in which he was encouraged by the "riff-raff" (*peritrimma*) Helicon and Apelles, who were acting as his advisors (203–6). When directions to proceed were given to Petronius, although he was afraid because he knew how fanatical the Jews were about their religion, he dared not disobey the orders of his emperor (207–19). He therefore delayed as much as possible by ordering the best craftsmen to take the greatest pains in their work. Because of the Jewish reaction and entreaties, he finally agreed to write to Caligula, using the excuse that the ripening harvest would be neglected and lost if he did not relent. Although Caligula was furious at this, he is alleged to have given a respectful reply that nevertheless urged Petronius to go on with the project (254–60). At about the same time Agrippa heard of the plan (261–75) and wrote a long rhetorical letter, at risk to his own life (276–330), which Caligula reluctantly heeded (331–33). He also ordered, however, that anyone outside Judah should be allowed to erect statues to him if they wanted to (334–36). Caligula did not abandon his plans, instead ordering another statue to be manufactured secretly in Rome, having in mind to take it with him when he later visited Egypt (337–38).

Although the three accounts, as well as the supplementary material in the Roman historians, broadly agree, Philo is generally given preference where there are differences, because he is the only writer contemporary with the events and in a position to know many of the details personally (Smallwood 1957; 1989; contra Bilde). He is also the only writer to explain the emperor's actions other than by Caligula's self-proclamation of divinity. By contast, as Bilde has recently noted, Philo's account is much more theologically and apologetically slanted than Josephus's. As with Antiochus IV, the sources put it down to the irrational actions of one man, combined with general animosity toward the Jews. Whereas even the Roman sources picture Caligula as mad, the trend among recent historians has been to see that portrayal as distorted, a picture to which the senatorial bias of the Roman sources has contributed a great deal (7.4.5). Although it is true that Caligula did some strange things, including proclaiming himself a god, he did not particularly penalize those who did not treat him as divine (cf. Bilde: 73–75). Even Philo's highly partisan account shows that he dismissed the Jewish delegation with the simple statement, "They seem to me to be people unfortunate rather than wicked and to be foolish in refusing to believe that I have got the nature of a god" (*Gaium* 367), hardly the words of a mad tyrant and rabid hater of the Jews.

The clue to Caligula's actions seems to lie in Philo's statement about an event in Jamnia. Roman policy was religious tolerance to Judaism, but it was expected that this tolerance would be reciprocated (Bilde: 74–75; cf. 7.3.8). When some local Jews tore down an altar to the emperor, they committed a serious breach not only against the local freedom of worship but also against Roman authority. Their actions could be taken as open rebellion. That Caligula responded with punishment is only to be expected. The Jews, including Philo and Josephus, found it convenient to interpret this as a sign of personal animosity against themselves, but this was only propaganda. The more likely explanation is further   .cated by the final outcome: Jews were allowed to worship unhindered, but they were not to interfere with emperor cults set up "outside the capital," probably meaning outside Judah itself (*Gaium* 334). The one thing still unexplained is why Caligula chose the idea of a statue in the Jerusalem temple as punishment for the Jewish political act in Jamnia, but D. R. Schwartz has pointed out a plausible reason: Judaism was tolerated on condition that it "had no political implications. If the Judaeans thought otherwise, then the Temple would have to be destroyed or Romanized; this is the rationale of Gaius' decision" (*82).

As both Josephus (*Antiquities*) and Philo state, the plan was abandoned because of the intervention of Agrippa. Although the exact details are uncertain because of differences between the accounts (e.g., Zeitlin has argued that Agrippa's long letter in Philo cannot be genuine; see also *D. R. Schwartz: 200–202), Agrippa would have had good reasons for requesting that Caligula abandon the project. As Bilde has noted, "Agrippa . . . had reason to fear a continued strike, and even more, an open revolt. Ultimately, his kingdom was at stake" (86). Philo's report that Caligula regretted his decision to cancel the project and gave secret orders to have another statue built in Rome seems unlikely, both because it does not fit Caligula's probable political motives and because it accords too closely with Philo's own biased picture of Caligula's madness and personal hatred toward the Jews. Perhaps there was such a rumor about, but it would have arisen for the same reasons that Philo had for believing and reporting it.

More of a problem is the chronology of the episode. Josephus puts it during sowing time, whereas Philo mentions the needs of the harvest (*Gaium* 248–49, 260). Many scholars have chosen to follow Josephus, putting the original actions of Caligula and Petronius in the late autumn. This fits with Petronius's plan to winter his troops in Ptolemais (*Ant.* 18.8.2 §262); the forty- (or fifty-) day delay in getting on with the planting (*War* 2.10.5 §200; *Ant.* 18.8.3 §272), which was usually carried out in October or November; and the delay of Caligula's message to Petronius, apparently because of winter sailing (*War* 2.10.5 §203). But how is this to be reconciled with Philo's statements? Furthermore, it ignores that autumn 40 to autumn 41 was a sabbatical year, so there would have been no sowing in the autumn of 40. Part of the problem is caused by the assumption that Caligula's interview with the Jewish mission led by Philo must have been later than May of 40 because of the mention of Jewish sacrifices for a victory in Germany (*Gaium* 357); the emperor returned to Rome from his expedition to Germany in May 40. However, D. R. Schwartz has argued that Philo's mission sailed in the winter of

38/39, and that both audiences with Caligula were in 39 (*196–99). In addition, he asserts that the order about setting up the statue was in summer 39 (*198). If so, then Philo's account fits into place better than Josephus's does (contra Bilde), although Josephus may have some events not recorded by Philo.

To summarize, Caligula planned to set up the statue in the Jerusalem temple as punishment for what he saw as an anti-Roman political act, the Jewish destruction of a Roman altar in Jamnia. It was politically motivated, not just a mad caprice or hatred for the Jews. He abandoned the project at the request of Agrippa, who not only had a duty as intermediary between the Romans and Jews but also realized that Jewish resistance would put his own rule at risk. Petronius evidently survived the emperor, although whether he was as bold or came as close to death as is implied in the Jewish apologetic tradition is uncertain.

7.3.7 Citizenship for Diaspora Jews?

Applebaum, S. *Jews and Greeks in Ancient Cyrene* (1979).
Goodman, M. Review of *Jews in Hellenistic and Roman Egypt* (Hebrew edition), by A. Kasher. *JJS* 32 (1981) 207–8.
Kasher, A. *The Jews in Hellenistic and Roman Egypt: The Struggle for Equal Rights* (1985).
Moehring, H. R. "The *Acta pro Judaeis* in the *Antiquities* of Flavius Josephus." *Christianity, Judaism and Other Greco-Roman Cults* (1975) 3.124–58.
Roux, J., and G. Roux. "Un décret du politeuma des Juifs de Bérénikè en Cyrénaïque au Musée Lapidaire de Carpentras." *REG* 62 (1949) 281–96.
Ruppel, W. "Politeuma." *Philologus* 82 (1926/27) 268–311, 433–54.
Tcherikover, V. *Hellenistic Civilization and the Jews* (1959) 296–332, 409–15.

The question of whether Jews were citizens of some of the Hellenistic cities in which they lived is one inherited from antiquity. In a number of passages Josephus implies that the Jews were citizens of such cities as Alexandria and Caesarea but that the Greeks refused to recognize this or attempted to disenfranchise them. His statements regarding citizenship follow.

War 2.18.7 §§487–88 says that Alexander the Great had given the Jewish inhabitants of Alexandria the right to live in the city "with equal status" (*ex isomoirias*) to the Greeks. His successors confirmed this, assigned a quarter of the city to them, and gave them the right to call themselves "Macedonians." *Antiquities* 12.1.1 §8 claims that Ptolemy I gave the Jews of Alexandria "equal civic rights" (*isopolitas*) with the Macedonians.

Antiquities 14.10.1–26 §§185–267 quotes a number of decrees of the Roman Senate and others with regard to the privileges of the Jews in various places, especially Asia Minor. Whether they are all authentic is a moot point (Moehring), but there is probably some basis for most of the rights granted, which are generally of a religious nature: permission to keep the Sabbath and festivals, exemption from military service (apparently only Roman citizens), the right to send the temple tax to Jerusalem, allowance of Jewish religious gatherings, and the like. Documents relating to Sardis (17 §235; 24 §§259–61) indicate that the community there was organized as a *politeuma* (see below). There are several references to "Jews who are Roman citizens" (13 §228; 14 §232; 16 §234; 18 §237; 19 §240). Finally, Josephus refers to a bronze tablet in Alexandria, set up by Julius Caesar, that declares the Jews are "citizens" (*politai*) of the city (1 §188).

Antiquities 16.6.1–7 §§160–73 also contains decrees on behalf of the Jews in Cyrene and in Asia, which Josephus claims regard the question of "equal civil rights" (*isonomia*). The specific issue is taxation and the allowance for the temple tax to be sent to Jerusalem. The basic religious rights are affirmed by Augustus and Agrippa, although citizenship is not specifically mentioned in the decrees.

Against Apion 2.4 §§35–41, in its polemic on Apion's attack, states that Alexander had given the Jews "equal privileges" (*isēs timēs*) with the Macedonians, that a stela in Alexandria records rights given to the Jews by Augustus ("Caesar the Great"), that the Jews in Antioch are called Antiochenes and have "citizenship" (*politeian*), and that those in Ephesus and the rest of Ionia are given the same name as "indigenous citizens" (*authigenesi politais*).

Because of these statements by Josephus, many scholars of the nineteenth century accepted that Jews were normally citizens of the Greek cities in which they resided. However, since that time many original documents have become available, especially among the papyri and inscriptions found in Egypt, which now seem to answer the question of citizenship decisively. It has long been known that certain Jews were citizens of their Greek city of residence; a prominent example from Alexandria was the family of Philo. Lists on which appeared the names of most future citizens of the city (the ephebate), from such diverse areas as Cyrene and Ptolemais, contain Jewish names (Applebaum: 167–68, 177–78).

Yet, as interesting as the individual examples are, they do not address the issue of the Jewish community as a whole. The Jews were not unusual in having communities with their own separate ethnic identities in the midst of Greek cities throughout the Hellenistic world. These communities were organized into *politeumata*. That is, each was granted a city charter that for the most part allowed them to maintain their own traditions and to regulate themselves internally. They were semi-autonomous entities within the Greek polis and had specific rights and privileges, but their members were not citizens of the city and did not possess those rights reserved for citizens. As already noted, a politeuma of the Jews is attested for Sardis in Josephus; inscriptions also mention politeumata for other cities, such as Cyrene, Alexandria, Memphis, Caesarea, and Antioch. Still, this fact alone suggests that the Jews as a whole did not have citizenship in these cities. Caesarea, for example, initially had few, if any, Jews, even though the city was founded by Herod. By about 60 C.E., when the Jewish population had grown significantly, the Jewish community began to agitate for equal rights, but this was refused by Nero, which contributed to the beginning of the war with Rome (*Ant.* 20.8.7, 9 §§173, 183–84).

Of particular importance to the question of citizenship is the position of the Alexandrian Jewish community. It also seems clear that at least part of the agitation in Alexandria in 38–41 was caused by a dispute over citizenship. Josephus quotes a letter from Claudius which confirms that the Jews were among the earliest inhabitants of the city and that they had "equal civic rights":

> Tiberius Claudius Caesar Augustus Germanicus, of tribunician power, speaks. Having from the first known that the Jews in Alexandria called Alexandrians were fellow colonizers from the very earliest times jointly with the Alexandrians and received equal civic rights [*isēs politeias*] from the kings, as is manifest from the documents in their possession and from the edicts; and that after Alexandria was made subject to our empire by Augustus their rights were preserved by the prefects sent from time to time, and that these rights of theirs have never been disputed. . . . I desire that none of their rights should be lost to the Jews on account of the madness of Gaius, but that their former privileges also be preserved to them, while they abide by their own customs; and I enjoin upon both parties to take the greatest precaution to prevent any disturbance arising after the posting of my edict. (*Ant.* 19.5.2 §§280–85)

If genuine, this letter would seem to settle the matter of citizenship, at least for the Alexandrian Jews. However, there are two reasons to suspect that the document is either a forgery or, more likely, a genuine edict altered by Jewish scribes for their own purposes: (1) Josephus is here writing in an apologetic mode, trying to defend the Jews who are under considerable threat in the Roman world; and (2) we now possess a genuine decree from Claudius which states plainly that the Jews as a whole were not citizens (*CPJ*: 2.36–55, text 153):

Tiberius Claudius Caesar Augustus Germanicus the Emperor, Pontifex Maximus, holder of the Tribunician Power, consul designate, to the city of Alexandria, greeting. . . . About the requests which you have made from me, my decision is this. To all those who have been registered as *epheboi* up to the time of my principate I guarantee and confirm their Alexandrian citizenship with all the privileges and benefits enjoyed by the city. . . . With regard to the responsibility for the disturbances and rioting, or rather, to speak the truth, the war, against the Jews, . . . I harbour within me a store of immutable indignation against those who renewed the conflict. I merely say that, unless you stop this destructive and obstinate mutual enmity, I shall be forced to show what a benevolent ruler can be when he is turned to righteous indignation. Even now, therefore, I conjure the Alexandrians to behave gently and kindly towards the Jews who have inhabited the same city for many years, and not to dishonour any of their customs in their worship of their god, but to allow them to keep their own ways, as they did in the time of the god Augustus and as I too, having heard both sides, have confirmed. The Jews, on the other hand, I order not to aim at more than they have previously had and not in future to send two embassies as if they lived in two cities, a thing which has never been done before, and not to intrude themselves into the games presided over by the *gymnasiarchoi* and the *kosmetai*, since they enjoy what is their own, and in a city which is not their own they possess an abundance of all good things. Nor are they to bring in or invite Jews coming from Syria or Egypt, or I shall be forced to conceive graver suspicions. (*CPJ*: 2.42–43)

This original document basically resolves the issue, even though the relationship between it and the letter of Claudius in Josephus is not completely clear. The simplest explanation is that the letter in Josephus is (part of) a genuine letter, perhaps sent on another occasion, which has been altered by Jewish apologists. D. R. Schwartz argues that it is a version of the genuine Claudius rescript (*99–106; contra Kasher: 262–309). As Tcherikover has pointed out, most of the ancient literature on the subject of citizenship falls into the category of Jewish apology (314–15). Whether Philo, Josephus, or 3 Maccabees, the apologists were all engaged in a vital battle against developing anti-Semitic attitudes. In order to prevent the erosion of past religious privileges traditionally granted to Jews, they used every weapon in their arsenal without worrying too much about whether their statements were strictly true. In contrast, the general decree about Jewish rights quoted by Josephus (*Ant.* 19.5.3 §§287–91) does not show the same defensive tendency. Although D. R. Schwartz points out the possibility that the decree in *Antiquities* might be forged, he ultimately sees no obstacles to its acceptance but, rather, finds several points which "support the authenticity of the second edict with perhaps some light Jewish editing" (*105). Therefore, the basic conclusions can be summarized as follows:

1. Some individual Jews were citizens of the Greek cities in which they resided. We know, for example, that Philo's family were citizens of Alexandria. Inscriptions, papyri, and some literary sources also indicate this for other Greek cities.
2. Nevertheless, the Jewish community as a whole in each city made up a semi-autonomous organization often called a politeuma or *katoikos*. The Jews were allowed to practice their own customs and religion and even to regulate themselves internally to a large extent. They were not citizens of the city, however, and did not enjoy the traditional civic rights.
3. The statements in Jewish literature that seem to contradict this are subject to several qualifications: (1) the terminology is often used loosely rather than according to strict legal definition, which can be confusing; (2) the statements are usually part of an apologetic context, in which an accurate description of the real status of the Jews is subordinated to defending traditional rights by whatever means possible; and (3) the writers themselves, when read closely, actually provide evidence that the Jews as a whole did not have the rights of citizens.

7.3.8 Anti-Semitism and Religious Tolerance

Daniel, J. L. "Anti-Semitism in the Hellenistic-Roman Period." *JBL* 98 (1979) 45–65.
Feldman, L. H. "Pro-Jewish Intimations in Anti-Jewish Remarks Cited in Josephus' *Against Apion*." *JQR* 78 (1987/88) 187–251.
Gager, J. G. *Moses in Greco-Roman Paganism* (1972).
Guterman, S. L. *Religious Toleration and Persecution in Ancient Rome* (1951).
Kasher, A. *Jews and Hellenistic Cities in Eretz-Israel* (1990).
Marshall, A. J. "Flaccus and the Jews of Asia (Cicero *Pro Flacco* 28.67–69)." *Phoenix* 29 (1975) 139–54.
Neusner, J., and E. S. Frerichs, eds. *"To See Ourselves as Others See Us"* (1985).
Rabello, A. M. "The Legal Condition of the Jews in the Roman Empire." *ANRW* 2 (1980) 13.662–762.
Rajak, T. "Was There a Roman Charter for the Jews?" *JRS* 74 (1984) 107–23.
Sevenster, J. N. *The Roots of Pagan Anti-Semitism in the Ancient World* (1975).

"Anti-Semitism" is a problematic word (Sevenster: 1–6). Some consider it a misnomer and would prefer another term (Feldman: 187 n.1), but so far no one has found a suitable English substitute (Daniel: 45–56). It has also been argued that anti-Semitism did not exist in the Greco-Roman period. This may be so, but I find it difficult to draw the line between the anti-Semitism of medieval and modern times and some of the attitudes expressed by Greco-Roman writers and individuals.

The earliest attitudes recorded in the literature indicate a reaction to the Jews similar to that toward other Near Eastern peoples coming into the Greek purview. There are those, such as Hecateus of Abdera, who found the Jews exotic and interesting (4.2.2; 4.4.4); against this must be weighed the generic contempt felt by the Greeks toward all "barbarians." It is not unusual, however, to find positive statements about the Jews in Greco-Roman literature, especially from the earlier period (Gager: 25–79; Feldman).

Furthermore, with the exception of the decrees of Antiochus IV, Judaism was tolerated throughout the Second Temple period. The Persians had allowed (and, according to biblical statements, even encouraged) the Jewish cult and traditional customs. There is no indication that anything changed with the Greek conquest. Similarly, under Roman rule the Jews enjoyed religious rights even over against their gentile neighbors. Although some of the alleged decrees in the Jews' favor are suspect (7.3.7), there are also unquestioned decrees permitting the free exercise of their traditional customs and way of life. For example, when the collegia were periodically banned, the Jewish synagogues were specifically exempted most of the time (7.3.4). Even during and after the 66–70 war, there is no indication of official persecution or restriction on Judaism as such (despite riots and mob action against the Jews in various Greek cities in the Syro-Palestinian region [7.4.11.1]). Therefore, the anti-Semitic attitudes and actions attested must be weighed against the official recognition and tolerance.

Anti-Semitism as such probably arose in the first century B.C.E. From this time on, the occasional positive statement about the Jews from pagan writers is quickly drowned in the cacophony of contempt, innuendo, invention, lie, and general antipathy. Why are the Jews so often caricatured and maligned by Greco-Roman writers? Was it because of their "odd" customs? Other local peoples had peculiar customs, some no less laughable to the educated Greco-Roman. Circumcision, for example, was practiced by a range of Oriental peoples. Therefore, strangeness of custom does not seem to be the primary cause of anti-Semitism. There are a number of possible explanations, but two stand out, one local and one general.

The local explanation has to do with the situation in Alexandria, where anti-Semitism seems first to have reared its head in the century or so before the Common Era. Many Jews lived in Alexandria, and the population increased proportionally as time went on. At various times, individual Jews are reported to have risen high in the Ptolemaic government (cf. 4.4.5; 5.4.7), although we have little indication that this caused any particular ethnic resentment. When Egypt was taken over by the Romans, however, the Jews favored the winning side. Antipater and Hyrcanus helped Julius Caesar with men and supplies (6.4.3). Not only was the Roman general grateful for this, but also he may have issued decrees about freedom for the Jews to practice their religion. Therefore, the Jews were seen—rightly or wrongly—by the Greek citizens of Alexandria and elsewhere in Egypt to be on the side of the Romans and, conversely, enemies of the Greek community. Then, when Jews began to agitate for Alexandrian citizenship or similar rights, smoldering resentment and hatred burst into full flame (7.3.5; 7.3.7).

The general reason for anti-Semitism was that the Jews were themselves seen as intolerant and misanthropic (cf. *Goodman: 97–99). This attitude was especially fostered by events that occurred under Hasmonean rule. After fighting and winning a bitter battle against religious persecution, the Maccabees proceeded to eliminate all other forms of worship in the territories under their control. The Idumeans and Itureans were converted to Judaism (6.3.6). Non-Jewish cults and cult places were destroyed. Even later under Roman rule, there were occasional acts of aggression by the Jews against non-Jewish cults which were illegal under Roman law (cf. 7.3.6).

The Jewish refusal to worship other gods was the occasion for astonishment and resentment among pagans and perhaps even an excuse to suspect subversive attitudes toward the state, but this by itself might have been accepted. It became the object not just of suspicion but also of fear and even hatred, however, when it was combined with an active attempt to suppress other forms of worship. To the Greeks and Romans, the Jews demanded religious tolerance, then denied it to others. The various lies about Jewish origins and worship (especially that of human sacrifice) were symbolic of the perception of the Jews as haters of all other peoples. The other factors often cited, although not the principal causes of anti-Semitism, would have contributed. The Jewish customs that the Greeks and Romans found laughable or barbaric were a convenient vehicle for the invention and dissemination of various slanders about Judaism. Proselytizing was probably never done on a large scale, but it happened frequently enough to have helped fuel the resentment (7.3.4; 8.3.2).

7.3.9 Causes of the War with Rome

Bilde, P. "The Causes of the Jewish War according to Josephus." *JSJ* 10 (1979) 179–202.

Kasher, A. *Jews and Hellenistic Cities in Eretz-Israel* (1990).

Rappaport, U. "Jewish-Pagan Relations and the Revolt against Rome in 66–70 C.E." *Jerusalem Cathedra* 1 (1981) 81–95.

It would be a mistake to assume that there was a simple cause of the war with Rome and that had one specific problem been eliminated, the war would have been averted. Good arguments have been made that confrontation with Rome was inevitable. This will naturally remain a moot point, but important aspects of Jewish history, as well as contemporary difficulties, worked together to bring war about. Josephus exercised himself with the causes of the war (Bilde), suggesting a number of the reasons which seem cogent to modern scholars; however, he gives no systematic discussion and frequently makes statements about "the cause" in one context, which contradicts what he says elsewhere. Five causes for the war are often cited, to which a sixth must be added:

1. Historical memory of an independent Israel under native rule. An independent state was generally an unrealized ideal, except for brief periods in Israel's history, primarily in the reigns of David and Solomon and for a portion of Hasmonean rule. For much of the period of the monarchy, Israel was dominated by foreign powers such as Egypt, Assyria, or Babylon; furthermore, Israel was split into two competing states after the death of Solomon. Nevertheless, this could easily be forgotten or the Scriptures misinterpreted, whereas the living memory of an independent Jewish state under Hasmonean rulers continued well into the first century. Given the importance of the monarchy as both a religious and political symbol, it is hardly surprising that a number of the rebel leaders under Herod and later were of royal descent or took on the trappings of royalty (see 7.4.11.2; 8.2.12).

2. Roman misrule. Rome's poor choice of governors for Judea, especially during the years 44–66 C.E., has often been emphasized, but Pilate is an example of an earlier governor whose stupidity lingered in the Jewish memory. The governors appointed after Agrippa I had many problems to contend with, but few showed even a modest ability to resolve the difficulties in a way that eased rather than exacerbated the situation (see 7.4.9).

3. Socioeconomic pressures both from within and without (see 7.3.10).

4. The religious tradition of Israel as God's chosen nation and people. As noted, recent study has shown the importance of socioeconomic factors in bringing about the confrontation between Judea and the Roman Empire. Nevertheless, it is important to keep in mind that religion is a powerful social force and may serve as a catalyst for changes toward which other social pressures are pushing. There is no doubt that religious ideology was an important factor, even though it was only one among many. Although various rebel groups may have emerged because of socioeconomic factors, religious ideology served to provide the justification for their activities and the hope that sustained them even in the face of a hopeless situation. Therefore, paramilitary activity often seemed to be associated with messianic pretensions and apocalyptic speculation. Perhaps no more telling illustration can be given than that in *War* 6.5.2 §§283–85: even with the Romans on their final assault, six thousand people assembled on a portico of the temple courtyard, with the expectation of imminent divine intervention on their behalf.

5. Bad relations with the neighboring Hellenistic cities (Kasher; Rappaport). Rappaport argues that this was the one inevitable cause of the war, that is, no cause but this one would inevitably lead to war if not resolved. No doubt this is a moot point, but Rappaport has thus pinpointed an important factor that has not often been recognized. The seriousness of the situation is shown by the incidents in Caesarea that sparked the revolt and by the slaughter of Jews in Greek cities and of non-Jews in Jewish cities.

6. The failure of the Jewish upper class (see further 7.3.10). This significant factor must now be added to those above. Indeed, this may be the decisive factor contributing to the outbreak of the war (*Goodman).

7.3.10 Socioeconomic Factors

Applebaum, S. "The Struggle for the Soil and the Revolt of 66–73 c.e." *EI* 12 (1975) 125–28 (Heb.) + 122*–23* (Eng. summary).

———. "Economic Life in Palestine." *The Jewish People in the First Century* (1976) 2.631–700.

———. "Judaea as a Roman Province: The Countryside as a Political and Economic Factor." *ANRW* 2 (1977) 8.355–96.

Brunt, P. A. "Josephus on Social Conflicts in Roman Judaea." *Klio* 59 (1977) 149–53.

Goodman, M. "The First Jewish Revolt: Social Conflict and the Problem of Debt." *JJS* 33 (1982) 417–27.

Hamel, G. *Poverty and Charity in Roman Palestine* (1990).
Jones, A.H.M. "Taxation in Antiquity." *The Roman Economy* (1974) 151–86.
Kreissig, H. "Die landwirtschaftliche Situation in Palästina vor dem judäischen Krieg." *Acta Antiqua* 17 (1969) 221–54.

Most of the socioeconomic forces which operated during Herod's reign (6.3.7) continued to have their place between 6 and 66 c.e. Jerusalem shopkeepers especially, but also others elsewhere in Judea, still benefited from the pilgrimage industry. The amount of money coming into the temple from the Diaspora Jews was enormous and served to enrich the economy indirectly. This had side effects, however, manifested in large surpluses which had no ready outlet (see below). The wealthy class was to a large extent made up of individuals from certain prominent priestly families, who obviously profited from their sacerdotal position. Continuing work on the temple also provided work for a considerable number of people. This is indicated by the severity of the problem when the work on the temple was finished, and a large surplus of labor was consequently dumped on the market. The problem was temporarily solved by putting these people to work paving the streets of Jerusalem, a project evidently paid for out of temple funds (*Ant.* 20.9.7 §§219–22).

It is debatable whether the tax burden under the Romans was more oppressive than it had been under Herod. According to Tacitus taxation was so high during the reign of Tiberius that "Syria and Judaea, exhausted by their burdens, were pressing for a diminution of the tribute" (*Ann.* 2.42.5). Both provinces were probably suffering from the cumulative effects of long years of taxation, rather than from any new measures under Tiberius. Although there were taxes on sales, imported goods, and the like, the backbone of the Roman tax system was the census (Jones: 164–68; Schürer: 1.401–4). On this were based the two main types of taxes: (1) a poll tax and a tax on property and possessions (*tributum capitis*), and (2) a tax on agricultural produce (*tributum soli*). All members of the household, including women and children (boys over fourteen, girls over twelve), were liable to the poll tax. The tax apparently varied according to time and place in the empire, but it has been estimated at one denarius per person in Tiberius's time (cf. Mark 12:13-17). Each head of the household had to make a yearly declaration of property, which was taxed at the rate of about 1 percent (Appian, *Syr.* 50.253). These taxes were usually collected on behalf of the Romans by the officials of the internal government rather than by the Romans directly. Many of the other taxes continued to be farmed out to tax farmers (*publicani*), however, as the majority of taxes had been in the early years of Roman rule (6.3.1). The reason for the distinction seems to be

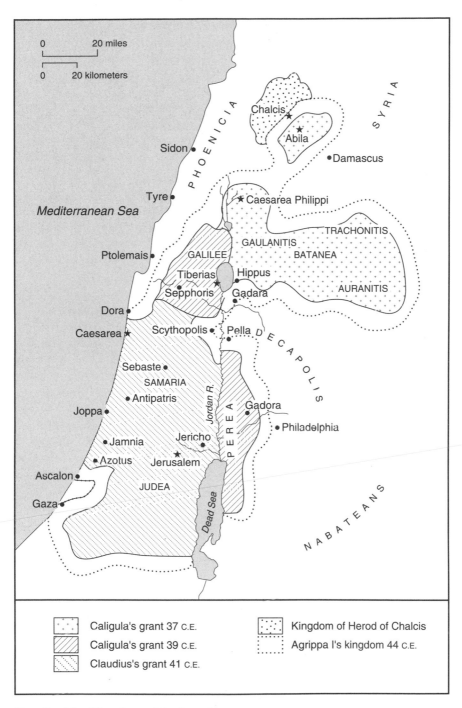

0   20 miles

0   20 kilometers

PHOENICIA

SYRIA

Chalcis

Abila

Sidon

Damascus

Tyre

Caesarea Philippi

Mediterranean Sea

TRACHONITIS

GAULANITIS

GALILEE   BATANEA

Ptolemais

Tiberias   Hippus

AURANITIS

Sepphoris   Gadara

Dora

Caesarea   Scythopolis   Pella   D
                                    E
                                    C
Sebaste   A
                                    P
SAMARIA   O
         Antipatris   L
Joppa   I
                               Gadora   S

Jamnia   Jericho   Philadelphia

Azotus   Jerusalem

Ascalon

JUDEA

Gaza

Jordan R.

PEREA

Dead Sea

NABATEANS

Caligula's grant 37 C.E.

Kingdom of Herod of Chalcis

Caligula's grant 39 C.E.

Agrippa I's kingdom 44 C.E.

Claudius's grant 41 C.E.

Map 6.   The Kingdom of Agrippa I

that the *tributum capitis* could be basically calculated in advance, but the other taxes were variable. Farming them out not only produced a guaranteed income but also the highest potential yield, because the farming rights were assigned to the highest bidder (Jones: 154–56).

The problem in Judea was not one primarily of wealth, because the province seems to have been prosperous on the whole, but of distribution. There is the obvious differential between the very wealthy few and the many poor who often bore the brunt of taxation, but a proper evaluation must go beyond this. Goodman has recently drawn attention to the problem of excess wealth that could not be readily reintroduced into the economy. The contributions from the Diaspora must have been enormous and may have found their way into the economy through the temple rebuilding program. Unfortunately, much of it could not be easily invested. Land was limited, which closed one obvious source of investment. Much of the wealth went into static stocks of gold and silver (*War* 6.5.2 §282). The one outlet was loans.

A number of references in Josephus indicate the depth of feeling many people had toward their creditors. For example, one of the earliest acts in the 66–70 war was the burning of debt records (*War* 2.17.6 §427). This and other examples show that one of the grievances felt by a large section of the population concerned repaying loans which seem to have been made without much care for the debtor's ability to repay. It has been asserted that one of the problems at this time was the lack of adequate farmland for the increasing population (Applebaum 1975; 1977: 379–85); however, we have no way of knowing whether this was really true (Hamel: 137–40). In particular, some recent population estimates are almost certainly too high. Many of those taking out loans were only tenants or even day laborers who had no property to secure the loan. Those who did own property were liable to lose it and thus move down to the status of tenant. Whether this would have made much of a difference in the actual lives of the people is debatable. (For the problems involved in reconstructing the situation, see 1.2.2.) Nevertheless, the great wealth which came in from loyal Jews outside Palestine in some ways created problems, rather than contributed to prosperity.

The socioeconomic divisions were not confined to the common people. Within the ranks of the priesthood, friction arose over the disparity of privilege between the various ranks and functions of priests, almost to the point of open warfare between factions (*Ant.* 20.8.8 §§179–81). A good deal of the contention seems to have arisen around the tithes. According to the Pentateuch, the people were to tithe to the Levites (lower clergy [2.4.5]), who in turn tithed to the priests (Num 18:21–32).

This was not the general practice in the first century, however, even if it once had been. Instead, the priests received tithes directly from the people, often bypassing the Levites, who had trouble finding an official function within the temple hierarchy. Josephus states:

> Such was the shamelessness and effrontery which possessed the high priests that they actually were so brazen as to send slaves to the threshing floors to receive the tithes that were due to the priests, with the result that the poorer priests starved to death. (*Ant.* 20.8.8 §181)

Exactly how to interpret this is difficult. On the one hand, it sounds like another example of hyperbole; on the other hand, it may illustrate a serious problem, namely, that the lower ranks of the priesthood increasingly had trouble receiving their traditional source of income from the tithes. This was no doubt partly because there were more priests than were needed to serve the temple and the priests comprised too large a percentage of the population to be readily supported by the rest of the people. Any greed on the part of the chief priests would only exacerbate the problem. Bitterness toward the wealthy, many of them priests, was one of the important causes of the civil war that arose out of the revolt against Rome (7.3.9).

The feeling of the Levites about their social status is further indicated by an incident shortly before the war. The Levitical temple singers agitated for permission to wear linen robes, which had been reserved for the priests (*Ant.* 20.9.6 §§216–18). When they appealed to Agrippa II, he obtained the consent of the Sanhedrin for the necessary permission. Exactly how this was done is not stated, although it seems likely that the priestly contingent of the Sanhedrin would have objected. If so, then the authority of the king was sufficient to carry the decision.

The discussion so far has covered a number of points which have related in part to the Judean upper class. It is to be expected that this group would be a major participant in the historical events of the time. Goodman has argued that many of the problems of Judea in the first century can be traced to the "failure of the ruling class" of Judeans, indeed, that a major cause of the revolt was theirs (*1987). The root of the problem goes back to the reign of Herod, when the old aristocracy was decimated by Herod, with many of the Hasmonean supporters (primarily of Aristobulus and his sons, but also of Hyrcanus) killed or disenfranchised. Furthermore, many of those on the Sanhedrin and in other high offices who opposed Herod were killed or removed. The Sanhedrin lost any real authority. With time, the wealthy and those high up in the administration all owed their position to Herod. There was, therefore, no natural leadership to which the people as a whole subscribed. The priest-hood might have been expected to fall into that category and no doubt did, to some extent. However, Herod began the practice of filling the office of high priest with his own nominee and also changing the incum-bent with some frequency. This practice continued under Roman admin-istration and later still, when filling the office became the prerogative of Agrippa I and Agrippa II. Therefore, the priesthood, which the people would naturally have looked up to, became an object of suspicion and was seen by many as staffed with Roman puppets.

It was Roman practice to administer through the local leadership. The Romans naturally turned to the Jewish upper class after the death of Herod, but this group did not have the confidence of the people and was not able to exert the influence and authority to keep the Judeans in line. Even though the Sanhedrin had been revived to some extent, its jurisdic-tion would have been primarily in religious matters. What was needed was what today might be called moral and political leadership; this the priesthood, the Sanhedrin, and other persons of position and wealth were evidently not able to provide. The divisions and animosities within Jewish society itself were a major contributing factor to the war, what-ever other causes there may have been.

Goodman's thesis is interesting and well argued. Some of the problems noted above about estimating and assessing the economic situation also apply in his case. He reasons from a number of assumptions about wealth and population that are still very uncertain. Nevertheless, as well as rep-resenting one particular reconstruction, his thesis is plausible from another perspective. There was, no doubt, some resentment over the overthrow of the Oniad priesthood in the time of the Maccabean revolt; however, the Maccabean success and territorial expansion would prob-ably have silenced many critics of the "upstart" Hasmonean priesthood and kingship. With the Roman destruction of the Hasmonean state, any feelings among the people would have had little chance of being expressed, except in the revolts surrounding Antigonus and his sons, which evidently had significant popular appeal. Under Herod, such resentments were also kept in severe check at the same time that impor-tant members of the old aristocracy were demoted or executed. Thus, it would have first been under the Roman governors that the new ruling class would have had a chance to exercise leadership and that popular attitudes toward this class manifested themselves. Even if some of Good-man's arguments may be difficult to prove at this stage of research, his overall thesis is a major contribution to our understanding of first-century Judean society and history.

7.4 SYNTHESIS

7.4.1 Overview

The story of Judea in the first century of the Common Era is tragic, yet events during this time changed the history of the world. Out of disaster grew two major religions and the roots of a third. Considering the country's past, it is hardly surprising that it eventually revolted against Roman rule, although the fault probably lies as much with one side as the other.

When Herod the Great died, a delegation of Jews appeared before Augustus to ask for direct Roman rule for Judea. A few years later they got their wish, and most of them doubtless lived to regret it. Through much of the first century of the Common Era Judea was a Roman province, and the consequences for most Jews were negative. Only for a few short years did they live under a Herodian ruler, but by all accounts they would have preferred to remain under such rule. Such are the ironies of history that Herodian rule looked very sweet once it had been lost.

The Roman governors were, by and large, an insensitive lot and frequently incompetent. The opportunity for the Jews to order their own affairs, as they did much of the time under Persian and Greek government, was lost for the most part. True, the Sanhedrin regained some of the powers taken away by Herod, but these seem to have been chiefly in the religious area. The Romans continued to depose high priests when they saw fit and even to keep the high priestly garments under their own jurisdiction (7.4.3). Thus the semi-autonomy that Judea had kept even as a subordinate state in pre-Roman times was gone. The Jews in Palestine, as elsewhere, had to take whatever the Roman government dished out. Several bright spots appear, however. The tetrarchies of Philip and Herod Antipas seem to have been at peace and flourishing for several decades, and they continued to do so under Agrippa I. Judea also had a brief respite under Agrippa. Although the kingdoms were ultimately subject to Rome, internal affairs could at least be administered by native rulers. Parts of the Jewish population also came under the rule of Agrippa II after Judea returned to provincial status.

Economic, social, and political trends all converged toward revolt, especially accelerating after the death of Agrippa I in 44, evidenced by a dramatic increase in the growth of banditry and revolutionary and terrorist groups; an accumulation of uninvested wealth in the temple, paralleled by growth in borrowing by the less well off; exacerbation of the gap between rich and poor, including between the upper and lower echelons of the priesthood; and increasing discontent with both the Roman governors and their collaborators among the Jews.

As far as the Romans were concerned, Judea was another border territory that needed to be kept stable, which it had been while a client kingdom under Herod and Agrippa. As a Roman province, however, any breach of the peace was a cause for concern, not to mention a full-scale revolt. Why the Jews thought they could win is not known, but their initial success in 66 gave them time to prepare, as well as confirming them in their determination to continue resisting. But much energy was expended in internal fighting. This is perhaps a commentary on the fractured state of Jewish society at the time: even in its darkest hour fellow Jews were often seen as the enemy, as long as the Romans were not actually battering at the gates. In Galilee, Josephus maneuvered against John of Gischala and others and was himself opposed by his superiors in Jerusalem. In the breathing space before the actual assault on Jerusalem, even with the city surrounded by the Roman army, a variety of Jewish factions freely shed the blood of fellow citizens in a quest for dominance.

The Jews had no chance of success. This quickly became clear when they were confronted by the well-planned campaign of Vespasian. In some areas opposition collapsed immediately, and resistance in others— brave as it was on occasion—was still not particularly effective. Jerusalem would probably have fallen in 68 except that the political situation in Rome made Vespasian delay the final assault on the city. When the siege of Jerusalem finally came under Titus's command in 70, the fanatical defense by the fighters was no match for the experienced, systematic siege of the Romans. The suicide defense at Masada has gone down in history, but it was equally futile—the war had been over for several years.

7.4.2 Tiberius (14–37 C.E.)

Balsdon, J.P.V.D. "The Principates of Tiberius and Gaius." *ANRW* 2 (1975) 2.86–92.

Downey, G. "Tiberiana." *ANRW* 2 (1975) 2.95–130.

Levick, B. *Tiberius the Politician* (1976).

Well before the end of Herod's reign, Augustus was concerning himself with the problem of succession. In an age when premature death was not unusual, several strong contenders were removed from the scene by this means (e.g., Herod's friend Marcus Agrippa). The lot eventually fell on Tiberius, the son of Augustus's wife Livia by a previous marriage, born in 42 B.C.E. Although Tiberius was not Augustus's first choice, he proved a capable military leader as well as administrator. Augustus made him essentially his co-ruler in 13. When he died in 14, Augustus had been co-leader or sole leader of the empire for over fifty years and his legacy was firmly established and would live on. Tiberius was a worthy successor.

Tiberius's bad image has come principally from the negative evaluation of Tacitus, whose account of his reign (*Ann.* 1–6) is one of our chief sources. Recent scholarship has seen Tiberius in a much more positive light, as a capable ruler but one whose personality was not of the sort to endear him to his associates. This combined with misfortunes in his personal life to make him a distant, melancholy person. Nor did he push himself personally, being reluctant to accept honors and unnecessary offices voted to him by the Senate and others (e.g., he consistently refused to allow an emperor cult to be established on his behalf). Although he continued Augustus's policy of treating the Senate with great respect, his personality prevented the maintenance of the delicate balance needed to keep up the fiction of senatorial rule. Therefore, it is hardly surprising that writers of the senatorial class, such as Tacitus, were not enthusiastic about him.

One of his early difficulties was with his nephew, Germanicus, a popular hero whom Tacitus cannot seem to praise enough. Modern scholarship sees Germanicus's qualities as much more modest, although he was a popular, dashing figure, in great contrast to Tiberius himself. There were even those who would have elevated him to the principat, but he seems to have remained loyal to Tiberius. Thus, when he died suddenly in Syria in 19 C.E., the legate of the province was accused of poisoning him and rumor even unfairly implicated Tiberius.

After the death of his son Drusus, who was being groomed to succeed him, Tiberius came under the influence of Sejanus, prefect over the Praetorian Guard. Sejanus persuaded the emperor to retire to the island of Capri in 27, a mistake which probably led to a breakdown in administration in the last years of his reign. Communication to the Senate was by message because he did not return to Rome. To make things worse, Tiberius found it difficult to make firm decisions, and provincial administrators and governors were often left in posts long after they should have been replaced (e.g., Pontius Pilate [7.3.3]). All this permitted vicious rumors to flourish. Many of these, such as sexual debauchery, can be dismissed as being without substance. More serious is Tacitus's charge that Tiberius inaugurated a reign of terror in which prominent individuals were prosecuted and executed on the basis of mere suspicion, rumor, or malicious, anonymous denunciation. There had been some treason trials (*maiestes*) earlier in his reign, although many accusations had been dismissed by Tiberius as having no substance. After his retirement to Capri, more trials took place. The actual number was not large, and Tacitus probably exaggerated to create the atmosphere of a "reign of terror." But even though Tiberius himself was probably not responsible for the increase in accusations, he seems to have resisted them less, with the result that a fair number of prominent individuals were executed or committed suicide during the last ten years of his reign.

Sejanus's power increased. Many modern scholars accept the allegations that his was a long-lived conspiracy to become emperor. But over time Tiberius began to believe the allegations secretly made against Sejanus. After seeing that Caligula, the third son of Germanicus, was safely in Capri, he sent a message to the Senate toward the end of 31 that denounced the unsuspecting Sejanus, who was actually present when it was read publicly. The succession fell on Caligula and Tiberius's grandson, Gemellus. The emperor died in March 37 and Caligula was proclaimed emperor because of Gemellus's youth.

Tiberius's reign was generally marked by restraint, fiscal thrift, and capable administrators. By reducing public spectacles and other unnecessary spending, he was able to cut the sales tax in half, and he left a large amount in the treasury when he died. Although Pilate is an exception, most of the administrators he appointed were good or even outstanding, and he kept a tight reign on them so that they did not exploit their provinces for personal gain, as had been the custom in earlier times. For the most part, the empire was quiet.

7.4.3   Judea a Roman Province (6–41 c.e.)

Prandi, L. "Una nuova ipotesi sull'iscrizione di Ponzio Pilato." *Civilta classica e cristiana* 2 (1981) 25–35.

Schwartz, D. R. "Pontius Pilate's Suspension from Office: Chronology and Sources." *Tarbiz* 51 (1981/82) 383–98 (Heb.) + VII (Eng. summary).

———. "Pontius Pilate's Appointment to Office and the Chronology of Josephus' *Jewish Antiquities*, Books XVIII–XX." *Zion* 48 (1982/83) 325–45 (Heb.) + XXI (Eng. summary).

———. "Josephus and Philo on Pontius Pilate." *Jerusalem Cathedra* 3 (1983) 26–45.

Smallwood, E. M. "The Date of the Dismissal of Pontius Pilate from Judaea." *JJS* 5 (1954) 12–21.

Syme, R. "The Titulus Tiburtinus." *Akten des VI. Internationalen Kongresses für Griechische und Lateinische Epigraphik* (1973) 585–601.

Sources: Josephus, *War* 2.8.1–9.4 §§117–77; *Ant.* 18.1.1–4.4 §§1–100.

Once Archelaus had been exiled in 6 c.e., it was necessary to set up the Roman administrative system in place of the Herodian one. This meant that taxation had to be done directly, rather than through the king or ethnarch (although it is doubtful whether there was Roman tribute under Herod [6.3.7]), and to determine the tax liability of each person required an assessment of personal property. Hence the first task of Quirinius, the Syrian legate, and Coponius, the governor of Judea, was to conduct a registration or census of persons and property. That this was an unprecedented action is quite clear because of the Jewish reaction. Many were very upset by it, although most acceded to the arguments of the high priest that there was nothing to do but submit. However, Judas the Galilean and Zaddok the Pharisee (the so-called Fourth Philosophy; see 8.2.8) led some sort of rebellion. Their view was that only God was their master and to accept the assessment was to submit to slavery. Josephus actually gives no details about the revolt, so it appears to have been either short-lived or only carried out by small bands using guerrilla tactics. The reference made to Judas in Acts 5:37 suggests a brief revolt, but this information may not be reliable because the movement survived Judas, contrary to the statement attributed to Gamaliel (cf. 7.2.5.2).

The next twenty years are almost a complete blank. In the *War*, Josephus simply skips to the beginning of the governorship of Pontius Pilate; however, in *Antiquities* he does give a list of the governors for this period of two decades: Coponius (6–ca. 9 C.E.), Marcus Ambivulus (ca. 9–12), Annius Rufus (ca. 12–15), and Valerius Gratus (ca. 15–26). He also notes that during Coponius's time, some Samaritans polluted the temple during the Passover festival by scattering human bones in it. A number of cities were also founded by the tetrarchs Herod Antipas and Philip (7.4.4): Caesarea Philippi, Autocratoris (the former Sepphoris), Julias (from Betharamphtha), Julias (Bethsaida), and Tiberias. The only other event recorded by Josephus was about not the Jews in Palestine but those in Rome: the expulsion of the noncitizen Jewish residents in 19 C.E., probably because of proselytizing activities (7.3.4).

Pontius Pilate's governorship (7.3.3) was a long one (26–36 C.E.), probably because it was the custom of Tiberius to leave provincial governors in their posts rather than to replace them frequently, as had been the former custom (*Ant.* 18.6.5 §§170–78; Tacitus, *Ann.* 1.80; Suetonius, *Tib.* 41). In addition to references by Josephus (*War* 2.9.2–4 §§169–77; *Ant.* 18.3.1–2 §§55–62; 18.4.1–2 §§85–89) and Tacitus (*Ann.* 15.44.3), an inscription has been found which refers to Pilate's governorship (Syme). According to the accounts of both Josephus and Tacitus, Pilate's term of office was not particularly successful. The charge that he was an anti-Semitic tool of Sejanus seems ill-founded (7.3.3.1); however, he had the ability, either through deliberate provocation or just plain stupidity, to upset the Jews. Josephus mentions three specific incidents.

The first was at the beginning of Pilate's governorship, when he moved the army from Caesarea to winter quarters in Jerusalem. Although previous Roman governors and military commanders had respected the Jewish objection to the imperial images, Pilate sent his men in with standards bearing such images. It was done at night and was thus a fait accompli by the time the Jews realized what had happened. Their entreaties and protests did no good, even though they journeyed to Caesarea to make them. Finally, Pilate had a large group of soldiers suddenly surround the importuning Jews and threaten them with death if they did not give up their demonstration. Their response was to lie down and expose their necks to the swords. This so astonished Pilate that he relented and removed the standards back to Caesarea. It is usually thought that this incident is different from the one concerning certain aniconic shields that Pilate set up in the palace in Jerusalem (7.3.3.2). In this case the Jews were offended even though there were no images, but Pilate refused to listen to them. When they appealed to Tiberius, however, the emperor ordered the shields removed.

A later protest was not so peacefully settled. Pilate took money from the temple treasury to build an aqueduct to bring water to Jerusalem. The large crowd that assembled while he was visiting Jerusalem raised an angry protest around his tribunal. This time Pilate had his soldiers in disguise, carrying cudgels instead of swords and mixing with the crowd. At a signal from Pilate they attacked the unarmed crowd, and many Jews were killed or injured.

Pilate went too far, however, in quelling a disturbance among the Samaritans. A man promised to show the Samaritans the sacred vessels of the tabernacle, which according to Samaritan tradition had been buried in a hidden site on Mount Gerizim. A large group gathered in a nearby village with the intention of climbing Mount Gerizim for the demonstration at a particular time. Whether it was anything more than a peaceful gathering is not indicated, but Pilate evidently interpreted it as the prelude of a revolt. Before they could actually make the ascent of the mountain, they were intercepted by Roman troops who killed and captured many and scattered the rest. The leaders and most prominent individuals among those captured were executed at Pilate's orders. This was too much for the Samaritan council, who protested to Vitellius, the governor of Syria. Exactly why he accepted their accusations is not clear, but he did, sending Marcellus to take over in Judea and ordering Pilate to return to Rome and appear for trial before Tiberius. This Pilate did, but Tiberius had died (March 37 c.e.) by the time he reached Rome. At this point our information ceases, and we know nothing further about Pilate's fate or subsequent activities.

Vitellius gained the goodwill of the Jews by two acts. One seems to have been earlier than the incident with Pilate (cf. *Ant.* 15.11.4 §§403–9 with *Ant.* 18.4.3 §§90–95): granting the Jews custody over the high priest's vestments. The special robes worn at the major festivals and on the Day of Atonement had traditionally been kept in a special building by the temple. Under Herod this building was turned into a fortress called the Antonia, and he took control of the vestments as a means of potential control of his Jewish subjects. After the exile of Archelaus, control of the vestments was assumed by the Romans. However, when Vitellius was well received by the people of Jerusalem at one point, he consented to place the sacred garments under the Jews' authority as a reciprocal gesture and even requested Tiberius's approval for this. A second act, probably made when he visited Jerusalem after deposing Pilate, was to remit the sales taxes on agricultural products for the inhabitants of Jerusalem.

7.4.4 The Tetrarchs Herod Antipas and Philip

Bowersock, G. W. *Roman Arabia* (1983).
Bultmann, R. *History of the Synoptic Tradition* (1968).
Fitzmyer, J. A. *The Gospel according to Luke I–IX* (1981).
—— ——. *The Gospel according to Luke X–XXIV* (1985).
Hoehner, H. W. *Herod Antipas* (1980).
Kasher, A. *Jews, Idumaeans, and Ancient Arabs* (1988).
Sullivan, R. D. "The Dynasty of Judaea in the First Century." *ANRW* 2 (1977) 8.306–8.

The two tetrarchs over portions of Herod the Great's old kingdom, Herod Antipas and Philip, are important for Jewish history at this time (even if few Jews lived in Philip's territory). Both were builders of noted cities, both made their way into the pages of the New Testament and Josephus, and both were succeeded by Agrippa I as king.

Philip (4 B.C.E.–34 C.E.) ruled over territories to the north and east of Galilee: Trachonitis, Auranitis, Gaulanitis, Batanea, and Paneas (*Ant.* 17.8.1 §189; 17.11.4 §319; 18.4.6 §106; *War* 2.6.3 §95). The statement that he also ruled Iturea (Luke 3:1) seems mistaken, because the bulk of the Itureans lived farther north, in Lebanon (Schürer: 1.338 n.2). Only a few Jews lived in his realm (e.g., at Bethsaida, as well as the colony of Babylonian Jews founded by Herod the Great at Batanea [6.3.7]). He rebuilt two cities. One was the ancient city of Paneas at the sources of the Jordan, which was named for its shrine to the god Pan. He named it after Augustus, but it became known as Caesarea-Philippi, to distinguish it from the city built by his father. The other was Bethsaida, which he renamed Julias after Augustus's daughter; whether it is identical to the Bethsaida of the Gospels is debated (cf. Schürer: 2.172).

According to Josephus, "In his conduct of the government he showed a moderate and easy-going disposition. Indeed, he spent all his time in the territory subject to him. . . . He fixed penalties for those who were convicted and released those who had been unjustly accused" (*Ant.* 18.4.6 §§106–7). No unrest is recorded during Philip's rule, which seems to have been a peaceful one. Because most of his subjects were non-Jews, he used the Roman model for his coins, including images of the emperors Augustus and Tiberius (7.2.8). We also know that he was married to the (in)famous Salome, daughter of Herodias, although this was possibly after the incident with John the Baptist (see below). When Philip died, in the twentieth year of Tiberius's rule (i.e., probably the winter of 33–34 B.C.E.), he had reigned thirty-seven years. His territory was put under the administration of the Syrian legate, but the income was kept in trust. A few years later, in 37 C.E., it was given to Agrippa I (7.4.6).

Herod Antipas (4 B.C.E.–39 C.E.) was tetrarch over Galilee and Perea (*War* 2.6.3 §§94–95; 2.9.1 §168; *Ant.* 18.2.1 §27; 18.2.3 §§36–38). We know something of his activities during the latter part of Tiberius's reign, although little before that. His building activities included the fortification of Betharamphtha (Beth-haram) east of the Jordan, which he renamed Livias or Julias, after Augustus's wife (who was Julia Livia). He also rebuilt Sepphoris (named Autocratoris), which served as an important administrative center and sometime-capital of the region. The jewel in the crown, however, was Tiberias, which he built as a new foundation on the western shores of the Sea of Galilee. Josephus states that the inhabitants were a "mixed lot" (*sygklydes*), including many poor people and some who were compelled to settle there by force. The reason for settling many undesirables at Tiberias was allegedly that the city was built on a site of tombs which many Jews would have avoided. Strangely, though, such objections nowhere appear in later Jewish literature, when the city became a rabbinic center. Tiberias was capital of Galilee much of the time, creating a rivalry between it and Sepphoris.

Antipas was also involved in negotiations between Vitellius, the Syrian legate, and Artabanus III, king of Parthia (*Ant.* 18.4.4–5 §§96–105). The dating of this incident is difficult, because Josephus puts it under Tiberius (ca. 35 C.E.) whereas there are reasons for thinking the final negotiations did not take place until Caligula's reign (37 C.E. [Schürer: 1.350–51]). The Roman appointee on the Armenian throne had died. This was occasion for the Parthian king, Artabanus III, to attempt to have his own favored candidate made king. After a series of unsuccessful maneuvers to unseat him, Tiberius decided the best course was to come to an agreement whereby a mutually acceptable individual was enthroned. Therefore, he had Vitellius negotiate with Artabanus on the Euphrates. Antipas was present at these negotiations and quickly sent an account of them to the emperor, before Vitellius had submitted his report. This angered Vitellius, who was to seek his revenge a few years later.

About 36 C.E. Antipas became involved in a war with Aretas IV, the king of Arabia (*Ant.* 18.5.1–2 §§109–19). The reason for the conflict is that Antipas planned to divorce his wife, who was Aretas's daughter, and marry Herodias, the wife of his half-brother (also named Herod). His Arabian wife got wind of his intentions and fled to her father, who launched an attack on Antipas at a disputed section of their common border. Josephus's narrative gives the impression that one event immediately followed the other; a closer look suggests otherwise (Kasher: 177–83; Bowersock: 65–67). Although the time when Antipas married Herodias is not clearly indicated, circumstances suggest that it was in the 20s, when John the Baptist was alive (see below), whereas the actual attack by Aretas was in about 36 C.E. Indeed, even though the divorce of Aretas's daughter was no doubt a contributing cause, the immediate occasion seems to have been the status of Philip's territory after his death in 34—both Aretas and Antipas hoped to get it, but the Roman directives about it seem to have been somewhat ambiguous. In the battle, Antipas's army was completely destroyed. When he reported this to Tiberius, the emperor ordered Vitellius to declare war on Aretas. Vitellius set out with the intention of marching through Judah but changed his route at the request of the Jews because it would have meant bringing the images of the emperor through their territory. Instead, he sent the army on another route and joined Antipas in Jerusalem for sacrifices at a festival (probably Passover). While there, he received word of Tiberius's death and cancelled the Arabian expedition.

Antipas's marriage to Herodias is supposed to have led to one of the most notorious episodes of his life. He arrested John the Baptist and had him executed (for which his defeat by Aretas was divine vengeance, according to the thinking of some). According to Mark 6:14-28 (followed by countless stories, sermons, passion plays, dramas, operas), the arrest was because of John's criticism for taking his brother's wife, and the execution was at the instigation of Herodias and her daughter Salome. Josephus knows nothing of this but ascribes the arrest and execution to Antipas's fear that John's popularity with the crowds might lead to sedition (*Ant.* 18.5.2 §§116–19). Although the two reasons are not necessarily mutually exclusive, the account in Mark is nevertheless suspect. For one thing, it states that Herodias was the wife of Philip, whereas her daughter Salome was Philip's wife. For another, the account of the plot by Herodias and Salome to have John beheaded looks very much like a folktale without historical foundation (cf. Bultmann: 301–2; Hoehner's attempt to save the Gospel account is predictably apologetic [110–71]). A similar problem occurs with Antipas's part in the trial of Jesus (Luke 23:6-12). This is not intrinsically improbable, because Antipas frequently came to Jerusalem for the festivals, but the story is found only in Luke, who may have had a literary purpose for including it (cf. Bultmann: 273). Like much in the passion narrative, the history behind the story is not easy to get at (cf. Fitzmyer 1985: 1478–80).

Antipas's downfall was due to ambition, according to Josephus, who principally blames Antipas's wife (*Ant.* 18.7.1–2 §§240–56). The irony is that the chief instigator was his brother-in-law Agrippa, whom he had helped at one point (7.4.6). Supposedly, Antipas was encouraged by Herodias to seek the title "king" (because of envy of her brother Agrippa) and sailed to Rome to appear before Caligula. Agrippa learned of what Antipas intended and wrote letters of accusation to Caligula, which arrived about the time that Antipas did. One charge was that Antipas was stockpiling arms with the intention of revolt. When he admitted to possessing the arms, Caligula took it as evidence of a conspiracy and removed him from office.

Getting behind this is not easy, especially with regard to the part played by Agrippa. Why he should accuse the man who had once helped him is left in the air. Was it fear of someone to whom he owed a favor? Was it rivalry? The charge of stockpiling arms, strictly a cause of concern to the Roman authorities, was not likely to be sufficient to remove him; the accusation therefore looks trumped up. Perhaps, in a desire to vilify Herodias, Josephus downplayed the part in this matter of the Syrian legate Vitellius, who had a grudge against Antipas. Vitellius's animosity may have been an important factor. In addition, there was a further charge of conspiring with the Parthians, the principal opponents of the Romans at this time; this would represent a more serious accusation and may have played a role in the decision (*D. R. Schwartz: 59). Whatever the ultimate reasons, Antipas was exiled either to Spain (*War* 2.9.6 §183) or Gaul (*Ant.* 18.7.2 §252) along with his wife. His territory was given to Agrippa.

7.4.5   Gaius Caligula (37–41 C.E.)

Balsdon, J.P.V.D. "The Principates of Tiberius and Gaius." *ANRW* 2 (1975) 2.92–94.
Barrett, A. A. *Caligula* (1989).

Caligula is one of the hardest of the emperors to evaluate dispassionately; in this, he is, perhaps, rivaled only by Nero. Son of the popular Germanicus, he spent much of his youth living in army camps, from which he got the nickname *caligula* ("little boots"). His two older brothers died in the later years of Tiberius's reign, allegedly as a part of Sejanus's plot, but Caligula was brought to Capri by Tiberius's order, where he spent five years.

Caligula's accession was greeted with enthusiasm because of the idiosyncracy of Tiberius's last years and the senatorial prejudice against Tiberius. The idyllic promise of the initial part of Caligula's reign is encapsulated in the rhetoric of the Jewish writer Philo:

> Indeed, the life under Saturn, pictured by the poets, no longer appeared to be a fabled story, so great was the prosperity and well-being, the freedom from grief and fear, the joy which pervaded households and people, night and day, and lasted continuously without a break through the first seven months. (*Gaium* 13)

The idyllic sentiment changed, however, at about the time the emperor was struck by an illness (which, according to Philo, marked the beginning of strange behavior). Opposition soon developed, including a conspiracy among officers in the army of the Rhine, which had to be suppressed. Like Tiberius, Caligula was accused of conducting a reign of terror against all sorts of alleged conspirators, but his actions have also been explained as a means of gaining money by confiscating the estates of those executed.

His efforts at foreign affairs were disastrous on the whole. For example, he removed the king of Armenia from the throne, which only provided an opportunity for Parthia to step in. He ordered the king of Mauretania to commit suicide, with the intention of making the region a Roman province, but it rebelled. He conducted his infamous campaigns in Germany and Britain (39–40 C.E.). The stories about his sorties in German territory make him appear ridiculous but must be evaluated as a part of the biased tradition. He then marched his forces to the English Channel, as if about to embark for Britain, but suddenly canceled whatever he had planned. Again, the anecdotal tradition may have distorted a reasonable decision (by stating, for instance, that he ordered his troops to gather seashells as the "spoils" of battle) and makes it difficult or impossible to determine the real events or intentions. In any case, he returned in May of 40 to celebrate a triumph in Rome. The events relating to his appointment of Agrippa I to a kingdom and the episode of the statue in the temple are dealt with at length elsewhere (7.4.6; 7.3.6).

Finally, in January 41, he was assassinated by some of his own Praetorian Guard while on his way to lunch from the theater. The episode is most fully preserved by Josephus (*Ant.* 19.1.1–2.5 §§1–211), although there are a number of confusions in his account.

Many of the anecdotes preserved about Caligula's reign are probably no more than slander (e.g., the stories that he made his horse a consul and that he had an incestuous relationship with his sister). There has been much psychologizing about him among historians over the years, but the recent study by Barrett goes a long way to explain the origin of much gossip. Caligula was hardly suited by his childhood experiences or training to be emperor. After a traumatic childhood, he was thrust into a position in which his word was law, and he was incapable of dealing with the situation. He had also developed a rather sarcastic sense of humor which others often misunderstood, no doubt the cause of many rumors about strange behavior. Despite the claims of many senators to have feared for their lives, the Senate as a whole fell into an obsequious role with relish and abandoned its duties of advice and even its opposition. Far from being a monster or psychopath, Caligula was a rather irresponsible young man placed in a role that he had neither the experience nor the psychological makeup to fill properly.

7.4.6   Agrippa I (41[37]–44 c.e.)

Lüdemann, G. *Early Christianity according to the Traditions in Acts* (1989).
*Schwartz, D. R.
Sullivan, R. D. "The Dynasty of Judaea in the First Century." *ANRW* 2 (1977) 8.322–29.
Wirgin, W. *Herod Agrippa I: King of the Jews* (1968).

Sources: Josephus, *War* 2.9.5–11.6 §§178–219; *Ant.* 18.5.3–8.9 §§126–309; 19.3.1–9.1 §§212–359.

Agrippa's full name was evidently Marcus Julius Agrippa, judging from the name of his son Agrippa II; therefore, the common reference to him as "Herod Agrippa" (based on Acts 12:1) is incorrect. It was thought recently that a coin had been found which used the name "Herod" for Agrippa, but this has now been shown to be a misinterpretation (*D. R. Schwartz: 120 n.50). Exactly why the author of Acts refers to Agrippa as "Herod" is uncertain, although it may be that he confused Agrippa I with his brother Herod of Chalcis (*D. R. Schwartz: 120 n.50, 215–16). Whatever the reason for the confusion, the name "Herod Agrippa" for Agrippa should be deleted from scholarly usage forthwith.

The son of the executed Aristobulus and grandson of Herod the Great, Agrippa was educated in Rome and lived there many years. After the death of his mother, however, he lived extravagantly and went through a fortune, giving expensive gifts to his Roman friends. His poverty became such that he believed it necessary to quit Rome, even then leaving behind large debts. Agrippa's sister Herodias was married to Herod Antipas. At the request of Agrippa's wife to Herodias, Antipas allowed Agrippa to live for a time in Tiberias and gave him the office of market commissioner (*agoranomia*), but the two brothers-in-law soon fell out. Agrippa then took money from Flaccus, the governor of Syria, until their friendship broke up (over a bribe paid to Agrippa to influence Flaccus's judgment in a particular case). Agrippa decided to return to Italy, managing to borrow money from his mother's freedman and from Alexander, the alabarch of Alexandria.

Arriving back in Italy, Agrippa was well received by Tiberius and stayed with him and his family on the island of Capri. Things went fairly smoothly for a time, although Agrippa's failure to repay a large debt to the imperial treasury caused a problem until he managed to borrow a further sum to pay it off. He developed a close association with Caligula at this time, which was to stand him in good stead later. However, it first cost him his freedom and may have endangered his life: he made a careless remark to Caligula that he hoped the latter would soon be ruling in place of Tiberius and was overheard by a freedman. Later, when this freedman was accused of theft by Agrippa, he told all to the emperor. Agrippa was put in prison, where he remained for six months, until Tiberius's death. When Caligula was declared emperor, he released Agrippa as soon as Tiberius's funeral had taken place and then turned over Philip's tetrarchy (7.4.4) to him, granting him the title "king" (37 C.E.). With Caligula's permission, Agrippa left Rome for his kingdom in 38 C.E. His fortunes had now considerably changed and, rather than being an importuner of his brother-in-law Antipas, as king, he was now his superior, for the other was only tetrarch. Antipas's attempts to change this led to his downfall, and his territory was given to Agrippa (7.4.4).

According to Josephus's *Antiquities* (but not the *War*) and Philo in their accounts of the attempt by Caligula to place his statue in the Jerusalem temple, Agrippa was instrumental in having the plans canceled. This would have been in 40 C.E., by which time Agrippa was evidently back in Rome. When he heard of Caligula's plan, he made a personal request that the project not proceed, and Caligula agreed, perhaps because of his close friendship with Agrippa (although there were no doubt other reasons). See 7.3.6 for a detailed account of this important event in Jewish history.

The next we hear of Agrippa is at the time of the assassination of Caligula and the succession of Claudius in January 41. The various sources agree that Agrippa was involved in the negotiations by which Claudius became recognized as emperor; the problem is his precise role, because the two most complete accounts (in Josephus) give somewhat different pictures. According to *War* 2.11.1–5 §§204–17, both Claudius and the Senate called on Agrippa as an intermediary between them, and his participation was mainly as an instrument of Claudius. *Antiquities* 19.3.1–4.6 §§212–73 gives Agrippa a much more active role, however, making him the one to convince Claudius to accept the declaration of the soldiers. Then, as the mediator between Claudius and the Senate, he acted as a skillful manipulator in helping to bring the senators around to accepting Claudius, despite their great reluctance. There is reason to think that a pro-Agrippa source, which exaggerated Agrippa's role in the affair, served as the basis of the *Antiquities* account (*D. R. Schwartz: 23–30, 91–93). The Roman writer Cassius Dio only notes Agrippa's help, without indicating details (60.8.2).

Claudius not only confirmed the territories given to Agrippa by Caligula but added to them Judea and Samaria, as well as land around Mount Hermon in southern Lebanon. Thus Agrippa's kingdom was even more extensive than that of his grandfather Herod the Great. To Agrippa's brother Herod was given the kingdom of Chalcis, located in the Lebanon valley. Even in his brief reign over Judea, Agrippa was able to accomplish some important projects and demonstrate that, despite his spendthrift ways, he could leave behind a rather happier memory than his grandfather had. He strengthened the walls of Jerusalem at its most vulnerable point, the north side, in the Bezetha district. Josephus suggests he would have made the city impregnable if he had been able to complete the project; whether that is true is perhaps a matter of speculation, but it would no doubt have caused even more problems for the Romans twenty-five years later. In any event, Marsus, the governor of Syria, reported the building to Claudius, who stopped it as potentially revolutionary (so *Ant.* 19.7.2 §§326–27; *War* 2.11.6 §§218–19 is less likely correct in stating only that his death stopped the project). Like his grandfather, Agrippa also supported building projects in the broader Hellenistic world, such as a theater and amphitheater in Berytus (Beirut).

Agrippa showed himself useful to the Jews once again when a statue of the emperor was placed in the synagogue of Dora by a young radical. Agrippa took up the matter with Petronius, who was still the Syrian governor at that time, and he wrote a letter to the leaders of Dora. On another occasion, however, he did not show the greatest sagacity. After presiding over games in Berytus, he entertained his brother and four other client kings in Tiberias. From the evidence given, the intent was only social and completely innocuous. Marsus, the Syrian governor, arrived during the celebrations and received a cordial reception from

Agrippa and the others, but he was suspicious and ordered the individual rulers back to their kingdoms. This caused a breach between him and Agrippa; nevertheless, it was the task of a Roman governor to anticipate trouble, and it is not particularly surprising that he viewed the situation with a critical eye. (D. R. Schwartz has made the plausible suggestion that Marsus saw Agrippa as a rival [*137–40].)

Most of the other information about Agrippa is anecdotal, although it does tend to confirm the positive picture and evaluation presented by Josephus. One story is that he was accused by a religious leader of entering the temple area while he was in a state of ritual impurity. Agrippa's diplomatic response was sufficient not only to show that there was no basis for the charge but also to win the man over. This is used to illustrate both Agrippa's lack of arrogance about his position and his devotion to the Jewish religion; he was said to be scrupulous in offering sacrifice and otherwise adhering to traditional practice. Interestingly, this does not seem to have prevented him from using his image on his coins outside the Jewish areas of his kingdom and from setting up statues of his daughters (*Ant.* 19.9.1 §357). However, unlike his grandfather Herod the Great, whose practice of Judaism was also somewhat selective, Agrippa has had a more popular image in ancient and modern literature.

Agrippa's relationship to the Pharisees was not a simple one. It is often alleged that he favored them and attempted to cultivate good relations with them (e.g., Schürer: 1.446). D. R. Schwartz has recently opposed this, arguing instead that it was the Sadducees who flourished under Agrippa, although this was in spite of, rather than because of, the king's policies (*116–30). The difficulty with both hypotheses is that they depend heavily on rabbinic traditions and questionable assumptions about the Pharisees and Sadducees (cf. 8.2.2–3). Nevertheless, there is some evidence of growing priestly power after the death of Agrippa, which might bear on Schwartz's thesis (*S. Schwartz: 58–70).

Agrippa's reign has been made notorious in Christian tradition in the Acts of the Apostles: Acts 12:1-19 makes him a persecutor of the Christians who killed James, the brother of John, and arrested Peter, although Peter was supposedly rescued from harm in a miraculous way. The persecution of Christians cannot be confirmed, although several recent studies accept it as having a basis in fact (Lüdemann: 139–46; *D. R. Schwartz: 119–24). There may be a genuine memory here, even if it also suits the theological motives of Luke. However, any arrests were likely to have been limited to a few individuals (only Peter and the sons of Zebedee are named) and to have been for reasons of "affairs of state" (*D. R. Schwartz: 122–23). A general persecution of the church is not indicated and is improbable.

Acts 12:20-23 states that Agrippa was acclaimed as a god by the people of Tyre and Sidon and was smitten by God for allowing the acclamation, and was then eaten by worms and died a painful death. One immediately recognizes both literary and theological stereotypes in this account. The story of his death in Josephus (*Ant.* 19.8.2 §§343–50) is similar enough to suggest a common origin, although a number of the details differ. According to Josephus, Agrippa appeared in a special garment at games in Caesarea, was proclaimed as more than human, and immediately was seized with an illness from which he died a few days later. Whatever the cause and whether or not worms had a hand in it, Agrippa was only fifty-four at his death. He had reigned for seven years, four of them over the territories of Philip and Antipas under Caligula and three over the rest of Herod the Great's kingdom under Claudius. In many ways his reign was probably a high point for Jews as a nation, not to be repeated for many centuries.

Agrippa's son, also named Agrippa (7.4.8), was only seventeen at his father's death. Claudius eventually decided not to enthrone Agrippa II over his father's realm, allegedly because of the boy's youth; however, this explanation sounds as if it were for public consumption, because a regency could easily have been established until Agrippa II was older. The most likely explanation is that the decision fitted the emperor's general policy of annexing vassal kingdoms at that time (*D. R. Schwartz: 149–53). Thus, the kingdom was divided up, as had happened in 6 c.e., with Judea turned once more into a Roman province.

7.4.7   Claudius (41–54 c.e.)

Levick, B. *Claudius* (1990).
Momigliano, A. *Claudius, the Emperor and His Achievement* (1934).
Scramuzza, V. M. *The Emperor Claudius* (1940).

Claudius was a most unlikely candidate for emperor. The uncle of Caligula, he had been pointedly kept out of public office and affairs by both Augustus and Tiberius, for reasons that are still somewhat obscure, although he is said to have had peculiar mannerisms which made him the object of ridicule. Nevertheless, he possessed a mind of unusual ability and had a positive reign on the whole, despite an ancient literary tradition which is often hostile. To distance himself from Caligula, Claudius made every attempt to reconcile the Senate with his rule and to show it respect, in the tradition of Augustus.

Where Claudius was both strongest and most controversial was in his development of the administrative structure. His motive seems chiefly to have been a concern with efficiency, but the result was a considerable step toward centralization, as well as the embryonic stage of a later bureaucracy. He put trusted freedmen in charge of several departments dealing with specific matters, such as petitions to the emperor or finances, that became the basis of a sort of civil service. In the same vein, he attempted to force the Senate to expedite its business, including a measure to resume the office of censor, by which he could add members to or remove them from the Senate. Both the removal of the traditional senatorial privilege and the use of freedmen were an affront to the upper classes and aroused their opposition. From a historical perspective, the actions led to increased power for the emperor and an upset of the balance which Augustus's settlements had tried to achieve.

Claudius was careful to cultivate the army, as it was important to maintaining his position. He also continued to push the frontiers of the empire outward. He made two new provinces from the former kingdom of Mauretania, which had been in revolt when he assumed office. He also traveled to Britain in 43, arriving in time to direct the final defeat of the rebellious tribe and to establish the new province of Britannia. Thrace and Lycia also became provinces. The Parthian problem was not fully resolved, although Claudius kept better control of it than Caligula had done.

The pro-senatorial tradition paints Claudius as the puppet of his wives and freedmen. Although to some extent this may have been true in the last few years of his reign, it has been exaggerated. He did, however, prove unlucky in his choice of wives. His first wife, Messalina, has become infamous as a model of promiscuity, and Claudius finally had to order her execution. His second wife was his niece Agrippina, the mother of Nero. She is alleged to have been a woman of such cruelty and malice as to destroy anyone whom she disliked. What is clear is that she worked hard to advance her son, pressuring Claudius to adopt him and appoint him as guardian of Claudius's own son Britannicus. In this she was supported by the philosopher Seneca and Claudius's freedman Pallas. When Claudius died suddenly in 54, the story was that she had given him a dish of poison mushrooms.

7.4.8 Agrippa II (44–94? c.e.)

Braund, D.C. "Berenice in Rome." *Historia* 33 (1984) 120–23.
Dittenberger, W. *Orientis graeci inscriptiones selectae* (1903) 1.630–39.
Groag, E., and A. Stein. *Prosopographia imperii Romani* (1952) 4.132–34.
Jones, B. W. *The Emperor Titus* (1984) 59–63.

Sullivan, R. D. "The Dynasty of Judaea in the First Century." *ANRW* 2 (1977) 8.329–345.

Named Marcus Julius Agrippa, like his father, Agrippa II was only seventeen when Agrippa I died in 44 c.e. (*Ant.* 19.9.1 §§354–55). Because he had been educated in Rome, he was well known to Claudius, who might have given him his father's kingdom; however, for various reasons Judea instead became once more a Roman province (*War* 2.11.6 §220; *Ant.* 19.9.2 §§360–62; cf. 7.4.6). Agrippa was able to serve the Jews, however, on a number of occasions, such as when a dispute arose with the Roman governor Fadus over the high priestly garments. Fadus ordered them to be placed in Roman custody, as had been the case in the period 6–41 c.e., but the Jews petitioned Claudius, who granted their request at Agrippa's instigation (*Ant.* 20.1.1–2 §§6–14). When in 48 c.e. Herod of Chalcis died, Claudius presented the kingdom to Agrippa II (*War* 2.12.1 §223; *Ant.* 20.5.2 §104). His privileges included appointing the high priests and he was given authority over the temple, even though he did not rule over any Judean territory (*Ant.* 20.1.3 §§15–16). In 53 c.e. Claudius assigned a new kingdom to the Jewish king, that of his great-uncle Philip (Trachonitis, Batanea, Gaulanitis) plus Abila, the former kingdom of Lysanias, and the former tetrarchy of Varus (*War* 2.12.8 §247; *Ant.* 20.7.1 §§137–38); however, rulership of Chalcis was taken away. When Nero came to office, he gave Agrippa the Galilean cities of Tiberias and Tarcheae, as well as Julias in Perea (*War* 2.13.2 §252; *Ant.* 20.8.4 §159).

Close to Agrippa for much of his life was his sister Berenice. She originally married Marcus Julius Alexander, the son of the Alexandrian alabarch named Alexander, in about 43/44 (*Ant.* 19.5.1 §§276–77). When he died, she was given by her father to Herod of Chalcis, who died in 48. She lived for a lengthy period with her brother, but a rumor began to circulate that she was having an incestuous affair with him. As a result of this she married Polemo, king of Cilicia, who agreed to be circumcised. This marriage lasted only a short time before she left him (*Ant.* 20.7.3 §§145–47). She bore the title "queen," as is known not only from Josephus but also from an inscription from Athens that actually uses the title "great queen" (*basilissan megalēn* [Dittenberger: 1:638–39, no. 428]). On her relationship with Titus, see 9.4.3.

Agrippa and Berenice are mentioned together in Acts 24:24—26:32 in conjunction with Festus, the governor of Judea. Although this may constitute original source material, there are reasons to be cautious. The actual data that can be checked are few, and the narrative significantly omits Berenice's title of queen. The omission of both any address to her and her title in the direct address of Acts 25:24 would have been an inexcusable breach of protocol. Whether Luke had any information at this point beyond a few commonplaces about the two is very questionable.

There is good reason to think that the priests had increased their power during this period and felt strong enough to oppose even the king, despite his nominal authority over the temple and its affairs (*S. Schwartz: 64–67). An example of this is an episode before the war involving a wall of the temple (*Ant*. 20.8.11 §§189–95). When in Jerusalem, Agrippa liked while dining to watch the proceedings within the temple court from a portion of his palace that overlooked the area. Certain "eminent men" (*prouchontes*) were incensed by this and erected a wall which blocked Agrippa's view. Because it also blocked the view of the Roman sentries posted to watch the crowds during the festivals, both Agrippa and Festus objected; however, Festus allowed the high priest Ishmael to lead a delegation to Nero over the matter. Nero's mistress Poppea, although probably not a Jewish convert, as sometimes alleged (7.4.10), interceded on behalf of the Jews, and Nero allowed the wall to remain in place.

When the war with Rome began, Agrippa attempted to dissuade the Jews from carrying through with their folly, but both he and Berenice were forced by the people to withdraw from the city. In the fighting that followed he led his own troops as an ally of the Romans and helped in crushing the revolt. After the war we hear only sporadic references to him. Josephus corresponded with him about his work and allegedly received his confirmation of their accuracy (*Life* 65 §§362–67). The date of his death has been disputed. Because of a statement by Photius, it has often been thought that Agrippa did not die until about 100 C.E., but more recent study suggests that the date of his death was closer to 96/97 (*S. Schwartz: 19–20).

7.4.9   Judea a Roman Province Again (44–66 C.E.)

Aberbach, M. "The Conflicting Accounts of Josephus and Tacitus concerning Cumanus' and Felix' Terms of Office." *JQR* 40 (1949/50) 1–14.

Sources: Josephus, *War* 2.11.6–14.3 §§220–83; *Ant*. 19.9.2 §363—20.11.1 §258.

7.4.9.1   Overview

The two decades following Agrippa I's death are the story of Judea's gradual slide into war. Some governors were reasonable; most were not, showing either a lack of personal integrity or gross insensitivity to the

Jewish subjects whom they governed, or often both. But even if diplomatic governors of great character had been put in place during this time, it might only have postponed the inevitable. Given their own history and religious assumptions, the Jews were bound in time to test themselves militarily against the Roman might (7.3.9). Although there had been rebellions and unruly elements at various times since Pompey, these seem to crescendo under the procurators: various bandit groups, sporadic appearances of prophets, the rise of terrorist gangs. Sociologically, these represent a complex set of responses to the general situation; those called "bandits" (lēₐstai) by Josephus were often this but sometimes more. That is, they were frequently disaffected people who took to brigandage both as an easier means of livelihood in a difficult situation and as a protest against Roman rule (see 8.2.12).

7.4.9.2 Cuspius Fadus (44–46? C.E.)

The first procurator, Cuspius Fadus, arrived to find a major problem of brigandage, which he soon eliminated, capturing Tholomeus, one of the chief leaders. It was also during his office that Theudas arose as a prophet and claimed to be able to divide the Jordan River, as had happened in the time of Joshua. He was killed and his following scattered before he had a chance to attempt the deed. This is probably the same person mentioned in Acts 5:36, although misdated there to a much earlier time (7.2.5.2). Fadus also had to sort out a dispute between the people of Philadelphia and the Jews of Perea, in which the Pereans had taken matters into their own hands. Probably because he thought it a means of control of the people, he ordered the high priest's vestments to come once more under Roman control. This was resisted by the Jews. They were allowed to send a delegation to Claudius, who acceded to the Jewish request, partly through the intercession of Agrippa II. About the same time Claudius also gave authority over the temple and the appointment of high priests to Herod of Chalcis. On the whole, though, Fadus supposedly kept the peace by respecting local customs (*War* 2.11.6 §220).

7.4.9.3 Tiberius Alexander (46?–48 C.E.)

CPJ: 2.188–97.
Reinmuth, O. W. "The Edict of Tiberius Julius Alexander." *TAPA* 65 (1934) 248–59.
Turner, E. G. "Tiberius Iulius Alexander." *JRS* 44 (1954) 54–64.

Tiberius Alexander was the son of the Alexandrian alabarch Alexander and nephew of the philosopher Philo of Alexandria whose tracate *De animalibus* consists of a dialogue between uncle and nephew. Tiberius Alexander's father was reputed to be one of the wealthiest men in the world at the time (*Ant.* 20.5.2 §§100–103). According to Josephus, the younger Alexander had abandoned the religion of his people, although exactly how that statement is to be interpreted is difficult because no details are given (8.3.2). Evidently he went through the normal offices of an upper-class Roman, because we first hear of him in adulthood when he was made governor of Judea. His term of office was basically peaceful because he understood the Jewish way of life (*War* 2.11.6 §220), although there is no indication that he was less than firm in his administration: He had James and Simon, the sons of Judas the Galilean, tried and crucified; the charge is not specified but was presumably that of revolution. Also during his governorship, a famine arose over a large area of the eastern Mediterranean. Helena, the queen mother of Adiabene and a convert to Judaism, was in Jerusalem at the time and spent a considerable sum importing grain from Egypt and figs from Cyprus to distribute to the needy (*Ant.* 20.2.5 §§49–53). In addition, her son Izates, king of Adiabene and also a convert, sent money to the leaders of Jerusalem to help with the famine.

The next time Tiberius Alexander appears in history is as governor of Egypt, to which he was appointed by Nero, evidently in 66 C.E. just before the Jewish revolt (*War* 2.15.1 §309). An edict of his outlines his administrative policy and is one of the most interesting of the surviving edicts from prefects of Egypt (Reinmuth; cf. *CPJ*: 2.195). A few months after the Jewish rebellion in Palestine began, riots broke out in Alexandria between the Greek citizens and the Jews, with the Jews seizing the initiative. At first Alexander tried to calm them without the use of force, but when that was unsuccessful, he turned his two legions loose on the Jewish quarter (*War* 2.18.7–8 §§487–98). According to Josephus's questionable figures, fifty thousand Jews were killed. A few years later, in 69 C.E., Alexander's legions were the first to declare for Vespasian as emperor (*CPJ*: 2.189); Josephus, who in *War* 4.10.6 §§616–18 has the legions in Judea declare first for Vespasian, is probably repeating—or engaged in—propaganda. The idea was to present the declaration as a spontaneous acclaim by Vespasian's own troops, whereas it was in fact a carefully managed affair, in which Tiberius Alexander played his part well. Although Vespasian turned over the continuation of the war to his son Titus, he requested that Alexander come from Egypt and be Titus's chief of staff (*War* 5.1.6 §§45–46; 6.4.3 §237). This is quite understandable because Titus, as a young and rather impetuous individual, could use the steadying influence and experience of the much older Alexander.

7.4.9.4 Ventidius Cumanus (48–52 c.e.)

Under Ventidius Cumanus a succession of incidents disturbed the order that had prevailed during Tiberius Alexander's governorship. As a precautionary measure, soldiers were posted on top of the temple portico during religious festivals to guard against any disturbances which might break out. During Passover, one soldier defiantly exposed himself to insult the celebrating Jews, and a riot soon followed. Cumanus sent additional troops to quell the disturbance. As they approached, the Jews attempted to flee through narrow exits, which resulted in many being crushed to death. Josephus lists a large number of deaths (*War* 2.12.1 §227; *Ant.* 20.5.3 §112; variant readings give ten thousand, twenty thousand, and thirty thousand deaths), which suggests a major revolt in the making. Shortly afterward, one of Caesar's servants was attacked and robbed outside Jerusalem on the road to Joppa. The Roman way of dealing with this was to punish the neighboring villages for not having intervened to help the Roman representative, also probably suspecting that some of the band were inhabitants of these same villages. However, during the attack on the villages, one of the soldiers defiled and destroyed a Torah scroll. Such a protest arose over this action that Cumanus hastily had the soldier brought out and publicly executed to appease Jewish anger.

A final episode was quite detrimental to Cumanus himself, as well as to the Jews. Some Samaritans attacked a group of Galileans who were on their way to Jerusalem for a festival and killed either many (*Ant.* 20.6.1 §118) or only one (*War* 2.12.3 §232). When the Jews appealed to Cumanus he did nothing, allegedly because he had been bribed by the Samaritans (a common accusation), so a mob of Jews took the law into their own hands and attacked some Samaritan villages. Josephus indicates the beginnings of a mass revolt, because the Galileans urged the Jews to assert their "freedom" (*eleutheria*). Cumanus intervened with troops, and the Jewish leaders attempted to persuade the rebels to return home; the two forms of persuasion eventually worked, but both Jews and Samaritans appealed to the Syrian governor, Quadratus. After a preliminary investigation and the execution of some of the chief participants in the fighting, Quadratus sent Cumanus, the military tribune Celer, some of the Samaritan notables, the high priests Jonathan and Ananias, and other Jewish leaders to Rome for trial before Claudius. The Jews were once again assisted by Agrippa II, who petitioned Claudius on their behalf. Claudius found in favor of the Jews, executing the Samaritan delegation and exiling Cumanus. The tribune Celer was taken back to Jerusalem and there publicly executed.

7.4.9.5 Antonius Felix (52–59? c.e.)

Antonius Felix, as is noted in a play on his name, "turned out not to be one of the happiest choices as governor" (*Smallwood: 269), despite the Christian tradition that he even showed an interest in the teachings of the apostle Paul (Acts 24:22-27). He was noted by Suetonius for having married "three queens" (*Claud*. 28), one of these being Drusilla, the sister of Agrippa II. Felix took stern measures against the widespread brigandage, with some success. For example, he captured and sent to Rome the bandit chief Eleazar, who was apparently also one of the leaders in the strife between the Jews and Samaritans under Cumanus (*War* 2.12.4 §235; 2.13.2 §253; *Ant*. 20.6.1 §121; 20.8.5 §161). But during his procuratorship another menace arose, which was much harder to deal with: the terrorists known as the Sicarii. Their name comes from *sica*, the curved dagger that was their favorite weapon. They could easily conceal the dagger under their clothes, and in a crowd, especially during a festival, it was no problem to get close to the victim, quickly dispatch him, and escape back into the crowd. Their targets were not usually the Romans but those of the Jews who cooperated with the Romans—primarily the leading priests, the wealthy, and those with an office in the administration of the country. One of the Sicarii's primary means of financial support was to act as professional assassins. Felix was rumored to have hired them to kill the high priest Jonathan because of a grudge.

Felix's period in office was also troubled by various prophets who emerged and gained followings. Many of these bands were revolutionary movements and not just religious cults. Josephus gives only one example to back up his blanket statement that there were many such groups: that of an unnamed Egyptian Jew who led a group to the Mount of Olives, where he was going to cause the walls of Jerusalem to fall down; one account states that this was a prelude to setting himself up as dictator of Jerusalem (*War* 2.13.5 §262). Felix quickly intervened to kill and scatter the Egyptian Jew's followers, although the prophet himself apparently escaped (cf. Acts 21:38). Josephus summarizes the escalation of revolt and disorder under Felix:

> No sooner were these disorders reduced than the inflammation, as in a sick man's body, broke out again in another quarter. The impostors and brigands, banding together, incited numbers to revolt, exhorting them to assert their independence, and threatening to kill any who submitted to Roman domination and forcibly to suppress those who voluntarily accepted servitude. Distributing themselves in companies throughout the country, they looted the houses of the wealthy, murdered their owners, and set the villages on fire. The effects of their

frenzy were thus felt throughout all Judaea, and every day saw this war being fanned into fiercer flame. (*War* 2.13.6 §§264–65)

Even allowing for a good deal of rhetorical exaggeration, this statement suggests an increase in the translation into action of popular sentiment against Roman rule. Ideological support came from nostalgia for better times in the past, feelings of nationalism, and religious teachings and prophecies of various sorts, but there were also important socioeconomic factors (7.3.9; 7.3.10).

One event toward the end of Felix's term of office was a forerunner of what was to happen at the beginning of the war with Rome. The Jews of Caesarea began to agitate for citizenship, arguing that they should have this by right because a Jew (Herod the Great) had founded the city. The Syro-Greek population opposed them, pointing out that if the city had been meant for Jewish residence, the various statues would not have been erected by Herod. It seems that over the years the noncitizen Jewish population, formerly in the minority, increased to the point that it outnumbered the Syrians, who were citizens. Despite attempts by the city magistrates to keep order by punishing any who started quarrels, they could not prevent physical clashes, in which the Jews prevailed. Felix intervened, killing and capturing a number of the rioting Jews. Because the issue was obviously not settled, Felix took representatives from both sides and sent them to Rome to present their case to Caesar. Shortly after this Felix was replaced as governor, and the Jews of Caesarea accused him of misdeeds in their presentation before Nero. The charge did not stick, allegedly because Felix's brother Pallas influenced Nero; Josephus also alleges that the Syrian delegation bribed Nero's secretary. Be that as it may, Nero sided with the Syro-Greek population of Caesarea against the Jews and issued a rescript with his ruling. Evidently, the Jews did not accept this and continued to press their quarrel with the Syrians until it came to a head a few years later.

7.4.9.6 Porcius Festus (59?–62 c.e.)

Porcius Festus attempted to deal with the major threat to Roman order: the numerous brigand groups and the Sicarii (although, according to Acts 25:1-6, his most urgent concern as soon as he arrived in Palestine was to hear the case of the apostle Paul!). He proceeded against the brigands and Sicarii, capturing and killing many, although to what extent he was able to achieve success in clearing the country of the menace is difficult to say. He also killed a "deceiver" (*goēs*) and scattered his following; the man had promised salvation to those who followed him into the desert (*Ant.* 20.8.10 §188). An issue developed at this time over a wall of the temple that had been raised to a new height by the priests, an action Agrippa II and Festus opposed (7.4.8). When delegations from both sides came before Nero, however, the emperor sided with the Jews and the wall remained in place. Festus died in office.

7.4.9.7 Lucceius Albinus (62–64)

The governorship of Lucceius Albinus is given two rather contrasting evaluations by Josephus. According to *War* 2.14.1 §§272–76, Albinus was nothing but an out-and-out villain who stole, plundered, accepted bribes to release criminals, and placed extra taxes on the people. *Antiquities* 20.9.2–3 §§204–10 gives what seems prima facie to be a more balanced picture: he attempted to clear the land of the Sicarii, who were the major problem. However, his efforts were in part thwarted by a new tactic, well known from modern terrorism: the kidnapping of prominent persons, who were then held hostage against the release of some of their own number from prison. A man named Eleazar, who seems to have been a temple official, was first to be kidnapped, and the former high priest Ananias b. Nedebaeus persuaded Albinus to meet the demands of the Sicarii. This only encouraged repeated kidnappings, until many of the Sicarii captured by Albinus were once more free to carry on their activities. As a final gesture before vacating his office, perhaps to leave some goodwill behind, Albinus is said to have cleared the prisons by executing those who deserved it but releasing those who had committed lesser offenses. Whether this made anything worse, as Josephus seems to conclude, is doubtful, and Albinus's rule probably consisted of making the best of a bad situation. During his rule there was also factionalism and strife within the priesthood, which at times even came to violence (7.3.10).

After the death of Festus but during the hiatus before Albinus arrived in Jerusalem, the high priest Ananus b. Ananus is said to have convened the Sanhedrin and condemned James, the brother of Jesus, and some others to death by stoning. Scholars generally accept this passage of Josephus (*Ant.* 20.9.1 §§197–200) as genuine and not a Christian interpolation. If this is the case, then the reaction of Albinus and Agrippa II would indicate that capital punishment was not the prerogative of the Sanhedrin at this time (7.3.2.4). As a result of his actions, Ananus was deposed from office by Agrippa.

During Albinus's term of office, Agrippa also enlarged Caesarea-Philippi and renamed it Neronias in honor of the emperor.

7.4.9.8 Gessius Florus (64–66 c.e.)

The last governor, during whose term of office the war with Rome began, was Gessius Florus. Josephus names him as the final cause of the collapse of the overstrained forces holding back chaos in the country; indeed, Florus is said to have made Albinus look positively virtuous by comparison. Despite a good deal of overblown rhetoric, however, Josephus gives us little in the way of specifics, although he does say that the Jews even complained to the Syrian legate Cestius Gallus about Florus.

Florus supposedly did nothing about brigandage because he was in league with the brigands and concerned only with getting his share. These charges, exaggerated and sweeping as they are, may be true. The important thing, however, is that whatever Florus's faults, he was only part of a long line of bad rule, coupled with a deteriorating social order. The precise situation is difficult to pinpoint from Josephus because of his hyperbole, but one does not need to know the details to appreciate that things were bad and leading up to some sort of explosion. This came in 66 and brought Florus's governorship to a violent end.

7.4.10 Nero (54–68 c.e.)

Griffin, M. T. *Nero: The End of a Dynasty* (1984).
Smallwood, E. M. "The Alleged Jewish Tendencies of Poppaea Sabina." *JTS* 10 (1959) 329–35.
Warmington, B. H. *Nero: Legend and Reality* (1969).

Like Gaius, Nero has been so vilified in the tradition that it is difficult to give a dispassionate assessment of his rule. Undoubtedly, many of the criticisms of him are justified, as even recent epigraphic finds indicate, but it is still difficult to penetrate the rumor, slander, and anecdote to reach the historical Nero. His reign began well and was very positive for about the first five years. Although the philosopher Seneca should perhaps receive credit for much of this, it is by no means certain that Nero's own thinking was not an important part of the success. However, even these years were clouded by his relationship with his mother. She had worked hard to secure the throne for him and then attempted to dominate him, even to the point of co-rulership; eventually, he ordered her execution in secret and forever entered history as a matricide (cf. *SibOr* 4.121).

A number of important events took place in the provinces during Nero's reign. The famous revolt of Boudicca (Boadicea) erupted in Britain in 61. In Armenia, Parthia placed its own choice of king on the throne and refused to negotiate with Rome, which regarded the act as a threat. The

Roman commander Corbulo invaded and enthroned the Romans' own choice of candidate in 58; Corbulo himself became the governor of Syria. A few years later the Roman puppet king provoked the Parthians and then requested Roman aid. The Roman commander sent by Nero in 62 was defeated and captured by the Parthians. When Corbulo came too late to rescue him, he was still able to negotiate a settlement in which both the Romans and Parthians would withdraw from Armenia, while the Parthian candidate would become king of Armenia but go to Rome to be crowned.

Nero had divorced his wife Octavia in 62 and married his longtime mistress, Poppea. She has been of considerable interest because of her peripheral place in Jewish history, but the idea that she was a Jewish convert is unlikely (Smallwood). At about the same time, Nero began to reign badly, at least according to the Roman historians. He is said to have reintroduced treason trials, with the usual consequences for various prominent individuals. He was also blamed for the great fire of Rome in the summer of 64, although this is probably slander provoked by his evident enthusiasm for rebuilding the city according to his own plans. No doubt the special taxes introduced to help pay for the rebuilding did not help his image. The persecution of the Christians that he instigated might have helped to divert attention to some extent, but it seems unlikely that many would have come to believe the Christians responsible for the fire, even if that was the aim of the persecution.

The final few years of Nero's reign were turbulent ones, marked by the outbreak of several real or imagined conspiracies in which a number of prominent individuals ended their lives (e.g., the philosopher Seneca and Nero's own arbiter of taste, the writer Petronius). The emperor had journeyed to Greece to take part in the Isthmian games when the revolt broke out in Judea in 66, but he did not return to Rome until early 68. Then his Gallic governor, Vindex, revolted. Although Vindex was defeated, Galba, the governor in Spain, had already taken the opportunity to declare himself a legate of "the Senate and people of Rome," rather than of Nero. Instead of taking firm action, Nero dithered, until finally one of the Praetorian prefects fled and the other bribed the Guard to declare for Galba. Nero was proclaimed an enemy by the Senate and took his own life in June 68, at the age of thirty.

7.4.11 Beginnings of the War with Rome (66–67 C.E.)

Avi-Yonah, M. "The Missing Fortress of Flavius Josephus." *IEJ* 3 (1953) 94–98.

Bar-Kochva, B. "Seron and Cestius Gallus at Beith Horon." *PEQ* 108 (1976)
   13–21.
Gichon, M. "Cestius Gallus's Campaign in Judaea." *PEQ* 113 (1981) 39–62.
Har-El, M. "The Zealots' Fortresses in Galilee." *IEJ* 33 (1972) 123–30.

7.4.11.1   Initial Events

Sources: Josephus, *War* 2.14.4–17.5 §§284–424; *Life* 4–5 §§17–23.

Most would agree that the war with Rome had a variety of causes;
perhaps the only debatable point is whether it was inevitable or not
(7.3.9): the long tradition of Israelite independence as a monarchy; the
belief that the Jews were God's chosen people; Roman misrule; socioeconomic forces; and the general discrediting of the upper class in the
eyes of the rest of the Jewish people. As with many wars, the Jewish war
with Rome did not begin suddenly with a single event. Events of twenty
years or more pushed the prospect continually closer, and it is difficult
to point to a specific moment when the war actually began. Nevertheless, Josephus gives special significance to an event in Caesarea in about
May 66 C.E.

According to Josephus, some years earlier the Caesarean Jewish community had argued for citizenship, even taking their case to Nero without
success (7.4.9.5). Many Jews would not accept this ruling, however, and
friction continued with the Syro-Greek community. When the Jews tried
to buy a piece of land adjoining the synagogue, the owners refused and
instead decided in 66 C.E. to build on the property in such a way as to
restrict access to the synagogue. Some angry Jews attempted to disrupt
the building by physical violence, appeals to Florus to take action were
unsuccessful, and, as a last straw, a Syrian insulted the Jews by sacrific-
ing birds on an upturned pot in front of the synagogue when they came
for worship. Violence broke out which the Roman commander was not
able to contain, so the Jewish community took their copy of the Torah
and withdrew to a place outside the city. A Jewish delegation tried once
more to gain Florus's help but was simply imprisoned by him.

Already agitated by this set of events, the people of Jerusalem were
further provoked when Florus took seventeen talents from the temple
treasury. The governor marched into Jerusalem with troops, refusing the
greetings of the people, and set up a tribunal to punish those individuals
who had publicly insulted his administration (by pretending to beg cop-
per coins for him after he took the money from the treasury). When the
Jewish leaders asserted that it was impossible to identify the culprits,
Florus sent his men to sack the upper city. Many Jews were killed in the

sacking or executed by crucifixion, including some of Roman equestrian rank, the total number being more than thirty-five hundred. Queen Berenice's attempts to make Florus halt the slaughter were ignored. Florus then inflamed the situation further by calling the chief priest and leaders and instructing them to greet two Roman cohorts who were being marched into Jerusalem; however, he had secretly commanded the soldiers not to return the greetings. When this happened, some of the Jews began to protest, thus giving an excuse to the soldiers to turn on them. In the fighting that followed, Florus tried to take possession of the Antonia with his men, the alleged reason being that he wanted to seize the temple treasury, but he was prevented from doing so.

In brief, this is Josephus's version of events in *War* 2.14.4–15.6 §§284–332. The problem is twofold: there is no parallel to compare with it, and this account sounds rather one-sided. Most of the blame falls on Florus personally, although unruly Jewish youths and other rash individuals are also blamed for some of the problems. Florus's guilt may have been quite real, but one suspects that he was not quite as monstrous, greedy, or stupid as here depicted. For example, no reason except greed is given for his seizing the seventeen talents from the temple treasury, but a little later it is stated that Jerusalem and its adjacent countryside alone were forty talents in arrears on tribute (*War* 2.17.1 §405). During the melee in Jerusalem, the reason for trying to take the Antonia was more likely to be military than just to confiscate the temple money. Furthermore, shortly after this incident, when Florus decided to leave Jerusalem, he called together the Sanhedrin to consult about the number of troops to leave behind to keep order. This is hardly the action of a man who is intent on bringing confusion and disorder to the city. Whatever Florus's failings—which were probably many—it seems that Josephus has given a very biased account of the events.

Shortly after Florus left Jerusalem, he sent a report to the Syrian governor, Cestius; on the Jewish side, too, letters came from the Jerusalem magistrates and from Berenice. At the same time as Cestius sent a tribune to investigate, Agrippa returned from a visit to Alexandria. Although feelings were running high, the two apparently found Jerusalem basically calm. In response to a request to send a delegation to Nero to accuse Florus, Agrippa responded with a public speech about the impossibility of fighting Rome and about the dangerous path on which the Jews had already embarked. According to Josephus, the initial response to this was favorable, with collection of the outstanding taxes and repair of the damage done to the temple porticos in the fighting against Florus. Suddenly the mood changed, however, and Agrippa and Berenice were actually formally expelled from Jerusalem. The exact reason for this is not clear, although Josephus says it was because Agrippa wanted the Jews to submit to Florus until Nero sent a new governor. Perhaps that was sufficient to sway opinion against Agrippa, but one wonders whether there was not more to the incident than Josephus reports. The reception of his speech may not really have been as favorable as Josephus implies, assuming such a speech was ever given. It is commonly recognized that the speech found in *War* 2.16.4 §§345–401 is Josephus's own composition (cf. *S. Schwartz: 133–36).

Up to this point wholesale war could probably have been avoided; however, things now moved rapidly. The Sicarii captured the fortress of Masada from its Roman garrison. Eleazar b. Ananias, the captain (*stratēgos*) of the temple, halted all sacrifices by foreigners, which meant that the daily offerings for Caesar were stopped. Although the chief priests and leading citizens were against this, according to Josephus, they failed to get the decision reversed. Therefore, for their own self-protection, they sent messages to both Florus, who did nothing, and Agrippa, who sent troops to their aid. With these they occupied the upper city, but the lower city and temple were in the hands of the "war party" led by Eleazar. Efforts to oust Eleazer and his supporters were unsuccessful, despite many casualties on both sides. How far to accept Josephus's picture is a major question, because there is evidence that the upper classes initially supported the war effort (see further at 7.4.11.3).

7.4.11.2 Defeat of Cestius

Kasher, A. *Jews and Hellenistic Cities in Eretz-Israel* (1990).

Sources: Josephus, *War* 2.17.6–19.9 §§425–555; *Life* 6 §§24–27.

By this time it was August 66 c.e. At the festival of wood-gathering, a number of Sicarii slipped into the city and joined the rebels, who were now strong enough to expel Agrippa's troops from the upper city. The troops and leaders fled to the palace, where they were besieged. Eventually, the Jews and the troops of Agrippa were allowed to leave, but exit was refused to the Roman soldiers, who continued under siege. However, the former high priest Ananias and his brother were found hiding and were slain by the insurgents. The leadership of the insurgents was now primarily in the hands of the Sicarius leader Menahem (8.2.8), who began to take on the trappings of royalty. This was too much for the followers of Eleazar, who attacked and killed Menahem and many of his followers, although some escaped to Masada under the leadership of Eleazar b. Jairus. The point of no return was reached by an action of the rebels that could have only one consequence: the besieged Roman garrison agreed to surrender with the promise of safe conduct out of Jerusalem, but once they had laid down their arms, they were massacred by the rebels. This was an act which Rome was bound to avenge.

The acts of the insurgents in Jerusalem had horrifying consequences for many Jewish communities elsewhere in the eastern Mediterranean, whose members were massacred by their gentile neighbors (cf. Kasher: 268–87; 7.3.8). There are probably a variety of reasons for the massacres: fear that the revolution would spread to Jews in their own area, greed for property, the chance to settle old scores, and general anti-Semitism. Another reason, however, is that Jewish bands were attacking and pillaging villages over a large area up and down Syria. Whatever the cause, the Jews were set upon and many slaughtered in Caesarea, Ascalon, Ptolemais, Tyre, Hippos, and Gadara. In Scythopolis the Jewish inhabitants actually fought back against the Jewish raiding bands but were attacked by their fellow inhabitants of the city. In Alexandria some Jews were recognized in a public gathering and were killed by a mob; when the Jews attempted to retaliate, however, war threatened to break out in the city. The governor Tiberius Alexander (7.4.9.3), unable to calm the Jews by entreaties, finally turned two Roman legions on them until they sued for peace. The cities that were exceptions to this Jewish-gentile friction were Antioch, Sidon, and Apamea, where no harm was permitted to befall the Jewish inhabitants.

It was September 66 when Cestius finally began military operations against the revolt. He had the equivalent of two legions, plus other infantry, cavalry, and auxiliaries; Agrippa was also with him. Galilee and Joppa were pacified in short order; then came the march to Jerusalem. The Roman forces approached the city during the Feast of Tabernacles, probably in early October 66. The Jews were able to mobilize a large body of fighters from the festival pilgrims and to halt temporarily the Roman advance. When an attempt by Agrippa to negotiate was met with an assault on the messengers, the Romans pushed on and laid siege. The city was only partially prepared to defend itself, and the defenders abandoned the suburbs and outer city along with the unfinished third wall, taking refuge in the temple and inner city.

According to Josephus, who may well be relying on Roman historians here, the city would have fallen and the war ended then and there if Cestius had pressed his advantage. Indeed, some of the citizens secretly negotiated, without success, to open the city gates to the Romans until they were discovered by the war party. Although Josephus states that Cestius was wrongly advised by his camp prefect (*stratopedarchēs*), who had been bribed by Florus, there may have been justifiable military reasons for his not pressing the siege. It could even have been a case of incorrect intelligence, which is not uncommon in battle conditions. Whatever the reason, Cestius suddenly broke off the siege and withdrew toward Caesarea. Harassed by the Jews, especially in the pass at Beth-horon (cf. Bar-Kochva), the withdrawal became more of a rout with the loss of the equivalent of a legion, according to Josephus's (normally unreliable) figures.

7.4.11.3 Preparations for War

Sources: Josephus, *War* 2.20.1–4 §§556–68.

The Jews now had the opportunity for war preparations, which, in hindsight, probably only prolonged the suffering and increased the casualties. At the time the opportunity undoubtedly seemed to be a much-needed breathing space for those who thought the Roman military machine could be taken on. The precise attitudes toward the war varied radically: whether Josephus's assessment is exactly correct is less important than that it indicates an expected range of opinion (*War* 2.20.1 §§556–57; 2.20.3 §§562–63; *Life* 4–5 §§17–23). He is probably correct in stating that the opposition to war was strongest among the upper classes, that is, the priests and municipal leaders, in Jerusalem. It is also probable that some of these felt strongly enough to flee the city, but many in this group clearly supported the war, even if some had private misgivings. The preparations for war were conducted under the leadership of the moderate party. As S. Schwartz's careful study shows, Josephus has discreetly played down the extent to which the priests were active supporters of the rebels (*82–87).

This is why the greatest suspicion falls on Josephus's own alleged intentions: even though it is possible that he was against the war and even a fifth columnist in Galilee, this is both too convenient for his later position and contrary to his conduct. The simplest interpretation of his actions is that, whatever initial reservations he may have had, he embarked on his task in Galilee with considerable enthusiasm and a constant eye to self-advantage. If he were really as much against the war as he states, then it would have been a simple matter for him to defect to Agrippa. It is also important not to allow the wealth of detail to accord his activities a place out of proportion to their actual value in the history of the war. Galilee was only secondary, a region to be secured so the Romans could concentrate on their real goal, which was Jerusalem.

Initially, the country was governed by a council which appointed various officers and generals. The overall leaders for Jerusalem were Joseph

b. Gorion and the former high priest Ananus b. Ananus. Eleazar b. Simon, despite his major part in the earlier events, was not trusted sufficiently to be given office, although this was later to change drastically. The rest of the country was divided into six districts, each one entrusted to a commander who acted in both military and civil capacity: (1) Idumea: Jesus b. Sapphas, Eleazar b. Neus, Niger the Perean; (2) Jericho: Joseph b. Simon; (3) Perea: Manasses; (4) Thamna, with Lydda, Joppa, and Emmaus: John the Essene; (5) Gophna and Acrabetta: John b. Ananias; and (6) Lower Galilee and Gamala: Josephus b. Matthias (he also claims to have been given Upper Galilee, but this is doubtful; see 7.4.11.4).

7.4.11.4   Josephus in Galilee

Rappaport, U. "John of Gischala in Galilee." *Jerusalem Cathedra* 3 (1983) 46–75.

Sources: Josephus, *War* 2.20.5–21.10 §§569–646; *Life* 7–73 §§28–406.

We are given little information about five of the districts, but the situation in Galilee is known from the detailed (if highly partisan and contradictory) narratives of its commander, Josephus (7.2.1). Galilee may not have been typical of the other sections of the country, but it certainly serves to highlight a major problem that the Jews faced: internal divisions and rivalries, which were probably as destructive as anything the Romans would do. A section of Galilee was not Jewish, and even some of the Jewish cities were basically pro-Roman or, at least, antiwar. For example, of three chief cities of Galilee, only Gabara seems to have been pro-revolt, whereas Sepphoris was pro-Roman and Tiberias prevaricated (*Life* 22 §§104–11; 25 §§123–24). Although Sepphoris cooperated sufficiently with Josephus to obtain help in building up its fortifications (*War* 3.4.1 §§61–62), the city did not give up trying to obtain help from the Romans (*War* 2.21.10 §§645–46; *Life* 8 §§30–31; 22 §104; 65 §§346–47; 67 §§373–80; 71 §§394–97). In spite of allegedly being punished by Josephus for pro-Roman activities (*War* 2.21.10 §646), Sepphoris asked Vespasian for military aid as soon as he arrived in the area, and it was willingly granted (*War* 3.2.4 §§30–34; 3.4.1 §59; *Life* 74 §411).

The situation was similar, although a bit more complicated, with Tiberias. Indeed, in his later account Josephus describes three different parties in Tiberias, each with a different view (*Life* 9 §§32–36): a pro-Roman group, made up principally of "respectable citizens" (*andrōn euschēmonōn*); a pro-war group, made up of "the most insignificant persons" (*asēmotatōn*); a third group, led by Justus b. Pistus (Justus of Tiberias [7.2.3]), that pretended to be reluctant to fight but was actually eager for revolution. Because Josephus is intent on denigrating Justus, it is likely that there was no "third party" but that Justus was aligned with the first group. Nevertheless, the subsequent events in Tiberias show that the city wavered between the Romans and the Jewish rebels, tending to side with the former until coerced by the presence of Josephus to join the latter but rapidly shifting back to the Romans when the opportunity arose. Rather incongruously, given his evocative language, Josephus received most of his support from the "insignificant persons" of the war party.

Josephus's first task was to appoint an administrative structure of seventy men over the whole of Galilee, plus other individuals within each city to settle minor affairs. He levied an army, allegedly of one hundred thousand men, but this is a grossly exaggerated figure. Although a partially trained irregular force was undoubtedly recruited in each town, these do not seem to have been very effective. The actual number of those fighting under Josephus's command at any one time is never more than a few thousand, and these seem to be chiefly his mercenaries and body-guards (about five thousand in all). A number of these mercenaries were "brigands" whom Josephus hired because he had little hope of controlling them directly. The major cities and defensible sites were also fortified. Most of Josephus's energy, however, seems to have been taken up with his rivalry with John of Gischala (also called John b. Levi).

Although Josephus states in the *Life* that Justus and his family were the major cause of the defeat in Galilee (9 §41), Justus is not even mentioned in the parallel account in *War*. Rather, the major opponent in both accounts is plainly John of Gischala. Josephus's tirade against John probably masks a political power struggle between two officially appointed commanders. That is, contrary to his own statement, Josephus was probably appointed commander only of Lower Galilee, and John was the commander of Upper Galilee. John was thus not straightforwardly the upstart, war profiteer, "brigand," or troublemaker that Josephus makes him out to be; on the contrary, there were many in Jerusalem (e.g., Simon b. Gamaliel [*War* 2.21.7 §§626–28; *Life* 38–39 §§189–98]) who viewed Josephus as the troublemaker who kept encroaching on John's command, instead of sticking to his own. The historian's responsibility is not to take sides but simply to recognize the complexity of the situation and the one-sided nature of Josephus's account. This means that the researcher must be agnostic about many of the individual episodes in which Josephus alleges John's treachery or propounds his own clever leadership; there is little point in recounting them here. (For a detailed analysis, see *Cohen; for a more credulous approach, contrast *Rajak.)

7.4.12 Galba, Otho, Vitellius (68–69 c.e.)

Wellesley, K. *The Long Year*, A.D. *69* (1976).

With the end of the Julio-Claudian line, one would have been surprised if a period of turmoil did not erupt in which various individuals staked a claim to the throne. Not long after Nero's suicide, Galba was in Rome and was generally accepted by the Senate and military. He faced large problems, however, and was very much on trial as to how well and how quickly he faced them. He immediately addressed the financial crisis by attempting to raise taxes and effect some economies. In a short time, however, his misadministration began to alienate many. At the beginning of January 69 the armies of the Rhine refused to renew their oath to him. Galba recognized the peril and tried to appease his opponents by associating a young senator with him in office. This did nothing for the military and alienated Otho, a close friend of Nero and governor of Lusitania, who would have considered himself an obvious choice to be Galba's associate.

Otho made arrangements for the usual bribe to the Praetorian Guard and was declared emperor in the middle of January. Although he immediately did away with Galba, the army of the Lower Rhine acclaimed their own commander, Vitellius, as emperor and began to march on Rome. Galba tried to come to an arrangement with Vitellius but failed. The stage was now set for another civil war. Superior tactics allowed the Vitellian army to make it safely over the Alps, even though it was still winter, and to surprise the supporters of Otho. The initial campaign went against Otho, who committed suicide rather than continue the fight.

However, it soon became clear that the new emperor's fight for his office was not at an end, for in July 69 the governor of Egypt, Tiberius Alexander, and the Eastern legions declared for Vespasian. This declaration was soon followed by that of the legions of the Danube, who had originally supported Otho. Antonius Primus, their commander, made a forced march on Italy, where he caught the Vitellians off guard. After Primus had gained two decisive victories, it was clear to Vitellius that he had little hope, and so he negotiated terms of abdication with Vespasian's elder brother who was in Rome. Before the agreement could be executed, however, the Praetorian Guard once again took matters into their own hands. They attacked and killed Vespasian's brother in the capitol, setting the temple of Jupiter on fire in the process.

Primus now arrived in Rome and fought with the remaining Vitellian resistance. Vitellius was captured and killed, and Vespasian's son Domitian was made vice-regent. Discipline was quickly breaking down, and it looked as if the Danube troops were about to sack the city. Vespasian's legate Mucianus appeared and established control, however, sending the legions of the Danube back to the frontier. Vespasian himself arrived in Rome a few months later, in the summer of 70.

7.4.13   The Rest of the War (67–73/74 C.E.)

Sources: apart from a few paragraphs in *Life* 74–76 §§407–23, the rest of the account of the war is based almost entirely on Josephus's single version in *War* 2.22.1 §647—7.11.5 §455. It is difficult for any history of this to be anything but some sort of paraphrase of Josephus, however critical one may be of his story.

7.4.13.1   Vespasian's Campaign against Galilee

Once the report of the scale of the Jewish revolt and Cestius's defeat came to Nero, he quickly recognized its seriousness and lost no time in appointing Vespasian to take charge. Vespasian sent his son Titus to Alexandria to bring the Fifteenth Legion, while he made his way to Antioch. There Vespasian was met by Agrippa, and they proceeded together to Ptolemais, which would serve as the staging center for the campaign, where Titus soon joined them. Vespasian by this time had at his disposal the Fifth, Tenth, and Fifteenth Legions; other cohorts and squadrons; and Agrippa's soldiers—about sixty thousand fighting men in all. It was then the spring of 67 C.E., just a year since the initial troubles in Caesarea.

The two sides had not been completely inactive during the months from November 66 to May 67. While Jews were fighting among themselves in Galilee, those in Jerusalem, flushed with their success against Cestius, attempted to take Ascalon. The attack force was led by men important in the fighting against Cestius, but the campaign was a complete disaster. Favored by the terrain, the Roman cavalry was able to mow down the Jewish foot soldiers with relative ease. Two of the Jewish generals were killed, including John the Essene, who had been commander over Thamna. Another general, Niger of Perea, barely escaped with his life. The slaughter at Ascalon was perhaps an ominous sign that the early success against Cestius was a fluke, not to be repeated.

The tribune Placidus had been sent by Cestius to harass the villages in the region of Ptolemais (*Life* 43 §§213–14). When the inhabitants of Sepphoris asked for a garrison from Vespasian, he dispatched this same Placidus, who made continual incursions into Galilee to soften up the opposition, even making an unsuccessful attack on Jotapata (*War* 3.4.1

§§59–63; 3.6.1 §§110–14). At this point Vespasian moved his forces out of Ptolemais and marched toward Galilee. Hardly had the Romans reached the neighborhood before the bulk of Josephus's men deserted him and fled, not a very propitious beginning to the real contest with Rome. Vespasian took Gabara on the first assault and killed all the males, probably both in revenge for the defeat of Cestius and as an example to the Jewish defenders of other cities.

Vespasian immediately proceeded to the siege of Jotapata, one of the major fortified cities in Galilee. Josephus had taken refuge there and managed to hold out for about six weeks during June and July 67. It was clearly an important target for the Romans, both because of its size and defenses and because of the Jewish general who was there. Although Josephus probably exaggerates his own reputation as a military leader (e.g., *War* 3.7.3 §143), his death or capture would have been a boost for the Romans and a setback for the Jews. Josephus managed to survive the final assault and hide in a cave with some other soldiers; when discovered by the Romans, they agreed on a suicide pact. Although Josephus describes this all in great detail, his account is extremely suspect, especially because he appears to have drawn the lot to be last to kill himself. In any case, he was taken captive by the Romans and brought before Vespasian, where he predicted that the Roman general would be emperor. His account at this point is believable in that something along these lines must have happened, not only to explain his subsequent treatment by Vespasian but also because the *War* was read (or at least, intended to be read) by Vespasian and Titus.

During the siege of Jotapata, Japha, the largest village of Galilee, had revolted. It was attacked and taken in short order at the time that Jotapata fell. About the same time a group of Samaritans assembled on Gerizim, for reasons which are unclear. The Romans interpreted this as a threat and sent in troops. When the Samaritans, allegedly numbering over eleven thousand, refused to lay down their arms, they were all slain. Although it was midsummer, Vespasian took his troops to Caesarea, evidently with the intention of wintering there and undertaking the invasion of Judea the next spring. He apparently believed that Galilee was sufficiently cowed to be a threat no longer. Word soon arrived, however, that both Tiberias and Taricheae were in revolt. As already noted, Tiberias's actions seem to have been due only to a minority faction, led at this time (if not before) by one of its magistrates named Jesus b. Saphat. Although a small force of Roman cavalry, which had been sent to offer terms to the city, was attacked and forced to flee, a delegation of citizens made haste to the Roman camp and offered the submission of the city to Vespasian. Jesus and his men withdrew to Taricheae. Even though this city offered much greater resistance than Tiberias, many of the native inhabitants (as opposed to refugees and fighters from elsewhere in Galilee) were against resistance. When this became known to the Romans, they were able to take the city in a surprise attack. Many of the defenders fled in boats onto the Sea of Galilee but were pursued and slain by the Roman soldiers on specially made war rafts. This occurred in September 67 c.e. At this time Vespasian also sent a force against a group of Jewish refugees in Joppa, who had turned to piracy. The pirates escaped safely in their ships, but an overnight storm wrecked the vessels and drowned most of the sailors, leaving only a few for the Romans to dispatch. Joppa itself was razed.

The next target was Gamala on the eastern side of the Sea of Tiberias, which continued to remain belligerent when most of the other cities had surrendered. Agrippa led his own troops alongside the Romans and was severely injured by a slingshot stone which hit him on the elbow. The siege lasted from early October to early November 67. When the city finally fell, many of the defenders threw themselves over the cliffs, but the rest, including women and children, were slaughtered by the attackers. During the siege, a task force was sent to capture the garrison on Mount Tabor, which had received support from Gamala.

The only city still holding out was the small town of Gischala, the hometown of John b. Levi (who later allied with the Zealots). Titus was sent with a cavalry unit to take it. He first offered terms. John agreed to think about them if left in peace over the Sabbath, but during the night he fled with many of his supporters. Although a large number of these were killed or captured when the Romans caught up with them the next day, John made it safely to Jerusalem. Gischala opened its gates to Titus, and Galilee was completely under Roman control.

7.4.13.2   Jerusalem Isolated and Surrounded

The arrival of John in Jerusalem was to lead to a series of internal fights and factions, which put Jew against Jew (see below). When news of this came back to Vespasian, there were those who advised an immediate march on Jerusalem, in hopes that they could take it quickly. It was decided, however, that the factional strife would weaken the defenders if they were left to themselves, and the policy of systematic reduction of the country was continued. Vespasian left his winter camp to march south in about March 68. He sent a contingent to Gadara, where the citizens opened the gates to the Romans and the rebel sympathizers were killed as they fled. Many people from the Perean area fled ahead of the advancing Romans toward Jericho, but they were cornered in the area of the Jordan and slaughtered.

Vespasian himself came down the western part of the country through Thamna, Lydda, and Jamnia. Then he turned east toward Idumea and reduced it. He retraced his steps back north, then turned east through Neapolis (Shechem) and down to Jericho, where he established a garrison. Jerusalem was then surrounded and isolated from the rest of the country. Vespasian returned to Caesarea and was preparing for the march on the city itself when word came of Nero's death. It would then have been July or August 68. Rather than continue the war, Vespasian decided to wait to see developments; to what extent he already had ideas of seeking the principat himself is difficult to say, but his judicious wait at this point would have been in line with such plans. When news came of Galba's acclamation, Vespasian sent Titus to salute the new emperor, with Agrippa II accompanying him. While apparently still in the area of Greece, however, they received word of Galba's death and Otho's accession (probably still January 69). Titus returned to his father in Caesarea.

The waiting apparently continued, but finally in June 69 Vespasian began once again his push to Jerusalem, which he had postponed for almost a year. Some areas north of Jerusalem were quickly reduced, whereas a detachment of cavalry took northern Idumea either because it had not been taken before or because it had returned to rebel control. The only fortresses left at this time in rebel hands were Herodium, Masada, and Macherus, and the Romans were at the walls of Jerusalem. Vespasian again returned to Caesarea, and again word came from Italy, this time to say that Vitellius had been successful against Otho and was now in Rome. Things developed rapidly. Tiberius Alexander, the governor of Egypt, acclaimed Vespasian as emperor in what was probably a carefully arranged move (contra Josephus, who says the acclamation came from Vespasian's own troops), followed shortly by other legions of the East and on the Danube (cf. 7.4.9.3). Both Titus and Vespasian moved to Egypt to secure the grain supply, while Mucianus the legate of Syria was dispatched with troops to Italy (7.4.12). As Vespasian prepared to embark for Rome, he sent Titus to finish the task of taking Jerusalem.

7.4.13.3 Jewish Infighting

In Jerusalem a considerable number of events had occurred during the year and a half since John of Gischala took refuge there. About the time that John arrived, a number of "brigand" chiefs and their men allied themselves to form a group known as the Zealots (*War* 4.3.4–9 §§138–61).

Although the term "zealot" has often been used as a general term to characterize any revolutionary group of this period, it is clear that Josephus confines it to the group which originated in 68 (8.2.7). The Zealots began a program of arrest and execution of those whom they considered obstacles and "democratized" the office of high priest in appointing by lot an individual from among the lower order of priests. The high priest Ananus and some of the leaders (including Simon b. Gamaliel) attempted to incite the citizens against the Zealots with some success, but they had taken over the inner court of the temple as their base and could not be dislodged. Attempts were made to arrange a treaty, although in the meantime the Zealots had sent to the Idumeans for help. What special relationship they had with the Idumeans is not stated, but the latter responded by marching with a large force on Jerusalem. They were not admitted and camped outside the walls until a group of Zealots opened the gates to them during a stormy night. The Zealots and Idumeans together attacked the followers of Ananus, who had taken over the outer court of the temple, and annihilated them. Ananus was caught and killed.

The Idumeans then aided the Zealots in a reign of terror against those perceived as enemies. With time, however, the Idumeans changed their minds, allegedly because of finding out the real crimes of the Zealots and learning that Ananus and others were not traitors as claimed (*War* 4.5.5 §§345–52). They are said all to have returned home (but this contradicts a later passage which mentions them; see below). John had apparently thrown his lot in with the Zealots, at least temporarily, but at this point created his own faction as a rival to them.

The Sicarii (8.2.8) had earlier taken Masada (7.4.11.1) and were using it as a base for raids on the countryside. They were joined by Simon b. Gioras. There Simon built up a following until he had a group large enough to overrun a considerable portion of Idumea. The Zealots began to fear (perhaps correctly) that he was planning to attack them in Jerusalem and made an anticipatory strike against him but were defeated. His private army grew until he was able to take Idumea, despite determined resistance by many of the citizens. He then made the threatened advance on Jerusalem and set up his camp before the gate.

At this point Josephus's narrative becomes confused (*War* 4.9.11 §§566–70). He says that the Idumeans mutinied against John (even though they were all said to have left Jerusalem some time earlier). John and the surviving "Zealots" fled into the temple, where other "Zealots" joined him to prepare to attack the people and the Idumeans. Who were the Idumeans? Presumably some who did not return to their homes. Who were the "Zealots"? As already noted, John is said to have broken with the Zealot party. Were these the followers of John only, or did the Zealots as a whole rally around John at this point? One wonders if Josephus is deliberately omitting important information. Whatever the precise situation with John, the chief priests decided to let Simon in to help them fight against John and the Zealots. Simon soon became master of the city and proceeded to attack John in the temple, although John had an advantage by being on higher ground.

The situation may be clarified by a later passage (*War* 5.1.1–4 §§1–26). Here it is stated that Eleazar b. Simon grew tired of John's tyranny and broke away with part of the Zealots. Because Eleazar was one of the original Zealot leaders (*War* 4.4.1 §225), it may be that a partial unity had at some point been achieved around John but that at this time the original division reasserted itself. In any event, a three-way split was now in evidence: Eleazar and his group were in the inner court of the temple; John and his group were in the outer court; and Simon and his group held the rest of the city. All three were fighting each other, with considerable bloodshed on all sides.

7.4.13.4 Fall of Jerusalem and End of the War

Alon, G. "The Burning of the Temple." *Jews, Judaism and the Classical World* (1977) 252–68.

This factional fighting was the state of things in Jerusalem when Titus marched on the city with four legions in the spring of 70. He set up camp on Mount Scopus and Mount Olivet and proceeded to attack the north side of the city, as had been traditional for invaders for centuries. The Jewish factions temporarily joined forces in making an initial sally on the Romans, as a foretaste of the hard fight ahead. Nevertheless, the three basic internal divisions continued until Passover time. Then, when Eleazar was allowing worshipers into the inner court, John was able to slip some of his men in secretly. They attacked Eleazar's faction and eventually won, uniting the two groups once more into one. John was in charge, but Eleazar also retained a position of command. The united group numbered about eighty-five hundred and maintained control of the temple, Ophla, and the Kedron valley. Simon's group of fifteen thousand continued to oppose them, having possession of the upper city and part of the lower. This was happening despite the progress of the Roman siege.

The details of the siege are given at length by Josephus and would be tedious to relate here. There were countless heroic deeds by ordinary soldiers on both sides. The noncombatants within the city suffered from famine and from the militants. Exactly how the many atrocities against innocent victims, often leaders and nobles, that are reported by Josephus are to be evaluated is problematic. If Josephus is to be believed, they must all have perished several times over: on several occasions his narrative describes things so that no one among the citizenry could have been left alive, yet the next episode reports more victims. That Josephus's father apparently lived through the siege without harm indicates that the insurgents were perhaps not the out-and-out monsters he makes them out to be (*War* 5.13.1 §533). Enough horrific things happened without need of recourse to exaggeration.

Josephus was himself sent to talk from a distance to the defenders, with the hope that some would desert or even that they could be parleyed into surrendering. Titus probably did feel some of the pity for the people that Josephus describes, but he was also a soldier with a task to do. When Josephus gives us a picture of the Roman commander trying to stop the fire that was destroying the temple, he is almost certainly engaging in fantasy, because other sources—and strategic sense—indicate that Titus saw the temple as a continuing instigation of rebellion and determined that it should be reduced to ruins, as the later writer Severus reports (*GLAJJ*: 2.64–67; cf. Alon).

The temple was destroyed sometime in August 70, although the traditional date of "the 9th of Ab" is a stereotype and doubtful. The city was finally taken completely during September. Most of the survivors were sold as slaves, but Titus (rather contradicting Josephus's description of his tenderness toward the besieged) kept a large number to throw to the beasts in shows at Caesarea-Philippi and Berytus (Beirut). Some were also taken back to Rome to be exhibited in his triumphal procession. Among them was Simon b. Gioras, who was then sent to be executed; however, John of Gischala was sentenced to life imprisonment.

Three fortresses still lay in Jewish hands. Lucilius Bassus, as the legate for Judea, had the task of taking them. Herodium was persuaded to surrender. Macherus held out, however, and had to be taken by siege. Bassus died soon after this and was replaced by Flavius Silva, whose task it was to reduce the remaining fortress, Masada, which was still held by the Sicarii. Masada has become a modern legend, in no small part because of the discoveries of the Dead Sea Scrolls and the excavations of the fortress by Yadin. The new information has been so interpreted as to expand the legend rather than demythologize it. Whether the defenders of Masada should be labeled "martyrs" or only "assassins" is a matter of opinion. Josephus would probably use the latter term, yet his account still makes heroes of them.

With the fall of Masada all Palestine was in Roman hands. Some of the Sicarii managed to flee to Egypt and began to try to stir up the Jewish community. The Jews feared that they might suffer the fate of their brothers in Judea, however, and captured as many Sicarii as they could, turning them over to the Romans. Some Sicarii made their way to Cyrene and repeated the familiar pattern of planning revolt, but again the leading local Jews betrayed their intentions to the Romans. When news of the Sicarii disturbances was conveyed to Vespasian, he sent orders for the closure of the temple of Onias at Leontopolis (5.3.8) as another potential focus for revolt. The former annual donation of all Jews to the Jerusalem temple was now converted into a Jewish tax of two drachmas, which paid for the reconstruction of Jupiter's temple on the capitol, which had been destroyed by the Vitellian forces.

Yet after all this Judaism was still a permitted religion, and there is no indication that Jewish worship was in any way infringed.

8

SECTS AND VIOLENCE: RELIGIOUS PLURALISM FROM THE MACCABEES TO YAVNEH

8.1 INTRODUCTION AND BIBLIOGRAPHICAL GUIDE

Bousset, W., and H. Gressmann. *Die Religion des Judentums im späthellenistischen Zeitaltar* (1925; 4th ed., 1966).

Cohen, S.J.D. "The Political and Social History of the Jews in Greco-Roman Antiquity: The State of the Question." *Early Judaism and Its Modern Interpreters* (1986) 33–56.

———. *From the Maccabees to the Mishnah* (1987).

Goodman, M. *State and Society in Roman Galilee, A.D. 132–212* (1983).

———. *The Ruling Class of Judaea* (1987).

Lightstone, J. N. *The Commerce of the Sacred* (1984).

———. *Society, the Sacred, and Scripture in Ancient Judaism* (1988).

Maccoby, H. *Judaism in the First Century* (1989).

Moore, G. F. *Judaism in the First Three Centuries of the Christian Era*. 3 vols. (1927–30).

Neusner, J. *The Rabbinic Traditions about the Pharisees before 70*. Vols. 1–3 (1971).

———. *From Politics to Piety: The Making of Pharisaic Religion* (1973).

———. *Judaism: The Evidence of the Mishnah* (1981).

———. *Judaism in the Beginning of Christianity* (1984).

———. *A Religion of Pots and Pans?* (1988).

Porton, G. G. "Diversity in Postbiblical Judaism." *Early Judaism and Its Modern Interpreters* (1986) 57–80.

Saldarini, A. J. "Reconstructions of Rabbinic Judaism." *Early Judaism and Its Modern Interpreters* (1986) 437–77.

———. *Pharisees, Scribes and Sadducees in Palestinian Society* (1988).

Segal, A. *Rebecca's Children* (1986).

Smith, M. "Palestinian Judaism in the First Century." *Israel: Its Role in Civilization* (1956) 67–81.

———. *Jesus the Magician* (1978).

Wilson, B. R. *Magic and the Millennium* (1973).

———. *The Social Dimensions of Sectarianism* (1990).

This chapter is laid out differently from most of the others. Instead of covering a particular time period, it covers a topic: the religious situation in Judea, primarily in the period from about 200 B.C.E. to the period of Yavneh (ca. 70–132 C.E.). Therefore, it is organized according to the various religious groups and institutions. Most of the sources have already been treated in previous chapters and need only cross-referencing here; those not treated elsewhere are discussed under each individual topic, rather than under a general heading of their own.

Secondary bibliography is especially a problem for this chapter, because some of the topics (e.g., Gnosticism) would require a great deal of space to be covered adequately. It is not my purpose to give a general introduction to such subjects; rather, I deal with them according to the needs of the topic at hand. Nevertheless, readers need some guidance for further reading in order to pursue the subject. To this end, I have attempted to list bibliographical guides and general discussions where appropriate.

Concerning the religious situation before 70, it is difficult to find general coverage that is not seriously flawed, especially for methodological reasons. For example, Moore's classic work, while valuable to one who understands its problems and can compensate for them, contains basic principles which must now be seriously questioned (Neusner 1981: 5–14). Another older study that has value if properly used is Bousset/Gressmann. Unfortunately, some recent useful surveys have such skimpy bibliographical references (e.g., Cohen; Segal) that the student has little way of checking or following up the discussion. For an introduction with references, especially to be recommended are the articles by Cohen, Porton, and Saldarini in *Early Judaism and Its Modern Interpreters* (1986). Neusner (1984) gives a very useful overview in a small compass. His earlier book (1973), although devoted to the Pharisees, also contains a good deal of passing comment on the pre-70 religious situation.

A very important book which covers a number of aspects of first-century Judaism is Saldarini (1988). I have benefited from and taken account of this study; however, because my treatments of the Pharisees, Sadducees, and scribes were originally written before his book became available, I have made only minimal changes to these sections to highlight the broad agreement between the two of us, despite different approaches at times and some differences of interpretation. Maccoby unfortunately makes little use of recent critical work on rabbinic literature, Josephus, the Pharisees, the New Testament, and so forth. It could have been written a century ago and not raised an eyebrow. Scholarship, however, has moved on. For further discussion of secondary bibliography, see the individual topics in this chapter, as well as chapter 1.

Some discussion is needed about terminology. I use the term "Judaism" in this chapter, as throughout the book, to refer to the umbrella religion, with all its subvarieties—parallel to the usage of the term "Christianity" to include everything from Jehovah's Witnesses to the Armenian Orthodox Church. Recently, some have preferred the term "Judaism" to mean a self-contained Jewish religious system, so that one speaks of "Judaisms" when referring to more than one system. There is much to be said for this, and I agree with the conceptualization; however, I retain the older usage for the time being because it tends to be more familiar. Nevertheless, readers should be aware that "Judaism" in this book covers all the various Jewish systems ("Judaisms") and implies no monolithic or "orthodox" view of the religion. What I emphasize here is the variety.

The term "sect" can also create difficulties. The word is obviously used in a variety of ways in scholarly discussion. As Wilson has pointed out, usage of the term has too often been influenced by the situation and bias of the Christian tradition (1973: 11–16). The term "sect" is often used in a pejorative sense, but some who use it neutrally nevertheless confine it to groups which withdraw from or reject the values of the wider society (e.g., Cohen: 124–27). This may fit many Christian sects but is not necessarily transferable to other societies (Wilson 1990: 1–3). Borrowing from Wilson's insights, I use the term "sect" here in a neutral and more encompassing sense to mean a minority religious movement (Wilson 1973: 11–18; cf. Greek *hairesis*). Therefore, it does not imply a "church" as its counterpart or assume that the group in question rejects the wider society. The problem with using organization as a criterion has been well discussed by Wilson. The problem with using ideology is that we often do not know enough about the ideology of various groups to make distinctions. Most of the groups we know of, including the Pharisees, were minority religious movements within the Jewish temple state of the time. In the usage here they are all sects.

8.2 INDIVIDUAL SECTS AND MOVEMENTS

8.2.1 Hasidim

Collins, J. J. *The Apocalyptic Vision of the Book of Daniel* (1977) 201–6.
Davies, P. R. "*Hasidim* in the Maccabean Period." *JJS* 28 (1977) 127–40.
Kampen, J. *The Hasideans and the Origins of Pharisaism* (1988).
Lightstone, J. N. "Judaism of the Second Commonwealth: Toward a Reform of the Scholarly Tradition." *Truth and Compassion* (1983) 31–40.
Sievers, J. *The Hasmoneans and Their Supporters* (1990) 38–40.

One who consults the handbooks will find all sorts of information about the Hasidim; unfortunately, most of it is imaginary. As Collins notes:

> The party of the Hasideans has grown in recent scholarship from an extremely poorly attested entity to the great Jewish alternative to the Maccabees at the time of the revolt. There has been no corresponding growth in the evidence. (201)

Thus the Hasidim are alleged to have been the ancestors of both the Pharisees and the Essenes, as well as the authors/editors of the book of Daniel. They are also described as the "orthodox" Jews who opposed the "Hellenizers" under the Hellenistic reform of Jason and Menelaus. The list of their characteristics goes on and on, little if any of it based on the actual original data. Most of the relevant passages have been critically studied in the seminal article by Davies (see also Lightstone 1983: 36–40; *Saldarini 1988: 251–54), of which the major texts are:

> When Mattathias and his friends learned of it [the massacre of some who refused to fight on the Sabbath], . . . they made this decision that day: "Let us fight against every man who comes to attack us on the sabbath day. . . ." Then there united with them a company of Hasideans, mighty warriors [*ischyroi dynamei*] of Israel, every one who offered himself willingly for the law. (1 Macc 2:39-42, RSV)

> Then a group of scribes [*synagōgē grammateōn*] appeared in a body before Alcimus and Bacchides to ask for just terms. The Hasideans were the first among the sons of Israel to seek peace from them, for they said, "A priest of the line of Aaron has come with the army, and he will not harm us." . . . So they trusted him; but he seized sixty of them and killed them in one day. . . . (1 Macc 7:12-16, RSV)

> [Speech by the high priest Alcimus to Demetrius I:] Those of the Jews who are called Hasideans, whose leader is Judas Maccabeus, are keeping up war and stirring up sedition, and will not let the kingdom attain tranquillity. (2 Macc 14:6, RSV)

It is generally assumed that a definite, coherent group is being referred to, because the Greek texts of 1 and 2 Maccabees transliterate the name as *Asidaioi*, universally agreed to reflect Hebrew *ḥăsîdîm* or Aramaic *ḥăsîdayyā'* ("the pious"). The Greek translator undoubtedly understood this to be a name, but this does not mean that the original Hebrew text of 1 Maccabees pointed to anything more than a miscellaneous group of "pious individuals" (Davies; Lightstone: 38–39; *Saldarini 1988: 252–53; contra Kampen). That is, because *ḥăsîdîm* was ambiguous in the Hebrew text of 1 Maccabees, it may well be that to read this as an organized group is a misunderstanding. Although either interpretation is possible, the uncertainty on this point further weakens the confidence with which one attempts to reconstruct the history of the alleged Hasidim.

The one concrete thing we know is that this group was composed of "mighty warriors." Far from being pacifist, they were fighters and thus to be dissociated from those who allowed themselves to be martyred (Davies: 134–35; Collins: 215–18). Such individuals should not be considered as authors of the book of Daniel, which encourages passive resistance through martyrdom rather than active armed resistance to persecution (Davies: 129–30; Collins: 198–210). Another point is that the statement of Alcimus to Demetrius (2 Macc 14:6) makes Judas the leader of the *Asadeans*. This is either an error of identification by Alcimus or another indication that the term was used only generally.

The only appropriate attitude is a skeptical one. We do not know for certain that the Hasidim were a definite, organized group; perhaps the authors of 1 and 2 Maccabees used the name only generally, to apply to a variety of groups. Even if only one particular group is in mind, however, we know little about it other than that it did not author Daniel 7–12 and that its relationship—if any—to the Essenes and Pharisees is unknown. Kampen has recently argued for a connection with the Pharisees; however, one of his main reasons is the supposition that the Hasidim formed a unified movement, and another is that the Pharisees had a position in Jewish society and religion that will be argued against in 8.2.2.

8.2.2 Pharisees

Baumgarten, A. I. "The Name of the Pharisees." *JBL* 102 (1983) 411–28.

———. "*Korban* and the Pharisaic *Paradosis*." *JANES* 16–17 (1984–85) 5–17.

———. "The Pharisaic *Paradosis*." *HTR* 80 (1987) 63–77.

Cohen, S.J.D. Review of *The Hidden Revolution*, by E. Rivkin. *JBL* 99 (1980) 627–29.

———. "The Significance of Yavneh: Pharisees, Rabbis, and the End of Jewish Sectarianism." *HUCA* 55 (1984) 27–53.

Cook, M. J. *Mark's Treatment of the Jewish Leaders* (1978a).

———. "Jesus and the Pharisees—The Problem as It Stands Today." *JES* (1978b) 441–60.

Davies, W. D., and D. C. Allison. *The Gospel according to Saint Matthew* (1988).

Ellenson, D. "Ellis Rivkin and the Problems of Pharisaic History: A Study in Historiography." *JAAR* 43 (1975) 787–802.

Goodblatt, D. "The Place of the Pharisees in First Century Judaism: The State of the Debate." *JSJ* 20 (1989) 12–30.

Gruber, M. I. "The Mishnah as Oral Torah: A Reconsideration." *JSJ* 15 (1984) 112–22.

Mason, S. N. "Priesthood in Josephus and the 'Pharisaic Revolution.'" *JBL* 107 (1988a) 657–61.

———. "Josephus on the Pharisees Reconsidered: A Critique of Smith/ Neusner." *SR* 17 (1988b) 455–69.

———. "Was Josephus a Pharisee? A Re-Examination of *Life* 10–12." *JJS* 40 (1989) 31–45.

Neusner, J. *Development of a Legend* (1970).

———. *1971.

———. "The Written Tradition in the Pre-rabbinic Period." *JSJ* 4 (1973) 56–65.

———. "'First Cleanse the Inside': The 'Halakhic' Background of a Controversy-Saying." *NTS* 22 (1975/76) 486–95.

———. "The Formation of Rabbinic Judaism: Yavneh (Jamnia) from A.D. 70 to 100." *ANRW* 2 (1979a) 19.2.3–24.

———. "From Scripture to Mishnah: The Origins of Mishnah's Fifth Division." *JBL* 98 (1979b) 269–83.

———. "Two Pictures of the Pharisees: Philosophical Circle or Eating Club." *ATR* 64 (1982) 525–38.

———. "Josephus' Pharisees: A Complete Repertoire." *Josephus, Judaism, and Christianity* (1987) 274–92.

———. "Money-Changers in the Temple: The Mishnah's Explanation." *NTS* 35 (1989) 287–90.

Neusner, J., with A. J. Avery-Peck. "The Quest for the Historical Hillel: Theory and Practice." *Formative Judaism* (1982) 45–63.

Rivkin, E. "Defining the Pharisees: The Tannaitic Sources." *HUCA* 43 (1972) 205–49.

———. *The Hidden Revolution: An Historical Reconstruction of the Pharisees* (1978).

Schwartz, D. R. "Josephus and Nicolaus on the Pharisees." *JSJ* 14 (1983) 157–71.

Schwartz, S. *Josephus and Judaean Politics* (1990).

Telford, W. R. Review of *Mark's Treatment of the Jewish Leaders*, by M. Cook. *JTS* 31 (1980) 154–62.

Wild, R. A. "The Encounter between Pharisaic and Christian Judaism: Some Early Gospel Evidence." *NovT* 27 (1985) 105–24.

Discussions about Judaism in the first century have tended to be dominated by the Pharisees. From a period when the Pharisees were denigrated by Christians, the tendency has passed into a sustained apologetic on their behalf by many Christian as well as Jewish scholars (cf. *Neusner 1971: 3.320–68). Like so many value judgments, neither approach is helpful. The revolution instigated by Neusner has meant that almost everything written about the Pharisees before about 1970—and much after that date—needs revision (1.1.4). There are essentially three sources of information, each with its own prejudices and problems: Josephus, the New Testament, and rabbinic literature.

8.2.2.1 Josephus

8.2.2.1.1 Texts. In *War* 2.8.14 §§162–63, 166, Josephus describes the Pharisees as follows (cf. *Ant.* 13.5.9 §172, which adds nothing):

> Of the two first-named schools, the Pharisees, who are considered the most accurate interpreters of the laws, and hold the position of the leading sect, attribute everything to Fate and to God; they hold that to act rightly or otherwise rests, indeed, for the most part with men, but that in each action Fate co-operates. Every soul, they maintain, is imperishable, but the soul of the good alone passes into another body, while the souls of the wicked suffer eternal punishment. . . . The Pharisees are affectionate to each other and cultivate harmonious relations with the community.

His account in *Ant.* 18.1.3 §§12–15, written some twenty years later, is rather different (see 8.2.2.4 for a discussion of possible reasons why):

> The Pharisees simplify their standard of living, making no concession to luxury. They follow the guidance of that which their doctrine has selected and transmitted as good, attaching the chief importance to the observance of those commandments which it has seen fit to dictate to them. They show respect and deference to their elders, nor do they rashly presume to contradict their proposals. Though they postulate that everything is brought about by fate, still they do not deprive the human will of the pursuit of what is in man's power, since it was God's good pleasure that there should be a fusion and that the will of man with his virtue and vice should be admitted to the council-chamber of fate. They believe that souls have power to survive death and that there are rewards and punishments under the earth for those who have led lives of virtue or vice: eternal imprisonment is the lot of evil souls, while the good souls receive an easy passage to a new life. Because of these views they are, as a matter of fact, extremely influential among the townsfolk; and all prayers and sacred rites of divine worship are performed according to their exposition. This is the great tribute that the inhabitants of the cities, by practising the highest ideals both in their way of living and in their discourse, have paid to the excellence of the Pharisees.

Scholarship has tended to concentrate on these two passages, but to do so is problematic. For one thing, the two accounts have some important differences; for another, they do not actually tell us very much. First, in *War*, after having spent a lengthy amount of space on the Essenes, Josephus briefly turns to the Pharisees and Sadducees (2.8.14 §§162, 166). The Pharisees are thought to be accurate interpreters of the law and hold the position of "first sect" (*tēn prōtēn hairesin*). They attribute everything to fate, although most of the initiative lies in human hands. The soul is immortal and is rewarded or punished. Finally, in a blatant piece of prejudicial writing, Josephus claims that the Pharisees are affectionate toward each other and the community, whereas the Sadducees are rude both to outsiders and one another.

According to *Ant*. 18.1.2–4 §§11–15, 17, the Pharisees live simply, respect their elders, and pay heed to traditional teachings. Josephus's discussion focuses on their stance on the question of fate and the soul, hardly the most vibrant topic among Jewish sects but one that gentile readers would have found of interest. He finally notes that prayers and other religious rites follow the Pharisees' dictates and that even Sadducees in high office must conform to Pharisaic customs (a claim parallel to that in *Ant*. 13.10.5 §288 but nowhere made in the *War*).

In *Life* 2 §§8–12 Josephus claims to have become a Pharisee at the age of nineteen, at least, as his statement is usually understood (but see 8.2.2.1.2); however, his account contains a number of improbabilities. He assures us that at the age of fourteen, he was so learned that chief priests and leading citizens would consult him about points of law—and he tells us this with a straight face. He also states that at sixteen he proceeded to "pass through" (*diēlthon*) the three major sects and, further, spend three years with a hermit in the desert. Nevertheless, after this arduous program of discipline, he was still only nineteen. The arithmetic is as hard to take in as his precocity.

Of considerable significance are those passages in which Josephus deals with actual historical incidents in which the Pharisees were involved. Surprisingly, there are not many of these, and they seem to cluster around two periods of time:

1. John Hyrcanus's break with the Pharisees (5.4.7). According to *Ant*. 13.10.5–7 §§288–99, the Pharisees became an issue at an early time, under John Hyrcanus (135–104 B.C.E.). They had such influence with the people that if they criticized even a king or high priest, they would be believed (a claim not found in the *War*). They had the support of the masses, in contrast to the Sadducees, who were supported by the wealthy. Hyrcanus was himself a disciple of the Pharisees but broke with them over the episode of Eleazar (a Pharisee who spoke out publicly about the offices which Hyrcanus held). Hyrcanus therefore abrogated their regulations for the people (regulations not found written in the Law of Moses) and quieted the resulting outbreak. Having dealt effectively with the opposition, he spent the rest of his reign in peace.

2. Pharisaic opposition to Alexander Janneus (5.4.9). In contrast to *Antiquities*, *War* 1.5.2–3 §§110–14 indicates that the Pharisees first came to prominence under Alexandra Salome (76–67 B.C.E.), who was very much under their thumb. The Pharisees, noted for their piety and ability to expound the law, at this time became the real administrators of state

and were able to impose their own regulations. The parallel passage in *Ant.* 13.15.5–16.6 §§398–432 shows considerable opposition to Alexander Janneus (103–76 B.C.E.). This is often assumed to be from the Pharisees, but Josephus actually does not say so. Rather, it seems that the Pharisees were only some of those among Janneus's opponents. On his deathbed, however, Janneus is alleged to have instructed his wife, Alexandra Salome, to make peace with the Pharisees. That she did, and the Pharisees were able to reestablish regulations which Hyrcanus had abrogated, to dominate the queen, and even to have some of their enemies executed. This section represents a considerable expansion of the account in *War* but does not seem to differ from it in character. Josephus (or his source) is not particularly pro-Pharisee at this point but also does not seem hostile to them (contra D. R. Schwartz: 158–62; Mason 1988b; Mason 1989: 35).

3. Conflict with Herod. The only information in the *War* is a brief statement that the wife of Pheroras (Herod's nephew) was accused of hiring the Pharisees against Herod (1.29.2 §571). The *Antiquities* is more detailed. Herod especially honored two Pharisees, Pollion and his disciple Samaias, because they had been useful to him in the past (*Ant.* 15.1.1 §§3–4). When Herod was besieging Jerusalem, they had advised admitting him. Pollion is also alleged to have predicted that if the Sanhedrin acquitted him of the charges against him, then Herod would eventually persecute them. Later, when Herod required an oath of loyalty from all citizens, Pollion and Samaias and their disciples refused to swear but were not punished, evidently because of Herod's goodwill toward them (*Ant.* 15.10.4 §370). The Essenes also escaped having to comply (§371).

However, the other Pharisees, six thousand in all (presumably the entire community), were fined (*Ant.* 17.2.4 3.1 §§41–47). They were said to dominate the women of the court; indeed, the wife of Pheroras paid the fine imposed on the Pharisees. Some were accused of plotting at court against Herod and were executed by him, as were others who agreed with them. The "Fourth Philosophy" is said to have been founded right at the end of Herod's reign by Judas of Gamala and Zadok (Saddokos) the Pharisee (*Ant.* 18.1.1 §4). This movement supposedly agreed with the Pharisees in all points except the view that God alone can be considered their master (*Ant.* 18.1.6 §23).

4. The war with Rome. As events were heating up toward war (*War* 2.17.2–3 §§410–11), the sacrifices for the Roman emperor were stopped by the ordinary priests, despite protests by many of the chief priests and the notables. Therefore, the principal citizens, together with the chief priests and "notable Pharisees" (*tois tōn Pharisaiōn gnōrimois*), assembled to discuss how they might forestall disaster. The *Life* seems compatible with this picture. Josephus consorted with the "leading Pharisees"

(*tois prōtois tōn Pharisaiōn*) and chief priests (*Life* 5 §21). One of the leaders in the early part of the revolt was Simon b. Gamaliel, a Pharisee (38 §190–91). Later, this same Simon dispatched a delegation to Josephus consisting of three Pharisees, one a priest, and another priest who was not a Pharisee (39 §197).

8.2.2.1.2 Analysis. We do not know Josephus's source(s). It is likely to have been Nicolaus of Damascus as far as Herod's reign, at least in part, although Josephus may well have supplemented Nicolaus with information from other sources. Whatever his source(s), however, the problem is knowing how much he altered them or added his own interpretation (cf. D. R. Schwartz). The accounts in the *War* are much briefer than those in *Antiquities*, but there is no clear difference of outlook in many of them (for exceptions, see below). Further, in many cases the writer does not seem to be a Pharisee or pro-Pharisee (exceptions below), but neither does he seem to be particularly hostile to the Pharisees. He thought they had too much influence with Alexandra Salome, yet such an opinion could come from a more or less neutral observer.

Striking, however, is the difference between the blanket statements about the influence of the Pharisees and the historical realities as described in the narrative: "So great is their influence with the masses that even when they speak against a king or a high priest, they immediately gain credence" (*Ant.* 13.10.5 §288). Such statements have often been seized on to show the power of the Pharisees—they can even force kings and priests to follow their bidding. The context itself, however, shows that such was not generally the case. Whatever Hyrcanus's original relationship to the Pharisees (the allegation that he was a disciple is suspect), when he turned against them, he prevailed: he abolished any Pharisaic regulations and punished those who followed them (§296) and stifled the outbreak (§299).

The nature of the Pharisaic opposition to Alexander Janneus is not clear, because Josephus does not identify Janneus's opponents as Pharisees. Pharisees must have been among them, however, because he supposedly recommended to his wife that she heal the breach. Again, whatever the opposition, it was not very successful (even if annoying to Janneus).

Under Alexandra Salome the Pharisees had genuine political power, were able to enforce specific regulations of their own as law (although what these were is never indicated), and even succeeded in driving out or having executed some of their opponents (*Ant.* 13.16.2 §§408–11). Nevertheless, things did not all go the Pharisees' way. Although they succeeded in having a few opponents executed, Alexandra was evidently reluctant to go too far (especially when some of the leading citizens complained) and kept many of the alleged enemies as guards in her fortresses (§§410–18). What is most astonishing, however, is that with her death, the Pharisees suddenly vanish from the scene. Nothing is said about a coup or mass roundup or any other drastic measure taken against them. They are simply not mentioned for the next several decades and seem to have no particular power in the struggles between Hyrcanus II and Aristobulus II.

Under Herod the Pharisees surface again, but only briefly. Apart from attempts at influence in the royal household, they are mainly presented as a group still having a reputation with regard to traditional laws. (The charge of conspiracy might have some validity, at least on the part of particular individuals, but was probably exaggerated in Herod's mind.) They then disappear once again until the beginnings of the war with Rome, at which time some Pharisees are among those leaders and figures who seem to be counseling moderation. It is the "notable" among them, however, who are part of the power structure. There is no indication that the Pharisees as a whole were more influential than any other grouping. For example, an individual such as Simon b. Gamaliel is an important figure in the revolt and a Pharisee, but it is nowhere stated that he is an important figure because he is a Pharisee.

Josephus's general descriptions of the sects are problematic. First, they tell us a lot about the Essenes but extremely little about the Pharisees or Sadducees. Second, they focus on questions which were probably of more concern to a Greco-Roman audience than to the sects themselves: the question of fate, whether the soul is immortal, the individual sect's "philosophical" way of life in general. Third, there are some important differences between *War* and *Antiquities* with regard to the Pharisees. Whereas in both cases Josephus mentions the reputation of the Pharisees for piety and the interpretation of the traditional laws, only in *Antiquities* does he assert that religious rites are conducted according to their precepts and that the Sadducees must obey them. This is a significant addition, and nowhere does anything in his writings demonstrate that such was the case. On the contrary, the priests seem to have carried out the cult according to priestly tradition (cf. Mason 1988a), and the high priest was quite willing to press decisions of which Pharisees might have disapproved. For example, the sentence of death passed by the Sanhedrin on James, the brother of Jesus, was instigated by the high priest Ananus b. Ananus (*Ant.* 20.9.1 §§199–200).

Mason (1989) has recently argued that, contrary to widespread interpretation, *Life* 2 §12 does not mean to indicate that Josephus himself became a Pharisee. The point about the peculiar wording of the passage is well taken, but Mason's main argument is not convincing, which is that

Josephus simply means to say that he followed the Pharisees in his public activities because they dominated public life. If everyone followed them, as Mason implies, would there be any point in Josephus making the statement? Mason also accepts without question Josephus's claim that public affairs were conducted according to Pharisaic dictates. As already noted, Josephus's claim is at odds with his data about actual practice. Indeed, Josephus himself happily opposed the leading Pharisee Simon and his embassy, which had three Pharisees on it.

The problem which Mason has correctly identified could be the result of Josephus trying to make a claim about his early life that is simply untrue. That is, his statement about following the Pharisees at age nineteen may be incongruous because he did no such thing (as noted in 8.2.2.1.1, the whole passage is self-serving and incredible). When one examines the passage in the context of the whole book, however, it is hard to believe that Josephus intended any other impression on the reader than that he joined the Pharisees at age nineteen.

A widely accepted thesis is that in the 90s Josephus was making a bid to throw in his lot with the Pharisees, who had become the dominant group in Israel (*Smith 1956: 74–78; *Neusner 1973: 45–66). Although the thesis is speculative (cf. D. R. Schwartz: 164–69), it is one way of explaining several passages in Josephus that show a pro-Pharisaic tendency not found elsewhere. Several scholars have recently argued against this view. Saldarini (*1988: 128–33) contends that Josephus's view in any one passage was determined primarily by his concern for order. Therefore, the Jewish historian approves of the Pharisees in one passage because they promote order but is hostile to them in another because they caused disruption. This is an interesting point which requires further study. It also illustrates the complexity of Josephus's thought and that one should be careful of trying to reduce his discussion to a single, overarching purpose. Similarly, Mason (1988b) attempts to show that, contrary to Smith and Neusner, Josephus was actually hostile to the Pharisees in the key passage (*Ant.* 13.15.5 §§399–402). Again, his comments show that Josephus was not univocal throughout his work. Nevertheless, one comes back to the central point, against both Saldarini and Mason, that Josephus makes a claim for the Pharisees at this (and other) points in *Antiquities* that occurs nowhere in *War*: that the Pharisees control both public life and religious worship. This claim remains true, despite the critics; the Smith-Neusner explanation cannot be proved but is still an important and viable hypothesis, as Goodblatt has also recently argued. (It should be noted, however, that a considerable difference exists between Saldarini and Mason; the former, on other grounds, argues forcibly against the idea that Pharisees dominated society and is thus in strong agreement with Smith and Neusner on the central issue.)

8.2.2.1.3 Conclusions. From Josephus the following points emerge:

1. One has to be careful to distinguish Josephus's claims about the Pharisees from the actual events he describes. The former are more likely to represent interpretation and even propaganda.
2. Although he claims that the Pharisees were able to gain credence when they spoke up against even a king or high priest, his narrative demonstrates no such thing. Only during the reign of Alexandra Salome did the Pharisees seem to have power to enforce their will to any major extent. During the war with Rome, certain Pharisees gained prominence (e.g., Simon b. Gamaliel), but they seem to have done so as individuals. Nowhere are the Pharisees as an undifferentiated group shown to control or dominate, either in the civil or the religious sphere.
3. On the whole, Josephus's narrative is fairly neutral toward the Pharisees, showing neither hostility nor particular favor (although in one passage he shows a marked prejudice against the Sadducees). However, twice in the *Antiquities* there appears an exceptional statement that seems to attribute powers to the Pharisees that are nowhere demonstrated by his narrative (see point 2). In a similar vein, Josephus's personal relationship to the Pharisees is somewhat puzzling. Although he seems to make the claim that he became a Pharisee at age nineteen, this appears only in a late writing, and there is little evidence elsewhere that he was a Pharisee for most of his life. It is not clear how to explain these difficulties, but the thesis that Josephus was making a bid to side with the Pharisees at a rather late date is a reasonable explanation.
4. The Pharisees appear in a number of passages as a group with a reputation for interpretation of the traditional laws, which were not written in the books of Moses. This is the one consistent thread throughout Josephus's references to the Pharisees (cf. Baumgarten 1984/85; 1987).

From these data, it is clear that Josephus does not discuss continuous activities of the Pharisees or consider the Pharisees the pervasive religious influence that his statements in *Ant.* 18.1.3–4 §§15–17 imply. Rather, they first came to public attention under Hyrcanus I and were active for the half century to the reign of Alexandra Salome. Then they seem almost to have disappeared, except for a couple of incidents during the reign of Herod. Otherwise, Josephus says nothing about Pharisees except for a brief mention in the *Life*, where he notes that the leader of the Jerusalem council was Simon b. Gamaliel, a Pharisee (§191), and that the committee sent to deal with Josephus was composed of four individuals, three of whom were Pharisees, one of these being a priest (§197). This suggests that the actual influence of the Pharisaic movement tended to be concentrated in particular periods, especially the latter part of the Hasmonean kingdom, after which their actual impact on society and history does not appear to have been great. Despite Josephus's claim, the Pharisees had not taken away the prerogatives of the priesthood; indeed, Josephus's statements elsewhere, in both *War* and *Antiquities*, show that he regarded the priests as preeminent in matters of law and cult (Mason 1988a). In addition, references to the temple and priesthood in his narratives nowhere show any indication that the Pharisees controlled these institutions.

8.2.2.2   New Testament

Here is a summary of the major statements in the New Testament about the Pharisees (see also *Saldarini 1988: 134–98; *Neusner 1973: 67–80; *Smith 1978: 153–57; Cook 1978a; Wild):

1. At various points in the Gospels, the Pharisees are associated with a variety of groups at one time or another, including scribes (Mark 7:1-23), Herodians (Mark 3:1-6; 12:13), Sadducees (Matt 3:7-10), and even the chief priests (Matt 21:45). Sometimes they oppose each other, but at other times they seem to be in an alliance against Jesus. There is good reason, however, to see the bulk of these as secondary ascriptions. Where Mark 2:6 and 12:38 mention only "scribes," Matt 23:2 and Luke 5:21 have "scribes and Pharisees." In what is generally assumed to be a Q-pericope, Matthew's "Pharisees and Sadducees" (3:7-10) is probably less original than Luke's "crowds" (3:7-9). Similarly, the Pharisees of Mark 8:11 become "the Pharisees and Sadducees" (Matt 16:1) or "scribes and Pharisees" (Matt 12:38). Therefore, there seems a tendency to inflate the opponents of Jesus in any episode, with the later sources more likely to add names.
2. They have "traditions from the elders" (Mark 7:5), although it is not stated that this is in the form of an "oral Torah."
3. Much is made of eating and ritual purity ("eating with unwashed hands") (Mark 2:15-17 // Matt 9:10-13 // Luke 5:29-32; Mark 7:1-23 // Matt 15:1-20 // Luke 11:37-41).

4. There are also some other questions, such as about the Sabbath (Mark 2:23-28 // Matt 12:1-8 // Luke 6:1-5; Mark 3:1-6 // Matt 12:9-14 // Luke 6:6-11), marriage (Mark 10:2-12 // Matt 19:3-12 // Luke 16:18), how to recognize the Messiah (Mark 12:35-37 // Matt 22:41-46 // Luke 20:41-44), and obedience to the Roman authorities (Mark 12:13-17 // Matt 22:15-22; Luke 20:20-26).

5. By and large, there is little attempt to give detailed information about the Pharisees. Rather, they (and others) serve simply as a foil to Jesus. They come to question Jesus, but then the focus is on his reply; the Pharisees usually have no comeback.

There are several possible ways of reading this evidence. One is to conclude that most of the statements about the Pharisees, especially those indicating Pharisaic dominance, are post-70 additions to the tradition and may well represent later controversies (cf. *Neusner 1973: 67–80; *Smith 1978: 28–29, 153–57; Cook 1978b: 453). It has also been suggested that the statements may represent intra-Pharisaic disputes between those who had become Christians and those who had not (Wild). Perhaps they even indicate intra-Christian debates, to some extent. Most New Testament scholars would agree, however, that there is some manifestation of the pre-70 situation in the statements, even if not always reaching back to the time of Jesus (*Saldarini 1988: 144–98). For example, Mark's traditions may reflect the mid-first century, whereas the role of the Pharisees in society as described by him is intrinsically probable (*Saldarini 1988: 145, 156–57).

8.2.2.3 The Rabbinic Traditions

It would be impossible even to survey the statements in rabbinic literature that could be connected with the Pharisees. Because much of the work not only of assembling the data but also of analyzing it has already been done by Neusner, however, it needs only to be summarized here (see also *Saldarini 1988: 199–237). (One of the problems is whom to include, because the individuals are not usually labeled Pharisees but "rabbi" or the like; see below for further comments.) Some of the major points to notice are:

1. The content of the Mishnah, the foundational rabbinic document, focuses on certain topics: laws of purity, eating, festivals, and agriculture; and laws relating to the exchange of women, such as betrothal, marriage, and divorce. The vast bulk of the traditions relate to these subjects.

2. An analysis of the early traditions about pre-70 figures and about the Houses of Shammai and Hillel reveals a preoccupation with the same topics that form the bulk of the traditions in the Mishnah.

3. The pre-70 traditions of the Mishnah, as well as the early traditions about pre-70 figures, do not indicate a concern with civil law, governance of the country, or the oversight of the temple cult. Rather, they relate to matters that would be under the control of an individual, the head of a family, or a small community: household affairs, family affairs, daily life, and the exchange of women. Exceptions are traditions of Gamaliel I and his son Simeon (Simon) b. Gamaliel, both of whom seem to have had some sort of civil office (*Neusner 1971: 3.291). Although a minority section of the Mishnah deals with civil law (*Neziqin*, "Damages"), there is no evidence of any part of it arising before 70 (*Neusner 1981: 62, 198–204). Similarly, the mishnaic order relating to the temple (*Qodašim*, "Holy Things") lacks one of the main components found in similar documents (e.g., Leviticus 1–15 and the Epistle to the Hebrews): a discussion of priestly law. That is, the expected contents of sacrifice, sources of cultic purity, and the temple are all in the Mishnah, but the priesthood as such is ignored (Neusner 1979b), a surprising omission if *Qodašim* arose in a group which allegedly controlled the priesthood.

4. A number of the important figures of pre-70 times seem to have had nothing to do with Hillel (or Shammai). The Gamaliel family (Gamaliel I, Simeon b. Gamaliel, Gamaliel II) is not associated with Hillel and not said to be descended from him (although later tradition makes Gamaliel I Hillel's grandson). Simeon does agree with the House of Shammai on one or two points and is likely to have been a Shammaite, as was his son Gamaliel II (*Neusner 1971: 1.380, 387; 3.274). Similarly, Yohanan b. Zakkai is not associated with Hillel, even though later tradition attempts to make him so; rather, he seems independent of the Houses (*Neusner 1970: 289–90; 1971: 3.275–77).

5. The size of the Houses of Hillel and Shammai seems to have been quite small (*Neusner 1971: 3.267). Their elders could all meet in one room (cf. *m. Suk.* 2.7). Even a sufficient quorum of the two Houses to make decisions affecting their entire membership could meet in an "upper room" ('*aliyyāh* [*m. Shab.* 1:4]). Evidently, all the ritual immersions of cooking utensils by the Pharisees in Jerusalem could be done at one trough (*m. Miq.* 4.5). In the Talmud, Hillel is alleged to have had only eighty disciples (or pairs of disciples: *y. Ned.* 5.6; *b. Suk.* 28a; *b. B. Batra* 134a). None of these accounts

may be historical, but why the later compilers would present the Houses as small if they remembered them as being quite large needs explaining. This suggests that the traditions available to them knew only of small groups around Hillel and Shammai.

These are important and valid points as far as they go; however, in more recent years Neusner has refined and extended his study so that further ramifications need to be taken into account. Some of these are the following:

6. Not all the pre-70 traditions of the Mishnah necessarily go back to Pharisees (*Neusner 1981: 70–71; cf. *Saldarini 1988: 201–2). Therefore, some of the laws and legal themes may have been created by groups other than the Pharisees.
7. The legal agenda of the Mishnah probably tells us a good deal about the pre-70 Pharisees, but it may not tell us all of their interests. That is, there may have been concerns which were not preserved, for one reason or another, by the framers of the Mishnah (*Saldarini 1988: 212–16).

8.2.2.4 Analysis

The picture given by the various sources is by no means a unified one; there are both striking similarities and sharp differences, which are too often ignored by writers on the Pharisees (e.g., Rivkin 1978; cf. the review by Cohen 1980). One might expect Josephus, who claims that he himself was a Pharisee, to be the best guide. The problem is that he actually gives little information in the two passages in which he describes the Pharisees (8.2.2.1). He concentrates on the Pharisaic view of fate, a topic which receives little or no concern in the other sources, probably because this would be of interest to his Greco-Roman audience. He also indicates that the Pharisees interpreted the traditional "laws" and had traditions not found written in Scripture.

More significant, however, are the discrepancies between his various accounts. In the *War* he gives a fairly short and factual, but by no means unfavorable, account (in contrast to his rendering of the Sadducees); in *Antiquities*, however, he makes the Pharisees the religious leaders of the country. The latter description does not fit with his own historical narratives, which describe actual events. How are we to account for these differences? That the description in *Antiquities* 18 fits well with his claim in *Life* 2 §12 to have become a Pharisee is clear. A legitimate conclusion is that Josephus's attitude toward the Pharisees changed at some point and that he decided to give the Pharisees a puff (in *Antiquities*) and to claim to have been a lifelong member of the sect (*Life*).

This much is evident, although the precise reason for the differences is not. Smith has given an explanation (*1956: 74–78): the Pharisees had become dominant by the time *Antiquities* was written, and Josephus— clever politician that he was—decided that it would be useful to help them and thus also help himself (see also *Neusner 1973: 45–66). This explanation cannot be proved, but it is plausible. It also reinforces the conclusion one must draw from Josephus's data: the Pharisees were not the religious leaders of the pre-70s, with the exception of a brief period during the reign of Alexandra Salome. Two recent studies tend to support this interpretation of Josephus's view of the Pharisees in *Antiquities*. Goodblatt provides explicit support for Smith's original thesis and rebuts the arguments of D. R. Schwartz. S. Schwartz examined a similar question, concluding that Josephus did indeed support a particular group, one not identical to Pharisees but related to them: the early rabbinic movement (172–200).

Both the named figures and unattributed sayings of the early rabbinic traditions represent a table-fellowship sect, a group that had control of its internal relations (home, eating, individual worship, marriage) but not of the country or the temple cult. There is indeed intent interest in particular priestly matters, but the application of them differs from that of priests on duty. The Old Testament cultic and purity regulations in Leviticus, Deuteronomy, and elsewhere relate primarily to the temple. In the temple the priest had to eat his food in a state of ritual purity. The laity bringing sacrifices to the temple also had to be cultically pure, yet it was not envisaged that they had to eat their daily food at home in this state. According to the traditions, however, the Pharisees did eat their meals— all of them, not just the cultic ones in the temple—in a state of ritual purity. In short, the Pharisee made his home into a miniature version of the temple: the Pharisee himself was analogous to the priest; his hearth, to the altar; his house, to the temple area.

The Pharisees discussed many points of law, but one subject not aired in the extant literature is Torah study. There is no reference to getting together to study Torah, which was so characteristic of rabbinic Judaism. Therefore, one can conclude that they did not engage in the study of the Torah as a religious act. This suggests that this aspect of rabbinic Judaism either evolved in the post-70 times or came from a group different from the Pharisees. Another concept that seems to be absent is the two-fold Torah from Moses, that is, the Written Torah and the Oral Torah (*Neusner 1971: 3.143–79; cf. Gruber). The Pharisees had traditions, as most sources affirm, but we are not told that these were transmitted orally, were regarded as a second Torah alongside the written one, or were alleged to originate with Moses.

Neusner has noted that there is a discrepancy between the way the Pharisees are presented in rabbinic literature compared to other sources. In Josephus the Pharisees are chiefly a political group seeking to influence government and sometimes succeeding, as in the reign of Alexandra Salome. In the Gospels the Pharisees appear as a group concerned about purity and agricultural regulations, very much parallel to the rabbinic traditions. Only in two main areas do they show a major interest which finds no counterpart in tannaitic literature: eschatology/messianism and the question of Roman rule. Neusner has explained the difference between the political picture of Josephus and the table-fellowship sect of the New Testament and the rabbinic tradition by hypothesizing a change of character under Herod. There are two reasons for this assumption: (1) Josephus presents the Pharisees as a group seeking political power throughout Hasmonean and early Herodian rule; and (2) the rabbinic traditions and the pre-70 figures, in contrast, are predominantly about Hillel, Shammai, and the Houses. The rabbinic traditions never refer to figures before Hillel and Shammai, however; it is as if the Pharisaic movement began with these two individuals. Because political activity could be dangerous (a number of Pharisees were executed by Herod for alleged involvement in a plot [8.2.2.1]), one can readily believe that a major reorientation of the sect is indicated by the sources, that is, that the Pharisees had moved from a politically activist group to a quietist religious sect (hence the title of Neusner's book, *From Politics to Piety* [*1973]). The ignoring of predecessors within the Hillel-Shammai-Houses traditions points to Hillel as a good candidate for the one who reoriented the Pharisees to purely religious views.

While developing and refining these arguments, Neusner kept much the same position for the decade after his main work in 1971 (cf. Neusner 1979a; 1987). Then his summary volume on the Mishnah presented, without discussing his earlier views, a much more noncommittal point of view that kept to the inductive approach used in that study (*1981: 70–71): the group producing the Mishnah before 70 had specific characteristics, but these could equally conform to a lay group attempting to imitate priests, a priestly group attempting to extend the cultic life to the home, or a mixture of the two. Although the characteristics could fit the Pharisees, they also have a good deal in common with the Essenes. In his 1981 work Neusner did not go on to draw further implications from these statements or to integrate them with the enormous number of his earlier writings (see also the criticisms of *Saldarini 1988: 212–16, 285–86).

Part of the difficulty is that the named sages of rabbinic literature are not found in other literature, for the most part, whereas the handful of Pharisees cited by name in Josephus and the New Testament are not found in rabbinic tradition. Some of those quoted in rabbinic sources are unlikely to have been Pharisees (Simon the Just, the high priest Alcimus, John Hyrcanus, Alexander Janneus). The two major exceptions, however, are Gamaliel (Gamliel) I and his son Simeon (b. Gamliel). The former is mentioned in Acts 5:34 as a leading Pharisee on the Sanhedrin, whereas the latter is referred to by Josephus as an important figure in the conduct of the war in Galilee (*Life* 38 §§190–94). Interestingly, Neusner's study has found that the only pre-70 figure who appears to have had public office and authority in the earliest rabbinic traditions is Gamaliel I (8.2.2.3). For example, Gamaliel made rules relating to the religious calendar, which was probably a function of the temple as long as it stood (8.3.3).

One of the initial difficulties is knowing which traditions to draw on. The term "Pharisees" (Hebrew, *perûšîm*) is seldom used in rabbinic literature, and when it is, its relationship to the Pharisees of the Greek sources is not always clear (Rivkin 1972; *Saldarini 1988: 220–25). Many early figures were claimed by the later rabbis, but is this only a later appropriation? In some cases there is reason to think so and to conclude that a non-Pharisee has been taken over by the tradition (e.g., Yohanan b. Zakkai). There may still be reason, however, to see a general connection between the pre-70 Pharisees and the tannaitic rabbis, even if the precise relationship is somewhat problematic (Cohen 1984). Some of the pre-70 figures could have become subsequently "Pharisaized" at a later date; nevertheless, the Yavneans do not make an issue of their Pharisaic roots. If those at Yavneh were seeking to form a grand coalition, they might not have been interested in emphasizing earlier sectarianism. Only the Amoraim (after 200) see themselves clearly as heirs of the Pharisees. Neusner has pointed out that there were several groups at Yavneh (1979a: 37), suggesting that the list of Yohanan b. Zakkai's five disciples (*m. Avot* 2:8) might be paradigmatic: Pharisee, priest, *am ha-aretz*, mystic, and a representative of rabbinism. This also fits in with his long-argued thesis that rabbinic Judaism originated primarily as a synthesis of Pharisaism and scribalism (1979a: 37–41).

8.2.2.5 History of the Pharisaic Movement

A tentative history is traced here, but it must always be subject to revision in the light of new study. As the preceding sections show, many points are uncertain because of lack of data, whereas others are controversial because of differences in interpretation. We have to be careful not to pretend we know more than we do.

The origins of the Pharisees are obscure. That they are first mentioned by Josephus in association with the reign of John Hyrcanus suggests that they may not have been around too long before then or, at least, that they only became important at that time, even if their existence was much older. Because we know little or nothing about the Hasidim, the relationship of the Pharisees with that entity is unknown. The one point which seems to occur consistently in traditions about the Pharisees is that they had their own religious traditions, which they claimed to derive "from the fathers" (Baumgarten 1987). Perhaps this is not unusual, because other religious sects also had their own traditions, but it does indicate a religious orientation of some sort throughout the history of the sect as we know it. Precisely what that tradition was is also uncertain. The rabbinic traditions about pre-70 figures relate to questions primarily of purity, eating, and the extension of cultic regulations to everyday life. Does this suggest that the characteristic Pharisaic "tradition" concerned such matters, as far back as they can be traced?

In contrast, the Pharisees' political outlook varied. In the time of Hyrcanus I they appeared as a party seeking political power (5.4.7). This continued under Alexander Janneus until they finally succeeded under the rule of his queen Alexandra Salome (5.4.10). We hear little of them in the next phase of their history, under the Romans and Herod the Great. They seem not to have been very active in politics. Nevertheless, at one point they refused to swear an oath of loyalty to Herod and were accused of meddling in the issue of the royal succession (8.2.2.1.1). This suggests political activity on the part of at least some Pharisees. Precisely at this point, when Josephus ceases to say anything about them, the rabbinic traditions become abundant with Hillel, Shammai, and the Houses. Was there a change in outlook at this point, a turning away from political activity for the sake of survival? Saldarini has argued that the answer should be in the negative (*1988: 214, 285–86). In his opinion, there is no reason to assume that the political goals of the Pharisees changed. In addition, they were not likely to have made a sharp distinction between the religious and the political.

This is valid up to a point, but we have to recognize also that people of the time were fully aware of what was likely to bring down Herod's wrath on their heads, whether one labels the behavior "political" or only "religious." Some groups of Pharisees may have been more political (in modern terms) than others. We have no further indication of involvement in politics after the time of Herod, apart from one or two individuals. Gamaliel I seems to have held a public office of some sort and to have sat on the Sanhedrin. His son Simon was one of the leaders during the revolt against Rome, and one or two other figures are named as Pharisees, but there seems to have been no unified Pharisaic position at the time. Was it that only the more inward-looking sections of the movement survived the

Roman conquest and the reign of Herod? In any event, it was only in the postwar period at Yavneh that Pharisees became prominent, especially the Houses of Hillel and Shammai. By the end of the Yavnean period the old Pharisaism seems to have been more or less subsumed into the new rabbinic Judaism.

8.2.3 Sadducees and Boethusians

Daube, D. "On Acts 23: Sadducees and Angels." *JBL* 109 (1990) 493–97.
LeMoyne, J. *Les Sadducéens* (1972).
Leszynsky, R. *Die Sadduzäer* (1912).
Lightstone, J. "Sadducees versus Pharisees." *Christianity, Judaism and Other Greco-Roman Cults* (1975) 3.206–17.
*Saldarini 1988: especially 105–23, 225–37, 298–308.

The only major study on the Sadducees is that of LeMoyne, though it does seem to be a solid and useful investigation of the little evidence we have. Also important (and sometimes more critical with regard to the evidence) is the briefer treatment by Saldarini (*1988). Leszynsky's work is skewed by dependence on the "Zadokite Work" (CD) and other writings which he identifies as Sadducean in origin.

The main problem with the Sadducees is that we have not a line of their own writings or thoughts—as far as we know—and the sources we do possess are generally hostile. Therefore, the Sadducees have tended to be the whipping boys of most writers, whether Jewish or Christian. In addition, the little information extant is very skimpy and tends to be overinterpreted by most who write on them. We have three main sources: Josephus, the New Testament, and some scattered references in rabbinic literature.

8.2.3.1 Sources

Josephus's description is often taken at face value, but it is clearly biased:

> The Pharisees are affectionate to each other and cultivate harmonious relations with the community. The Sadducees, on the contrary, are, even among themselves, rather boorish in their behaviour, and in their intercourse with their peers are as rude as to aliens. (*War* 2.8.14 §166)

Most modern historians would quickly pounce on a single statement that categorized Democrats (Labour party members) as being polite to each other, but Republicans (Tories), on the contrary, as boorish and rude. Therefore, the number of historians who have accepted an equivalent statement by Josephus without question is surprising.

The later statement in *Antiquities* is in keeping with Josephus's increased bias toward the Pharisees:

> The Sadducees hold that the soul perishes along with the body. They own no observance of any sort apart from the laws; in fact, they reckon it a virtue to dispute with the teachers of the path of wisdom that they pursue. There are but few men to whom this doctrine has been made known, but these are men of the highest standing. They accomplish practically nothing, however. For whenever they assume some office, though they submit unwillingly and perforce, yet submit they do to the formulas of the Pharisees, since otherwise the masses would not tolerate them. (*Ant.* 18.1.4 §§16–17; see also 13.5.9 §§171–72)

As will be seen, Josephus gives no evidence for his last point about the Sadducees submitting to Pharisaic rule. Not only is it incredible in itself, but there are other data that oppose his statement.

Apart from these general descriptions, Josephus refers to individual Sadducees and activities of the Sadducees hardly at all. One of the few important episodes he discusses concerns the reign of John Hyrcanus (*Ant.* 13.10.6 §§293–98). Hyrcanus, who was himself a Pharisee (so Josephus claims), fell out with the Pharisees and sided with the Sadducees for the rest of his reign because of undiplomatic criticism by one of the Pharisees. Opposition to the Pharisees continued under Alexander Janneus, although Josephus says nothing further about the Sadducees during this period or during the reign of Alexandra Salome, when the Pharisees became the dominant influence in her government (8.2.2.1; 5.4.10). Much later, just before the war with Rome, the high priest Ananus, who managed to have James, the brother of Jesus, condemned, is said to have been one of the Sadducees, "who are indeed more heartless than any of the other Jews . . . when they sit in judgement" (*Ant.* 20.9.1 §199). Otherwise, no other specific persons are said to be Sadducees.

In the New Testament, Acts 5 (ostensibly ca. 33 C.E.) associates the Sadducees with the high priest: "But the high priest rose up and all who were with him, that is, the party of the Sadducees" (5:17; also 4:1). They are evidently the dominant group on the Sanhedrin, even though there are also Pharisees, such as Gamaliel. According to the picture in Acts 23:6–10 (dated by the author to about 59 C.E.), the Sanhedrin is more evenly divided; nevertheless, the Sadducees are able to enforce their own will to keep Paul under arrest. They are also said not to believe in angels or the resurrection (v 8; but cf. Daube on the question of angels). The Sadducees are mentioned in the Gospels as well but without much specificity. They may be little more than ciphers to fill out the quota for "opponents of Jesus" (cf. 8.2.2.2).

Rabbinic literature is uniformly hostile to the Sadducees. There is also a further problem in that the term "Sadducee" seems to be interchangeable (at least at times) with "Boethusian" and even occasionally with "Samaritan." The latter is clearly an assimilation to later opponents. "Boethusian" is more difficult (LeMoyne: 101–2, 337–40). It is often explained as a reference to the family of Boethus, which provided a number of the high priests from the time of Herod on. If this is the case, then the association of Sadducees and Boethusians is explicable without assuming a precise identity. (Saldarini argues, however, that because we know so little, the two groups should be kept apart [*1988: 227–28].) A few religious beliefs are mentioned as coming up in debates between Pharisees and Sadducees/Boethusians, some of which follow.

The Sadducees/Boethusians reckoned Pentecost as being the Sunday following the seventh weekly Sabbath after the wavesheaf day (LeMoyne: 177–90). That is, they interpreted the term "Sabbath" in Lev 23:15-16 as the weekly Sabbath, whereas the Pharisees took it to mean the annual holy day. The Sadducean Pentecost always fell on a particular day of the week (Sunday), whereas the Pharisaic view would assign it to a particular day of the month (either 5, 6, or 7 Sivan on a calendar determined by observation). The most natural reading of the Hebrew text is that of the Sadducees, a conclusion confirmed by the practice of other Jewish sects (Samaritans; Karaites; cf. Qumran).

The Sadducees also rejected the concept of the *eruv*, which was a means of extending the limits of a Sabbath day's journey (LeMoyne: 201–4). They may also have objected to the popular customs of pouring water and beating with willow branches at the Feast of Tabernacles (LeMoyne: 192–95, 283–89).

It is often asserted that the Sadducees accepted only the Pentateuch as canonical, but this is only a deduction from their supposed rejection of beliefs in angels and spirits (on this, see Daube). It may be that a late book such as Daniel, with an elaborate angelology and the concept of resurrection, was not accepted, but it is not clear that the Old Testament canon was closed at this time in any case. The Sadducees may well have accepted the Pentateuch, Prophets, and some of the Writings just as, apparently, many other Jews did (cf. LeMoyne: 357–79).

8.2.3.2 Analysis

Evaluation of the data is very difficult. The earliest references to the Sadducees (in Josephus) indicate that they were a political party and that the Pharisees were their primary rivals, but no particular religious beliefs are specified. Otherwise, the Sadducees tend to be characterized by particular religious positions, but these have a rather miscellaneous character about them, that is, they do not form a coherent set of beliefs. We could take individual points from a variety of sources and create an artificial system, but this takes little account of the nature of our evidence. The best we can do is advance cautiously from the surest conclusions to the less certain to attempt some sort of hypothesis, recognizing, however, that it is only a reconstruction, whose tentative nature has always to be acknowledged.

1. The most certain conclusion is that the group first appeared as a political entity (whatever its origin and other characteristics) and continued to exist in some form until after the fall of Jerusalem, possibly even into the second century C.E. (Lightstone).

2. Several data suggest some sort of connection between the group and the priestly establishment: (1) The name "Sadducees" is often thought to be derived from "Zadok," the family that held the high priestly line until the Hasmoneans. If the "Boethusians" are to be associated in some way with the Sadducees, their name is also suggestive (assuming it derives from the family of Boethus, which provided a number of high priests). (2) Several beliefs, such as their rejection of the afterlife, connect the Sadducees with the older Israelite religion (on whether they rejected angels, see Daube). These beliefs would be compatible with the conservatism of the priesthood. (3) The Sadducees' restriction of themselves to the authority of the written word seems also a priestly characteristic (however, even the priests were likely to have their own tradition of interpretation [cf. *Saldarini 1988: 303–4]). (4) Their method of reckoning Pentecost is not only the most natural one from the biblical text (cf. the Karaites) but also coincides with that of the Samaritans. This points to a priestly practice. (5) Other beliefs associated with the Sadducees seem to concern rituals relating to the temple (e.g., objections to certain popular practices at Sukkot). (6) Acts 5 makes them the high priestly party and gives them a majority on the Sanhedrin, which was dominated by the high priest; Josephus also notes that one high priest in the 60s was a Sadducee, but he does not seem to be suggesting that this was unique.

3. Josephus states that the Sadducees were to be identified with the upper socioeconomic class (and thus were not popular with the masses). This is not confirmed in other sources, but it is compatible with an association with the priestly establishment and membership on the Sanhedrin. This is not to suggest, however, that the two were coextensive. Not all Sadducees were priests or perhaps even wealthy, and not all priests or upper-class individuals were Sadducees.

8.2.4 Scribes

Cook, M. J. *Mark's Treatment of the Jewish Leaders* (1978).

Ellenson, D. "Ellis Rivkin and the Problems of Pharisaic History: A Study in Historiography." *JAAR* 43 (1975) 787–802.

Harrington, D. J. "The Wisdom of the Scribe according to Ben Sira." *Ideal Figures in Ancient Judaism* (1980) 181–88.

Jeremias, J. *Jerusalem in the Time of Jesus* (1969).

Lührmann, D. "Die Pharisäer und die Schriftgelehrten im Markusevangelium." *ZNW* 78 (1987) 169–85.

*Neusner 1981: 230–48.

Rivkin, E. "Scribes, Pharisees, Lawyers, Hypocrites: A Study in Synonymity." *HUCA* 49 (1978) 135–42.

*Saldarini 1988: 144–87, 241–76.

*Smith 1978: 30–66.

The word "scribe" (*grammateus*) is widely used in Greek literature to mean "secretary, recorder, clerk," and those of similar function, which involved writing, often in the context of a civic or public office. A parallel usage is found in Jewish literature. Josephus frequently applies the term to a public official or a secretary: village clerks (*War* 1.24.3 §479), secretary to Herod (*War* 1.26.3 §529), secretary of the Sanhedrin (*War* 5.13.1 §532), and scribes of the temple (*Ant.* 12.3.3 §142). The same usage occurs in other Jewish literature (cf. 1 Macc 5:42; Ben Sira 10:5), but there are hints that another usage might be developing: one learned in the Jewish law. First Maccabees 7:12 speaks of a delegation of scribes who appeared before Alcimus to ask for terms. Although the delegation may have represented the learned among the anti-Seleucid opposition (the scholars among the Hasidim?—v 13), it is also possible that they were professional scribes (it is also not clear that they had anything to do with the Hasidim). Second Maccabees 6:18-31 describes the martyrdom of Eleazar. Again, his title possibly comes from his knowledge of divine law, but he may have been a scribe in the normal sense (4 Macc 5:4 states that he was a priest).

The issue of a religious entity called "the scribes" arises primarily from the New Testament, because any earlier hints that one learned in Jewish law could be called a scribe are not certain. The Gospels and Acts, however, definitely use the term in that way, which is a bit puzzling. In rabbinic literature the term "scribe" (*sôfēr*) is usually used not of rabbis or those skilled in the law but of copyists and those who deal with the biblical text. If it were not for the New Testament, there might be no question of thinking about scribes as a religious grouping. Therefore, we have to be careful not to create a problem that in fact did not exist.

Several recent attempts at investigating the issue have reached rather different conclusions (cf. Cook: 71–73). Rivkin has identified the scribes with the Pharisees, arguing that the terms are mutually interchangeable, but his use of the New Testament passages is uncritical (cf. *Saldarini 1988: 228–34; Ellenson). Furthermore, Josephus never associates the two. Jeremias presents probably the most widely accepted thesis: the term "scribe" applies to all those learned in the law. Thus the Pharisees had their scribes but so did the Sadducees and other groups, and there were scribes who adhered to no particular party. The problem with such theories is that they generally founder on an uncritical approach to either the New Testament, rabbinic literature, or both.

Cook's recent treatment is therefore important because of its critical use of sources. He argues that Mark brought the scribes and Pharisees into conjunction in chapters 1 to 13 (by inserting the word "scribes" to go with "Pharisees") so that the presence of the scribes in the passion narrative would relate to the activities of the Pharisees in the first part of the book. This leads to two significant conclusions: (1) Mark was writing at a time when a precise knowledge of many of the Jewish leaders of the early tradition had been lost; and (2) the "scribes" in Mark are often simply a surrogate for "Pharisee" (although Cook thinks that Mark assumed the scribes and Pharisees were actually distinct).

Cook's analysis suggests that the Gospel writers lived at a time when only the Pharisees were known and the other terms for Jewish leaders were merely names with little meaning. If so, we cannot rely on the Gospels' usage to tell us anything of historical value about an actual group. This is the most significant result of Cook's study. The accuracy of this conclusion can be left to New Testament scholars to debate (Saldarini, for one, disagrees that Mark was quite so ignorant [*1988: 146–48, 154–57]), but for our purposes there are two areas in which Cook's analysis is problematic. First, Cook admits that the phrase "scribes of the Pharisees" (Mark 2:16) is unusual and probably the correct reading, but then he dismisses it as Mark's creation. This is unlikely because Mark's contribution would be "scribes *and* the Pharisees," and this phrase is therefore likely to be pre-Markan. Second, he dismisses the existence of Q, whereas most New Testament scholars accept it.

Mark 2:16, then, suggests that the Pharisees had their scribes but that the two were not coextensive. Acts 23:9 uses a similar expression: "several of the scribes of the Pharisees' party." Cook may be correct in dismissing the expression in Acts as simply a creation of Luke (90–91); on the other hand, Luke sometimes has independent information about pre-70 Judaism (7.2.5), which means that one should take seriously this information, even if one cannot be certain (see also *Saldarini 1988: 184–87). To this may be added a passage in Luke on the "lawyers" (*nomikoi*) and Pharisees (Luke 7:30 = Q?). Finally, the scribes who occur in the passion narrative could be non-Pharisees. Cook more or less dismisses the idea that they could be "Sadducean scribes" (89–91, 94) but then admits that the term is amorphous and cannot be defined (94). If the term is amorphous, then why not accept that they might be Sadducean scribes? They may well be nothing but a construct of the evangelist, but their likely presence in pre-Markan material at least raises the possibility that there is genuine historical memory.

With a much more detailed analysis (and also taking a somewhat different approach from mine), Saldarini has come to similar conclusions. One of the most important conclusions concerns the scribes as presented in the Gospels. As just noted, they seem something of an anomaly there when compared with other sources. Saldarini concludes that the scribes of the Gospels are indeed professional scribes, but the difficulty arises because the New Testament presents them as a unifed group, which they were not. When this is recognized, usage of the term falls into line with what we know of scribes in the world at that time (*1988: 266–68, 273–76). The discussion thus leads to the following possibilities and conclusions:

1. The term "scribe" was widely used in the Hellenistic world, including Palestine, to refer to personal secretaries and to public officials who functioned as village clerks, recorders and registrars, and scribes of the temple.

2. Although the term was also used of those skilled in Jewish law, they seem normally to have held the professional scribal office that is mentioned in point 1. The scribes of the Gospels are an exception to this, because they appear as almost a sectarian grouping. However, this seems to be only an artificial construct created by the Gospel writers. In reality, the scribes were probably professional scribes, and the impression of unity of belief is due to the theological aims of the Christian tradents (bearers of tradition) and writers.

3. Scribes as such seem to be referred to in the pre-Markan tradition and in Q. If their presence is historical, then it suggests that they were not to be identified with the Pharisees but constituted those learned in the Torah, regardless of their sectarian affiliation. This would lead to the conclusion that those who postulate Sadducean and other scribes, as well as Pharisaic scribes, have some justification for their view. But we need to recognize that scribalism generally represented a profession, and those labeled "scribes" in these

sources are not to be confused with the later rabbinic figures for whom knowledge of the Torah was an avocation, not a public office.

8.2.5 Essenes

Baumgarten, A. I. "Josephus and Hippolytus on the Pharisees." *HUCA* 55 (1984) 1–25.

Beall, T. S. *Josephus' Description of the Essenes Illustrated by the Dead Sea Scrolls* (1988).

Brownlee, W. H. "The Wicked Priest, the Man of Lies, and the Righteous Teacher—The Problem of Identity." *JQR* 73 (1982/83) 1–37.

Burchard, C. "Die Essener bei Hippolyt." *JSJ* 8 (1977) 1–41.

Davies, P. R. "The Ideology of the Temple in the Damascus Document." *JJS* 33 (1982) 287–301.

———. *The Damascus Covenant: An Interpretation of the "Damascus Document"* (1983).

———. "Eschatology at Qumran." *JBL* 104 (1985) 39–55.

———. *Behind the Essenes: History and Ideology in the Dead Sea Scrolls* (1987).

———. "How Not to Do Archaeology: The Story of Qumran." *BA* 51 (1988) 203–7.

———. "Halakhah at Qumran." *A Tribute to Geza Vermes* (1990) 37–50.

Dimant, D. "Qumran Sectarian Literature." *JWSTP* (1984) 483–550.

Grabbe, L. L. "Chronography in Hellenistic Jewish Historiography." *SBLSP* (1979) 2.43–68.

Kampen, J. "A Reconsideration of the Name 'Essene' in Greco-Jewish Literature in Light of Recent Perceptions of the Qumran Sect." *HUCA* 57 (1986) 61–81.

Murphy-O'Connor, J. "The Essenes and Their History." *RB* 81 (1974) 215–44.

———. "The Essenes in Palestine." *BA* 40 (1977) 100–124.

———. "The *Damascus Document* Revisited." *RB* 92 (1985) 223–46 = *SBLSP* (1986) 369–83.

———. "The Judean Desert." *Early Judaism and Its Modern Interpreters* (1986) 119–46.

Rabinowitz, I. "A Reconsideration of 'Damascus' and '390 Years' in the 'Damascus' ('Zadokite') Fragments." *JBL* 73 (1954) 11–35.

Smith, M. "The Description of the Essenes in Josephus and the Philosophumena." *HUCA* 29 (1958) 273–313.

Vaux, R. de. *Archaeology and the Dead Sea Scrolls* (1973).

Vermes, G. "The Etymology of 'Essenes.'" *RevQ* 2 (1960) 427–43.

Vermes, G., and M. D. Goodman, eds. *The Essenes according to Classical Sources* (1989).

There are several ancient descriptions of the Essenes. After the Qumran scrolls were discovered, it was argued the group that produced them was to be identified with the Essenes. This remains the strongest consensus after forty years, despite some dissent (indeed, this is probably the area of greatest consensus concerning the Qumran scrolls). Therefore, the Qumran scrolls are listed below as a source for the Essenes, but the arguments for associating the two groups are given in 8.2.5.4.1.

8.2.5.1 Pliny the Elder

Pliny (ca. 24–79 C.E.) makes the following statement:

> On the west side of the Dead Sea, but out of range of the noxious exhalations of the coast, is the solitary tribe of the Essenes, which is remarkable beyond all the other tribes in the whole world, as it has no women and has renounced all sexual desire, has no money, and has only palm-trees for company. . . . Lying below [*infra*] the Essenes was formerly the town of Engedi. . . . Next comes Masada. . . . (*Hist. nat.* 5.73)

The approximate location of the Essenes' habitation is made clear by Pliny's geographical description. Although the term "below" may be ambiguous, the sequence of listing is from north to south. Therefore, the Essenes evidently lived on the northern part of the west coast of the Dead Sea, north of Engedi, that is, somewhere in the region of the ruins discovered at Qumran.

8.2.5.2 Philo and Josephus

The accounts of the Essenes that Philo gives in *Quod omnis probus* 75–87 and *Hypothetica* (LCL 9.437–43, as quoted by Eusebius, *Praep. evang.* 8) are both very close to those in Josephus (*War* 2.8.2–13 §§120–61; *Ant.* 18.1.5 §§18–22). This leads to the supposition that the two used a common source, at least in part. In addition, Josephus's principal account (*War* 2.8.2–13 §§120–61) has much in common with the patristic antiheretical writing by Hippolytus (*Philosophumena* 9.18.2–9.29.4). Although it is often assumed that Hippolytus simply copied from Josephus, Smith has argued that is not the case, because the patristic writer differs verbally from the Jewish. Burchard challenged this and argued for a direct borrowing. Baumgarten (although specifically on the Pharisees) supported Smith in seeing no direct borrowing from Josephus but concluded that Josephus is nevertheless Hippolytus's source, via an intermediary. Regardless of the answer to the question of Hippolytus's source, it seems likely that Josephus and Philo used an earlier source rather than personal knowledge in their descriptions of the Essenes (despite Josephus's claim to have been initiated into the sect [*Life* 2 §§10–11]. Both Josephus and

Philo (in one or more accounts) agree on a number of points about the Essene community:

1. Approximately four thousand members, all male (Josephus, *Ant.* 18.1.5 §20; Philo, *Probus* 75).
2. Live in many towns and villages (Josephus, *War* 2.8.4 §124; Philo, *Probus* 76; *Hyp.* 11.1).
3. No wives, women, or marriage (Josephus, *War* 2.8.2 §§120–21; *Ant.* 18.1.5 §21; Philo, *Hyp.* 11.14–17).
4. A community of goods and communal meals (*War* 2.8.3 §122; *Ant.* 18.1.5 §20; Philo, *Probus* 85–86; *Hyp.* 11.4–5).
5. The primary work is in agriculture and crafts (Josephus, *Ant.* 18.1.5 §19; Philo, *Probus* 76; *Hyp.* 11.6, 8–9).
6. No swearing of oaths (Josephus, *War* 2.8.6 §135; Philo, *Probus* 84).
7. No changing of clothes (Josephus, *War* 2.8.4 §126; Philo, *Hyp.* 11.12).
8. No slaves (Josephus, *Ant.* 18.1.5 §21; Philo, *Probus* 79).

Two characteristics are found in *War* and *Antiquities* but not in either of Philo's accounts:

9. The election of overseers and officials (*War* 2.8.3 §123; *Ant.* 18.1.5 §22).
10. The belief in the immortality of the soul (*War* 2.8.11 §§154–58; *Ant.* 18.1.5 §18).

The *War* mentions a number of topics not found in *Antiquities* or Philo:

11. Oil is defiling (*War* 2.8.3 §123).
12. Prayers to the sun (*War* 2.8.5 §128).
13. Daily schedule of work (*War* 2.8.5 §§128–32).
14. Bathing before eating (*War* 2.8.5 §129) and after being touched by an outsider (*War* 2.8.10 §150).
15. Speaking in turn (*War* 2.8.5 §132).
16. Studying medicines and the writings of the ancients (*War* 2.8.6 §136).
17. Regulations for admission to (*War* 2.8.7 §§137–42) and expulsion from the order (*War* 2.8.8 §§143–44).
18. Preserving the names of angels (*War* 2.8.7 §142).
19. Forbidding spitting in company or to the right (*War* 2.8.8 §147).
20. Strictness in observing the Sabbath (*War* 2.8.8 §147).
21. Foretelling the future (*War* 2.8.12 §159).
22. One particular group of Essenes marries (*War* 2.8.13 §160).

Philo's two accounts are very moralizing, and most of what he gives is paralleled in Josephus and has already been listed.

8.2.5.3 Qumran Scrolls

There is a major methodological problem with attempting to reconstruct any sort of schema from the Qumran scrolls (5.2.6). First, the writings found in the Qumran caves were not all the products of the community, even if they all belonged to its "library." Most of the sectarian writings can be identified and separated from those taken in from outside, but there is still dispute over a number. Second, and more importantly, is the question of whether the major sectarian writings are to be read as unified compositions from the community itself or as writings that, perhaps, originated in other times, places, and circumstances and were taken over and reedited by the community. Especially Murphy-O'Connor and Davies have drawn attention to this problem, although there is no consensus on even the significance of this, much less on source analysis.

The major sectarian writings from Qumran are listed briefly at 5.2.6, with bibliography. In the discussion in the next section, only two Qumran writings will be cited: the *Damascus Document* (CD) and the *Community Rule* (1QS). Both of these contain regulations about the organization of a community and are generally agreed to be related to the Essenes in some way and to have been given their final form by the Qumran group (cf. Davies 1990).

8.2.5.4 Analysis

Only those issues directly relating to the Essenes as such are dealt with here; also, I am able to include only a very brief discussion of some of the important topics. For further bibliographical guidance and treatment of some of the issues relating to Qumran, see 5.2.6.

8.2.5.4.1 The first question is that of the identity of the Qumran community. If there is one central agreement among Qumran scholars, it is that the Qumran community is in some way to be associated with the Essenes. The basic reasons for this are:

1. The location of Qumran. The statement of Pliny the Elder regarding the location of the Essene community seems incompatible with any interpretation other than Qumran and perhaps one or two other sites on the northwest shore of the Dead Sea. Philo (*Probus* 76; *Hyp.*

11.1), Josephus (*War* 2.8.4 §124), and CD (7.6; 12.19–14.16; 19.2) also indicate communities in a variety of towns and villages, but this is not incompatible with the idea of a "headquarters," "monastic center," or breakaway community located at Qumran.

2. A community of goods. Philo (*Probus* 85–86; *Hyp.* 11.4), Josephus (*War* 2.8.3 §122; *Ant.* 18.1.5 §20), and 1QS (1.11–12; 5.1–22; 6.16–23) agree that property was held in common. All new entrants turned over their property to the community on attaining full membership. However, certain passages in the *Damascus Document* can be interpreted as allowing at least some private ownership (CD 9.10–16; 14.12–16).

3. Common meals, preceded by bathing (Philo, *Probus* 86; *Hyp.* 11.5, 11; Josephus, *War* 2.8.5 §129; CD 10.10–13; 1QS 3.4–5; 5.13–14; 6.2, 25; 7.2–3).

4. Regulations for assemblies. The members were to sit according to a particular order (Philo, *Probus* 81; 1QS 6.8–10), to speak in turn (Josephus, *War* 2.8.5 §132; 1QS 6.10–13), and not to spit (Josephus, *War* 2.8.9 §147; 1QS 7.13).

5. Procedures for entry. The sources agree that a period of probation was required. Josephus (*War* 2.8.7 §137–42) describes it in two or three stages, over three years. The *Community Rule* (1QS) 6.13–23 mentions two stages, each of a year, although a further, less formal stage preceding these is perhaps not incompatible with Josephus's data.

6. Rigor in keeping the Sabbath. Josephus (*War.* 2.8.9 §147) states that the Essenes were more particular in their Sabbath observances than any other group. This seems to be confirmed by such regulations as those found in CD 10.14–11.18.

The foregoing are the most solid arguments. The ones I now list are potentially more controversial, though many scholars would accept them as valid.

7. Worship at the temple. Overall, the Qumran documents seem to oppose the Jerusalem cult as being polluted (e.g., CD 6.11–20). In addition, Philo indicates that the Essenes had no interest in physical sacrifice (*Probus* 75). Josephus, however, says that the Essenes would send votive offerings to the temple, although he immediately adds that they had their own cultic rites (*Ant.* 18.1.5 §19). Certain passages appear to support the view that some offerings were allowed (CD 11.18–21; 12.1–2; 16.13). One explanation is that the Essenes as a whole, including the pre-Qumran community, allowed

a minimal amount of participation in the temple cult, but that the Qumran group forbade even that (cf. Davies 1982; Davies 1983: 134–40; Murphy-O'Connor 1985).

8. Women and marriage. The ancient sources agree that the Essenes were celibate. Burial excavations undertaken to date seem to support this: a few skeletons of women and children have been found, but so few as to confirm the absence of women in the community (de Vaux 1973: 47–48); however, future work may change this picture. The *Community Rule* is silent on the subject, but the *Damascus Document* (7.6–7; 12.1–2; 15.5; 16.10–12; 7.6–7 // 19.2–3), the *War Scroll* (7.3), and 1QSª 1.4, 9–11 all indicate the presence of women. Various suggestions have been made to explain this. One argues that Qumran was a celibate community but the Essene communities in the villages were not. The important thing is that Josephus acknowledges marriage among at least some Essenes for purposes of procreation, which seems also the intent of CD 4.10–5.2 (cf. Davies 1987: 73–85).

These are some of the principal arguments that have caused the majority of scholars to associate the Qumran community with the Essenes. But this does not mean that the two are coextensive; on the contrary, it seems that Qumran represented only one group. References in Josephus, Philo, and perhaps the *Damascus Document* all indicate that Essene communities were found in various towns and villages (point 1). Therefore, Qumran could be seen as any of a number of possibilities: a sort of headquarters of the Essene movement; an Essene monastery; simply another branch of the Essene movement; or a breakaway group with specific disagreements. There is no reason, however, to think of the Essenes as a tightly knit group with a hierarchical structure or organization. It could have been a much more diffuse movement with different branches or communities that were only loosely associated with one another.

8.2.5.4.2 The word "Essene" has exercised scholars. It has often been explained as deriving from the Aramaic *ḥasayyā'/ḥāsîn* ("pious"), related to the Hebrew *ḥăsîdîm*. But this explanation has been strongly influenced by assumptions about the Hasidim that cannot be supported in the light of current scholarship (8.2.1). Furthermore, the word is known from Syriac but is not attested in Jewish Aramaic. Vermes (1960; cf. Schürer: 2.559–60) suggested that the name "Essene" was from *'āsyā'*, an Aramaic word for "healer," and connected the name with that of the Therapeutae (8.2.6), which means "healers" in Greek; however, this explanation does not seem to have attracted many adherents. These and other suggestions have usually assumed a Semitic etymology of some sort, but most recently Kampen has argued for a Greek origin, from *essēn*, the name for a cultic official of Artemis.

8.2.5.4.3 The identity of several figures mentioned in the Qumran documents has been the object of considerable speculation, the main problem being that they are cited under sobriquets in the texts. One of the principal ones is the "Wicked Priest" (*hakkôhēn hārāšā'*), who has usually been equated with a high priest in the Jerusalem temple. Most have identified him with one of the Hasmonean priest-kings, but the variety of identifications has been wide: Jonathan, Simon, Hyrcanus, Janneus, a succession of Hasmonean figures. The "Man of Lies" has often been identified with the Wicked Priest, but others have argued that there is little reason to think they are the same person. For example, the Man of Lies has been equated with the Essene leader with whom the Teacher of Righteousness broke.

The identity of the Teacher of Righteousness himself has occasioned many hypotheses but no consensus: examples of his identification include an otherwise unknown high priest during the interregnum after Alcimus's death (5.4.5) or Judas the Essene (although Murphy-O'Connor sees Judas as the Essene opponent of the Teacher!). Similarly, the "Seekers after Smooth Things" are often confidently asserted to be the Pharisees, but this is not at all certain. See 5.2.6 for a more detailed discussion of all these issues.

The adoption of one, as opposed to another, of these various identifications is often of some significance in reconstructing the history of the movement. Davies has done a useful service in pointing out how particular titles of generic enemies found in the *Thanksgiving Hymns* may have been appropriated by different later writers to apply to specific groups that were known to them (1987: 87–105). This demonstrates how much is still not known about Qumran, despite the unqualified statements often found in handbooks.

8.2.5.5 Historical Reconstruction

A few individual Essenes are mentioned by Josephus: Judas, who was noted for his successful foretelling of events in the time of Aristobulus I (*Ant.* 13.11.2 §311); Manaemus, who predicted Herod's rise to rule and was rewarded by him (*Ant.* 15.10.5 §373); Simon, who interpreted a dream of Archelaus (*Ant.* 17.13.3 §§347–48); and John, who was one of the commanders during the war against Rome (*War* 2.20.4 §567; 3.2.1 §11). Otherwise, any history of the Essenes is chiefly confined to what we know of the Qumran community and its history, which may be somewhat less than appears in many standard treatments. The most certain information on the history of the Qumran community is archeological. Unfortunately, this source has too often been subordinated to reconstructions made from the documents themselves (Davies 1988; 1985: 46). Redaction criticism of such works as the *Damascus Document* may also provide some insight into the pre-Qumran movement, although this process remains controversial.

Two points seem clear from the archeological evidence: Qumran was settled in the late second (or early first) century B.C.E.; and the original community consisted of only about fifty individuals, though later it seems to have expanded to about two hundred. Was this the beginning of the Essene movement? A number of scholars think not, for a variety of reasons. Murphy-O'Connor, Davies, and others argue that the movement began outside Judah, perhaps in Babylon, perhaps at the time of the Exile. This argument is based especially on the source-critical analysis of CD and 1QS, as well as on the identification of "Damascus" with Babylon.

Dimant argues from the 390 years of CD 1.5–6 that the Essene movement began just before 200 B.C.E. (1984: 543–44). There seem to be several problems with this: (1) the 390 years is a stereotyped number from Ezekiel 4 (as Dimant recognizes); (2) all other Jewish chronographical sources from this period show great ignorance about the chronology of the Persian period (Grabbe: 2.55–58); and (3) it has been argued that the 390 years ends with the Exile and is thus to be interpreted as it is in Ezekiel 4 (Rabinowitz).

There seem to be good arguments that the Qumran community began as a separate movement within the Essenes. A number of statements in CD, 1QS, and 1QpHab can be interpreted in this way. The small size of the Qumran community in its first foundation does not suggest that all Essenes lived there, if the group existed when Qumran was established. The 4000 members mentioned in both Philo and Josephus were too many to fit into Qumran, which suggests that the bulk of the sect lived elsewhere. If Murphy-O'Connor is right, the Teacher of Righteousness founded a breakaway group that moved to Qumran. As anyone with experience of a religious sect knows, the most bitter polemic is usually reserved for internal enemies. The strong polemic against the Man of Lies could well be aimed at one who was once associated with the Teacher, possibly the leader of a group that did not follow the Teacher.

We can trace the history of the Qumran group to some extent. They survived the (real or imagined) attacks of the Wicked Priest and the death of the Teacher, continued to flourish until the destruction of the settlement (probably by the earthquake of 31 B.C.E.), later rebuilt it (how long it was abandoned is debated), and finally fell to the Romans, who overran the area of Qumran in 68 C.E. What happened to the rest of the Essenes is unknown, although they do not seem to have survived the catastrophe of 70 as an organized group.

8.2.6 Therapeutae

Riaud, J. "Les Thérapeutes d'Alexandrie dans la tradition et dans la recherche critique jusqu'aux découvertes de Qumran." *ANRW* 2 (1987) 20.2.1189–1295.
Schürer: 2.593–97.

There are resemblances between the Essenes as described by Philo, whom he places in Palestine, and a group in Egypt known as the Therapeutae (*De vita contemplativa*). Philo seems to keep them apart, but we have to bear in mind that he was probably working from written sources rather than direct knowledge, so his failure to connect them directly cannot be taken as definitive. The suggestion that the Therapeutae were a branch of the Essenes is not farfetched. Indeed, as noted in 8.2.5.4.2, Vermes has connected the Therapeutae with the Essenes on the basis of both having a name meaning "healers." Regardless of the name, the resemblance of the Therapeutae to the Essenes suggests some sort of connection.

8.2.7 Zealots

Applebaum, S. "The Zealots: The Case for Revaluation." *JRS* 61 (1971) 155–70.
Borg, M. "The Currency of the Term 'Zealot.'" *JTS* 22 (1971) 504–12.
Hengel, M. *The Zealots* (1989).
Horsley, R. A. "The Zealots: Their Origin, Relationships and Importance in the Jewish Revolt." *NovT* 28 (1986) 159–92.
Nikiprowetzky, V. "Sicaires et Zélotes—Une reconsidération." *Semitica* 23 (1973) 51–64.
Smith, M. "Zealots and Sicarii, Their Origins and Relation." *HTR* 64 (1971) 1–19.

Our knowledge of the Zealots comes entirely from Josephus, who does not mention them until the revolt against Rome was well underway. They first appear in 68 and seem to have formed as an amalgamation of several groups of "social bandits" (8.2.12) who had come into Jerusalem in the face of Vespasian's advance. They were only one of several groups in

Jerusalem at the time (7.4.13.3). Most of their effort was spent in fighting other Jewish revolutionary groups until the Romans finally surrounded Jerusalem, at which time they all presented a united front and, for the most part, died fighting.

One of the principal scholarly debates concerns the use of the term "zealot" to mean any revolutionary group or person in the last century or two before the fall of Jerusalem. This has become common terminology (e.g., Hengel) but is now being attacked as contrary to Josephus's usage; he mainly confines the term to a particular group in Jerusalem for the brief period from 68 to 70 C.E. (Smith; Horsley; Borg). To use the term for any anti-Roman group or individual is not only unjustified by our most important source but is also confusing, because it fails to notice the different motives, modi operandi, and socioreligious bases of the different groups. Hengel replied to Smith in the Appendix (380–404) of the later edition of his work, but not convincingly (cf. Horsley on the 1976 German edition).

8.2.8   Fourth Philosophy and the Sicarii

Black, M. "Judas of Galilee and Josephus's 'Fourth Philosophy.' " *Josephus-Studien* (1974) 45–54.
Horsley, R. A. "The Sicarii: Ancient Jewish 'Terrorists.' " *JR* 59 (1979) 435–58.
———. "Menahem in Jerusalem: A Brief Messianic Episode among the Sicarii—Not 'Zealot Messianism.' " *NovT* 27 (1985) 334–48.
Michel, O. "Studien zu Josephus: Simon bar Giora." *NTS* 14 (1967–68) 402–8.
Rhoads, D. M. *Israel in Revolution: 6–74 C.E.* (1976).

Our major source for the Fourth Philosophy is Josephus (*Ant.* 18.1.1 §§4–10; 18.1.6 §23). He states that the group was essentially the same as the Pharisees, except for its belief that only God should be recognized as king and ruler, the founders being Judas the Galilean and Zadok (Saddokos) the Pharisee. He goes on to say that in the latter part of the 40s the Fourth Philosophy gave rise to the Sicarii, a group that specialized in assassinating Jewish officials (the name apparently comes from *sica*, the name of a type of dagger). There is good reason to question Josephus's statement about Judas the Galilean as the founder of the Sicarii, however, because it was probably based partly on his deductions and partly on his bias against the "insurgents," blaming them for the war (Rhoads: 52–60).

As with "zealot," *sicarii* could be used as a common noun to mean "assassins." Therefore, there is no reason to think that all the groups in the 40s, 50s, and early 60s that are referred to by this term were part of a single organization. Their targets seem to have been primarily Jews who were seen as collaborators with the Roman administration, not Roman officials. They also attacked the estates of pro-Roman Jewish notables, killing the inhabitants and looting and destroying their property. Later on, the Sicarii resorted to kidnapping, principally to obtain the release of some of their number who had been arrested.

The activities of the Sicarii were very important in the events leading up to the revolt (7.4.9). They destabilized Roman rule, especially as it was administered by native Jews. Without attacking the Romans, they were able to bring about a mounting state of chaos, in which public officials feared for their lives and were unable to carry out their duties. In contrast, once the fight against Rome began, they played only a minor part (7.4.11.3; 7.4.13.4). One of their leaders, Menahem, grandson of Judas the Galilean, led a group in Jerusalem for a period of time in 66; however, he and many of his followers were killed by the Zealots under Eleazar. The survivors fled to Masada, where they remained aloof from the war until besieged by the Romans after the fall of Jerusalem. Some of the Sicarii escaped the destruction and caused difficulties in Egypt and Cyrene in the early 70s. This is the last we hear of the group.

The Sicarii are good candidates for sociological investigation. Horsley puts them in the category of "urban terrorists" and compares them with a number of modern groups who have used both assassination and kidnapping to further their political goals, but they should not be seen as solely political. There are some indications that the Sicarii were in part motivated by eschatological and messianic expectations. For example, Menahem took on royal trappings and evidently set himself up as a messianic figure, which was one of the reasons for his assassination by the Zealots (*War* 2.17.8–9 §§433–34, 443–46). The Sicarii should not be confused with the Zealots, although they often are (8.2.7), for they form a distinct group with a different history and goals.

8.2.9 Herodians

Bickerman, E. J. [E. Bikerman]. "Les Hérodiens." *RB* 47 (1938) 184–97.
Daniel, C. "Les 'Hérodiens' du Nouveau Testament sont-ils des Esséniens?" *RevQ* 6 (1967/69) 31–53.
Rowley, H. H. "The Herodians in the Gospels." *JTS* o.s. 41 (1940) 14–27.

The specific form of the name *Hērōdianoi* is found only in the New Testament (Mark 3:6; 12:13; Matt 22:16); however, there is good reason to believe that this is only another form of the name *Hērōdeioi*, found in

Josephus (*War* 1.16.6 §319). This would make the Herodians simply members of Herod's household, that is, officials of the court, which is indeed the contention of Bickerman, who also argues that the *-ian* ending is a Latinism. Such forms for adjectives are infrequent in Greek, the main ones being *Christianoi* ("followers of Christ") and *Kaisarianoi* ("adherents of Caesar"). Rowley, who gives a wide survey of patristic opinions on the subject, eventually agrees with Bickerman that the Herodians were a political group, not a religious sect; however, he concludes that they consisted of any supporters of Herodian rule, rather than specifically members of the court.

Daniel develops the thesis that "Herodians" is another name for the Essenes. His evidence is primarily circumstantial: Herod was fascinated by the Essenes and favored particular members of the sect. His arguments are ingenious but unconvincing. Nevertheless, he does point out that certain statements regarding Herod in the Gospels seem strange (e.g., "beware the leaven of the Pharisees and of Herod" [Mark 8:15]). Smith (*28–29) argues that these statements reflect the time during the 40s when the Pharisees persecuted the Christians with Agrippa's approval (like Bickerman, he supposes that the Herodians were members of Herod's household). Statements such as Mark 8:15 would be out of place in the 30s, when there was no Herodian ruler in Judea, but would fit well the early 40s when Agrippa I was king. This assumes that statements about the persecution of Christians by Jews at this early time and the favoring of the Pharisees by Agrippa have a historical basis, which may be questionable (7.4.6).

8.2.10   The Samaritans

Adler, E. N., and M. Seligsohn. "Une nouvelle chronique samaritaine." *REJ* 44 (1902) 188–222; 45 (1902) 70–98; 223–54; 46 (1903) 123–46.

Bowman, J. *Transcript of the Original Text of the Samaritan Chronicle Tolidah* (1954).

———. *Samaritan Documents relating to Their History, Religion and Life* (1977).

Coggins, R. J. *Samaritans and Jews* (1975).

———. "The Samaritans in Josephus." *Josephus, Judaism, and Christianity* (1987) 257–73.

Crown, A. D. "New Light on the Interrelationships of Samaritan Chronicles from Some Manuscripts in the John Rylands Library." *BJRL* 54 (1971/72) 282–313; 55 (1972/73) 86–111.

———, ed. *The Samaritans* (1989).

Grabbe, L. L. "Josephus and the Reconstruction of the Judean Restoration." *JBL* 106 (1987) 231–46.

Isser, S. J. *The Dositheans: A Samaritan Sect in Late Antiquity* (1976).
Macdonald, J. *Memar Marqah: The Teaching of Marqah* (1963).
————. *The Theology of the Samaritans* (1964).
————. *The Samaritan Chronicle No. II* (1969).
Montgomery, J. A. *The Samaritans: The Earliest Jewish Sect* (1907).
Neubauer, A. "Chronique samaritaine, suivie d'un appendice contenant de courtes notices sur quelques autres ouvrages samaritains." *Journal asiatique* 14 (1869) 385–470.
Pummer, R. "The Present State of Samaritan Studies." *JSS* 21 (1976) 39–61; 22 (1977) 27–47.
————. *The Samaritans* (1987).
Purvis, J. D. "The Samaritans and Judaism." *Early Judaism and Its Modern Interpreters* (1986) 81–98.
Schiffman, L. H. "The Samaritans in Tannaitic Halakhah." *JQR* 75 (1984/85) 323–50.
Waltke, B. K. "The Samaritan Pentateuch and the Text of the Old Testament." *New Perspectives on the Old Testament* (1970) 212–39.

In much Jewish polemic of antiquity, the Samaritans are out-and-out pagans. In their own writings, however, they are simply Israelites who have faithfully preserved the ancestral religion of Moses, and indeed, in various references in rabbinic literature, this is tacitly recognized in that the Samaritans are regarded as observing most of the Torah (*b. Qid.* 76a; cf. Schiffman). Tracing the history of the Samaritans has been bedeviled by two problems: (1) much of our data from early sources comes from hostile witnesses; and (2) the Samaritan writings are generally very late; this includes both the manuscript witnesses and the literary contents. (The important manuscripts are no more than a few centuries old at the most.) In addition, because of the small number of Samaritan specialists, little work has been done so far on the traditio-historical analysis of the literature. Although a number of surveys are available (e.g., Montgomery, Macdonald, Bowman), they can be unreliable in parts because of faulty methodology in attempting to reconstruct Samaritan history, and should be read in the light of studies by Coggins (1975), Pummer (1987), and now the imposing study edited by Crown (1989); see also the recent survey by Purvis. Only the briefest of introductions to Samaritan studies can be given here, and that will relate principally to the historical question. See especially Pummer (1976; 1977; 1987) and Crown (1989) for a summary of scholarship.

8.2.10.1 Non-Samaritan Sources

Second Kings 17. This has been the locus of much of the early Jewish comment on the Samaritans and has even been accepted as normative by many modern scholars. The essence of the chapter is that all the inhabitants of the Northern Kingdom (except for some of the very poor) were deported and replaced with pagans from various parts of the Assyrian Empire. Yahwism was introduced only as a superstitious gesture and then only by an illegitimate priest from one of the forbidden northern shrines. The polemical nature of this account becomes clear when other Old Testament passages and the Assyrian records are consulted, because only a small portion of the population (some of the upper class) was deported and the bulk of the population remained in the land (Coggins 1975: 13–18).

Ezra/Nehemiah. The inhabitants of Samaria are consistently presented as hostile to the returnees from the Exile. Sanballat in particular is taken as an enemy, specifically to Nehemiah. See further at 2.4.3.3.

Ben Sira 50:25-26. This makes the enigmatic statement, "With two nations my soul is vexed, and the third is no nation: Those who live on Mount Seir, and the Philistines, and the foolish people that dwell in Shechem." The precise meaning is difficult, although it seems to be anti-Samaritan (Coggins 1975: 82–86).

Josephus, *Ant*. 11.7.2–8.7 §§302–47. He reports that at the time of Alexander, the Samaritan priesthood was founded by a renegade priest from Jerusalem. Although Josephus may have had some independent information, the whole of the story is pervaded by anti-Samaritan bias (Coggins 1975: 93–99; Coggins 1987; Grabbe 1987).

Quintus Curtius 4.8.9–11. Shortly after Syro-Palestine submitted to Alexander and after Alexander had carried his campaign further east, Samaria revolted against the Greek-appointed governor and killed him. Alexander had the city of Samaria attacked, the inhabitants massacred or sold into slavery, and the city razed. There are problems with this report in that it has no confirmation elsewhere in the Alexander material and is not considered reliable by some classical scholars (Coggins 1975: 106–9). However, it is partially confirmed in the Wadi Daliyeh papyri (2.2.2).

Second Maccabees 6:1-2. The Samaritans also had their temple dedicated to Zeus by Antiochus IV. Although Josephus gives the impression that they desired this, other considerations suggest that it was a preventive measure to make sure their cult could continue unharmed (5.4.3.3).

8.2.10.2   Samaritan Sources

The Samaritan writings preserved by the present-day Samaritan community give a quite different picture from that gleaned from non-Samaritan sources. This information is found mainly in the Samaritans' chronicles, all of which seem interrelated despite some difference of detail. The chronicles mentioned in our discussion follow. The relationship between them is complicated; for an attempt to sort them out, see Crown (1971/72; 1972/73).

Chronicle 2. Published only in part by Macdonald (1969). The entire chronicle apparently extends from the death of Moses to medieval times.

The Tolidah (Chronicle 3). This is a simple list of the Samaritan high priests, the best edition of which is that edited by Bowman (1954). Bowman has argued that it is the earliest and most original source, but studies by Crown (1971/72; 1972/73) have suggested that it is, in fact, an abbreviation of the fuller chronicle(s) that lie(s) behind Chronicle 7.

Samaritan Book of Joshua (Chronicle 4). Although about half of this is a paraphrase of the MT Joshua, the rest of the book takes the story as late as the time of Baba Rabba (about the fourth century C.E.).

The Shalshalah (Chronicle 5). This is the shortest of the chronicles, even shorter than the Tolidah, being a bare list of the high priests, with the lengths of reign correlated with various world eras. It goes from Adam to the nineteenth century in its present form.

Abu'l Fath (Chronicle 6). This differs from the other chronicles in being a composite history that was composed in the fourteenth century in Arabic by a single person. Much of it is based on the Arabic version of the Samaritan Book of Joshua, although at times the historian seems to have had better manuscripts than those now available. For the rest he had a chronicle similar to the Tolidah and the Adler Chonicle (below) but often much more expansive than these.

Adler Chronicle (Chronicle 7). This is similar to the Tolidah in being principally a list of the high priests, but most of the figures are accompanied by a small block of material that relates the events of each priest's term of office. Although its present form is recent, the core of the work seems to have a respectable antiquity (Crown 1971/72; 1972/73, contra Bowman 1977: 87).

In addition to the chronicles, two other writings are of some importance, especially for the development of theology. These are the *Defter*, an early liturgical collection, and the *Memar Marqa*. The latter is hard to characterize but is chiefly a midrashic collection from the fourth century C.E. Macdonald has produced an edition and translation (1963), but there are evidently some problems with it (Pummer 1976: 57).

In spite of differences in detail between the various chronicles, they all agree on an overall picture which is considerably different from that found in the non-Samaritan (mostly Jewish and anti-Samaritan) sources. According to their version of events, a parting of the ways came in the time of Eli. He became a renegade, moving the ark from its proper place at Gerizim to Shiloh. The Jerusalem priesthood was descended from this breakaway faction of Eli, whereas the true Aaronic line continued at Gerizim. Although there were several captivities and exiles, as well as much persecution, the true Israelite priesthood continued as a pure line through the centuries and remains true to the faith at Shechem (Nablus) and God's holy mountain, Gerizim, today. Far from having a pagan or syncretized worship, the Samaritans are descendants of Joseph and Levi who have preserved the true worship.

8.2.10.3   Analysis

Just as it would be foolish to take the anti-Samaritan polemic at face value (although it often has been), it would be equally naive to accept the Samaritan apologetic without question. Elements of the tradition look suspiciously like an adaptation of portions of the Old Testament, although the Samaritan tradition could be explained as a parallel history that sometimes intertwined with Old Testament history, rather than depended on it. But the sources are so far removed from the original events and so little study has been done to date that one should be very skeptical of the Samaritan version of events. Nevertheless, this version demonstrates the unreliability of most of the non-Samaritan sources.

What can be said is that the Samaritan religious community, as far back as it can be traced, represents a conservative Yahwistic cult, with few major differences from Judaism of the Second Temple period (cf. Purvis: 90–95). Although both Judaism and Samaritanism have absorbed various elements from the surrounding culture over the centuries, there is no more evidence of a pagan origin to Samaritan worship than there is to Jewish worship. The main differences are five: the Samaritans (1) use only the Pentateuch of the Old Testament (and that in a form slightly different from the MT, although a good portion of Joshua also has authoritative status in the chronicles); (2) worship at Mount Gerizim as "the place that Yahweh shall choose"; (3) sacrifice a lamb at Passover; (4) follow a slightly different calendar; and, (5) naturally, have their own liturgy as well. Intercourse between the Samaritan and Jewish communities continued quite freely through much of the Second Temple period. Some would see the decisive break as occurring with the destruction of the Gerizim temple by John Hyrcanus in 128 B.C.E. (Purvis: 89–90), but others would see it as coming rather later and perhaps being gradual, not abrupt (Pummer 1976: 48–55; Coggins 1975: 162–64; Schiffman).

8.2.11 Baptismal Sects

Cameron, R., and A. J. Dewey. *The Cologne Mani Codex (P. Colon. inv. nr. 4780): "Concerning the Origin of His Body"* (1979).

Collins, J. J. "The Place of the Fourth Sibyl in the Development of the Jewish Sibyllina." *JJS* 25 (1974) 365–80.

Coxon, P. W. "Script Analysis and Mandaean Origins." *JSS* 15 (1970) 16–30.

Henricks, A. "Mani and the Babylonian Baptists: A Historical Confrontation." *HSCP* 77 (1973) 23–59.

———. "The Cologne Mani Codex Reconsidered." *HSCP* 83 (1979) 339–67.

Henricks, A., and L. Koenen. "Ein griechischer Mani-Codex." *ZPE* 5 (1970) 97–216.

———. "Der kölner Mani-Kodex (P. Colon. inv. nr. 4780)." *ZPE* 19 (1975) 1–85; 32 (1978) 87–199; 44 (1981) 201–312; 48 (1982) 1–59.

Luttikhuizen, G. P. *The Revelation of Elchasai* (1985).

Macuch, R. "Anfänge der Mandäer." *Die Araber in der Alten Welt* (1965) 2.76–190.

———. "The Origins of the Mandaeans and Their Script." *JSS* 16 (1971) 174–92.

———. "Gnostische Ethik und die Anfänge der Mandäer." *Christentum am Roten Meer* (1973) 2.254–73.

Naveh, J. "The Origin of the Mandaic Script." *BASOR* 198 (1970) 32–37.

Rudolph, K. *Die Mandäer*, 2 vols. (1960–61).

———. *Theogonie, Kosmogonie, und Anthropogonie in den mandäische Schriften* (1965).

———. "Zum gegenwärtigen Stand der mandäischen Religionsgeschichte." *Gnosis und neues Testament* (1973) 121–48 = revision of "Problems of a History of the Development of the Mandaean Religion." *HR* 8 (1968/69) 210–35.

———. "Quellenprobleme zum Ursprung und Alter der Mandäer." *Christianity, Judaism and Other Greco-Roman Cults: Studies for Morton Smith at Sixty* (1975) 4.112–42.

———. *Mandaeism* (1978).

———. *Antike Baptisten: Zu den Überlieferungen über frühjüdische und -christliche Taufsekten* (1981).

Segelberg, E. *Masbūtā* (1958).

Thomas, J. *Le mouvement baptiste en Palestine et Syrie* (1935).
Yamauchi, E. M. *Gnostic Ethics and Mandaean Origins* (1970).

8.2.11.1 Sources and Arguments

Although one might assume from reading only the Gospels that John the
Baptist was unique, other sources indicate that there were probably a
variety of sects that placed emphasis on the ritual of baptism, whether
for regular ritual purification, initiation, or both. The evidence for the
existence of baptismal sects comes from several arguments (Thomas;
Rudolph 1981). A principal source of support is the surviving baptismal
sect of the Mandeans (8.2.11.2). Other possibilities include:

1. John the Baptist. Although nothing is said about John's being only
   one of a number of groups or persons calling for repentance and its
   concomitant symbol of baptism, it is interesting that the audience is
   not pictured as seeing his actions as strange or different.
2. *Sibylline Oracle* 4. This places a strong emphasis on baptism and
   repentance as the keys to salvation (*SibOr* 4.163–69); in fact, they
   replace the temple and its cult, a most unusual feature for a Jewish
   sect of this time. Thomas had already suggested that this writing
   was the product of a Jewish baptismal sect (59), a view confirmed
   by Collins.
3. Baptismal sect of the Cologne Mani Codex. The recently discovered
   life of Mani shows that he lived to the age of twenty-four in a
   Jewish-Christian group that had many characteristics in common
   with Qumran: male only; ascetic (vegetarian); strict observance of
   Old Testament purity laws; Sabbath; daily baptism; coming of the
   True Prophet (Henricks 1973: 47–56).
4. Patristic references to baptismal sects. Justin Martyr (*Dial. Trypho*
   80.4), Eusebius (*Hist. eccl.* 4.22.5, 7), the *Apostolic Constitutions*
   (6.6), and Epiphanius (*Panarion* 17) all included baptismal groups
   (*Hēmerobaptistai, Masbōtheoi, Sebouaioi*) among their lists of Jewish sects. Unhappily, the data are skimpy and little study has so far
   been devoted to the brief reports extant (Rudolph 1981: 8–10). This
   makes reconstruction difficult and the end product rather hypothetical; nevertheless, taken with the other evidences we have, patristic
   references at least add to the argument for postulating such sects.
5. Elchesaites. According to some ancient sources, at least as often
   asserted in secondary literature, an ascetic Jewish-Christian group
   flourished in the first few centuries C.E., named after its founder
   Elchasai or Elxai. The most recent study on the subject calls a

number of these assumptions into question (Luttikhuizen). A book titled *The Revelations of Elchasai* (named for the revelatory angel) was used by certain groups, but this was a Jewish book written about 115 C.E. Whether there was a founder named Elchasai is debatable, but the groups called Elchesaites or Elcheseans were evidently not baptismal groups (Luttikhuizen: 222). Therefore, if Luttikhuizen is correct, the Elchesaites should be eliminated as evidence for baptismal sects.

When the evidence just summarized is taken together with the Mandeans, there is sufficient reason to assume that there were several Jewish baptismal groups in existence before 70 (not counting the Essenes, which many would also include in this category). The groups were probably small and most likely preferred an area such as the Jordan Valley, where running water was readily available, but beyond the bare conclusion of their existence, we can only speculate.

8.2.11.2 Mandeans

The small sect of the Mandeans still survives (apparently) in Iraq and Iran. It is neither Jewish nor Christian, although it has specific features in common with both. Rather, it is the sole surviving gnostic group (8.2.13). Its central religious myth has a great deal in common with the gnostic myths known from antiquity. The major cultic ceremony is baptism, which is done periodically in cultic enclosures with running water. A further description of the group is found in the many writings of Rudolph (see especially 1960–61; 1978; 1983 [8.2.13]: 343–66).

The Mandeans originated in pre-Islamic times. One of the main questions is whether they date back to the pre-70 period. The overwhelming majority of the small number of Mandaic specialists agree that they do. The following eight arguments are accepted by researchers as noted:

1. They retain a tradition of having left Palestine to settle in the Babylonian area (Rudolph 1978: 268–71; Macuch 1965: 110–37).
2. The Aramaic baptismal terminology reflects Western rather than Eastern usage (Macuch 1965: 82–109; 1973: 255–57; Rudolph 1973: 129–30; 1978: 265–66).
3. The baptismal ceremony itself is Jewish at the core, even though various peripheral features have been added as a result of Christian influence (Segelberg: 182–84; Rudolph 1960: 1.222–52; 1961: 2.367–80; 1973: 139–40; 1975: 139–41).
4. Many of the major ideas and practices of the group are Jewish,

suggesting a Jewish origin, despite a hostility to Judaism from a fairly early period (Rudolph 1973: 141–42, plus references in points 2 and 3).

The following arguments (5–8) have also been used by Macuch but have not been accepted by other specialists:

5. The *Haran-Gawaita* legend shows that the Mandeans migrated eastward before 70, probably during the reign of Artabanus III (ca. 12–38 C.E. [1965: 110–37; 1973: 258–59]). Rudolph feels there is too much legendary material in the work to put any confidence in the details (1973: 131–34; 1975: 119–25). He would put the migration in the second century C.E., perhaps in the reign of Artabanus V (ca. 213–224 C.E.).

6. The details about an association with John the Baptist are to be accepted as reliable, again showing a pre-70 date (Macuch 1965: 105–9). Rudolph argues that John the Baptist was only secondarily adopted by the sect at a rather late date (1960: 1.66–80; 1975: 140; 1978: 270).

7. Macuch judges that the development of the Mandaic script shows that it originated earlier than the Elamite inscriptions which are dated to the second to third centuries C.E. (1967: 139–58). This has been opposed by other paleographers (Naveh; Coxon), but Macuch has strongly defended his position (1971). Rudolph points to Macuch's own admission that certainty is not possible and prefers to reserve judgment until experts on the script are agreed (1973: 134–35).

8. The colophons have been used to show an early dating (Macuch 1965: 158–65). These are important, but the value of their evidence for Macuch's position is not necessarily demonstrated (Rudolph 1973: 136–37).

The main opponent of an early origin for the community within Judaism has been Yamauchi. Although he does not clearly distinguish the more important objections from the minor ones, Yamauchi's main arguments seem to be the following:

1. None of the texts is early; therefore, a pre-Christian origin of the sect cannot be proved (4–10). However, he rejects the use of traditio-historical criticism which many believe allows scholars to trace some traditions back much earlier than the final form of the text.

2. The Mandeans' own history is too garbled and legendary to be given

any credence (68–71). (But why would they have come up with a consistent tradition that traces them back to the Palestinian area, granted that the details may not be trustworthy?)
3. Because the Mandeans are hostile to the Jews, it makes no sense to argue for a Jewish origin (64–67). In addition, the traits alleged to show a connection with Judaism, such as marriage, could have come from elsewhere. After all, particular Jewish characteristics can also be found in Islam (53–56). (The influence of Judaism on Islam from its very foundation, however, is well known. Were the Jews likely to have influenced the Mandeans so much if they were consistently hostile to them, as Yamauchi believes?)

Some of Yamauchi's points are well taken; indeed, it should be noted that a number of them were anticipated by Rudolph, and some of the positions that Yamauchi argues against are not held by most Mandaic experts. His arguments have not changed many minds, however, partly because his "hidden agenda" is well recognized (see 8.2.13). A full evaluation of the Mandeans has to take account of the history of Gnosticism as a movement. Although Yamauchi has found objections to various individual points, part of the cogency of a hypothesis is how well it explains a diversity of data. He argues for an origin in a Mesopotamian cult that syncretized with gnostic and Jewish ideas:

> Mandaeanism is basically a Gnostic interpretation of an indigenous Mesopotamian cult . . . the result of an assimilation of Gnostic ideas from the west into an eastern mythology, accompanied by a reinterpretation of the indigenous Mesopotamian cult. (82, 86)

To many, Yamauchi's explanation of the origins is more complicated and less convincing than that of those he criticizes: a Jewish baptist group that evolved gnostic ideas in its Western homeland and then absorbed other elements in its new home in Mesopotamia. It seems significant that most Mandean experts—few as they are—are willing to see the origin of the Mandeans in Jewish baptismal circles in the Palestinian area before 70. This origin is fully consistent with the widespread view in modern scholarship that Gnosticism as such has its root in pre-70 Judaism (8.2.13).

8.2.12 Revolutionaries and Other Popular Movements

Applebaum, S. "The Zealots: The Case for Revaluation." *JRS* 61 (1971) 155–70.
Dyson, S. L. "Native Revolts in the Roman Empire." *Historia* 20 (1971) 239–74.

————. "Native Revolt Patterns in the Roman Empire." *ANRW* 2 (1975) 3.138–75.

Hengel, M. *The Zealots* (1989).

Horsley, R. A. "Josephus and the Bandits." *JSJ* 10 (1979) 37–63.

————. "Ancient Jewish Banditry and the Revolt against Rome, A.D. 66–70." *CBQ* 43 (1981) 409–32.

————. "Popular Messianic Movements Around the Time of Jesus." *CBQ* 46 (1984) 471–95.

————. "Popular Prophetic Movements at the Time of Jesus: Their Principal Features and Social Origins." *JSNT* 26 (1986) 3–27.

————. *Jesus and the Spiral of Violence* (1987).

Horsley, R. A., and J. S. Hanson. *Bandits, Prophets, and Messiahs* (1985).

Isaac, B. "Bandits in Judaea and Arabia." *HSCP* 88 (1984) 171–203.

Macmullen, R. *Enemies of the Roman Order* (1967).

Rengstorf, K. H. ληστής. *TDNT* (1967) 4.257–62.

Shaw, B. D. "Bandits in the Roman Empire." *Past and Present* 105 (Nov. 1984) 3–52.

There are several movements which have tended to be lumped together (often under the term "zealot") but that actually represent diverse socioreligious movements. Josephus refers to a number of these, which may well represent only the tip of the iceberg. Most were short-lived and little is known of them, but what little is known is sufficient to indicate the ferment among the people during this period and to show that the "philosophies" of Josephus were hardly a full summary of the religious situation at the time. Some of these movements become intelligible in the light of sociological studies, as Horsley and others have shown, but one must keep in mind that a rigid distinction cannot easily be made between a social and a religious movement of this period. There are often religious overtones even when the movement in question can be described in the sociological terms applied to secular movements in modern times. More important, the nature of our sources does not always allow a fine distinction.

One such phenomenon was the growth of banditry. Horsley has done a sociological analysis of the "bandits" that are mentioned by Josephus as being troublesome at various times during the Roman period, especially during the early days of Herod's rule and in the years from 44 to the revolt. As Hengel and Rengstorf have recognized, Josephus often uses the term "bandit" (*lēistēs*) when more than just a straightforward criminal or thief is in question; however, where they go wrong is in assuming that "bandit" is simply a pejorative term for revolutionary. On the contrary, Horsley argues that they were genuine bandits but of a particular sort: those engaged in "social banditry." Horsley does not appear to be aware of Applebaum, who has also pointed out the importance of a proper sociological understanding of the Zealot movement, although Applebaum suffers from lumping Zealots, Sicarii, and others together. Social banditry has four major characteristics (Horsley 1979: 42–47):

1. It arises in traditionally rural societies, as opposed to urban ones, when actions of the rulers (whether national or local) are felt to be unjust or intolerable. It generally occurs when the peasant population is in a poor or vulnerable socioeconomic situation, such as famine, heavy taxation, oppression by foreign rulers, or times of a new, imposed, ruling social class and structure.
2. The bandits generally have the support of the local people. They are no threat to the poor because they prey on the upper classes and the wealthy; indeed, they often arise from a local community and continue to live in the same basic area. The local people will not betray them or cooperate in their capture, and on occasion they will even provide active support toward helping the bandits to elude capture and to continue their activities.
3. It is not unusual for the social bandit to have a Robin Hood image of helping the poor, meting out justice, righting wrongs, and, in some cases, redistributing wealth or, at least, providing for certain of the needy. In the same way, those on whom the social bandits prey are often the very ones whom the poor see as their oppressors: the wealthy, the landlords, the ruling classes.
4. They usually share the same religious and other basic values of the peasant society. In many cases they are quite devout and, conversely, are backed by the prayers of the devout peasants.

Thus, the "bandits" mentioned by Josephus seem to be genuine bandits in most cases, but they emerged because of the oppressive and troubled circumstances of the time. There are instances in which banditry among the peasant population developed into a popular revolt. This is precisely what seems to have happened in first-century Judea. Under Roman rule, either direct or through a client king, there were times when large numbers took to banditry as a means of survival. Most of these groups were short-lived, but in the late 40s and 50s this practice began to crescendo. To use Josephus's words, "the land was infested with brigands" (*Ant.* 20.9.5 §215). The bandits were not responsible for the outbreak of the war itself, but once it had begun, they were an important motivator behind it. A number of the independent bandit groups coalesced into the Zealots in the year 68 (8.2.7; 7.4.13.3).

There are also references to popular "messianic" movements in both Josephus and Acts in the New Testament. These generally looked to a particular leader as God's anointed, the exact definition of "anointed" varying. In some cases the leader was proclaimed (or proclaimed himself) king (Horsley 1984). On the subject of messianism and messiahs, see further at 8.3.5.

8.2.13   Gnostic Tendencies

Alexander, P. S. "Comparing Merkavah Mysticism and Gnosticism: An Essay in Method." *JJS* 35 (1984) 1–18.
Fossum, J. E. *The Name of God and the Angel of the Lord* (1985).
———. "The Magharians: A Pre-Christian Jewish Sect and Its Significance for the Study of Gnosticism and Christianity." *Henoch* 9 (1987) 303–44.
Gershenzon, R., and E. Slomovic. "A Second Century Jewish-Gnostic Debate: Rabbi Jose ben Halafta and the Matrona." *JSJ* 16 (1985) 1–41.
Gruenwald, I. *Apocalyptic and Merkavah Mysticism* (1980).
———. "Aspects of the Jewish-Gnostic Controversy." *The Rediscovery of Gnosticism* (1981a) 2.713–23.
———. "The Problem of the Anti-Gnostic Polemic in Rabbinic Literature." *Studies in Gnosticism and Hellenistic Religions Presented to Gilles Quispel on the Occasion of His 65th Birthday* (1981b) 171–89.
———. "Jewish Merkavah Mysticism and Gnosticism." *Studies in Jewish Mysticism* (1982) 41–55.
Lüdemann, G. *Untersuchungen zur simonianischen Gnosis* (1975).
———. "The Acts of the Apostles and the Beginnings of Simonian Gnosis." *NTS* 33 (1987) 420–26.
Meeks, W. A. "Simon Magus in Recent Research." *RSR* 3 (1977) 137–42.
Pearson, B. A. "Jewish Sources in Gnostic Literature." *JWSTP* (1984) 443–81.
Rudolph, K. *Gnosis, the Nature and History of an Ancient Religion* (1983).
Scholem, G. G. *Jewish Gnosticism, Merkabah Mysticism, and Talmudic Tradition* (1965).
Segal, A. F. *Two Powers in Heaven* (1977).
Stroumsa, G.A.G. "Aher: A Gnostic." *The Rediscovery of Gnosticism* (1981) 2.808–18.
———. *Another Seed: Studies in Gnostic Mythology* (1984).
Yamauchi, E. M. *Pre-Christian Gnosticism: A Survey of the Proposed Evidences* (1973).

Two current streams of thought under discussion are Gnosticism and Jewish mysticism. Mysticism is well known from later Judaism, and we have many texts from medieval times; however, Scholem, one of the chief pioneers in the scholarly study of the subject, has argued that some of the literature goes back to the second century C.E. and the roots of *merkavah* mysticism even further. Several recent studies (e.g., Gruenwald 1980) have found many of the features of the later mysticism in the apocalyptic literature and hypothesize a direct connection. Nevertheless, the association of *merkavah* mysticism with Gnosticism should probably be avoided in the current discussion. Scholem's "Jewish Gnosticism" actually has little in common with the Jewish Gnosticism hypothesized by many gnostic specialists, and *merkavah* mysticism does not seem to have arisen in gnostic circles as such (Alexander). Therefore, this section will confine itself to the gnostic question.

A major discussion centers on whether a Jewish Gnosticism existed and, if so, whether it was pre-Christian. A considerable number of scholars now answer "yes" to both questions. Two prima facie reasons can be given initially (cf. Pearson):

1. A number of gnostic texts show no Christian content or appear to be only secondarily Christianized.
2. Particular Jewish interpretations of passages in Genesis are heavily used in some gnostic writings, which appear to exhibit not only interpretations of the Old Testament text but also detailed knowledge of extrabiblical Jewish tradition and interpretation. Furthermore, such interpretations seem to lie at the heart of certain central gnostic myths.

Two major counterarguments have been advanced (cf. Yamauchi; Gruenwald 1980, 1981):

1. Actual gnostic texts are post-Christian, many of them (such as the Nag Hammadi writings) dating to centuries after the beginnings of Christianity.
2. The strong anti-Jewish and anti-Old Testament polemic of the gnostic texts is inconceivable for Jews. Therefore, the idea that Gnosticism could have originated in Judaism is ridiculous.

Both of these objections are important and must not be dismissed lightly. That no pre-Christian gnostic texts are known is an obstacle, but it may be possible to overcome this problem by traditio-historical analysis. There are also attestations in the Christian heresiologists about some early Gnostics who date back to the first century C.E. Despite the thorny problems that often plague the use of the heresiological data, study has indicated that these reports are not always fabricated (see below).

The objection that Gnosticism is anti-Jewish and therefore could not have originated in Judaism can be countered by reference to Christianity: Christianity became strongly anti-Jewish at a particular point in its history, but no one asserts that it did not originate in Judaism. Christianity did not reject the Old Testament, although it should not be forgotten that this was not a foregone conclusion: certain Christians, such as Marcion, made a determined case for doing just that. More of a problem, however, is that the God of the Old Testament is made the wicked demiurge in gnostic interpretation. This is not just rejection of Judaism but a complete inversion of its central beliefs: Yahweh is seen as wicked and ignorant and his act of creation as evil. This is why some have argued that Gnostics simply took over the Old Testament and distorted it for their polemical purposes. In contrast, Gruenwald has argued just the opposite; the Gnostics used Jewish tradition as a means of wooing Jews as converts to Gnosticism (Gruenwald 1981a: 718–20).

Unfortunately, one of the main defenses against a pre-Christian Gnosticism (Yamauchi) is not well argued on the whole. First, there seems to be a clear "hidden agenda" in the argument: the desire to dissociate Christian beginnings from any possibility of gnostic influence. Second, Yamauchi does not argue his defense so much as juxtapose quotations of scholarly opinions, countering those who favor a pre-Christian origin with the opinions of those who oppose it. Careful analysis of the arguments is lacking for the most part. Yamauchi has written a useful survey of study of the subject. Reviewers have also recognized the persuasiveness of his arguments when it comes to the theories of Reitzenstein, Bultmann, and others. But the major reasons for deriving Gnosticism from Judaism have not been really dealt with, and a persuasive alternative theory has not been developed.

Several recent studies tip the debate in the direction of seeing Gnosticism as an outgrowth of Judaism. Segal examines the rabbinic attack on the "two powers in heaven" belief. At a later point, the polemic becomes directed at any "heretical" group, including Christians, but the earlier discussions (early second century) are against beliefs that seemed to compromise divine unity by the acceptance of an angelic power alongside God. Predecessors of such beliefs can be found in Philo and pre-70 apocalyptic literature which is rooted in earlier speculation on the figure of Wisdom; even though these were still regarded as fully compatible with God's unity, they were straining the boundaries of monotheism, and the "two powers in heaven" concept developed from this. Full-blown Gnosticism, with its dualism between the inferior creator God and the good higher God, "was a product of the battle between the rabbis, the Christians and various other 'two powers' sectarians who inhabited the outskirts of Judaism" (Segal: 265).

Stroumsa (1984) points out that one of the principal questions for the Gnostics, as already recognized by the heresiologists, concerned the origin of evil. The answer to the question was the gnostic myth about the two races or divisions of humanity into the wicked and the righteous. Essential for these beliefs were the early Jewish traditions about the intercourse between angels and women (Enochic traditions) and between Satan and Eve (Adamic traditions). The development of Gnosticism shows that its basic myth could only have originated within Judaism:

> Time and again, I have insisted upon the importance of the Jewish elements, which were thoroughly reinterpreted or inverted in Gnosticism. These elements came not only from apocalyptic texts, but also from traditions later recorded in rabbinic literature; they appeared not as merely discrete mythologoumena, but rather pervaded all of early Gnosis, before its double encounter with Christianity and Middle Platonism. These Jewish elements could hardly be later influences upon a movement further and further estranged from anything Jewish; they must point to Jewish roots of Gnosticism, roots which appear to have run very deep. . . . Every piece of evidence seems to confirm the conjecture that the cradle of some of the earliest Gnostic groups was among Palestinian or Syrian baptist sects of Jewish background. (Stroumsa 1984: 170, 172)

Stroumsa (1981) also addresses the subject of the early rabbinic figure of Yavneh, Elisha b. Abuya, one of the four rabbis who "entered paradise" (*t. Hag.* 2.3). Elisha is called *Aher* ("other, stranger"). This nickname has been given various explanations, but Stroumsa relates it to the title "Allogenes" (from Greek *allogenēs*, "another race, stranger") which was adopted by some Gnostics. This and other elements of the tradition lead Stroumsa to the conclusion that Elisha probably turned to some sort of gnostic teaching, if not to becoming a Gnostic himself (1981: 815).

Fossum (1985) has a similar theme to Segal but is specifically interested in the idea of angels as intermediaries. He also breaks new ground in carrying his investigation into Samaritan literature. Unfortunately, the study is not well organized and has no concluding summary, which makes it difficult to sort out Fossum's important arguments and presuppositions from the mass of detail. The following seem to be his important themes: (1) in both Judaism and Samaritanism, the concepts of the name of God and the angel of Yahweh developed into a hypostasis which acted as an intermediary of revelation between God and his people; (2) the earlier gnostic systems (Simon, Menander, Justin, Carpocrates) did not show the radical dualism and anti-Judaism of the later systems (1985: 213–20); and (3) the dualistic, anti-Old Testament form of Gnosticism came only at the end of a long development, which began with concepts quite at home within Judaism and Samaritanism. Fossum's argumentation has certain weaknesses: for example, he has to depend on Samaritan literature which is relatively late, especially the *Memar Marqa* (fourth century C.E. [8.2.10.2]), and he uses the Pseudo-Clementine writings rather extensively despite their complex and problematic tradition history. His study should have been founded on a much more explicit and detailed analysis of sources than he provides. Nevertheless, Fossum's is an important book which seems to establish the main theses already listed.

The question of Simon Magus (Acts 8:9-24) is vexing. The earliest source is a piece of Christian polemic with little information. It was well over a century before Justin Martyr referred to Simon and described his theological system in detail. Other heresiologists provide further information but are even later, whereas such sources as the Pseudo-Clementine writings are very problematic. The Simonism described by the heresiologists (Justin Martyr; Hippolytus) is a gnostic system. The question is whether it developed from the Simon of Acts 8 or was simply assigned his name at some point (Meeks). Can the missing century be bridged? Lüdemann (1975; 1987) has argued that it can be and that the original Simon had already propounded a gnostic (proto-gnostic?) set of beliefs. He emphasizes in particular the expression "thought of the heart" (*epinoia tēs kardias* [Acts 8:22]), unique in the New Testament but an important technical term in the later Simonian system (1987: 424–25). Lüdemann takes it to be a reference to Simon's consort Helen, who was called Simon's "first thought" (*ennoia*), according to Hippolytus's report.

Although Lüdemann sees nothing particularly Samaritan about Simon's teachings, Fossum has been able to explain terms and concepts from the Samaritan tradition (1985: 162–91). In particular, he argues that the expression "the great power of god" (*hē dynamis tou theou hē megalē* [Acts 8:10]) was a Samaritan theological expression, and Simon's use of it "apparently was a claim to the office of being the Glory of God or the Angel of the Lord" (1985: 190). If Fossum is correct, there is nothing incompatible with Simon's being both an early Gnostic and a Samaritan. Thus the debate about Simon seems to be drifting in the same direction as many gnostic studies: identification of an early form of non-Christian Gnosticism rooted in the Jewish-Samaritan tradition.

No doubt the question will continue to be disputed for a long time to come, but among specialists there is increasingly a consensus that Gnosticism had its roots in pre-70 Judaism. The anti-Jewish and anti-Old Testament polemics found in many gnostic texts, as indeed in the Christian forms of Gnosticism, seem to be a later development. But one also has to reckon with a long period of development; the phenomenon, although still a part of Judaism, might be better labeled "proto-Gnosticism" or "gnostic trends." What is called "Jewish Gnosticism" was probably far removed from the radical dualism of developed systems, such as was taught by Valentinius or found in some of the Nag Hammadi documents. By contrast, to recognize the concept of "Jewish Gnosticism" is to recognize another strand within early Judaism that has largely disappeared from the known Jewish sources.

8.2.14 Charismatics, Preachers, and Miracle Workers

Aune, D. E. "Magic in Early Christianity." *ANRW* 2 (1980) 23.2.1507–57.

———. *Prophecy in Early Christianity and the Ancient Mediterranean World* (1983).

Barnett, P. W. "The Jewish Sign Prophets—A.D. 40–70: Their Intentions and Origin." *NTS* 27 (1980/81) 679–97.

Berman, D. "Hasidim in Rabbinic Traditions." *SBLSP* (1979) 15–33.

Betz, H. D. "Jesus as Divine Man." *Jesus and the Historian* (1969) 114–33.

Bokser, B. M. "Wonder-Working and the Rabbinic Tradition: The Case of Hanina ben Dosa." *JSJ* 16 (1985) 42–92.

Charlesworth, J. H. "Jewish Interest in Astrology during the Hellenistic and Roman Period." *ANRW* 2 (1987) 20.2.926–50.

Freyne, S. "The Charismatic." *Ideal Figures in Ancient Judaism* (1980) 223–58.

Gerhardsson, B. *Memory and Manuscript* (1961).

Green, W. S. "Palestinian Holy Men: Charismatic Leadership and Rabbinic Tradition." *ANRW* 2 (1979) 19.2.619–47.

Hill, D. *New Testament Prophecy* (1979).

Holladay, C. H. *Theios Aner in Hellenistic-Judaism: A Critique of the Use of This Category in New Testament Christology* (1977).

Horsley, R. A. " 'Like One of the Prophets of Old': Two Types of Popular Prophets at the Time of Jesus." *CBQ* 47 (1985) 435–63.

———. "Popular Prophetic Movements at the Time of Jesus: Their Principal Features and Social Origins." *JSNT* 26 (1986) 3–27.

Horsley, R. A., and J. S. Hanson. *Bandits, Prophets, and Messiahs* (1985).

Koester, H. "The Divine Human Being." *HTR* 78 (1985) 243–52.

Macmullen, R. *Enemies of the Roman Order* (1967).

Meeks, W. A. *The Prophet-King: Moses Traditions and the Johannine Christology* (1967).

Neusner, J. *The Wonder-Working Lawyers of Talmudic Babylonia* (1987) = *A History of the Jews in Babylonia* (1966) 2.251–87; (1968) 3.95–194; (1969) 4.179–402; (1970) 5.244–342.

Segal, A. F. "Hellenistic Magic: Some Questions of Definition." *Studies in Gnosticism and Hellenistic Religions* (1981) 349–75.

Smith, M. "A Comparison of Early Christian and Early Rabbinic Tradition." *JBL* 82 (1963) 169–76.

———. *1978.

———. "On the Lack of a History of Greco-Roman Magic." *Althistorische Studien* (1983) 251–57.

Strange, J. F. "Archaeology and the Religion of Judaism in Palestine." *ANRW* 2 (1979) 19.1.646–85.

Teeple, H. M. *The Mosaic Eschatological Prophet* (1957).

Tiede, D. L. *The Charismatic Figure as Miracle Worker* (1972).

Vermes, G. "Hanina ben Dosa'. A Controversial Galilean Saint from the First Century of the Christian Era." *JJS* 23 (1972) 28–50; 24 (1973a) 51–64.

——. *Jesus the Jew* (1973b).

We know of a number of teachers and sages whose adherence to a particular group or movement is not recorded, although in some cases they may have belonged to such. At other times the person appears to be a loner who had, perhaps, only a disciple or two. The best known of these is Jesus. Josephus refers in passing to a number of figures whom he does not identify with any particular sect. One is Onias the Rainmaker (see below). Others are the "scribes" Judas and his disciple Matthias, who tore down the eagle that Herod had placed over the temple entrance (*War* 1.33.2–4 §§648–55; *Ant.* 17.6.2–4 §§149–67; see 6.4.9.4). Both Josephus and the New Testament also mention various prophets who drew a following for a period of time, although generally not for long if their actions caught the Romans' attention (*War* 2.13.4–5 §§258–63; *Ant.* 20.8.6 §§167–72; Acts 21:37-38).

The esoteric arts were widely practiced. Astrology was as ubiquitous among the Jews as in the Greco-Roman world in general: horoscopes have been found at Qumran and also in later phases of Judaism; astrological motifs are well known from the synagogue decorations of the talmudic age (Strange: 670–71). What we today would call "magic" was also a widespread feature of popular religion in antiquity (*Smith: 68–80); however, we have to be careful what we are talking about: in many cases, it represented a perfectly repectable craft, such as healing and exorcism. The term "magic" was used in antiquity, as today, in a pejorative sense to label what one did not like, whereas the same sort of practice might be given a respectable description if one approved it (Aune 1980: 1510–23; Segal; Macmullen: 95–127). Exorcism and control of the spirit world were accepted practice in Jewish society and even can be traced back to Solomon (Josephus, *Ant.* 8.2.5 §§45–49; cf. the *Testament of Solomon*); such skills were a common feature of the miracle worker. Healing and exorcism were closely associated because it was thought that many diseases were the result of demonic possession. A number of individuals with these or other "miraculous" powers are sufficiently well attested from antiquity to demonstrate this.

Honi the Circle-Drawer, for example, is known from rabbinic literature as an individual who could make rain by symbolic action (*m. Ta'an.*

3.8). Although the description of him is legendary, a development in the tradition can be discerned (*Neusner 1971: 1.176–82; Green). He does not fit the early rabbinic image of the sage and was thus evidently something of an embarrassment. For some reason the tannaitic sources seem to downplay miracle-working, unlike the Babylonian Talmud, which shows no sign of suppressing such claims (cf. Neusner: 46–70, 190–262). Green has shown that Honi has been "rabbinized" but his charismatic origins still shine through. The rabbinic tradition seems in some way related to Onias the Rainmaker, mentioned by Josephus (*Ant.* 14.2.1 §§22–24).

Another such individual is Hanina b. Dosa (Vermes 1972; 1973a; to be corrected in light of Neusner [*1971: 1.394–96], Freyne, Bokser). Like Honi, he does not appear as a typical rabbinic sage but is noted for his miraculous powers. Probably a pre-70 figure, he too becomes rabbinized over a period of time.

This brings us to the important figure of Jesus. He should not be assimilated to the rabbinic model (contra Gerhardsson; see the criticisms of Smith 1963); rather, he fits well with the general image of a traveling exorcist and miracle-worker (Aune 1980: 1523–44; *Smith; Vermes 1973b: 58–82). The Gospels are unanimous that he healed, cast out demons, and did other marvelous works. These traits seem to have been ascribed to the historical Jesus and are not simply a later development of the tradition, but whether they are or not, the significant thing is that the early Christian tradition is happy to present him as an exorcist and miracle-worker.

The basic question does not really concern the "historical" Honi or Hanina or Jesus, even if it is possible to find them underneath the tradition. The ascription of extraordinary powers seems to occur in the earliest layer of the tradition in each case, although this layer naturally already represents interpretation. But even if this should be only a secondary development, it still demonstrates that the concept of the charismatic miracle-worker was widely known and accepted. For the purposes here, that is all that is necessary to know.

Whether there was a model of the charismatic is perhaps a moot question (cf. Freyne: 247–49), but this may be more a problem of semantics than substance, at least for present concerns. The issue is whether various sorts of "charismatic holy men" were known and accepted. The answer to this seems to be yes, even if we should think of various types rather than a single model. (One could perhaps invoke the Weberian ideal type, recognizing that it is only a scholarly construct for heuristic purposes and not to be confused with precise existence in the real world.) The term *ḥāsîd* has sometimes been used of such figures (Vermes 1972;

Vermes 1973a; Vermes 1973b), but this is probably inappropriate (Berman: 2.16–17; Freyne: 224–27). The rabbinic image of the *ḥāsîd* is rather different.

This brings us to the controversy over the *theios anēr*. It has long been argued that Jesus is to be understood as modeled on this idea (e.g., Betz). The gestalt of the *theios anēr* comes from the Greek philosophical tradition and consists of an individual who partakes of both the image of philosophical sage and the more popular role of the miracle-worker (Tiede; Holladay). The appropriateness of the term in its application to Jesus has been disputed (Tiede). Nevertheless, such an image was evidently widespread in the Greco-Roman world, with at least some features in common with charismatic types accepted in Judaism (Koester). Whether it should be applied to Jesus is for New Testament scholars to debate, but it serves as another illustration of a cluster of figures well known in the pre-70 culture of Judea.

"Prophet" and "prophecy" are also terms found in the sources for this period. The modern scholarly distinction between "forthteller" and "foreteller" is not maintained in the use of the term "prophet," but that distinction is to some extent a scholarly fiction because examples of both sorts of proclaiming can be found in the Old Testament prophets. Although there had developed a tradition that prophecy had ceased, many references to "prophet" are still found in the literature (Aune 1983: 103–6). Josephus, one of those who tells of the cessation of prophecy (*Ag. Ap*. 1.8 §41), goes on to claim himself to be a prophet (*War* 3.8.9 §§399–407). In two long passages Josephus also describes a variety of prophecies and prophetic types of figures (7.4.9). One can add to this his claim that the Essenes had a reputation for foretelling events accurately (8.2.5.5; 5.4.8). The Teacher of Righteousness at Qumran seems to have been thought of as a prophet and perhaps even expected to return as the eschatological prophet at the end of days (1QS 9:11). Jesus himself emerges as a prophet from the Gospel portraits. This may be partly an assimilation of the role of the "eschatological prophet" on the model of Moses (Teeple; Meeks), Elijah, and so on, but arguments have been made that Jesus' self-identification and the evaluation of his contemporaries included that of prophet (Hill: 50–69; Aune 1983: 153–88).

A word of caution should be added here. Horsley (in criticism of Aune 1983: 121–29) has pointed out that literary descriptions of prophets ("prophet like Moses," etc.) should not be lumped in with the social phenomena (1986: 25 n.15). He divides the social prophets into two main types (although also mentioning a third). The attempt at a sociological analysis is commendable, but it must not be forgotten that we do not have sociological field data. All we have are descriptions in ancient literature, and our sociological analyses represent an attempt to extract socio-logical data from literature. This suggests two points to which Horsley does not seem to give sufficient attention in his useful studies: (1) the descriptions themselves may be influenced to a lesser or greater extent by literary-theological models; and (2) the social phenomena may have been influenced by, or even inspired by, the literary-theological models extant at the time. A further problem is that the data in the ancient sources are far from complete. That certain elements are lacking in the description (e.g., religious motives or messianic expectations) does not mean that they were not present in the actual historical situation. One has no right to read them in without evidence, but the incompleteness of the data complicates any task of classification and makes one cautious about accepting any system that is overly schematic.

It can be concluded that a variety of charismatic figures practiced (individually or in combination) magic, exorcism, healing, and other "miraculous" arts. Some of these also preached religious messages and even engaged in prophetism. One could perhaps argue that such figures were only on the fringe or had only a marginal influence. This is difficult to decide because of the episodic nature of our data, but no description of first-century Palestine can ignore them, any more than a description of the Church of England today can ignore such practices as Satanism and exorcism, as embarrassing as they may be to some of the clergy. Further, a comparison with various historical and contemporary traditional cultures argues that such beliefs were an integral part of first-century Jewish society. The "superstitions" of the Middle Ages are hardly likely to have been a "degeneration" from the Greco-Roman world; on the contrary, they were only the continuation of popular religion and culture, whether accepted or not by the dominant church. For example, magical practices and oracles are a way of life in many parts of Africa, even among the well-educated and the firm Christians. The data available to us suggest that such was no less the case in first-century Palestine.

8.2.15 The Ammei ha-Aretz and the Haverim

Cohen, S.J.D. Review of *'Am ha-Aretz*, by A. Oppenheimer. *JBL* 97 (1978) 596–97.

Neusner, J. "The Fellowship (חבורה) in the Second Jewish Commonwealth." *HTR* 53 (1960) 125–42.

———. "ḤBR and N'MN." *RevQ* 5 (1964/66) 119–22.

Nicholson, E. W. "The Meaning of the Expression עם הארץ in the Old Testament." *JSS* 10 (1965) 59–66.

Oppenheimer, A. *The 'Am ha-Aretz* (1977).

Peli, P. H. "The Havurot That Were in Jerusalem." *HUCA* 55 (1984) 55–74.
*Saldarini 1988: 216–20.

Tannaitic literature has many references to the "person of the land" (*'am hā'āreṣ*; plural *'ammê hā'āreṣ*), by which is meant a Jew who is not strictly observant in particular matters that the rabbis regarded as required. This usually involved tithing and purity regulations. The problem is that no equivalent term is found in the pre-70 Jewish literature. In the Old Testament *'am hā'āreṣ* is a collective ("people of the land") that apparently designated citizens or landowners (Nicholson). In the post-exilic period, however, the term seems already to have begun to carry the connotation of those who were not properly observant (cf. Ezra 10:2), although it initially seems to have referred to Palestinian residents who were non-Jews. In early rabbinic literature it is often used in opposition to a member (*ḥāber*) of a "fellowship" (*ḥăbûrāh*). The *havurot* were associations of Jews who had pledged strict observance of particular halakic regulations, especially with regard to tithing and cultic purity (Neusner 1960). Many Pharisees were probably *haverim* but the precise relationship is still in need of study (cf. Neusner's article [1960], which was written before his critical method had developed; see also *Goodman 1987: 82–85).

The term *am ha-aretz* is widely used in scholarship to refer to the ordinary Jew of late antiquity who did not follow rabbinic prescriptions in every detail. Unfortunately, the most recent studies (Oppenheimer; Peli) suffer from methodological deficiencies (cf. Cohen): a harmonized picture drawn from rabbinic literature is projected back into pre-70 times and the rabbinic data often read into the earlier sources. It is wrong to assume Pharisaic dominance before 70 in the same way that it is wrong to assume rabbinic dominance during the late first and early second centuries. Yet there is a genuine problem, because the Pharisees may well have viewed non-Pharisees as *ammei ha-aretz* in the later sense and may even have used that term (although this cannot be demonstrated). The term itself is a useful one for modern scholarship as long as it does not have a pejorative connotation and the assumption is not made that Judaism was to be measured against a Pharisaic or rabbinic "orthodoxy" (8.3.1).

8.2.16 Art, Artifacts, and Archeology

Frerichs, E. S., and J. Neusner, eds. *Goodenough on the History of Religion and on Judaism* (1986).
Goodenough, E. R. *By Light, Light* (1935).

———. *Jewish Symbols in the Greco-Roman Period.* 13 vols. (1953–65).

———. *Jewish Symbols in the Greco-Roman Period,* ed. J. Neusner (1988).

Henten, J. W. van, ed. *Die Entstehung der jüdischen Martyrologie* (1989).

Lease, G. "Jewish Mystery Cults since Goodenough." *ANRW* 2 (1987) 20.2.858–80.

Meyers, E. M. *Jewish Ossuaries: Reburial and Rebirth* (1971).

———. "Galilean Regionalism as a Factor in Historical Reconstruction." *BASOR* 221 (1976) 93–101.

———. "Galilean Regionalism: A Reappraisal." *Approaches to Ancient Judaism* (1985) 5.115–31.

Meyers, E. M., and J. F. Strange. *Archaeology, the Rabbis and Early Christianity* (1981).

Neusner, J. "Preface." *Goodenough on the History of Religion and on Judaism* (1986) ix–xix.

Strange, J. F. "Archaeology and the Religion of Judaism in Palestine." *ANRW* 2 (1979) 19.1.646–85.

This section differs from the previous in that it is devoted to a type of data rather than a group or movement: the nonliterary data. The name most associated with Jewish art is that of Erwin Goodenough, whose monumental thirteen-volume work attempted to assemble the bulk of early Jewish art and interpret it on its own terms (cf. Neusner 1986 and his introduction to the abridged volume of Goodenough's *Symbols* [1988] with the literature assembled there).

The importance of this material is that it helps to round out the religious picture of the times. Literary sources not only are too sparse and episodic to give a full picture of the religious situation but also often represent a partisan point of view and even an attempt to palm off an entirely spurious status quo on the reader. If people are told that such and such is the case—even if it is not—then many may still come to believe it in time. Thus the picture of Judaism often accepted for pre-70 times is that of rabbinic literature, partly because the documents wish the reader to believe that their own view of the world is the one believed by everyone, not only now but also in the past.

Goodenough was able to show from the art and artifacts that there was another side to religion among the Jews in the first few centuries of the Common Era. His name is often associated with the theory of "mystical Hellenistic Judaism" (cf. Goodenough 1935). The fact that this has been widely rejected (cf. Lease) has meant that Goodenough's greater and more basic contribution is often overlooked. One does not have to accept his thesis about mystical Hellenistic Judaism to recognize the fundamental way in which his study has shown a pluralistic and even fragmented Judaism, in which many different currents still flowed at a time when it was thought that the rabbis were fully in charge (see the evaluation in Neusner 1986 [also in Goodenough 1988]).

Other aspects of popular religion are not so easily discovered. Popular religion is often frowned on by the established religious authorities and may therefore be ignored or quietly swept under the carpet in the preserved sources. Archeology is probably the biggest help (Strange; cf. Meyers 1976; 1985; Meyers/Strange), although only certain elements survive in the form of artifacts. Ossuaries and other burial customs may show some sort of views about afterlife (Meyers 1971). As already noted, astrology was widespread and eventually surfaced in synagogue motifs of the later Roman period. There is also some evidence of the veneration of holy sites, such as Mamre (Strange: 671–72), which may well have its origins in pre-Israelite times. Tombs of holy men were also made the object of veneration and perhaps even pilgrimage (Strange: 667–70), a fact well known from Christianity but not usually associated with Judaism of this period (cf. van Henten).

8.3   SYNTHESIS

8.3.1   Overview: Judaism at the Turn of the Era

Aune, D. E. "Orthodoxy in First-Century Judaism? A Response to N. J. McEleney." *JSJ* 7 (1976) 1–10.

Bauer, W. *Orthodoxy and Heresy in Earliest Christianity* (1934; Eng. trans. 1971).

Brown, R. E. *The Gospel according to John* (1966).

Grabbe, L. L. "Orthodoxy in First Century Judaism: What Are the Issues?" *JSJ* 8 (1977) 149–53.

Kraft, R. A. "The Multiform Jewish Heritage of Early Christianity." *Christianity, Judaism and Other Greco-Roman Cults* (1975) 3.174–99.

McEleney, N. J. "Orthodoxy in Judaism of the First Christian Century." *JSJ* 4 (1973) 19–42.

———. "Orthodoxy in Judaism of the First Christian Century: Replies to David E. Aune and Lester L. Grabbe." *JSJ* 9 (1978) 83–88.

Neusner, J. "The Demise of 'Normative Judaism.'" *Judaism* 15 (1966) 230–40.

———. "'Covenantal Nomism.' The Piety of Judaism in the First Century." *Major Trends in Formative Judaism*. 3d series (1985) 9–34.

Smith, J. Z. "Native Cults in the Hellenistic Period." *HR* 11 (1971/72) 236–49.

———. "Hellenistic Religions." *Encyclopaedia Britannica* (1975) 8.749–51.

Strange, J. F. "Archaeology and the Religion of Judaism in Palestine." *ANRW* 2 (1979) 19.1.646–85.

Describing the religious situation in Palestine from the Maccabees to the fall of Jerusalem is a complicated task that requires a description and an understanding of the history and society of the period (cf. Kraft). Any characterization is likely to contain such terms as "pluralistic," "diverse," "complex," "great variety," "not monolithic," and "many-sided." This has led some scholars to prefer the term "Judaisms" to describe the many different Jewish religious systems around at the time (see 8.1).

There were many Jewish religious systems ("Judaisms") extant in the Land of Israel before 70. For a proper understanding, we ought to examine each one on its own terms. Lamentably, we do not have sufficient information for a coherent description of most of them. Instead, we find only partial information or even no more than hints in the extant literary and material remains. Many discussions of the past have grouped the sources together to describe *the* Jewish belief or practice with regard to eschatology, messianism, worship, and so on. Although in some cases this was carefully done, the tendency has been to present a monolithic portrait (often with assumptions about "orthodoxy" underlying the reconstruction) so that the description of one system or form of Judaism—or even no actual system but only an artificial construct—masquerades as a portrait of all Judaism.

The importance of recognizing what one is doing is exemplified in Neusner's description of rabbinic Judaism (*1981). Each document should be understood in its own historical and literary context before extrapolating to a religious system. Then the particular system must be understood in itself before attempting to compare it with other systems. But whereas the Mishnah and other rabbinic documents are of sufficient length to make description a reasonable enterprise, many of the pre-70 sources are simply not extensive enough for a proper sketching out of the underlying religious ideology.

One should immediately put aside any model based on the idea of Christian orthodoxy. To what extent "orthodoxy" is a useful term in any period of Christianity is for church historians to debate, but the term is out of place in the first century or so of the Christian church, as Bauer demonstrated half a century ago (1934). A fortiori, the term "orthodox" is of little use as a concept for Judaism before 70 (Aune; Grabbe; contra McEleney 1973; McEleney 1978; cf. Neusner 1985: 19–20).

Although a more useful term might be "orthopraxy" (Aune), even that can be misleading, because it implies a widely accepted standard against which halakic practice could be measured. Is there evidence for such a standard? If we have in mind only the few most basic concepts (below), then we can agree that such beliefs and practices were almost universal. Beyond this handful of points, which for practical purposes were almost a definition of what it was to be a Jew, however, there was wide variation in matters of purity, festival observance, and interpretation of the Pentateuch. One can find exceptions to some or perhaps all of the basic characteristics to be noted, but this only illustrates the problem.

Therefore, when we describe Judaism of the time, we should not focus on particular groups or sects, such as the Pharisees or Essenes. These groups ought to be described and understood on their own terms (to the extent that there are sufficient data to do so), but once this is done we still have only a small bit of the mosaic, for their contribution to common Judaism was not primarily as sectarians. That is, each sect had its own peculiar beliefs and observances which may tell us much about it but little about other versions of Judaism. In contrast, each sect held much in common with other Jews. Instead of concentrating on groups, we need to think about institutions and ideals. In Palestine, the central institution was the cult, which also represented a spiritual center for Jews in the Diaspora. Closely tied to this was the concept of the land as a possession and home for individuals but also as the place which God had chosen and had made his own abode, in some sense. The land as divine inheritance had been a part of Israelite thinking from an early period. These were ideals important to practically every Jew.

Personal Jewish identity was usually bound up with specific items: belief in one God, the concept of being a part of the "chosen people," the rejection of images in worship, the Torah (i.e., those traditions and interpretations of the Old Testament seen as important for religious identity and observance), and circumcision. Most of these characteristics are straightforward; they seem to occur in almost all groups, as far as we can determine; and Greco-Roman writers often remark on them. It is difficult to find persons identifying themselves as Jews who lacked one or more of these. The most problematic item is Torah, because there is evidence that different Jews had different ideas about what should be included in the concept (canon), about the interpretation of that which was included (exegesis), and about the relative importance of the accepted traditions (authority).

A person was a Jew whether in the Land of Israel or outside it. The basic religious heritage was the same for Jews of every stripe. That legacy was essentially the story—the myth—of Israel. God had been involved in the life of the people since creation. A line connected each Jew back to the first man, Adam, and the first woman, Eve, but it was Abraham who had been chosen from all the other nations and peoples to be the father of God's people. A special covenant had been made with Abraham, and a special covenant had been made with his descendants, the people of Israel. "We are Abraham's seed and heirs according to the promise" is a claim which every Jew could make and most would. The Torah told them about the promise, and circumcision was the sign in the flesh confirming it. Certain practices also marked them off from the surrounding peoples: the refusal to eat particular meats, the observance of the Sabbath or other festivals, and, perhaps, purity regulations. These points were universal. Nevertheless, there were some interesting distinctions between the natives of Judea and those living in the Diaspora.

Worship and religion in the Land of Israel was dominated by the annual festival calendar and the pilgrimage to the temple in Jerusalem. According to the Torah, each male Israelite was to "appear before the Lord" three times during the year (Deut 16:16), that is, at Passover, Pentecost (*Shavuot*), and the festivals of the month of Tishri: the festival of Trumpets, the Day of Atonement (*Yom ha-Kippurim*), and, especially, the Feast of Tabernacles (*Sukkot*). This was a time when vows would be made, sin- and thanksgiving-offerings brought to the altar, the regular sacrifices solemnly observed, and other ceremonies associated with the festival celebrated. This was not an optional extra or a side issue to being a Jew. For most Jews, this was the primary form of worship. There were additional aspects to being a Jew, including ethical and moral conduct, private devotions, and theological speculation, but participation in the temple cult was the sine qua non of service to God. This was how sins were forgiven and how one renewed the relationship with God. This is what it meant to be a temple-centered religion.

It seems likely, however, that many Jews did not abide by the command to come to Jerusalem to worship three times a year (cf. John 7:2-9). For those who lived a distance from the city, it was simply impractical. Nevertheless, it was probably the custom for many or most of those living in such neighboring areas as Galilee to make a regular journey to the temple during one of the festivals, even if not several times a year. This fact does not preclude other aspects of worship and practice, such as private prayer, the public observance of the Sabbath, and annual festivals in the local area. Synagogues seem to be a late introduction into the Palestinian area, not very long before the destruction of the temple (8.3.3). They probably first appeared in the more remote parts of the country before spreading to Judea itself. The place of synagogue worship in Palestinian Judaism before 70 does not seem to have been a large one, however, even though there are grounds for thinking the synagogue had become an established institution by the first century C.E. (8.3.3).

There were also other traditional observances which were probably adhered to by most Jews, such as some purity laws, especially those clearly laid down in the Pentateuch, and the agricultural priestly dues. The average Jew did not attempt to make his home into a model of the temple, as the Pharisee did. The Pharisees may have had a reputation for learning and knowledge of the law—although they were not the only ones with such a reputation—but they hardly controlled how people practiced their Judaism. How people were educated in their religion is not completely clear. According to the Old Testament, the primary duty lay with the family, especially the father. There was undoubtedly some instruction in the temple during the festivals because the cult would otherwise have been meaningless. The scribes may have been primary offical communicants regarding religious law. If many of them were schoolmasters, as Smith argues, then this role for them would make sense (*1978: 30–31). Just as the magistrate and schoolmaster in a small village may have the primary duty of instructing in government, so the schoolmaster and village clerk—the scribe—would have been the symbol of instruction in religious law.

Even though most people were not members of a religious sect, a religious outlook was frequently influenced by teachers and groups who may not have had a large number of actual followers. People who were ill or "had a demon" would seek out those whom they thought could help them, whether it was the priest in the temple, the local Jerusalem Lourdes (John 5:2-7, cf. the textual variant; Brown: 1.205–7), or the traveling healer-cum-exorcist. Astrologers probably did not starve in Judea any more than they did elsewhere in the Greco-Roman world. The peripatetic preacher—whether Pharisee, Essene, ascetic, mystic, or whatnot—could always draw a crowd. It was a diversion and one of the few forms of entertainment available. There were always a few curious persons in these crowds who would then experience personal enlightenment. These people might continue to follow the preacher when he moved on, perhaps abandoning their home and livelihood. Such periods of discipleship were probably brief for all but the hard-core believers, but usually a few individuals in any village would become engaged in such discipleship, even if for a short time.

Thus the various teachers, preachers, and sectarians made their mark on society, even though only a few had permanent followers or devotees. Jesus was only one of many; the difference was that his movement survived and grew. The same seems to be true of the Pharisees. Small in numbers before 70, their traditions formed an important component in the first rabbinic document, the Mishnah, and their attitudes were a major component in the rabbinic Judaism which developed in the Yavnean period.

The average Jew was probably what the later rabbis referred to as an *am ha-aretz* (8.2.15). That is, they were men and women who were pious in their own way but whose main focus of attention was making a living.

They could not afford the luxury of devoting a great portion of their time and energy to the picayune details of religious observance which some sectarians may have regarded as essential. Other aspects of religion are not so easily discovered. Popular religion is often frowned on by the established religious authorities and may thus be ignored or quietly swept under the carpet in the preserved sources. Archeology and art are probably the biggest help (8.2.16), although only some elements show up in the form of artifacts. Ossuaries and other burial customs may reveal some views about the afterlife. Synagogue motifs are very important, as shown by Goodenough's study of Dura-Europa and other sites, and demonstrate such overlooked facts as the widespread belief in and practice of the "science" of astrology. There is also some evidence of the veneration of holy sites, including the tombs of holy men, with pilgrimages made to them. All this gives a picture rather different from that often drawn from the interpretation of "pious literature" alone.

The differences between the Jews of Israel and the Diaspora Jews fall largely into two areas: (1) the great distance between the temple as center of worship and the Diaspora Jew's actual home; and (2) the fact that Diaspora Jews were a minority community in a largely pagan setting. In the Diaspora, Jerusalem and its temple were also an object of concern, interest, and identity. Members of the community paid the half-shekel temple tax, a not inconsiderable sum which represented about two days' wages for the ordinary worker. For many the temple represented an ideal; the pilgrimage to worship there, a dream; and ultimate burial in the land, a strong desire. Nevertheless, the realities of daily religious practice tended to be the community, the synagogue, and the home. Synagogues are attested in Egypt as early as the mid-third century B.C.E. and seem to have been equally important in other areas at an early date (8.3.3).

There is a tendency to assume that Jews of antiquity saw their life and identity primarily in religious terms. In most cases, however, we do not know one way or the other. The writings preserved are mostly religious literature and show us what was important to the writers, but we cannot assume that Philo was the model for Alexandrian Jews or that the apocalypses show us where most Jews of Palestine concentrated their energies. If we look at a writer such as Josephus, we see an interesting mixture. His writings contain a large religious element, but they are not just religious. He saw his identity in the broad context of Judaism but also in Jewish history and ethnicity. It would be wrong to define Josephus's view of himself in purely religious terms. Indeed, his outlook is very much parallel to that which we find in many Greco-Roman writers of the time, such as Cicero or Plutarch. Religion and personal piety were very important but they did not dominate these writers' lives. One might correctly observe that the Jews then did not make a sharp distinction between religion and other aspects of life, such as politics and profession. That outlook was not unique to the Jews, however—no self-respecting Roman or Greek would have regarded himself as "secular" in the modern sense. To be thought of as an "atheist" was a serious stigma.

Indeed, religion meant different things to different Jews, and to assume that all took the same view is to misapprehend. For the average Jew—farmer, day laborer, craftsman, beggar—making a living was not easy. Earning enough for food, as well as for clothing and housing, was sufficient concern for many. This would not make them irreligious, for most were probably quite pious by their own estimation; it was simply a matter of emphasis. The piety of the sectarian was not the piety of most Israelites, and what was slackness or impiety in the eyes of the sect member might be normal, accepted behavior for other Jews. Some individuals had the means and the leisure to practice a strenuous form of religion; most did not.

Of course, poverty was no barrier to intense devotion, and even those living on the edge of subsistence might well turn to religion for solace and hope. Judging from the preserved literature, many had a keen expectation that God would bring a better future. Few could have been fully content with the status quo throughout most of the Second Temple period (with perhaps the exception of the early Hasmonean period). For much of that time Judah was a subject nation, yet according to tradition it had once been a proud, independent country and even a great empire by the grace of God.

Some Jews could think on this subject only with extreme bitterness at the current state of their nation. They believed that the correct action, either by God alone or by human agents with God's help, might put the situation right. Some espoused revolution as the appropriate means of rectifying the situation. There were plenty of Old Testament precedents, and in the post-Hasmonean period the Maccabees served as exemplars. "By God and my right hand" might be their motto.

Others felt just as passionately but saw the human role as being more passive: prayer, obedience, patient waiting for God to fulfill his will—even the shedding of one's own blood in martyrdom. God would do what needed to be done; it was not up to humans to take matters into their own hands. They had a part to play, but their part was waiting on the Lord. They could also calculate and speculate, and these calculations and speculations fill many extant, and presumably some lost, apocalypses. Although the exact moment of God's wrath might be uncertain, there was never any doubt that God would descend in fury, when the time was right, to punish the wicked, reward the righteous, and bring about new heavens and a new earth.

How many Jews were caught up in this apocalyptic worldview at the turn of the era? Some scholars have assumed that the vast majority were, but we really do not know. In Palestine many Jews had enough with their daily struggle to make a living, so that any involvement with apocalypticism was not their first concern, although it may have served as a diversion from a life of misery for some people. Outside Palestine we know there were Jews who saw the future life not in apocalyptic terms but in personal salvation of the soul. It is impossible to quantify the number of people who took the different approaches, but the literature and other indications are sufficient to recognize a variety of paths followed.

The Hellenistic period was characterized by religions of personal salvation. Contrary to some older religions of the Greco-Roman period, Judaism retained many of its ancient Near Eastern characteristics as a national religion. That is, it continued to be primarily an ethnic religion, even in the Diaspora, whereas other national religions developed much more universalistic tendencies during the Hellenistic period (Smith 1971/ 72; 1975). Isis worship, for example, was transformed from a national cult of Egypt to a Hellenistic religion of salvation which actively sought converts and penetrated into many parts of society in the Roman Empire. Nevertheless, Judaism in the Greco-Roman world fitted the category of salvation religion in some respects. Although the extent of Jewish influence might be debated, there seems no question that many Romans and others were attracted by the religion, and we find sporadic examples of outright conversion to Judaism, although Jewish sympathizers seem to have been more common (8.3.2).

This overview has touched on many points and several major areas important to first-century Judaism. Some of these need a more detailed look, even though none of them can be considered in isolation but must be related to each other for a full picture. Individual studies take up the rest of this chapter.

8.3.2 To Be—or Not to Be—a Jew

Cohen, S.J.D. "Conversion to Judaism in Historical Perspective: From Biblical Israel to Postbiblical Judaism." *Conservative Judaism* 36 (1983) 31–45.

———. "The Origins of the Matrilineal Principle in Rabbinic Law." *AJS Review* 10 (1985) 19–53.

———. "Was Timothy Jewish (Acts 16:1-3)? Patristic Exegesis, Rabbinic Law, and Matrilineal Descent." *JBL* 105 (1986) 251–68.

———. "Respect for Judaism by Gentiles according to Josephus." *HTR* 80 (1987) 409–30.

Feldman, L. H. "Jewish 'Sympathizers' in Classical Literature and Inscriptions." *TAPA* 81 (1950) 200–208.

————. "The Omnipresence of the God-Fearers." *BAR* 12, no. 5 (Sept./Oct. 1986) 58–69.

Gager, J. G. "Jews, Gentiles, and Synagogues in the Book of Acts." *HTR* 79 (1986) 91–99.

Kraabel, A. T. "The Disappearance of the 'God-Fearers.'" *Numen* 28 (1981) 113–26.

McEleney, N. J. "Conversion, Circumcision and the Law." *NTS* 20 (1973/74) 319–41.

MacLennan, R. S., and A. T. Kraabel. "The God-Fearers—A Literary and Theological Invention." *BAR* 12, no. 5 (Sept./Oct. 1986) 46–53.

Nolland, J. "Uncircumcised Proselytes?" *JSJ* 12 (1981) 173–94.

Reynolds, J., and R. Tannenbaum. *Jews and Godfearers at Aphrodisias* (1987).

Smith, J. Z. "Fences and Neighbors: Some Contours of Early Judaism." *Approaches to Ancient Judaism* (1980) 2.1–25.

Tannenbaum, R. F. "Jews and God-Fearers in the Holy City of Aphrodite." *BAR* 12, no. 5 (Sept./Oct. 1986) 54–57.

What did it mean to be a Jew? The question is much debated in modern times, with the rise of the state of Israel, but it seems unlikely that it was a problem for many in antiquity. Then, you were a Jew if you were born a Jew. Problems arose primarily in three situations: (1) categorizing the offspring of a marriage between a Jew and a Gentile; (2) with regard to a proselyte; and (3) in the case of a person who had renounced Judaism.

1. For children of mixed marriages, identification as a Jew probably depended on how the offspring was brought up. Those raised as Jews—and circumcised if boys—were not likely to have had their Jewishness called into question. If this had not happened, however, could one claim to be a Jew simply by having a Jewish mother? The matrilinear transfer of Jewishness is well known from later Judaism until the present day and seems to go back as far as the Amoraic period, but there is no evidence of such a practice operating before 70. On the contrary, both rabbinic evidence and such examples as Acts 16:1-3 indicate that ethnic identity tended to be passed on from the father (Cohen 1983; 1985; 1986).

2. The issue of proselytes has occasioned much discussion in recent times. As already noted, even in the Diaspora, Judaism continued to be primarily an ethnic religion, rather than a religion of conversion such as were the Isis cult and Mithraism (8.3.1). Nevertheless, the idea of someone renouncing paganism and joining the Jewish community is an old one, with its roots in the Old Testament tradition. Ruth is a prime example (2.2.1.9.2). We also have various references to proselytizing in the literature (7.3.4), showing that converts were made and—in some cases—actively sought. It seems unlikely, however, that there was a major "mission" on the part of the Jews to gain gentile converts, and there was

nothing on the missionary scale of Christians. Although such has been postulated at different times, there is simply no evidence for it (see further below).

What was involved in becoming a Jew? The one element which occurs wherever we have any actual details is circumcision for men (cf. Smith: 10–15). The only example in which conversion seems to be envisaged without circumcision is related by Josephus and concerns the royal house of Adiabene (*Ant.* 20.2.3–4 §§34–48). This is a rather special case, however, in that Izates, who wanted to become a full convert by circumcision, was king over a non-Jewish people. He was advised by the Jewish merchant who had converted his mother that he could

> worship God even without being circumcised if indeed he had fully decided to be a devoted adherent of Judaism, for it was this that counted more than circumcision. He told him, furthermore, that God Himself would pardon him if, constrained thus by necessity and by fear of his subjects, he failed to perform this rite. Afterwards, however, since he had not completely given up his desire, another Jew . . . urged him to carry out the rite. (*Ant.* 20.2.3–4 §§41–43)

When this story is read in context, there seems no reason to believe in the general practice of conversion without circumcision. Rather, this was a special case involving a king with potentially hostile subjects (cf. Nolland: 192–94). Therefore, circumcision seems to have been a universal practice for male proselytes. We have no information about female proselytes. It is frequently asserted in handbooks and commentaries that both men and women had to undergo a ritual bath ("baptism"), and men had to be circumcised as well (Schürer: 3.173–74). Although this is a practice referred to in rabbinic literature (e.g., *b. Yeb.* 46a), we have no evidence for it before 70 (Cohen 1987: 430). Indeed, the silence of Josephus and other sources suggests that such was not the practice.

There were more Jewish sympathizers than outright converts (cf. Feldman 1950), circumcision no doubt being the major obstacle for men; not surprisingly, one has the impression that female converts were more common. Therefore, a topic very much in current debate concerns the question of "God-fearers." Were there non-Jews, especially men, who adopted Judaism in many or all respects except for circumcision? Older sources argued that this was so. Studies in the last few decades noted that the term "God-fearer" (*sebomenoi, phoboumenoi*) was not necessarily a term for sympathizers and could not be taken as such without a clear context (Feldman 1950); the term was sometimes used for those who were unquestionably Jews, as simply an indication of piety. Recently, Kraabel has argued that the terms "God-fearer" and "semi-proselyte" should be dropped as nonexistent categories. His major points are well taken: (1) the claim, often made in the context of New Testament studies and based on passages such as Acts 16:14, that there was an extensive Jewish mission to the Gentiles that created a large pool of uncircumcised sympathizers is wrong; and (2) the many synagogue inscriptions, which one would expect to mention such sympathizers, are silent on the subject. The discovery of the Aphrodisias inscription casts doubt on his second point (Reynolds/Tannenbaum), however, and many scholars are now of the opinion that "God-fearer" did often have the technical meaning of one who adhered to Judaism, was even a member of a synagogue, without having undergone circumcision (Schürer: 3.1.150–76; Tannenbaum). One can recognize that sympathizers were referred to in a variety of sources without endorsing the idea of a wholesale mission to the Gentiles (Feldman 1986; Gager; contra MacLennan/Kraabel), although we do have some examples of Jews who sought converts (7.3.4). One term should be eliminated, however: "proselyte of the gate," still occasionally found in New Testament scholarship as a term for a Jewish sympathizer, occurs only in a few late rabbinic texts (Schürer: 3.171–72).

Finally, we should consider the question of whether converts could be accepted without circumcision. Such has been argued (e.g., McEleney 1973–74), but apart from the example of Adiabene, it is difficult to find passages to support this. That his was a very exceptional case must also be recognized. Although Philo seems to say that there were Jews who thought physical circumcision was unnecessary as long as the spiritual (allegorical) intent was noted, he does not suggest that Gentiles were being converted without circumcision (cf. Nolland: 173–79). Circumcision was and long remained the universal sign of Jewish identity.

3. The question of those who abandoned Judaism is more difficult than it might seem. For example, Josephus says that Philo's nephew Tiberius Julius Alexander (7.4.9.3) had abandoned his ancestral religion (*Ant.* 20.5.2 §100). We are given insufficient data to make sense of this, however. Is this a judgment by Josephus, which Tiberius Alexander would have hotly disputed? Did Tiberius Alexander renounce his Judaism? Or did he quietly ignore Jewish practices when not in the Jewish community? Was he never circumcised, or did he submit to epispasm, or was the circumcision simply ignored as if it were a physical blemish? Similarly, those judged to be evildoers by the authors of 1 and 2 Maccabees would probably have considered themselves fully Jewish (5.4.3.2). Even those (few!) who disguised their circumcision may have regarded themselves as practitioners of an enlightened Judaism. We can only guess, because we do not have their side of the story. Third Maccabees 1:3 mentions a Jew named Dositheus who had "abandoned the law and left the customs

of his fathers" (*metabalōn ta nomima kai tōn patriōn dogmatōn apēl-lotriōmenos*), but no details are given and precise interpretation is impossible.

8.3.3 Temple and Torah

Beckwith, R. *The Old Testament Canon of the New Testament Church* (1985).
Bickerman, E. J. *The Jews in the Greek Age* (1988).
Blenkinsopp, J. *Prophecy and Canon* (1977).
———. "Temple and Society in Achemenid Judah." *Studies in the Second Temple: The Persian Period* (1991) 22–53.
Brown, R. E. *The Gospel according to John (i–xii)* (1966).
Chiat, M.J.S. "First-Century Synagogue Architecture: Methodological Problems." *Ancient Synagogues Revealed* (1981) 49–60.
———. *Handbook of Synagogue Architecture* (1982).
Davies, P. R. "The Social World of the Apocalyptic Writings." *The World of Ancient Israel* (1989) 251–71.
Douglas, M. *Purity and Danger* (1966).
Flesher, P.V.M. "Palestinian Synagogues before 70 C.E.: A Review of the Evidence." *Approaches to Ancient Judaism* (1989) 6.68–81.
Forster, G. "The Synagogues at Masada and Herodium." *Ancient Synagogues Revealed* (1981) 24–29.
Grabbe, L. L. "Synagogues in Pre-70 Palestine: A Re-assessment." *JTS* 39 (1988) 401–10.
———. "The Social Setting of Early Jewish Apocalypticism." *JSP* 4 (1989) 27–47.
Hüttenmeister, F., and G. Reeg. *Die antiken Synagogen in Israel* (1977).
Lundquist, J. M. "What Is a Temple? A Preliminary Typology." *The Quest for the Kingdom of God* (1983) 205–19.
———. "The Common Temple Ideology of the Ancient Near East." *The Temple in Antiquity* (1984) 53–76.
Neusner, J. "Emergent Rabbinic Judaism in a Time of Crisis." *Judaism* 21 (1972) 313–27.
———. *The Idea of Purity in Ancient Judaism* (1973).
———. *Torah* (1985).
———. *The Wonder-Working Lawyers of Talmudic Babylonia* (1987) = *A History of the Jews in Babylonia* (1966) 2.251–87; (1968) 3.95–194; (1969) 4.179–402; (1970) 5.244–342.
Patai, R. *Man and Temple* (1947).
Roberts, J.J.M. "Zion Tradition." *IDBSup* (1976) 985–87.
Smith, J. Z. "Sacred Persistence: Towards a Redescription of Canon." *Approaches to Ancient Judaism: Theory and Practice* (1978) 11–28.
———. *To Take Place* (1987).
Sundberg, A. C. *The Old Testament of the Early Church* (1964).

Judaism before 70 was temple-centered, a characteristic of Israelite religion since the time of the monarchy. For close to a millennium or more, the heart of Israelite religious practice resided in the cult in Jerusalem. Even for those in the Diaspora, the ideal was to make a yearly pilgrimage to participate in the cult at one of the major festivals, such as Passover or Sukkot (cf. Tob 1:6-8). This was not all there was to Judaism by any means, whether in or outside Palestine, but all the other aspects were only branches and twigs. The foliage might at times seem to overwhelm the tree, but the trunk was always there, the vital support for the rest. The essential place of the temple is demonstrated by the extreme reaction to its pollution in the time of the Maccabees so that the goal of its restoration was the immediate cause of the Maccabean revolt.

The destruction of the First Temple in 587/586 B.C.E. was a traumatic event that jolted Israelite thinking and theology in a way never done before. There had been those under the influence of the "Zion tradition" who assumed that God would never allow foreigners to desecrate his sanctuary (cf. Roberts). But the destruction of the First Temple did not change the basic religious outlook; the temple was still much needed and desired. One of the first objectives of those who returned from captivity in Babylon was to rebuild the temple (Haggai; Ezra 1–6). A basic continuum in practice and ideology united the First and Second temples, but some important differences existed on a subtle level. One major difference was the lack of a monarch. The place of the king in the service of the First Temple has been much debated (e.g., the theory of an annual new year festival involving the reenthronement of the king) and is beyond our purpose; however, it seems clear that the king was an important component of the cultic service.

This changed with the Second Temple. In spite of hope in some sections of the community, the kingship was not restored. The high priest became the chief theological figurehead, a responsibility which was generally combined with the position of de facto head of state. Thus some of the aspects of the monarchy were absorbed by the priesthood; eventually, this led to the Hasmonean position of the high priest also taking on the office of king.

The importance of the temple in the regular practice of religion is frequently overlooked in modern writings, in part because of the bias against ritual in general and blood sacrifice in particular. There has been a tendency to concentrate on those institutions parallel to present-day forms of worship: prayer, hymns and other liturgical features, preaching, synagogues. There are two dangers in this: on the one hand, it fails to give a true description of the historical worship and what it meant to worshiping Jews of the time; on the other hand, it can lead to a misconstrual of actual practice by emphasizing elements important today, rather than at the time. For example, scholars have often focused on the synagogue as the center of worship in first-century Judea. This appears to be a mistake because the synagogue as an institution came late to Judea itself and was not the primary outlet for worship before 70 (see below).

In the New Testament, Jesus' parents are depicted as going to Jerusalem for the Passover on a regular basis (Luke 2:41). According to the Gospel of John, Jesus himself often went to Jerusalem and the temple for annual festivals, although evidently not on every occasion (2:23; 5:1; 7:2-11; 10:22). And according to Acts, the early church began its teaching at the temple and continued to see it as important, some members allegedly even taking vows that could be fulfilled only with particular ceremonies in the cult (Acts 18:18; 21:23).

The precise form of the regular temple cult cannot be reconstructed with certainty. The one thing we do know is that animal and other forms of sacrifice at the altar was the central activity. Priests were butchers. Their job was to slay animals efficiently and commit parts or all of them to the roaring flames of an altar that stood five meters high and measured about ten-by-ten meters. Wine and bread were also offered on the altar. Like all things sacred, however, it was not the activity itself that was holy but the meaning invested in it. The temple site was holy because it had been declared holy, not because of some innate quality (Smith 1987: 22–23). Slaughter of bulls, sheep, and goats was sacred in the temple because this was what God had commanded. The sacrifice was *ex opera operato*—the action itself had been vested with sacral meaning by age-old tradition, and performing the sacrifice was a holy and efficacious act in and of itself. The offering of a sin offering resulted in the forgiveness of sin (Lev 4:26, 31, 35; 5:10, 13, 16, 18, etc.). Guilt was removed, the proper relationship with God reestablished, and the cosmic balance correctly realigned.

Unfortunately, Protestant polemic has obscured these basic facts with such sobriquets as "empty ritual" or "meaningless form" or "legal instead of ethical." Such a prejudiced view fails to recognize that the mundane physical acts of the daily temple cult were invested with deep symbolic meaning (cf. *Neusner [1988] whose general points apply to the temple cult as well as to early rabbinic Judaism). This meaning is not usually discussed in ritual texts, which focus on the correct performance of the ritual, however, and we are often left to guess at the meaning that the worshiper saw in the acts. We gain some idea of the cosmic, mythical significance of the temple and its worship from various hints in early texts and rather more detail in later texts (cf. Patai; Lundquist 1983; Lundquist 1984). Doubtless, however, both priests and worshipers would have stood aghast at the thought that the sacrifice itself could be jettisoned once one appreciated its spiritual meaning. On the contrary, loss of the daily offering of flesh and blood to God was an event that shook heaven and earth to their foundations and heralded the eschaton itself, according to a contemporary witness (Daniel 7–12).

The liturgy was not limited to sacrifice but included prayers and singing, although the exact place of these in the cult is uncertain. According to the *Letter of Aristeas,* the sacrifices were performed in silence (95), yet we also know that singers were an important part of the temple personnel (2.4.5). Prayers and hymns may have been a part of the sacrificial ritual, but they could just as well have occupied another part of the regular worship. The worshiper approached the sacred site with reverence, in a state of cultic purity. Although the issue of ritual purity or pollution probably had a long history in the life of Israel, during the Second Temple period it seems to have concerned primarily the temple itself (Neusner 1973). Priests had to be cultically pure to carry out their duties; likewise, the Israelites who came to worship had to be in a state of cultic purity. One may debate the origins of such regulations (cf. Douglas; also her contribution to Neusner 1973: 137–41), but they were deemed vital for proper veneration of the deity. Nevertheless, most regarded the regulations as being necessary only for the temple itself. Only some sects insisted on cultic purity for the eating of common meals outside the temple as well as the sacral meals within.

This does not mean that the Jerusalem cult was universally revered, to the exclusion of any other. At least, some groups regarded it and the current priesthood as polluted (e.g., the Essenes [8.2.5.4.1]). A temple flourished at Leontopolis in Egypt (5.3.8), as did a cult, if not a temple, on Mount Gerizim (8.2.10). It also seems that, in some circles, the idea of a "temple made with hands" was already being questioned or even rejected. *Sibylline Oracle* 4 is one of the few examples—if not the sole one—of a total rejection of the temple in a Jewish source (9.2.3.2). More problematic is Stephen's speech in Acts 7, which castigates a physical, earthly temple. Stephen's tirade is found in a post-70 Christian source and is therefore suspect; nevertheless, it has parallels with *Sibylline Oracle* 4 and may represent the ideas of an early Jewish or related group.

Despite these exceptions (which are few enough to prove the rule), the temple at Jerusalem served as the center of Judaism, and to reject it was usually a sign of having moved beyond the pale. Despite the rejection of the temple by such individuals as Stephen—and it is not clear that he represented any Jewish faction—and the fact that Christians theoretically no longer stood in need of the physical temple, one would gather that the decisive break between Jews and Christians came about only with the temple's destruction in 70, if not even much later.

For example, the real difference between the Samaritans and Jews was in how each regarded the temples at Gerizim and Jerusalem; otherwise, the differences in actual practice were no greater than within Judaism itself. The loss of the temple was a major crisis for Judaism as a whole, as is evidenced by such writings as the Apocalypses of Ezra and Baruch (9.2.3.1). Even though there was probably hope of its rebuilding, as had happened in the case of the First Temple, the passage of even a few decades was the cause of tremendous soul-searching about matters of theodicy. Some Jewish groups had the potential for replacing the temple as their theological center: the Christians, the Pharisees, and the scribes (Neusner 1972). The Christians had early on reached the position of considering the physical temple unnecessary, an important step in separating from Judaism proper. The Pharisees were apparently attempting to replicate the temple environment in their own homes, with their hearth as a model of the altar; the actual temple was superfluous to this practice. The activities of the scribes were focused on the written word of God. Study and exegesis could continue apart from the physical cult and the buildings that housed it.

To what extent synagogues played a part in weekly Sabbath worship away from the temple remains a question. The reason is that synagogues, although an institution of Diaspora Judaism from at least the middle of the third century B.C.E., were a late development in Palestine itself—post-Maccabean, from the data currently available (Grabbe 1988; Flesher). Although it has been accepted by many that pre-70 synagogues have been found during the excavations of Herodium, Gamla, Masada, and perhaps one or two other places (Forster), this has also been queried (Chiat 1981; 1982: 116–18, 204–7, 248–51, 282–84). There was definitely a synagogue in Caesarea (*War* 2.14.4 §285), as well as in Tiberias (*Life* 54 §277). The Theodotus inscription is a Greek text about the establishment of a synagogue for purposes of learning the law and providing hospitality to travelers (Hüttenmeister/Reeg: 192–94). Although it was not discovered in its original architectural context, it has generally been accepted as coming from the synagogue itself and being pre-70 in origin.

Although no conclusion can be certain, these data all suggest that the number of synagogues in Palestine before 70 was rather limited, and the size of those that existed was insufficient to take more than a fraction of the local population. The Theodotus inscription indicates that at least some were private foundations (see also Luke 7:1-5). Thus the synagogue may have served as the religious center for some, but whether for any more than a small minority seems doubtful. Any sort of central hierarchy over synagogues as a whole is even more unlikely for this period. The ruler(s) of individual synagogues could probably keep out those whom they did not like, but the picture of excommunication from all the synagogues, as given in John 9:13-34, is probably anachronistic, based on later church or synagogue practice (Brown: 1.380). Furthermore, the idea that synagogues were usually controlled by the Pharisees is a modern scholarly myth, in no way supported by the sources (Grabbe 1988: 408).

Long before the destruction of the temple, the Jews were also a "people of the book." Not much needs to be said about this subject here because so much scholarly writing has focused on it rather than on the centrality of the temple cult. The Bible was an important component of Judaism throughout the Second Temple period. This was the case in the Diaspora because the temple and priesthood were not readily accessible; but many of the writings which probably originated in Palestine also show the importance of the Old Testament tradition on the continuing practice of religion.

We must be careful about thinking in terms of a closed canon before 70, because emphasis on the tradition does not always indicate a use of the precise form of the text found in the MT. Not only was the text of most books available in more than one version, but precisely which books were authoritative was by no means agreed (Sundberg; contra Beckwith). All known Jewish groups accepted the Pentateuch. Large sections of the Prophets and Writings also seem to have been regarded by much of Judaism as having some measure of religious weight. At this point, however, one must recognize enormous diversity of outlook. Although Philo quotes from various parts of the Old Testament, this is infrequent, and his concentration is on the Pentateuch. Even if the Samaritans used a form of Joshua, only the Pentateuch was really canonical for them. Qumran, in contrast, apparently invested a variety of books with authority, books not generally accepted by other sections of Judaism (e.g., Jubilees and *1 Enoch*). The many apocalyptic and other pseudepigraphic writings were probably taken as divine revelation by many Jews, although the extent of this is difficult to estimate because the precise social context of the writings is not known in most cases (Davies; Grabbe 1989).

The Jewish people as a whole during this period were familiar with many of the Old Testament traditions. To what extent the actual text was read by the average Jew is uncertain. The signatures of witnesses in preserved legal documents show that many Jews were illiterate (although they do not indicate that women were less literate than men [cf. *Goodman 1983: 72]), but knowledge of the basic contents of the Bible could have come through a variety of modes other than direct reading. Synagogue public reading (to the extent that it existed) would have been one such means. Some individuals and groups made study of the text a religious duty, and this resulted in the production of commentaries and other works which heavily depended on or reworked the biblical text (cf. 1QS 6.6–8 and the Qumran pĕšārîm). It would be a mistake, however, to take the later rabbinic ideal of the Torah scholar as characteristic of Judaism before 70. It was not even a correct description of Judaism in the talmudic period, much less earlier (Neusner 1987: 1–37; *Goodman 1983: 93–118).

Even though the canon for most groups seems to have been somewhat fluid, by the first century certain books seem to have been in practically all canons, whereas others were widely accepted, even if not by everyone. This has crucial implications for the use of Scripture. It seems that a feature of being human is to restrict oneself to a particular area of concern, then to create great diversity within this restriction by ingenuity (Smith 1978). So it is with a canonized or semicanonized sacred literature. There were at least four different ways of interpreting and using the holy books within the different forms of Judaism:

1. The simplest is as a source of information for the cult, festival observance, purity regulations, theological concepts, religious ideals. It would be expected that God's revelation generally included such vital information. However, it is often assumed that this was the primary function of Scripture—as a source of information. In fact, other purposes were often more important to the individual person or group.

2. A justification or authorization for beliefs and practices which arose from quite other sources. To take the example of the Mishnah, much of its contents either did not arise from the Old Testament, even though it is often parallel, or is related to Pentateuchal regulations only tangentially (*Neusner 1981). Nevertheless, the authors of the Tannaitic Midrashim were concerned that these teachings be seen as exegeses of Scripture, and they arranged the material as commentary rather than as an autonomous legal collection, as in the Mishnah. Another example is the Christian apostle Paul. The book of 1 Corinthians represents an example of how personal rulings about a particular situation (that in the Corinthian church) are justified by appeal to the Old Testament writings. Paul did not say that he was studying his Bible one day and noticed a couple of things which he wished to share with the brothers and sisters at Corinth. On the contrary, he reacted with considerable emotion to the state of the church as he saw it, and he proceeded to set them straight in no uncertain terms. As justification for his commands, he referred to particular biblical passages; however, his exegesis is plainly post hoc. He was seeking biblical authority for decisions which he thought were right for quite other reasons.

It is in this light that many of the so-called exegetical rules are to be seen. That is, much of ancient exegesis was not an attempt to understand the text in its own right. On the contrary, the "rules" served to bridge the gap between teachings that were considered (or desired to be) authoritative and the sacred text. Therefore, Philo, as a Middle Platonist, would hardly accept that his views about the soul and the Logos were mere borrowings from Greek philosophy; instead, he exercised great ingenuity in finding all the different elements in the text of the LXX (7.2.2). Various rules or devices can be extrapolated from his activity, but it would be erroneous to take these as a neutral attempt to understand the text. He understood the text before he started.

A related idea is found at Qumran. Again, certain exegetical techniques can be extracted from the commentaries and other writings, but the ultimate source of understanding was evidently thought to have been direct inspiration from God. As is stated in 1QpHab 7:1–5: "God told Habakkuk to write down that which would happen to the final generation, but He did not make known to him when time would come to an end. . . . [It is] the Teacher of Righteousness, to whom God made known all the mysteries of the words of His servants the Prophets" (Vermes' translation [5.2.6]). The prophets wrote but did not understand; God who inspired the prophets to write now inspired the Teacher with the correct understanding of the prophecies.

3. A "magical" function (Neusner 1987; *Lightstone 1984; *Lightstone 1988). The words of the Bible were not a means of communication but of efficacy. They would "do" things if properly employed. They could be used as amulets or the like.

4. Adding to the canon. This may seem to be a misnomer because "canon" implies restriction. Nevertheless, various groups emerging in Judaism found the means of overcoming the constraints of the Old Testament canon by adding to it. Christians added what they called the New Testament; rabbinic Judaism created its own "new testament" in the talmudic literature (even if never officially canonical). It is uncertain how other groups regarded the canon of Scripture, but there is reason to think that the Qumran community regarded some of their own sectarian and other writings on the same level as many of the Old Testament books.

In sum, the religious life of pre-70 Jews in Palestine was dominated by the priesthood and the cult. Apart from the Romans and the Herodian dynasty (when Herodian rulers were actually over Judea proper), the chief civil—as well as religious—authority was the priesthood. This does not mean that all those of priestly descent exercised this authority, but the civil institutions below emperor and king were dominated by the priesthood, especially the "chief priests" (*archiereis*). The Sanhedrin was the supreme governing and judicial body, composed of both priests and nonpriests but with the high priest at its head (7.3.2.3). Beyond this there was no central religious authority. The only religious issues likely to be brought before the Sanhedrin, however, were such serious matters as blasphemy or perhaps desecration of the temple (cf. Josephus, *Ant.* 20.9.1 §§199–200, in which James the brother of Jesus was tried and executed). That this happened very often is highly unlikely, given that only one or two actual examples are found in the sources. The Sanhedrin also determined the calendar, which was essential for religious observance and reckoned by the observation of the new moon each month (cf. *m. Rosh ha-Shan.* 1.7, which mentions that witnesses reported to the priests). Otherwise, the people were basically free to choose their religious observances, and the opportunities for the development of sects were readily available.

8.3.4 Sects and Teachers

Rhoads, D. M. *Israel in Revolution: 6–74 C.E.* (1976).

There were many different teachers, sects, movements, and tendencies within society. Some sought a public means of propagating their message and attracting followers. Others withdrew and lived apart from society at large. Still others lived within society but primarily in enclaves, thus maintaining separateness while not withdrawing altogether. Some teachers remained primarily lone individuals, whereas others built a following which eventually formed a sect or movement. Religion was in a constant state of flux: teachers rose up and disappeared; sects began, flourished, withered, and died; small beginnings led to large followings—or to nothing; some movements were peaceful, others, revolutionary, still others potentially revolutionary. Those that caught the eye of the Romans were viewed through narrowed lids, and the slightest hint of sedition could lead to a severe crackdown. Single men and entire groups came and went without leaving a mark in history; at least, the few that we know about lead us to guess at those who once existed but have left no trace.

The advantage of being a sect (on the term, see 8.1) was that it gave autonomy. A sect could regulate its own affairs according to its lights: matters of internal regulation, halakah, initiation, and excommunication were sectarian. If Essenes wanted to accept members only after a three-year initiation period and expel members for apparently small infractions, then that was their business. A Pharisee could pronounce anathema on ex-Pharisees, but it would mean something only to other Pharisees and perhaps not even to all of them. Questions such as ordination, authorization to teach, and excommunication, which some associate with a national or established church, simply did not arise. The one example we have of an alleged religious attempt to suppress dissidents required the authority of the high priest (and, by implication, the Sanhedrin), not Pharisees or other sectarians (Acts 9:1-2). Even this attempt is suspect, however, because the high priest of Jerusalem would have no powers to authorize the arrest of citizens of Damascus, which was not even under Judean jurisdiction. The one New Testament account of excommunication from the synagogues is equally unlikely (John 9; see further at 8.3.3).

The Pharisees (8.2.2) were probably the largest single group and were evidently influential, when their size is taken into account. But there were only six thousand of them in the time of Herod (*Ant.* 17.2.4 §42), hardly an overwhelming percentage of the population. Besides, how do we measure influence? Today many religious leaders and even ordinary clergy are "influential," that is, they are looked up to and respected, but this does not suggest that the majority of the population orders its life by their views. The influence of the Pharisees does not seem to have gone far in concrete terms. They have often been described in almost Marxist terms: a lay group of the common people (proletariat?), as opposed to the upper-crust, wealthy Sadducees (capitalists?). In contrast, the actual Pharisees named in Josephus seem to come from various strata of society. A delegation sent by the Sanhedrin during the war with Rome was composed of three Pharisees, two from the lower ranks and one a priest, plus another priest from the high priest's family, who is not said to belong to any party (*Life* 39 §§196–98). Therefore, although many Pharisees may have been poor and "laymen," this is hardly a complete description of them. Josephus seems to have joined them in some sense at some point (although probably not at age nineteen, as he alleges), and he was not a poor peasant. We have too few data to make categorical socioeconomic judgments concerning the Pharisees.

Indeed, one of the main problems in scholarly study has been to ignore the absence of data and to read the Pharisees in wherever one feels like it. Not untypical of scholars in this regard is a particular example found in what is often a careful study by Rhoads (91–92). After noting, "There is little direct evidence [i.e., no evidence!] for the involvement of Pharisees in resistance against Rome in this period," he then goes on for a page or so about how the Pharisees are "likely" to have been involved in an episode or were "probably" participants in another—all without a scrap of data. Similarly, there are the figures of Judas and Matthias, who removed the image of an eagle which Herod had placed over the entrance to the temple (6.4.9.4). They are frequently identified as Pharisees (e.g., Rhoads: 37), again without the slightest reason. Even in *Antiquities*, where Josephus tends to expand the activities of the Pharisees, he gives no hint that Judas and Matthias were Pharisees (*War* 1.33.2–4 §§648–55; *Ant.* 17.6.2–4 §§149–64).

Rabbinic literature puts special emphasis on Hillel and Shammai and their disciples (the Houses) before 70. One would gather that most Pharisees must have belonged to one or the other; however, there is also the indication that a considerable portion of the Houses of Hillel and Shammai could all meet in one reasonably sized room, suggesting that they numbered in the dozens, not in the hundreds or thousands. Although the later rabbinic tradition has constructed a chain of descent, in which the major pre-70 figures succeed one another in the office of the patriarch (*nāśî'*), this is most likely an anachronism because the office did not exist before the late second century (^Goodman 1983: 111–18). Neusner has found no evidence that Gamaliel (I) or his son Simon (b. Gamaliel) had any relationship to Hillel, much less succeeded him as patriarch (8.2.2.3; 8.2.2.4). Therefore, evidence exists for a variety of Pharisaic teachers, each with his own band of disciples, rather than for a tightly knit organization or authoritarian hierarchy. There is even the possibility that Hillel and Shammai were not very important in their own time and dominate the tradition only because their houses happened to have become dominant at Yavneh, with the House of Hillel eventually winning out. In any event, the tradition does indicate that the House of Shammai was actually more influential before 70 than that of Hillel (8.2.2.3).

The teachings of Pharisees were primarily for other Pharisees, although doubtless they would be pleased if non-Pharisees also listened. They did not generally expect others to follow them, because the sources do not preserve discussions about matters outside the sect. Their traditions, which can be demonstrated to be pre-70, concern only internal matters, including regulations and rulings about purity, marriage, agriculture, eating, festivals, and personal worship. There are no civil laws, questions of government, or regulations for running and maintaining the temple cult. The Pharisees had no control over such things, at least as Pharisees, so they had no need to discuss them. When the situation changed and such matters came into their power of jurisdiction (even if only theoretically; e.g., the regulation of the temple), they proceeded to thrash them out.

Before 70, however, there was no need or opportunity to do so. A Pharisaic priest conducted himself in the temple according to priestly regulations, even if in his own home he lived by Pharisaic rules. Despite a few statements to the effect that the people looked to the Pharisees for guidance (8.2.2.1), there is no evidence that this happened in practice. The rabbis of the second century complained that the *ammei ha-aretz* did not listen to them (*Goodman 1983: 102–4). Why should the people of the first century have been any different?

Not much smaller in number than the Pharisees were the Essenes (8.2.5), numbering four thousand in the time of Herod, according to Josephus and Philo. Accepting the consensus that Qumran was an Essene community, one might think it likely that the site also served as an organizational and spiritual center of the movement; however, some see Qumran as only a split from or breakaway movement within Essenism. Whatever is correct, Qumran could by no means accommodate several thousand adherents as permanent residents. Rather, the bulk of the Essenes lived all over Palestine in local towns and villages, according to both Josephus and Philo. They were evidently one of the groups which lived in society for the most part but were not of it. Even in the local communities they apparently had their own enclaves or communes, organized along communistic lines. They would work in the community but put their earnings in the common fund. There may have been periodic pilgrimages to Qumran for festivals, but the relationship of the Qumran community to the rest of the Essene movement is by no means established. Although, from extant knowledge, the beliefs and organization of the order appear to be fairly rigid, we still should probably not think of absolute unity but consider some differences within the movement and perhaps even subsects. Many think that Philo's Therapeutae (8.2.6) represent a local Essene group in Egypt. We also know of Essenes who were apparently known to the public, such as Judas, who had a reputation for prophecy, and John, who was one of the military leaders in the war against Rome. Therefore, the Essenes, despite an exclusivistic approach to religion, were apparently well known to the wider community and were not an unknown fringe group as they are sometimes pictured.

The number of Sadducees (8.2.3) is nowhere given, although Josephus indicates that the group was smaller than either the Pharisees or Essenes. Whether or not the image of the Sadducees as a party of the aristocrats is fully justified, it does seem that some of the most prominent of the priests and national leaders belonged to the party. Although it presumably was not composed exclusively of priests and not all priests belonged to it, it seems to have been dominated by priests, especially the high priest and other leading members in the hierocracy. The handful of beliefs that antiquity has preserved under the name "Sadducean" for the most part represent priestly belief and practice (e.g., the question of how to reckon Pentecost).

The Herodians (8.2.9) were evidently not really a religious sect but were either the followers of or, more likely, members of the household of Herod. If either of these is the case, then reference to the Herodians in the Gospels is probably anachronistic because they would not have been on the scene except when a Herodian ruler was in Jerusalem, which was the case only under Herod the Great (to 4 B.C.E.), Archelaus (until 6 C.E.), and Agrippa I (41–44 C.E.). During Jesus' ministry there would not have been any "Herodians" about, certainly not in Jerusalem, if this interpretation is correct.

The "movement" founded by Judas the Galilean (Josephus's Fourth Philosophy) may not have been a movement as such but a sort of family tradition (8.2.8). If it was a movement, it seems not to have been particularly active for the first half century C.E. In about 50 C.E., however, a terrorist organization (or, more likely, "organizations") sprang to life to fight against Roman rule by targeting "collaborator" Jews of the ruling class, who were seen as the most compromised in doing the Romans' bidding. These Sicarii (as they came to be called) originated with Judas the Galilean, according to Josephus, but this seems only a surmise on Josephus's part. In any case, they continued their activities until the actual revolt was underway but then withdrew from the fighting after the assassination of their leader in Jerusalem. Although Josephus gives little direct information, he hints that they were inspired by messianic and perhaps even eschatological beliefs. The Jerusalem leader Menahem seems to have declared himself king or was building to the point of doing so when he and many followers were killed by the Zealots.

The Zealots proper (8.2.7)—despite the frequent use and abuse of the term to denote any anti-Roman group from the time of the Maccabees—originated in about 68 from the coalescense of several "bandit" groups into a popular revolt in the path of the invading Roman army. Social banditry was a frequent response to the socioeconomic stresses and oppressions of the time, as it is in many societies of various periods. Although bandit groups were often short-lived, they were a continuing phenomenon at intermittent periods, if not all along. We are especially informed of such appearing in the early Roman period and in the two decades before the First Revolt. Social banditry is usually just an attempt to survive in difficult circumstances and does not necessarily imply any intent to start a widespread revolt, but such occasionally develops when conditions become oppressive enough and large numbers take to the practice. Social banditry reached such proportions that the Roman invasion acted as the catalyst for a popular revolt, which in turn served to bring the Zealots into being. They were evidently inspired by popular eschatological views, which kept them going in the face of the imminent Roman victory. Even as the Roman armies were breaking down the last defenses, six thousand people poured into the temple court to await God's deliverance (Josephus, *War* 6.5.2 §§283–87).

These major sects and movements were only part of the socioreligious picture, however, because the individual teacher, miracle-worker, and prophet were evidently as ubiquitous in Palestine then as the soapbox is in Hyde Park today. Some prophets succeeded in acquiring a large following for a short time, but because large followings equaled sedition to the Roman police, the larger the following the shorter the life, as a general rule. Whether or not some of the prophets we know of were genuinely attempting to start a revolt, the Romans were not too interested in precise inquiries and quickly executed the shepherd and scattered the flock in most cases. One alleged miracle-worker, Theudas, gathered a group which he promised to take across the Jordan dry-shod; his miraculous powers were never tested (or perhaps they were) because Fadus's soldiers intervened (Josephus, *Ant.* 20.5.1 §§97–99; Acts 5:36). A number of other prophets and popular leaders are referred to for the last decade or so before the revolt, such as an Egyptian Jew who evidently intended to take direct action against the Romans, again without success (Josephus, *War* 2.13.4–6 §§258–65; *Ant.* 20.8.6 §§167–72; Acts 21:38).

Individual teachers are mentioned a number of times by Josephus (8.2.14). For example, there was an Onias noted for his ability to make rain at the time that the Romans extended their hegemony over Palestine. Another, named Judas, was known as a prophet during the reign of Aristobulus I. Judas was an Essene, and other individual Essenes were known for their ability to predict the future, such as Manaemus and Simon (8.2.5.5). The two individuals Judas and Matthias, who showed their zeal for God by removing the eagle that Herod had erected (see above), apparently had some disciples, although we are not told precisely how many, but the figure "forty" in the narrative may indicate dozens, even if it is only a round figure.

Although the data are skimpy, there are tantalizing hints of the existence of other spiritual trends and groups. John the Baptist was not an isolated individual, as the Gospels might imply, but only one of a number of baptismal movements that connected physical washing of one sort or another with spiritual purity and salvation (8.2.11). There is some evidence that the Jordan Valley, with its readily available supply of running water, was the home of several such groups, and one of these is thought by many to exist still in the small sect of the Mandeans. The issue of origin and history is a complicated one, as are others concerning Jewish Gnosticism and mysticism. Mystical trends are found early in apocalyptic writings, with their speculations on the mysteries of the heavens and God's universal plan for the earth. It is only a matter of emphasis. Some apocalypses focus on the culmination of world history and the events of the end-time, but others, similar to later *merkavah* mysticism, seem to concentrate more on the geography of the heavens and the vision of God's throne. For one who can gain direct access to the divine vision, issues of eschatology might seem somewhat inconsequential.

Gnosticism (8.2.13) has usually been taken as anti-Old Testament and, consequently, anti-Jewish. This may be a correct assessment of Gnosticism in its developed form but still does not answer the question of whether Gnosticism may not have had a home in Judaism. The tendency of "two powers in heaven" is strong in the wisdom tradition, with its speculation about Wisdom (*sōphia*) and Word (*logos*). Philo, the Wisdom of Solomon, and even such earlier writings as Proverbs 8 can be used to argue that particular developed features of Gnosticism were known in incipient form in Judaism. There is almost universal agreement that a number of features of the gnostic mythology have come from Judaism by some path or other, even if there was never anything which could be labeled "Jewish Gnosticism." Nevertheless, a number of scholars have long argued that Gnosticism grew out of "heterodox" Judaism. The terminology is problematic, as noted in 8.3.1, and one might ask whether a full Gnostic would not have gone beyond the pale in the eyes of most Jews. The question is one of academics, however, not apologetics. Gnosticism could have sprung up within Judaism even if it eventually separated from it, which is also the conclusion of many gnostic specialists.

The matter is still in current debate. It does seem to be established that non-Christian gnostic texts exist, and a good case has been made for non-Christian Gnosticism. That is not quite the same as establishing the existence of pre-Christian or Jewish Gnosticism, but for many the circumstantial evidence is strong enough to warrant such a hypothesis. Even if such Gnosticism did not exist in the sense of later gnostic groups, at least gnostic trends can be documented from Jewish texts, many of them probably or certainly pre-Christian.

A description of Judaism in the first century must take account of all these trends and teachers, of the kaleidoscopic nature of the overall religious scene. It must also assess the extent to which the average Jew was affected by them, and the state of religious practice in the population as a whole. Most Jews were not Gnostics, mystics, magicians, revolutionaries. Neither were they Pharisees. Later rabbinic literature—at a time when Judaism was much more monolithic—makes it clear that the average Jew was an *am ha-aretz*, one who could not be trusted to practice the strict laws of agriculture and purity laid down by rabbinic law (*Smith 1956: 73–74; *Goodman 1983: 102–4). So much the more before 70. The average Jewish man and woman had such important things on their minds as keeping body and soul together (assuming they believed in a soul). For the peasant farmer, life was generally hard, and good years were offset by years of droughts and famine, as well as heavy taxation. Tithing mint and cumin was probably not the first priority in life.

8.3.5   Messiahs, "Bandits," and Eschatology

Cavallin, H.C.C. *Life after Death* (1974).
Fischer, U. *Eschatologie und Jenseitserwartung im hellenistischen Diasporajudentum* (1978).
Neusner, J. *Messiah in Context* (1984).
Neusner, J., W. S. Green, and E. S. Frerichs, eds. *Judaisms and Their Messiahs at the Turn of the Christian Era* (1987).
Nickelsburg, G.W.E. *Resurrection, Immortality, and Eternal Life in Intertestamental Judaism* (1972).
Schiffman, L. H. *The Eschatological Community of the Dead Sea Scrolls: A Study of the Rule of Congregation* (1989).
Trump, S., ed. *Millennial Dreams in Action* (1962).

Eschatological expectations played an important role in the lives of many Jews, but not in the lives of many other Jews. Beliefs in this area were as complex and diverse as in any other aspect of Judaism of this time. Not all Jews expected a messiah; not all Jews looked forward to an eschatological event; and not all those Jews who entertained both ideas allowed it to affect their lives in any way.

The messianic idea probably owes its origins to the monarchy of ancient Israel. As particular Israelites despaired of the current king or, after 587/586, of the lack of a king, hope began to be placed in a future, idealized figure, modeled on David (whose picture in Samuel and Kings is also idealized). But the form these expectations and speculations took was by no means uniform. Many looked forward to a human king—a larger-than-life king, perhaps, but a human figure, nevertheless (*PssSol* 2; 17–18). The majority of those who looked for a messiah probably thought along these lines. There were others, however, who seem to have thought of a heavenly figure (11QMelch; perhaps 4 Ezra 13). Alongside this diversity within messianic speculation was a similar assortment of views on eschatology. Some Jews, in line with much of the Old Testament, saw death as the end of the individual. Others believed in a resurrection of the body, the spirit, or perhaps both. This could be combined with a cosmic eschatology, in which the world came to a catastrophic end or gradually slipped over into the "Messianic Age" with a minimum of trauma.

A proper survey of the different opinions would take a good deal of space and has already been done, at least in part (Neusner/Green/ Frerichs; Neusner; Cavallin; Schiffman; cf. Schürer: 2.488–554). The conclusion to be drawn is that no consistent idea of eschatology or messianism can be invoked wherever convenient to explain incidents, movements, or ideology. Both concepts could be powerful ideological forces at times, as has already been noted in several of the groups surveyed. Each case, however, must be critically examined on its own merits. There was no "Jewish view" on any of these subjects, although there were plenty of Jews with views.

Perhaps less important than the different individual beliefs about eschatology are the consequences of such beliefs. What did they lead the believer to do? Here there is not always a one-to-one correspondence between ideology and action; nor is the action undertaken necessarily motivated by religious ideology. In a number of cases the response has nonreligious causes, whether or not the actor uses religious arguments to justify it. The potential outcomes are three:

1. Quietism. If one believed in an eschatology in which all was done by God (or even if one had no belief in eschatology), the person might well do nothing overtly. Such individuals did see themselves as being very busy in the service of the Lord: prayer, temple worship, service to others, and good deeds of all sorts. In some cases this might even lead to martyrdom, in which the individual saw the shedding of innocent blood as the catalyst for God to take a direct hand in human affairs. The outward activity for such people was basically no different from that of people with no belief in eschatology. The majority of Jews generally fell into this grouping.
2. Peaceful political activity. Although the ruling class participated in the 66–70 revolt, it seems clear from Josephus that many of them did so reluctantly (7.4.11.3). They were more at home with cooperation and compromise with their ultimate rulers. Armed revolt was not to Roman advantage, and with skillful diplomacy much could be gained by combining willingness to help and defuse troublesome situations with heavily veiled demands for concessions. On other occasions, passive resistance proved quite useful (7.3.6; 7.4.3). In the face of growing fanaticism and moral failure on the part of the leading classes, this resistance eventually broke down, but there

were times it proved effective. It should be noted that religious ideology need not be—and probably usually was not—involved in this sort of response.

3. Armed resistance and revolt. The sources tell us that in some cases refusal to accept Roman rule was tied up specifically with beliefs about God's rule. Nevertheless, one did not have to believe in a messiah or a particular form of eschatology to revolt against the Romans. Much of the time we have no way of knowing one way or the other, but the analogy of the Middle Ages may be helpful: although there were millenarian revolts and movements at that time, revolts also took place that had no such motivation: "In the vast majority of the many hundreds of medieval peasant revolts and urban revolutions on record there is no evidence of any millennial influence" (Trump: 23). No one can say that medieval Europe made any sharper distinction between the religious and the secular than did the Jews of late antiquity.

9

EPILOGUE:
TO BAR KOKHBA
(70–135 C.E.)

9.1 BIBLIOGRAPHICAL GUIDE

Applebaum, S. *Prolegomena to the Study of the Second Jewish Revolt (A.D. 132–135)* (1976).
Cary, M., and H. H. Scullard. *A History of Rome* (1975).
Fitzmyer, J. A. "The Bar Cochba Period." *Essays on the Semitic Background of the New Testament* (1971) 305–54.
Garzetti, A. *From Tiberius to the Antonines* (1974).
Meshorer, Y. *Ancient Jewish Coinage.* Vol. 2: *Herod the Great through Bar Kokhba* (1982).
Mildenberg, L. "Bar Kokhba Coins and Documents." *HSCP* 84 (1980) 311–35.
———. *The Coinage of the Bar Kokhba War* (1984).
Schäfer, P. *Der Bar Kokhba-Aufstand* (1981).
Schürer: 1.514–57.
Smallwood, E. M. *The Jews under Roman Rule* (1981).

Both Schürer and Smallwood cover in detail the period between 70 and 135, providing relevant sources and listing secondary literature. The extent of scholarly research since both were published, however, requires that they be updated by a number of more recent studies. Because of the lack of a literary history of the period, archeology and coins are extremely important resources. Two major collections are Mildenberg (1984) and Meshorer. Mildenberg does not limit himself to the coins but goes on to discuss many other aspects of the Bar Kokhba revolt in detail.

The major study of the Bar Kokhba revolt is Schäfer, which assembles all the original sources and analyzes them in detail. Naturally, there is disagreement with some of his conclusions, but little escaped his eye before 1980. Other useful studies are Applebaum and Fitzmyer. The principal literature on the 115–117 C.E. revolts is at 9.4.8; that on the Bar Kokhba revolt, at 9.4.10.

For Roman history in general, probably the best general survey for the period is Garzetti. More general, although more up-to-date, is Cary/Scullard.

9.2 SOURCES

An important collection of the major literary sources relating to the revolt of 132–135 C.E. can be found in *Schäfer. References to the Jews in the non-Christian Greco-Roman writers are found in *GLAJJ*. On Greek and Latin writers in general, see *CHCL* and *OCD*.

9.2.1 Greco-Roman Writers

9.2.1.1 Cassius Dio

GLAJJ: 2.385–405.
Millar, F. *A Study of Cassius Dio* (1964) especially 60–72.

For a general introduction to Dio, see 5.2.13.4. Dio's history is one of the few sources to mention the 115–117 C.E. revolts, and the only source that gives any sort of description of the Bar Kokhba revolt and its results. His account of Hadrian's reign is noteworthy in that he seems to have used Hadrian's autobiography as a source. In addition, the account of the Jewish war may have come from Hadrian's own report to the Senate (Millar: 62). Although we now possess only a medieval epitome of Dio's account, there is no reason to assume that the epitomist has extensively distorted or rewritten it, only shortened it by omission. Dio's surviving reference to the revolts of 115–117 is as follows:

> Trajan therefore departed thence, and a little later began to fail in health. Meanwhile the Jews in the region of Cyrene had put a certain Andreas at their head, and were destroying both the Romans and the Greeks. They would eat the flesh of their victims, make belts for themselves of their entrails, anoint themselves with their blood and wear their skins for clothing; many they sawed in two, from the head downwards; others they gave to wild beasts, and still others they forced to fight as gladiators. In all two hundred and twenty thousand persons perished. In Egypt, too, they perpetrated many similar outrages and in Cyprus under the leadership of a certain Artemion. There, also, two hundred and forty thousand perished, and for this reason no Jew may set foot on this island, but if one of them is driven upon its shores by a storm he is put to death. Among others who subdued the Jews was Lusius, who was sent by Trajan. (68.32.1–3)

He also makes much lengthier comments about the Bar Kokhba revolt:

> At Jerusalem he founded a city in place of the one which had been razed to the ground, naming it Aelia Capitolina, and on the site of the temple of the god he raised a new temple to Jupiter. This brought on a

war of no slight importance nor of brief duration, for the Jews deemed it intolerable that foreign races should be settled in their city and foreign religious rites planted there. So long, indeed, as Hadrian was close by in Egypt and again in Syria, they remained quiet, save in so far as they purposely made of poor quality such weapons as they were called upon to furnish, in order that the Romans might reject them and that they themselves might thus have the use of them; but when he went farther away, they openly revolted. To be sure, they did not dare try conclusions with the Romans in the open field, but they occupied the advantageous positions in the country and strengthened them with mines and walls, in order that they might have places of refuge whenever they should be hard pressed, and might meet together unobserved under ground; and they pierced these subterranean passages from above at intervals to let in air and light.

At first the Romans took no account of them. Soon, however, all Judaea had been stirred up, and the Jews everywhere were showing signs of disturbance, were gathering together, and giving evidence of great hostility to the Romans, partly by secret and partly by overt acts; many outside nations, too, were joining them through eagerness for gain, and the whole earth, one might almost say, was being stirred up over the matter. Then, indeed, Hadrian sent against them his best generals. First of these was Julius Severus, who was dispatched from Britain, where he was governor, against the Jews. Severus did not venture to attack his opponents in the open at any one point, in view of their numbers and their desperation, but by intercepting small groups, thanks to the number of his soldiers and his under-officers, and by depriving them of food and shutting them up, he was able, rather slowly, to be sure, but with comparatively little danger, to crush, exhaust and exterminate them. Very few of them in fact survived. Fifty of their most important outposts and nine hundred and eighty-five of their most famous villages were razed to the ground. Five hundred and eighty thousand men were slain in the various raids and battles, and the number of those that perished by famine, disease and fire was past finding out. Thus nearly the whole of Judaea was made desolate, a result of which the people had had forewarning before the war. For the tomb of Solomon, which the Jews regard as an object of veneration, fell to pieces of itself and collapsed, and many wolves and hyenas rushed howling into their cities. Many Romans, moreover, perished in this war. Therefore Hadrian in writing to the senate did not employ the opening phrase commonly affected by the emperors, "If you and your children are in health, it is well; I and the legions are in health." (69.12.1–14.13)

9.2.1.2 *Historia Augusta*

Barnes, T. D. *The Sources of the Historia Augusta* (1978).
Momigliano, A. "An Unsolved Problem of Historical Forgery: The *Scriptores*

Historiae Augustae." Secondo contributo alla storia degli studi classici (1960)
105–43.
Syme, R. Historia Augusta Papers (1983).

Scriptores Historiae Augustae (Historia Augusta) is a collection of biographies of emperors and pretenders from Hadrian to Numerian. Some have argued it was meant as a continuation of Suetonius's Lives of the Twelve Caesars and originally contained lives of Nerva and Trajan, but if so, then these have been lost. Although the Historia Augusta claims to have been written by a variety of individuals and appears to quote many original documents, these claims are now generally rejected. The uniformity of style suggests that it was largely written by one person, although dating varies from the early fourth to the early fifth centuries. Much of the material is gossip, rumor, and invention, including the supposedly original documents now thought to be forgeries, making the work untrustworthy as a source. Nevertheless, it covers a period for which there is often little other material, although some of the biographies, especially the earlier lives (including Hadrian's), seem to be of better quality than others. Its value for Jewish history lies in its brief statements about the later Jewish revolts (Hadr. 5.2; 14.2; quoted at 9.3.2 and 9.3.3, below).

9.2.1.3 Suetonius

Suetonius gives the lives of the three Flavians: Vespasian, Titus, and Domitian. For a general introduction to Suetonius, see 6.2.4.5.

9.2.1.4 Pliny the Younger

Sherwin-White, A. N. The Letters of Pliny: A Historical and Social Commentary
(1966).

Nephew of Pliny the Elder who perished in the eruption of Vesuvius, Pliny the Younger served as legate in Bithynia-Pontus under Trajan and apparently died there in 112 c.e. His collected letters contain correspondence with Trajan and include the famous Epistles 10.96 concerning the Christians and their worship. Also preserved is his Panegyricus on Trajan, which contrasts Trajan's reign with Domitian's. Pliny is an important source for general Roman history, but he does not mention the Jews.

9.2.2 Christian Writers and Chronographers

9.2.2.1 Eusebius

Barnes, T. D. *Constantine and Eusebius* (1981).
Helm, R., ed. *Die Chronik des Hieronymus* (1956).
Karst, J. *Die Chronik aus dem Armenischen übersetzt* (1911).
Mosshammer, A. A. *The Chronicle of Eusebius and Greek Chronographic Tradition* (1979).

Because there is so little information on the revolts after 70, the simple statements in the later chronographers are of greater significance than they are for earlier periods. The best and most reliable source is Eusebius, specifically his comments in both his *Chronicle* and his *Ecclesiastical History*. Two versions of the *Chronicle* have been preserved, one in the Latin translation and revision by Jerome (Helm) and the other in Armenian translation, generally cited according to the German translation of Karst. In *Ecclesiastical History* (conveniently available in LCL) he writes about the Jewish revolts of 115–117:

> In the course of the eighteenth year of the reign of the Emperor [Trajan] a rebellion of the Jews again broke out and destroyed a great multitude of them. For both in Alexandria and in the rest of Egypt and especially in Cyrene, as though they had been seized by some terrible spirit of rebellion, they rushed into sedition against their Greek fellow citizens, and increasing the scope of the rebellion in the following year started a great war while Lupus was governor of all Egypt. In the first engagement they happened to overcome the Greeks, who fled to Alexandria and captured and killed the Jews in the city, but though thus losing the help of the townsmen, the Jews of Cyrene continued to plunder the country of Egypt and to ravage the districts in it under their leader Lucuas. The Emperor sent against them Marcius Turbo with land and sea forces including cavalry. He waged war vigorously against them in many battles for a considerable time and killed many thousands of Jews, not only those of Cyrene but also those of Egypt who had rallied to Lucuas, their king. The emperor suspected that the Jews of Mesopotamia would also attack the inhabitants and ordered Lusius Quietus to clean them out of the province. He organized a force and murdered a great multitude of the Jews there, and for this reform was appointed governor of Judaea by the Emperor. (*Hist. eccl.* 4.2.1–5)

Eusebius has the following to say about the Bar Kokhba revolt:

> The rebellion of the Jews once more progressed in character and extent, and Rufus, the governor of Judaea, when military aid had been sent him by the Emperor, moved out against them, treating their madness without mercy. He destroyed in heaps thousands of men, women, and children, and, under the law of war, enslaved their land. The Jews were

at that time led by a certain Bar Chochebas, which means "star," a man who was murderous and a bandit, but relied on his name, as if dealing with slaves, and claimed to be a luminary who had come down to them from heaven and was magically enlightening those who were in misery. The war reached its height in the eighteenth year of the reign of Hadrian in Beththera, which was a strong citadel not very far from Jerusalem; the siege lasted a long time before the rebels were driven to final destruction by famine and thirst and the instigator of their madness paid the penalty he deserved. Hadrian then commanded that by a legal decree and ordinances the whole nation should be absolutely prevented from entering from thenceforth even the district round Jerusalem, so that not even from a distance could it see its ancestral home. Ariston of Pella tells the story. Thus when the city came to be bereft of the nation of the Jews, and its ancient inhabitants had completely perished, it was colonized by foreigners, and the Roman city which afterwards arose changed its name, and in honour of the reigning emperor Aelius Hadrian was called Aelia. (*Hist. eccl.* 4.6.1–4)

9.2.2.2 Orosius

Deferrari, R. J., ed. *Paulus Orosius, The Seven Books of History against the Pagans* (1964).
Zangemeister, C. *Pauli Orosii historiarum adversum paganos libri VII* (1882).

Orosius's history, *Seven Books against the Pagans*, written about 418 C.E., is useful because it has been completely preserved. Unfortunately it contains gross errors of both history and chronology along with important and useful information. The difficulty lies in sorting the errors from the accurate and unique information. For example, he quotes Josephus as saying that the expulsion of the Jews from Rome occurred in Claudius's ninth year (7.6.15–16); but no such statement is found in Josephus, and it seems unlikely that Orosius possessed a text of his works significantly different from ours. Is his statement a misinterpretation of Josephus, perhaps combined with a calculation from Acts 18:2, or does Orosius indeed have additional information?

In contrast, his statements about the revolts in 115–117 seem to be largely confirmed by archeological and other evidence. Orosius says about the 115–117 revolts:

Then, all at once, the Jews in different parts of the world, as if enraged with madness, burst forth in an incredible revolution. For throughout all Libya, they carried on most violent wars against the inhabitants, and Libya was, then, so forsaken by the killing of the cultivators of the soil that, unless Hadrian afterwards had not gathered colonists from without and brought them there, the land would have remained completely destitute and without an inhabitant. Indeed, they threw into confusion all Egypt, Cyrene, and the Thebaid with bloody seditions. But in Alexandria, in a pitched battle, they were conquered and crushed. In Mesopotamia also, when they rebelled, by order of the emperor, war was introduced against them. And thus many thousands of them were destroyed in a vast slaughter. Indeed, they did destroy Salamis, a city of Cyprus, after killing all the inhabitants. (7.12.6–8, Deferrari's translation)

He also wrote about the Bar Kokhba revolt:

Indeed, he [Hadrian] overcame the Jews in a final slaughter, who were disturbed by the disorders of their own crimes and were laying waste the province of Palestine, once their own, and thus avenging the Christians whom the Jews, under the leadership of Cochebas, were torturing because they would not join them against the Romans; and he gave orders that no Jew should be permitted to enter Jerusalem, that the city be open only to Christians; and he restored the city to high prosperity by rebuilding the walls, giving orders that it be called Aelia after his own first name. (7.13.4–5)

9.2.2.3 Other Christian Writers

The later Christian chronographers, such as John Malala(s) and the *Passover Chronicle*, are either dependent on Eusebius or not at all reliable; however, they do occasionally have useful information. For the references to the Bar Kokhba revolt in these works, see *Schäfer (especially 35, 97, 134), who discusses their value in each instance.

9.2.3 Jewish Writings

9.2.3.1 Apocalypses of Ezra and Baruch

Bogaert, P. *L'Apocalypse syriaque de Baruch* (1969).
Charles, R. H. *The Apocalypse of Baruch* (1896).
Grabbe, L. L. "Chronography in 4 Ezra and 2 Baruch." *SBLSP* (1981) 49–63.
JLBM: 287–94.
JWSTP: 408–10, 412–14.
Klijn, A.F.J. "Recent Developments in the Study of the Syriac Apocalypse of Baruch." *JSP* 4 (1989) 3–17.
Murphy, F. J. *The Structure and Meaning of Second Baruch* (1985a).
———. "*2 Baruch* and the Romans." *JBL* 104 (1985b) 663–69.
Myers, J. M. *I and II Esdras* (1974).
OTP: 1.517–59, 615–52.

Schürer: 3.294–306, 750–56
Stone, M. E. *Features of the Eschatology of IV Ezra* (1989).
————. *Fourth Ezra* (1990).

The Apocalypse of Ezra, or 4 Ezra (also sometimes referred to as 3 Ezra or 2 Esdras), is preserved in Latin and Syriac translations; the original (probably in Hebrew) is entirely lost. Fourth Ezra forms chapters 3 to 14 in the work called 2 Esdras in the Apocrypha (chaps. 1–2 are usually referred to as 5 Ezra, chaps. 15–16 as 6 Ezra). It is generally dated to about 100 C.E. because of the statement in 3:1 that Ezra had a vision in the thirtieth year after the destruction of Jerusalem. This dating is confirmed by the "eagle vision" in 4 Ezra 11–12, which seems to show the emperors to about the time of Domitian.

The Apocalypse of Baruch, or 2 Baruch, is preserved only in a Syriac translation from a lost original (presumably in Hebrew). From the number of passages which closely parallel 4 Ezra, scholars have tended to see it as dependent on 4 Ezra, but the recent commentary by Bogaert argues that the converse is true: 2 Baruch is the prior work, and 4 Ezra is dependent on it.

Regardless of which is the earlier, both works seem to represent the situation some years after the Roman destruction of Jerusalem and the Second Temple. In both books the destruction is a major theological problem, and both address the issue of theodicy. Although the books deal with a variety of questions, the most important answer is that God will shortly intervene to right matters. The victorious conqueror (the "eagle" of 4 Ezra 11–12) has not much longer to enjoy its evil gains, because God will take a hand to destroy the Roman Empire. This will commence the end-time process which will include the temporary Messianic Age and, finally, the creation of a new heaven and new earth. Indeed, Murphy (1985b) has recently argued that 2 Baruch opposes any armed struggle against Rome, preferring to leave the action to God. Other Jews of the time took a different view. One of the interesting features of 4 Ezra is its apparent attempt to calculate the time of the end (Grabbe).

9.2.3.2 The *Sibylline Oracles*

Collins, J. J. *The Sibylline Oracles of Egyptian Judaism* (1974a).
————. "The Place of the Fourth Sibyl in the Development of the Jewish Sibyllina." *JJS* 25 (1974b) 356–80.
————. *Between Athens and Jerusalem* (1986).
JLBM: 162–65 (*Sibylline Oracle* 3 only).
JWSTP: 357–81.

OTP: 1.317–472.
Schürer: 3.618–54.

The original *Sibylline Oracles* were preserved by the Romans and con-sulted in times of crisis. Only a few fragments of these have survived, but there was an active production of fake *Sibylline Oracles* in Jewish and Christian circles for their own propaganda. Most of those extant are either Christian in origin or present form (although several of the latter were created by reworking an originally Jewish composition). Three of the oracles are commonly accepted as Jewish: *Sibylline Oracles* 3, 4, and 5.

The original core of *Sibylline Oracle* 3 (vv 97–349, 489–829) was com-posed during the second century B.C.E. (Collins 1974a: 21–34; Collins 1986: 61–72). There are possible references to Antiochus IV, but the most decisive factor is the "king from the Sun" (v 652), who is also referred to as the "seventh" (vv 193, 318, 608). It is generally agreed that this refer-ence is to one of the Ptolemaic rulers, although Ptolemy VI, Ptolemy VII, and Ptolemy VIII are all candidates. Perhaps the most likely is Ptolemy VI Philometor, who had good relations with the Jews. The oracles against various nations (vv 350–488) allude to the last Cleopatra of Egypt and were therefore written after the battle of Actium (31 B.C.E.). Verses 1–96 contain a reference to Nero *redivivus*, indicating a time not long after the fall of Jerusalem in 70.

Sibylline Oracle 4 was composed in about 80 C.E. At its core is an old Hellenistic oracle, probably non-Jewish, dating from the second century B.C.E. An unusual feature of the book is its antitemple polemic, perhaps unique in Jewish literature to this point. This and other theological points suggest the document's origin in a Jewish baptismal sect (cf. 8.2.11), most likely in the Palestinian area. Again, the expectation of the immi-nent end seems to be part of the message.

Sibylline Oracle 5 was composed about the time of the Bar Kokhba revolt, although probably in Egypt rather than Palestine. It shows an open hostility to Rome and places its hope in a messianic figure who comes from heaven. Even after the revolts under Trajan and Hadrian, in Egypt, at least, Jews still hoped for deliverance from God in the not-too-distant future.

The *Sibylline Oracles* are of historical interest primarily because of their eschatology. Not only do various passages describe and predict the end-time but there is also a messianic figure who seems to be a Ptole-maic ruler. This demonstrates a remarkably positive view toward the dominant Greco-Egyptian culture, at least in pre-Roman times, as well as a form of eschatology somewhat different from that found in other Jewish writings of the period. Nevertheless, there is a fierce loyalty to the temple and its service, showing how Jews of the Diaspora still looked to it as their religious focal point.

9.2.3.3 Rabbinic Literature

For a general introduction and bibliography to rabbinic literature, see 1.4.4. For further bibliography and discussion as it relates to the period of Yavneh, see 9.4.6. A variety of statements relating to the Bar Kokhba revolt is also found in rabbinic literature. Other statements, although not specifically mentioning the revolt, have been connected with it by modern scholars. Almost all of these passages have been collected and discussed in *Schäfer, which should be consulted for further details and bibliography.

9.2.4 Archeology and Literary Discoveries

9.2.4.1 General Archeology and Coins

Barag, D. "The Palestinian 'Judaea Capta' Coins of Vespasian and Titus and the Era on the Coins of Agrippa II Minted under the Flavians." *Numismatic Chronicle* 138 (1978) 14–23.
Kuhnen, H.-P. *Palästina in griechisch-römischer Zeit* (1990).
*Meshorer.
———. "A Coin Hoard of Bar-Kokhba's Time." *Israel Museum Journal* 4 (1985) 43–50.
*Mildenberg 1984.
———. "Der Bar-Kochba-Krieg im Lichte der Münzprägungen." In H.-P. Kuhnen, *Palästina in griechisch-römischer Zeit* (1990) 357–66.

Archeological evidence is extremely important for this period because of the paucity of literary evidence. In this category are not only artifacts as such but also a number of epigraphic sources: Roman milestones, drain tiles, and other brief inscriptions of various sorts. Relevant discussion and bibliography are found in various sections of this chapter (e.g., 9.2.4.2–3; 9.3.1; 9.4.8; 9.4.10).

*Meshorer not only catalogues all Jewish coins known at the time of his publication but also includes those of the Roman governors. Coins important for the Bar Kokhba revolt have been conveniently collected in *Mildenberg. These can be supplemented by the more recent articles by Meshorer (1985) and Mildenberg (1990); see also Barag. More on the coins, especially as they relate to chronology, can be found at 9.3.4.

9.2.4.2 Judean Desert Manuscripts

Benoit, P., et al., eds. *Les grottes de Murabba'at* (1961).

Fitzmyer, J. A., and D. J. Harrington. *A Manual of Palestinian Aramaic Texts* (1978).

Lewis, N., ed. *The Documents from the Bar Kokhba Period in the Cave of Letters: Greek Papyri* (1989).

Lifshitz, B. "The Greek Documents from Nahal Seelim and Nahal Mishmar." *IEJ* 11 (1961) 53–62.

———. "The Greek Documents from the Cave of Horror." *IEJ* 12 (1962a) 201–7.

———. "Papyrus grecs du désert de Juda." *Aegyptus* 42 (1962b) 240–58.

Pardee, D., et al. *Handbook of Ancient Hebrew Letters* (1982).

Polotsky, H. J. "The Greek Papyri from the Cave of Letters." *IEJ* 12 (1962) 258–62.

Yadin, Y. "Expedition D." *IEJ* 11 (1961) 36–52.

———. "Expedition D—The Cave of Letters." *IEJ* 12 (1962) 227–57.

———. *Bar-Kokhba* (1971).

Manuscripts deposited in the aftermath of the Bar Kokhba revolt have been found in several sites in the Judean desert west of the Dead Sea. These were, for the most part, personal archives evidently taken by refugees from the Romans to their hiding places in wilderness caves. Most of these refugees were probably found and killed, but their personal documents remained hidden. These documents consist of business records (deeds of the sale and rental of property), marriage certificates, and letters in Hebrew, Aramaic, and Greek. A number of these letters were written during the revolt, some of them by Bar Kokhba himself. The finds from Murabba'at have been published by Benoit, et al. The documents from the Israeli expeditions have been made available only in preliminary form (Yadin 1961; Yadin 1962; Lifshitz 1961; Lifshitz 1962a; Lifshitz 1962b; Polotsky; cf. Yadin 1971); however, one volume of the definitive edition has now appeared (Lewis), and more are promised in the near future. The published Hebrew letters are now available with translation and commentary in Pardee, et al., and the Aramaic documents are collected in Fitzmyer/Harrington. Some of the documents are from an earlier time, even before the 66–70 war.

9.2.4.3 Egyptian Papyri on the Revolt of 115–117 C.E.

In *CPJ* 2.225–60 Tcherikover and Fuks have collected all the material available to them that relates to the Jewish revolt in Egypt in 115–117 C.E. Because this is an event for which so little information is preserved, the papyri provide valuable firsthand data. For the interpretation of the material, see 9.4.8.

9.3 HISTORICAL STUDIES AND PROBLEMS

9.3.1 Administration of Judea (70 to Post-135)

Avi-Yonah, M. "When Did Judea Become a Consular Province?" *IEJ* 23 (1973) 209–13.

Geva, H. "The Camp of the Tenth Legion in Jerusalem: An Archaeological Reconsideration." *IEJ* 34 (1984) 239–54.

Goodman, M. *State and Society in Roman Galilee,* A.D. *132–212* (1983).

Isaac, B., and I. Roll. "Judaea in the Early Years of Hadrian's Reign." *Latomus* 38 (1979a) 54–66.

———. "Legio II Traiana in Judaea." *ZPE* 33 (1979b) 149–56.

Keppie, L.J.F. "The Legionary Garrison of Judaea under Hadrian." *Latomus* 32 (1973) 859–64.

Lifshitz, B. "Sur la date du transfert de la legion VI Ferrata en Palestine." *Latomus* 19 (1960) 109–11.

Negev, A. "The High Level Aqueduct at Caesarea." *IEJ* 14 (1964) 237–49.

———. "A New Inscription from the High Level Aqueduct at Caesarea." *IEJ* 22 (1972) 52–53.

Pflaum, H.-G. "Remarques sur le changement de statut administratif de la province de Judée." *IEJ* 19 (1969) 225–33.

Safrai, S. "Jewish Self-Government." *The Jewish People in the First Century* (1974) 1.377–419.

Smallwood, E. M. "Atticus, Legate of Judaea under Trajan." *JRS* 52 (1962) 131–33.

Tzori, N. "An Inscription of the Legio VI Ferrata from the Northern Jordan Valley." *IEJ* 21 (1971) 53–54.

After the First Revolt, because a legion (X Fretensis) was stationed there permanently Judea was now administered by governors of senatorial rank. Later, when the single legion was increased to two, Judea became a consular province. For a long time it was thought that the consular status did not come about until after the revolt of 132–135 C.E., but recent studies have now pushed that time back by a considerable number of years. First, Lifshitz suggested that the conversion came as early as 130 (109–11); then Pflaum maintained that it occurred as early as 123. The most recent studies argue that consular status came about in 117 or immediately afterward (Avi-Yonah; Keppie; Isaac/Roll 1979a), a conclusion now confirmed by the discovery of a milestone which shows that the II Traiana legion was also in Palestine by 120 at the latest (Isaac/Roll 1979b).

Otherwise, the governing of the province seems to have been carried on much as it had been before 66. There is no evidence that Judaism as a religion was suppressed. Although it has been argued that much of the land was taken away from the Jewish owners, this is a moot point (see 9.3.7). The names and dates of only a few of the governors are known (Schürer: 1.515–19; Pflaum; Avi-Yonah: 212–13; Smallwood).

The local administration by the Jews themselves also seems to have continued, as was customary under Roman rule, but details are uncertain. The Sanhedrin had been destroyed and perhaps much of the pre-66 structure ruptured by the war. We know that in time Palestine came increasingly under rabbinic control, until finally the Jewish patriarch had considerable power even over Jewish communities outside Palestine. Just as it is now clear that the Pharisees did not control the administration and temple before 66 (8.2.2), however, it is also plain that the extension of rabbinic control after 70 was slow. Neusner's investigation of the mishnaic order of *Nezikin* ("damages") finds little systematic discussion or evidence of the practical application of regulations in the sphere of civil law for the period between the First and Second Revolts (9.4.6). Goodman comes to similar conclusions, pointing out that, not only for the Yavnean period but also for much of the second century after the Second Revolt, the evidence is against widespread rabbinic influence in Galilee (93–118). Local administration was in the hands of others than the rabbis, and the advice of the rabbis was only occasionally sought and then only in specific areas of religious law. Thus, contrary to common assumption (e.g., Safrai: 404–12), the movement of civil control into the hands of the rabbis was only a slow development, probably first making itself felt not earlier than the early third century and becoming significant only in the late third century (Goodman: 110).

9.3.2 Judea in the 115–117 Revolt

Applebaum, S. "Notes on the Jewish Revolt under Trajan." *JJS* 2 (1950/51) 26–30.
———. *Jews and Greeks in Ancient Cyrene* (1979).
Rokeah, D. "The War of Kitos: Towards the Clarification of a Philological-Historical Problem." *Scripta Hierosolymitana* 23 (1972) 79–84.
Smallwood, E. M. "Palestine *c.* A.D. 115–118." *Historia* 11 (1962) 500–510.

Although the Jews in widely separated areas arose against the Romans at the end of Trajan's reign, it has generally been assumed that Palestine itself was quiet during this period. According to several scholars, however, there is evidence to show that Palestine itself participated in this revolt (Applebaum 1950/51: 29; Applebaum 1979: 300–308; Smallwood), although the evidence is all indirect. The arguments of Applebaum and Smallwood are essentially as follows:

1. Various rabbinic texts mention a "war of Quietus" (Quietus was governor of Judea in 117–118 c.e.) and fighting in the time of Trajan. The problem is that these texts are often late and admittedly legendary in many cases. For example, the story of Pappus and Lulianus (*Eccles. Rabba* on Eccles 3:17; *Meg. Ta'an.* 12) has Trajan killed by Roman officials. Is it really convincing to say that Trajan is a substitution for his governor Quietus and that the historical allusion is correct, even though the rest is legendary? Does this not evade the real problem, which is whether it is ever legitimate to use such legendary anecdotes in a reconstruction? See Rokeah for further criticisms.

2. The *Historia Augusta* (*Hadr.* 5.2) states: "For the nations which Trajan had conquered began to revolt: . . . and finally Libya and Palestine showed the spirit of rebellion." Apart from the untrustworthy nature of this source (9.2.1.2), the interpretation of this specific passage is not clear-cut.

3. Several Roman inscriptions seem to indicate the presence of part of the III Cyrenaica legion in Palestine at this time. In addition, an epitaph mentions that a particular soldier who served in Judea could have been there in 117. Neither of these is very solid proof.

4. Some medieval Syriac sources mentioned that the leader of the Cyrene revolt eventually made his way to Judea, where he made his final stand against the Romans. The lateness of the reports makes them suspect, although these writers sometimes had earlier material available which has been lost.

5. An excavation at Jaffa indicates a destruction during the reign of Trajan. But why this should be connected with a revolt in 115–117 and not any number of other causes is not made clear by Applebaum, who mentions it (1979: 306).

6. In the Decapolis city of Gerasa an arch from the time of Hadrian seems to have incorporated fragments which could have come from a synagogue. Because Gerasa protected its Jewish inhabitants in the 66–70 war, the synagogue must have been destroyed at another time, perhaps in the 115–117 period. There are dozens of reasons, however, why a synagogue might have been destroyed and portions of its architecture incorporated into the Hadrianic arch, apart from a revolt in 115–117.

7. A fragment by Hippolytus, known only in a Syriac source, states that "Traianus Quintus" set up a pagan statue in Jerusalem. This has been interpreted to mean "Quietus" in the time of "Trajan," which seems to read a great deal into the statement.

8. The *Seder Olam Rabbah* gives fifty-two years as the time between the war of Vespasian and the "war of Titus," although some manuscripts have the "war of Quietus." Similarly, the Palestinian Talmud mentions that "Bethar lasted 52 years after the destruction of the Temple" (*y. Ta'an.* 4.5, 69a). Because there was no "event" in 122 C.E. that fits, the counting must be from 66 C.E. In addition to recalculating the figures to make them correspond, however, it is assumed that Quietus's war must refer to something in Palestine (it is known that he put down the insurrection in Mesopotamia) and that the reference to Bar Kokhba (where the last battle occurred at Bethar) is actually a reference to 115–117. Such argumentation, which proceeds by first making extensive emendation to the data and then interpreting the emendations, is unconvincing.

9. It seems unlikely that the Jews of Palestine would have remained neutral when their compatriots were fighting Rome elsewhere. Yet why not? The Jews of Palestine did not rebel when the Alexandrians suffered in 38; nor did the Diaspora Jews rise up in 66–70. We know too little about the causes of the 115–117 revolts to say whether the Judeans would have had cause to join their brethren in Egypt and elsewhere.

Some of these arguments are extremely weak and depend on data which have been overinterpreted and even emended. Others, although not strong in themselves, could perhaps have a cumulative effect if taken together. Against them one must note the silence of the early historians: none of the surviving accounts—Dio, Eusebius, Orosius—mentions Palestine, which seems strange despite the general brevity of these accounts. The only Greco-Roman source hinting at a Palestinian revolt is the *Historia Augusta*. In light of arguments advanced so far, it seems best to allow for the possibility of a Palestinian revolt but to recognize that the evidence is uncertain. And if such unrest did occur, it was probably quickly stamped out.

9.3.3 Causes of the Bar Kokhba Revolt

Boer, W. den. "Religion and Literature in Hadrian's Policy." *Mnemosyne* 8, Series 4 (1955) 123–44.

Bowersock, G. W. "A Roman Perspective on the Bar Kochba War." *Approaches to Ancient Judaism* (1980) 2.131–41.

Golan, D. "Hadrian's Decision to Supplant 'Jerusalem' by 'Aelia Capitolina.' " *Historia* 35 (1986) 226–39.

Lifshitz, B. "Jérusalem sous la domination romaine. Histoire de la ville depuis la conquête de Pompée jusqu'à Constantin (63 A.C.–325 P.C.)." *ANRW* 2 (1977) 8.444–89.

Mantel, H. "The Causes of the Bar Kokba Revolt." *JQR* 58 (1967/68) 224–42, 274–96.

Mommsen, T., and A. Watson, eds. *The Digest of Justinian* (1985).

Neusner, J. *The Tosefta, Translated from the Hebrew.* Vols. 1–6 (1977–86).

Perowne, S. *Hadrian* (1960).

Schäfer, P. "The Causes of the Bar Kokhba Revolt." *Studies in Aggadah, Targum and Jewish Liturgy in Memory of Joseph Heinemann* (1981) 74–94.

———. "Hadrian's Policy in Judaea and the Bar Kokhba Revolt: A Reassessment." *A Tribute to Geza Vermes* (1990) 281–303.

Scott, S.P. *Justinian, Corpus Juris Civilis, the Civil Law, the Digest or Panadects* (1973).

Smallwood, E. M. "The Legislation of Hadrian and Antoninus Pius against Circumcision." *Latomus* 18 (1959) 334–47; 20 (1961) 93–96.

So little information is available about the reasons for the Bar Kokhba rebellion that speculation has been inevitable. Most modern attempts at explaining the causes have been based on two short passages of Roman literature and a few isolated passages in rabbinic and Christian literature.

According to one explanation, which had a number of adherents in the past, Hadrian at first gave permission for the Jews to rebuild the temple but then withdrew that permission. The principal text for this is from *Midrash Rabbah* (*Gen. Rab.* 64.10), although the Epistle of Barnabas 16:4 is also cited in support. This explanation is now generally dismissed (Schürer: 1.535–36; cf. *Schäfer: 75–81) because the rabbinic passage is unlikely to have any historical basis (nor does it refer specifically to the Bar Kokhba revolt, as Schäfer has pointed out [*76]). Moreover, the passage in Barnabas is ambiguous and not at all certain to be a reference to a contemporary rebuilding of the temple.

Recent debate has tended to center on two causes, either singly or in combination (*Smallwood: 428–38; Schürer: 1.536–43; *Mildenberg 1984: 102–9):

1. Hadrian issued a decree against castration that was interpreted to include circumcision, thus constituting a serious attack on Jewish religious practice. This interpretation comes principally from the *Historia Augusta*, which states, "At that time the Jews also waged war because they had been forbidden to mutilate their genitals [*mutilare genitalia*]" (*Hadr.* 14.2). This statement has been confirmed, it is argued (Small-

wood 1959), by the decree of Hadrian's successor, Antoninus Pius, who explicitly exempted Jewish circumcision from the prohibition (Justinian). There are also rabbinic passages concerning those who underwent recircumcision after having undergone epispasm to cover a previous circumcision (*t. Shab.* 15[116]:9).

There are several problems with this explanation, however (*Schäfer: 85–92). First, Hadrian's decree regarding castration was not a new one but only the renewal of a decree already issued by Domitian and renewed by Trajan.

Second, previous rulers had almost always been sensitive to the practices of the Jews and caused no unnecessary infringement of Jewish religious rights. Hadrian could hardly have been unaware of the implications of an order which would bring him into conflict with Judaism, and he was not the type of ruler likely to engineer such a conflict. The explanation that Hadrian may not have been aware of the consequences of his renewal of the decree is very weak.

Third, the sources which suggest that such an act preceded the war are suspect. The rabbinic sources are generally late and only reiterate a commonplace charge about the prohibition of Judaism (i.e., persecution was automatically thought to take the form of suppressing circumcision, the Sabbath, and similar rites); and *Historia Augusta* is not the most reliable of sources, not least because of its origin in a rather late period (9.2.1.2).

Fourth, Antoninus's permission does not prove that there had been an actual ban at all, much less one which preceded the Jewish war. If Hadrian ever issued such a decree—which is not proved—then it could have been after the war began or even after it was won.

Part of the difficulty seems to be linguistic. The crucial phrase in Justinian's *Digesta* 48.8.11 has often been understood as the abolition of an earlier prohibition, as in Scott's translation: "By Rescript of the Divine Pius, Jews are permitted to circumcise only their own children, anyone who performs this operation upon persons of a different religion will incur the penalty for castration" (Scott: 11.71). But it should probably be understood only as a standard exemption of the Jews from anti-castration legislation, without implying a previous ban, as the more recent translation by Watson indicates: "By a rescript of the deified Pius it is allowed only to Jews to circumcise their own sons; a person not of that religion who does so suffers the penalty of one carrying out a castration" (Mommsen/Watson: 4.821). In sum, even though many recent handbooks accept the theory concerning Hadrian's prohibition of circumcision as a cause of the revolt, there seems good reason to doubt it.

2.	Hadrian attempted to rebuild Jerusalem as the Roman city Aelia Capitolina. This depends primarily on Cassius Dio 69.12 (see 9.2.1.1):

> When he [Hadrian] founded a city of its own at Jerusalem on the site of
> the destroyed one, calling it Aelia Capitolina, and erected on the site of
> the Temple of God another to Zeus, a great and protracted war resulted.
> (trans. Schäfer 1981: 81)

One difficulty with this explanation is that it seems to be contradicted
by Eusebius, who states that Aelia Capitolina was founded *after* the Jewish defeat, making it a consequence rather than a cause of the revolt
(*Hist. eccl.* 4.6.4; see 9.2.2.1, above). Modern scholars, however, have
generally seen these two statements as complementary rather than contradictory (*Schürer: 1.540–43; *Smallwood: 431–34); that is, Hadrian's
plans to found Aelia sparked the revolt so that the actual execution of the
project was postponed until the revolt was put down. Coins more recently
discovered show that Aelia Capitolina was definitely planned before the
revolt (*Mildenberg 1980: 333; *Mildenberg 1984: 99–101): (1) Aelia Capitolina coins have been found together with Jewish coins minted during
the revolt; (2) Hadrian's title on these (*Imp Caes Traiano Hadriano*) is an
early one which was abandoned and would not have been used after the
end of the revolt; (3) some of these coins have the name of Hadrian's
consort, Sabina Augusta; because she died in 136 and received the epithet Diva Sabina, these coins were minted before her death; and (4)
several Aelia Capitolina coins were overstruck by the Jews during the
revolt (Lifshitz: 481). From this, it seems definitively established that
Jerusalem was refounded as Aelia Capitolina *before* the revolt. However, one
group of Aelia coins seems to have been minted after the revolt (*Mildenberg 1984: 100–101), perhaps suggesting that the real process of building did
indeed come afterward, even though the official founding preceded it.

One difficulty concerns why Hadrian would have founded a city with a
pagan temple on the site of the former Jewish temple, when to do so
would have provoked a strong reaction. Again, the explanation that
Hadrian was not aware of the Jewish reaction is facile. Because no archeological evidence for a temple has been found (Bowersock: 137), it may
be that Hadrian did not envisage having a temple in the new city. This
would assume that he changed his mind after the revolt, erecting at least
a statue of Jupiter, and that Dio mistakenly assumed that the statue was
put up in the original foundation.

A suggestion by Schäfer, however, may contribute toward a solution to
the problem. In the context of a broader discussion of the causes of the
revolt, Schäfer (*1981; 1990) has developed a thesis which not only
explains why Hadrian planned a new city on the site of Jerusalem but
also takes account of strange rabbinic statements that particular Jews
were "recircumcised" at the time of Bar Kokhba. According to a passage
of the Tosefta,

A. One who has the prepuce drawn forward has to be circumcised.

B. R. Judah says, "One who has his prepuce drawn forward should not be circumcised, because it is dangerous."

C. They said to him, "Many were circumcised in the time of Ben Koziba, and they had children and did not die." (*t. Shab.* 15[16]:9, trans. J. Neusner)

This has been taken by some scholars to mean that Jews had their circumcision reversed when Hadrian forbade the practice (Smallwood 1959: 337–39; *Smallwood: 430–31), but, as Schäfer has pointed out, this is absurd: the ban applied only to the circumcision of children or converts. It would hardly have affected circumcised adults, of whom there were tens of thousands. So who were these individuals who had their circumcision disguised by an operation (called *měšûkîm* in Hebrew) and were then recircumcised? Schäfer suggests they were assimilated Jews who acted just as some had in Maccabean times (5.4.3.2), and their recircumcision may not have been voluntary but carried out under threat or even by force. The existence of such individuals, however, again using the analogy with Maccabean times, also suggests that they would not only have approved but even positively encouraged a plan to have Jerusalem made into a Hellenistic center. If Hadrian planned to refound Jerusalem, it was only one of many such projects which he carried out in the East during his reign. And the existence of assimilated Jews encouraging the project could well have made him overlook the possibility of serious opposition on the part of other Jews.

Schäfer's explanation is highly suggestive (but cf. the strong opposition of *Mildenberg 1984: 103–5 nn.286, 297), not only because it resolves the difficulties surrounding the statement of Dio, who gives the most coherent account of the revolt, but also because it develops an integrated hypothesis which fits with the broader context of Hadrian's rule. As noted with regard to the Hellenistic policy of Jason in Seleucid times, many educated Jews saw no contradiction between their Judaism and the acceptance of Hellenistic ideals (5.3.3; 5.4.3.2).

Here the analogy runs into problems, however. The number who actually abandoned Judaism by undergoing epispasm during Hadrian's reign is not likely to have been great, any more than it was under the Maccabees (5.4.3.2), but these would not have been the only people to welcome the idea of a Hellenistic city on the site of Jerusalem. The erection of a statue of Jupiter is also problematic, because even most pro-Roman Jews would have strongly opposed the idea (but cf. Schäfer 1990: 288–89). As already noted, it may be that it was not originally planned but took place only after the revolt. Assimilated Jews may also have caused Hadrian to assume that the erection of a statue of Jupiter on the former temple site would have been tolerated. Finally, the rabbinic sources which mention recircumcision say nothing about any connection with Hadrian or the city of Aelia. Schäfer has answered his critics (1990), although I do not believe that all the points mentioned above are adequately dealt with. Nevertheless, he has drawn attention to some important issues and clarified many points surrounding Hadrian's policies and actions with regard to Jerusalem.

A recent twist regarding the foundation of Aelia has been given by Golan. He argues that Hadrian, as a cultured and enlightened product of Greek civilization, was prepared to allow various religious views, within the bounds of Roman law. Christianity, however, intolerant of other religions and unwilling to support the ruling powers, would have been perceived as a growing threat. To Hadrian a possible solution seemed to be to destroy an important Christian symbol, namely, Jerusalem, which the sect focused on as the place of Christ's crucifixion as well as his expected return. Jerusalem's replacement by a Roman city would both weaken Christianity directly and provide the Roman public with a symbol of the revitalized state religion and culture. This was a calculated risk, because a side effect of this action would be to offend the Jews; nevertheless, Hadrian took that risk and had to contend with a Jewish revolt, even though the Jews were not the object of his actions.

Thus, the founding of Aelia Capitolina emerges as, in some way or other, the major cause of the revolt. Nevertheless, it seems likely that there were a variety of factors and that Hadrian's plans for Aelia served only as the catalyst which brought things to a head. Many of the factors that led to the 66–70 revolt were still in existence in the early second century, including economic pressures, strong feelings of nationalism, and resentment against Roman rule, all of which were further fueled by messianic expectations and apocalyptic prophecies in some circles. The Apocalypses of Baruch and Ezra were probably completed not long before the Bar Kokhba revolt and show that speculation about the supernatural destruction of Roman rule was still much in evidence (9.2.3.1; 9.2.3.2). These and the New Testament book of Revelation allow us to surmise the existence of other such apocalypses which have not survived. Although specific accounts are lacking, there are various hints that Judea remained an unruly province during the years 70 to 132, with periodic, minor resurgences against the Roman occupation (*Applebaum: 17–22). The upgrading of the province to consular level and the extensive road building under Hadrian support this (9.3.1; however, note the cautionary remarks of Schäfer 1990: 285–87).

A further factor leading to the revolt was a series of actions taken by

Hadrian while on his tour of the East, which could have been interpreted by some Jews as plans for him to become a second suppressor of Judaism:

> First, he had declared himself the successor to Antiochus Epiphanes. He had finished Antiochus' own temple in Athens. Secondly, like Antiochus, he had adopted, or allowed others to adopt in addressing him, the style of god, of Zeus Olympios. Thirdly, he had permitted this style to appear on coins which circulated among Jewish communities. (Perowne: 149)

It seems rather farfetched to assume that many Jews not only knew of such actions but also were familiar enough with the specific events of the Maccabean revolt to interpret them as Perowne suggests. His point about the coins is the most cogent. More important, however, is another action that would have occurred closer to Palestine and thus would have been more likely to become known to Judeans: Hadrian honored Pompey by visiting his tomb as he traveled from Palestine to Egypt.

9.3.4 Chronology of the Bar Kokhba Revolt

Follet, S. "Hadrien en Egypte et en Judée." *Revue de philologie* 42 (1968) 54–77.

Helm, R., ed. *Die Chronik des Hieronymus* (1956).

Kanael, B. "Notes on the Dates Used during the Bar Kokhba Revolt." *IEJ* 21 (1971) 39–46.

Kennedy, D. L. "*Legio VI Ferrata*: The Annexation and Early Garrison of Arabia." *HSCP* 84 (1980) 283–309.

Parker, H.M.D. *The Roman Legions* (1928).

Stinespring, W. F. "Hadrian in Palestine, 129/130 A.D." *JAOS* 59 (1939) 360–65.

Until recently, the chronology of the revolt was determined by the journeys of Hadrian (Stinespring; Follet) and by contradictory statements in Christian and rabbinic literature. Unfortunately, the imperial coinage, which normally provides valuable information on the course of the reign, is not very helpful because Hadrian did not hold the office of consul after the third year of his reign. This means that on most of the coins from his reign appears *co(n)s(ul) III* (*Mildenberg 1980: 317). Now a much firmer chronology is possible because of coins and dates in the Judean desert manuscripts, but there are still uncertainties. According to Cassius Dio (9.2.1.1), the Jews were peaceful as long as Hadrian was nearby, but as soon as he left the area, fighting began. The chronology of Hadrian's journeys is generally imprecise; however, it appears that his second major journey began in 128 and that he spent the winter of 128/129 in Greece. From there he crossed to Asia, spending much of 129 in the region of Antioch and also traveling south to Gaza and Damascus. The winter of 129/130 was passed in either Antioch or another city, such as Gerasa. It was probably in 130 that he visited Jerusalem, refounding it as Aelia Capitolina (9.3.3), on his way to Egypt where he stayed until mid-131. From Egypt he sailed to Athens to spend the winter of 131/132. Therefore, Dio's statement suggests the spring of 132 as the earliest date for the beginning of the rebellion. This would appear to agree with Eusebius, who dates the beginning of the revolt to Hadrian's sixteenth year (132/133: *Chronicle* [Helm: 200–201]).

Dates on Jewish coins and documents help to determine the length of the revolt (9.2.4.1–2). Coins discovered to date are of three types. One type is dated to "year 1 of the redemption of Israel"; another type to "year 2 of the freedom of Israel." A third type of coin, undated but with the inscription "for the freedom of Jerusalem," is likely to belong to year 3 and later. Dates in documents range from "1 Iyyar [April–May], year 1 of the freedom of Israel" (5/6Hev, document 42 = Yadin 1962: 249) to "21 Tishri [September–October], year 4" (Mur 30 = DJD 2.144–48). This suggests that the war began at the latest in the spring of 132 and ended no sooner than the autumn of 135. Roman inscriptions indicate that Hadrian was proclaimed *imperator* for the second time in the year between 10 December 134 and 10 December 135 (*Schäfer: 14–15), implying that the war was finished or nearly finished by this time. Putting this together with the Jewish material suggests that the war ended sometime in late 135 or early 136. This is not too far from Eusebius's date of Hadrian's eighteenth year (134/135).

There is still a slight problem with the time for the beginning of the revolt, however, because of some dated coins of Gaza that were overstruck by the Jews (*Mildenberg 1980: 318). One undated Jewish coin was struck over a coin from Gaza with the double date of 131 and 132; another overstrike is alleged to have the original date 132/133 on it. From these, Mildenberg concludes that the revolt did not begin earlier than the autumn of 132. He also points out that the latest document in the archive of Babata is dated to August 132, deducing from this that the war could not have begun in the spring because Babata could not have reached Engedi from her residence in Nabatea at that late date (*1980: 319). This requires the rather narrow assumption that the Jews could not possibly have obtained a Gaza coin after the revolt began; in addition, the reading of 132/133 on the Gaza coin has been challenged (*Schäfer: 27 n.92). As for the Babata archive, Mildenberg's interpretation presupposes that we have exact information on the course of the war, which we do not. Considering the few data we have, the argument that Babata could not have traveled from Nabatea to Engedi after the war broke out seems tenuous. In contrast, 5/6Hev 42 seems difficult to explain in the light of a dating which begins the revolt as late as the autumn of 132.

The date of 132–135 for the war has generally been accepted, but an exception is Mantel (9.3.3), who argues that Bar Kokhba's kingdom existed for this period but that the fighting had begun a number of years before. In other words, 132 marked not the start of the war but the time at which the Jews had more or less pushed the Romans out and established their independent rule under Bar Kokhba. Mantel's argument depends on dubious datings in Christian and rabbinic literature, hints of unrest in Judea before 132, and surmises about the movements of Roman legions in 125–132. Especially important to this last point is the argument that a legion (XXII Deiotariana) had been wiped out and replaced in 127 by another (II Trajana) from Egypt. The arguments against Mantel's thesis are (cf. *Schäfer: 12–14):

1. The slight evidence for unrest in Judea before 132 does not support the concept of an all-out war.
2. Recent studies on the posting of legions in the East go against Mantel. There has long been a problem with the XXII Deiotariana. This legion is last listed on an inscription of 119 but not in the army list of Antoninus Pius, leading many to speculate that it was wiped out in the Judean war (Parker: 162–63). Now, Kennedy's study, utilizing newly discovered inscriptions and some new decipherments, indicates that the XXII Deiotariana had disappeared by 123, lending weight to the older alternative explanation that it had been disgraced (in the Alexandrian riots of 121–122?) and was disbanded as a result (Kennedy: 303–7). Furthermore, we now know that the II Traiana legion was in Palestine by 120 at the latest (9.3.1). Therefore, this and other of Mantel's proposals about the sending of legions to Palestine in the period 125–132 do not seem likely in light of recent investigations.
3. The datings of rabbinic literature and such Christian writers as Epiphanius and the *Passover Chronicle* should not be preferred to that of Eusebius.

The conclusion from the known data is, therefore, that the revolt began early in 132 and was concluded only in late 135 or possibly early 136.

9.3.5   Territory in Bar Kokhba's Kingdom

An important clue to the nature of the revolt is found in the territory held by Bar Kokhba. Significantly, this does not appear to have included the whole of Palestine or even the whole of Judea, suggesting that much of the war was a guerrilla action, which seems to accord well with the statements of Dio (9.2.1.1). Manuscript finds occur only along the west coast of the Dead Sea. More important are the sites actually mentioned in the documents and those where coins have been found; these include Hebron, Latrun, Herodium, Tekoa, Ir Nahash, and Engedi (Mildenberg *1980: 320–23; *Mildenberg 1984: 84–94). These all are located roughly in a rectangle bounded on the north by Jerusalem and Latrun, on the east by the Dead Sea, on the south by Nahal Hever, and on the west by a line running south from Latrun. Most of these sites border on the Judean desert, and Engedi is an important oasis on the Dead Sea. Thus the territory held by Bar Kokhba was not very accessible to the Romans; moreover, the wilderness would have provided the Jews with a quick place of retreat after guerrilla raids or if a pitched battle went against them. Surprisingly, there is no evidence that the Jews held Masada, but this could be explained by the suggestion that they were also concerned not to defend fortresses from which there was no possible retreat (*Mildenberg 1980: 323).

An important question is whether Bar Kokhba took and held Jerusalem for any length of time. The coin inscriptions "for the freedom of Jerusalem" and the temple symbolism have suggested to many that Bar Kokhba held the city for a period of up to two years (e.g., Schürer: 1.545–46; *Smallwood: 443–45). Jerusalem is not mentioned in any documents, however, and no Bar Kokhba coins have been found there, surprising if the city was held for a considerable period of time by the rebels (*Schäfer: 78–101). These facts could be interpreted to mean that the possession of Jerusalem was a goal rather than an actuality (*Mildenberg 1980: 324). The temple symbolism is not decisive, although the existence of Aelia Capitolina would explain Bar Kokhba's goal to take and cleanse the city of its pagan occupation, just as the Maccabees had done. Because the city was held by the tenth legion, however, it would have required a large and disciplined force over many months to take the city under normal circumstances. But if it had been besieged, then other forces could have been called in to attack the besiegers from behind. It would have been an unprecedented military victory if Bar Kokhba had been able even to take the city, much less hold it for two years.

9.3.6 The Question of Bar Kokhba's Messiahship and R. Aqiva's Part in the Revolt

Aleksandrov, G. S. "The Role of Aqiba in the Bar Kokhba Rebellion." *Eliezar ben Hyrcanus* (1973) 2.428–42.

Finkelstein, L. *Akiba: Scholar, Saint and Martyr* (1970).

Schäfer, P. "R. Aqiva und Bar Kokhba." *Studien zur Geschichte und Theologie des rabbinischen Judentums* (1978) 65–121.

———. "Aqiva and Bar Kokhba." *Approaches to Ancient Judaism* (1980) 2.113–30.

It has become a part of modern scholarly tradition that R. Aqiva declared Bar Kokhba the messiah and was active in preparations for the revolt which broke out under the latter's leadership (see Aleksandrov: 422–23). The first part of this common assumption comes from the statement in *y. Ta'an.* 4.8 68a:

> R. Simeon b. Yohai taught, "My teacher Aqiva used to expound, 'There shall step forth a star out of Jacob* (Num. 24:17)—thus Koziva steps forth out of Jacob!' When R. Aqiva beheld Bar Koziva, he exclaimed, 'This is the king Messiah.'" R. Yohanan b. Torta retorted, "Aqiva, grass will grow between your cheeks and he still will not have come." (trans. Schäfer 1980: 117)

The idea that the purpose of Aqiva's alleged travels was to raise money and gain arms for the war is a modern reconstruction but has, nevertheless, appeared widely in literature on the subject (cf. Aleksandrov: 422–23).

In an article which originally appeared in Russian, Aleksandrov points out that the modern theories about Aqiva's position as ideologist and organizer of the revolt have little foundation and "ignored factual material in the sources and preferred to build hypotheses, for which, by their own admission, there is no basis in the sources" (427). He also argues that Bar Kokhba had never claimed to be the messiah, although he accepts that Aqiva was a "calculator of the end of days" who, after the initial victories against the Romans, may have given moral support to the revolt and even declared Bar Kokhba a "king-messiah." A later generation who had suffered seriously from the war remembered this with bitterness; hence the castigation of such "calculators of the end of days."

Other recent scholars have also denied that Bar Kokhba thought of himself as the messiah (*Mildenberg 1980: 313–15; *Mildenberg 1984: 73–76). They cite two reasons: (1) none of the Judean desert manuscripts suggests anything about messiahship, and (2) the symbolism on the coins is ambiguous at best and has been overinterpreted. Aleksandrov's investigation was principally a critical look at the arguments advanced for particular theories and did not constitute a systematic analysis of the sources. More recently, Schäfer has taken such a systematic look at the relevant texts in detail (1978; 1980); his study supports Aleksandrov's conclusion that there is no evidence to suggest that Aqiva undertook journeys to prepare for the war. It is very possible, however, that Aqiva looked on Bar Kokhba as messiah and was therefore involved in the revolt. Schäfer's conclusions may be summarized as follows (Schäfer 1978: 119–21; 1980: 124–25):

1. The textual analysis suggests that in some cases the goal of the journey was not specified, and in others there is a question whether the journey really took place. The only possible dating for a journey is about 110 c.e. The most likely purpose of any trips was religious; to suggest any military or political purpose is simply speculation.

2. If the texts which interpret Num 24:17 are correctly ascribed to him, then there seems little doubt that Aqiva understood the Bar Kokhba rebellion as messianic and approved it.

3. The sparse number of sayings on the subject suggest that Aqiva held a nationalistic messianic expectation which he anticipated being fulfilled in the near future.

4. The alleged discussions between Aqiva and Tineius Rufus are a part of the apologetic that makes use of pagan-Jewish dialogue and have no historical value.

5. The texts about Aqiva's imprisonment are unlikely to provide historical information beyond a general connection with the Bar Kokhba revolt. When, for how long, and precisely why Aqiva was imprisoned cannot be determined.

6. Similarly, the texts about the death and burial of Aqiva provide little reliable information beyond a connection with the Bar Kokhba rebellion. The core of the traditions is a cycle of legends that cannot be expected to give trustworthy historical data.

It is impossible to pronounce on Bar Kokhba's self-understanding of his role. His letters and other documents give no indication of a claim to messiahship. Coin legends are difficult to interpret and may hint at messiahship, although even this is by no means certain (*Meshorer: 2.138–50). Nevertheless, we do know that apocalyptic and messianic speculation continued during this period, as it had before 70 (contra *Mildenberg 1980: 314; see 9.2.3.1; 9.2.3.2; 9.4.1). It seems clear that some, including probably Aqiva, identified Bar Kokhba as the messiah. One indication of this is his epithet ("son of the star"), which was attested in the mid-second century (Justin Martyr, *Apologia* 1.31.6; Mildenberg's doubts about the textual reading [*1984: 78 n.191; 80 n.210] seem purely *ex hypothesi* and based on no tangible evidence). We must keep in mind, however, that the concept of the messiah varied considerably, from a full-blown heavenly figure to little more than a human hero (8.3.5). Later rabbinic literature seems concerned to brand Bar Kokhba a false messiah, a rather strange thing to do if no one ever thought him the true one. A final point to keep in mind, however, is that the opinion of Aqiva and other rabbis may have had little influence on the Jewish population (9.4.6). They were part of a group whose tradition became dominant within a century or so, but whether Aqiva's opinion about Bar Kokhba made much difference at the time is another matter. Hence we should not necessarily be surprised at the absence of the rabbi's name in the Bar Kokhba manuscripts (cf. *Mildenberg 1984: 75 n.176: "It remains, however, an astonishing and remarkable fact that Akiba does not occur in the documents").

9.3.7 Socioeconomic Matters

Applebaum, S. "Economic Life in Palestine." *The Jewish People in the First Century* (1976) 2.692–99.

———. "Judaea as a Roman Province: The Countryside as a Political and Economic Factor." *ANRW* 2 (1977) 8.385–95.

Bruce, I.A.F. "Nerva and the *Fiscus Iudaicus*." *PEQ* 96 (1964) 34–45.

Carlebach, A. "Rabbinic References to Fiscus Judaicus." *JQR* 66 (1975/76) 57–61.

Goodman, M. "Nerva, the *Fiscus Judaicus* and Jewish Identity." *JRS* 79 (1989) 40–44.

Isaac, B. "Judaea after A.D. 70." *JJS* 35 (1984) 44–50.

Mandell, S. "Who Paid the Temple Tax When the Jews Were under Roman Rule?" *HTR* 77 (1984) 223–32.

Smallwood, E. M. "Domitian's Attitude toward the Jews and Judaism." *Classical Philology* 51 (1956) 1–13.

Thompson, L. A. "Domitian and the Jewish Tax." *Historia* 31 (1982) 329–42.

It has generally been argued that the 66–70 war left Judea desolate and in a desperate economic plight. This argument is based on the assumption of widespread destruction caused by the revolt and the seizure of land by the Romans (e.g., Applebaum 1976: 692–99; Applebaum 1977: 385–95; *Applebaum 9–15). Indeed, it is inferred from Josephus (see below) that Vespasian took much of the land as his own, as a result of which many Jews who had been landowners became tenants. There is no question that Jerusalem and the surrounding area suffered greatly; in fact, for the siege of Jerusalem, the countryside as far away as ten to twelve miles from the city was scoured for siege materials (*War* 5.12.4 §523). Vespasian also founded a colony of discharged soldiers at Emmaus, not far from Jerusalem (*War* 7.6.6 §217); further, we have the example of

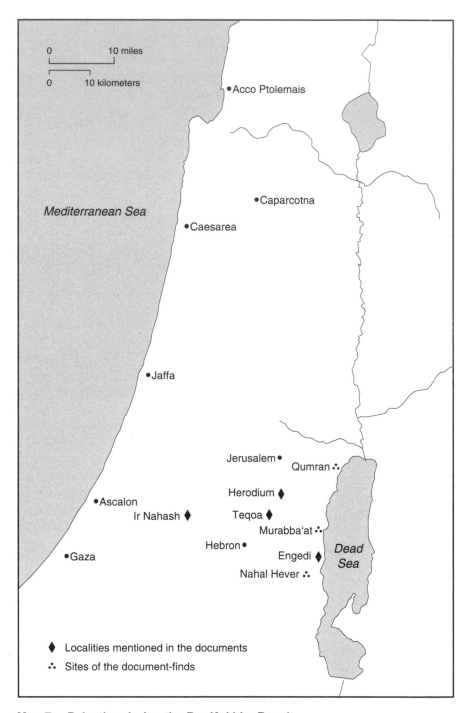

Map 7.   Palestine during the Bar Kokhba Revolt

his gift of land to Josephus in compensation for property made unprofitable by the Roman garrison near Jerusalem (*Life* 76 §422). It has even been argued that an important cause of the Second Revolt was peasant poverty, and thus Bar Kokhba's principal supporters were found among the peasantry (*Applebaum: 15–17).

This, however, is not the only assessment of the situation. Some scholars argue that only the area in the immediate vicinity of Jerusalem suffered heavily. Galilee did not suffer because most cities quickly capitulated, and only Jotapata required an extended siege. Most of the rebels fled to Jerusalem in the face of the Roman advance, which meant that the actual destruction by fighting was at a minimum throughout much of the country, making it possible to recover in a reasonably short period of time. Thus, Mildenberg has pointed out, in the decades just before the Second Revolt there are all the signs of widespread Jewish ownership of the land and relative prosperity (*1984: 84–94).

Nevertheless, the question about the possession of land for farming has revolved around Josephus's statement, which has been interpreted as evidence that Vespasian took over much of the country (*War* 7.6.6 §§216–17). Recently, Isaac has argued that the passage has been so misinterpreted that the text has even been emended to support the standard interpretation. When read correctly, without emendation, he concludes that it should be translated as follows:

> About the same time Caesar sent instructions to Bassus and Laberius Maximus, the procurator, to dispose of all Jewish land. For he founded there no city of his own while keeping their territory, but only to eight hundred veterans did he assign a place for settlement called Emmaus. . . . (Isaac: 46)

Of course the land of rebels was confiscated and became Vespasian's property; it is to this that "all Jewish land" refers, not to the whole of Judea. Those not directly involved in the revolt continued to own their property and make a living from it, as they had in the years before 66. Thus, the climb from the postwar depression to the former level of agrarian prosperity would have been a matter of years rather than decades, with the area around Jerusalem being the last to recover.

There seems little doubt that Judea as a whole had reverted much more to a subsistence economy that consisted chiefly of tenant farmers, hired laborers, crafts workers, and small businesses. This was the case regardless of whether the destruction and effects of the 66–70 war were as great as often asserted. But one should be cautious in building on the assumption that the whole of Palestine suffered economic and agrarian disaster as a result of the First Revolt.

In those areas relating to the temple, however, there is no question that the former revenues were lost. Thousands of pilgrims no longer came each year to celebrate the festivals at Jerusalem. The entire industry that catered for and depended on the multitudes coming annually from the Diaspora to visit the temple was at an end. Thus an important element in the pre-66 economy of Judea was gone. Gone also was the contribution to the temple, which had theoretically been the responsibility of every male Jew above a certain age; after the First Revolt, this was forfeited to the Roman exchequer as the *fiscus Judaicus* and was evidently levied on every Jew—man, woman, child, and slave, even Roman citizens (Goodman: 40; contra Mandell: although many eligible Jews may not have paid the contribution to the temple, as she notes, the evidence indicates that the Romans did not make fine distinctions about who had or had not paid before). Both the large sums that had poured into the temple coffers and the resultant "trickle-down" no longer had any place in the economy. It is possible that this had an impact, which was not completely negative, because one problem of the pre-70 economy had been the large amount of uninvested wealth accumulating in the temple and among a few individuals or families (7.3.10). Nevertheless, the overall result was a much more subsistence-level economy with a smaller surplus.

Under Domitian a regulation had extended the Jewish tax even further, and Nerva made a point of abolishing this additional measure (as shown by an inscription on some of his coins). Precisely what constituted Domitian's decree has been debated (Bruce). The theory has recently been defended, however, that Domitian's ruling extended the tax to all those circumcised, even those who had abandoned the Jewish religion (Thompson; Goodman). If so, Domitian's measure probably had not affected most Jews one way or the other; in contrast, Nerva's decree placed the tax on all who practiced Judaism, whether born Jewish or not. An unintended side effect was the equating of Jewish identity with religion rather than ethnic origin and tacitly recognizing, for the first time, the existence of proselytes to Judaism (Goodman).

9.4 SYNTHESIS

9.4.1 Overview

Neusner, J. "Emergent Rabbinic Judaism in a Time of Crisis: Four Responses to the Destruction of the Second Temple." *Judaism* 21 (1972) 313–27.
Schwartz, S. *Josephus and Judaean Politics* (1990).

Stone, M. E. "Reactions to Destructions of the Second Temple." *JSJ* 13 (1982) 195–204.

One of the major problems with writing a history of the Jews after 70 C.E. is that Josephus's narrative—an invaluable survival from antiquity, despite all its problems—ceases, and the history must be pieced together from scattered bits of information. Most of what we know of specific events revolves around two periods of revolt, yet, despite recent important discoveries, even today only a few data are known regarding the extremely important rebellion under Bar Kokhba. We have a good deal of what might be called prosopographic material about rabbis for the entire period, but the nature of the rabbinic literature which preserves these data is problematic: in spite of the amount of material regarding particular persons, it is still doubtful whether we could write their biographies in a rigorously historical sense (1.1.2; 9.4.6).

The years following the 66–70 revolt were bad ones for many Jews in Palestine. Not only had thousands been killed and sold into slavery but portions of Judea, especially around Jerusalem, had suffered the ravages of war. Some interpret the data to mean that the economic situation was desperate, and assume that large tracts of land had been taken over by the emperor and redistributed to Roman supporters or kept under his direct ownership, so that little land was available for purchase, even by one with the means (9.3.7).

Recently, others have argued that this picture needs revision. Rather than taking much of Judea into his personal possession, Vespasian confiscated only the property of rebels and founded just the one colony of soldiers in Judea itself. Furthermore, much of the country had suffered little direct damage from the war because most of the fighting had been in Judea proper, primarily around Jerusalem. By contrast, the annual donations for the temple from the Diaspora were lost by being converted to a Jewish tax. Further, the basis for the significant industry which catered for the thousands of pilgrims who came for the annual festivals was gone forever. Judea was evidently reduced to an agrarian and basically subsistence economy.

There was definitely a major crisis from a religious perspective. The Jerusalem temple, until this time the center of Judaism, was in ruins. Because such destruction had happened once before and the temple had been rebuilt, no doubt many hoped that it was only a matter of time before a new edifice was erected on Zion. Nevertheless, the destruction of Jerusalem and the temple was an important theological problem, as attested by the writer of the Apocalypse of Ezra:

> Because of my grief I have spoken; for every hour I suffer agonies of heart, while I strive to understand the way of the Most High and to search out part of his judgment. . . . Why then was I born? Or why did not my mother's womb become my grave, that I might not see the travail of Jacob and the exhaustion of the people of Israel? (4 Ezra 5:34-35)

Therefore, as long as Jerusalem and the temple remained in ruins, a serious religious problem existed for many Jews. Some, like the writers of the Ezra and Baruch Apocalypses (9.2.3.1), sought to resolve the difficulty through the medium of apocalypticism and the expectation that divine intervention would destroy Rome and exalt the faithful Jews in the near future. Needless to say, such expectations were doomed to failure and could be satisfying only in the short term. Not only were those whose hope was in the temple affected but also those whose power base lay there—primarily the priests but probably such groups as the Sadducees as well (8.2.3). This does not mean that the identity of the priestly families was forgotten, for even today many Jews maintain a tradition that they are "Cohen" or "Levi," but this identification is and was of little use when no temple existed. Most privileges formerly possessed by the priestly families were removed, and their worth could be established only when they found a part in the new order. (There is evidence that the priests tried unsuccessfully to regain their pre-66 influence in the last decades of the century [Schwartz: 210–16].)

The groups that survived and flourished were those with built-in mechanisms that allowed them to provide substitutes for the temple and its cult, primarily the Pharisees and the Christians (Neusner; Stone). Christians had long substituted Christ for the temple and its sacrificial system. Although Luke (rightly or wrongly) pictures the Jewish members of the early church as continuing to observe temple and ritual practice (Acts 2:1; 21:17-26), he also preserves a tradition that rejects the temple completely (Acts 7:44-50). The Epistle to the Hebrews includes a long exposition on how the temple cult was a detailed symbol of the sacrifice of Christ. There is little indication that the destruction of the temple was in any way a theological problem for the early church.

Although Pharisees would have participated in the official temple worship, as did other Jews, their religious system was evidently capable of operation without a physical temple. According to one interpretation, the first-century Pharisees were a table-fellowship sect, in which the home represented the temple; the hearth, the altar; and the Pharisee himself, the priest (8.2.2). If this is so, then a Pharisaic layman in his home was able to reenact the temple cult in symbol. It is therefore hardly surprising that the Pharisees were an important factor in the post-70 religious reconstruction (9.4.6). Coincidentally, the situation was also favorable to the Pharisees and other groups in that it had removed many rivals from the scene. The Essenes seem to have been more or less wiped out: their center at Qumran was overrun, and many of those who escaped from that destruction ended their lives at Masada. And, as noted, the priests (and Sadducees) had derived much of their influence from the temple as a functioning institution, even though there are traditions that (if credible) suggest that remnants of the Sadducees survived into the second century C.E. (8.2.3).

Contrary to the developing rabbinic tradition, coming to terms with the new situation was not to the taste of all Jews, as events in the early second century demonstrate. Trajan's conquests in Mesopotamia were followed by a rebellion against the new overlord, in which the Jews of the region also participated. This was followed by uprisings in Cyrene, Egypt, and Cyprus, and possibly some unrest in Judea. Hadrian's measures after these revolts were put down included strengthening the occupying force in Judea, establishing Judea as a consular province, and instituting a program of road building that would have made control of the region easier. Nevertheless, the Jews of Palestine rose up once again in 132–135 under the leadership of a man whom some called "son of the star" and identified as the messiah. This was the last revolt: Jerusalem was made off-limits to Jews, and the official name of the province became "Syria Palaestina" instead of "Judaea."

9.4.2 Vespasian (69–79 C.E.)

Nicols, J. *Vespasian and the Partes Flavianae* (1978).

Vespasian was above all a military man who had campaigned in Britain and Africa before being appointed commander for the Judean campaign by Nero. His family was newly arrived into the ranks of the *equites*, and he had never been in the Senate. Thus, his appointment was innovative in several ways. To lessen the impact of these differences, he attempted to create the fiction of a relationship to the Julio-Claudians. In any case, he came at a time when Rome was desperate for peace and calm, and he proved a good administrator and ruler, becoming perhaps the most popular emperor since Augustus.

His handling of the economic crisis was an example of his ability; he was able to cut spending and raise new taxes without alienating his supporters or provoking major discontent in the provinces which bore the brunt of increased imposts. Although still making some use of freedmen, he avoided the problems created by Claudius and Nero by appointing most governmental officials from the equestrian ranks. Like Augustus, he kept enough of the forms of republican government to satisfy the senators while continuing to reduce the Senate's power.

He began his reign by putting down a revolt which had arisen in the chaos of 69 on the German frontier, in which a German chieftain and a Gallic Roman commander declared an "empire of the Gauls." Despite some initial successes, however, the Gauls as a whole refused to join the revolt, and the new "empire" was soon dissolved. Some expansion of the frontiers occurred under Vespasian: a push west and north in Britain, which eventually ended in bringing northern England, southern Scotland, and much of Wales under Roman control by Domitian's time; and initiatives to bring further areas of Germany, specifically the Black Forest, into the defense system.

Perhaps one of Vespasian's greatest contributions to peace was his establishment of the dynastic principle. He made it quite clear from the beginning that his older son, Titus, was to be his successor and Domitian, his second son, after that if Titus had no children. (The fact that Vespasian had two suitable sons was indeed one of the reasons many supported him.) When Vespasian died in 79, Titus was thus able to make the transition into the office without incident.

9.4.3   Titus (79–81 C.E.)

Jones, B. W. *The Emperor Titus* (1984).

The reign of Titus was short but popular, and there are those who argue that if it had been longer, it would have been different in character. The greatest of his achievements were accomplished before his reign, most notably the conquest of Judea, which was left to him by Vespasian (7.4.13.4). Between 70 and 79 Titus obtained a variety of high offices, including consulship, censorship, priesthood, and tribuneship, many of which he occupied jointly with Vespasian to the point that he was practically co-ruler with his father.

Born in 39, Titus was educated alongside the stepbrother of Nero and was not yet thirty when he took up a command post under Vespasian during the Jewish war. He had by then been a military tribune in Germany; in the Jewish war he showed himself to be a skilled diplomat when acting on his father's behalf, especially in the events related to Vespasian's being declared emperor, notable behavior in a young man still in his twenties. One of our main sources for Titus's activities during the war is Josephus, who lost no opportunity to praise his abilities as a soldier, general, and man. Josephus's picture is clearly exaggerated. Doubtless Titus had ability and was an individual of courage and action; but he was also impetuous to the point of foolhardiness in battle, and he was no great strategist. The credit for taking Jerusalem rightly belonged to him, yet the superiority of the Roman military machine made victory a foregone conclusion. He also had in the enterprise the steadying hand of Tiberius Alexander (7.4.9.3).

Titus's behavior after victory led to misunderstanding and rumor. He celebrated with lavish spectacles, accepted the acclaim of the troops and countries of the East, and even allowed the title *imperator* to be put on coinage for a time. This was probably innocent enough behavior, even if a sign of poor judgment, but it gave the impression that he was trying to become a rival to his father. When Titus learned of developing opinion, he immediately sailed for Rome and reported to Vespasian, dispelling rumors of a power play. Vespasian, for his part, gladly shared many of his offices and responsibilities to ensure that Titus would succeed him. Indeed, Titus became the first Roman emperor to receive the throne from his natural (as opposed to adoptive) father.

One of the most important posts held by Titus was that of prefect of the Praetorian Guard. Reports are that he was a stern officeholder and did not hesitate to punish with death those suspected of disloyalty or danger to the state. This made him, on the one hand, popular with the guard itself and the military in general but, on the other hand, feared and disliked by the upper classes and those likely to suffer from his policies. (It has been suggested that attempting to change this attitude is the reason for his later public generosity when emperor.) He accused of conspiracy and put to death people such as Marcellus and Caecina, who had once been close to him and had served his father well.

Of special interest is his relationship with Berenice, the sister of Agrippa II (7.4.8). They first met when he came to Syria with his father to put down the Jewish revolt, and their affair was carried on fairly openly until he returned to Rome in 71. Because of regard for public opinion, and probably on the advice of his father, he did not invite her to Rome until 75 and then with Agrippa. How long she remained is not recorded, but he sent her away at some point because of public animosity. No doubt there were serious reminders of Mark Antony's affair with Cleopatra. After Titus became emperor and Berenice once more returned to Rome, he could only send her away again, firmly and finally, although evidently to their mutual regret.

His brief reign included the completion of both the famous Colosseum, which Vespasian had begun, and the baths built in his own honor. Titus is reported to have been generous to the point of extravagance in giving gifts to the Roman public and to many individuals. After the destruction of Pompeii in 79 and a fire and plague in Rome in 80, he gave considerable aid to the survivors. Dio nevertheless states that Titus governed frugally, so that precise judgment is difficult. It is also difficult to judge because his time in office was so short. Dio thought that his rule would have gone downhill with time, but because he died at age forty-one, after a little more than two years in office, this is conjecture.

9.4.4 Domitian (81–96 c.e.)

Keresztes, P. "The Jews, the Christians, and Emperor Domitian." *VigChr* 27 (1973) 1–28.
Smallwood, E. M. "Domitian's Attitude toward the Jews and Judaism." *Classical Philology* 51 (1956) 1–13.

The third Flavian and the second son of Vespasian to rule, Domitian has gone down in both Christian and Roman history as a bad ruler. This is due principally to control over the tradition by those who benefited from Domitian's murder (especially the supporters of Nerva). It is in this light that one must evaluate the alleged strict measures he took to maintain the throne, especially the revival of treason trials. Domitian was actually an efficient administrator of the empire and essentially continued the policies of Vespasian. The opposition came because of personality traits that in large part were due to his position as the younger son who had been overshadowed by Titus all his life. Although Domitian had even functioned briefly as vice-regent in late 69, after the Vitellians were defeated (7.4.12), he was not given any office or honor of substance. Whereas Titus was groomed for government by a succession of appointments with real responsibility, Domitian received only empty honors. Therefore, when he had the chance to govern, he took the reins firmly in hand and did not bother to keep up the appearances of respecting the Senate, as his father had done.

Continuing Vespasian's policies of entrusting the administration to professionals of equestrian rank, Domitian began the practice of dividing the governance of large provinces between a civilian official (*iuridicus*) and a military governor (this may have been begun by Vespasian). He completed the reorganization of the frontier defenses in several areas. In Britain, Roman control was extended over much of Wales and as far as northern Scotland. When a legion had to be withdrawn to serve on the Danube, Domitian decided that the three remaining legions were too thinly stretched and established the defenses further south. The British commander Agricola was dismayed by this, as his son-in-law Tacitus makes plain, but this decision was probably correct from a strategic point of view.

The reason for the withdrawal of a legion was the unification of the Dacians under Decebalus and that leader's invasion of Moesia in 85. Domitian himself took to the field in the crisis. He hastily arranged a treaty in 88, however, because of a rebellion by two legions of the Rhine and unrest in Pannonia. The Rhine mutiny was suppressed even before Domitian arrived; precisely what happened in Pannonia is not known, but matters seem to have been peacefully settled. On both the Rhine and Danube, a series of permanent fortresses and accompanying defenses were built. Vespasian had already absorbed the Black Forest; now Domitian extended Roman control to the heights of the Taunus Mountains, the most strategic location for his line of fortification on the German border.

After the Rhine rebellion of 88, Domitian began to fear conspiracies, and he revived prosecutions for treason. It had last been under Nero that the senatorial class had suffered condemnation of many of its own. From a historical perspective, this action does not negate the positive nature of much of Domitian's administration, but it is hardly surprising that it colored his entire reign for those upper-class writers who suffered through the period (or at least claim to have suffered). His wife, Domitia, instigated his assassination in 96, and his memory was condemned by the Senate. It has been speculated that he was planning an attack on the Jews which only his death prevented (Smallwood), but this hypothesis does not seem well founded. He did extend the Jewish tax (*fiscus Iudaicus*) in various ways, though the nature of his change is a subject still debated (9.3.7).

9.4.5 Nerva (96–98 c.e.)

The choice of Domitian's successor fell to the Senate, who appointed Nerva because of his seniority (he was already over sixty-five) rather than any personal distinction. He was popular with the Senate as one of its own and took an oath not to execute any senator except after a free trial by the Senate itself, a vow later repeated by both Trajan and Hadrian.

Nevertheless, Nerva clearly led a caretaker government. He had no military prowess to claim the loyalty of the army, and he soon had trouble with the Praetorian Guard, which was angry about the murder of Domitian and demanded that one of their prefects who was privy to the plot be punished. Nerva was forced to accede to their demands, an action which showed how vulnerable he was to the whims of the military and invoked images of "the year of the four emperors." He had the sense to resolve the problem by gaining the support of Trajan, who was commander in northern Germany. Nerva adopted him and named him co-ruler, thus ensuring stability for the few months left in his reign. Trajan then took the throne in a smooth transition. One interesting decree during Nerva's reign was a change in the Jewish tax, which he commemorated by an inscription on some of his coins (9.3.7).

9.4.6   Yavneh (ca. 70–130 c.e.)

Cohen, S.J.D. "The Significance of Yavneh: Pharisees, Rabbis, and the End of Jewish Sectarianism." *HUCA* 55 (1984) 27–53.

Gereboff, J. *Rabbi Tarfon* (1979).

Goodblatt, D. "Towards the Rehabilitation of Talmudic History." *History of Judaism: The Next Ten Years* (1980) 31–44.

Green, W. S., ed. *Persons and Institutions in Early Rabbinic Judaism* (1977).

———. "What's in a Name?—The Problematic of Rabbinic 'Biography.'" *Approaches to Ancient Judaism: Theory and Practice* (1978) 1.77–96.

———. "Context and Meaning in Rabbinic 'Biography.'" *Approaches to Ancient Judaism* (1980) 2.97–111.

Kanter, S. *Rabban Gamaliel II* (1979).

Neusner, J. *Development of a Legend* (1969).

———. *Eliezer ben Hyrcanus* (1973a).

———. *From Politics to Piety: The Making of Pharisaic Religion* (1973b).

———. *A History of the Mishnaic Law of Purities.* Vols. 1–22. (1974–77).

———. *A History of the Mishnaic Law of Holy Things.* Vols. 1–6. (1978–80).

———. "The Formation of Rabbinic Judaism: Yavneh (Jamnia) from A.D. 70 to 100." *ANRW* 2 (1979) 19.2.3–42.

———. "The Present State of Rabbinic Biography." *Hommage à Georges Vajda* (1980a) 85–91.

———. *A History of the Mishnaic Law of Women.* Vols. 1–5. (1980b).

———. *A History of the Mishnaic Law of Appointed Times.* Vols. 1–5. (1981–83).

———. *Judaism: The Evidence of the Mishnah* (1981).

———. *A History of the Mishnaic Law of Damages.* Vols. 1–5. (1983–85).

———. "Varieties of Judaism in the Formative Age." *Formative Judaism II: Religious, Historical, and Literary Studies* (1983) 59–89.

Porton, G. G. *The Traditions of Rabbi Ishmael.* 4 vols. (1976–82).

Saldarini, A. J. "Johanan ben Zakkai's Escape from Jerusalem: Origin and Development of a Rabbinic Story." *JSJ* 6 (1975) 189–204.

Zahavy, T. *The Traditions of Eleazar Ben Azariah* (1977).

According to legend, Yohanan ben Zakkai was given permission to establish an academy in the city of Yavneh (Jamnia) by the emperor Vespasian (Neusner 1969; Saldarini). Whatever the origins of the academy, the episode is extremely important in Jewish history. We know very little of the details, despite the many uncritical accounts in older secondary studies, because almost all of our knowledge of what happened comes from rabbinic literature, which has little or no interest in historiographic matters. Events may even have gone largely unnoticed by many Jews at the time. During the last twenty years much analysis has been done by Neusner and his students of the basic works in the Mishnah and Tosefta (see Neusner, *A History of the Mishnaic Law* [1974–77; 1980b; 1981–83; 1983–85], much of it summarized in his *Judaism: The Evidence of the Mishnah*), as well as the prosopographic traditions in rabbinic literature (e.g., Yohanan b. Zakkai, Eliezar b. Hyrcanus, Gamaliel II, Ishmael). It is impossible to peruse all the research which has gone into the Yavnean period, and the reader must consult the specialized works for further information. Suffice it to say that much of the picture reconstructed by an older scholarship must be discarded or extensively revised.

As an area which had come into Roman possession, Yavneh represented an important concession to Judaism by the Romans: the reconstruction which began under Yohanan had, if not Roman sanction, at least Roman tolerance. Yavneh is often misrepresented as a "synod," as if it were analogous to a church council. It was actually more like an academy, and the number of participants seems to have been quite small at first. Nor were its members necessarily recognized as representatives of Jews of the country. This group behind the Mishnah came to be influential in Jewish society, but its success took well over a century.

Although neither biography nor narrative history is possible because of the nature of the traditions (Green 1978; Green 1980; Neusner 1980), there is material of value to the historian in the rabbinic literature (Goodblatt). Most importantly, source analysis shows the development of religious ideas in the major stages of growth of the Mishnah (Neusner 1981). Before 70 the areas of most interest to the religion—at least as they have left their mark on the literature—were purity, agriculture, festivals, and women. These were the most important concerns of this table-fellowship sect which had control of its internal affairs but not of society as a whole.

The Yavnean layer represents an interesting transitional phase in the Mishnah as it moved toward its final form. There is little development in the order's dealings with civil law (*Neziqin*), indicating the group was not administering society at large. The considerable discussion about the cult does not seem to have been rooted in the experience of cultic personnel but in the biblical text alone; that is, the interest was in creating a new, idealized cult according to the sect's principles, not in extending or developing the old Second Temple practices. Understanding the situation at

Yavneh should bury a lot of myths, such as the notion that here the Old Testament was canonized (8.3.3) or that the leaders of the academy ran society, whether in the civil or religious sphere. Rather, Yavneh presents only a transitional period on the way toward the dominance of Jewish life by the rabbis.

Developing Judaism at Yavneh appears to owe a great deal to the pre-70 Pharisaic tradition (Cohen), yet it was also a synthesis of a variety of elements. Yohanan shows little evidence of being a Pharisee according to the early traditions (Neusner 1979: 30–32, 36–37); rather, he shows all the characteristics of a scribe whose religion centered on Scripture. Because this is an important feature of rabbinic Judaism, it was probably Yohanan who gave direction to the reconstruction and reorientation at Yavneh. Yohanan seems to have outlived the destruction of the temple by only a few years. Whether or not he was a Pharisee or interested in the Pharisaic tradition, figures associated with the Pharisees soon dominated the discussions.

The major concern of pre-70 Pharisaism, at least in the first century, was religious law (8.2.2). Therefore, most of the preserved pre-70 tradition centers on legal discussions and disputes. Pharisaism itself was divided into a variety of schools, of which two of the dominant ones at Yavneh were those of Hillel and Shammai. Moreover, there was no unity of tradition or legal ruling. Each school had its own rulings, some or many of which may have differed from those of other schools. These traditions also represented the interests and sphere of authority of the Pharisees, namely, their own homes and intersectarian concerns. At Yavneh the differences had to be thrashed out among the various schools and whatever non-Pharisaic parties were represented there. The maneuverings which went on can only be guessed at, but at some point agreement was reached that the opinions of both the school of Hillel and the school of Shammai would be preserved. Eventually, the school of Hillel became dominant, although this seems to have taken time because the school of Shammai was apparently more influential in pre-70 Pharisaism.

The important factor in the development of rabbinic Judaism was the injection of a new perspective—the concept of Torah-centeredness and the religious efficacy of study. The early rabbinic traditions about named figures do not indicate that these people were a group whose focus was on the study of the Torah. Rather, they comprised a table-fellowship sect for whom legal concerns and debate were important but for whom study was not a religious act. In the developing rabbinic Judaism, the center definitely became Torah study. Neusner has suggested that this element most logically came from the scribes, whose preoccupation was with the written law. Although there were scribes who were also Pharisees, the two were not synonymous; indeed, scribes were probably to be found in the other sects as well, because scribalism was principally a profession (8.2.4).

Despite our ignorance of the detailed events and our inability to reconstruct a narrative history, we know enough to appreciate how vital the Yavnean period was in the history of Judaism. During this time the roots of modern Judaism were first put down. A period of about sixty years saw the reconstruction of Judaism after the disaster of 70 and the birth of a new phenomenon previously unknown to history: rabbinic Judaism.

9.4.7 Trajan (98–117 c.e.)

According to our (pro-Trajan) sources, Trajan had many of the qualities of Vespasian. The army considered him one of them, and he maintained the outward forms of the republic sufficiently to keep the Senate happy. To the personal contrast with Domitian was added Trajan's administrative ability, which permitted him to inaugurate a period of relative order and peace that lasted through a good portion of the second century (but not at the frontiers). Indeed, Trajan began his reign by deciding to deal with the Dacians, who were still led by Decebalus. Trajan was victorious in the two Dacian wars (101–102, 105–106 c.e.), and the territory became a province. This was the start of Trajan's policy of expansion. The boundaries of the Roman Empire, which had remained more or less intact since the time of Augustus, were now being pushed by Trajan to their widest limits.

After the Dacians, Trajan turned to the East. In 106 he annexed Arabia to form a new province, but this was only a prelude to the campaigns which came near the end of his reign, his wars in the East. Although the precise reason behind the wars has been debated, they were undoubtedly undertaken primarily for strategic reasons, whatever secondary aims there may have been. Certainly Trajan felt the situation with the Parthians needed to be settled, and it served as a convenient excuse to renew expansion. When Pacorus II died in 109/110, the Parthian throne was taken by his brother Chosroes. Pacorus had intended that the throne of Armenia go to his younger son, Axidares, with Roman approval, but Chosroes now supported Pacorus's elder son, Parthamasiris, who had seized the Armenian throne. Trajan left Rome in October 113 for Antioch, where he spent several months preparing for war. He probably had the equivalent of eleven legions (plus auxiliaries) when he set out in the spring of 114 for Armenia. Parthamasiris submitted, but the crown was removed from him (he later died under mysterious circumstances) and Armenia—at least, the western part of it—became a Roman province. In the Caucasus, Trajan established a number of client kings to help hold the frontier.

In the autumn of 114, Trajan turned south into Mesopotamia. His precise course of events for the next year is uncertain, but he obtained the submission of various peoples, including Nisibus, Edessa, and Singra, and he acquired territory beyond the Tigris. He did not return until late in 115 but was in Antioch when the earthquake of 13 December 115 occurred. There was by this time a new province of Mesopotamia, but Trajan was not finished. In the spring of 116 he set out to conquer Assyria and Babylonia. He took Adiabene, Seleucia, and Ctesiphon by the summer, establishing the new province of Assyria, sailed downriver to the Persian Gulf to add additional client kings and then returned to the site of ancient Babylon to spend the winter. A counterattack by the Parthians, combined with revolts in Mesopotamia, threatened to reverse his successes, but they were effectively suppressed and most of the conquered areas remained under Roman control. Lusius Quietus received much of the credit for this.

It was now 117, however, and the serious situation with the Jews in Cyprus, Cyrene, and Egypt required attention, which included returning to the West those military units removed for the Parthian invasion. It was time to stop advancing and consolidate. Trajan left this task to Hadrian and began to make his way back to Rome. He died on the way, in August 117.

9.4.8   The Revolts under Trajan

Applebaum, S. *Jews and Greeks in Ancient Cyrene* (1979).

Barnes, T. D. "Trajan and the Jews." *JJS* 40 (1989) 145–62.

Fuks, A. "The Jewish Revolt in Egypt (A.D. 115–117) in the Light of the Papyri." *Aegyptus* 33 (1953) 131–58.

———. "Aspects of the Jewish Revolt in A.D. 115–117." *JRS* 51 (1961) 98–104.

Hengel, M. "Messianische Hoffnung und politischer 'Radikalismus' in der 'jüdisch-hellenistischen Diaspora': Zur Frage der Voraussetzungen des jüdischen Aufstandes unter Trajan 115–117 n. Chr." *Apocalypticism in the Mediterranean World and the Near East* (1983) 655–86.

Kasher, A. "Some Comments on the Jewish Uprising in Egypt in the Time of Trajan." *JJS* 27 (1976) 147–58.

Pucci, M. *La rivolta ebraica al tempo di Traiano* (1981).

———. "Sullo sfondo politico dei moti insurrezionali ebraici del 116–117 d.C." *Atti dell'Istituto Veneto di Scienze, Lettere ed Arti*. Classe di scienze morali, lettere ed arti 141 (1982/83) 241–77.

———. "C.P.J. II 158, 435 e la Revolta Ebraica al tempo di Traiano." *ZPE* 51 (1983) 95–103.

During the years 115–117, Jewish revolts broke out in Cyrenaica, Egypt, Mesopotamia, and, according to some, even in Palestine. The brief statements we have by Eusebius (9.2.2.1) and Dio (9.2.1.1) give few data. These can be filled out to some extent by papyri in Egypt, especially the personal archive of Apollonius, who served as *stratēgos* of the Apollinopolis-Heptakomias district ca. 113–120 (*CPJ*: 2.226), and by archeological evidence. For Mesopotamia almost nothing is known, and the situation in Palestine is little more than scholarly hypothesis (9.3.2).

Something of a consensus has come about on the chronology and development of the revolt (Schürer: 1.529–34; *Smallwood: 389–427): it began in 115 in Egypt, and spread from there; only later did Mesopotamia rise up against the Romans who had just conquered it. Barnes has challenged several elements of the consensus. His principal points are that (1) the revolt began not in Egypt but in Mesopotamia, and (2) this was not until 116. With so little data, any consensus may be nothing more than a confession of ignorance. Moreover, there is a grave danger of overinterpreting what little evidence there is (e.g., as is done at times by Pucci).

The Mesopotamian revolts seem to have begun in the wake of Trajan's eastern conquests (Barnes: 152–53). After he sailed down the Tigris to the Persian Gulf in mid-116, a general revolt occurred in the newly created provinces of Mesopotamia and Assyria during his absence. Although Trajan put it down, he died soon afterward. Jewish participation seems to have been only part of a broader backlash against the Roman conquest that included the Parthians and other native inhabitants of Mesopotamia. Apart from the knowledge that Jews were among those trying to throw off the recently acquired Roman yoke, we know nothing about the Mesopotamian revolts. To what extent the Jewish uprisings in Mesopotamia should be directly connected with the ones in the Mediterranean is a topic of debate.

Although the revolt in the West may not have begun in Cyrene, it reached a critical mass there first and spilled over into Egypt. Archeological and inscriptional evidence (Applebaum: 269–94) has tended to bear out the statements of Orosius (quoted in 9.2.2.2). Although excavation has concentrated on sacred and public buildings, sufficient evidence has been found to suggest that the city of Cyrene was completely destroyed. Preliminary study also shows some damage at Apollonia, Balagrae, Teucheira, and possibly Messa, and the devastation of the coastal area between Teucheira and Berenice. The situation at Berenice, as well as at

Barka and Ptolemais, is not clear. Multiple inscriptions tell of buildings and temples that were rebuilt to replace those torn down by the Jews, who seem to have concentrated their efforts on pagan temples and statues. According to literary sources, the fight was led by a "king" named Lukuas (Eusebius) or Andreius (Dio). This is important because the proclamation of a king not only shows a desire for national independence but also suggests messianic impulses.

The revolt in Egypt eventually was countrywide, judging from the places mentioned (*CPJ*: 1.88; Kasher: 154 n.36). A riot or larger civil action took place in Alexandria and was put down straightaway, before October 115 (*CPJ*: 2.228–33 [no. 435]). The Greeks then used this opportunity to attack the pacified Jews, who required the Romans to intervene on their behalf. Such periodic friction was not unusual, however, and it does not seem to have led to a general revolt because taxes continued to be paid until the summer of 116 (Barnes: 157–58). The real revolt, when it came, lasted approximately a year and was put down only after Roman reinforcements arrived. Even then suppression was not easy because in anticipation of the legions' arrival, the Jews seem to have concentrated their forces around Memphis to prevent the Romans from crossing the river, and they even succeeded in defeating one legion. Not until a second legion joined the first were the Romans able to overcome the Jews in about January 117 (*CPJ*: 2.236–40 [nos. 438–39]; Kasher: 155–56).

The ferocity of the fighting is indicated by records of new recruits into the Roman centuries in the months after the battle. Recruitment seems to average about one-third of total strength, which suggests a high rate of casualties (Kasher: 157). Areas of Egypt were so devastated by the fighting that they were unfruitful many decades later (*CPJ*: 2.257 [no. 449]; Kasher: 148–49, 153). But the Jews suffered more. They are said to have been "exterminated" (Appian, *Bell. Civ.* 2.90.380), undoubtedly true in many areas for local references to Jews practically cease after this. Because the revolt was quickly stifled in Alexandria, there were survivors there. Many of them were resettled in an area adjacent to the city, but the magnificent, great synagogue had been destroyed, and the Jewish court seems to have been suspended (*CPJ*: 1.92–93).

The rebellion in Cyprus was led by a "king" named Artemion, and this, too, has overtones of a messianic movement. Dio's number of 240,000 slain by the Jews is incredible, as are his figures for Cyrene, but the numbers suggest widespread killing and destruction. Unfortunately, archeology has not yet provided much to add to the brief literary evidence (Applebaum: 297–99). A few building inscriptions could be interpreted as representing rebuilding after the fighting in Cyprus, but nothing is specifically said to show this. A potentially more telling find is a heavily damaged statue, possibly of a Flavian emperor, with divine images on the cuirass especially mutilated. According to Dio, when the Jews were finally defeated, an edict was issued forbidding Jews to settle on the island.

The revolts were probably due to a variety of factors. In Egypt there had been continual friction between the Jews and the Greek population for at least a century (7.3.5; 7.3.8). In addition, the strength of the Roman military forces in Egypt had always been low because of the lack of significant unrest throughout much of Roman rule and was at this time further reduced by Trajan's call for units to aid in his Parthian War (9.4.7; Kasher: 150–54). Scholars have often suggested a connection between Trajan's Parthian War and the Jewish uprisings in the West. The idea that the Parthians themselves fomented the uprisings directly seems far-fetched, although an indirect connection is possible; that is, the realization that troops had been dispatched elsewhere, leaving a significantly reduced garrison, and the hope that the Parthians might be victorious may have combined to encourage the revolts.

The revolts in Cyprus and Cyrene had definite catalysts in the "kings," evidently messianic figures of some sort, who took the lead. Tcherikover has suggested that the cause in Egypt was similarly messianic or eschatological, because the Jews could not rationally have hoped to win by ordinary military means (*CPJ*: 1.90–91; see also Hengel). This has prima facie merit, especially if the Cyrene uprising was the cause of the uprisings in the Egyptian countryside; but arguing against it is the lack of any reference to a specific leader in the sources available to us. Possibly the combination of socioeconomic factors (especially the Jewish tax and the continual friction with the Greeks) provided ample fuel which only needed the spark of revolt in Cyrene to set off the Egyptian Jews' own attempt for freedom. Barnes is no doubt correct to be skeptical about the messianic cause of the revolt (161–62), but it could still be an important element because eschatological speculation was significant at this time (cf. 9.2.3.1; 9.2.3.2).

The situation in Palestine is difficult to ascertain (see 9.3.2). The evidence for revolts in the province seems extremely skimpy and is indirect at best, yet it is possible that there were attempts at an uprising. If there were, then they seem to have been quickly put down by the governor, Quietus (cf. Barnes: 160).

9.4.9 Hadrian (117–138 c.e.)

A protégé of Trajan, Hadrian had been well trained for his role as emperor. He had campaigned with Trajan and was in charge of the army in the East at Trajan's death. He was already in his early forties and had apparently been designated as Trajan's heir. His initial acts kept him on good terms with the Senate by allowing them to maintain the appearance of power by declaring him emperor. Although voted a number of honors immediately, as was customary, he initially declined most. Hadrian halted the extension of the borders of the empire further east; he quickly abandoned the recent conquests in Mesopotamia as too difficult to defend and came to terms with the Parthians. This meant that most of his reign was a time of peace, which allowed him to exercise his considerable skills to overhaul the administration and establish formal procedures for regular military training. It also let him take a number of tours of the empire, which occupied the bulk of his twenty-one-year reign.

After three years in Rome working on the administration of the empire, Hadrian began his first tour of the empire in 120 or 121. He proceeded initially to Gaul, then to the legions on the Rhine, sailing from there for Britain and wintering finally in Spain. After a visit to Mauretania, he sailed directly to the East, spending considerable time in Greece and Asia Minor, although he seems to have paid a visit to Syria as well. Back in Rome by 126, his second tour most likely began in early 128 with a visit to Carthage and a tour of Roman Africa, then to Greece, which he reached in late 128. After wintering in Athens, he crossed to Asia Minor for a tour through the southern provinces, ending at Antioch about mid-129. Using Antioch as a base, he made further excursions to such places as Damascus and Palmyra and possibly even Petra (although this may have been in the next year).

It was most likely in the spring of 130 that he set out again from Antioch on his journey south. At this time (rather than in 129) he visited Jerusalem and probably gave the order that it be rebuilt as Aelia Capitolina (cf. 9.3.3). The occasion was marked by the issue of a series of coins with the inscription "for the arrival of Augustus [Hadrian] in Judea" (*Adventui Aug[usti] Iudaeae* [*Mildenberg 1984: 97–99]). Moving on, he restored Pompey's tomb at Pelusium before entering Egypt, where he remained for the next year. In late summer 131 he returned to Syria, apparently spending some time there. He wintered in Athens in 131–132. The next visit of which we are sure was to Rome in 134, and his actions in the intervening time are uncertain. Plaques and dedications in various Greek and Eastern cities show his generosity to them, but dating his presence in these cities is often a matter of speculation. It seems probable, however, that he personally inspected the theater of war in Judea sometime in 133–134. It may have been the exertions of his tours that brought on an illness in 136 that only worsened during the final years of his reign. He died in July 138.

9.4.10   The Bar Kokhba Revolt (132–135 c.e.)

Applebaum, S. "The Second Jewish Revolt (A.D. 131–35)." *PEQ* 116 (1984) 35–41.

Gichon, M. "The Bar Kokhba War: A Colonial Uprising against Imperial Rome." *Revue internationale d'histoire militaire* 42 (1979) 82–97.

———. "New Insight into the Bar Kokhba War and a Reappraisal of Dio Cassius 69.12–13." *JQR* 77 (1986/87) 15–43.

Goodblatt, D. "A Contribution to the Prosopography of the Second Revolt: Yehudah bar Menasheh." *JJS* 38 (1987) 38–55.

Isaac, B. "Roman Colonies in Judaea: The Foundation of Aelia Capitolina." *Talanta* 12–13 (1980–81) 31–54.

Isaac, B., and A. Oppenheimer. "The Revolt of Bar Kokhba: Ideology and Modern Scholarship." *JJS* 36 (1985) 33–60.

Isaac, B., and I. Roll. *Roman Roads in Judaea* (1982).

Kloner, A. "Underground Hiding Complexes from the Bar Kokhba War in the Judean Shephelah." *BA* 46 (1983a) 210–21.

———. "The Subterranean Hideaways of the Judean Foothills and the Bar-Kokhba Revolt." *Jerusalem Cathedra* 3 (1983b) 114–35.

Laperrousaz, E. M. "L'Hérodium, quartier général de Bar Kokhba?" *Syria* 41 (1964) 347–58.

Mildenberg, L. "The Eleazar Coins of the Bar Kochba Rebellion." *Historia Judaica* 11 (1949) 77–108.

Mor, M. "The Bar-Kokhba Revolt and Non-Jewish Participants." *JJS* 36 (1985) 200–209.

Oppenheimer, A. "The Bar Kokhba Revolt." *Immanuel* 14 (1982) 58–76.

Roll, I. "The Roman Road System in Judaea." *Jerusalem Cathedra* 3 (1983) 136–61.

We know a bit more about the Palestinian revolt of 132–135 than about the earlier revolts in Egypt, Cyrene, and Cyprus, thanks in large part to recent discoveries of manuscripts and coins. Again, though, there is not enough information to give a history of the war or even a rough sequence of events. The only account of consequence preserved is that of Cassius Dio (see 9.2.1.1 for the text), although Eusebius has some additional information (9.2.2.1). This can now be supplemented by data from letters, documents, and coins recently discovered, as well as a fair amount of archeological information (9.2.4). These fit together to give an overall chronology for the revolt but not much in the way of detail (9.3.4).

The causes of the revolt were multiple and complex (9.3.3). Early suggestions, such as the claim that Hadrian gave, then withdrew, permission for the temple to be rebuilt should probably no longer be seriously entertained. Recent studies have tended to center on two causes, both Hadrianic decrees, one to prohibit circumcision, the other to rebuild Jerusalem as the Hellenistic city Aelia Capitolina. Both reasons have generally been accepted, but a number of scholars have called into question the thesis of a prohibition of circumcision by Hadrian as a cause of the revolt, although it may have been a consequence. The main source of the theory is a single statement in the unreliable *Historia Augusta*. It has been argued that this statement is supported by passages in rabbinic literature, but closer investigation shows that the passages are not only late, on the whole, but subject to more than one interpretation. There is no doubt that a decree prohibiting circumcision would have been a significant reason for the revolt, but the questions are whether such a decree conforms with Hadrian's general character and policies and whether the single source for this allegation should be believed.

More secure is the proposal that the plan to build Aelia Capitolina preceded the revolt. This would not only have fitted Hadrian's program of founding Hellenistic cities but now seems confirmed by evidence from coins. It has also been argued that some Jews may have encouraged him in the plan. Nevertheless, this is probably not the only cause. A recent suggestion is that Hadrian's primary concern was a perceived threat from growing Christianity (9.3.3). Many of the factors that led to the 66–70 rebellion were still in existence. There is some evidence of periodic unrest in Judea after the fall of Jerusalem in 70. Economic difficulties were another potential source of discontent, although these may not have been as dire as sometimes assumed (9.3.7). Jewish literature of the time shows that messianic and apocalyptic expectations were still entertained in some circles (9.2.3.1–2). Finally, various actions taken by Hadrian on his tour of the eastern Mediterranean, although innocent in themselves, could have been interpreted by Jews as a slur on their status and history (e.g., the honor paid by Hadrian to the tomb of Pompey). All that was needed was the right catalyst. Whether that catalyst was a single action of Hadrian, the rise of Bar Kokhba as a leader, or something else, the Jews were not willing to remain under the Roman yoke without one more try for independence.

The war was evidently preceded by unrest in Palestine, which would explain why the Romans felt it necessary to bring a second legion into the area sometime before 120 (9.3.1). This could also explain the intense period of road building in the decade 120–130 (Isaac/Oppenheimer: 50–51). Dio's statement about the Jewish manufacture of weapons (if at all credible) would also indicate advance preparation for the war. Although exactly when the revolt began is unclear, coins and the dates on various documents suggest that it had started by the spring of 132 (9.3.4). The precise course of the war is very uncertain, although attempts at reconstruction have been proposed (see below).

Whereas the First Revolt produced a number of leaders but no single outstanding one, the Second Revolt was dominated by the name of its leader. In rabbinic literature he is referred to as Shim'on ben Koziba, which has usually been considered a denigratory play on words (*koziba* means "lie" in Aramaic). Some rabbinic passages also refer to him as *bar kôkĕvā'*, "son of the star," a name also found in Eusebius (*barchōchebas*). The explanation that this is a title, based on the messianic interpretation of Num 24:17, is probably correct, especially as documents have recently been found which contain his actual name. In various Hebrew letters he is called *šm'wn bn kwsbh*, "Simon son of Kosiva." The correct vocalization of the name is now confirmed by a Greek letter which gives it as *simōn chōsiba* (5/6HevEp gr 6 [9.2.4.2]). Apart from his father's name and his personal name, however, we know extremely little about this unusual man, despite the discovery of his personal letters. There is no indication in documents or on coinage that he claimed to be the messiah (although some of the coin symbolism has been so interpreted [cf. *Meshorer: 2.138–50]). Nevertheless, rabbinic and Christian traditions show that his role was interpreted messianically by some, including most likely by R. Aqiva. Hence the title Bar Kokhba ("son of the star"), which became attached to him at some point. The exact significance of the title "prince" (*nāśî'*) found on coins and in one or two documents is uncertain (as to whether it has messianic overtones or represents simply a refusal to take the title "king").

The coins are an important though sometimes ambiguous source of information. Meshorer (*2.132–65) and Mildenberg (*1984: 69–72) agree that Bar Kokhba put high value on the coins as a medium of propaganda. Both the number of coin finds and the quality of their manufacture indicate significant support among the people. All the coins are over-strikes, but the Roman coins, both silver and bronze, that were over-struck were apparently already in circulation among the Jewish people themselves. (No gold overstrikes have been found, suggesting that any Roman gold coins were used by the rebels for external purchases rather than internal trade.) The only name on the coins other than Simon b. Kosiva is "Eleazar the priest" (*'l'zr hkwhn*). Although it is not known who he was, a reasonable assumption is that he was the individual who had assumed the office of high priest. It is common to identify him with Eleazar of Modein of rabbinic legend, who was said to be Bar Kokhba's uncle, but to what extent such tradition should be trusted is a moot point (*Schäfer: 173–74). Because his name disappears from the silver coinage after year 1, it has been suggested that he was deposed by Bar Kokhba (again, drawing on rabbinic legend), yet this seems a rather precarious conclusion because the name is found on all years of the bronze coins.

Bar Kokhba's military strategy is revealed by (1) the location of his "kingdom" or territory in the area to the south of Jerusalem and west of the Dead Sea, bordering on the Judean desert (9.3.5); and (2) the discovery of a number of man-made hideouts tunneled into the rock in the Shephelah and elsewhere (Kloner). These discoveries and the information in Dio suggest that Bar Kokhba's men waged primarily a guerrilla war rather than pitched battles with the Romans. The denlike dwellings dug into the rock formed bases of operation that allowed the Jewish fighters to hide undetected, emerge when the opportunity presented itself for a swift blow at the enemy, and then disappear once more, as if into thin air. Even if hideouts were discovered, they were constructed so as to make it difficult to attack those within.

Gichon (1979; 1986/87) has attempted to go beyond this general conclusion by relating the hideouts to his excavations at Horvat Eqed and other archeological data, and to the statements of Dio. He concludes that the hideouts were constructed surreptitiously over a period of time preceding the war and used with considerable success to make a surprise attack on the Romans at the beginning of the uprising. A second construction stage involved more conventional fortifications aboveground, to meet the Roman counterattack. Gichon's interpretation makes good military sense and also fits various of the archeological data. However, his conclusion that the Jews successfully occupied a large part of the country (including Galilee, because hideouts have been found there) is more problematic (9.3.5). Such hideouts were used in many periods, and the attempt to relate them all to the Bar Kokhba revolt is disputed (Isaac/Oppenheimer: 42–43, 53–54).

The location of the territory also made invasion difficult, except from predictable directions. The wilderness was at Bar Kokhba's back and was a refuge of last resort (which some seem to have made use of in the end). The oasis of Engedi served as a point of provisioning and a communications center. Whether there was one central headquarters is debatable, although it has been argued that Herodium served this purpose for at least part of the war (Laperrousaz). Another important site was Betar (Bethar), six to seven miles southwest of Jerusalem, which eventually served as the site of Bar Kokhba's last stand against the Romans. Several other places appear in the documents, all from the area to the south of Jerusalem and west of the Dead Sea.

Although it has often been asserted that the Jews took Jerusalem, there is actually little hard evidence for this beyond hints in minor literary sources and a particular interpretation of the phrase "Year ____ of the liberation of Jerusalem" on some coins. A strong argument against Jewish seizure of Jerusalem is the lack of any Bar Kokhba coin finds from the extensive archeological excavations in Jerusalem (9.2.4.1). There is also no evidence of the occupation of Masada, another surprising fact. Perhaps the Jews had learned from the experience of the First Revolt that success lay in hit-and-run tactics and that making a stand in fortresses meant inevitable defeat after a lengthy siege. If so, it seems that things went wrong at the end of the Bar Kokhba revolt, because a final stand was made in the hilltop fortress of Betar in 135.

The letters and other documents of Bar Kokhba show neither a messianic figure nor a fighter in action. Instead, they mirror a mundane world in which land is leased (Mur 24), the Sabbath observed (Mur 44), the festivals scrupulously celebrated (5/6ḤevEp 15), and the ownership of a cow disputed (Mur 42). A couple of letters assert Bar Kokhba's authority because he had apparently not been obeyed (Mur 43; 5/6ḤevEp 1), and another mentions something not done because the "Gentiles" (Romans) were near (Mur 42). These appear to be the closest references to military activity found in the contemporary records. An intriguing statement by Dio is that non-Jews also participated in the fight against the Romans. Although evidence presented to substantiate this assertion (such as names in the Bar Kokhba manuscripts) has not been very cogent, there may be a basis to it; Mor has argued that those who joined the Jews would have been slaves and others on the low end of the socioeconomic scale, who had good reason to fight against the Romans. Some may also have done so as mercenaries.

According to Dio, five hundred thousand Jews died in the fighting alone, not counting those who perished from famine and disease and those who were enslaved. This seems an exaggerated figure but at least indicates the serious cost of the Second Revolt in Jewish lives. After the defeat, the glut of slaves was so great that the price dropped drastically in the Eastern markets for a time. Judging from the comments of Dio, however, the Roman casualties were also very high, such that Hadrian in his report to the Senate dropped the customary formula "I and the legions are well." Aelia Capitolina became a reality, and Jews were long excluded at least officially, even from entry into the city. Only in the fourth century were Jews again formally allowed access to the temple site, and then only once a year on the ninth of Ab, the traditional date of its destruction (*Fitzmyer: 352).

10

THE JEWISH THEOCRACY FROM CYRUS TO HADRIAN

If there is one word to characterize the nation of Judah throughout the Second Temple period, it is "theocracy." During most of this time the country was ruled by priests, primarily the high priest. This was both its strength and its weakness, and, ironically, Judah's high point politically and economically came under the rule of Herod the Great, when the high priest and Sanhedrin were at their weakest. Yet the priestly rule allowed for a union of the civil and the religious when Judah was under foreign rule and a native king might not have been acceptable to the overlords. This theocratic rule began during the Persian period when the administration was at first a dyarchy, that is, joint rule between a governor appointed by the Persians (who was often, if not always, Jewish) and the high priest. Whether that practice continued throughout the Persian period is unknown. Under Greek rule, however, the Jewish official responsible for the nation in the eyes of the Seleucid and Ptolemaic governments was the high priest himself.

Israelite religion—as far back as it can be traced—had centered on the sacrificial cult. Perhaps responsibility for this rite had once rested with the head of the clan or family. At some point, though, a professional priesthood developed, initially at several cultic sites but eventually centered in Jerusalem. Although it was probably only late in the monarchial period that a concerted attempt was made to eliminate worship outside of Jerusalem, by the time of Cyrus (ca. 540 B.C.E.) we hear little of other cultic sites (with one or two notable exceptions, such as Mount Gerizim). Jerusalem was the place Yahweh had chosen; here was Yahweh's temple, sanctuary, and holy place.

At the heart of the cult was blood sacrifice. By such sacrifice, breaches of social and cultic order could be rectified and harmony reestablished. Blood purified and restored. Without the shedding of blood there was no forgiveness of sin. Sacrifice was also a social and communal act, for in most cases the victim became the basis of a cultic meal: only certain parts were burned on the altar; other parts went to the priests; and the rest was for the worshiper and family to consume in a state of ritual purity. There were other elements in worship and other means to worship, but until 70 C.E. the central act of devotion remained the slaying of a sacrificial animal.

Music and singing also constituted a part of worship, although their precise roles can only be guessed at. The temple-singers formed a specific group of temple personnel (2.4.5). Many of the canonical and other psalms and hymns no doubt had their places in the liturgy, but precisely how and where is not found in the extant Second Temple sources (8.3.3). Special ceremonies were also associated with certain dates in the cultic calendar. For example, the most solemn rite of the year was the Day of Atonement (Yom ha-Kippurim), when the high priest entered into the most mystical and sacred part of the temple, the Holy of Holies (Leviticus 16; cf. Ben Sira 50:5-21).

The emphasis of Israelite religion and early Judaism was, therefore, on public worship at the altar. However, private devotions could also be included and were especially important for those unable to present themselves regularly at the temple. Private worship especially included prayer, but other activity could also be considered a part of religious devotion: charity to the poor and other acts of kindness associated with a concern for one's fellow Jew—in short, love of one's neighbor. Observance of the law—obedience to the Torah in all its forms—counted as a religious service to God. Eventually, even various acts of asceticism (fasting, celibacy) took on a pious value, at least in some circles. In the Diaspora the synagogue developed into a major communal place of instruction and worship, probably first in the early Greek period. The institution eventually spread to the homeland itself, but even though synagogues are sparsely attested in Judea before 70 C.E., from all archeological and literary evidence they seem to have been a late introduction there, well after the Maccabean revolt. The temple was still the religious center of the Land of Israel.

Thus, the first concern of the exiles returning from the Babylonian captivity was the rebuilding of the temple. Because of the nature of our historical sources, it is difficult to be precise, but building seems to have begun in earnest early in Darius's reign. The date of the temple's completion is unknown (very unlikely is the sixth year of Darius [Ezra 6:15]), as is much of the history of Judah for the next seventy-five years.

Then, sometime around the middle of the fifth century B.C.E., a new force was unleashed on the province, a compulsion to isolate the people from the surrounding nations and cultures. In one sense, this isolationist push was not new since the idea that mixing with Gentiles was bad for religious purity had long been common in some circles. But the zealot Nehemiah came not only with a single-minded view of what Judaism should be but also with powers backed by Persian authority. In this he may have been preceded or followed by Ezra, although assessment of the Ezra tradition is much more difficult and controversial; in any event, the measures ascribed to Ezra look very similar to those of Nehemiah. Suddenly the Jewish community became very narrowly defined. Boundaries were drawn and non-Jews excluded as far as possible. Nehemiah could enforce his rulings as law and evidently did, to the consternation of not a few of his fellow Jews. The community became exclusivistic and inward-looking, and barriers kept the outside world as far away as possible.

How long this approach lasted after the passing of Nehemiah (and Ezra?) is uncertain, although there is evidence that at least some—perhaps many—of the community did not share Nehemiah's vision. For almost four hundred years after the exile, however, Judea was a small, economically backward country with little impact on the wider world. Many of the more prosperous areas of the old Israelite kingdoms were outside these new borders, and Jews now lived in regions outside the province of Judea and especially in Galilee. Individual Jews rose to important positions in the Hellenistic world. Several are said to have become generals in the Egyptian army under the Ptolemies. The Tobiad legend, even discounting its romantic exaggerations, attests to a Jewish family with important connections to the Ptolemaic court and considerable political and economic influence in the region of Coele-Syria. Clearly, some Jews were people of wealth and influence, but the Jews as a whole and Judea in particular formed a backwater in the Greek empires, eking out a daily living and paying the regular tribute. In such circumstances, Nehemiah's narrow vision may have seemed highly appropriate. During this isolation, religious literature was produced, some of it of considerable interest and value, evidencing the continued spiritual development and growth of Judaism, and not all of it likely to have been approved by the exclusivists and conservative members of the community. Qohelet (Ecclesiastes, or "The Preacher") created a unique work of skeptical inquiry, challenging the traditional religious shibboleths while perhaps also affirming basic providence in spite of human uncertainty. Other Jews contemplated "true reality" (as they saw it), divorced from the grind of mundane living under a colonial power. They thought on the world above and the world to come: the heavenly order with the progression of the celestial bodies and the divine calendar (*1 Enoch* 72–82); the realms of angels and demons in whose hands the earthly powers and potentates were mere puppets; the place of the souls of the dead, awaiting the eventual eschaton and the final judgment. To them, the movements of armies, the decisions of emperors, the debasement of God's chosen people were temporary and trivial. It would all end with a cosmic bang.

The high priest presided over the nation. He was responsible to the colonial authorities, especially in the matter of the annual tribute (4.3.1). Certain taxes were farmed out to the highest bidder, but fixed tribute also seems to have been demanded, for which the high priest was held accountable. Advising the priestly head of state was a council which seems to have been made up of priests and lay members of the aristocracy. This Sanhedrin (*synedrion*, also known as the *boulē* or *gerousia*) may have been only advisory or it may have had actual powers—probably being sometimes one and sometimes the other during its long history (7.3.2.3).

For three centuries, from the time of Ezra-Nehemiah (mid-fifth century B.C.E.) to the Maccabean revolt (mid-second century B.C.E.), we hear little about the internal affairs of the small province of Judah. It seems to have remained quiet for the most part—although some scholars have seen hints of the odd revolt (2.3.9)—to have paid its taxes and got along as best it could in the circumstances. The transition from Persian to Greek rule (ca. 330 B.C.E.) apparently took place without major trauma or significant change for the Jews. Perhaps more unhappy was the period of the Diadochi when armies marched back and forth over the entire Near East for almost forty years. We do not know the details, but Jerusalem seems to have been taken at least once, and to have experienced a transfer of population to Egypt on one or more occasions. In any case, Palestine came permanently under Ptolemaic rule by about 300 B.C.E., and Judea was more or less at peace for the next century. Egypt possessed Coele-Syria, but the Seleucids had a legal claim to it. During the first four Syrian wars, the Seleucids tried but failed to take the territory that they argued was rightfully theirs. As far as we know, little if any of this struggle affected the little Jewish province, isolated as it was from the main invasion routes and the most fertile areas of the region.

Some Jews no doubt served in the Ptolemaic army because they were members of a military colony such as the Tobiads (4.3.2) or were even mercenaries. Otherwise, we hear little about the Jews. Underneath the calm surface, however, changes were taking place. Slowly, quietly, but inexorably, the developing Hellenistic culture was making its impact felt in even the remote and mainly rural province of Judea. The only urban area, Jerusalem, had an upper class and cosmopolitan residents; and there was regular contact with the outside world—perhaps not least because of the large Jewish Diaspora which still looked to Jerusalem and the temple, as well as the not insignificant number of pilgrims coming at each of the major festival periods. The small upper class would have watched developing events with some interest. For a few, the potential commercial advantages would have excited attention. The political question of whether the region might come under Seleucid control was a concern for many. These were practical matters, but no doubt various members of the priestly and lay aristocracy also found themselves intrigued by the novelties of Hellenistic culture, an attraction perhaps enhanced by communication with relatives who actually lived in Greek cities. For such people, the vision of Nehemiah must have seemed decidedly blinkered.

After a century or so of quiet development and influence, attitudes changed and new interests were kindled. Hellenization had its impact. Then Coele-Syria changed hands; sometime around 200 B.C.E. Antiochus III was finally able to take Judea as the southern part of his empire, something his ancestors had been trying to do for almost a century. Judea was now under Seleucid rule, but the old constitution was affirmed by official decree and nothing seems to have changed immediately. After the stormy period under Antiochus III, Seleucus IV reigned for a few quiet years, to be succeeded in 175 B.C.E. by his vigorous brother, Antiochus IV.

Suddenly, what had been building for decades burst forth in the so-called Hellenistic reform. This was not imposed from above by the Seleucid king but blossomed naturally from below out of seeds long nurtured in an environment stimulated by the proximity of Greek institutions. When Jason, the brother of the high priest Onias, went to Antiochus IV and asked that Jerusalem become a Greek polis, it could hardly have been startling—because this sentiment had been growing for years. Many if not most Jews apparently took it in their stride, at least, we hear of no adverse reaction. Even the most potentially scandalous act—the king deposing the serving high priest in favor of another—seems to have been accepted without overt protest.

It would be difficult to overestimate the importance of the Hellenistic reform for the subsequent history of Judea, for it brought the full impact of a more sophisticated culture and its economic benefits onto an economically and culturally backward nation. Judea could no longer exist quietly and let the rest of the world pass it by. Not only did the bright light of a new way of living fall on the Jews, but its glare also exposed them to the rest of the world. The long relative isolation had come to an end. If changes had been allowed to occur in a steady, peaceful manner, it is hard to predict how things may have developed. However, with the Maccabean revolt, and its subsequent success, enormous change took place which culminated in two disastrous revolts and the end of Judah as a nation until the present day.

With one important exception, Jewish religious rights were officially respected throughout the Second Temple period. The widespread feeling today that religious tolerance is a product of modern enlightenment is due to the experience of centuries of monotheistic persecution. In fact, the polytheism common in the ancient world was by nature tolerant. Other gods and forms of worship were accepted and permitted. The Persian, Greek, and Roman governments did not restrict the practice of Judaism as a religion, whatever the personal feelings of individuals. Thus, Judaism was sometimes ridiculed and eventually even attacked under Roman rule, but official tolerance persisted.

The one exception to this general policy remains inexplicable, although a number of important and ingenious suggestions have been offered in explanation. In 168 B.C.E. the Seleucid king Antiochus IV forbade both the daily sacrifice in the temple and all practice of Jewish worship. For three years Judaism was officially proscribed. This action is puzzling because it was unprecedented: for the first time in its history, Judaism was persecuted as a religion. Much about the persecution and the events surrounding it do not make sense, but a number of older and frequently repeated assumptions can no longer be entertained. That Antiochus should have taken such a drastic step was out of keeping with his normally shrewd administration. Whatever else Antiochus IV was, he was no fool; indeed, he seems to have been one of the most able of the Seleucid rulers. His attack on the Jewish religion was a serious miscalculation, however, and plunged him into an unnecessary war which took valuable resources at a time when finances were a problem.

The Hellenistic reform has often been blamed for the persecution. This is probably wrong in the strict sense because the reform did not affect the practice of Judaism. (The reform is to be dissociated from the fight over the high priesthood, which is a separate issue.) There is no evidence of pagan worship or infringement of traditional Jewish worship while Jerusalem was a Greek polis under Jason, despite the impression given by 1 and 2 Maccabees. Nothing in Jewish law prohibited the measures taken to adopt the constitution of a polis. No images were set up in the temple and no pagan rites were introduced. The regular, traditional cultic service in the temple went on as before, and the presence of a gymnasium in no way altered this. In fact, it would not have been in the interest of the priesthood, dependent as it was on the tithes and offerings of the people, to antagonize the ordinary worshiper. Jason's innovations were political and cultural, not religious.

Things may have been different under Menelaus. It was rumored, with considerable plausibility, that his brother sold off some of the silver temple vessels to raise money. Menelaus was alleged to have conducted Antiochus into the temple itself; if true, this was a clear disregard for cultic law. Thus, those who argue that Menelaus was somehow the cause of the persecution have a point, even if the precise motivation and sequence of events have not been clarified. Menelaus has often been labeled an "extreme Hellenist," but whether his actions had anything in common with Jason's Hellenistic measures is debatable. Once he had obtained the priesthood, Menelaus's subsequent actions, which were often opposed by Jason's supporters, seem to have been aimed at maintaining his position. If Menelaus was interested in the Hellenistic reform, it is not immediately clear from the sources.

Thus, it is correct to stress the importance of the Hellenistic reform. On the other hand, it must also be recognized that the reform was itself an almost inevitable development brought about by insistent forces of Hellenization. It is doubtful that Judea could have remained aloof from the new environment, even if it wanted to. The Hellenistic reform was in many ways natural and expected. Nevertheless, it marks a watershed in Jewish history and itself set in motion relentless forces that shaped Israelite history for many centuries. Judaism and Judea would never be the same afterward.

The high point of the theocracy probably occurred under Hasmonean rule, when the Maccabean successors adopted the title "king." For less than half a century the one who presided at the temple was also the monarch and chief administrator of the country, presiding at the head of the governing council (Sanhedrin). The Hasmoneans were truly "priest-kings" at this time, with all which that implies. The success of the Maccabean revolt allowed Judea to become an independent nation for the first time in perhaps half a millennium.

Yet the Israel of old had been able to maintain its independence only when the major powers of Egypt and Mesopotamia were not on the scene. The Seleucid empire was fragmenting, and this allowed the Hasmonean kingdom to emerge, but the Seleucid decline was in part due to the rise of Rome. Basically, Israel's short-lived freedom did nothing but kindle a consuming desire to regain that freedom when the people came once more under colonial domination, this time by Rome. Perhaps if Judea had remained a small backwater, the two revolts against Rome might not have taken place. However, coming under renewed foreign rule after some decades of independence made eventual revolt almost inevitable.

The first few decades of imposed Roman rule were difficult for the nation. The renewed servitude chafed. The instability created by the Roman civil war encouraged nationalistic movements and revolts. One part of the nation—or its leadership, at least—accepted compromise with the Romans as unavoidable; another part tried to restore Hasmonean rule under Aristobulus II. Several times it appeared possible that Aristobulus would shake off the Roman yoke and renew the Hasmonean kingdom. Hope continued even after the declaration of Herod as king in 40 B.C.E.; however, once Octavian prevailed at the battle of Actium (31 B.C.E.), the fate of the nation was sealed: life was possible only by recognizing the overlordship of Rome. Whether as a client kingdom or as a province, Judea was a subject people.

Despite centuries of criticism, Herod was, on balance, good for Judea and amidst the inevitability of Roman rule was able to champion many Jewish causes. A ruthless response to any challenge to his power could be taken for granted even without striking examples (e.g., his decimation of the Sanhedrin [7.3.2.3]), but those who suffered directly from his measures to maintain power were few, primarily a few families of the priesthood and aristocracy. The charge that he conducted a reign of terror against the people as a whole is unsubstantiated and unlikely. The claim that he bled the nation financially is often repeated but seldom argued. Like all rulers, Herod collected taxes, but there is no evidence that he was more exploitative than the Hasmoneans and certainly no more so than the Romans when they ruled directly. His friendship with Augustus, his good works for the Greek world, his building program in Judea, and especially his refashioning of the temple to make it one of the most famous edifices of the time could only have enhanced the prestige of the nation and people as a whole, even if few benefited directly. Herod saw to it that Jewish religious privileges were restored in Asia Minor, where they had been eroded by local opposition. He established peace and unified the country into a kingdom as large as Solomon's, respecting Jewish sensibilities and apparently living as a Jew himself, albeit on the permissive wing of the faith (although in this he was hardly alone).

But bad feeling there was, if unquantifiable, and Herod largely destroyed general confidence in the traditional priestly and lay aristocracy. This was to have important consequences in the middle decades of the first century. On the other hand, once the Jews had a chance to experience direct Roman rule (as some had indeed requested after the king's death) they were glad to welcome a Herodian ruler once more only a few decades later. The Romans were clearly going to rule, so there were advantages in having a Herodian as a buffer between them and the Roman machine. Thus, the kingship of Agrippa I (41–44 C.E.) was greeted with enthusiasm. Unfortunately, his rule ended all too quickly. Whether he could have maintained the good will of both the people and Rome, and whether he might even have prevented the 66–70 war, is a matter of interesting speculation. Some examples of tensions in both areas were already evident during his short reign, yet he, more than anyone else, might have kept both sides placated.

Agrippa's early death had a further consequence: his son Agrippa II was quite young and, for whatever reasons, the emperor Claudius did not choose to have him succeed his father. Judea once more found itself a Roman province. Agrippa II maintained connections with Jerusalem, eventually acquiring various rights with regard to the temple, such as the power to appoint the high priest. However, those in the upper echelons of the priesthood also asserted themselves, coming in conflict with Agrippa on more than one occasion. If he had been king of Judea, events might have been different, but his authority was more indirect and his influence had its limits. Thus, during the earliest stages of the First Revolt (66–70 C.E.) when he was actually present in Jerusalem, his attempts to intervene and change the minds of the leading citizens and priests were ineffectual, and he was hounded from the city. Had his father lived longer, Agrippa II might have been mature enough in Roman eyes to become king of Judea, with sufficient actual and moral authority to avert the impending crisis. But that is not what happened. Instead, the Jews took the path of revolt and, when the first attempt failed, tried again some decades later with even more disastrous consequences.

The 66–70 revolt, despite the bitter results, need not have been the end of the temple state. The destruction of population and property was minimal except for Jerusalem itself, and many in the higher priesthood survived. However, for reasons still unclear, the priests were not able to gain sufficient Roman confidence to resume the temple cult and their traditional place within it. A new power structure and a new form of Judaism began shortly after the destruction that was a synthesis of various forms, factions, and sects of pre-70 Judaism. Although descriptions of Second Temple Judaism have been dominated by discussions of the various sects, this emphasis is wrong. Most Judaism of the time fell within certain parameters and shared a broad common ground. But the cult-centeredness and other characteristics of Judaism then meant there was no "orthodoxy" as such. This fact encouraged various sects to flourish.

We know that many groups existed for shorter or longer periods of time, including the Pharisees, Sadducees, and Essenes. But in investigating them we discover that, like watching a fan dancer, we see less than we initially thought we did. Apart from the Essenes (and depending on how one relates them to Qumran), we know little about the three sects so often referred to. This includes the Pharisees, about which so much has been written with so little evidence. There is, for example, despite the silence of the sources, a tendency to insert the word "Pharisaic" wherever the word "piety" occurs and to identify all pious or learned individuals as Pharisees (e.g., the individuals who tore down Herod's eagle from the temple). In fact, about all we know with reasonable certainty is that they had traditions from the fathers and that from Maccabean times on they attempted on several occasions to gain political power. But we are told very little about what they actually believed and what these traditions from the fathers were. Recent scholarship has made considerable progress in separating the earlier layers of tradition from the later in the Mishnah. If the pre-70 strata can be associated with the Pharisees, this would give us some idea of their beliefs. If so, the description of "table fellowship" sect seems accurate, as far as it goes (although they could have believed other things omitted from the Mishnah).

Whatever the precise beliefs of the Pharisees, the long-prevalent view that they dominated the society and religion of first-century Judaism can no longer be maintained, whether this view comes from Josephus, the New Testament, or the earlier traditions of rabbinic literature. Still, the Pharisees were an important component of pre-70 Judaism and probably of the Judaism that developed afterward. The Judaism after 70 was a synthesis, a new creation, an entity that had not existed before and is thus not to be identified with any Second Temple group. Yet it seems to have made use of various elements of the pre-70 scene. One of the more important of these was probably the old Pharisaic legal traditions. But this new Judaism also included other traditions and interests, especially priestly and scribal ones. At Yavneh, rabbinic Judaism was born.

The main power base of the priests and the aristocracy evidently disappeared with the temple. There is reason to think that they tried unsuccessfully to regain their old position with the Romans. Whether the failure of the old elite was significant in the Second Revolt (132–135 C.E.) is difficult to know, partly because we know so little about the revolt itself. Perhaps this effeteness of the traditional upper classes was irrelevant to the forces that pushed toward another revolt. As long as the real cause of the revolt is itself more or less obscure, we can only speculate on how much the changed situation in the sixty years between the two revolts had to do with it.

What is clear is that the period between 70 and 130—the Yavneh period in rabbinic literature—was a watershed in the history of Judaism. The Judaism arising after 135 was new and different in many essential ways from that before 70. However much the temple and cult may have formed the basis of theoretical discussion in the emerging rabbinic Judaism, the Jewish temple state had ceased forever. Jewish identity was ethnic and religious. A Jewish state of any kind would have to wait another nineteen hundred years.

CHRONOLOGY

Date	Ancient Near East	Judah	Date
B.C.E.			
600	Nebuchadnezzar (604–562)		**600**
590		Fall of Jerusalem (587/586)	**590**
580			**580**
570			**570**
	Amel-Marduk (562–560)	Jehoiachin released from prison	
560	Nabonidus (558–539)		**560**
	Cyrus ([556]539–530)		

CHRONOLOGY

Date	Ancient Near East	Judah	Date
B.C.E.			
550			**550**
•			•
•			•
•			•
•			•
•			•
•			•
•			•
•			•
540			**540**
•	Fall of Babylon (539)		•
•		Beginning of return to Judah	•
•		under Cyrus (?)	•
•			•
•			•
•		Mission of Sheshbazzar (?)	•
•			•
•			•
•			•
530	Cambyses (530–522)		**530**
•			•
•			•
•			•
•	Cambyses invades Egypt		•
•			•
•		Joshua and Zerubbabel	•
•	Darius I (522–486)	Prophets Haggai/Zechariah	•
•	Revolts under Darius	Rebuilding of temple begun	•
520			**520**
•			•
•			•
•			•
•			•
•			•
•			•
•			•
•			•
510			**510**
•			•
•			•
•			•
•			•
•			•
•			•
•			•
•			•

CHRONOLOGY

Date	Ancient Near East	Judah	Date
B.C.E.			
500			500
•			•
•			•
•			•
•			•
•			•
•			•
•			•
•			•
•			•
490	Battle of Marathon		490
•			•
•			•
•			•
•	Xerxes (486–465)		•
•		Destruction layer at	•
•		various sites	•
•			•
•			•
•			•
480	Battle of Salamis		480
•			•
•			•
•			•
•			•
•			•
•			•
•			•
•			•
470			470
•			•
•			•
•			•
•	Artaxerxes I (465–424)		•
•			•
•			•
•			•
•			•
460	Inarus's revolt (460–454)		460
•			•
•		(Mission of Ezra ?)	•
•			•
•			•
•			•
•			•
•			•
•			•

CHRONOLOGY

Date	Ancient Near East	Judah	Date
B.C.E.			
450			**450**
•	Peace of Callias		•
•			•
•			•
•		Mission of Nehemiah	•
•			•
•			•
•			•
•			•
440			**440**
•			•
•			•
•			•
•			•
•			•
•			•
•			•
•			•
430			**430**
•			•
•			•
•			•
•			•
•	Darius II (424–404)		•
•			•
•			•
•			•
420			**420**
•			•
•			•
•			•
•			•
•			•
•			•
•			•
•			•
410		Bagohi governor of Judah	**410**
•			•
•		Letter from Elephantine to	•
•		high priest Johanan and to	•
•		Shelemyah/Delayah	•
•			•
•	Artaxerxes II (404–359)		•
•			•
•			•
•	Revolt of Cyrus the Younger		•

CHRONOLOGY

Date	Ancient Near East	Judah	Date
B.C.E.			
400		(Episode of Johanan and Joshua in the temple) (Mission of Ezra?)	400
•			•
•			•
•			•
•			•
•			•
•			•
•			•
•			•
•			•
390			390
•			•
•			•
•			•
•			•
•			•
•			•
•			•
•			•
•			•
380			380
•			•
•			•
•			•
•			•
•			•
•			•
•	Satraps' Revolt (373–359)		•
•			•
•			•
370			370
•			•
•			•
•			•
•			•
•			•
•			•
•			•
•			•
•			•
360			360
•	Artaxerxes III (359–338)		•
•			•
•			•
•			•
•			•
•			•
•			•
•			•
•			•

CHRONOLOGY

Date	Ancient Near East	Judah	Date
B.C.E.			
350			**350**
•	Rebellion of Tennes (349–343)		•
•			•
•			•
•			•
•			•
•			•
•			•
•			•
•			•
340			**340**
•			•
•	Arses (338–336)		•
•			•
•	Darius III (336–331)		•
•			•
•	Alexander (336–323)		•
•	Battle of Issus		•
•		Samaria razed	•
•	Battle of Gaugamela		•
330			**330**
•			•
•			•
•			•
•			•
•			•
•	Diodochi (323–281)		•
•			•
•			•
320			**320**
•			•
•		(Jerusalem taken by	•
•		Ptolemy I?)	•
•			•
•			•
•			•
•	Seleucus (I) retakes Babylon		•
•	(Seleucid Era begins)		•
310			**310**
•			•
•			•
•			•
•		(High priest [and governor?]	•
•	Ptolemy I (305–282)	Hezekiah [Ezekias])	•
•	Seleucus I (304–281)		•
•			•
•	Battle of Ipsus and division		•
•	of Alexander's empire		•

CHRONOLOGY

Date	Ancient Near East	Judah	Date
B.C.E.			
300			300
•			•
•			•
•			•
•			•
•			•
•			•
•			•
•			•
•			•
290			290
•			•
•			•
•			•
•			•
•			•
•			•
•	Ptolemy II (282–246)		•
•	Antiochus I (281–261)		•
280			280
•			•
•			•
•			•
•	First Syrian War (274–271)		•
•			•
•			•
270			270
•			•
•			•
•			•
•			•
•	First Punic War (264–241)		•
•			•
•			•
•	Antiochus II (261–246)		•
260	Second Syrian War		260
•	(ca. 260–253)	Tobias "sheik" of Araq el-Emir	•
•	Zenon's tour of Palestine		•
•			•
•			•
•			•
•			•
•			•
•			•

CHRONOLOGY

Date	Ancient Near East	Judah	Date
B.C.E.			
250			250
•			•
•			•
•			•
•	Ptolemy III (246–221)		•
•	Seleucus II (246–226)		•
•	Third Syrian War (246–241)		•
•			•
•			•
•			•
240	War of the Brothers		240
•	(ca. 240–237)		•
•			•
•			•
•			•
•			•
•			•
•			•
•			•
•			•
230			230
•			•
•			•
•			•
•	Seleucus III (226–223)		•
•		Onias (II?) high priest	•
•		Joseph Tobiad becomes tax	•
•	Antiochus III (223–187)	farmer over Syro-Palestine	•
•			•
•	Ptolemy IV (221–204)		•
220	Fourth Syrian War (221–217)		220
•			•
•	Second Punic War (218–202)	Simon II high priest (?–ca. 190)	•
•	Battle of Raphia		•
•			•
•			•
•			•
•			•
•			•
•			•
210			210
•			•
•			•
•			•
•			•
•		Hyrcanus Tobiad	•
•	Ptolemy V (204–180)		•
•			•
•	Fifth Syrian War (202–200)		•
•			•

CHRONOLOGY

Date	Ancient Near East	Judah	Date
B.C.E.			
200	Battle of Paneion	Judea comes under Seleucid rule	**200**
•			•
•			•
•			•
•			•
•			•
•			•
•			•
•			•
•			•
190		Onias III high priest (ca. 190–175)	**190**
•			•
•	Seleucus IV (187–175)		•
•			•
•			•
•			•
•			•
•			•
•			•
180			**180**
•			•
•			•
•			•
•	Antiochus IV (175–164)	Jason high priest (175–172)	•
•			•
•		Antiochus visits Jerusalem	•
•		Menelaus high priest	•
•		(172–163)	•
170	Sixth Syrian War (170–168)		**170**
•	First invasion of Egypt		•
•	Second invasion of Egypt	Jason attacks Menelaus	•
•		Judaism prohibited	•
•		Maccabean revolt (168–165)	•
•		Temple cleansed	•
•	Antiochus V (164–162)		•
•		Alcimus high priest (162–160)	•
•	Demetrius I (162–150)	Death of Judas Maccabee	•
•		Jonathan Maccabee (161–143)	•
160			**160**
•			•
•			•
•			•
•			•
•			•
•			•
•			•
•			•

CHRONOLOGY

Date	Ancient Near East	Judah	Date
B.C.E.			
150	Alexander Balas (150–145)		**150**
•	Third Punic War (149–146)		•
•			•
•			•
•	Achean War and fall of		•
•	Greece		•
•	Demetrius II (145–140,		•
•	first reign)	Simon Maccabee (143–135)	•
•	Trypho (ca. 142–138)		•
•			•
140	Parthians take Babylon		**140**
•			•
•	Antiochus VII (138–129)		•
•			•
•			•
•		John Hyrcanus I (135–104)	•
•			•
•			•
•			•
•			•
130			**130**
•	Demetrius II (129–126,		•
•	second reign)		•
•			•
•	Antiochus VIII (126–113)		•
•			•
•			•
•			•
•			•
•			•
120			**120**
•			•
•			•
•			•
•			•
•			•
•			•
•	Antiochus IX (113–95)		•
•			•
•			•
110			**110**
•			•
•			•
•			•
•			•
•		Aristobulus I (104–103)	•
•		Alexander Janneus (103–76)	•
•			•
•			•

CHRONOLOGY

Date	Ancient Near East	Judah	Date
B.C.E.			
100			100
•			•
•			•
•			•
•			•
•			•
•			•
•	Demetrius III	Demetrius III attacks Janneus	•
•			•
•			•
90			90
•			•
•	First Mithridatic War		•
•	(88–84)		•
•			•
•			•
•			•
•	Second Mithridatic War		•
•	(83–81)		•
•			•
80			80
•			•
•			•
•			•
•		Alexandra Salome (76–67)	•
•			•
•	Third Mithridatic War (74–63)		•
•			•
•			•
•			•
70			70
•			•
•			•
•		Hyrcanus II and Aristobulus II	•
•		(67–63)	•
•			•
•			•
•	Pompeian settlement in Syria	Pompey takes Jerusalem	•
•			•
•			•
60			60
•			•
•			•
•		Gabinius governor	•
•			•
•			•
•		Cassius governor	•
•			•
•			•
•			•

CHRONOLOGY

Date	Ancient Near East	Judah	Date
B.C.E.			
50			**50**
•			•
•	Caesar defeats Pompey	Caesar rewards Hyrcanus	•
•		and Antipater	•
•		Herod governor of Galilee	•
•			•
•	Assassination of Julius		•
•	Caesar		•
•	Antony takes rule in East		•
•		Parthian invasion	•
40	Treaty of Brundisium	Herod made king (40–4)	**40**
•			•
•			•
•		Herod takes Jerusalem;	•
•		Aristobulus executed	•
•			•
•			•
•			•
•			•
•	Battle of Actium/Roman	Herod confirmed in office;	•
30	Empire begins	territory expanded	**30**
•			•
•			•
•	Octavian becomes Augustus		•
•	(27 B.C.E.–14 C.E.)		•
•			•
•			•
•			•
•			•
•			•
20		Territory expanded further	**20**
•		Rebuilding of temple begins	•
•		Further land to Herod	•
•			•
•			•
•			•
•			•
•			•
•			•
•			•
10			**10**
•		Trouble with Augustus over	•
•		Arab conflict	•
•			•
•			•
•			•
•		Archelaus (4 B.C.E.–6 C.E.)	•
•		Herod Antipas (4 B.C.E.–39 C.E.)	•
•		Philip (4 B.C.E.–34 C.E.)	•
•			•

CHRONOLOGY

Date	Ancient Near East	Judah	Date
C.E.			
		Judea becomes Roman province (6–41)	
10			10
	Tiberius (14–37)		
		Jews expelled from Rome	
20			20
		Pilate governor (26–36)	
30			30
	Caligula (Gaius [37–41])	Agrippa I ([37]41–44) Riots in Alexandria Philo leads mission to Caligula	
40	Claudius (41–54)	Attempt to place statue in Jerusalem temple	40
		Fadus governor (44–46?)	
		Tiberius Alexander governor (46?–48) Cumanus governor (48–52)	

CHRONOLOGY

Date	Ancient Near East	Judah	Date
C.E.			
50			**50**
•			•
•		Felix governor (52–59?)	•
•			•
•	Nero (54–68)		•
•			•
•			•
•			•
•			•
•		Festus governor (59?–62)	•
60			**60**
•			•
•		Albinus governor (62–64)	•
•			•
•		Florus governor (64–66)	•
•			•
•		War against Rome (66–70)	•
•	Galba (68–69)		•
•	Otto (69)/Vitellius (69)		•
•	Vespasian (69–79)		•
70		Fall of Jerusalem	**70**
•			•
•			•
•		Fall of Masada (73/74)	•
•			•
•			•
•			•
•			•
•			•
•	Titus (79–81)		•
80			**80**
•	Domitian (81–96)		•
•			•
•			•
•			•
•			•
•			•
•			•
•			•
•			•
90			**90**
•			•
•			•
•			•
•			•
•			•
•	Nerva (96–98)		•
•			•
•	Trajan (98–117)		•
•			•

CHRONOLOGY

Date	Ancient Near East	Judah	Date
C.E.			
100			**100**
•			•
•			•
•			•
•			•
•			•
•	Province of Arabia created		•
•			•
•			•
•			•
110			**110**
•			•
•			•
•			•
•			•
•		Revolts in Mesopotamia and	•
•		Egypt (115–17)	•
•	Hadrian (117–38)		•
•			•
•			•
120			**120**
•			•
•			•
•			•
•			•
•			•
•			•
•			•
•			•
•			•
130			**130**
•			•
•		Bar-Kokhba revolt (132–35)	•
•			•
•			•
•			•
•			•
•			•
•	Antonius Pius (138–61)		•
•			•
140			**140**
•			•

BIBLIOGRAPHY

Abel, F.-M. *Les libres des Maccabées.* Etudes bibliques. Paris: Lecoffre, 1949.

Ackroyd, P. R. "Two Old Testament Historical Problems of the Early Persian Period." *JNES* 17 (1958) 13–27.

——. *Exile and Restoration.* OTL. Philadelphia: Westminster; London: SCM, 1968.

——. *The Age of the Chronicler.* Supplement to *Colloquium—The Australian and New Zealand Theological Review* (1970).

——. *Israel under Babylon and Persia.* New Clarendon Bible, Old Testament 4. London: Oxford University Press, 1970.

——. *I and II Chronicles, Ezra, Nehemiah.* Torch Bible Commentaries. London: SCM, 1973.

——. "God and People in the Chronicler's Presentation of Ezra." *Bibliotheca Ephemeridum Theologicarum Lovaniensium* 41 (1976) 145–62.

——. "Archaeology, Politics and Religion: The Persian Period." *Iliff Review* 39 (1982) 5–24, 51.

——. "Historical Problems of the Early Achaemenian Period." *Orient* 20 (1984) 1–15.

——. "Problems in the Handling of Biblical and Related Sources in the Achaemenid Period." In *Achaemenid History III: Method and Theory.* Proceeding of the London 1985 Achaemenid History Workshop, 33–54. Edited by A. Kuhrt and H. Sancisi-Weerdenburg. Leiden: Nederlands Instituut voor het Nabije Oosten, 1988.

——. "Chronicles-Ezra-Nehemiah: The Concept of Unity." *ZAW* 100 *Supplement* (1988) 189–201.

Aharoni, Y. *The Land of the Bible: A Historical Geography.* 2d ed.; edited by A. F. Rainey. Philadelphia: Westminster, 1979.

Ahlström, G. W. *Joel and the Temple Cult in Jerusalem.* VTSup 21. Leiden: E. J. Brill, 1971.

Albrektson, B. *History and the Gods.* ConBOT 1. Lund: Gleerup, 1967.

Albright, W. F. *The Biblical Period from Abraham to Ezra.* New York: Harper & Row, 1965.

Aleksandrov, G. S. "The Role of Aqiba in the Bar Kokhba Rebellion." In J. Neusner, *Eliezar ben Hyrcanus* 2.428–42. SJLA 4. Leiden: E. J. Brill, 1973; and *REJ* 132 (1973) 65–77.

BIBLIOGRAPHY

Alexander, P. S. "Comparing Merkavah Mysticism and Gnosticism: An Essay in Method." *JJS* 35 (1984) 1–18.

Allrik, H. L. "The Lists of Zerubbabel (Nehemiah 7 and Ezra 2) and the Hebrew Numeral Notation." *BASOR* 136 (Dec. 1954) 21–27.

Alon, G. "The Burning of the Temple." In idem, *Jews, Judaism and the Classical World: Studies in Jewish History in the Times of the Second Temple and Talmud*, 252–68. Jerusalem: Magnes, 1977.

Alt, A. "Die Rolle Samarias bei der Entstehung des Judentums." In idem, *Kleine Schriften zur Geschichte des Volkes Israel* 2.316–37. Munich: Beck, 1953. Reprinted from *Festschrift Otto Procksch zum 60. Geburtstag*. Leipzig: Deichert und Hinrichs, 1934.

Altheim, F., and R. Stiehl. "Antiochos IV. Epiphanes und der Osten." In *Geschichte Mittelasiens im Altertum*, edited by F. Altheim and R. Stiehl, 553–71. Berlin: de Gruyter, 1970.

Andrewes, A. "Diodorus and Ephoros: One Source of Misunderstanding." In *The Craft of the Ancient Historian: Essays in Honor of Chester G. Starr*, edited by J. W. Eadie and J. Ober, 189–97. Lanham, Md.: University Press of America, 1985.

Applebaum, S. "Notes on the Jewish Revolt under Trajan." *JJS* 2 (1950/51) 26–30.

———. "The Zealots: The Case for Revaluation." *JRS* 61 (1971) 155–70.

———. "The Struggle for the Soil and the Revolt of 66–73 c.e." *EI* 12 (1975) 125–28 (Heb.); 122*–23* (Eng. summary).

———. "Economic Life in Palestine." In *The Jewish People in the First Century: Historical Geography, Political History, Social, Cultural and Religious Life and Institutions*, edited by S. Safrai and M. Stern. CRINT 1/2. Assen: Van Gorcum; Philadelphia: Fortress, 1976, 2.631–700.

———. *Prolegomena to the Study of the Second Jewish Revolt (A.D. 132–135)*. British Archaeological Reports Supplementary Series 7. Oxford: BAR, 1976.

———. "Judaea as a Roman Province: The Countryside as a Political and Economic Factor." *ANRW* 2 (1977) 8.355–96.

———. *Jews and Greeks in Ancient Cyrene*. SJLA 28. Leiden: E. J. Brill, 1979.

———. "The Second Jewish Revolt (A.D. 131–35)." *PEQ* 116 (1984) 35–41.

———. "The Beginnings of the Limes Palaestinae." In idem, *Judaea in Hellenistic and Roman Times: Historical and Archaeological Essays*, 132–42. SJLA 40. Leiden: E. J. Brill, 1989.

———. "The Troopers of Zamaris." In *Judaea in Hellenistic and Roman Times: Historical and Archaeological Essays*, 47–65. SJLA 40. Leiden: E. J. Brill, 1989.

Arav, R. *Hellenistic Palestine: Settlement Patterns and City Planning, 337–31 B.C.E.* British Archaeological Reports International Series 485. Oxford: BAR, 1989.

Archer, G. L. *Jerome's Commentary on Daniel*. Grand Rapids: Baker, 1958.

Archer, L. J. *Her Price Is beyond Rubies: The Jewish Woman in Graeco-Roman Palestine*. JSOTSS 60. Sheffield: JSOT Press, 1990.

Atkinson, K.T.M. "The Legitimacy of Cambyses and Darius as Kings of Egypt." *JAOS* 76 (1956) 167–77.

————. "A Hellenistic Land-Conveyance: The Estate of Mnesimachus in the Plain of Sardis." *Historia* 21 (1972) 45–74.

Attridge, H. W. "Josephus and His Works." *JWSTP* (1984) 185–232.

————. "Jewish Historiography." In *Early Judaism and Its Modern Interpreters*, edited by R. A. Kraft and G.W.E. Nickelsburg, 311–43. Atlanta: Scholars Press; Philadelphia: Fortress, 1986.

Aune, D. E. "Orthodoxy in First-Century Judaism? A Response to N. J. McEleney." *JSJ* 7 (1976) 1–10.

————. "Magic in Early Christianity." *ANRW* 2 (1980) 23.2.1507–57.

————. *Prophecy in Early Christianity and the Ancient Mediterranean World.* Grand Rapids: Wm. B. Eerdmans, 1983.

Austen, M. M. *The Hellenistic World from Alexander to the Roman Conquest: A Selection of Ancient Sources in Translation.* Cambridge: Cambridge University Press, 1981.

Avigad, N. "New Light on the MSH Seal Impressions." *IEJ* 8 (1958) 113–19.

————. "The Burial-Vault of a Nazirite Family on Mount Scopus." *IEJ* 21 (1971) 185–200.

————. "A Bulla of Jonathan the High Priest." *IEJ* 25 (1975) 8–12.

————. *Bullae and Seals from a Post-Exilic Judean Archive.* Qedem 4. Jerusalem: Hebrew University Press, 1976.

————. "The Burnt House Captures a Moment in Time." *BAR* 9, no. 6 (Nov./ Dec. 1983) 66–72.

————. *Discovering Jerusalem.* Oxford: Blackwell, 1984.

————. "The Upper City." In *Biblical Archaeology Today: Proceedings of the International Congress on Biblical Archaeology, Jerusalem, April 1984*, edited by J. Amitai, 469–75. Jerusalem: Israel Exploration Society, 1985.

Avi-Yonah, M. "The Missing Fortress of Flavius Josephus." *IEJ* 3 (1953) 94–98.

————. "Syrian Gods at Ptolemais-Accho." *IEJ* 9 (1959) 1–12.

————. *The Holy Land from the Persian to the Arab Conquests (536 B.C.E. to A.D. 640): A Historical Geography.* Grand Rapids: Baker, 1966.

————. "The Third and Second Walls of Jerusalem." *IEJ* 18 (1968) 98–125.

————. "When Did Judea Become a Consular Province?" *IEJ* 23 (1973) 209–13.

————. "Historical Geography of Palestine." In *The Jewish People in the First Century: Historical Geography, Political History, Social, Cultural and Religious Life and Institutions*, edited by S. Safrai and M. Stern. CRINT 1/1. Assen: Van Gorcum; Philadelphia: Fortress, 1974, 1.91–113.

————. "Archaeological Sources." In *The Jewish People in the First Century: Historical Geography, Political History, Social, Cultural and Religious Life and Institutions*, edited by S. Safrai and M. Stern. CRINT 1/1. Assen: Van Gorcum; Philadelphia: Fortress, 1974, 1.46–62.

————, ed. *The Herodian Period.* WHJP. First series, vol. 7. New Brunswick, N.J.: Rutgers University Press, 1975.

————. *Hellenism and the East: Contacts and Interrelations from Alexander to the Roman Conquest.* Jerusalem: Institute of Languages, Literature and the Arts, Hebrew University, 1978; available from University Microfilms, Ann Arbor, Mich.

Avi-Yonah, M., and E. Stern, eds. *Encyclopedia of Archaeological Excavations in the Holy Land.* Vols. 1–4. Jerusalem: Israel Exploration Society; London: Oxford University Press, 1975–78.

Aymard, A. "Autour de l'avènement d'Antiochos IV." *Historia* 2 (1953–54) 49–73.

Bagatti, B., and J. T. Milik. *Gli scavi del "Dominus Flevit" (Monte Oliveto-Gerusalemme): I. La necropoli del periodo romano.* Pubblicazioni dello Studium Biblicum Franciscanum 13. Jerusalem: Franciscan Printing Press, 1958.

Bagnall, R. S. *The Administration of the Ptolemaic Possessions Outside Egypt.* CSCT 4. Leiden: E. J. Brill, 1976.

Bagnall, R. S., and P. Derow. *Greek Historical Documents: The Hellenistic Period.* SBLSBS 16. Atlanta: Scholars Press, 1981.

Bailey, H. H. *Zoroastrian Problems in the Ninth-Century Books: Ratanbai Katrak Lectures.* Oxford: Clarendon, 1943.

Balcer, J. M. *Herodotus and Bisitun: Problems in Ancient Persian Historiography.* Historia Einzelschriften 49. Stuttgart: Steiner, 1987.

Balsdon, J.P.V.D. "The Principates of Tiberius and Gaius." *ANRW* 2 (1975) 2.86–92.

Bammel, E. "Die Blutgerichtsbarkeit in der römischen Provinz Judäa vor dem ersten jüdischen Aufstand." *JJS* 25 (1974) 35–49.

Bar-Adon, P. "Another Settlement of the Judean Desert Sect at 'En el-Ghuweir on the Shores of the Dead Sea." *BASOR* 227 (1977) 1–25.

Barag, D. "The Effects of the Tennes Rebellion on Palestine." *BASOR* 183 (Oct. 1966) 6–12.

———. "The Palestinian 'Judaea Capta' Coins of Vespasian and Titus and the Era on the Coins of Agrippa II Minted under the Flavians." *Numismatic Chronicle* 138 (1978) 14–23.

———. "Some Notes on a Silver Coin of Johanan the High Priest." *BA* 48 (1985) 166–68.

———. "A Silver Coin of Yohanan the High Priest and the Coinage of Judea in the Fourth Century B.C." *Israel Numismatic Journal* 9 (1986–87) 4–21.

Barag, D., and D. Flusser. "The Ossuary of Yehoḥanah Granddaughter of the High Priest Theophilus." *IEJ* 36 (1986) 39–44.

Barber, G. L. *The Historian Ephorus.* Cambridge: Cambridge University Press, 1935.

Bar-Kochva, B. "Hellenistic Warfare in Jonathan's Campaign near Azotos." *Scripta Classica Israelica* 2 (1975) 83–96.

———. "Sēron and Cestius Gallus at Beith Ḥoron." *PEQ* 108 (1976) 13–21.

———. *The Seleucid Army: Organization and Tactics in the Great Campaigns.* Cambridge Classical Studies. Cambridge: Cambridge University Press, 1976.

———. *Judas Maccabaeus: The Jewish Struggle against the Seleucids.* Cambridge: Cambridge University Press, 1989.

Barker, M. "The Two Figures in Zechariah." *Heythrop Journal* 18 (1977) 38–46.

Barnes, T. D. "The Date of Herod's Death." *JTS* 19 (1968) 204–9.

———. *The Sources of the Historia Augusta.* Collection Latomus 155. Brussels: Latomus, 1978.

———. *Constantine and Eusebius.* Cambridge: Harvard University Press, 1981.

———. "Trajan and the Jews." *JJS* 40 (1989) 145–62.

Barnett, P. W. "The Jewish Sign Prophets—A.D. 40–70: Their Intentions and Origin." *NTS* 27 (1980–81) 679–97.

Barr, J. "Philo of Byblos and His 'Phoenician History.'" *BJRL* 57 (1974–75) 17–68.

———. "Story and History in Biblical Theology." *JR* 56 (1976) 1–17.

———. "The Question of Religious Influence: The Case of Zoroastrianism, Judaism, and Christianity." *JAAR* 53 (1985) 201–35.

Barrett, A. A. *Caligula: The Corruption of Power.* London: Batsford, 1989.

Bartlett, J. R. *Edom and the Edomites.* JSOTSS 77. Sheffield: JSOT Press, 1989.

Batten, L. W. *A Critical and Exegetical Commentary on Ezra and Nehemiah.* ICC. Edinburgh: T. & T. Clark, 1913.

Bauer, W. *Orthodoxy and Heresy in Earliest Christianity.* German original, 1934. English translation with evaluative essays by G. Strecker, et al. Philadelphia: Fortress, 1971.

Baumgarten, A. I. "The Name of the Pharisees." *JBL* 102 (1983) 411–28.

———. "Josephus and Hippolytus on the Pharisees." *HUCA* 55 (1984) 1–25.

———. "*Korban* and the Pharisaic *Paradosis.*" *JANES* 16–17 (1984–85) 5–17.

———. "The Pharisaic *Paradosis.*" *HTR* 80 (1987) 63–77.

Beall, T. S. *Josephus' Description of the Essenes Illustrated by the Dead Sea Scrolls.* SNTSMS 58. Cambridge: Cambridge University Press, 1988.

Beckwith, R. *The Old Testament Canon of the New Testament Church and Its Background in Early Judaism.* London: SPCK, 1985.

Ben-Arieh, S., and E. Netzer. "Where Is the Third Wall of Agrippa I?" *BA* 42 (1979) 140–41.

Ben-David, A. *Talmudische Ökonomie: Die Wirtschaft des jüdischen Palästina zur Zeit der Mischna und des Talmud.* Band 1. Hildesheim: Olms, 1974.

Ben-Dor, M. "Herod's Mighty Temple Mount." *BAR* 12, no. 6 (Nov./Dec. 1986) 40–49.

Bengtson, H. *Die Strategie in der hellenistischen Zeit.* 3 vols. Münchener Beiträge zur Papyrusforschung und antiken Rechtsgeschichte 26, 32, 36. Munich: Beck, 1937 (1964_2), 1944, 1952.

Benoit, P., et al., eds. *Les grottes de Murabba'ât.* DJD 2. 2 vols. Oxford: Clarendon, 1961.

Berg, S. B. *The Book of Esther: Motifs, Themes and Structure.* SBLDS 44. Atlanta: Scholars Press, 1979.

Berger, P.-R. "Zu den Namen שׁשׁבצר und שׁנאצר (Esr $1_{8.11}$ $5_{14.16}$ bzw. I Chr 3_{18}." *ZAW* 83 (1971) 98–100.

———. "Der Kyros-Zylinder mit dem Zusatzfragment BIN II Nr. 32 und die akkadischen Personennamen im Danielbuch." *ZA* 64 (1975) 192–234.

Berman, D. "Hasidim in Rabbinic Traditions." *SBLSP* 1979, edited by P. J. Achtemeier, 15–33. Missoula, Mont.: Scholars Press, 1979.

Bernard, P. "Aï Khanum on the Oxus: A Hellenistic City in Central Asia." *Proceedings of the British Academy* 53 (1967) 71–95.

Bernegger, P. M. "Affirmation of Herod's Death in 4 B.C." *JTS* 34 (1983) 526–31.

Betz, H. D. "Jesus as Divine Man." In *Jesus and the Historian: Written in Honor of Ernest Cadman Colwell,* edited by F. T. Trotter, 114–33. Philadelphia: Westminster, 1969.

Beyse, K.-M. *Serubbabel und die Königserwartungen der Propheten Haggai und Sacharja: Eine historische und traditionsgeschichtliche Untersuchung.* Arbeiten zur Theologie 48. Stuttgart: Calwer, 1972.

Bickerman, E. J. [Bickermann, E. J.]. "Makkabäerbücher." *PW* 14 (1930) 779–800.

———. [Bickermann, E. J.]. "Ein jüdischer Festbrief vom Jahre 124 v. Chr. (II Macc 1₁.₉." *ZNW* 32 (1933) 233–54.

———. [Bikerman, E.]. *Institutions des Séleucides.* Paris: Geuthner, 1938.

———. [Bikerman, E.]. "Les Hérodiens." *RB* 47 (1938) 184–97.

———. "The Warning Inscriptions of Herod's Temple." *JQR* 37 (1946/47) 387–405.

———. *From Ezra to the Last of the Maccabees: Foundations of Postbiblical Judaism.* New York: Schocken, 1962.

———. "The Jewish Historian Demetrius." In *Christianity, Judaism, and Other Greco-Roman Cults* 3.72–84. Edited by J. Neusner. SJLA 12. Leiden: E. J. Brill, 1975.

———. "The Edict of Cyrus in Ezra 1." In *Studies in Jewish and Christian History* 1.72–108. AGAJU 9. Leiden: E. J. Brill, 1976 = partial revision of *JBL* 65 (1946) 244–75.

———. *The God of the Maccabees: Studies on the Meaning and Origin of the Maccabean Revolt.* SJLA 32. Leiden: E. J. Brill, 1979.

———. "Une question d'authenticité: les privilèges juifs." In *Studies in Jewish and Christian History* 2.24–43. AGAJU 9. Leiden: E. J. Brill, 1980.

———. "La charte séleucide de Jérusalem." In *Studies in Jewish and Christian History* 2.44–85. AGAJU 9. Leiden: E. J. Brill, 1980. Original pub.: *REJ* 100 (1935).

———. "Une proclamation séleucide relative au temple de Jérusalem." In *Studies in Jewish and Christian History* 2.86–104. AGAJU 9. Leiden: E. J. Brill, 1980. Originally published in *Syria* 25 (1946–48).

———. "Les Maccabées de Malalas." In *Studies in Jewish and Christian History* 2.192–209. Leiden: E. J. Brill, 1980 = *Byzantion* 21 (1951) 63–83.

———. *Chronology of the Ancient World.* Rev. ed. Aspects of Greek and Roman Life. Ithaca, N.Y.: Cornell University Press, 1980.

———. "The Generation of Ezra and Nehemiah." In *Studies in Jewish and Christian History* 3.299–326. AGAJU 9. Leiden: E. J. Brill, 1986. Reprinted from *PAAJR* 46–47 (1979–80).

———. *The Jews in the Greek Age.* Cambridge: Harvard University Press, 1988.

Bickerman, E. J., and H. Tadmor. "Darius I, Pseudo-Smerdis, and the Magi." *Athenaeum* 56 (1978) 241–61.

Bigwood, J. M. "Ctesias as Historian of the Persian Wars." *Phoenix* 32 (1978) 19–41.

———. "Diodorus and Ctesias." *Phoenix* 34 (1980) 195–207.

Bilde, P. "The Roman Emperor Gaius (Caligula)'s Attempt to Erect His Statue in the Temple of Jerusalem." *Studia Theologica* 32 (1978) 67–93.

———. "The Causes of the Jewish War according to Josephus." *JSJ* 10 (1979) 179–202.

———. *Flavius Josephus between Jerusalem and Rome: His Life, His Works, and Their Importance*. JSPSS 2. Sheffield: JSOT Press, 1988.

Biran, A. "Tel Dan." *RB* 84 (1977) 256–63.

Black, M. "Judas of Galilee and Josephus's 'Fourth Philosophy.'" In *Josephus-Studien: Untersuchungen zu Josephus, dem antiken Judentum und dem Neuen Testament, Otto Michel zum 70. Geburtstag gewidmet*, edited by O. Betz, et al., 45–54. Göttingen: Vandenhoeck & Ruprecht, 1974.

———. *The Book of Enoch or I Enoch: A New English Edition with Commentary and Textual Notes*. SVTP 7. Leiden: E. J. Brill, 1985.

Bleckmann, F. "Die erste syrische Statthalterschaft des P. Sulpicius Quirinius." *Klio* 17 (1920/21) 104–12.

Blenkinsopp, J. "Interpretation and the Tendency to Sectarianism: An Aspect of Second Temple History." In *Jewish and Christian Self-Definition*. Vol. 2: *Aspects of Judaism in the Graeco-Roman Period*, edited by E. P. Sanders, et al., 1–26. London: SCM, 1981.

———. *A History of Prophecy in Israel*. London: SPCK, 1984.

———. "The Mission of Udjahorresnet and Those of Ezra and Nehemiah." *JBL* 106 (1987) 409–21.

———. *Ezra-Nehemiah*. OTL. London: SCM, 1988.

———. "A Jewish Sect of the Persian Period." *CBQ* 52 (1990) 5–20.

———. "The Sage, the Scribe, and Scribalism in the Chronicler's Work." In *The Sage in Israel and the Ancient Near East*, edited by J. G. Gammie and L. G. Perdue, 307–15. Winona Lake, Ind.: Eisenbrauns, 1990.

———. "Temple and Society in Achemenid Judah." In *Studies in the Second Temple: The Persian Period*, edited by P. R. Davies, 22–53. JSOTSS 117. Sheffield: JSOT Press, 1991.

Blinzler, J. *The Trial of Jesus*. 2d ed. Cork: Mercier, 1959.

———. *Der Prozess Jesus*. 4th ed. Regensburg: Friedrich Pustet, 1969.

Boer, W. den. "Religion and Literature in Hadrian's Policy." *Mnemosyne* 8, series 4 (1955) 123–44.

Boffo, L. "La lettera di Dario I [*sic*] a Gadata: i privilegi del tempio di Apollo a Magnesia sul Meandro." *Bulletino dell' Istituto di Diritto Romano, "Vittorio Scialojo"* 81 (1978) 267–303.

Bogaert, P. *L'Apocalypse syriaque de Baruch*. 2 vols. SC 144. Paris: Editions du Cerf, 1969.

Bokser, B. M. "Wonder-Working and the Rabbinic Tradition: The Case of Hanina ben Dosa." *JSJ* 16 (1985) 42–92.

Borg, M. "The Currency of the Term 'Zealot.'" *JTS* 22 (1971) 504–12.

Borger, R. "An Additional Remark on P. R. Ackroyd, *JNES*, XVII, 23–27." *JNES* 18 (1959) 74.

Bousset, W., and H. Gressmann. *Die Religion des Judentums im späthellenistischen Zeitaltar*. 1925. 4th ed. HNT 21. Tübingen: J.C.B. Mohr (Paul Siebeck), 1966.

Bowersock, G. W. "A Roman Perspective on the Bar Kochba War." In *Approaches to Ancient Judaism*, vol. 2, edited by W. S. Green, 131–41. BJS 9. Atlanta: Scholars Press, 1980.

———. *Roman Arabia*. Cambridge: Harvard University Press, 1983.

Bowker, J. *The Targums and Rabbinic Literature.* Cambridge: Cambridge University Press, 1969.

Bowman, J. *Transcript of the Original Text of the Samaritan Chronicle Tolidah.* Leeds: University of Leeds, 1954.

———. *Samaritan Documents Relating to Their History, Religion and Life.* Pittsburgh Original Texts and Translations 2. Pittsburgh: Pickwick, 1977.

Bowman, R. A. *Aramaic Ritual Texts from Persepolis.* University of Chicago, Oriental Institute Publication 91. Chicago: University of Chicago Press, 1970.

Box, G. H. *The Ezra-Apocalypse, Being Chapters 3–14 of the Book Commonly Known as 4 Ezra (or II Esdras).* London: Pitman, 1912.

———. *Philonis Alexandrini In Flaccum.* London: Oxford University Press, 1939.

Boyce, M. *A History of Zoroastrianism.* Vols. 1– . HdO I.8.1. Leiden: E. J. Brill, 1975– .

———. *Zoroastrians: Their Religious Beliefs and Practices.* Library of Religious Beliefs and Practices. London: Routledge & Kegan Paul, 1979.

———, ed. *Textual Sources for the Study of Zoroastrianism.* Textual Sources for the Study of Religion. Manchester: Manchester University Press, 1984.

———. "On the Antiquity of Zoroastrian Apocalyptic." *BSOAS* 47 (1984) 57–75.

———. *Zoroastrianism: A Shadowy but Powerful Presence in the Judaeo-Christian World.* Friends of Dr. Williams's Library Lecture. London: Dr. Williams's Trust, 1987.

Brandstein, W., and M. Mayrhofer. *Handbuch des Altpersischen.* Wiesbaden: Harrassowitz, 1964.

Braun, R. *Koheleth und die frühhellenistische Popularphilosophie.* BZAW 130. Berlin and New York: de Gruyter, 1973.

Braun, R. L. "Solomonic Apologetic in Chronicles." *JBL* 92 (1973) 503–16.

———. "Chronicles, Ezra, and Nehemiah: Theology and Literary History." In *Studies in the Historical Books of the Old Testament,* 52–64. VTSup 30. Leiden: E. J. Brill, 1979.

———. *1 Chronicles.* WBC 14. Waco, Tex.: Word, 1986.

Braund, D. C. "Gabinius, Caesar, and the *publicani* of Judaea." *Klio* 65 (1983) 241–44.

———. *Rome and the Friendly King: The Character of Client Kingship.* New York: St. Martin's; London: Croom Helm, 1984.

———. "Berenice in Rome." *Historia* 33 (1984) 120–23.

———. *Augustus to Nero: A Sourcebook on Roman History 31 B.C.-A.D. 68.* London and Sydney: Croom Helm, 1985.

Braverman, J. *Jerome's Commentary on Daniel: A Study of Comparative Jewish and Christian Interpretations of the Hebrew Bible.* CBQMS 7. Washington, D.C.: Catholic Biblical Association, 1978.

Brawley, R. L. *Luke-Acts and the Jews: Conflict, Apology, and Conciliation.* SBLMS 33. Atlanta: Scholars Press, 1987.

Breitenbach, W. "Xenophon." *PW* (1967) 9A2.1709–18.

Brenner, A. *The Song of Songs.* Society for Old Testament Study; Old Testament Guides. Sheffield: JSOT Press, 1989.

Bresciani, E., and M. Kamil. "Le lettere aramaiche di Hermopoli." *Atti della Accademia Nazionale dei Lincei.* Series 8, vol. 12 (1965–66) 358–428.

Briant, P. *Rois, tributs et paysans: Etudes sur les formations tributaire du Moyen-Orient ancien.* Annales littéraires de l'Université de Besan 269, Centre de Recherches d'Histoire Ancienne 43. Paris: Les Belles Lettres, 1982.

Bright, J. *A History of Israel.* 3d ed. Philadelphia: Westminster, 1980.

Bringmann, K. *Hellenistische Reform und Religionsverfolgung in Judäa.* AAWG. Philologische-historische Klasse, 3te Folge, Nr. 132. Göttingen: Vandenhoeck & Ruprecht, 1983.

Briscoe, J. *A Commentary on Livy, Books XXXI–XXXIII.* Oxford: Clarendon, 1973.

Brock, S. P., et al. *A Classified Bibliography of the Septuagint.* ALGHJ 6. Leiden: E. J. Brill, 1973.

Brooke, G. J. *Exegesis at Qumran: 4Q Florilegium in Its Jewish Context.* JSOTSS 29. Sheffield: JSOT Press, 1985.

———, ed. *Temple Scroll Studies: Papers Presented at the International Symposium on the Temple Scroll, Manchester, December 1987.* JSPSS 7. Sheffield: JSOT Press, 1989.

Broshi, M. "La population de l'ancienne Jérusalem." *RB* 82 (1975) 5–14.

———. "Estimating the Population of Ancient Jerusalem." *BAR* 4/3 (June 1978) 10–15.

———. "The Role of the Temple in the Herodian Economy." *JJS* 38 (1987) 31–37.

Broughton, T.R.S. "Roman Asia Minor." In *An Economic Survey of Ancient Rome* 4.499–918. Edited by T. Frank. Baltimore: Johns Hopkins University Press, 1938.

———. "New Evidence on Temple-Estates in Asia Minor." In *Studies in Roman Economic and Social History in Honor of Allan Chester Johnson,* edited by P. R. Coleman-Norton, et al., 236–50. Princeton, N.J.: Princeton University Press, 1951.

Brown, R. E. *The Gospel according to John I–XII.* AB 29. Garden City, N.Y.: Doubleday, 1966.

———. *The Gospel according to John XIII–XXI.* AB 29A. Garden City, N.Y.: Doubleday, 1970.

Brown, T. S. *The Greek Historians.* Civilization and Society. Lexington, Mass.: Heath, 1973.

———. "Herodotus' Portrait of Cambyses." *Historia* 31 (1982) 387–403.

Brownlee, W. H. "The Wicked Priest, the Man of Lies, and the Righteous Teacher—The Problem of Identity." *JQR* 73 (1982/83) 1–37.

Bruce, I.A.F. "Nerva and the *Fiscus Iudaicus.*" *PEQ* 96 (1964) 34–45.

Bruggen, J. van. "The Year of the Death of Herod the Great." In *Miscellanea Neotestamentica,* edited by T. Baarda, et al., 1–15. NovTSup 48. Leiden: E. J. Brill, 1978.

Brunt, P. A. "Josephus on Social Conflicts in Roman Judaea." *Klio* 59 (1977) 149–53.

Büchler, A. "La Relation de Josèphe concernant Alexandre le Grand." *REJ* 36 (1898) 1–26.

————. *Die Tobiaden und die Oniaden.* VI. Jahresbericht der Israelitisch-Theologischen Lehranstalt. Vienna: Israelitisch-Theologische Lehranstalt, 1899.

Bull, R. J. "er-Ras, Tell (Mount Gerizim)." In *Encyclopedia of Archaeological Excavations in the Holy Land* 4.1015–22. Edited by E. Stern. Jerusalem: Israel Exploration Society, 1978.

Bultmann, R. *History of the Synoptic Tradition.* 2d ed. San Francisco: Harper & Row, 1968.

Bunge, J. G. "Der 'Gott der Festungen' und der 'Liebling der Frauen': Zur Identifizierung der Götter in Dan. 11,36-39." *JSJ* 4 (1973) 169–82.

————. "Münzen als Mittel politischer Propaganda: Antiochos IV. Epiphanes von Syrien." *Studii Clasice* 16 (1974) 43–52.

————. " 'Theos Epiphanes': Zu den ersten fünf Regierungsjahren Antiochos' IV. Epiphanes." *Historia* 23 (1974) 57–85.

————. " 'Antiochos-Helios': Methoden und Ergebnisse der Reichspolitik Antiochos' IV. Epiphanes von Syrien im Spiegel seiner Münzen." *Historia* 24 (1975) 164–88.

————. "Zur Geschichte und Chronology des Untergangs der Oniaden und des Aufstiegs der Hasmonäer." *JSJ* 6 (1976) 1–46.

————. "Die Feiern Antiochos' IV. Epiphanes in Daphne im Herbst 166 v. Chr." *Chiron* 6 (1976) 53–71.

Burchard, C. "Die Essener bei Hippolyt." *JSJ* 8 (1977) 1–41.

Burgmann, H. "Das umstrittene Intersacerdotium in Jerusalem 159–152 v. Chr." *JSJ* 11 (1980) 135–76.

Burrows, M. "The Literary Category of the Book of Jonah." In *Translating and Understanding the Old Testament: Essays in Honor of Herbert Gordon May,* edited by H. T. Frank and W. L. Reed, 80–107. Nashville: Abingdon, 1970.

Burstein, S. M. *The Babyloniaca of Berossus.* SANE. Vol. 1, no. 5. Malibu, Calif.: Undena, 1978.

————. *The Hellenistic Age from the Battle of Ipsus to the Death of Kleopatra VII.* Translated Documents of Greece and Rome 3. Cambridge: Cambridge University Press, 1985.

Byatt, A. "Josephus and Population Numbers in First-Century Palestine." *PEQ* 105 (1973) 51–60.

Callaway, P. R. *The History of the Qumran Community.* JSPSS 3. Sheffield: JSOT Press, 1988.

Cameron, G. G. *Persepolis Treasury Tablets.* Chicago: University of Chicago Press, 1948.

————. "Ancient Persia." In idem, *The Idea of History in the Ancient Near East,* 77–97. New Haven: Yale University Press, 1955.

————. "New Tablets from the Persepolis Treasury." *JNES* 24 (1965) 167–92.

————. "The Persian Satrapies and Related Matters." *JNES* 82 (1973) 47–56.

Cameron, R., and A. J. Dewey. *The Cologne Mani Codex (P. Colon. inv. nr. 4780): "Concerning the Origin of His Body."* SBLTT 15; ECL 3. Atlanta: Scholars Press, 1979.

Campbell, E. F. *Ruth.* AB 7. Garden City, N.Y.: Doubleday, 1975.

Cardascia, G. *Les archives des Murašû*. Paris: Imprimerie Nationale, 1951.

Cardauns, B. "Juden und Spartaner: Zur hellenistisch-jüdischen Literatur." *Hermes* 95 (1967) 317–24.

Cargill, J. "The Nabonidus Chronicle and the Fall of Lydia: Consensus with Feet of Clay." *AJAH* 2 (1978) 97–116.

Carlebach, A. "Rabbinic References to Fiscus Judaicus." *JQR* 66 (1975/76) 57–61.

Carlo, Z. "Patterns of Mobility among Ancient Near Eastern Craftsmen." *JNES* 42 (1983) 245–64.

Carroll, R. P. "Twilight of Prophecy or Dawn of Apocalyptic?" *JSOT* 14 (1979) 3–35.

Cary, M. *A History of the Greek World 323 to 146 B.C.* 2d ed. London: Methuen, 1951. Reprint, with new bibliography, 1963.

Cary, M., and H. H. Scullard. *A History of Rome*. 3d ed. London: Macmillan, 1975.

Catchpole, D. R. *The Trial of Jesus: A Study in the Gospels and Jewish Historiography from 1770 to the Present Day*. SPB 22. Leiden: E. J. Brill, 1971.

Cavallin, H.C.C. *Life after Death: Paul's Argument for the Resurrection of the Dead in I Cor 15. Part I: An Enquiry into the Jewish Background*. ConBNT 7:1. Lund: Gleerup, 1974.

Cazelles, H. "La mission d'Esdras." *VT* 4 (1954) 113–40.

———. Review of *Israel in the Books of Chronicles*, by H.G.M. Williamson. *VT* 29 (1979) 375–80.

Charles, R. H. *The Apocalypse of Baruch. Edited with Introduction, Notes, and Indices*. London: Black, 1896.

———. *The Book of Jubilees or the Little Genesis*. Oxford: Clarendon, 1902.

———, ed. *Apocrypha and Pseudepigrapha of the Old Testament*. 2 vols. Oxford: Clarendon, 1913.

———. *The Book of Enoch*. Oxford: Clarendon, 1913.

———. *A Critical and Exegetical Commentary on the Book of Daniel*. Oxford: Clarendon, 1929.

Charlesworth, J. H. *The Pseudepigrapha and Modern Research: New Edition with a Supplement*. SBLSCS 75. Atlanta: Scholars Press, 1981.

———, ed. *The Old Testament Pseudepigrapha*. 2 vols. Garden City, N.Y.: Doubleday, 1983–85.

———. "Jewish Interest in Astrology during the Hellenistic and Roman Period." *ANRW* 2 (1987) 20.2.926–50.

Charlesworth, J. H., with J. R. Mueller. *The New Testament Apocrypha and Pseudepigrapha: A Guide to Publications, with Excursuses on Apocalypses*, 20–24. Metuchen, N.J., and London: Scarecrow, 1987.

Chiat, M.J.S. "First-Century Synagogue Architecture: Methodological Problems." In *Ancient Synagogues Revealed*, edited by L. I. Levine, 49–60. Jerusalem: Israel Exploration Society, 1981.

———. *Handbook of Synagogue Architecture*. BJS 29. Atlanta: Scholars Press, 1982.

Childs, B. S. *Introduction to the Old Testament as Scripture*. Philadelphia: Fortress, 1979.

Clements, R. E. "The Purpose of the Book of Jonah." In *Congress Volume, Edinburgh 1974*, 16–28. VTSup 28. Leiden: E. J. Brill, 1975.

Clines, D.J.A. "Nehemiah 10 as an Example of Early Jewish Biblical Exegesis." *JSOT* 21 (1981) 111–17.

———. *The Esther Scroll: The Story of the Story.* JSOTSS 30. Sheffield: JSOT Press, 1984.

———. *Ezra, Nehemiah, Esther.* NCB. Grand Rapids: Wm. B. Eerdmans; London: Marshall, Morgan & Scott, 1984.

———. *Job 1–20.* WBC 17. Dallas: Word, 1989.

———. "The Nehemiah Memoir: The Perils of Autobiography." In *What Does Eve Do to Help? and Other Readerly Questions to the Old Testament*, 124–64. JSOTSS 94. Sheffield: Sheffield Academic, 1990.

———. "In Quest of the Historical Mordecai." *VT* 41 (1991) 129–36.

Cody, A. *A History of Old Testament Priesthood.* AnBib 35. Rome: Biblical Institute, 1969.

Coggins, R. J. *Samaritans and Jews: The Origins of Samaritanism Reconsidered.* Growing Points in Theology. Atlanta: John Knox; London: Blackwell, 1975.

———. *Haggai, Zechariah, Malachi.* OT Guides. Sheffield: JSOT Press, 1987.

———. "The Samaritans in Josephus." In *Josephus, Judaism, and Christianity*, edited by L. H. Feldman and G. Hata, 257–73. Leiden: E. J. Brill, 1987.

Cohen, G. M. *The Seleucid Colonies.* Historia Einzelschrift 30. Wiesbaden: Steiner, 1978.

Cohen, S.J.D. Review of *The 'Am ha-Aretz*, by A. Oppenheimer. *JBL* 97 (1978) 596–97.

———. *Josephus in Galilee and Rome: His Vita and Development as a Historian.* CSCT 8. Leiden: E. J. Brill, 1979.

———. Review of *The Hidden Revolution*, by E. Rivkin. *JBL* 99 (1980) 627–29.

———. "Masada: Literary Tradition, Archaeological Remains, and the Credibility of Josephus." *JJS* 33 (1982) 385–405.

———. "Alexander the Great and Jaddus the High Priest according to Josephus." *AJS Review* 7–8 (1982/83) 41–68.

———. "Conversion to Judaism in Historical Perspective: From Biblical Israel to Postbiblical Judaism." *Conservative Judaism* 36 (1983) 31–45.

———. "The Significance of Yavneh: Pharisees, Rabbis, and the End of Jewish Sectarianism." *HUCA* 55 (1984) 27–53.

———. "The Origins of the Matrilineal Principle in Rabbinic Law." *AJS Review* 10 (1985) 19–53.

———. "The Political and Social History of the Jews in Greco-Roman Antiquity: The State of the Question." In *Early Judaism and Its Modern Interpreters*, edited by R. A. Kraft and G.W.E. Nickelsburg, 33–56. Atlanta: Scholars Press; Philadelphia: Fortress, 1986.

———. "Was Timothy Jewish (Acts 16:1-3)? Patristic Exegesis, Rabbinic Law, and Matrilineal Descent." *JBL* 105 (1986) 251–68.

———. "Respect for Judaism by Gentiles according to Josephus." *HTR* 80 (1987) 409–30.

———. *From the Maccabees to the Mishnah.* Library of Early Christianity. Philadelphia: Westminster, 1987.

Colella, P. "Les abréviations ☻ et ✗ (XP)." *RB* 80 (1973) 547–58.

Colledge, M. "Greek and Non-Greek Interaction in the Art and Architecture of the Hellenistic East." In *Hellenism in the East*, edited by A. Kuhrt and S. Sherwin-White, 134–62. London: Duckworth, 1987.

Collins, J. J. *The Sibylline Oracles of Egyptian Judaism.* SBLDS 13. Atlanta: Scholars Press, 1974.

———. "The Place of the Fourth Sibyl in the Development of the Jewish Sibyllina." *JJS* 25 (1974) 365–80.

———. *The Apocalyptic Vision of the Book of Daniel.* HSM 16. Atlanta: Scholars Press, 1977.

———, ed. *Apocalypse: The Morphology of a Genre.* Semeia 14. Atlanta: Scholars Press, 1979.

———. "Persian Apocalypses." In *Apocalypse: The Morphology of a Genre*, edited by J. J. Collins, 207–17. Semeia 14. Atlanta: Scholars Press, 1979.

———. *The Apocalyptic Imagination: An Introduction to the Jewish Matrix of Christianity.* New York: Crossroad, 1984.

———. *Between Athens and Jerusalem: Jewish Identity in the Hellenistic Diaspora.* New York: Crossroad, 1986.

———. "The Origin of the Qumran Community: A Review of the Evidence." In *To Touch the Text: Biblical and Related Studies in Honor of Joseph A. Fitzmyer, S.J.*, edited by M. P. Horgan and P. J. Kobelski, 159–78. New York: Crossroad, 1989.

Coogan, M. D. *West Semitic Personal Names in the Murašu Documents.* HSM 7. Atlanta: Scholars Press, 1976.

Cook, J. M. *The Persian Empire.* London: J. M. Dent, 1983.

Cook, M. J. "Jesus and the Pharisees—The Problem as It Stands Today." *JES* (1978) 441–60.

———. *Mark's Treatment of the Jewish Leaders.* NovTSup 51. Leiden: E. J. Brill, 1978.

Cousin, G., and G. Deschamps. "Lettre de Darius, fils d'Hystaspes." *Bulletin de correspondence hellénique* 13 (1889) 529–42.

Cowley, A. *Aramaic Papyri of the Fifth Century B.C.* 1923. Reprint. Osnabrück: Otto Zeller, 1967.

Coxon, P. W. "Script Analysis and Mandaean Origins." *JSS* 15 (1970) 16–30.

Craven, T. *Artistry and Faith in the Book of Judith.* SBLDS 70. Atlanta: Scholars Press, 1983.

Crawford, M. H. *The Roman Republic.* Sussex, Eng.: Harvester, 1978.

Crenshaw, J. "The Birth of Skepticism in Ancient Israel." In *The Divine Helmsman: Studies on God's Control of Human Events. Presented to Lou H. Silberman*, edited by J. L. Crenshaw and S. Sandmel, 1–19. New York: Ktav, 1980.

———. *Ecclesiastes.* OTL. London: SCM, 1988.

Cross, F. M. *The Ancient Library of Qumran.* 2d ed. Garden City, N.Y.: Doubleday, 1961.

———. "Aspects of Samaritan and Jewish History in Late Persian and Hellenistic Times." *HTR* 59 (1966) 201–11.

———. "Papyri of the Fourth Century B.C. from Daliyeh." In *New Directions in Biblical Archaeology*, edited by D. N. Freedman and J. C. Greenfield, 45–69. Garden City, N.Y.: Doubleday, 1969.

———. "Judean Stamps." *EI* 9 (1969) 20–27.

———. "The Papyri and Their Historical Implications." In *Discoveries in the Wadi ed-Daliyeh*, edited by P. W. Lapp and N. L. Lapp, 17–24. AASOR 41. Cambridge: ASOR, 1974.

———. "A Reconstruction of the Judean Restoration." *JBL* 94 (1975) 4–18. Reprinted in *Int* 29 (1975) 187–203.

———. "An Aramaic Ostracon of the Third Century B.C.E. from Excavations in Jerusalem." *EI* 15 (1981) 67*–69*.

———. "Samaria Papyrus 1: An Aramaic Slave Conveyance of 335 B.C.E. Found in the Wâdī ed-Dâliyeh." *EI* 18 (1985) 7*–17*.

———. "A Report on the Samaria Papyri." In *Congress Volume: Jerusalem 1986*, edited by J. A. Emerton, 17–26. VTSup 40. Leiden: E. J. Brill, 1988.

Crown, A. D. "New Light on the Interrelationships of Samaritan Chronicles from Some Manuscripts in the John Rylands Library." *BJRL* 54 (1971/72) 282–313; 55 (1972/73) 86–111.

———, ed. *The Samaritans*. Tübingen: J.C.B. Mohr (Paul Siebeck), 1989.

Dalman, G. *Arbeit und Sitte in Palästina*. Vols. 1–7. 1928–42. Reprint. Hildesheim: Olms, 1964.

Dandamaev, M. A. *Persien unter den ersten Achämeniden (6. Jahrhundert v. Chr.)*. Beiträge zur Iranistik 8. Wiesbaden: Reichert, 1976.

———. *Slavery in Babylonia: From Nabopolassar to Alexander the Great (625–331 B.C.)*. Rev. ed. DeKalb: Northern Illinois University Press, 1984.

———. *A Political History of the Achaemenid Empire*. Leiden: E. J. Brill, 1989.

Dandamaev, M. A., and V. G. Lukonin. *The Culture and Social Institutions of Ancient Iran*. Cambridge: Cambridge University Press, 1989.

Daniel, C. "Les 'Hérodiens' du Nouveau Testament sont-ils des Esséniens?" *RevQ* 6 (1967/69) 31–53.

Daniel, J. L. "Anti-Semitism in the Hellenistic-Roman Period." *JBL* 98 (1979) 45–65.

Daube, D. "On Acts 23: Sadducees and Angels." *JBL* 109 (1990) 493–97.

Davies, J. K. "Cultural, Social and Economic Features of the Hellenistic World." *CAH*² (1984) 7.1.257–320.

Davies, P. R. *1QM, the War Scroll from Qumran: Its Structure and History*. BibOr 32. Rome: Biblical Institute, 1977.

———. "*Ḥasidim* in the Maccabean Period." *JJS* 28 (1977) 127–40.

———. *Qumran*. Cities of the Biblical World. Guildford, Surrey: Lutterworth, 1982.

———. "The Ideology of the Temple in the Damascus Document." *JJS* 33 (1982) 287–301.

———. *The Damascus Covenant: An Interpretation of the "Damascus Document."* JSOTSS 25. Sheffield: JSOT Press, 1983.

———. *Daniel*. Society for Old Testament Study, Old Testament Guides. Sheffield: Academic Press, 1985.

———. "Eschatology at Qumran." *JBL* 104 (1985) 39–55.

———. *Behind the Essenes: History and Ideology in the Dead Sea Scrolls*. BJS 94. Atlanta: Scholars Press, 1987.

―――. "The Social World of the Apocalyptic Writings." In *The World of Ancient Israel: Sociological, Anthropological and Political Perspectives. Essays by Members of the Society for Old Testament Study*, edited by R. E. Clements, 251–71. Cambridge: Cambridge University Press, 1989.

―――. "Halakhah at Qumran." In *A Tribute to Geza Vermes: Essays on Jewish and Christian Literature and History*, edited by P. R. Davies and R. T. White, 37–50. JSOTSS 100. Sheffield: JSOT Press, 1990.

Davies, P. S. "The Meaning of Philo's Text about the Gilded Shields." *JTS* 37 (1986) 109–14.

Davies, W. D. *The Gospel and the Land: Early Christianity and Jewish Territorial Doctrine*. Berkeley and Los Angeles: University of California Press, 1974.

―――. *The Territorial Dimensions of Judaism*. Berkeley and Los Angeles: University of California Press, 1982.

Davies, W. D., and D. C. Allison. *The Gospel according to Saint Matthew*. Vols. 1– . ICC. Edinburgh: T & T Clark, 1988– .

Davis, N., and C. M. Kraay. *The Hellenistic Kingdoms: Portrait Coins and History*. London: Thames & Hudson, 1973.

Day, P. L. *An Adversary in Heaven: sāṭān in the Hebrew Bible*. HSM 43. Atlanta: Scholars Press, 1988.

Deferrari, R. J., ed. *Paulus Orosius: The Seven Books of History against the Pagans*. The Fathers of the Church 50. Washington, D.C.: Catholic University of America Press, 1964.

Delavault, B., and A. Lemaire. "La tablette ougaritique RS 16.127 et l'abréviation 'T' en Nord-Ouest Sémitique." *Semitica* 25 (1975) 31–41.

Delcor, M. "Le temple d'Onias en Égypte." *RB* 75 (1968) 188–205. Reprinted in *Études bibliques et orientales de religions comparées*, 328–45. Leiden: E. J. Brill, 1979.

Demsky, A. "*Pelekh* in Nehemiah 3." *IEJ* 33 (1983) 242–44.

Dentzer, J. M., F. Villeneuve, and F. Larché. "Iraq el Amir: Excavations at the Monumental Gateway." *Studies in the History and Archaeology of Jordan* 1 (1982) 201–7.

Dequeker, L. "The City of David and the Seleucid Acra in Jerusalem." *Orientalia Lovaniensia Analecta* 19 (1985) 193–210.

Deselaers, P. *Das Buch Tobit: Studien zu seiner Entstehung, Komposition und Theologie*. Orbis biblicus et orientalis 43. Freiburg: Universitätsverlag, 1982.

Dessau, H. "Zu den neuen Inschriften des Sulpicius Quirinius." *Klio* 17 (1920/21) 252–58.

Diakonov, I. M., ed. *Ancient Mesopotamia: Socio-Economic History. A Collection of Studies by Soviet Scholars*. Moscow: Nauka, 1969.

Diamond, F. H. *Hecataeus of Abdera: A New Historical Approach*. Ph.D. diss., University of California, Los Angeles, 1974; available from Xerox University Microfilms.

―――. "Hecataeus of Abdera and the Mosaic Constitution." In *Panhellenica: Essays in Ancient History and Historiography in Honor of Truesdell S. Brown*, edited by S. M. Burstein and L. A. Okin, 77–95. Lawrence, Kan.: Coronado, 1980.

Dillon, J. *The Middle Platonists: A Study of Platonism 80 B.C. to A.D. 220*. London: Duckworth, 1977.

Dimant, D. "Qumran Sectarian Literature." *JWSTP* (1984) 483–550.

Dion, P. E. "שבצר‎ and סנורי‎." *ZAW* 95 (1983) 111–12.

Dittenberger, W. *Orientis graeci inscriptiones selectae*. Leipzig: 1903. Reprint. Hildesheim: Olms, 1960.

Doran, R. *Temple Propaganda: The Purpose and Character of 2 Maccabees*. CBQMS 12. Washington, D.C.: Catholic Biblical Association, 1981.

———. "The Jewish Hellenistic Historians before Josephus." *ANRW* 2 (1987) 20.1.246–97.

———. "The Non-Dating of Jubilees: Jub 34–38; 23:14-32 in Narrative Context." *JSJ* 20 (1989) 1–11.

Doty, L. T. "The Archive of the Nanâ-Iddin Family from Uruk." *JCS* 30 (1980) 65–90.

Douglas, M. *Purity and Danger: An Analysis of the Concepts of Pollution and Taboo*. London: Routledge & Kegan Paul, 1966.

Downey, G. "Tiberiana." *ANRW* 2 (1975) 2.95–130.

Drews, R. "Diodorus and His Sources." *AJP* 83 (1963) 383–92.

———. *The Greek Accounts of Eastern History*. Center for Hellenic Studies. Cambridge: Harvard University Press, 1973.

Driver, G. R. *Aramaic Documents of the Fifth Century B.C.* Rev. ed. Oxford: Clarendon, 1957.

Dubberstein, W. H. "The Chronology of Cyrus and Cambyses." *AJSL* 55 (1930) 417–19.

Due, B. *The Cyropaedia: Xenophon's Aims and Methods*. Aarhus: University Press, 1989.

Dumbrell, W. J. "The Tell el-Maskhuṭa Bowls and the 'Kingdom' of Qedar in the Persian Period." *BASOR* 203 (Oct. 1971) 33–44.

Dunn, S. P. *The Fall and Rise of the Asiatic Mode of Production*. London: Routledge & Kegan Paul, 1982.

Dupont-Sommer, A., et al. "La stele trilingue recemment decouverte au letoon de Xanthos." *CRAIBL* (1974) 82–93, 115–25, 132–49.

Dyson, S. L. "Native Revolts in the Roman Empire." *Historia* 20 (1971) 239–74.

———. "Native Revolt Patterns in the Roman Empire." *ANRW* 2 (1975) 3.138–75.

Eddy, S. K. *The King Is Dead: Studies in the Near Eastern Resistance to Hellenism 334–31 B.C.* Lincoln: University of Nebraska Press, 1961.

Edwards, O. "Herodian Chronology." *PEQ* 114 (1982) 29–42.

Efron, J. *Studies on the Hasmonean Period*. SJLA 31. Leiden: E. J. Brill, 1987.

Eilers, W. "Le texte cunéiforme du cylindre de Cyrus." In *Commémoration Cyrus: Actes du congrès de Shiraz 1971 et autres études rédigées à l'occasion du 2500e anniversaire de la fondation de l'empire perse* 2.25–34. Acta Iranica 2. Leiden: E. J. Brill, 1974.

Eissfeldt, O. *The Old Testament: An Introduction*. New York: Harper, 1965.

Ellenson, D. "Ellis Rivkin and the Problems of Pharisaic History: A Study in Historiography." *JAAR* 43 (1975) 787–802.

Emerton, J. A. "Did Ezra Go to Jerusalem in 428 B.C.?" *JTS* 17 (1966) 1–19.

Endres, J. C. *Biblical Interpretation in the Book of Jubilees.* CBQMS 18. Washington, D.C.: Catholic Biblical Association, 1987.

Eph'al, I. *The Ancient Arabs: Nomads on the Borders of the Fertile Crescent, Ninth–Fifth Centuries B.C.* Jerusalem: Magnes, 1982.

Epp, E. J., and G. W. Macrae, eds. *The New Testament and Its Modern Interpreters.* Atlanta: Scholars Press; Philadelphia: Fortress, 1989.

Eskenazi, T. C. "The Chronicler and the Composition of 1 Esdras." *CBQ* 48 (1986) 39–61.

———. *In an Age of Prose: A Literary Approach to Ezra-Nehemiah.* SBLMS 36. Atlanta: Scholars Press, 1988.

———. "The Structure of Ezra-Nehemiah and the Integrity of the Book." *JBL* 107 (1988) 641–56.

Fehling, D. *Herodotus and His "Sources."* Arca 21. Leeds: Cairns, 1989.

Feldman, L. H. "Jewish 'Sympathizers' in Classical Literature and Inscriptions." *TAPA* 81 (1950) 200–208.

———. "Hengel's *Judaism and Hellenism* in Retrospect." *JBL* 96 (1977) 371–82.

———. *Josephus and Modern Scholarship (1937–1980).* Berlin and London: de Gruyter, 1984.

———. "How Much Hellenism in Jewish Palestine?" *HUCA* 57 (1986) 83–111.

———. "The Omnipresence of the God-Fearers." *BAR* 12, no. 5 (Sept./Oct. 1986) 58–69.

———. "Pro-Jewish Intimations in Anti-Jewish Remarks Cited in Josephus' *Against Apion.*" *JQR* 78 (1987/88) 187–251.

Feldman, L. H., and G. Hata, eds. *Josephus, Judaism, and Christianity.* Leiden: E. J. Brill, 1987.

———, eds. *Josephus, the Bible, and History.* Leiden: E. J. Brill, 1989.

Filmer, W. E. "The Chronology of the Reign of Herod the Great." *JTS* 17 (1966) 283–98.

Finkelstein, L. *Akiba: Scholar, Saint and Martyr.* New York: Jewish Theological Society, 1936.

Finley, M. I. *The Ancient Economy.* 2d ed. London: Hogarth, 1985.

Fischel, H. A. *Rabbinic Literature and Greco-Roman Philosophy: A Study of Epicurea and Rhetorica in Early Midrashic Writings.* SPB 21. Leiden: E. J. Brill, 1973.

———, ed. *Essays in Greco-Roman and Related Talmudic Literature.* Library of Biblical Studies. New York: Ktav, 1977.

Fischer, T. "Zu den Beziehungen zwischen Rom und den Juden im 2. Jahrhundert v. Chr." *ZAW* 86 (1974) 90–93.

———. "Johannes Hyrkan I. auf Tetradrachmen Antiochos' VII?" *ZDPV* 91 (1975) 191–96.

———. "Zur Seleukideninschrift von Hefzibah." *ZPE* 33 (1979) 131–38.

———. *Seleukiden und Makkabäer: Beiträge zur Seleukidengeschichte und zu den politischen Ereignissen in Judäa während der 1. Hälfte des 2. Jahrhunderts v. Chr.* Bochum: Brockmeyer, 1980.

Fischer, U. *Eschatologie und Jenseitserwartung im hellenistischen Diasporajudentum.* Berlin and New York: de Gruyter, 1978.

Fitzmyer, J. A. "The Bar Cochba Period." In *Essays on the Semitic Background of the New Testament,* 305–54. London: Chapman, 1971. Originally published in *The Bible in Current Catholic Thought: Gruenthaner Memorial Volume,* edited by J. L. McKenzie, 133–68. New York: Herder, 1962.

———. *The Gospel according to Luke I–IX.* AB 28. Garden City, N.Y.: Doubleday, 1981.

———. *The Gospel according to Luke X–XXIV.* AB 28A. Garden City, N.Y.: Doubleday, 1985.

———. *The Dead Sea Scrolls: Major Publications and Tools for Study.* Rev. ed. SBLRBS 20. Atlanta: Scholars Press, 1990.

Fitzmyer, J. A., and D. J. Harrington. *A Manual of Palestinian Aramaic Texts.* BibOr 34. Rome: Biblical Institute, 1978.

Flesher, P.V.M. "Palestinian Synagogues before 70 C.E.: A Review of the Evidence." In *Approaches to Ancient Judaism VI: Studies in the Ethnography and Literature of Judaism,* edited by J. Neusner and E. Frerichs, 68–81. BJS 192. Atlanta: Scholars Press, 1989.

Flusser, D. *Sefer Yosippon.* Vols. 1–2. Jerusalem: Bialik Institute, 1978–80.

———. "Hystaspes and John of Patmos." In *Irano-Judaica: Studies relating to Jewish Contacts with Persian Culture throughout the Ages,* edited by S. Shaked, 12–75. Jerusalem: Ben Zvi Institute, 1982 = D. Flusser, *Judaism and the Origins of Christianity,* 390–453. Jerusalem: Magnes, 1988.

Fohrer, G. *Introduction to the Old Testament.* Nashville: Abingdon, 1968.

Follet, S. "Hadrien en Egypte et en Judée." *Revue de Philologie* 42 (1968) 54–77.

Forrer, E. *Die Provinzeinteilung des assyrischen Reiches.* Leipzig: Hinrichs, 1920.

Forster, G. "The Synagogues at Masada and Herodium." In *Ancient Synagogues Revealed,* edited by L. I. Levine, 24–29. Jerusalem: Israel Exploration Society, 1981.

Fossum, J. E. *The Name of God and the Angel of the Lord: Samaritan and Jewish Concepts of Intermediation and the Origin of Gnosticism.* WUNT 36. Tübingen: J.C.B. Mohr (Paul Siebeck), 1985.

———. "The Magharians: A Pre-Christian Jewish Sect and Its Significance for the Study of Gnosticism and Christianity." *Henoch* 9 (1987) 303–44.

Fox, M. *The Song of Songs and the Ancient Egyptian Love Songs.* Madison: University of Wisconsin Press, 1985.

France, R. T. "Herod and the Children of Bethlehem." *NovT* 21 (1979) 98–120.

Frank, T., ed. *An Economic Survey of Ancient Rome.* Vols. 1–5. Baltimore: Johns Hopkins University Press, 1933–40.

Frerichs, E. S., and J. Neusner, eds. *Goodenough on the History of Religion and on Judaism.* BJS 121. Atlanta: Scholars Press, 1986.

Freyne, S. *Galilee from Alexander the Great to Hadrian: A Study of Second Temple Judaism.* Notre Dame, Ind.: University of Notre Dame Press, 1980.

———. "The Charismatic." In *Ideal Figures in Ancient Judaism,* edited by G.W.E. Nickelsburg and J. J. Collins, 223–58. SBLSCS 12. Atlanta: Scholars Press, 1980.

Frye, R. N. "Qumran and Iran: The State of Studies." In *Christianity, Judaism and Other Greco-Roman Cults: Studies for Morton Smith at Sixty,* 3.167–73. Edited by J. Neusner. SJLA 12. Leiden: E. J. Brill, 1975.

———. *History of Ancient Iran.* Handbuch der Altertumswissenschaft, 3.7. Berlin and New York: de Gruyter, 1984.

Fuks, A. "The Jewish Revolt in Egypt (A.D. 115–117) in the Light of the Papyri." *Aegyptus* 33 (1953) 131–58.

———. "Aspects of the Jewish Revolt in A.D. 115–117." *JRS* 51 (1961) 98–104.

Fuks, G. "Again on the Episode of the Gilded Roman Shields at Jerusalem." *HTR* 75 (1982) 503–7.

Funk, R. W. "The 1957 Campaign at Beth-Zur." *BASOR* 150 (April 1958) 8–20.

Gager, J. G. *Moses in Greco-Roman Paganism.* SBLMS 16. Nashville: Abingdon, 1972.

———. "Jews, Gentiles, and Synagogues in the Book of Acts." *HTR* 79 (1986) 91–99.

Galili, E. "Raphia, 217 B.C.E., Revisited." *Scripta Classica Israelica* 3 (1976–77) 52–126.

Galling, K. *Studien zur Geschichte Israels im persischen Zeitalter.* Tübingen: J.C.B. Mohr (Paul Siebeck), 1964.

———. "Die Liste der aus dem Exil Heimgekehrten." *Studien* (1964): 89–108 = revision of "The 'Gōlā-List' according to Ezra 2//Nehemiah 7." *JBL* 70 (1951) 149–58.

Garnsey, P., ed. *Non-Slave Labour in the Greco-Roman World.* Cambridge Philological Society, Supplementary Volume 6. Cambridge: Cambridge Philological Society, 1980.

Garnsey, P., and R. Saller. *The Roman Empire: Economy, Society, and Culture.* London: Duckworth, 1987.

Garnsey, P., and C. R. Whittaker, eds. *Trade and Famine in Classical Antiquity.* Cambridge Philological Society, Supplementary Volume 8. Cambridge: Cambridge Philological Society, 1983.

Garnsey, P., et al., eds. *Trade in the Ancient Economy.* London: Chatto & Windus, 1983.

Garzetti, A. *From Tiberius to the Antonines: A History of the Roman Empire A.D. 14–192.* London: Methuen, 1974.

Gauger, J.-D. *Beiträge zur jüdischen Apologetik: Untersuchungen zur Authentizität von Urkunden bei Flavius Josephus und im I. Makkabäerbuch.* Bonner Biblische Beiträge 49. Cologne and Bonn: Peter Hanstein, 1977.

———. "Zitate in der jüdischen Apologetik und die Authentizität der Hekataios-Passagen bei Flavius Josephus und im Ps. Aristeas-Brief." *JSJ* 13 (1982) 6–46.

Gelston, A. "The Foundations of the Second Temple." *VT* 16 (1966) 232–35.

Gelzer, H. *Sextus Julius Africanus und die byzantinische Chronographie.* 2 vols., 1885–98. Reprint. New York: Burt Franklin, n.d.

Gera, D. "Tryphon's Sling Bullet from Dor." *IEJ* 35 (1985) 153–63.

Geraty, L. T. "The Khirbet el-Kôm Bilingual Ostracon." *BASOR* 220 (Dec. 1975) 55–61.

———. "Recent Suggestions on the Bilingual Ostracon from Khirbet el-Kôm." *AUSS* 19 (1981) 137–40.

———. "The Historical, Linguistic, and Biblical Significance of the Khirbet el-Kôm Ostraca." In *The Word of the Lord Shall Go Forth: Essays in Honor of David Noel Freedman in Celebration of His Sixtieth Birthday*, edited by C. L. Meyers and M. O'Connor, 545–48. ASOR Sp. Vol. Series 1. Winona Lake, Ind.: Eisenbrauns, 1983.

Gereboff, J. *Rabbi Tarfon*. BJS 6. Atlanta: Scholars Press, 1979.

Gerhardsson, B. *Memory and Manuscript*. Acta seminarii neotestamentici upsaliensis 22. Lund: Gleerup, 1961.

Gershenzon, R., and E. Slomovic. "A Second-Century Jewish-Gnostic Debate: Rabbi Jose ben Halafta and the Matrona." *JSJ* 16 (1985) 1–41.

Gese, H. "Zur Geschichte der Kultsänger am Zweiten Tempel." In *Abraham unser Vater: Juden und Christen im Gespräch über die Bibel, Festschrift für Otto Michel zum 60. Geburtstag*, edited by O. Betz, et al., 222–34. Leiden: E. J. Brill, 1963.

Geva, H. "The 'Tower of David'—Phasael or Hippicus?" *IEJ* 31 (1981) 57–65.

———. "The Camp of the Tenth Legion in Jerusalem: An Archaeological Reconsideration." *IEJ* 34 (1984) 239–54.

Gichon, M. "Idumea and the Herodian Limes." *IEJ* 17 (1967) 27–42.

———. "The Bar Kokhba War: A Colonial Uprising against Imperial Rome." *Revue internationale d'histoire militaire* 42 (1979) 82–97.

———. "Cestius Gallus's Campaign in Judaea." *PEQ* 113 (1981) 39–62.

———. "New Insight into the Bar Kokhba War and a Reappraisal of Dio Cassius 69.12-13." *JQR* 77 (1986/87) 15–43.

Gilboa, A. "The Intervention of Sextus Julius Caesar, Governor of Syria, in the Affair of Herod's Trial." *Scripta Classica Israelica* 5 (1979/80) 185–94.

Glasson, T. F. *Greek Influence in Jewish Eschatology, with Special Reference to the Apocalypses and Pseudepigraphs*. London: SPCK, 1961.

Glazier-McDonald, B. *Malachi: The Divine Messenger*. SBLDS 98. Atlanta: Scholars Press, 1987.

Golan, D. "Hadrian's Decision to Supplant 'Jerusalem' by 'Aelia Capitolina.'" *Historia* 35 (1986) 226–39.

Goldingay, J. E. *Daniel*. WBC 30. Dallas: Word, 1989.

Goldschmidt-Lehmann, R. P. "The Second (Herodian) Temple: Selected Bibliography." *Jerusalem Cathedra* 1 (1981) 336–59.

Goldstein, J. A. "The Tales of the Tobiads." In *Christianity, Judaism and Other Greco-Roman Cults* 3.85–123. Edited by J. Neusner. SJLA 12. Leiden: E. J. Brill, 1975.

———. *I Maccabees*. AB 41. Garden City, N.Y.: Doubleday, 1976.

———. *II Maccabees*. AB 41A; Garden City, N.Y.: Doubleday, 1983.

———. "The Date of the Book of Jubilees." *PAAJR* 50 (1983) 63–86.

Goldwasser, O., and J. Naveh. "The Origin of the Ṭet-Symbol." *IEJ* 26 (1976) 15–19.

Goodblatt, D. "Towards the Rehabilitation of Talmudic History." In *History of Judaism: The Next Ten Years*, edited by B. Bokser, 31–44. BJS 21. Atlanta: Scholars Press, 1980.

———. "A Contribution to the Prosopography of the Second Revolt: Yehudah bar Menasheh." *JJS* 38 (1987) 38–55.

———. "Sanhedrin." In *The Encyclopedia of Religion* 13.60–63. New York and London: Macmillan, 1987.

————. "The Place of the Pharisees in First-Century Judaism: The State of the Debate." *JSJ* 20 (1989) 12–30.

Goodenough, E. R. *By Light, Light: The Mystic Gospel of Hellenistic Judaism.* New Haven: Yale University Press, 1935.

————. *Jewish Symbols in the Greco-Roman Period.* Vols. 1–13. Bollingen Series 37. New York: Pantheon, 1953–65.

————. *An Introduction to Philo Judaeus.* Rev. ed. Oxford: Clarendon, 1962.

————. *Jewish Symbols in the Greco-Roman Period.* Abridged ed., edited by J. Neusner. Bollingen Series. Princeton: Princeton University Press, 1988.

Goodenough, E. R., with H. L. Goodhart. *The Politics of Philo Judaeus, Practice and Theory: With a General Bibliography of Philo.* New Haven: Yale University Press, 1938.

Goodman, M. Review of *Jews in Hellenistic and Roman Egypt,* by A. Kasher. *JJS* 32 (1981) 207–8.

————. "The First Jewish Revolt: Social Conflict and the Problem of Debt." *JJS* 33 (1982) 417–27.

————. *State and Society in Roman Galilee,* A.D. *132–212.* Oxford Centre for Postgraduate Hebrew Studies. Totowa, N.J.: Rowman & Allanheld, 1983.

————. *The Ruling Class of Judaea: The Origins of the Jewish Revolt against Rome* A.D. *66–70.* Cambridge: Cambridge University Press, 1987.

————. "Nerva, the *Fiscus Judaicus* and Jewish Identity." *JRS* 79 (1989) 40–44.

Grabbe, L. L. "Orthodoxy in First-Century Judaism: What Are the Issues?" *JSJ* 8 (1977) 149–53.

————. "Chronography in Hellenistic Jewish Historiography." *SBLSP* 17. Edited by P. J. Achtemeier, 2.43–68. Missoula, Mont.: Scholars Press, 1979.

————. "Chronography in 4 Ezra and 2 Baruch." *SBLSP* 1981. SBLASP. Chico: Scholars Press, 1981.

————. "Josephus and the Reconstruction of the Judean Restoration." *JBL* 106 (1987) 231–46.

————. "The Jewish Theocracy from Cyrus to Titus: A Programmatic Essay." *JSOT* 37 (1987) 117–24.

————. "The Scapegoat Ritual: A Study in Early Jewish Interpretation." *JSJ* 18 (1987) 152–67.

————. "Synagogues in Pre-70 Palestine: A Reassessment." *JTS* 39 (1988) 401–10.

————. *Etymology in Early Jewish Interpretation: The Hebrew Names in Philo.* BJS 115. Atlanta: Scholars Press, 1988.

————. "Another Look at the *Gestalt* of 'Darius the Mede.'" *CBQ* 50 (1988) 198–213.

————. "The Social Setting of Early Jewish Apocalypticism." *JSP* 4 (1989) 27–47.

————. "Josephus." In *Dictionary of Biblical Interpretation,* edited by R. J. Coggins and J. L. Houlden, 365–68. London: SCM, 1990.

————. "Maccabean Chronology: 167–164 or 168–165 B.C.E.?" *JBL* 110 (1991) 59–74.

————. "Who Was the Bagoses of Josephus (*Ant.* 11.7.1 §§297–301)?" *Transeuphratène* 5 (1991) 49–55.

————. Review of *Persia and the Bible*, by E. M. Yamauchi. *JSJ* (1991).

————. "Reconstructing History from the Book of Ezra." In *Studies in the Second Temple: The Persian Period*, edited by P. R. Davies, 98–107. JSOTSS 117. Sheffield: JSOT Press, 1991.

————. "What Was Ezra's Mission?" In *Studies in the Second Temple: The Persian Period.* Vol. 2. Forthcoming.

Graf, D. F. "Medism: The Origin and Significance of the Term." *JHS* 104 (1984) 15–30.

Grayson, A. K. *Assyrian and Babylonian Chronicles.* Texts from Cuneiform Sources 5. Locust Valley, N.Y.: J. J. Augustin, 1975.

Green, W. S., ed. *Persons and Institutions in Early Rabbinic Judaism.* BJS 3. Atlanta: Scholars Press, 1977.

————. "What's in a Name?—The Problematic of Rabbinic 'Biography.'" In *Approaches to Ancient Judaism: Theory and Practice*, edited by W. S. Green, 77–96. BJS 1. Atlanta: Scholars Press, 1978.

————. "Palestinian Holy Men: Charismatic Leadership and Rabbinic Tradition." *ANRW* 2 (1979) 19.2.619–47.

————. "Context and Meaning in Rabbinic 'Biography.'" In *Approaches to Ancient Judaism*, Vol. 2, edited by W. S. Green, 97–111. BJS 9. Atlanta: Scholars Press, 1980.

Greenfield, J. C., and B. Porten. *The Bisitun Inscription of Darius the Great: Aramaic Version.* Corpus Inscriptionum Iranicarum. Part I: Inscriptions of Ancient Iran; Vol. V: The Aramaic Versions of the Achaemenian Inscriptions, Texts I. London: Humphries, 1982.

Grelot, P. "Etudes sur le 'Papyrus Pascal' d'Eléphantine." *VT* 4 (1954) 349–84.

————. "Sur le 'Papyrus Pascal' d'Eléphantine." In *Mélanges bibliques et orientaux en l'honneur de M. Henri Cazelles*, edited by A. Caquot and M. Delcor, 163–72. Neukirchen-Vluyn: Neukirchener Verlag, 1981.

Gressmann, H. "Die ammonitischen Tobiaden." *SPAW* (1921) 663–71.

Griffin, M. T. *Nero: The End of a Dynasty.* London: Batsford, 1984.

Griffiths, J. G. "Hellenistic Religions." In *The Encyclopedia of Religion.* New York and London: Macmillan, 1987.

Grimal, P., ed. *Hellenism and the Rise of Rome.* Delacorte World History. English trans. of *Fischer Weltgeschichte.* New York: Delacorte, 1968.

Groag, E., and A. Stein. *Prosopographia imperii Romani: Saec. I.II.III.* Vols. 1–5. Berlin: de Gruyter, 1933–87.

Gruber, M. I. "The Mishnah as Oral Torah: A Reconsideration." *JSJ* 15 (1984) 112–22.

Gruen, E. S. *The Hellenistic World and the Coming of Rome.* 2 vols. Berkeley and Los Angeles: University of California Press, 1984.

Gruenwald, I. *Apocalyptic and Merkavah Mysticism.* AGAJU 14. Leiden: E. J. Brill, 1980.

————. "Aspects of the Jewish-Gnostic Controversy." In *The Rediscovery of Gnosticism* 2.713–23. Edited by B. Layton. Studies in the History of Religions: Numen Sup 41. Leiden: E. J. Brill, 1981.

————. "The Problem of the Anti-Gnostic Polemic in Rabbinic Literature." In *Studies in Gnosticism and Hellenistic Religions Presented to Gilles Quispel on the Occasion of His Sixty-fifth Birthday,* edited by R. van den Broek and M. J. Vermaseren, 171–89. Leiden: E. J. Brill, 1981.

———. "Jewish Merkavah Mysticism and Gnosticism." In *Studies in Jewish Mysticism,* edited by J. Dan and F. Talmage, 41–55. Cambridge, Mass.: Association for Jewish Studies, 1982.

Guelich, R. A. *Mark 1—8:26.* WBC 34A. Dallas: Word, 1989.

Gunneweg, A.H.J. *Leviten und Priester: Hauptlinien der Traditionsbildung und Geschichte des israelitisch-jüdischen Kultpersonals.* FRLANT 89. Göttingen: Vandenhoeck & Ruprecht, 1965.

———. "Zur Interpretation der Bücher Esra-Nehemiah: Zugleich ein Beitrag zur Methode der Exegese." In *Congress Volume, Vienna 1980,* 146–61. VTSup 32. Leiden: E. J. Brill, 1981.

———. "Die aramäische und die hebräische Erzählung über die nachexilische Restauration—ein Vergleich." *ZAW* 94 (1982) 299–302.

———. *Esra.* KAT 19.1. Gütersloh: Mohn, 1985.

———. *Nehemia.* KAT 19.2. Gütersloh: Mohn, 1987.

Guterman, S. L. *Religious Toleration and Persecution in Ancient Rome.* London: Aiglon, 1951.

Habicht, C., ed. *II. Makkabäerbuch.* JSHRZ 1/3. Gütersloh: Mohn, 1976.

———. "Royal Documents in Maccabees II." *Harvard Studies in Classical Philology* 80 (1976) 1–18.

———. "The Seleucids and Their Rivals." *CAH*² (1989) 8.324–87.

Hachlili, R. "A Jerusalem Family in Jericho." *BASOR* 230 (1978) 45–56.

———. "The Goliath Family in Jericho: Funerary Inscriptions from a First Century A.D. Jewish Monumental Tomb." *BASOR* 235 (1979) 31–65.

Hachlili, R., et al. "The Genealogy of the Goliath Family." *BASOR* 235 (1979) 66–73.

Hadas, M. *Aristeas to Philocrates.* Dropsie College Jewish Apocryphal Literature. New York: Harper, 1951. Reprint. New York: Ktav, 1973.

Haenchen, E. *The Acts of the Apostles.* Philadelphia: Westminster; Oxford: Blackwell, 1971.

Hall, R. G. "Epispasm and the Dating of Ancient Jewish Writings." *JSP* 4 (1989) 71–86.

Hallock, R. T. *Persepolis Fortification Tablets.* Chicago: University of Chicago Press, 1969.

———. "The Evidence of the Persepolis Tablets." *CHI* (1985) 2.588–609.

Halpern, B. "Ritual Background of Zechariah's Temple Song." *CBQ* 40 (1978) 167–90.

Halpern-Zylberstein, M.-C. "The Archeology of Hellenistic Palestine." *CHJ* (1989) 2.1–34.

Hamel, G. *Poverty and Charity in Roman Palestine, First Three Centuries C.E.* University of California Publications; Near Eastern Studies 23. Berkeley and Los Angeles: University of California Press, 1990.

Hann, R. R. "The Community of the Pious: The Social Setting of the Psalms of Solomon." *SR* 17 (1988) 169–89.

Hansen, E. V. *The Attalids of Pergamon.* 2d ed. Cornell Studies in Classical Philology 36. Ithaca, N.Y.: Cornell University Press, 1971.

Hansen, O. "The Purported Letter of Darius to Gadates." *Rheinisches Museum* 129 (1986) 95–96.

Hanson, P. D. *The Dawn of Apocalyptic.* Philadelphia: Westminster, 1973.

———. "Apocalypticism." *IDBSup* (1976) 29–31.

———. "From Prophecy to Apocalyptic: Unresolved Issues." *JSOT* 15 (1980) 3–6.

Hanson, R. S. "Toward a Chronology of the Hasmonean Coins." *BASOR* 216 (1974) 21–23.

———. *Tyrian Influence in the Upper Galilee.* Meiron Excavation Project 2. Cambridge, Mass.: American Schools of Oriental Research, 1980.

Har-El, M. "The Zealots' Fortresses in Galilee." *IEJ* 33 (1972) 123–30.

Harmatta, J. "Irano-Aramaica (Zur Geschichte des frühhellenistischen Judentums in Agypten)." *Acta Antiqua* 7 (1959) 337–409.

Harper, C. M., Jr. "A Study in the Commercial Relations between Egypt and Syria in the Third Century Before Christ." *AJP* 49 (1928) 1–35.

Harper, G. M. "Village Administration in the Roman Province of Syria." *YCS* 1 (1928) 105–68.

Harrelson, W. "The Trial of the High Priest Joshua: Zechariah 3." *EI* 16 (1982) 116*–24*.

Harrington, D. J. "The Wisdom of the Scribe according to Ben Sira." In *Ideal Figures in Ancient Judaism: Profiles and Paradigms,* edited by J. J. Collins and G.W.E. Nickelsburg, 181–88. SBLSCS 12. Atlanta: Scholars Press, 1980.

———. *The Maccabean Revolt: Anatomy of a Biblical Revolution.* Old Testament Studies 1. Wilmington, Del.: Michael Glazier, 1988.

Hartman, L. F., and A. A. Di Lella. *The Book of Daniel.* AB 23. Garden City, N.Y.: Doubleday, 1978.

Hasel, G. F. *The Remnant: The History and Theology of the Remnant Idea from Genesis to Isaiah.* Andrews University Monographs, Studies in Religion 5. Berrien Springs, Mich.: Andrews University, 1974.

———. "Remnant." *IDBSup* (1976) 735–36.

Hausmann, J. *Israels Rest: Studien zum Selbstverständnis der nachexilischen Gemeinde.* BWANT 124. Stuttgart: Kohlhammer, 1987.

Hay, D. M. "Philo's References to Other Allegorists." *Studia Philonica* 6 (1979/80) 41–75.

Hayes, J., and J. M. Miller, eds. *Israelite and Judaean History.* OTL. Philadelphia: Westminster; London: SCM, 1977.

Hayward, R. "The Jewish Temple at Leontopolis: A Reconsideration." *JJS* 33 (1982) 429–43.

Heichelheim, F. M. "Roman Syria." In *An Economic Survey of Ancient Rome* 4.121–257. Edited by T. Frank. Baltimore: Johns Hopkins University Press, 1938.

Heinemann, I. "Wer veranlasste den Glaubenszwang der Makkabäerzeit?" *MGWJ* 82 (1938) 145–72.

Hellholm, D., ed. *Apocalypticism in the Mediterranean World and the Near East.* Tübingen: J.C.B. Mohr (Paul Siebeck), 1983.

Helm, R., ed. *Die Chronik des Hieronymus.* Eusebius Werke 7. GCS. Berlin: Akademie-Verlag, 1956.

Hemer, C. J. *The Book of Acts in the Setting of Hellenistic History.* WUNT 49. Tübingen: J.C.B. Mohr (Paul Siebeck), 1989.

Hengel, M. *Judaism and Hellenism: Studies in Their Encounter in Palestine during the Early Hellenistic Period.* 2 vols. Philadelphia: Fortress; London: SCM, 1974.

———. *Acts and the History of Earliest Christianity.* London: SCM, 1979.

———. *Jews, Greeks and Barbarians: Aspects of the Hellenization of Judaism in the Pre-Christian Period.* Philadelphia: Fortress; London: SCM, 1980.

———. "Messianische Hoffnung und politischer 'Radikalismus' in der 'jüdisch-hellenistischen Diaspora': Zur Frage der Voraussetzungen des jüdischen Aufstandes unter Trajan 115–117 n. Chr." In *Apocalypticism in the Mediterranean World and the Near East,* edited by D. Hellholm, 655–86. Tübingen: J.C.B. Mohr (Paul Siebeck), 1983.

———. *The "Hellenization" of Judaea in the First Century after Christ.* Philadelphia: Trinity Press International; London: SCM, 1989.

———. *The Zealots: Investigations into the Jewish Freedom Movement in the Period from Herod I until 70 A.D.* Edinburgh: T. & T. Clark, 1989.

Henricks, A. "Mani and the Babylonian Baptists: A Historical Confrontation." *HSCP* 77 (1973) 23–59.

———. "The Cologne Mani Codex Reconsidered." *HSCP* 83 (1979) 339–67.

Henricks, A., and L. Koenen. "Ein griechischer Mani-Codex." *ZPE* 5 (1970) 97–216.

——— ——. "Der kölner Mani-Kodex (P. Colon. inv. nr. 4780)." *ZPE* 19 (1975) 1–85; 32 (1978) 87–199; 44 (1981) 201–312; and 48 (1982) 1–59.

Henry, K. H. "Land Tenure in the Old Testament." *PEQ* 86 (1954) 5–15.

Hensley, L. V. *The Official Persian Documents in the Book of Ezra.* Ph.D. diss., University of Liverpool, 1977.

Henten, J. W. van, ed. *Die Entstehung der jüdischen Martyrologie.* SPB 38. Leiden: E. J. Brill, 1989.

Hieronymus (Jerome). *Commentariorum in Danielem.* 1964.

Hilgert, E. "Bibliographia Philoniana 1935–1981." *ANRW* 2 (1984) 21.1.47–97.

Hill, A. E. "Dating the Book of Malachi: A Linguistic Reexamination." In *The Word of the Lord Shall Go Forth: Essays in Honor of David Noel Freedman in Celebration of His Sixtieth Birthday,* edited by C. L. Meyers and M. O'Connor, 77–89. ASOR Sp. Vol. Series 1. Winona Lake, Ind.: Eisenbrauns, 1983.

Hill, D. *New Testament Prophecy.* Basingstoke, Eng.: Marshall, Morgan, & Scott, 1979.

Hinnells, J. "The Zoroastrian Doctrine of Salvation in the Roman World." In *Man and His Salvation: Studies in Memory of S.G.F. Brandon,* edited by E. J. Sharpe and J. R. Hinnells, 125–48. Manchester, Eng.: Manchester University Press, 1973.

Hirsch, S. W. *The Friendship of the Barbarians: Xenophon and the Persian Empire.* Hanover, N.H., and London: University Press of New England, 1985.

Hoehner, H. W. *Herod Antipas: A Contemporary of Jesus Christ.* 1972. Reprint, with corrections. Grand Rapids: Zondervan, 1980.

Holladay, C. R. *Theios Aner in Hellenistic-Judaism: A Critique of the Use of This Category in New Testament Christology.* SBLDS 40. Atlanta: Scholars Press, 1977.

――――. *Fragments from Hellenistic Jewish Authors.* Vol. 1: *Historians.* TT 20; Pseudepigrapha Series 10. Atlanta: Scholars Press, 1983. Vol. 2: *Poets: The Epic Poets Theodotus and Philo and Ezekiel the Tragedian.* TT 30; Pseudepigrapha Series 12. Atlanta: Scholars Press, 1989.

Hölscher, G. *Die Hohenpriesterliste bei Josephus und die evangelische Chronologie. SAWH.* Philologische-historische Klasse, Jahrgang 1939/40, 3 Abhandlung. Heidelberg (Winter, 1940) 1–33.

Hopkins, K. "Taxes and Trade in the Roman Empire (200 B.C.–A.D. 400)." *JRS* 70 (1980) 101–25.

Horgan, M. P. *Pesharim: Qumran Interpretations of Biblical Books.* CBQMS 8. Washington, D.C.: Catholic Biblical Association, 1979.

Hornblower, S. *Mausolus.* Oxford: Clarendon, 1982.

――――. *The Greek World 479–323 B.C.* New York and London: Methuen, 1983.

Horowitz, G. "Town Planning of Hellenistic Marisa: A Reappraisal of the Excavations after Eighty Years." *PEQ* 112 (1980) 93–111.

Horsley, G.H.R. *New Documents Illustrating Early Christianity: A Review of the Greek Inscriptions and Papyri Published in 1976.* Ancient History Documentary Research Centre. Sydney, Australia: Macquarie University Press, 1981.

Horsley, R. A. "Josephus and the Bandits." *JSJ* 10 (1979) 37–63.

――――. "The Sicarii: Ancient Jewish 'Terrorists.' " *JR* 59 (1979) 435–58.

――――. "Ancient Jewish Banditry and the Revolt against Rome, A.D. 66–70." *CBQ* 43 (1981) 409–32.

――――. "Popular Messianic Movements around the Time of Jesus." *CBQ* 46 (1984) 471–95.

――――. " 'Like One of the Prophets of Old': Two Types of Popular Prophets at the Time of Jesus." *CBQ* 47 (1985) 435–63.

――――. "Menahem in Jerusalem: A Brief Messianic Episode among the Sicarii—Not 'Zealot Messianism.' " *NovT* 27 (1985) 334–48.

――――. "Popular Prophetic Movements at the Time of Jesus: Their Principal Features and Social Origins." *JSNT* 26 (1986) 3–27.

――――. "The Zealots: Their Origin, Relationships and Importance in the Jewish Revolt." *NovT* 28 (1986) 159–92.

――――. *Jesus and the Spiral of Violence: Popular Jewish Resistance in Roman Palestine.* San Francisco: Harper & Row, 1987.

Horsley, R. A., and J. S. Hanson. *Bandits, Prophets, and Messiahs: Popular Movements in the Time of Jesus.* New Voices in Biblical Studies. Minneapolis: Winston, 1985.

Hout, M. van den. "Studies in Early Greek Letter-Writing." *Mnemosyne.* Series 4, vol. 2 (1949) 19–41, 138–53.

Houtman, C. "Ezra and the Law: Observations on the Supposed Relation between Ezra and the Pentateuch." *OTS* 21 (1981) 91–115.

Hughes, G. R. "The So-called Pherendates Correspondence." In *Grammata*

Demotika: Festschrift für Erich Lüddeckens zum 15. Juni 1983, edited by H.-J. Thissen and K.-T. Zauzich, 75–86. Würzburg: Zauzich, 1984.

Hultgård, A. "Das Judentum in der hellenistisch-römischen Zeit und die iranische Religion—ein religionsgeschichtliches Problem." *ANRW* 2 (1979) 512–90.

Humphries, W. L. "A Life-Style for Diaspora: A Study of the Tales of Esther and Daniel." *JBL* 92 (1973) 211–23.

Hurvitz, A. "Dating the Priestly Source in Light of the Historical Study of Biblical Hebrew: A Century after Wellhausen." *ZAW* 100 *Supplement* (1988) 88–100.

Hüttenmeister, F., and G. Reeg. *Die antiken Synagogen in Israel.* 2 vols. Beihefte zum Tübinger Atlas des Vorderen Orients. Reihe B, Nr. 12. Wiesbaden: Reichert, 1977.

In der Smitten, W. T. "Historische Probleme zum Kyrosedikt und zum Jerusalemer Tempelbau von 515." *Persica* 6 (1972–74) 167–78.

———. *Esra: Quellen, Überlieferung und Geschichte.* Studia Semitica Neerlandica 15. Assen: Van Gorcum, 1973.

Isaac, B. "Roman Colonies in Judaea: The Foundation of Aelia Capitolina." *Talanta* 12–13 (1980–81) 31–54.

———. "A Donation for Herod's Temple in Jerusalem." *IEJ* 33 (1983) 86–92. Hebrew version in *EI* 18 (1985) 1–4.

———. "Bandits in Judaea and Arabia." *HSCP* 88 (1984) 171–203.

———. "Judaea after A.D. 70." *JJS* 35 (1984) 44–50.

Isaac, B., and A. Oppenheimer. "The Revolt of Bar Kokhba: Ideology and Modern Scholarship." *JJS* 36 (1985) 33–60.

Isaac, B., and I. Roll. "Judaea in the Early Years of Hadrian's Reign." *Latomus* 38 (1979) 54–66.

———. "Legio II Traiana in Judaea." *ZPE* 33 (1979) 149–56.

———. *Roman Roads in Judaea.* Vol. 1: *The Legio-Scythopolis Road.* British Archaeological Reports International Series 141. Oxford: BAR, 1982.

Isser, S. J. *The Dositheans: A Samaritan Sect in Late Antiquity.* SJLA 17. Leiden: E. J. Brill, 1976.

Jacobson, H. *The "Exagoge" of Ezekiel.* Cambridge: Cambridge University Press, 1983.

Jacoby, F. *Die Fragmente der griechischen Historiker.* Parts 1–17. Berlin: Weidman, 1926–58.

———. "Ktesias." In idem, *Griechische Historiker,* 311–32. Stuttgart: Alfred Druckenmuller, 1956. Reprinted from *PW* 11.2032–73.

Jagersma, H. *A History of Israel in the Old Testament Period.* London: SCM, 1982.

———. *A History of Israel from Alexander the Great to Bar Kochba.* London: SCM, 1985.

Japhet, S. "The Supposed Common Authorship of Chronicles and Ezra-Nehemiah Investigated Anew." *VT* 18 (1968) 330–71.

———. "Sheshbazzar and Zerubbabel—Against the Background of the Historical and Religious Tendencies of Ezra-Nehemiah." *ZAW* 94 (1982) 66–98; 95 (1983) 218-29.

————. *The Ideology of the Book of Chronicles and Its Place in Biblical Thought.* Beiträge zur Erforschung des Alten Testaments und des antiken Judentums 9. Frankfurt: Lang, 1989.

Jellicoe, S. *The Septuagint and Modern Study.* Oxford: Clarendon, 1968.

Jeremias, J. *Jerusalem in the Time of Jesus: An Investigation into Economic and Social Conditions during the New Testament Period.* London: SCM, 1969.

Jeselsohn, D. "A New Coin Type with Hebrew Inscription." *IEJ* 24 (1974) 77–78.

————. "Hever Yehudim—A New Jewish Coin." *PEQ* 112 (1980) 11–17.

Johnson, J. H. "The Demotic Chronicle as an Historical Source." *Enchoria* 4 (1974) 1–17.

————. "Is the Demotic Chronicle an Anti-Greek Tract?" In *Grammata Demotika: Festschrift für Erich Lüddeckens zum 15. Juni 1983*, edited by H.-J. Thissen and K.-T. Zauzich, 107–24. Würzburg: Zauzich, 1984.

Johnson, M. D. *The Purpose of the Biblical Genealogies.* 2d ed. SNTSMS 8. Cambridge: Cambridge University Press, 1988.

Jones, A.H.M. *The Cities of the Eastern Roman Provinces.* 2d ed. Oxford: Clarendon, 1971.

————. "Taxation in Antiquity." In *The Roman Economy*, edited by P. A. Brunt, 151–86. Oxford: Blackwell, 1974.

Jones, B. W. *The Emperor Titus.* New York: St. Martin's; London: Croom Helm, 1984.

Kampen, J. "A Reconsideration of the Name 'Essene' in Greco-Jewish Literature in Light of Recent Perceptions of the Qumran Sect." *HUCA* 57 (1986) 61–81.

————. *The Hasideans and the Origins of Pharisaism: A Study in 1 and 2 Maccabees.* SBLSCS 24. Atlanta: Scholars Press, 1988.

Kanael, B. "The Partition of Judea by Gabinius." *IEJ* 6 (1956) 98–106.

————. "Ancient Jewish Coins and Their Historical Importance." *BA* 26 (1963) 38–62.

————. "Altjüdische Münzen." *Jahrbuch für Numismatik und Geldgeschichte* 17 (1967) 159–298.

————. "Notes on the Dates Used during the Bar Kokhba Revolt." *IEJ* 21 (1971) 39–46.

Kanter, S. *Rabban Gamaliel II.* BJS 8. Atlanta: Scholars Press, 1979.

Karst, J. *Die Chronik aus dem Armenischen übersetzt.* Eusebius Werke 5. GCS. Leipzig: Hinrichs, 1911.

Kasher, A. "Some Comments on the Jewish Uprising in Egypt in the Time of Trajan." *JJS* 27 (1976) 147–58.

————. *The Jews in Hellenistic and Roman Egypt: The Struggle for Equal Rights.* TSAJ 7. Tübingen: J.C.B. Mohr (Paul Siebeck), 1985.

————. *Jews, Idumaeans, and Ancient Arabs: Relations of the Jews in Eretz-Israel with the Nations of the Frontier and the Desert during the Hellenistic and Roman Era (332 B.C.E.–70 C.E.).* TSAJ 18. Tübingen: J.C.B. Mohr (Paul Siebeck), 1988.

————. *Jews and Hellenistic Cities in Eretz-Israel: Relations of the Jews in Eretz-Israel with the Hellenistic Cities during the Second Temple Period (332 B.C.E.–70 C.E.).* TSAJ 21. Tübingen: J.C.B. Mohr (Paul Siebeck), 1990.

Katzoff, R. "Jonathan and Late Sparta." *AJP* 106 (1985) 485–89.

Kazis, I. J. *The Book of the Gests of Alexander of Macedon.* Cambridge, Mass.: Medieval Academy of America, 1962.

Kellermann, D. לֵוִי *TWAT* (1984) 4.499–521.

Kellermann, U. "Die Listen in Nehemia 11: eine Dokumentation aus den letzten Jahren des Reiches Juda?" *ZDPV* 82 (1966) 209–27.

———. *Nehemia: Quellen, Überlieferung und Geschichte.* BZAW 102. Berlin: Töpelmann, 1967.

Kennedy, D. L. "*Legio VI Ferrata*: The Annexation and Early Garrison of Arabia." *HSCP* 84 (1980) 283–309.

Kent, R. G. *Old Persian.* 2d ed. AOS 33. New Haven, Conn.: American Oriental Society, 1953.

Keppie, L.J.F. "The Legionary Garrison of Judaea under Hadrian." *Latomus* 32 (1973) 859–64.

Keresztes, P. "The Jews, the Christians, and Emperor Domitian." *VigChr* 27 (1973) 1–28.

Kervran, M., et al. "Une statue de Darius découverte à Suse." *Journal asiatique* 260 (1972) 235–66.

Kindler, A. "The Jaffa Hoard of Alexander Jannaeus." *IEJ* 4 (1954) 170–85.

———. "Addendum to the Dated Coins of Alexander Janneus." *IEJ* 18 (1968) 188–91.

———. "Silver Coins Bearing the Name of Judea from the Early Hellenistic Period." *IEJ* 24 (1974) 73–76.

Kippenberg, H. G. *Religion und Klassenbildung im antiken Judäa: Eine religionssocialogische Studie zum Verhältnis von Tradition und gesellschaftlicher Entwicklung.* 2d ed. SUNT 14. Göttingen: Vandenhoeck & Ruprecht, 1982.

Klijn, A.F.J. "Recent Developments in the Study of the Syriac Apocalypse of Baruch." *JSP* 4 (1989) 3–17.

Kloner, A. "A Tomb of the Second Temple Period at French Hill, Jerusalem." *IEJ* 30 (1980) 99–108.

———. "The Subterranean Hideaways of the Judean Foothills and the Bar-Kokhba Revolt." *Jerusalem Cathedra* 3 (1983) 83–96.

———. "Underground Hiding Complexes from the Bar Kokhba War in the Judean Shephelah." *BA* 46 (1983) 210–21.

Knibb, M. A. "The Exile in the Literature of the Intertestamental Period." *Heythrop Journal* 18 (1977) 253–72.

———. *The Ethiopic Book of Enoch.* Vols. 1–2. Oxford: Clarendon, 1978.

———. "Prophecy and the Emergence of the Jewish Apocalypses." In *Israel's Prophetic Tradition: Essays in Honour of Peter R. Ackroyd,* edited by R. Coggins, et al., 161–65. Cambridge: Cambridge University Press, 1982.

———. *The Qumran Community.* CCWJCW 2. Cambridge: Cambridge University Press, 1987.

———. *Jubilees and the Origins of the Qumran Community.* Inaugural Lecture in the Department of Biblical Studies. London: King's College, 1989.

Knight, D. A., and G. M. Tucker, eds. *The Hebrew Bible and Its Modern Interpreters.* Atlanta: Scholars Press; Philadelphia: Fortress, 1985.

Kobelski, P. J. *Melchizedek and Melchireša*. CBQMS 10. Washington, D.C.: Catholic Biblical Association, 1981.

Koch, K. "Haggais unreines Volk." *ZAW* 79 (1967) 52–66.

———. "Ezra and the Origins of Judaism." *JSS* 19 (1974) 173–97.

———. *The Prophets*. Vol. 2: *The Babylonian and Persian Periods*. London: SCM, 1983.

Koester, C. "A Qumran Bibliography: 1974–1984." *BTB* 15 (1985) 110–20.

Koester, H. "The Divine Human Being." *HTR* 78 (1985) 243–52.

Koffmahn, E. *Die Doppelurkunden aus der Wüste Juda: Recht und Praxis der jüdischen Papyri des 1. und 2. Jahrhunderts n. Chr.* STDJ 5. Leiden: E. J. Brill, 1968.

König, F. W. *Die Persika des Ktesias von Knidos*. Archiv für Orientforschung Beiheft 18. Graz: Archiv für Orientforschung, 1972.

Koopmans, J. J. *Aramäische Chrestomathie: Ausgewählte Texte (Inschriften, Ostraka und Papyri) bis zum 3. Jahrhundert n. Chr.* 2 vols. Leiden: Nederlands Instituut voor het Nabije Oosten, 1962.

Kraabel, A. T. "The Disappearance of the 'God-Fearers.'" *Numen* 28 (1981) 113–26.

Krader, L. *The Asiatic Mode of Production: Sources, Development and Critique in the Writings of Karl Marx*. Dialect and Society 1. Assen: Van Gorcum, 1975.

Kraeling, E. G. *The Brooklyn Museum Aramaic Papyri*. New Haven: Yale University Press, 1953.

Kraft, R. A. "The Multiform Jewish Heritage of Early Christianity." In *Christianity, Judaism and Other Greco-Roman Cults: Studies for Morton Smith at Sixty* 3.174–99. 4 vols. Edited by J. Neusner. SJLA 12. Leiden: E. J. Brill, 1975.

Kraft, R. A., and G.W.E. Nickelsburg, eds. *Early Judaism and Its Modern Interpreters*. Atlanta: Scholars Press; Philadelphia: Fortress, 1986.

Krauss, S. *Talmudische Archäologie*. Vols. 1–2. Grundriss der Gesamtwissenschaft des Judentums. Leipzig: Fock, 1910–11.

Kreissig, H. "Der Makkabäeraufstand zur Frage seiner Socialökonomischen Zusammenhänge und Wirkungen." *Studii Clasice* 4 (1962) 143–75.

———. "Die landwirtschaftliche Situation in Palästina vor dem judäischen Krieg." *Acta Antiqua* 17 (1969) 223–54.

———. *Die sozialökonomische Situation in Juda zur Achämenidenzeit*. Akademie der Wissenschaften der DDR Zentralinstitut für Alte Geschichte und Archäologie, Schriften zur Geschichte und Kultur des Alten Orients 7. Berlin: Akademie-Verlag, 1973.

———. "Landed Property in the 'Hellenistic' Orient." *Eirene* 15 (1977) 5–26.

———. "Tempelland, Katoiken, Hierodulen im Seleukidenreich." *Klio* 59 (1977) 375–80.

———. *Wirtschaft und Gesellschaft im Seleukidenreich: Die Eigentums- und die Abhängigkeitsverhältnisse*. Akademie der Wissenschaften, Schriften zur Geschichte und Kultur der Antike 16. Berlin: Akademie-Verlag, 1978.

Kuhn, H.-W. "Zum Gekreuzigten von Giv'at ha-Mivtar: Korrektur eines Versehens in der Erstveröffentlichung." *ZNW* 69 (1978) 118–22.

Kuhnen, H.-P. *Palästina in griechisch-römischer Zeit.* HdA, Vorderasien 2, Band 2. Munich: Beck, 1990.

Kuhrt, A. "Assyrian and Babylonian Traditions in Classical Authors: A Critical Synthesis." In *Mesopotamien und seine Nachbarn.* XXV. Rencontre Assyriologique Internationale, edited by H.-J. Nissen and J. Renger, 539–53. Berlin: Dietrich Reimer, 1982.

———. "The Cyrus Cylinder and Achaemenid Imperial Policy." *JSOT* 25 (1983) 83–97.

———. "Berossus' *Babyloniaka* and Seleucid Rule in Babylonia." In *Hellenism in the East,* edited by A. Kuhrt and S. Sherwin-White, 32–56. London: Duckworth, 1987.

———. "Survey of Written Sources Available for the History of Babylonia under the Later Achaemenids (Concentrating on the Period from Artaxerxes II to Darius III)." In *Achaemenid History I: Sources, Structures and Synthesis.* Proceeding of the Groningen 1983 Achaemenid History Workshop, 147–57. Edited by H. Sancisi-Weerdenburg. Leiden: Nederlands Instituut voor het Nabije Oosten, 1987.

———. "Babylonia from Cyrus to Xerxes." *CAH²* (1988) 4.112–38.

Kuhrt, A., and H. Sancisi-Weerdenburg, eds. *Achaemenid History III: Method and Theory.* Proceeding of the London 1985 Achaemenid History Workshop. Leiden: Nederlands Instituut voor het Nabije Oosten, 1988.

Kuhrt, A., and S. Sherwin-White, eds. *Hellenism in the East: The Interaction of Greek and Non-Greek Civilizations from Syria to Central Asia after Alexander.* London: Duckworth, 1987.

———. "Xerxes' Destruction of Babylonian Temples." In *Achaemenid History II: The Greek Sources.* Proceeding of the Groningen 1984 Achaemenid History Workshop, 69–78. Edited by H. Sancisi-Weerdenburg and A. Kuhrt. Leiden: Nederlands Instituut voor het Nabije Oosten, 1987.

Kümmel, W. G. *Introduction to the New Testament.* Rev. ed. London: SCM, 1975.

Kvanig, H. S. *Roots of Apocalyptic: The Mesopotamian Background of the Enoch Figure and the Son of Man.* WMANT 6. Neukirchen-Vluyn: Neukirchener, 1988.

La Barre, W. "Materials for a History of Studies of Crisis Cults: A Bibliographic Essay." *Current Anthropology* 12 (1971) 3–44.

Ladouceur, D. J. "The Death of Herod the Great." *Classical Philology* 76 (1981) 25–34.

———. "Josephus and Masada." In *Josephus, Judaism and Christianity,* edited by L. H. Feldman and G. Hata, 95–113. Leiden: E. J. Brill, 1987.

Lambert, W. G. *The Background of Jewish Apocalyptic.* Ethel M. Wood Lecture, University of London, delivered on 22 February 1977. London: Athlone, 1978.

Landau, Y. H. "A Greek Inscription Found Near Hefzibah." *IEJ* 16 (1966) 54–70.

Landes, G. M. "Linguistic Criteria and the Date of the Book of Jonah." *EI* 16 (1982) 147*–70*.

Landsberger, B., and T. Bauer. "Zu neuveröffentlichten Geschichtsquellen der Zeit von Asarhaddon bis Nabonid." *ZA* 37 (1927) 61–98.

Laperrousaz, E. M. "L'Hérodium, quartier général de Bar Kokhba?" *Syria* 41 (1964) 347–58.

———. "Le problème du 'premier mur' et du 'deuxième mur' de Jérusalem après la réfutation décisive de la 'minimalist view.' " In *Hommage à Georges Vajda*, edited by G. Nahon and C. Touati, 13–35. Louvain: Peeters, 1980.

———. "Le régime théocratique juif a-t-il commencé a l'époque perse, ou seulement a l'époque hellénistique?" *Semitica* 32 (1982) 93–96.

———. "Jérusalem á l'époque perse (étendue et statut)." *Transeuphratène* 1 (1989) 55–65.

Lapp, N. L., ed. *The Excavations at Araq el-Emir.* Vol. 1. AASOR 47. Winona Lake, Ind.: Eisenbrauns, 1983.

Lapp, P. W. " 'Iraq el-Emir." In *Encyclopedia of Archaeological Excavations in the Holy Land* 2.527–31. Edited by M. Avi-Yonah. Jerusalem: Israel Exploration Society, 1976.

Lapp, P. W., and N. L. Lapp, eds. *Discoveries in the Wadi ed-Dâliyeh.* AASOR 41. Cambridge, Mass.: ASOR, 1974.

Laqueur, R. *Der jüdische Historiker Flavius Josephus.* Giessen: Munchow, 1920.

Lease, G. "Jewish Mystery Cults since Goodenough." *ANRW* 2 (1987) 20.2.858–80.

Lebram, J.C.H. "Perspektiven der Gegenwärtigen Danielforschung." *JSJ* 5 (1974) 1–33.

———. "König Antiochus im Buch Daniel." *VT* 25 (1975) 737–72.

———. "Die Traditionsgeschichte der Ezragestalt und die Frage nach dem historischen Esra." In *Achaemenid History I: Sources, Structures and Synthesis.* Proceeding of the Groningen 1983 Achaemenid History Workshop, 103–38. Edited by H. Sancisi-Weerdenburg. Leiden: Nederlands Instituut voor het Nabije Oosten, 1987.

Lecoq, P. "Observations sur le sens du mot *dahyu* dans les inscriptions achéménides." *Transeuphratène* 3 (1990) 131–39.

Lemaire, A. "Un nouveau roi arabe de Qedar dans l'inscription de l'autel à encens de Lakish." *RB* 81 (1974) 63–72.

———. "Populations et territoires de Palestine à l'époque perse." *Transeuphratène* 3 (1990) 31–74.

Lémonon, J.-P. *Pilate et le gouvernement de la Judée: Textes et monuments.* Etudes Bibliques. Paris: Lecoffre, 1981.

LeMoyne, J. *Les Sadducéen.* EB. Paris: Lecoffre, 1972.

Lenger, M.-T. *Corpus des Ordonnances des Ptolémées.* Académie Royale de Belgique, Classe Des Lettres, Mémoires, t. 56/5. Brussels: Palais des Académies, 1964.

Lesky, A. H. *A History of Greek Literature.* London: Methuen, 1966.

Leszynsky, R. *Die Sadduzäer.* Berlin: Mayer & Muller, 1912.

Leuze, O. *Die Satrapieneinteilung in Syrien und im Zweistromlande von 520–320.* Schriften der Königsberger Gelehrten Gesellschaft, 11. Jahr, Heft 4. Halle: Niemeyer, 1935.

Levick, B. *Tiberius the Politician.* Aspects of Greek and Roman Life. London: Thames & Hudson, 1976.

———. *Claudius.* London: Batsford, 1990.

Levine, B. A. "The Temple Scroll: Aspects of Its Historical Provenance and Literary Character." *BASOR* 232 (1978) 5–23.

Levine, L. I. *Roman Caesarea: An Archaeological-Topographical Study.* Qedem 2. Jerusalem: Hebrew University Press, 1975.

————. "Archaeological Discoveries from the Greco-Roman Era." In *Recent Archaeology in the Land of Israel*, edited by H. Shanks and B. Mazar, 75–88. Washington, D.C.: Biblical Archaeology Society; Jerusalem: Israel Exploration Society, 1981.

Lewis, D. M. *Sparta and Persia.* CCS 1. Leiden: E. J. Brill, 1977.

Lewis, N., ed. *The Documents from the Bar Kokhba Period in the Cave of Letters: Greek Papyri*, with Y. Yadin and J. C. Greenfield, eds. *Aramaic and Nabatean Signatures and Subscriptions.* Jerusalem: Israel Exploration Society, 1989.

Lichtenstein, H. "Die Fastenrolle: Eine Untersuchung zur jüdisch-hellenistischen Geschichte." *HUCA* 8–9 (1931–32) 257–351.

Lichtheim, M. *Ancient Egyptian Literature.* Vol. 3: *The Late Period.* Berkeley and Los Angeles: University of California Press, 1980.

Lieberman, S. *Hellenism in Jewish Palestine.* Texts and Studies of the Jewish Theological Seminary 18. New York: Jewish Theological Seminary, 1962.

————. "How Much Greek in Jewish Palestine?" In *Biblical and Other Studies*, edited by A. Altmann, 123–41. Philip W. Lown Institute of Advanced Judaic Studies: Studies and Texts 1. Cambridge: Harvard University Press, 1963.

————. *Greek in Jewish Palestine.* 2d ed. New York: P. Feldheim, 1965.

Liebesny, H. "Ein Erlass des Königs Ptolemaios II Philadelphos über die Deklaration von Vieh und Sklaven in Syrien und Phönikien (PER Inv. Nr. 24.552 gr.)." *Aegyptus* 16 (1936) 257–91.

Lifshitz, B. "Sur la date du transfert de la legion VI Ferrata en Palestine." *Latomus* 19 (1960) 109–11.

————. "The Greek Documents from Naḥal Ṣeelim and Naḥal Mishmar." *IEJ* 11 (1961) 53–62.

————. "Papyrus grecs du désert de Juda." *Aegyptus* 42 (1962) 240–58.

————. "The Greek Documents from the Cave of Horror." *IEJ* 12 (1962) 201–7.

————. "Notes philologiques et epigraphiques." *SCI* 2 (1975) 97–112.

————. "Jérusalem sous la domination romaine. Histoire de la ville depuis la conquête de Pompée jusqu'à Constantin (63 A.C.–325 p.C.)." *ANRW* 2 (1977) 8.444–89.

Lightstone, J. N. "Sadducees versus Pharisees." In *Christianity, Judaism and Other Greco-Roman Cults: Studies for Morton Smith at Sixty* 3.206–17. SJLA 12. Leiden: E. J. Brill, 1975.

————. "Judaism of the Second Commonwealth: Toward a Reform of the Scholarly Tradition." In *Truth and Compassion: Essays on Judaism and Religion in Memory of Rabbi Dr. Solomon Frank*, edited by H. Joseph, et al., 31–40. Ontario: Wilfrid Laurier University Press, 1983.

————. *The Commerce of the Sacred: Mediation of the Divine among Jews in the Graeco-Roman Diaspora.* BJS 59. Atlanta: Scholars Press, 1984.

————. *Society, the Sacred, and Scripture in Ancient Judaism.* Studies in Christianity and Judaism 3. Ontario: Wilfrid Laurier University Press, 1988.

Lloyd, A. B. "Nationalist Propaganda in Ptolemaic Egypt." *Historia* 31 (1982) 33–55.

———. "The Inscription of Udjaḥorresnet: A Collaborator's Testament." *JEA* 68 (1982) 166–80.

Loretz, O. *Qohelet und der alte Orient.* Freiburg: Herder, 1964.

Lüdemann, G. *Untersuchungen zur simonianischen Gnosis.* GTA 1. Göttingen: Vandenhoeck & Ruprecht, 1975.

———. "The Acts of the Apostles and the Beginnings of Simonian Gnosis." *NTS* 33 (1987) 420–26.

———. *Early Christianity according to the Traditions in Acts: A Commentary.* London: SCM, 1989.

Lührmann, D. "Die Pharisäer und die Schriftgelehrten im Markusevangelium." *ZNW* 78 (1987) 169–85.

Lundquist, J. M. "What Is a Temple? A Preliminary Typology." In *The Quest for the Kingdom of God: Studies in Honor of George E. Mendenhall,* edited by H. B. Huffmon, et al., 205–19. Winona Lake, Ind.: Eisenbrauns, 1983.

———. "The Common Temple Ideology of the Ancient Near East." In *The Temple in Antiquity,* edited by T. G. Madsen, 53–76. Religious Studies Monograph Series 9. Provo, Utah: Brigham Young University Press, 1984.

Lust, J. "The Identification of Zerubbabel with Sheshbassar." *Ephemerides Theologicae Lovanienses* 63 (1987) 90–95.

Luther, H. *Josephus und Justus von Tiberias.* Inaugural dissertation. Halle: Friedrichs-Universitat, 1910.

Luttikhuizen, G. P. *The Revelation of Elchasai: Investigations into the Evidence for a Mesopotamian Jewish Apocalypse of the Second Century and Its Reception by Judeo-Christian Propagandists.* TSAJ 8. Tübingen: J.C.B. Mohr (Paul Siebeck), 1985.

Maccoby, H. *Judaism in the First Century.* Issues in Religious Studies. London: Sheldon, 1989.

McConville, J. G. "Ezra-Nehemiah and the Fulfilment of Prophecy." *VT* 36 (1986) 205–24.

McCown, C. C. "The 'Araq el-Emir and the Tobiads." *BA* 20 (1957) 63–76.

Macdonald, J. *Memar Marqah: The Teaching of Marqah.* 2 vols. BZAW 84. Berlin: Töpelmann, 1963.

———. *The Theology of the Samaritans.* New Testament Library. London: SCM, 1964.

———. *The Samaritan Chronicle No. 2.* BZAW 107. Berlin: de Gruyter, 1969.

McEleney, N. J. "Orthodoxy in Judaism of the First Christian Century." *JSJ* 4 (1973) 19–42.

———. "Conversion, Circumcision and the Law." *NTS* 20 (1973/74) 319–41.

———. "Orthodoxy in Judaism of the First Christian Century: Replies to David E. Aune and Lester L. Grabbe." *JSJ* 9 (1978) 83–88.

McEvenue, S. E. "The Political Structure in Judah from Cyrus to Nehemiah." *CBQ* 43 (1981) 353–64.

McKenzie, S. L. *The Chronicler's Use of the Deuteronomistic History.* HSM 33. Atlanta: Scholars Press, 1985.

MacLennan, R. S., and A. T. Kraabel. "The God-Fearers—A Literary and Theological Invention." *BAR* 12, no. 5 (Sept./Oct. 1986) 46–53, 64.

Macmullen, R. *Enemies of the Roman Order: Treason, Unrest, and Alienation in the Empire.* Cambridge, Mass.: Harvard University Press, 1967.

McNamara, M. "Nabonidus and the Book of Daniel." *ITQ* 37 (1970) 131–49.

McNulty, I. B. "The North Wall outside Jerusalem." *BA* 42 (1979) 141–44.

Macuch, R. "Anfänge der Mandäer." In *Die Araber in der Alten Welt* 2.76–190. Edited by F. Altheim and R. Stiehl. Berlin: de Gruyter, 1965.

———. "The Origins of the Mandaeans and Their Script." *JSS* 16 (1971) 174–92.

———. "Gnostische Ethik und die Anfänge der Mandäer." In *Christentum am Roten Meer* 2.254–73. Edited by F. Altheim and R. Stiehl. Berlin and New York: de Gruyter, 1973.

Magie, D. *Roman Rule in Asia Minor, to the End of the Third Century after Christ.* 2 vols. Princeton: Princeton University Press, 1950.

Maier, J. *Zwischen den Testamenten: Geschichte und Religion in der Zeit des Zweiten Tempels.* Neue Echter Bibel, Ergänzungsband zum AT 3. Würzburg: Echter, 1990.

Maier, P. L. "The Episode of the Golden Roman Shields at Jerusalem." *HTR* 62 (1969) 109–21.

Mallau, H. H. "The Redaction of Ezra 4–6: A Plea for a Theology of Scribes." *Perspectives in Religious Studies* 15 (1988) 67–80.

Mandell, S. "Who Paid the Temple Tax When the Jews Were under Roman Rule?" *HTR* 77 (1984) 223–32.

Mantel, H. *Studies in the History of the Sanhedrin.* Cambridge: Cambridge University Press, 1961.

———. "The Causes of the Bar Kokba Revolt." *JQR* 58 (1967/68) 224–42, 274–96.

———. "Sanhedrin." *IDBSup* (1976) 784–86.

Marcus, R. "Appendix D. Antiochus III and the Jews (*Ant.* xii. 129–153)" 7.743–66. In *Josephus.* LCL. London: Heinemann; Cambridge: Harvard University Press, 1943.

Margalith, O. "The Political Role of Ezra as Persian Governor." *ZAW* 98 (1986) 110–12.

Marshall, A. J. "Flaccus and the Jews of Asia (Cicero *Pro Flacco* 28.67–69)." *Phoenix* 29 (1975) 139–54.

Marshall, I. H. *The Gospel of Luke.* NIGTC. Exeter: Paternoster, 1978.

Mason, R. "The Purpose of the 'Editorial Framework' of the Book of Haggai." *VT* 27 (1977) 415–21.

———. "The Prophets of the Restoration." In *Israel's Prophetic Tradition: Essays in Honour of Peter R. Ackroyd,* edited by R. Coggins, et al., 137–54. Cambridge: Cambridge University Press, 1982.

Mason, S. N. "Josephus on the Pharisees Reconsidered: A Critique of Smith/Neusner." *SR* 17 (1988) 455–69.

———. "Priesthood in Josephus and the 'Pharisaic Revolution.'" *JBL* 107 (1988) 657–61.

———. "Was Josephus a Pharisee? A Re-examination of *Life* 10–12." *JJS* 40 (1989) 31–45.

Mattill, A. J., Jr. "The Value of Acts as a Source for the Study of Paul." In *Perspectives on Luke-Acts,* edited by C. H. Talbert, 76–98. Edinburgh: T. & T. Clark, 1978.

May, H. G. " 'This People' and 'This Nation' in Haggai." *VT* 18 (1968) 190–97.

Mayer, G. *Die jüdische Frau in der hellenistisch-römischen Antiken.* Stuttgart: Kohlhammer, 1987.

———. *Index Philoneus.* Berlin and New York: de Gruyter, 1974.

Mayrhofer, M. *Supplement zur Sammlung der altpersischen Inschriften.* Veröffentlichungen der iranischen Kommission 7; Sitzungsberichte der Österreichischen Akademie der Wissenschaften, philologisch-historische Klasse 338. Vienna: Akademie der Wissenschaften, 1978.

Mazar, B. "The Tobiads." *IEJ* 7 (1957): 137–45, 229–38. Revision of articles in *Tarbiz* 12 (1941) 109–23; and *EI* 4 (1956) 249–51.

———. "Herodian Jerusalem in the Light of the Excavations South and South-West of the Temple Mount." *IEJ* 28 (1978) 230–37.

———. "Josephus Flavius and the Archaeological Excavations in Jerusalem." In *Josephus, the Bible, and History,* edited by L. H. Feldman and G. Hata, 325–29. Leiden: E. J. Brill, 1989.

Mazar, B., et al. *Beth She'arim.* 3 vols. New Brunswick, N.J.: Rutgers University Press; Jerusalem: Massada, 1973–76.

Meeks, W. A. *The Prophet-King: Moses Traditions and the Johannine Christology.* NovTSup 14. Leiden: E. J. Brill, 1967.

———. "Simon Magus in Recent Research." *RSR* 3 (1977) 137–42.

Meiggs, R., and D. Lewis. *A Selection of Greek Historical Inscriptions to the End of the Fifth Century B.C.* Oxford: Clarendon, 1969.

Mendels, D. "Hecataeus of Abdera and a Jewish 'patrios politeia' of the Persian Period (Diodorus Siculus XL, 3)." *ZAW* 95 (1983) 96–110.

———. *The Land of Israel as a Political Concept in Hasmonean Literature.* TSAJ 15. Tübingen: J.C.B. Mohr (Paul Siebeck), 1987.

Mendelson, A. *Philo's Jewish Identity.* BJS 161. Atlanta: Scholars Press, 1988.

Meshorer, Y. *Jewish Coins of the Second Temple Period.* Tel-Aviv: Am Hassefer, 1967.

———. *Nabataean Coins.* Qedem 3. Jerusalem: Hebrew University Press, 1975.

———. *Ancient Jewish Coinage.* Vol. 1: *Persian Period through Hasmonaeans.* Vol. 2: *Herod the Great through Bar Cochba.* New York: Amphora, 1982.

———. "A Coin Hoard of Bar-Kokhba's Time." *Israel Museum Journal* 4 (1985) 43–50.

———. "Jewish Numismatics." In *Early Judaism and Its Modern Interpreters,* edited by R. A. Kraft and G.W.E. Nickelsburg, 211–20. Atlanta: Scholars Press; Philadelphia: Fortress, 1986.

Metzger, H., et al. *La stèle trilingue du Létôon.* Fouilles de Xanthos, Tome VI; Institute français d'études anatoliennes. Paris: Klincksieck, 1979.

Meyer, E. *Die Entstehung des Judenthums: Eine historische Untersuchung.* Halle: Niemeyer, 1896. Reprint. Hildesheim: Olms, 1965.

Meyers, C. L., and E. M. Meyers. *Haggai, Zechariah 1–8.* AB 25B. Garden City, N.Y.: Doubleday, 1987.

Meyers, E. M. *Jewish Ossuaries: Reburial and Rebirth. Secondary Burials in Their Ancient Near Eastern Setting.* BibOr 24. Rome: Biblical Institute, 1971.

———. "Galilean Regionalism as a Factor in Historical Reconstruction." *BASOR* 221 (1976) 93–101.

———. "Galilean Regionalism: A Reappraisal." In *Approaches to Ancient Judaism*. Vol. 5: *Studies in Judaism and Its Greco-Roman Context*, edited by W. S. Green, 115–31. BJS 32. Atlanta: Scholars Press, 1985.

———. "The Shelomith Seal and the Judean Restoration: Some Additional Considerations." *EI* 18 (1985) 33*–38*.

Meyers, E. M., and A. T. Kraabel. "Archaeology, Iconography, and Nonliterary Written Remains." In *Early Judaism and Its Modern Interpreters*, edited by R. A. Kraft and G.W.E. Nickelsburg, 175–210. Atlanta: Scholars Press; Philadelphia: Fortress, 1986.

Meyers, E. M., and J. F. Strange. *Archaeology, the Rabbis and Early Christianity*. Nashville: Abingdon, 1981.

Meyshan, J. "The Coinage of Agrippa the First." *IEJ* 4 (1954) 186–200.

Michel, O. "Studien zu Josephus: Simon bar Giora." *NTS* 14 (1967–68) 402–8.

Mielziner, M. *Introduction to the Talmud*. 1902. 5th ed. with new bibliography from 1925–67. New York: Bloch, 1968.

Mildenberg, L. "The Eleazar Coins of the Bar Kochba Rebellion." *Historia Judaica* 11 (1949) 77–108.

———. "Yehud: A Preliminary Study of the Provincial Coinage of Judaea." In *Greek Numismatics and Archaeology: Essays in Honor of Margaret Thompson*, edited by O. Mørkholm and N. M. Waggoner, 183–96. Wetteren: Editions NR, 1979.

———. "Bar Kokhba Coins and Documents." *HSCP* 84 (1980) 311–35.

———. *The Coinage of the Bar Kokhba War*. Typos 6. Aarau, Frankfurt and Salzburg: Sauerlander, 1984.

———. "*Yehūd* Münzen." In H. Weippert, *Palästina in vorhellenistischer Zeit*, 721–28. HdA, Vorderasien 2, Band 1. Munich: Beck, 1988.

———. "Der Bar-Kochba-Krieg im Lichte der Münzprägungen." In H.-P. Kuhnen, *Palästina in griechisch-römischer Zeit*, 357–66. HdA. Vorderasien 2, Band 2. Munich: Beck, 1990.

Milik, J. T. *Ten Years of Discovery in the Wilderness of Judaea*. SBT 26. London: SCM, 1959.

———. *The Books of Enoch: Aramaic Fragments of Qumran Cave 4*. Oxford: Clarendon, 1976.

Millar, F. *A Study of Cassius Dio*. Oxford: Clarendon, 1964.

———. "The Background to the Maccabean Revolution: Reflections on Martin Hengel's 'Judaism and Hellenism.'" *JJS* 29 (1978) 1–21.

———. "The Phoenician Cities: A Case-Study of Hellenisation." *Proceedings of the Cambridge Philological Association* 209 (1983) 55–71.

———. "The Problem of Hellenistic Syria." In *Hellenism in the East*, edited by A. Kuhrt and S. Sherwin-White, 110–33. London: Duckworth, 1987.

Millar, F., and E. Segal, eds. *Caesar Augustus: Seven Aspects*. Oxford: Clarendon, 1984.

Mills, W. E., ed. *A Bibliography of the Periodical Literature on the Acts of the Apostles, 1962–1984*. NovTSup 58. Leiden: E. J. Brill, 1986.

Mitchell, H. G., et al. *Haggai, Zechariah, Malachi, Jonah*. ICC. Edinburgh: T. & T. Clark, 1912.

Mittwoch, A. "Tribute and Land-Tax in Seleucid Judaea." *Bib* 36 (1955) 352–61.

Moehring, H. R. "The Persecution of the Jews and the Adherents of the Isis Cult at Rome A.D. 19." *NovT* 3 (1959) 293–304.

―――. "The Census in Luke as an Apologetic Device." In *Studies in New Testament and Early Christian Literature: Essays in Honor of Allen P. Wikgren*, edited by D. E. Aune, 144–60. Leiden: E. J. Brill, 1972.

―――. "The *Acta pro Judaeis* in the *Antiquities* of Flavius Josephus." In *Christianity, Judaism and Other Greco-Roman Cults* 3.124–58. Studies in Judaism in Late Antiquity 12. Edited by J. Neusner. Leiden: E. J. Brill, 1975.

―――. Review of *Josephus in Galilee and Rome*, by S.J.D. Cohen. *JJS* 31 (1980) 240–42.

―――. "Joseph ben Matthia and Flavius Josephus: The Jewish Prophet and Roman Historian." *ANRW* 2 (1984) 21.2.864–944.

Momigliano, A. "Josephus as a Source for the History of Judaea." *CAH* (1934) 10.884–87.

―――. "Richerche sull' organizzazione della Giudea sotto il dominio romano (63 a. C.–70 d. C.)." *Annali della Scuola Normale Superiore di Pisa*. Classe di Lettere 3 (1934) 183–221, 347–96.

―――. "An Unsolved Problem of Historical Forgery: The *Scriptores Historiae Augustae.*" *Secondo contributo alla storia degli studi classici*, 105–43. Rome: Edizione di Storia e Letteratura, 1960 = *Journal of the Warburg and Courtauld Institutes* 17 (1954) 22–46.

―――. *Claudius, the Emperor and His Achievement*. 1934. Reprint. London: Oxford University Press, 1961.

―――. "M. I. Rostovtzeff." *Studies in Historiography*, 91–104. London: Weidenfeld, 1966 = *The Cambridge Journal* 7 (1954) 334–46.

―――. "Tradizione e invenzione in Ctesia." In *Quarto contributo alla storia degli studi classici e del Mondo Antico*. Storia e Letteratura 115, 181–212. Rome: Edizioni di Storia e Letteratura, 1969.

―――. Review of *Judentum und Hellenismus*, by M. Hengel. *JTS* 21 (1970) 149–53 = *Quinto contributo alla storia degli studi classici e del Mondo Antico*. Storia e Letteratura 136, 931–36. Rome: Edizioni di Storia e Letteratura, 1975 = Fischel, H. A., ed. *Essays in Greco-Roman and Related Talmudic Literature*, 495–99. Library of Biblical Studies. New York: Ktav, 1977.

―――. "The Second Book of Maccabees." *Classical Philology* 70 (1975) 81–88.

―――. *Alien Wisdom: The Limits of Hellenization*. Cambridge: Cambridge University Press, 1975.

―――. "I Tobiadi nella preistoria del Moto Maccabaico." In *Quinto contributo alla storia degli studi classici e del Mondo Antico*, 597–628. Storia e Letteratura 135. Rome: Edizioni di Storia e Letteratura, 1975. Originally published in *Atti della Reale Accademia delle Scienze di Torino* 67 (1931–32) 165–200.

―――. "Flavius Josephus and Alexander's Visit to Jerusalem." *Athaeneum* 57 (1979) 442–48.

―――. "Greek Culture and the Jews." In *The Legacy of Greece: A New Appraisal*, edited by M. I. Finley, 325–46. Oxford: Clarendon, 1981.

―――. Review of *Beiträge zur jüdischen Apologetik*, by J.-D. Gauger. *Classical Philology* 77 (1982) 258–61.

Mommsen, T., P. Krueger, and A. Watson, eds. *The Digest of Justinian*. Vols. 1–4. Philadelphia: University of Pennsylvania Press, 1985.

Montgomery, J. A. *The Samaritans: The Earliest Jewish Sect*. 1907. Reprint, with introduction by A. S. Halkin. New York: Ktav, 1968.

———. *A Critical and Exegetical Commentary on the Book of Daniel*. ICC. Edinburgh: T. & T. Clark, 1927.

Moore, C. A. *Esther*. AB 7B. Garden City, N.Y.: Doubleday, 1971.

———. *Daniel, Esther and Jeremiah: The Additions*. AB 44. Garden City, N.Y.: Doubleday, 1977.

———. "Esther Revisited Again: A Further Examination of Certain Esther Studies of the Past Ten Years." *HAR* 7 (1983) 169–86.

———. "Esther Revisited: An Examination of Esther Studies over the Past Decade." In *Biblical and Related Studies Presented to Samuel Iwry*, edited by A. Kort and S. Morschauser, 163–72. Winona Lake, Ind.: Eisenbrauns, 1985.

———. *Judith*. AB 40. Garden City, N.Y.: Doubleday, 1985.

Moore, G. F. *Judaism in the First Three Centuries of the Christian Era*. 3 vols. Cambridge: Harvard University Press, 1927–30.

Mor, M. "The Bar-Kokhba Revolt and Non-Jewish Participants." *JJS* 36 (1985) 200–209.

Morgenstern, J. "Jerusalem—485 B.C." *HUCA* 27 (1956) 101–79; 28 (1957) 15–47; and 31 (1960) 1–29.

———. "Further Light from the Book of Isaiah upon the Catastrophe of 485 B.C." *HUCA* 37 (1966) 1–28.

Mørkholm, O. *Antiochus IV of Syria*. Classica et Mediaevalia, Dissertationes 8. Copenhagen: Gyldendalske Boghandel, 1966.

Mosshammer, A. A. *The Chronicle of Eusebius and Greek Chronographic Tradition*. Lewisburg: Bucknell University Press, 1979.

Mowinckel, S. " 'Ich' und 'Er' in der Ezrageschichte." In *Verbannung und Heimkehr: Beiträge zur Geschichte und Theologie Israels im 6. und 5. Jahrhundert v. Chr., Wilhelm Rudolph zum 70. Geburtstage*, edited by A. Kuschke, 211–33. Tübingen: J.C.B. Mohr (Paul Siebeck), 1961.

———. *Studien zu dem Buche Ezra-Nehemiah I*. Skrifter utgitt av Det Norske Videnskaps-Akademi i Oslo II. Hist.-Filos. Klasse. Ny Serie. No. 3; Oslo: Universitetsforlaget, 1964; *II* (No. 5, 1964); *III* (No. 7, 1965).

Müller, H.-P. "Magisch-mantische Weisheit und die Gestalt Daniels." *Ugarit-Forschungen* 1 (1969) 79–94.

———. "Mantische Weisheit und Apokalyptik." In *Congress Volume, Uppsala 1971*, 268–93. VTSup 22. Leiden: E. J. Brill, 1972.

Murphy, F. J. "2 Baruch and the Romans." *JBL* 104 (1985) 663–69.

———. *The Structure and Meaning of Second Baruch*. SBLDS 78. Atlanta: Scholars Press, 1985.

Murphy, R. *The Song of Songs*. Hermeneia. Minneapolis: Fortress, 1990.

Murphy-O'Connor, J. "La genèse littéraire de la Règle de la Communauté." *RB* 76 (1969) 528–49.

———. "The Essenes and Their History." *RB* 81 (1974) 215–44.

———. "Demetrius I and the Teacher of Righteousness (I Macc., x, 25–45)." *RB* 83 (1976) 400–420.

————. "The Essenes in Palestine." *BA* 40 (1977) 100–124.

————. "The *Damascus Document* Revisited." *RB* 92 (1985) 223–46 = *SBLSP* 1986, edited by K. H. Richards, 369–83. SBLASP 25. Atlanta: Scholars Press, 1986.

————. "The Judean Desert." In *Early Judaism and Its Modern Interpreters*, edited by R. A. Kraft and G.W.E. Nickelsburg, 119–46. Atlanta: Scholars Press; Philadelphia: Fortress, 1986.

Murray, O. "Hecataeus of Abdera and Pharaonic Kingship." *JEA* 56 (1970) 141–71.

Musti, D. "Syria and the East." *CAH*² (1984) 7.1.175–220.

Musurillo, H. A., ed. *The Acts of the Pagan Martyrs: Acta Alexandrinorum.* Oxford: Clarendon, 1954.

Myers, J. M. *I and II Esdras.* AB 42. Garden City, N.Y.: Doubleday, 1974.

Naveh, J. "Dated Coins of Alexander Janneus." *IEJ* 18 (1968) 20–25.

————. "The Origin of the Mandaic Script." *BASOR* (1970) 32–37.

————. "An Aramaic Tomb Inscription Written in Paleo-Hebrew Script." *IEJ* 23 (1973) 82–91.

————. "The Aramaic Ostraca from Tel Beer-sheba (Seasons 1971–1976)." *Tel Aviv* 6 (1979) 182–98.

Naveh, J., and S. Shaked. "Ritual Texts or Treasury Documents?" *Orientalia* 42 (1973) 445–57.

Negev, A. "The High Level Aqueduct at Caesarea." *IEJ* 14 (1964) 237–49.

————. "A New Inscription from the High Level Aqueduct at Caesarea." *IEJ* 22 (1972) 52–53.

————. "The Nabateans and the Provincia Arabia." *ANRW* 2 (1977) 8.520–686.

Neill, S., and T. Wright. *The Interpretation of the New Testament 1861–1986.* 2d ed. New York and Oxford: Oxford University Press, 1988.

Neirynck, F. "Recent Developments in the Study of Q." In *Logia: Les paroles de Jésus—The Sayings of Jesus*, edited by J. Delobel, 29–75. BETL 69. Leuven: Leuven University, 1982.

Nestle, E. "Der Greuel der Verwüstung." *ZAW* 4 (1884) 248.

————. "The Hasmonean and Herodian Winter Palaces at Jericho." *IEJ* 25 (1975) 89–100.

————. "The Winter Palaces of the Judean Kings at Jericho at the End of the Second Temple Period." *BASOR* 228 (1977) 1–13.

————. *Greater Herodium.* Qedem 13. Jerusalem: Hebrew University Press, 1981.

Netzer, E. "Ancient Ritual Baths (*Miqvaot*) in Jericho." *Jerusalem Cathedra* 2 (1982) 106–19.

Netzer, E., et al. "Symposium: Herod's Building Projects." *Jerusalem Cathedra* 1 (1981) 48–80.

Neubauer, A., "Chronique samaritaine, suivie d'un appendice contenant de courtes notices sur quelques autres ouvrages samaritains." *Journal asiatique* 14 (1869) 385–470.

Neuhaus, G. O. "Quellen im 1. Makkabäerbuch? Eine Entgegnung auf die Analyse von K.-D. Schunck." *JSJ* 5 (1974) 162–75.

Neusner, J. "The Fellowship (חבורה) in the Second Jewish Commonwealth." *HTR* 53 (1960) 125–42.

———. "*ḤBR* and *N'MN*." *RevQum* 5 (1964–66) 119–22.

———. "The Demise of 'Normative Judaism.'" *Judaism* 15 (1966) 230–240. In *Early Rabbinic Judaism: Historical Studies in Religion, Literature and Art*, 139–51. SJLA 13. Leiden: E. J. Brill, 1975.

———. *Development of a Legend: Studies on the Traditions Concerning Yohanan ben Zakkai*. SPB 16. Leiden: E. J. Brill, 1970.

———. *The Rabbinic Traditions about the Pharisees before 70*. 3 vols. Leiden: E. J. Brill, 1971.

———. "Emergent Rabbinic Judaism in a Time of Crisis: Four Responses to the Destruction of the Second Temple." *Judaism* 21 (1972) 313–27. Reprinted in idem, *Early Rabbinic Judaism: Historical Studies in Religion, Literature and Art*, 34–49. SJLA 13. Leiden: E. J. Brill, 1975.

———. *Eliezer ben Hyrcanus*. 2 vols. Leiden: E. J. Brill, 1973.

———. *From Politics to Piety: The Emergence of Pharisaic Judaism*. Englewood Cliffs, N.J.: Prentice-Hall, 1973.

———. *Invitation to the Talmud*. New York: Harper & Row, 1973.

———. "The Written Tradition in the Pre-rabbinic Period." *JSJ* 4 (1973) 56–65.

———. *The Idea of Purity in Ancient Judaism: The Haskell Lectures, 1972–1973*. With critique and commentary by M. Douglas. SJLA 1. Leiden: E. J. Brill, 1973.

———. *A History of the Mishnaic Law of Purities*. Vols. 1–22. SJLA 6. Leiden: E. J. Brill, 1974–77.

———. "'First Cleanse the Inside': The 'Halakhic' Background of a Controversy-Saying." *NTS* 22 (1975/76) 486–95.

———. *The Tosefta, Translated from the Hebrew*. Vols. 1–6. New York: Ktav, 1977–86.

———. *A History of the Mishnaic Law of Holy Things*. Vols. 1–6. SJLA 30. Leiden: E. J. Brill, 1978–80.

———. "From Scripture to Mishnah: The Origins of Mishnah's Fifth Division." *JBL* 98 (1979) 269–83.

———. "The Formation of Rabbinic Judaism: Yavneh (Jamnia) from A.D. 70 to 100." *ANRW* 2 (1979) 19.2.3–42.

———. *A History of the Mishnaic Law of Women*. Vols. 1–5. SJLA 33. Leiden: E. J. Brill, 1980.

———. "The Present State of Rabbinic Biography." In *Hommage à Georges Vajda: Etudes d'histoire et de pensée juive*, edited by G. Nahon and C. Touati, 85–91. Louvain: Peeters, 1980.

———. *A History of the Mishnaic Law of Appointed Times*. Vols. 1–5. SJLA 34. Leiden: E. J. Brill, 1981–83.

———. *Judaism: The Evidence of the Mishnah*. Chicago: University of Chicago Press, 1981.

———. "Two Pictures of the Pharisees: Philosophical Circle or Eating Club?" *ATR* 64 (1982) 525–38.

———. *A History of the Mishnaic Law of Damages*. Vols. 1–5. SJLA 35. Leiden: E. J. Brill, 1983–85.

———. "Varieties of Judaism in the Formative Age." In *Formative Judaism II: Religious, Historical, and Literary Studies*, 59–89. BJS 41. Atlanta: Scholars Press, 1983.

———. *Judaism in the Beginning of Christianity*. London: SPCK, 1984.

———. *Messiah in Context: Israel's History and Destiny in Formative Judaism*. Philadelphia: Fortress, 1984.

———. *Torah: From Scroll to Symbolism in Formative Judaism*. Philadelphia: Fortress, 1985.

———. " 'Covenantal Nomism.' The Piety of Judaism in the First Century." In *Major Trends in Formative Judaism*. Third Series: *The Three Stages in the Formation of Judaism*, edited by J. Neusner, 9–34. BJS 99. Atlanta: Scholars Press, 1985.

———. "Preface." In *Goodenough on the History of Religion and on Judaism*, edited by E. S. Frerichs and J. Neusner, ix–xix. BJS 121. Atlanta: Scholars Press, 1986 = "Introduction." E. R. Goodenough, *Jewish Symbols in the Greco-Roman Period* (abridged ed., 1988).

———. "Josephus' Pharisees: A Complete Repertoire." In *Josephus, Judaism, and Christianity*, edited by L. H. Feldman and G. Hata, 274–92. Leiden: E. J. Brill, 1987.

———. *The Wonder-Working Lawyers of Talmudic Babylonia: The Theory and Practice of Judaism in Its Formative Age*. Studies in Judaism. Lanham, Md.: University Press of America, 1987 = *A History of the Jews in Babylonia*. Leiden: E. J. Brill (1966) 2.251–87; (1968) 3.95–194; (1969) 4.179–402; (1970) 5.244–342.

———. *A Religion of Pots and Pans? Modes of Philosophical and Theological Discourse in Ancient Judaism: Essays and a Program*. BJS 156. Atlanta: Scholars Press, 1988.

———. *Invitation to Midrash: The Workings of Rabbinic Bible Interpretation*. San Francisco: Harper & Row, 1989.

———. "Money-changers in the Temple: The Mishnah's Explanation." *NTS* 35 (1989) 287–90.

Neusner, J., and E. S. Frerichs, eds. *"To See Ourselves as Others See Us": Christians, Jews, "Others" in Late Antiquity*. SPSH. Atlanta: Scholars Press, 1985.

Neusner, J., W. S. Green, E. S. Frerichs, eds. *Judaisms and Their Messiahs at the Turn of the Christian Era*. Cambridge: Cambridge University Press, 1987.

Neusner, J., with A. J. Avery-Peck. "The Quest for the Historical Hillel: Theory and Practice." In J. Neusner, *Formative Judaism: Religious, Historical, and Literary Studies*, 45–63. BJS 37. Atlanta: Scholars Press, 1982.

Nicholson, E. W. "The Meaning of the Expression עם הארץ in the Old Testament." *JSS* 10 (1965) 59–66.

Nickelsburg, G.W.E. *Resurrection, Immortality, and Eternal Life in Intertestamental Judaism*. HTS 26. Cambridge: Harvard University Press, 1972.

———. *Jewish Literature between the Bible and the Mishnah*. Philadelphia: Fortress, 1981.

———, ed. *Studies on the Testament of Moses*. SBLSCS 4. Atlanta: Scholars Press, 1973.

Nicols, J. *Vespasian and the Partes Flavianae*. Historia Einzelschrift 28. Wiesbaden: Steiner, 1978.

Nikiprowetzky, V. "Sicaires et Zélotes—une Reconsidération." *Semitica* 23 (1973) 51–64.

Nolland, J. "Uncircumcised Proselytes?" *JSJ* 12 (1981) 173–94.

Noth, M. *The Chronicler's History*. Translation of *Überlieferungs Geschichte*, chaps. 14–25. Translated and edited by H.G.M. Williamson. Sheffield: JSOT Press, 1987.

Oden, R. A. *Studies in Lucian's De Syria Dea*. HSM 15. Atlanta: Scholars Press, 1976.

———. "The Persistence of Canaanite Religion." *BA* 39 (1976) 31–36.

———. "Ba'al Šāmēm and 'El." *CBQ* 39 (1977) 457–73.

Ogilvie, R. M. *A Commentary on Livy, Books 1–5*. Oxford: Clarendon, 1965.

O'Leary B. *The Asiatic Mode of Production: Oriental Despotism, Historical Materialism and Indian History*. Explorations in Social Structures. Oxford: Blackwell, 1989.

Olmstead, A. T. "Tattenai, Governor of 'Across the River.'" *JNES* 3 (1944) 46.

———. *History of the Persian Empire*. Chicago: University of Chicago Press, 1948.

Oppenheim, A. L. "The Babylonian Evidence of Achaemenian Rule in Mesopotamia." *CHI* (1985) 2.529–87.

Oppenheimer, A. *The 'Am ha-Aretz: A Study in the Social History of the Jewish People in the Hellenistic-Roman Period*. ALGHJ 8. Leiden: E. J. Brill, 1977.

———. "The Bar Kokhba Revolt." *Immanuel* 14 (1982) 58–76.

Otto, E. *Die biographischen Inschriften der ägyptischen Spätzeit*. Leiden: E. J. Brill, 1954.

Otto, W. "14) Herodes I." *PWSup* (1913) 2.1–202.

Pardee, D. "A Restudy of the Commentary on Psalm 37 from Qumran Cave 4." *RevQ* 8 (1972–73) 163–94.

Pardee, D., et al., *Handbook of Ancient Hebrew Letters*. SBLSBS 15. Atlanta: Scholars Press, 1982.

Parente, F. "The Third Book of Maccabees as Ideological Document and Historical Source." *Henoch* 10 (1988) 143–82.

Parker, H.M.D. *The Roman Legions*. 1928. Reprint. Cambridge: Heffer, 1971.

Patai, R. *Man and Temple in Ancient Jewish Myth and Ritual*. Edinburgh: Thomas Nelson, 1947.

Patrich, J. "Inscriptions araméennes juives dans les grottes d'El-'Aleiliyât: Wadi Suweinit (Naḥal Michmas)." *RB* 92 (1985) 265–73.

Pauritsch, K. *Die neue Gemeinde: Gott sammelt Ausgestossene und Arme (Jesaia 56–66)*. Analecta Biblica 47. Rome: Pontifical Biblical Institute, 1971.

Pearson, B. A. "Jewish Sources in Gnostic Literature." *JWSTP* (1984) 443–81.

Pearson, L. *The Lost Historians of Alexander the Great*. American Philological Association Monograph 20. New York: American Philological Association; Oxford: Blackwell, 1960.

Peli, P. H. "The Havurot That Were in Jerusalem." *HUCA* 55 (1984) 55–74.

Pelletier, A. *Lettre d'Aristée à Philocrate*. SC 89. Paris: Editions du Cerf, 1962.

Peremans, W. "Les révolutions égyptiennes sous les Lagides." *Das ptole-mäische Ägypten: Akten des Internationalen Symposions 27.–29. September 1976 in Berlin*, edited by H. Maehler and V. M. Strocka, 39–50. Mainz: Zabern, 1978.

Perowne, S. *Hadrian.* London: Hodder & Stoughton, 1960.

Perrot, J., and D. Ladiray. "La porte de Darius à Suse." *Cahiers de la délégation archéologique française en Iran* 4 (1974) 43–56.

Petersen, D. L. *Haggai and Zechariah 1–8.* OTL. London: SCM, 1984.

Petersen, H. "Real and Alleged Literary Projects of Josephus." *AJP* 79 (1958) 259–74.

Petit, T. "L'évolution sémantique des termes hébreux et araméens *phh* et *sgn* et accadiens *pāḫatu* et *šaknu*." *JBL* 107 (1988) 53–67.

Pfister, F. *Eine jüdische Gründungsgeschichte Alexandrias.* SAWH. Heidelberg: Carl Winters, 1914.

Pflaum, H.-G. "Remarques sur le changement de statut administratif de la province de Judée." *IEJ* 19 (1969) 225–33.

Pietersma, A. Review of *Palestinian Parties and Politics*, by M. Smith. *JBL* 91 (1972) 550–52.

Plöger, O. "Hyrkan im Ostjordanland." *ZDPV* 71 (1955) 70–81.

———. *Theocracy and Eschatology.* Oxford: Blackwell, 1968.

Plümacher, E. "Lukas als griechischer Historiker." *PWSup* (1974) 14.235–64.

Pohlmann, K.-F. *Studien zum dritten Esra: Ein Beitrag zur Frage nach dem ursprünglichen Schluss des chronistischen Geschichtswerkes.* FRLANT 104. Göttingen: Vandenhoeck & Ruprecht, 1970.

Polotsky, H. J. "The Greek Papyri from the Cave of Letters." *IEJ* 12 (1962) 258–62.

Pope, M. *Job.* 3d ed. AB 15. Garden City, N.Y.: Doubleday, 1973.

———. *Song of Songs.* AB 7C. Garden City, N.Y.: Doubleday, 1977.

Porten, B. *Archives from Elephantine: The Life of an Ancient Jewish Military Colony.* Berkeley and Los Angeles: University of California Press, 1968.

———. "Aramaic Papyri and Parchments: A New Look." *BA* 42 (1979) 74–104.

———. "Baalshamem and the Date of the Book of Jonah." In *De la Tôrah au Messie: Etudes d'exégèse et d'herméneutiques bibliques offertes à Henri Cazelles*, edited by M. Carrez, et al., 237–44. Paris: Desclée, 1981.

Porten, B., with J. C. Greenfield. *Jews of Elephantine and Arameans of Syene (Fifth Century B.C.E.).* Department of the History of the Jewish People, Texts and Studies for Students. Jerusalem: Hebrew University Press, 1976.

Porten, B., and J. C. Greenfield. "Hermopolis Letter 6." *IOS* 4 (1974) 14–30.

Porten, B., and A. Yardeni. *Textbook of Aramaic Documents from Ancient Egypt: 1 Letters.* Hebrew University, Department of the History of the Jewish People, Texts and Studies for Students. Jerusalem: Hebrew University Press, 1986.

Porter, J. R. "Son or Grandson (Ezra X. 6)?" *JTS* 17 (1966) 54–67.

Porton, G. G. *The Traditions of Rabbi Ishmael.* SJLA 19. Parts 1–4. Leiden: E. J. Brill, 1976–82.

———. "Diversity in Postbiblical Judaism." In *Early Judaism and Its Modern Interpreters*, edited by R. A. Kraft and G.W.E. Nickelsburg, 57–80. Atlanta: Scholars Press; Philadelphia: Fortress, 1986.

Posener, G. *La première domination perse en Égypte*. Bibliotheque d'Etude de l'Institute Francais d'Archeologie Orientale 11. Cairo: Institut Francais d'Archeologie Orientale, 1936.

Prandi, L. "Una nuova ipotesi sull'iscrizione di Ponzio Pilato." *Civilta classica e cristiana* 2 (1981) 25–35.

Pucci, M. *La rivolta ebraica al tempo di Traiano*. Biblioteca di Studi Antichi 33. Pisa: Giardini Editori e Stamatori, 1981.

————. "Sullo sfondo politico dei moti insurrezionali ebraici del 116–117 d.C." *Atti dell'Istituto Veneto di Scienze, Lettere ed Arti*. Classe di scienze morali, lettere ed arti, 141 (1982/83) 241–77.

————. "C.P.J. II 158, 435 e la Revolta Ebraica al tempo di Traiano." *ZPE* 51 (1983) 95–103.

Puech, E. "Inscriptions funéraires palestiniennes: tombeau de Jason et ossuaires." *RB* 90 (1983) 481–533.

Pugliese Carratelli, G., and G. Garbini. *A Bilingual Graeco-Aramaic Edict by Asoka: The First Greek Inscription Discovered in Afghanistan*. Serie Orientale Roma 29. Rome: Istituto Italiano per il Medio ed Estremo Oriente, 1964.

Pummer, R. "The Present State of Samaritan Studies." *JSS* 21 (1976) 39–61; 22 (1977) 27–47.

————. "The *Book of Jubilees* and the Samaritans." *Eglise et théologie* 10 (1979) 147–78.

————. *The Samaritans*. Iconography of Religion, sect. 23: Judaism, Fascicle 5. Leiden: E. J. Brill, 1987.

————. "Samaritan Material Remains and Archaeology." In *The Samaritans*, edited by A. Crown, 135–77. Tübingen: J.C.B. Mohr (Paul Siebeck), 1989.

Purvis, J. D. "The Samaritans and Judaism." In *Early Judaism and Its Modern Interpreters*, edited by R. A. Kraft and G.W.E. Nickelsburg, 81–98. Atlanta: Scholars Press; Philadelphia: Fortress, 1986.

Qimron, E., and J. Strugnell. "An Unpublished Halakhic Letter from Qumran." In *Biblical Archaeology Today: Proceedings of the International Congress on Biblical Archaeology, Jerusalem, April 1984*, 400–407. Jerusalem: Israel Exploration Society, 1985.

Raban, A., ed. *The Harbours of Caesarea Maritima: Results of the Caesarea Ancient Harbour Excavation Project, 1980–1985*. Vol. 1: *The Site and the Excavations*. Parts 1–2, British Archaeological Reports International Series 491. Center for Maritime Studies, University of Haifa, Pub. no. 3. Oxford: BAR, 1989.

Rabello, A. M. "The Legal Condition of the Jews in the Roman Empire." *ANRW* 2 (1980) 13.662–762.

Rabin, C. "Alexander Jannaeus and the Pharisees." *JJS* 7 (1956) 3–11.

Rabinowitz, I. "A Reconsideration of 'Damascus' and '390 Years' in the 'Damascus' ('Zadokite') Fragments." *JBL* 73 (1954) 11–35.

————. "Aramaic Inscriptions of the Fifth Century B.C.E. from a North-Arab Shrine in Egypt." *JNES* 15 (1956) 1–9.

Radice, R., and D. T. Runia. *Philo of Alexandria: An Annotated Bibliography 1937–1986*. VigChrSupp 8. Leiden: E. J. Brill, 1988.

Rainey, A. F. "The Satrapy 'Beyond the River.'" *AJBA* 1 (1969) 51–78.

Rajak, T. "Justus of Tiberias." *Classical Quarterly* 23 (1973) 345–68.

———. "Roman Intervention in a Seleucid Siege of Jerusalem?" *GRBS* 22 (1981) 65–81.

———. *Josephus: The Historian and His Society.* London: Duckworth, 1983.

———. "Was There a Roman Charter for the Jews?" *JRS* 74 (1984) 107–23.

———. "Josephus and Justus of Tiberias." In *Josephus, Judaism, and Christianity*, edited by L. H. Feldman and G. Hata, 81–94. Leiden: E. J. Brill, 1987.

———. "The Hasmoneans and the Uses of Hellenism." In *A Tribute to Geza Vermes: Essays on Jewish and Christian Literature and History*, edited by P. R. Davies and R. T. White, 261–80. JSOTSS 100. Sheffield: JSOT Press, 1990.

Rappaport, U. "Les Iduméens en Egypte." *Revue de philologie, d'histoire et de littératures anciennes*, 3d series, 43 (1969) 73–82.

———. "Gaza and Ascalon in the Persian and Hellenistic Periods in Relation to Their Coins." *IEJ* 20 (1970) 75–80.

———. "The Emergence of Hasmonean Coinage." *AJS Review* 1 (1976) 171–86.

———. "The First Judean Coinage." *JJS* 32 (1981) 1–17.

———. "Jewish-Pagan Relations and the Revolt against Rome in 66–70 C.E." *Jerusalem Cathedra* 1 (1981) 81–95.

———. "John of Gischala in Galilee." *Jerusalem Cathedra* 3 (1983) 46–75.

———. "Numismatics." *CHJ* (1984) 1.25–59.

Ratner, B., ed. *Seder Olam Rabba: Die Grosse Weltchronik.* Vilna: Romm, 1897.

Ray, J. D. *The Archive of Ḥor.* Texts from Excavations, Second Memoir. London: Egypt Exploration Society, 1976.

Redditt, P. L. "Once Again, the City in Isaiah 24–27." *HAR* 10 (1986) 317–35.

———. "The Book of Joel and Peripheral Prophecy." *CBQ* 48 (1986) 225–40.

———. "Israel's Shepherds: Hope and Pessimism in Zechariah 9–14." *CBQ* 51 (1989) 632–42.

Reggiani, C. K. "I rapporti tra l'impero romano e il mondo ebraico al tempo di Caligola secondo la 'Legatio ad Gaium' di Filone Alessandrino." *ANRW* 2 (1984) 21.1.554–86.

Reich, R. "Archaeological Evidence of the Jewish Population at Hasmonean Gezer." *IEJ* 31 (1981) 48–52.

Reif, S. Review of *Koheleth*, by C. Whitley. *VT* 31 (1981) 120–26.

Reinhardt, K. "Herodots Persergeschichten: Östliches und Westliches im Übergang von Sage zu Geschichte." In *Herodot*, edited by W. Marg, 320–69. Munich: Beck, 1962.

Reinhold, M. "Historian of the Classic World: A Critique of Rostovtzeff." *Science and Society* 10 (1946) 361–91.

Reinmuth, O. W. "The Edict of Tiberius Julius Alexander." *TAPA* 65 (1934) 248–59.

Rendtorff, R. "Esra und das >>Gesetz<<" *ZAW* 96 (1984) 165–84.

Rengstorf, K. H. *A Complete Concordance to Flavius Josephus.* 4 vols. Leiden: E. J. Brill, 1973–83.

————. λῃστής. *TDNT* (1967) 4.257–62.

Reynolds, J., and R. Tannenbaum. *Jews and Godfearers at Aphrodisias: Greek Inscriptions with Commentary.* Cambridge Philological Society, Supplement 12. Cambridge: Cambridge Philological Society, 1987.

Rhoads, D. M. *Israel in Revolution: 6–74 c.e.: A Political History Based on the Writings of Josephus.* Philadelphia: Fortress, 1976.

Riaud, J. "Les Thérapeutes d'Alexandrie dans la tradition et dans la recherche critique jusqu'aux découvertes de Qumran." *ANRW* 2 (1987) 20.2.1189–1295.

Richardson, P. "Religion and Architecture: A Study in Herod's Piety, Power, Pomp and Pleasure." *Bulletin of the Canadian Society of Biblical Studies* 45 (1985) 3–29.

————. "Law and Piety in Herod's Architecture." *SR* 15 (1986) 347–60.

Rigby, K. J. "Seleucid Notes." *TAPA* 110 (1980) 233–54.

Rivkin, E. "Defining the Pharisees: The Tannaitic Sources." *HUCA* 43 (1972) 205–49.

————. "Beth Din, Boule, Sanhedrin: A Tragedy of Errors." *HUCA* 46 (1975) 181–99.

————. "Scribes, Pharisees, Lawyers, Hypocrites: A Study in Synonymity." *HUCA* 49 (1978) 135–42.

————. *The Hidden Revolution: An Historical Reconstruction of the Pharisees.* Nashville: Abingdon, 1978.

Roaf, M. "The Subject Peoples on the Base of the Statue of Darius." *Cahiers de la délégation archéologique française en Iran* 4 (1974) 73–160.

Roberts, J.J.M. "Myth versus History: Relaying the Comparative Foundations." *CBQ* 38 (1976) 1–13.

————. "Zion Tradition." *IDBSup* (1976) 985–87.

Rofé, A. "Isaiah 66:1-4: Judean Sects in the Persian Period as Viewed by Trito-Isaiah." In *Biblical and Related Studies Presented to Samuel Iwry,* edited by A. Kort and S. Morschauser, 205–17. Winona Lake, Ind.: Eisenbrauns, 1985.

Rokeah, D. "The War of Kitos: Towards the Clarification of a Philological-Historical Problem." *Scripta Hierosolymitana* 23 (1972) 79–84.

Roll, I. "The Roman Road System in Judaea." *Jerusalem Cathedra* 3 (1983) 136–61.

Rosenthal, E. S. "The Giv'at ha-Mivtar Inscription." *IEJ* 23 (1973) 72–81.

Rostovtzeff, M. [Rostowzew, M.] *Studien zur Geschichte des römischen Kolonates.* Beiheft zum Archiv für Papyrusforschung 1. Leipzig: Teubner, 1910.

————. *A Large Estate in Egypt in the Third Century b.c.* University of Wisconsin Studies in the Social Sciences and History 6. Madison: University of Wisconsin Press, 1922.

————. "Seleucid Babylonia: Bullae and Seals of Clay with Greek Inscriptions." *YCS* 3 (1932) 1–114.

————. *The Social and Economic History of the Hellenistic World.* 3 vols. Oxford: Clarendon, 1941.

————. *The Social and Economic History of the Roman Empire.* 1926. 2d ed., rev. by P. M. Fraser. Oxford: Clarendon, 1957.

Roueché, C., and S. M. Sherwin-White. "Some Aspects of the Seleucid Empire: The Greek Inscriptions from Failaka, in the Arabian Gulf." *Chiron* 15 (1985) 1–39.

Roux, J., and G. Roux. "Un décret du politeuma des Juifs de Bérénikè en Cyrénaïque au Musée Lapidaire de Carpentras." *REG* 62 (1949) 281–96.

Rowley, H. H. *Darius the Mede and the Four World Empires in the Book of Daniel.* Cardiff: University of Wales, 1935.

———. "The Herodians in the Gospels." *JTS* o.s. 41 (1940) 14–27.

———. "The Chronological Order of Ezra and Nehemiah." In idem, *The Servant of the Lord and Other Essays on the Old Testament,* 131–59. London: Lutterworth, 1952. Reprinted from *The Ignace Goldziher Memorial Volume,* edited by S. Lowinger and J. Somogyi. Budapest: Globus, 1948.

Rudolph, K. *Die Mandäer.* 2 vols. FRLANT 56–57 (1960); FRLANT 75–76 (1961). Göttingen: Vandenhoeck & Ruprecht.

———. *Theogonie, Kosmogonie, und Anthropogonie in den mandäische Schriften: Eine literarkritische und traditions-geschichtliche Untersuchung.* FRLANT 88. Göttingen: Vandenhoeck & Ruprecht, 1965.

———. "Zum gegenwärtigen Stand der mandäischen Religionsgeschichte." In *Gnosis und Neues Testament: Studien aus Religionswissenschaft und Theologie,* edited by K.-W. Tröger, 121–48. Gütersloh: Mohn, 1973 = revision of "Problems of a History of the Development of the Mandaean Religion." *HR* 8 (1968/69) 210–35.

———. "Quellenprobleme zum Ursprung und Alter der Mandäer." In *Christianity, Judaism and Other Greco-Roman Cults: Studies for Morton Smith at Sixty* 4.112–42. Edited by J. Neusner. SJLA 12. Leiden: E. J. Brill, 1975.

———. *Mandaeism.* Iconography of Religions 21. Leiden: E. J. Brill, 1978.

———. *Antike Baptisten: Zu den Überlieferungen über frühjüdische und -christliche Taufsekten.* SSAW, Philologische-historische Klasse, 121.4. Berlin: Akademie-Verlag, 1981.

———. *Gnosis, the Nature and History of an Ancient Religion.* Edinburgh: T. & T. Clark, 1983.

Rudolph, W. *Ezra und Nehemia.* HAT 20. Tübingen: J.C.B. Mohr (Paul Siebeck), 1949.

Ruhl, F. "Justus von Tiberias." *Rheinisches Museum* 71 (1916) 289–308.

Ruppel, W. "Politeuma." *Philologus* 82 (1926/27) 268–311, 433–54.

Sachs, A. J., and D. J. Wiseman. "A Babylonian King List of the Hellenistic Period." *Iraq* 16 (1954) 202–11.

Safrai, S. "Jewish Self-government." In *The Jewish People in the First Century: Historical Geography, Political History, Social, Cultural and Religious Life and Institutions,* edited by S. Safrai and M. Stern. CRINT 1/1. Assen: Van Gorcum; Philadelphia: Fortress, 1974, 1.377–419.

Safrai, Z. "The Administrative Structure of Judea in the Roman and Byzantine Periods." *Immanuel* 13 (1981) 30–38.

Saldarini, A. J. "Johanan ben Zakkai's Escape from Jerusalem: Origin and Development of a Rabbinic Story." *JSJ* 6 (1975) 189–204.

———. "'Form Criticism' of Rabbinic Literature." *JBL* 96 (1977) 257–74.

———. "Reconstructions of Rabbinic Judaism." *Early Judaism and Its Mod-*

ern Interpreters, edited by R. A. Kraft and G.W.E. Nickelsburg, 437–77. Atlanta: Scholars Press; Philadelphia: Fortress, 1986.

————. *Pharisees, Scribes and Sadducees in Palestinian Society: A Sociological Approach.* Wilmington, Del.: Michael Glazier, 1988.

Saley, R. J. "The Date of Nehemiah Reconsidered." In *Biblical and Near Eastern Studies: Essays in Honor of William Sanford LaSor,* edited by G. A. Tuttle, 151–65. Grand Rapids: Wm. B. Eerdmans, 1978.

Samuel, A. E. *From Athens to Alexandria: Hellenism and Social Goals in Ptolemaic Egypt.* Studia Hellenistica 26. Louvain: Imprimerie Orientaliste, 1983.

San Nicolò, M. *Beiträge zu einer Prosopographie neubabylonischer Beamten der Zivil- und Tempelverwaltung.* SBAW, Philologisch-historische Abteilung, Jahrgang 1941, Band II, Heft 2.

Sancisi-Weerdenburg, H., ed. *Achaemenid History I: Sources, Structures and Synthesis.* Proceeding of the Groningen 1983 Achaemenid History Workshop. Leiden: Nederlands Instituut voor het Nabije Oosten, 1987.

Sancisi-Weerdenburg, H., and A. Kuhrt, eds. *Achaemenid History II: The Greek Sources.* Proceeding of the Groningen 1984 Achaemenid History Workshop. Leiden: Nederlands Instituut voor het Nabije Oosten, 1987.

Sanders, E. P. "The Genre of Palestinian Jewish Apocalypses." In *Apocalypticism in the Mediterranean World,* edited by D. Hellholm, 447–59. Tübingen: J.C.B. Mohr (Paul Siebeck), 1983.

Sanders, J. T. *Ben Sira and Demotic Wisdom.* SBLMS 28. Atlanta: Scholars Press, 1983.

Sandmel, S. *Herod: Profile of a Tyrant.* Philadelphia: Lippincott, 1967.

————. "Palestinian and Hellenistic Judaism and Christianity: The Question of the Comfortable Theory." *HUCA* 50 (1979) 137–48.

————. *Philo of Alexandria: An Introduction.* Oxford and New York: Oxford University Press, 1979.

Sarkisian, G. K. "Greek Personal Names in Uruk and the *Graeco-Babyloniaca* Problem." *Acta Antiqua* 22 (1974) 495–503.

Sasson, J. M. *Ruth: A New Translation with a Philological Commentary and a Formalist-Folklorist Interpretation.* 2d ed. Biblical Seminar. Sheffield: JSOT Press, 1989.

Sauer, G. "Serubbabel in der Sicht Haggais und Sacharjas." In *Das ferne und nahe Wort: Festschrift Leonhard Rost zur Vollendung seines 70. Lebensjahres am 30. November 1966 gewidmet,* edited by F. Maass, 199–207. BZAW 105. Berlin: Töpelmann, 1967.

Saulnier, C., with C. Perrot. *Histoire d'Israël. III: De la conquête d'Alexandre à la destruction du temple.* Paris: Editions du Cerf, 1985.

Schaeder, H. H. *Esra der Schreiber.* Beiträge zur historischen Theologie 5. Tübingen: J.C.B. Mohr (Paul Siebeck), 1930.

————. *Iranische Beiträge I.* Schriften der Königsberger Gelehrten Gesellschaft, 6. Jahr: Geisteswissenschaftliche Klasse, Heft 5. Halle[Saale]: Niemeyer, 1930.

Schäfer, P. "R. Aqiva und Bar Kokhba." In idem, *Studien zur Geschichte und Theologie des rabbinischen Judentums.* AGAJU 15. Leiden: E. J. Brill, 1978, 65–121.

―――. "Aqiva and Bar Kokhba." In *Approaches to Ancient Judaism,* vol. 2, edited by W. S. Green, 113–30. BJS 9. Atlanta: Scholars Press, 1980.

―――. *Der Bar Kokhba-Aufstand.* TSAJ 1. Tübingen: J.C.B. Mohr (Paul Siebeck), 1981.

―――. "The Causes of the Bar Kokhba Revolt." In *Studies in Aggadah, Targum and Jewish Liturgy in Memory of Joseph Heinemann,* edited by J. Petuchowski and E. Fleischer, 74–94. Jerusalem: Magnes, 1981.

―――. *Geschichte der Juden in der Antike: Die Juden Palästinas von Alexander dem Grossen bis zur arabischen Eroberung.* Stuttgart: Katholisches Bibelwerk, 1983.

―――. "Hadrian's Policy in Judaea and the Bar Kokhba Revolt: A Reassessment." In *A Tribute to Geza Vermes: Essays on Jewish and Christian Literature and History,* edited by P. R. Davies and R. T. White, 281–303. JSOTSS 100. Sheffield: JSOT Press, 1990.

Schalit, A. "Josephus und Justus: Studien zur Vita des Josephus." *Klio* 26 (1933) 67–95.

―――. "The Letter of Antiochus III to Zeuxis regarding the Establishment of Jewish Military Colonies in Phrygia and Lydia." *JQR* 50 (1959–60) 289–318.

―――. "Die frühchristliche Überlieferung über die Herkunft der Familie des Herodes." *ASTI* 1 (1962) 109–60.

―――. "Die Eroberungen des Alexander Jannäus in Moab." *Theokratia* 1 (1967–69) 3–50.

―――. *König Herodes: Der Mann und sein Werk.* Studia Judaica 4. Berlin: de Gruyter, 1969.

―――. "A Clash of Ideologies: Palestine under the Seleucids and Romans." In *The Crucible of Christianity: Judaism, Hellenism and the Historical Background to the Christian Faith,* edited by A. Toynbee, 47–76. London: Thames & Hudson, 1969.

―――, ed. *The Hellenistic Age.* World History of the Jewish People. Series 1, vol. 6. New Brunswick, N.J.: Rutgers University Press, 1972.

―――. *Untersuchung zur "Assumptio Mosis."* ALGHJ 17. Leiden: E. J. Brill, 1989.

Scharbert, J. "*Bēyt 'Āb* als soziologische Grösse im Alten Testament." In *Von Kanaan bis Kerala: Festschrift für Prof. Mag. Dr. Dr. J. P. M. van der Ploeg O.P. zur Vollendung des siebzigsten Lebensjahres am 4. Juli 1979,* edited by W. C. Delsman, et al., 213–37. AOAT. Neukirchen-Vluyn: Neukirchener Verlag, 1982.

Schein, B. E. "The Second Wall of Jerusalem." *BA* 44 (1981) 21–26.

Schiffman, L. H. "The Samaritans in Tannaitic Halakhah." *JQR* 75 (1984/85) 323–50.

―――. *The Eschatological Community of the Dead Sea Scrolls: A Study of the Rule of the Congregation.* SBLMS 38. Atlanta: Scholars Press, 1989.

―――. "The New Halakhic Letter (4QMMT) and the Origins of the Dead Sea Sect." *BA* 53 (1990) 64–73.

―――. "*Miqṣat Ma'aseh Ha-Torah* and the *Temple Scroll.*" *RevQ* 14 (1990) 435–57.

Schnabel, P. *Berossos und die babylonische-hellenistische Literatur.* Berlin and Leipzig: Teubner, 1923.

Scholem, G. G. *Jewish Gnosticism, Merkabah Mysticism, and Talmudic Tradition.* New York: Jewish Theological Seminary, 1965.

Schottroff, W. "Zur Sozialgeschichte Israels in der Perserzeit." *Verkündigung und Forschung* 27 (1982) 46–68.

Schreckenberg, H. *Bibliography zu Flavius Josephus.* ALGHJ 1. Leiden: E. J. Brill, 1968.

———. *Bibliography zu Flavius Josephus: Supplementband mit Gesamtregister.* ALGHJ 12. Leiden: E. J. Brill, 1979.

———. "Flavius Josephus und die lukanischen Schriften." In *Wort in der Zeit: Neutestamentliche Studien, Festgabe für Karl Heinrich Rengstorf zum 75. Geburtstag,* edited by W. Haubeck and M. Bachmann, 179–209. Leiden: E. J. Brill, 1980.

Schüller, S. "Some Problems Connected with the Supposed Common Ancestry of Jews and Spartans and Their Relations during the Last Three Centuries B.C." *JSS* 1 (1956) 257–68.

Schunck, K.-D. *Die Quellen des I and II Makkabäerbuches.* Halle: Niemeyer, 1954.

Schürer, E. *The History of the Jewish People in the Age of Jesus Christ.* Revised by G. Vermes, et al. 3 vols. in 4. Edinburgh: T. & T. Clark, 1973–87.

Schwartz, D. R. "Pontius Pilate's Suspension from Office: Chronology and Sources." *Tarbiz* 51 (1981/82) 383–98 (Heb.) + VII (Eng. summary).

———. "Ishmael ben Phiabi and the Chronology of Provincia Judaea." *Tarbiz* 52 (1982/83) 177–200 (Heb.) + V–VI (Eng. summary).

———. "Pontius Pilate's Appointment to Office and the Chronology of Josephus' *Jewish Antiquities*, Books XVIII–XX." *Zion* 48 (1982/83) 325–45 (Heb.) + XXI (Eng. summary).

———. "Josephus and Philo on Pontius Pilate." *Jerusalem Cathedra* 3 (1983) 26–45.

———. "Josephus and Nicolaus on the Pharisees." *JSJ* 14 (1983) 157–71.

———. "Philo's Priestly Descent." In *Nourished with Peace: Studies in Hellenistic Judaism in Memory of Samuel Sandmel,* edited by F. E. Greenspahn, et al., 155–71. SPHS 9. Atlanta: Scholars Press, 1984.

———. *Agrippa I: The Last King of Judaea.* TSAJ 23. Tübingen: J.C.B. Mohr (Paul Siebeck), 1990.

Schwartz, E. "Diodoros." *Griechische Geschichtschreiber,* 35–97. Leipzig: Koehler & Amelang, 1957. Reprint from *PW* 5.663–704.

Schwartz, S. "The Composition and Publication of Josephus's 'Bellum Judaicum' Book 7." *HTR* 79 (1986) 373–86.

———. *Josephus and Judaean Politics.* CSCT 18. Leiden: E. J. Brill, 1990.

———. "Israel and the Nations Roundabout: 1 Maccabees and the Hasmonean Expansion." *JJS* 42 (1991) 16–38.

Scott, S. P. *Justinian, Corpus Juris Civilis, the Civil Law, the Digest or Pandects.* 1932. Reprint. New York: AMS, 1973.

Scramuzza, V. M. *The Emperor Claudius.* Cambridge: Harvard University Press, 1940.

Scullard, H. H. *From the Gracchi to Nero: A History of Rome from 133 B.C. to A.D. 68.* 5th ed. New York and London: Methuen, 1982.

Seel, O., ed. *M. Iuniani Iustini epitoma Historiarum Philippicarum Pompei Trogi.* Leipzig: Teubner, 1985.

———, ed. *Pompei Trogi Fragmenta.* Leipzig: Teubner, 1956.

Segal, A. "Archaeological Research in Israel: 1960–1985." *BTB* 16 (1986) 73–77.

Segal, A. F. *Two Powers in Heaven.* SJLA 25. Leiden: E. J. Brill, 1977.

———. "Hellenistic Magic: Some Questions of Definition." In *Studies in Gnosticism and Hellenistic Religions Presented to Gilles Quispel on the Occasion of His Sixty-fifth Birthday,* edited by R. van den Broek and M. J. Vermaseren, 349–75. Leiden: E. J. Brill, 1981.

———. *Rebecca's Children: Judaism and Christianity in the Roman World.* Cambridge: Harvard University Press, 1986.

Segal, J. B. *Aramaic Texts from North Saqqâra with Some Fragments in Phoenician.* Texts from Excavations 6. London: Egyptian Exploration Society, 1983.

Segelberg, E. *Masbūtā: Studies in the Ritual of the Mandaean Baptism.* Uppsala: Almquist & Wiksells, 1958.

Sellers, O. R. "Coins of the 1960 Excavation at Shechem." *BA* 25 (1962) 87–96.

Sellers, O. R., et al. *The 1957 Excavation at Beth-Zur.* AASOR 38. Cambridge, Mass.: American Schools of Oriental Research, 1968.

Sevenster, J. N. *The Roots of Pagan Anti-Semitism in the Ancient World.* NovTSup 41. Leiden: E. J. Brill, 1975.

Seybold, K. "Die Königserwartung bei den Propheten Haggai und Sacharja." *Judaica* 28 (1972) 69–78.

Shaked, S. "Qumran and Iran: Further Considerations." *IOS* 2 (1972) 433–46.

———. "Iranian Influence on Judaism: First Century B.C.E. to Second Century C.E." *CHJ* (1984) 1.308–25.

Shanks, H. "The Jerusalem Wall That Shouldn't Be There." *BAR* 13, no. 3 (May/June 1987) 46–57.

Shaw, B. D. "Bandits in the Roman Empire." *Past and Present* 105 (Nov. 1984) 3–52.

Shedl, C. "Nabuchodonosor, Arpaksad und Darius: Untersuchungen zum Buch Judit." *ZDMG* 115 (1965) 242–54.

Sherk, R. K. *Rome and the Greek East to the Death of Augustus.* Translated Documents of Greece and Rome 4. Cambridge: Cambridge University Press, 1984.

Sherwin-White, A. N. *Roman Society and Roman Law in the New Testament.* Sarum Lectures, 1960–61. Oxford: Clarendon, 1963.

———. "The Trial of Jesus." In *Historicity and Chronology in the New Testament,* edited by D. E. Nineham, 97–116. Theological Collections 6. London: SPCK, 1965.

———. *The Letters of Pliny: A Historical and Social Commentary.* Oxford: Clarendon, 1966.

———. *Roman Foreign Policy in the East, 168 B.C. to A.D. 1.* London: Duckworth, 1984.

Sherwin-White, S. "A Greek Ostrakon from Babylon of the Early Third Century B.C." *ZPE* 47 (1982) 51–70.

———. "Ritual for a Seleucid King at Babylon?" *JHS* 103 (1983) 156–59.

———. "Seleucid Babylonia: A Case Study for the Installation and Development of Greek Rule." In *Hellenism in the East*, edited by A. Kuhrt and S. Sherwin-White, 1–31. London: Duckworth, 1987.

Shiloh, Y. *Excavations at the City of David.* Vol. 1: *1978–1982.* Qedem 19. Jerusalem: Hebrew University Press, 1984.

Shutt, R.J.H. *Studies in Josephus.* London: SPCK, 1961.

Sievers, J. *The Hasmoneans and Their Supporters: From Mattathias to the Death of John Hyrcanus I.* SFSHJ 6. Atlanta: Scholars Press, 1990.

Skaist, A. "A Note on the Bilingual Ostracon from Khirbet el-Kôm." *IEJ* 28 (1978) 106–8.

Skeat, T. C. "Notes on Ptolemaic Chronology: II. 'The Twelfth Year which is also the First': The Invasion of Egypt by Antiochus Epiphanes." *JEA* 47 (1961) 107–12.

Skehan, P. W., and A. A. Di Lella. *The Wisdom of Ben Sira.* AB 39. Garden City, N.Y.: Doubleday, 1987.

Smallwood, E. M. "The Date of the Dismissal of Pontius Pilate from Judaea." *JJS* 5 (1954) 12–21.

———. "Domitian's Attitude toward the Jews and Judaism." *Classical Philology* 51 (1956) 1–13.

———. "The Chronology of Gaius' Attempt to Desecrate the Temple." *Latomus* 16 (1957) 3–17.

———. "The Legislation of Hadrian and Antoninus Pius against Circumcision." *Latomus* 18 (1959) 334–47; 20 (1961) 93–96.

———. "The Alleged Jewish Tendencies of Poppaea Sabina." *JTS* 10 (1959) 329–35.

———. *Philonis Alexandrini Legatio ad Gaium.* Leiden: E. J. Brill, 1961.

———. "Atticus, Legate of Judaea under Trajan." *JRS* 52 (1962) 131–33.

———. "Palestine *c.* A.D. 115–118." *Historia* 11 (1962) 500–510.

———. "Gabinius' Organisation of Palestine." *JJS* 18 (1967) 89–92.

———. *The Jews under Roman Rule.* SJLA 20. Leiden: E. J. Brill, 1976. Corrected reprint, 1981.

———. "Philo and Josephus as Historians of the Same Event." In *Josephus, Judaism, and Christianity*, edited by L. H. Feldman and G. Hata, 114–29. Leiden: E. J. Brill, 1987.

Smith, J. Z. "Native Cults in the Hellenistic Period." *HR* 11 (1971/72) 236–49.

———. "Wisdom and Apocalyptic." In *Religious Syncretism in Antiquity*, edited by B. A. Pearson, 131–56. Atlanta: Scholars Press, 1975.

———. "Sacred Persistence: Towards a Redescription of Canon." In *Approaches to Ancient Judaism: Theory and Practice*, edited by W. S. Green, 11–28. BJS 1. Atlanta: Scholars Press, 1978.

———. "Fences and Neighbors: Some Contours of Early Judaism." In *Approaches to Ancient Judaism, Volume II*, edited by W. S. Green, 1–25. BJS 9. Atlanta: Scholars Press, 1980.

———. "European Religions, Ancient: Hellenistic Religions." In *Encyclopae-*

dia Britannica. 15th ed. *Macropaedia* 18.925–27. Chicago: Encyclopaedia Britannica, 1985.

————. *To Take Place: Toward Theory in Ritual*. Chicago Studies in the History of Judaism. Chicago: University of Chicago Press, 1987.

Smith, M. "Palestinian Judaism in the First Century." In *Israel: Its Role in Civilization*, edited by M. Davis, 67–81. New York: Harper, 1956.

————. "The Description of the Essenes in Josephus and the Philosophumena." *HUCA* 29 (1958) 273–313.

————. "A Comparison of Early Christian and Early Rabbinic Tradition." *JBL* 82 (1963) 169–76.

————. "Palestinian Judaism in the Persian Period." In *The Greeks and the Persians*, edited by H. Bengtson, 386–401. Delacorte World History. New York: Delacorte, 1968.

————. *Palestinian Parties and Politics That Shaped the Old Testament*. New York: Columbia University Press, 1971.

————. "Zealots and Sicarii, Their Origins and Relation." *HTR* 64 (1971) 1–19.

————. *Jesus the Magician*. San Francisco: Harper & Row, 1978.

————. "On the Lack of a History of Greco-Roman Magic." In *Althistorische Studien: Hermann Bengtson zum 70. Geburtstag dargebracht von Kollegen und Schülern*, edited by H. Heinen, et al., 251–57. Historia Einzelschriften 40. Wiesbaden: Steiner, 1983.

————. "Jewish Religious Life in the Persian Period." *CHJ* (1984) 1.219–78.

Smith, R. L. *Micah-Malachi*. WBC 32. Waco, Tex.: Word, 1984.

Smith, S. *Babylonian Historical Texts Relating to the Capture and Downfall of Babylon*. London: Methuen, 1924.

Soden, W. von. "Eine babylonische Volksüberlieferung von Nabonid in den Danielerzählungen." *ZAW* 53 (1935) 81–89.

Soggin, J. A. *Introduction to the Old Testament*. 3d ed. London: SCM, 1988.

Sokoloff, M. "The Giv'at ha-Mivtar Aramaic Tomb Inscription in Paleo-Hebrew Script and Its Historical Implications." *Immanuel* 10 (1980) 38–46.

Spaer, A. "Jaddua the High Priest?" *INJ* 9 (1986–87) 1–3.

Sparks, H., ed. *The Apocryphal Old Testament*. Oxford: Clarendon, 1984.

Speidel, M. P. "The Roman Army in Judaea under the Procurators: The Italian and the Augustan Cohort in the Acts of the Apostles." *Ancient Society* 13/14 (1982/83) 233–40.

Spek, R. J. van der. "The Babylonian City." In *Hellenism in the East*, edited by A. Kuhrt and S. Sherwin-White, 57–74. London: Duckworth, 1987.

Sperber, D. "A Note on Hasmonean Coin-Legends. Heber and Rosh Heber." *PEQ* 97 (1965) 85–93.

Spiegelberg, W. *Die sogenannte demotische Chronik des Pap. 215 der Bibliothèque Nationale zu Paris: nebst den auf der Rückseite des Papyrus stehenden Texten*. Demotische Studien 7. Leipzig: Hinrichs, 1914.

————. "Drei demotische Schreiben aus der Korrespondenz des Pherendates, des Satrapen Darius' I., mit den Chnum-Priestern von Elephantine." *SPAW*, philologisch-historische Klasse (1928) 604–22.

Stadelmann, H. *Ben Sira als Schriftgelehrter: einer Untersuchung zum Berufs-bild des vor-makkabäischen Sofer unter Berücksichtigung seines Verhältnisses zu Priester-, Propheten- und Weisheitslehrertum.* WUNT 2. Reihe, Nr. 6. Tübingen: J.C.B. Mohr (Paul Siebeck), 1980.

Starr, C. G. "Greeks and Persians in the Fourth Century B.C.: A Study in Cultural Contacts before Alexander." *Iranica Antiqua* 11 (1975) 39–99; 12 (1977) 49–115.

Ste. Croix, G.E.M. de. *The Class Struggle in the Ancient Greek World from the Archaic Age to the Arab Conquests.* London: Duckworth, 1981.

Steckoll, S. H. "The Qumran Sect in Relation to the Temple of Leontopolis." *RevQ* 6 (1967–69) 55–69.

Stegemann, H. "Is the Temple Scroll a Sixth Book of the Torah—Lost for 2,500 Years?" *BAR* 13, no. 6 (Nov./Dec. 1987) 28–35.

———. "The Literary Composition of the Temple Scroll and Its Status at Qumran." In *Temple Scroll Studies: Papers Presented at the International Symposium on the Temple Scroll, Manchester, December 1987,* edited by G. J. Brooke, 123–48. JSPSS 7. Sheffield: JSOT Press, 1989.

Stern, E. *Material Culture of the Land of the Bible in the Persian Period 538–332 B.C.* Jerusalem: Israel Exploration Society; Warminster, Wiltshire: Aris & Phillips, 1982.

———. "The Archeology of Persian Palestine." *CHJ* (1984) 2.88–114.

———. "The Walls of Dor." *IEJ* 38 (1988) 6–14.

Stern, M. "A. Schalit's Herod." 1960 Heb. ed. *JJS* 11 (1960) 49–58.

———. "Chronology." In *The Jewish People in the First Century: Historical Geography, Political History, Social, Cultural and Religious Life and Institu-tions,* edited by S. Safrai and M. Stern. CRINT 1/1. Assen: Van Gorcum; Philadelphia: Fortress, 1974, 1.62–68.

———. "The Greek and Roman Literary Sources." In *The Jewish People in the First Century: Historical Geography, Political History, Social, Cultural and Religious Life and Institutions,* edited by S. Safrai and M. Stern. CRINT 1/1. Assen: Van Gorcum; Philadelphia: Fortress, 1974, 1.18–36.

———. "The Province of Judaea." In *The Jewish People in the First Century: Historical Geography, Political History, Social, Cultural and Religious Life and Institutions,* edited by S. Safrai and M. Stern. CRINT 1/1. Assen: Van Gorcum; Philadelphia: Fortress, 1974, 1.308–76.

———. *Greek and Latin Authors on Jews and Judaism.* 3 vols. Jerusalem: Israel Academy of Arts and Sciences, 1974–84.

———. "The Province of Yehud: The Vision and the Reality." *The Jerusalem Cathedra* 1 (1981) 9–21.

———. "Judaea and Her Neighbors in the Days of Alexander Jannaeus." *The Jerusalem Cathedra* 1 (1981) 22–46.

Stern, M., and O. Murray. "Hecataeus of Abdera and Theophrastus on Jews and Egyptians." *JEA* 59 (1973) 159–68.

Stinespring, W. F. "Hadrian in Palestine, 129/130 A.D." *JAOS* 59 (1939) 360–65.

Stolper, M. W. "The Governor of Babylon and Across-the-River in 486 B.C." *JNES* 48 (1989) 283–305.

————. "Bēlšunu the Satrap." In *Language, Literature, and History: Philological and Historical Studies Presented to Erica Reiner*, edited by F. Rochberg-Halton, 389–402. AOS 67. New Haven: American Oriental Society, 1987.

Stone, M. E. "Lists of Revealed Things in the Apocalyptic Literature." In *Magnalia Dei: Essays on the Bible and Archaeology in Memory of G. Ernest Wright*, edited by F. M. Cross, et al., 439–43. Garden City, N.Y.: Doubleday, 1976.

————. "The Book of Enoch and Judaism in the Third Century B.C.E." *CBQ* 40 (1978) 479–92.

————. "Reactions to Destructions of the Second Temple." *JSJ* 13 (1982) 195–204.

————. *Features of the Eschatology of IV Ezra*. HSS 35. Atlanta: Scholars Press, 1989.

————. *Fourth Ezra*. Hermeneia. Minneapolis: Fortress, 1990.

Strack, H. L., and G. Stemberger. *Introduction to the Talmud and Midrash*. Edinburgh: T. & T. Clark, 1991.

Strange, J. F. "Late Hellenistic and Herodian Ossuary Tombs at French Hill, Jerusalem." *BASOR* 219 (1975) 39–67.

————. "Archaeology and the Religion of Judaism in Palestine." *ANRW* 2 (1979) 19.1.646–85.

Stronach, D. "La statue de Darius le Grand découverte à Suse." *Cahiers de la délégation archéologique française en Iran* 4 (1974) 61–72.

Stroumsa, G.A.G. "Aher: A Gnostic." In *The Rediscovery of Gnosticism* 2.808–18. Edited by B. Layton. *Numen* Supplement 41. Leiden: E. J. Brill, 1981.

————. *Another Seed: Studies in Gnostic Mythology*. NHS 24. Leiden: E. J. Brill, 1984.

Sullivan, R. D. "The Dynasty of Judaea in the First Century." *ANRW* 2 (1977) 8.296–354.

Sundberg, A. C. *The Old Testament of the Early Church*. HTS 20. Cambridge: Harvard University Press, 1964.

Svencickaja, I. S. "Some Problems of Agrarian Relations in the Province of Asia." *Eirene* 15 (1977) 27–54.

Swete, H. *An Introduction to the Old Testament in Greek*. Revised by R. R. Ottley. Cambridge: Cambridge University Press, 1914.

Syme, R. *Tacitus*. 2 vols. Oxford: Clarendon, 1958.

————. "The Titulus Tiburtinus." In *Akten des VI. Internationalen Kongresses für Griechische und Lateinische Epigraphik, München 1972*, 585–601. Vestigia 17. Munich: Beck, 1973.

————. *Historia Augusta Papers*. Oxford: Clarendon, 1983.

Taeubler, E. "Jerusalem 201 to 199 B.C.E. on the History of a Messianic Movement." *JQR* 37 (1946–47) 1–30, 125–37, 249–63.

Talmon. S. "The Emergence of Jewish Sectarianism in the Early Second Temple Period." In idem, *King, Cult and Calendar in Ancient Israel*, 165–201. Jerusalem: Magnes, 1986 = idem, in *Ancient Israelite Religion: Essays in Honor of Frank Moore Cross*, edited by P. D. Miller, et al., 587–616. Philadelphia: Fortress, 1987 = trans. of German version in *Max Webers Sicht des antiken Christentums*, edited by E. Schluchter, 233–80. Frankfurt: Suhrkamp, 1985.

Talshir, D. "A Reinvestigation of the Linguistic Relationship between Chronicles and Ezra-Nehemiah." *VT* 38 (1988) 165–93.

Tannenbaum, R. F. "Jews and God-Fearers in the Holy City of Aphrodite." *BAR* 12, no. 5 (Sept./Oct. 1986) 54–57.

Tarn, W. W., and G. T. Griffith. *Hellenistic Civilisation*. 3d ed. London: Arnold, 1952.

Tcherikover, V. A. [Tscherikower, V. A.]. "Palestine under the Ptolemies: (A Contribution to the Study of the Zenon Papyri)." *Mizraim* 4–5 (1937) 9–90.

———. "The Ideology of the Letter of Aristeas." *HTR* 51 (1958) 59–85.

———. *Hellenistic Civilization and the Jews*. New York: Jewish Publication Society, 1959.

———. "The Third Book of Maccabees as a Historical Source of Augustus' Time." *Scripta Hierosolymitana* 7 (1961) 1–26. Heb. *Zion* 10 (1945) 1–20.

———. "Was Jerusalem a 'Polis'?" *IEJ* 4 (1964) 61–78.

Tcherikover, V. A., A. Fuks, and M. Stern. *Corpus Papyrorum Judaicarum*. 3 vols. Cambridge: Harvard University Press; Jerusalem: Magnes, 1957–64.

Teeple, H. M. *The Mosaic Eschatological Prophet*. SBLMS 10. Atlanta: Scholars Press, 1957.

Teixidor, J. *The Pagan God: Popular Religion in the Greco-Roman Near East*. Princeton: Princeton University Press, 1977.

Telford, W. R. Review of *Mark's Treatment of the Jewish Leaders*, by M. Cook. *JTS* 31 (1980) 154–62.

Terian, A. *Philonis Alexandrini De Animalibus: The Armenian Text with an Introduction, Translation, and Commentary*. Studies in Hellenistic Judaism 1. Atlanta: Scholars Press, 1981.

Thackeray, H. St. J., et al. *Josephus*. LCL. London: Heineman; Cambridge: Harvard University Press, 1926–65.

Thomas, J. *Le mouvement baptiste en Palestine et Syrie*. Universitas Catholica Lovaniensis, Dissertationes, Series II, Tomus 28. Bembloux: Duclot, 1935.

Thompson, L. A. "Domitian and the Jewish Tax." *Historia* 31 (1982) 329–42.

Throntveit, M. A. "Linguistic Analysis and the Question of Authorship in Chronicles, Ezra and Nehemiah." *VT* 32 (1982) 201–16.

Tiede, D. L. *The Charismatic Figure as Miracle Worker*. SBLDS 1. Atlanta: Scholars Press, 1972.

Timpe, D. "Der römische Vertrag mit den Juden von 161 v. Chr." *Chiron* 4 (1974) 133–52.

Torrey, C. C. *The Composition and Historical Value of Ezra-Nehemiah*. BZAW 2. Giessen: Ricker, 1896.

———. *Ezra Studies*. 1910. Edited with a prolegomenon by W. F. Stinespring. New York: Ktav, 1970.

Tov, E. *The Text-Critical Use of the Septuagint in Biblical Research*. Jerusalem Biblical Studies. Jerusalem: Simor, 1981.

———. "The Septuagint." In *Mikra: Text, Translation, Reading and Interpretation of the Hebrew Bible in Ancient Judaism and Early Christianity*, edited by M. J. Mulder. CRINT 2/1. Assen: Van Gorcum; Minneapolis: Fortress, 1988, 1.161–88.

Tov, E., et al. *The Greek Minor Prophets Scroll from Naḥal Ḥever (8ḤevXIIgr)*. DJD 8. Oxford: Clarendon: 1990.

Townsend, J. T. "Rabbinic Sources." In *The Study of Judaism*, 35–80. New York: Anti-defamation League of B'nai B'rith, 1972.

Trump, S., ed. *Millennial Dreams in Action.* Comparative Studies in Society and History, Supplement 2. Hague: Mouton, 1962.

Tsafrir, Y. "The Location of the Seleucid Akra." *RB* 82 (1975) 501–21.

———. "The Desert Fortresses of Judaea in the Second Temple Period." *Jerusalem Cathedra* 2 (1982) 120–45.

Tuland, C. G. "'*Uššayyā*' and '*uššarnâ*: A Clarification of Terms, Date, and Text." *JNES* 17 (1958) 269–75.

Tuplin, C. "The Administration of the Achaemenid Empire." In *Coinage and Administration in the Athenian and Persian Empires: The Ninth Oxford Symposium on Coinage and Monetary History*, edited by I. Carradice, 109–66. BAR International Series 343. Oxford: BAR, 1987.

Turner, E. G. "Tiberius Iulius Alexander." *JRS* 44 (1954) 54–64.

Tushingham, A. D. "The Western Hill of Jerusalem: A Critique of the 'Maximalist' Position." *Levant* 19 (1987) 137–43.

Tzori, N. "An Inscription of the Legio VI Ferrata from the Northern Jordan Valley." *IEJ* 21 (1971) 53–54.

Urman, D. *The Golan: A Profile of a Region during the Roman and Byzantine Periods.* British Archaeological Reports International Series 269. Oxford: BAR, 1985.

Vallat, F. "Les textes cunéiformes de la statue de Darius." *Cahiers de la délégation archéologique française en Iran* 4 (1974) 161–70.

———. "L'inscription trilingue de Xerxès à la porte de Darius." *Cahiers de la délégation archéologique française en Iran* 4 (1974) 171–80.

VanderKam, J. C. *Textual and Historical Studies in the Book of Jubilees.* HSM 14. Atlanta: Scholars Press, 1977.

———. "The Origin, Character and Early History of the 364-day Calendar: A Reassessment of Jaubert's Hypotheses." *CBQ* 41 (1979) 390–411.

———. "2 Maccabees 6, 7a and Calendrical Change in Jerusalem." *JSJ* 12 (1981) 52–74.

———. "The Putative Author of the Book of Jubilees." *JSS* 26 (1981) 209–17.

———. *Enoch and the Growth of an Apocalyptic Tradition.* CBQMS 16. Washington, D.C.: Catholic Biblical Association, 1984.

———. "The Prophetic-Sapiential Origins of Apocalyptic Thought." In *A Word in Season: Essays in Honour of William McKane*, edited by J. D. Martin and P. R. Davies, 163–76. JSOTSS 42. Sheffield: Sheffield Academic Press, 1986.

———, ed. *The Book of Jubilees: Text and English Translation.* 2 vols. CSCO 510–11, Scriptores Aethiopici 87–88. Leuven: Peeters, 1989.

Vaux, R. de. "The Cults of Adonis and Osiris: A Comparative Study." In *The Bible and the Ancient Near East*, 210–37. London: Darton, Longman & Todd, 1971 = French original in *RB* 42 (1933) 3–56.

———. "The Decrees of Cyrus and Darius on the Rebuilding of the Temple." In *The Bible and the Ancient Near East*, 63–96. London: Darton, Longman & Todd, 1971 = trans. from *RB* 46 (1937) 29–57.

———. *Archaeology and the Dead Sea Scrolls.* Schweich Lectures of the British Academy 1959. London: Oxford University Press, 1973.

Vermes, G. "The Etymology of 'Essenes.'" *RevQ* 2 (1960) 427–43 = *Post-biblical Jewish Studies*, 8–29. SJLA 8. Leiden: E. J. Brill, 1975.

———. "Hanina ben Dosa': A Controversial Galilean Saint from the First Century of the Christian Era." *JJS* 23 (1972) 28–50; and 24 (1973) 51–64.

———. *Jesus the Jew: A Historian's Reading of the Gospels*. New York: Macmillan, 1973.

———. *The Dead Sea Scrolls: Qumran in Perspective*. London: Collins, 1977.

———. *The Dead Sea Scrolls in English*. 3d ed. London: Penguin, 1987.

Vermes, G., and M. D. Goodman, eds. *The Essenes according to Classical Sources*. Oxford Centre for Postgraduate Hebrew Studies Textbook 1. Sheffield: JSOT Press, 1989.

Vermeylen, J. *Du prophète Isaïe à l'apocalyptique: Isaïe I–XXXV, miroir d'un demi-millenaire d'experience religieuse en Israël* 2.1–517. 2 vols. EB. Paris: Lecoffre, 1977.

Vidal-Naquet, P. "Flavius Josèphe et Masada." *Revue historique* 260 (1978) 3–21.

Villalba i Varneda, P. *The Historical Method of Flavius Josephus*. ALGHJ 19. Leiden: E. J. Brill, 1986.

Vincent, L. H. "La Palestine dans les papyrus Ptolemaiques de Gerza." *RB* 29 (1920) 161–202.

Vogel, E. K. "Bibliography of Holy Land Sites: Part I." *HUCA* 42 (1971) 1–96.

———. "Bibliography of Holy Land Sites: Part II." *HUCA* 52 (1981) 1–92.

———. "Bibliography of Holy Land Sites: Part III, 1981–1987." *HUCA* 58 (1987) 1–63.

Voigtlander, E. N. von. *The Bisitun Inscription of Darius the Great. Babylonian Version*. Corpus Inscriptionum Iranicarum; Part I: Inscriptions of Ancient Iran, Vol. 2: The Babylonian Versions of the Achaemenian Inscriptions, Texts 1. London: Humphries, 1978.

Wacher, J. *The Roman Empire*. London: J. M. Dent, 1987.

Wacholder, B. Z. *Nicolas of Damascus*. Berkeley and Los Angeles: University of California Press, 1962.

———. *Eupolemus: A Study of Judaeo-Greek Literature*. HUC Monograph 3. Cincinnati: Hebrew Union College, 1974.

———. "The Letter from Judah Maccabee to Aristobulus: Is 2 Maccabees 1:10b—2:18 Authentic?" *HUCA* 49 (1978) 89–133.

Walbank, F. W. *A Historical Commentary on Polybius*. 3 vols. Oxford: Clarendon, 1957–79.

———. *The Hellenistic World*. Fontana History of the Ancient World. London: Fontana, 1981.

Waldmann, H. *Die kommagenischen Kultreformen unter König Mithradates I. Kallinikos und seinem Sohne Antiochos I.* Etudes préliminaires aux religions orientales dans l'Empire romain 34. Leiden: E. J. Brill, 1973.

Walter, N. *Der Thoraausleger Aristobulus*. TU 86. Berlin: Akademie-Verlag, 1964.

Waltke, B. K. "The Samaritan Pentateuch and the Text of the Old Testament." *New Perspectives on the Old Testament*, edited by J. B. Payne, 212–39. Waco, Tex.: Word, 1970.

Warmington, B. H. *Nero: Legend and Reality.* London: Chatto & Windus, 1969.

Waterman, L. "The Camouflaged Purge of Three Messianic Conspirators." *JNES* 13 (1954) 73–78.

Watson, J. S. *Justin, Cornelius Nepo, and Eutropius Literally Translated, with Notes and a General Index.* London: Bell & Daldy, 1872.

Weinberg, J. P. "Demographische Notizen zur Geschichte der nachexilischen Gemeinde in Juda." *Klio* 54 (1972) 45–59.

———. "Das *Bēit 'Āḇōt* im 6.-4. Jh. v. u. Z." *VT* 23 (1973) 400–414.

———. "Die Agrarverhältnisse in der Bürger-Tempel-Gemeinde der Achämenidenzeit." *Acta Antiqua* 22 (1974) 473–86.

———. "Die soziale Gruppe im Weltbild des Chronisten." *ZAW* 98 (1986) 72–95.

Weippert, H. *Palästina in vorhellenistischer Zeit.* HdA. Vorderasien 2, Band 1. Munich: Beck, 1988.

Weissbach, F. H. *Die Keilinschriften der Achameniden.* Vorderasiatische Bibliothek 3. Leipzig: Hinrichs, 1911. Reprint. Leipzig: Zentral-Antiquariat der DDR, 1968.

Welles, C. B. *Royal Correspondence in the Hellenistic Period: A Study in Greek Epigraphy.* New Haven: Yale University Press, 1934.

Wellesley, K. *The Long Year, A.D. 69.* Boulder, Colo.: Westview; London: Paul Elek, 1976.

Wells, C. M. *The Roman Empire.* Fontana History of the Ancient World. Isle of Man: Fontana, 1984.

Welwei, K. W. "Abhängige Landbevölkerungen auf <<Tempelterritorien>> im hellenistischen Kleinasien und Syrien." *Ancient Society* 10 (1979) 97–118.

Wenning, R. "Das Nabatäerreich: seine archäologischen und historischen Hinterlassenschaften." In H. P. Kuhnen, *Palästina in griechisch-römischer Zeit,* 367–415. HdA. Vorderasien 2, Band 2. Munich: Beck, 1990.

Westermann, C. *Isaiah 40–66.* OTL. Philadelphia: Westminster; London: SCM, 1969.

Whitley, C. F. *Koheleth: His Language and Thought.* BZAW 148. Berlin and New York: de Gruyter, 1979.

Whittaker, C. R. "Rural Labour in Three Roman Provinces." In *Non-slave Labour in the Greco-Roman World,* edited by P. Garnsey, 73–99. Cambridge Philological Society Supplementary Volume 6. Cambridge: Cambridge Philological Society, 1980.

Whybray, R. N. *Isaiah 40–66.* NCB. Grand Rapids: Wm. B. Eerdmans; London: Marshall, Morgan & Scott, 1975.

———. *The Making of the Pentateuch: A Methodological Study.* JSOTSS 53. Sheffield: JSOT Press, 1987.

———. *Ecclesiastes.* NCB. Grand Rapids: Wm. B. Eerdmans; London: Marshall, Morgan & Scott, 1989.

Widengren, G. "The Persian Period." In *Israelite and Judaean History,* edited by J. Hayes and J. Miller, 489–538. Philadelphia: Fortress, 1977.

Wiesehöfer, J. "Zur Frage der Echtheit des Dareios-Briefes an Gadatas." *Reinisches Museum* 130 (1987) 396–98.

Wild, R. A. "The Encounter between Pharisaic and Christian Judaism: Some Early Gospel Evidence." *NovT* 27 (1985) 105–24.

Wilkinson, J. "The Streets of Jerusalem." *Levant* 7 (1975) 118–36.

Will, E. *Histoire politique du monde hellénistique (323–30 av. J.-C.).* Rev. ed. 2 vols. Annales de l-Est, Mémoire 30. Nancy: Publications de l'Université, 1979–82.

————. "Un Monument Hellénistique de Jordanie: Le Qasr el 'abd d"Iraq al Amir." *Studies in the History and Archaeology of Jordan* 1 (1982) 197–200.

————. "Pour une 'Anthropologie Coloniale' du Monde Hellénistique." In *The Craft of the Ancient Historian: Essays in Honor of Chester G. Starr,* edited by J. W. Eadie and J. Ober, 273–301. New York: University Press of America, 1985.

Will, E., et al. *Le monde grec et l'Orient.* 2 vols. Paris: Presses Universitaires de France, 1975.

Willi, T. *Die Chronik als Auslegung.* FRLANT 106. Göttingen: Vandenhoeck & Ruprecht, 1972.

Williams, R. S. "The Role of Amicitia in the Career of A. Gabinius (Cos. 58)." *Phoenix* 32 (1978) 195–210.

Williamson, H.G.M. *Israel in the Books of Chronicles.* Cambridge: Cambridge University Press, 1977.

————. "Eschatology in Chronicles." *Tyndale Bulletin* 28 (1977) 115–54.

————. "The Historical Value of Josephus' *Jewish Antiquities* XI.297–301." *JTS* 28 (1977) 49–66.

————. *1 and 2 Chronicles.* NCB. Grand Rapids: Wm. B. Eerdmans; London: Marshall, Morgan & Scott, 1982.

————. "The Composition of Ezra i-vi." *JTS* 34 (1983) 1–30.

————. "Nehemiah's Walls Revisited." *PEQ* 116 (1984) 81–88.

————. *Ezra, Nehemiah.* WBC 16. Waco, Tex.: Word, 1985.

————. *Ezra and Nehemiah.* Society for Old Testament Study, Old Testament Guides. Sheffield: JSOT Press, 1987.

————. "The Governors of Judah under the Persians." *Tyndale Bulletin* 39 (1988) 59–82.

Wilson, B. R. *Magic and the Millennium: A Sociological Study of Religious Movements of Protest among Tribal and Third-World Peoples.* London: Heinemann, 1973.

————. *The Social Dimensions of Sectarianism: Sects and New Religious Movements in Contemporary Society.* Oxford: Clarendon, 1990.

Winston, D. "The Iranian Component in the Bible, Apocrypha, and Qumran: A Review of the Evidence." *HR* 5 (1965–66) 183–216.

Winter, P. *On the Trial of Jesus.* 2d ed. Studia Judaica 1. Berlin and New York: de Gruyter, 1974.

Wirgin, W. *Herod Agrippa I: King of the Jews.* Leeds University Oriental Society Monograph Series 10A/10B. Leeds: Leeds University Press, 1968.

————. "Judah Maccabee's Embassy to Rome and the Jewish-Roman Treaty." *PEQ* 101 (1969) 15–20.

Wiseman, T. P. "The Census in the First Century B.C." *JRS* 59 (1969) 59–75.

————. " 'There Went Out a Decree from Caesar Augustus . . . ' " *NTS* 33 (1987) 479–80.

Wolff, H. W. *Hosea and Joel.* Hermeneia. Philadelphia: Fortress, 1977.

———. *Obadiah and Jonah: A Commentary.* Minneapolis: Augsburg, 1986.

———. *Haggai: A Commentary.* Minneapolis: Augsburg, 1988.

Worsley, P. *The Trumpet Shall Sound: A Study of "Cargo" Cults in Melanesia.* London: Macgibbon & Kee, 1957.

Woude, A. S. van der. "Malachi's Struggle for a Pure Community: Reflections on Malachi 2:10-16." In *Tradition and Re-Interpretation in Jewish and Early Christian Literature: Essays in Honour of Jürgen C. H. Lebram,* edited by J. W. van Henten, et al., 65–71. SPB 36. Leiden: E. J. Brill, 1986.

———. Review of *Studies on the Hasmonean Period,* by J. Efron. *JSJ* 20 (1989) 91–94.

Wright, J. S. "The Historicity of the Book of Esther." In *New Perspectives on the Old Testament,* edited by J. B. Payne, 37–47. Waco: Word, 1970.

Yadin, Y. "Expedition D." *IEJ* 11 (1961) 36–52.

———, ed. *The Scroll of the War of the Sons of Light against the Sons of Darkness.* Oxford: Clarendon, 1962.

———. "Expedition D—The Cave of Letters." *IEJ* 12 (1962) 227–57.

———. *The Ben Sira Scroll from Masada: With Introduction, Emendations and Commentary.* Jerusalem: Israel Exploration Society, 1965.

———. "The Excavation of Masada—1963/64: Preliminary Report." *IEJ* 15 (1965) 1–120.

———. *Masada: Herod's Fortress and the Zealots' Last Stand.* New York: Random House, 1966.

———. *Bar-Kokhba.* London: Weidenfeld & Nicolson, 1971.

———. "Epigraphy and Crucifixion." *IEJ* 23 (1973) 18–22.

———, ed. *Jerusalem Revealed: Archaeology in the Holy City (1968–1974).* Jerusalem: Israel Exploration Society, 1975.

———, ed. *The Temple Scroll: Hebrew and English.* 3 vols. in 4. Jerusalem: Israel Exploration Society, 1983.

Yamauchi, E. M. *Gnostic Ethics and Mandaean Origins.* HTS 24. Cambridge: Harvard University Press; London: Oxford University Press, 1970.

———. *Pre-Christian Gnosticism: A Survey of the Proposed Evidences.* Grand Rapids: Wm. B. Eerdmans, 1973.

———. *Persia and the Bible.* Grand Rapids: Baker, 1990.

Yarbro Collins, A., ed. *Early Christian Apocalypticism: Genre and Social Setting.* Semeia 36. Atlanta: Scholars Press, 1986.

Zahavy, T. *The Traditions of Eleazar Ben Azariah.* BJS 2. Atlanta: Scholars Press, 1977.

Zangemeister, C. *Pauli Orosii historiarum adversum paganos libri VII.* CSEL 5. Vienna: Temsky, 1882.

Zeitlin, S. "Did Agrippa Write a Letter to Gaius Caligula?" *JQR* 56 (1965/66) 22–31.

Zeitlin, S., and S. Tedesche, eds. *The First Book of Maccabees.* Dropsie College Jewish Apocryphal Literature. New York: Harper, 1950.

Zias, J., and E. Sekeles. "The Crucified Man from Giv'at ha-Mivtar: A Reappraisal." *IEJ* 35 (1985) 22–27.

Zimmermann, F. *The Book of Tobit.* Dropsie College Jewish Apocryphal Literature. New York: Harper, 1958.

INDEX OF PASSAGES

HEBREW BIBLE (OLD TESTAMENT)

APOCRYPHA AND PSEUDEPIGRAPHA

QUMRAN AND JUDEAN DESERT MANUSCRIPTS

PHILO

JOSEPHUS

NEW TESTAMENT

EARLY CHRISTIAN LITERATURE

RABBINIC LITERATURE

GREEK AND ROMAN WRITINGS

INSCRIPTIONS

INDEX OF
NAMES AND SUBJECTS

714

INDEX OF MODERN AUTHORS

INDEX OF MODERN AUTHORS